Second Edition

Fundamental Concepts of Educational Leadership

Taher A. Razik
State University of New York–Buffalo

Austin D. Swanson
State University of New York–Buffalo

Merrill
Prentice Hall

Upper Saddle River, New Jersey
Columbus, Ohio

Library of Congress Cataloging-in-Publication Data
Razik, Taher A.
   Fundamental concepts of educational leadership / Taher A. Razik,
Austin D. Swanson.—2nd ed.
      p. cm.
   Rev. ed. of: Fundamental concepts of educational leadership and
management. 1st ed. c1995.
   Includes bibliographical references and index.
   ISBN 0-13-014491-6
   1. School management and organization—United States. 2. Educational
leadership—United States. I. Swanson, Austin D. II. Razik, Taher A.
Fundamental concepts of educational leadership and management. III.
Title.
   LB2805 .R29 2001
   371.2'00973—dc21   00-036120

Vice President and Publisher: Jeffery W. Johnston
Executive Editor: Debra A. Stollenwerk
Editorial Assistant: Penny S. Burleson
Production Editor: Linda Hillis Bayma
Production Coordination: WordCrafters Editorial Services, Inc.
Design Coordinator: Diane C. Lorenzo
Cover Designer: Rod Harris
Cover art: Hugh M. Neil, Ed. D., Professor of Art Education, State University of New York College at Buffalo
Production Manager: Pamela D. Bennett
Director of Marketing: Kevin Flanagan
Marketing Manager: Amy June
Marketing Services Manager: Krista Groshong

This book was set in ITC Garamond by Carlisle Communications, Ltd. It was printed and bound by R.R.
Donnelley & Sons Company. The cover was printed by Phoenix Color Corp.

10 9 8 7 6 5 4 3 2 1
ISBN: 0-13-014491-6

Preface

Perspective

If there was ever a time when educational institutions required effective leadership, it is now. This is the first time in the history of the United States that the quality of the education provided for our citizens has been recognized politically as being strategically important to national success and survival. Educational issues are among the major concerns of voters; therefore, not surprisingly, they are debated vigorously by candidates for public office at all levels of government and they are covered regularly on the front pages of major newspapers.

Today's educational leaders need to possess a broad variety of skills that enable them to function comfortably and effectively in changing environments and under highly politicized conditions. In these new circumstances, change is the only constant. The mission of this book is to foster understanding of this reality among those preparing for careers in leading educational institutions and to help develop skills necessary for working competently within them. For better or for worse, this is a dynamic and exciting period in human history. Because of the fluidity of the situation, it is a period of unparalleled opportunity and of potential danger. To capitalize on the opportunities and to minimize the dangers demands extraordinarily wise leadership in all sectors and in all enterprises, including education.

While pervasive social change affects persons in all walks of life, there is bound to be greater impact upon those in positions of great social visibility and concern—such as persons holding administrative and supervisory responsibility for educational systems. Society has a right to expect adept performance from people in those positions. Under these conditions, proficient leadership cannot be a matter of copying conventional behavior. To advance education, there is a clear need for educational leaders to have and exercise: the ability to comprehend the dynamics of human affairs as a basis for relevant action under novel conditions; a better understanding of issues and processes in educational institutions; and greater originality and collaboration in designing strategic policies. Their approach to the opportunities and problems confronting them must remain hypothetical and open-ended so that more may be learned by what is done.

Graham (1999) saw the accomplishments of the new public schools during the first quarter of the twentieth century concentrating on assimilating the flood of immigrants pouring into the country. The middle years focused on broadening the curriculum, especially at the secondary level, to include vocational subjects and courses in social and personal adjustment that enabled secondary schools to address the educational needs of most of the student population. The 1960s and 1970s addressed issues of equity and access among genders and ethnic groups. *During the first three-quarters of the century, Graham concluded, the schools were much more successful in enrolling students than in teaching them* (emphasis added). This practice is no longer acceptable. Schools must now set out to correct the situation by focusing on raising the achievement levels of *all* students.

Past assumptions used by educators in designing schools and school curricula no longer hold across the board. Children are less likely to come from majority backgrounds, they are more likely to be members of nontraditional families, and they are more likely to be poor. Education through high school and beyond is essential if graduates are to be employed in other than menial jobs and to enjoy comfortable standards of living. Well-paying employment opportunities increasingly require sophisticated intellectual skills. Educational leadership is being challenged to design new curricula that recognize the multicultural nature of students, provide institutional support for those at risk, and link schooling to employment and citizenship. Solving our "educational" crisis will require coordination of schools' efforts with those of other social agencies in the community.

Not only will school leaders of the future be working with a student body markedly different from that of the past, the organizational structures and professional and political relationships will also be quite different. These changes will produce a new climate for school organizations that demands a transformational rather than hierarchical leadership. Parents and community members are likely to have greater influence on the organization and operation of schools through membership on school councils or through parental choice of schooling. The relationships between teachers and administrators are likely to be collegial, not authoritarian. Principals and teachers are likely to have greater professional discretion as many decisions formerly made at the district, state, and federal levels are left to schools. Nevertheless, local, state, and federal authorities will continue to set certain parameters. We can expect states, in particular, to set achievement standards, to design curricula to meet those standards, and to administer examinations to identify schools failing to meet those standards.

For several years, the authors co-taught an introductory course for students of educational administration. We sought in vain to find an appropriate text that would be comprehensive in coverage, yet have sufficient depth to lead students to a fundamental understanding of relevant issues. We wanted a text that was eclectic, not ideological, in approach, and that would emphasize an "action-research" perspective, compelling readers to consider critically the theoretical underpinnings of current educational practice and motivating them to seek practical alternative approaches. Not finding such a text, we set out to create our own: *Fundamental Concepts of Educational Leadership* is the result.

The careful reader will quickly detect that we do not subscribe entirely to any particular philosophy of education. We attempt to report the best of what has been produced by researchers regardless of their paradigm and orientation. We view the study of leadership as a multiple-perspective activity. Theories of leadership should not be viewed as competing with one another in the quest for the "one best view" (Sergiovanni, 1984). Each approach, each theory, has inherent strengths and weaknesses. Each theory is better able to illuminate and explain *certain* aspects of each concept. Taken together, a more complete understanding of the concept is possible through the power of triangulation and perspective.

New to This Edition

The second edition continues to set forth principles undergirding the knowledge base of educational leadership, updated to address new and evolving thinking, learning, and organizational paradigms that are in a significant period of transformation. The book is still highly applicable to introductory courses in programs that prepare educational administrators, but is also recommended as a basic guide for all educational practitioners. As with the first edition, leadership principles are presented within a systems framework. The second edition maintains the thorough coverage of relevant theory of the first, but is more consistent in relating that theory to practice.

In the previous edition, we defined *leadership* as influencing the actions of others in achieving desirable ends. While that definition is historically based on a significant and important body of knowledge, new definitions reflect a major rethinking of the concept. Today, *leadership* is also thought of as an overall action/change orientation—a transformation occurring in and across numerous educational environments. Leadership in this new arena of transformation becomes less role-specific in the traditional sense, while it amasses broad new elements that expand its overall character.

Today a leader (in whatever situation that might involve) can be thought of as a teacher, steward, facilitator, pathfinder, aligner, empowerer, appraiser, forecaster, enabler, and/or advisor. As this incomplete list expands to engulf a multitude of possibilities, you begin to sense the critical themes that further define leadership for the educational practitioner today. Under evolving conditions, leadership takes on an action-rich perspective. Leadership becomes the capacity to generate, operationalize, and evaluate a continuously changing environment—to build feedback into environments in the process of continuous improvement.

With these new considerations becoming more apparent, we have reorganized the divisions of the book as our examination of the various aspects of leadership unfolds. Part One, whose title remains "Leadership in a Period of Dynamic Change," presents the current and projected contexts of educational leadership and discusses systems theory and leadership theory, which continue to serve as the undergirding concepts of the book. Parts Two, Three, Five, and Six carry new titles reflecting added content and different organization and emphases: "Schools as Learning Organizations: Communication and Human Interaction," "The Generation and Use of Information in a Learning Organization," "Strategy Formulation and Implementation," and "Leadership for a New Millennium."

In Chapter 7, addressing processes of inquiry and analysis, more attention is given to naturalistic and action research orientations, supplementing the already strong discussion of quantitative approaches that appeared in the first edition. Theory development is de-emphasized relative to the first edition, while greater application is developed to provide a stronger connection to ongoing organizational functioning.

Chapter 8, focusing on evaluation, is an updated version of the original chapter with a significant new section giving the essence of the quality movement and its relation to program evaluation, student achievement, and staff evaluation. Another addition is a section of commentary about national and state standards and assessment activities.

Chapter 9 approaches the topic of educational policy from an economic perspective as well as the political perspective of the first edition. The discussion of universal principles (Chapter 12) gives more attention to the importance of personal reflection by educational leaders and proposes professional platforms as a vehicle for doing so. In Chapter 13, the discussion of strategy formation and planning is essentially new, with greater coverage of school-based decision making. In Chapter 14, additional attention is given to school-based budgeting.

A new chapter (15) has been added, addressing the role of information and technology in a constantly changing environment. As the information age progresses, numerous traditional roles in schools may change. A discussion of this possibility devotes particular attention to the evolving nature of leadership as information and technology become more pervasive.

Chapter Descriptions

Part I: Leadership in a Period of Dynamic Change

Chapter 1, "The Context for Leadership," highlights some of the causes for concern over public education. The failure of the nation's public schools to meet the expectations set forth by Goals 2000 is examined, followed by an exploration of the future needs of the educational enterprise and the challenges they pose for reformers of today's educational environment. The chapter concludes with a presentation of the structure of precollegiate education in the United States and a description of the problems that must be corrected.

Chapter 2, "The Power of Systems Thinking for Educational Change," presents a modified version of systems theory as a lens for perceiving the many facets of leadership and as a framework for understanding the interrelationships of those facets. It traces the history of systems theory, including creating significant detail about systems frameworks and properties in general terms. The discussion includes organizational implications of a systems perspective and speaks to issues surrounding the post-industrial paradigm.

In Chapter 3, "Leadership in a Reform Environment," theories of leadership are discussed, emphasizing leadership's many dimensions. Transformational leadership and other current theoretical models are explored to demonstrate the complexity and variety of components of leadership.

Part II: Schools as Learning Organizations: Communication and Human Interaction

Chapter 4, "Schools as Organizational Systems," considers organizational theory and practice relating to educational enterprises. Depending on one's view, organizational activity may be linked to values, effectiveness, integration, and more. Metaphors are examined to help the reader envision the broad nature of how we think about, use, and evaluate organizational performance today.

Chapter 5, "Communication: The Breath of Organizational Life," examines this key ingredient of effective leadership: communication is the conduit for inquiry that develops understanding within and across environments. As the information age progresses, communication theory becomes increasingly important. This chapter explores communication concepts as applied to social systems, with particular emphasis on educational systems.

Chapter 6, "Human Relations: The Base for Educational Leadership," discusses human relations as the integration of people that allows them to work together productively and cooperatively. This chapter broadens the understanding of teamwork and team learning applications, and explains how mental states affect the human component of educational enterprises. Each individual's ability to work harmoniously and to understand the educational organization is a key to organizational effectiveness.

Part III: The Generation and Use of Information in a Learning Organization

Chapter 7, "The Process of Inquiry and Analysis," presents theory-based quantitative and naturalistic approaches to inquiry and analysis. Common errors made in human inquiry are discussed, as is the development of safeguards to ensure that fundamental issues are considered and observed. Theory is developed with emphasis on practical applications intended to provide a strong connection to the effective functioning of organizations.

Chapter 8, "Evaluation in Education: Theories, Models, and Processes," discusses the means by which leaders pursue the process of mobilizing resources to enable organizations to function effectively. Judgments of effective functioning are based on monitoring outcomes and measuring them against established goals and objectives. The quality movement and its relation to program evaluation, student achievement, and staff evaluation are considered. Also included is a discussion of national and state standards and assessment activities.

Part IV: Decision Making and Change

Policies are sets of rules for guiding the operation of an organization that have been formally adopted through a prescribed process. Chapter 9, "Educational Policy Formulation in a Mixed Economy," focuses on policy formulation as collective decision-making through the market (economics) and through governments (politics). A number of public policy models are described and critiqued. Special attention is given to assessing the impact of current proposals for decentralizing decision-making in education; placing more authority at the school level; and involving teachers, parents, and students.

Chapter 10, "Organizational Decision Making," focuses on decisions as made in school organizations. Decision making, the process of choosing among alternatives, is one of the most crucial skills needed by an effective educational leader. We criticize the common practice of viewing decision making as a linear process (identifying a problem, defining the problem, weighing alternative solutions, and making a choice). Instead, we propose a circular process that is more compatible with the inherent dynamics of the educational environment.

The ultimate objective of educational organizations (or any organization, for that matter) is to maintain internal stability. To maintain stability while existing within turbulent environments requires constant change—the focus of Chapter 11, "Systemic Change." Educational leaders of the new millennium must be prepared to develop, articulate, and bring to fruition new educational systems, and to do so in such a way that the new systems meet societal demands for flexibility and quality.

Part V: Strategy Formulation and Implementation

Chapter 12, "Impact of Universal Principles, Social Expectations, and Personal Values on Leadership," surveys various philosophical points of view and then turns to social science perspectives on values. A person's philosophy determines how that person interprets what is experienced. To be an effective tool of administrative behavior, however, it is preferable that this philosophy be understood and intellectualized and that the values and beliefs that it implies to be made explicit. The importance of values and beliefs held by an individual and how these values and beliefs are integrated into the visions, missions, and goals of an organization are examined. The role of megavalues held by society as a whole in shaping the policy-making process is also explored.

Chapter 13, "Strategy Formation and Planning at the District and School Levels," seeks to produce an understanding of how educational institutions develop a sense of direction and purpose, make decisions about organizing themselves in order to realize their purposes, and allocate resources available to them in order to further their purposes. While the process is usually referred to as *strategic planning,* we distinguish between strategy formation and planning as two separate but equally important procedures. Because planning is an analytical process and strategy formulation is a synthesizing process, they must happen separately. We take the position that strategy is not the consequence of planning; rather, planning takes place within the framework formed by strategy. Planning helps to translate intended strategies into realized ones by laying out the steps necessary for effective implementation.

An essential part of planning and implementation is allocation of resources. Demands for resources always exceed their availability; therefore it is incumbent upon educators to use available resources to maximize productivity within the context of organizational priorities. Chapter 14, "The Allocation of Resources for Education: Adequacy, Equity, and Efficiency," addresses issues concerning the allocation of resources to the educational sector and within educational enterprises.

The availability of appropriate information is critical to the development of wise strategies, effective plans, and efficient allocation of resources. Chapter 15, "The Role of Information and Technology," considers the nature and importance of information systems to these processes. Note is taken of the astounding advances in information and communication technologies, and the relevance of these changes to the organization of schools, a major segment of the information industry, is explored. Particular attention is paid to the changing nature of leadership because information technology has an impact across educational systems.

Part VI: Leadership for a New Millennium

Chapter 16, "Educational Leadership for Systemic Change," builds a composite view of the complete work of the book by synthesizing the highlights of the previous chapters. This last discussion provides further illustrations of how education must contend with emerging issues and conditions. The discussion points to possible scenarios that may demonstrate the future of education.

References

Graham, P. A. (1999). Delineating the boundaries of a people's aspiration: Our rhetoric of educational access often has belied a contradictory reality. *Education Week, 18,* 20, 44–45, 50.

Sergiovanni, T. J. (1984). Cultural and competing perspectives in administrative theory and practice. In T. J. Sergiovanni & J. E. Corbally (Eds.), *Leadership and organizational culture* (pp. 1–17). Urbana, IL: University of Illinois Press.

Acknowledgments

We express our appreciation to the following reviewers of the second edition of this book: Keith E. Crawley, University of Arizona, Phoenix; Jitsuo Furusawa, California State University; Larry W. Hughes, University of Houston; and Donna M. Schmitt, Eastern Michigan University. We also thank those persons who used the book as a text for the study of educational leadership. And we extend our appreciation to Bruce Hilyard of Genesee Community College, James Jacobs of Paul Smith College, Zahid Khairullah of St. Bonaventure University, and Verna Willis of Georgia State University for taking the time to read various chapters of the new edition and for making valuable suggestions.

Brief Contents

Part I Leadership in a Period of Dynamic Change   1

Chapter 1   The Context for Leadership   3

Chapter 2   The Power of Systems Thinking for Educational Change   29

Chapter 3   Leadership in a Reform Environment   60

**Part II Schools as Learning Organizations: Communication
and Human Interaction   85**

Chapter 4   Schools as Organizational Systems   87

Chapter 5   Communication: The Breath of Organizational Life   121

Chapter 6   Human Relations: The Base for Educational Leadership   156

Part III The Generation and Use of Information in a Learning Organization   195

Chapter 7   The Process of Inquiry and Analysis   197

Chapter 8   Evaluation in Education: Theories, Models, and Processes   222

Part IV Decision Making and Change   255

Chapter 9   Educational Policy Formulation in a Mixed Economy   257

Chapter 10   Organizational Decision Making   281

Chapter 11   Systemic Change   315

Part V Strategy Formulation and Implementation   347

Chapter 12   Impact of Universal Principles, Social Expectations, and
Personal Values on Leadership   349

Chapter 13   Strategy Formation and Planning at the District and School Levels   381

Chapter 14   The Allocation of Resources for Education: Adequacy, Equity,
and Efficiency   417

Chapter 15   The Role of Information and Technology   450

Part VI Leadership for a New Millennium   467

Chapter 16   Educational Leadership for Systemic Change   469

Contents

Part I   Leadership in a Period of Dynamic Change   1

Chapter 1   The Context for Leadership   3
                   Causes for Concern   6
                        Declining Achievement   6
                        The Making of an Underclass   9
                        Family Influences on School Success   11
                        Peer Influences on Student Achievement   15
                   The Education Reform Movement   16
                        Waves of Educational Reform   16
                        Emerging Patterns of Reform   18
                   The Scope and Structure of School Governance   19
                        The Historical Development of Public Education   19
                        The Current Organization of School Governance   22
                   Summary   24
                   Activities   25
                   References   26

Chapter 2   The Power of Systems Thinking for Educational Change   29
                   Conceptualizing Systems   30
                        The Development of Systems Thinking   30
                        Systems Definitions   31
                        Systems Frameworks   33
                        Systems Properties Explored   35
                        Other Properties of Systems   37
                   The Organizational Implications of Systems Thinking   39
                        Groundbreaking: Early Organizational Theories   39
                        Changing in Management Roles and Contexts   41
                        Organizational Change   41
                        Systemic Interventions   42
                        Feedback Requirements   43
                   Looking Toward the Future   44
                        Unrest in Organizations   44
                        Regulating Variety in Organizations   46
                        Metaphor and System Modeling in Educational Administration   47
                        Systems Thinking as a Wave of the Future in Education   49
                        Liberating Systems Theory: The Critical Stance   52
                   Case Study   54
                   References   56

Chapter 3   Leadership in a Reform Environment   60
             Leadership or Management   61
                  Leadership Trait Theories   62
                  Behavioral Theory   62
                  Power Influence   64
                  Leadership Styles   68
                  Contingency and Situational Theories and Models   70
                  Situational Determinants Theories and Models   75
                  Transformational and Transactional Leadership   75
                  Leadership within a Culture Context   77
             Women in Authority   80
             A New Paradigm for Leadership   81
             Case Study   82
             References   83

Part II   Schools as Learning Organizations: Communication
and Human Interaction   85

Chapter 4   Schools as Organizational Systems   87
             Ways of Thinking About Organizations   88
             Organizational Learning and Learning Organizations   92
             Decision Making in Organizations   92
             Power in Organizations   93
             Culture in Organizations   94
             Leadership in Organizations   95
             Communication in Organizations   96
             Size, Structure, and Complexity in Organizations   97
             Organizational Health and Effectiveness   98
             Change in Organizations   99
             Images of Organizations   100
                  The Machine   100
                  The Organism   101
                  The Brain   102
             Political Systems and Power   103
             Organizations as Culture   104
             Organizations as Psychic Prisons   105
             Mirrors of Organizations   106
             Mirrors of Education as Organizations   106
             Portraits of Contemporary Schooling   108
             Future Organizations and Schools of the Future   110
             Case Study   114
             References   116

Chapter 5   Communication: The Breath of Organizational Life   121
             Systemic Metaphors of Communication   122
             Theory Building and Judgment   123

Diversity in Communication Theories: A Twenty-First Century
    Paradox   124
Theory Genres in Communication   125
Metaphors and Assumptions in Organizational Communication   126
Distinguishing Features of Organizational Communication   128
Factors Affecting Clarity, Credibility, and Directionality of Organizational
    Messages   130
Types of Message Directionality   133
Other Factors Affecting Organizational Communication   135
A Sampling of Approaches to Organizational Communication   136
    Structure and Functional Approaches   136
    Behavioral Approaches   138
    Approaches Related to the Process of Organizing   139
    *Sociopsychological Perspective on Individual Communication in
        Organizations   140*
Pathway to the Future   142
Synthesizing Known Principles of Organizational Communication   144
Combining the Metaphors   146
Moving Forward: Potential New Directions   148
Case Study   151
References   153

Chapter 6   **Human Relations: The Base for Educational Leadership   156**
The Development of Human Relations Concepts   157
Conceptualizing Human Relations Theories   159
    Definitions of Human Relations   159
    Optimistic Assumptions of Human Nature   160
    Clinical and Ethical Dimensions   160
    The Importance of Human Needs   160
    Human Motivation and Human Behavior   161
    The Role of Motivation in Performance   161
    Morale and Productivity   162
    The Significance of Informal Organizations   162
    The Application of Human Relations Concepts   162
Theoretical Perspectives of Human Relations   162
    Human Nature   163
Human Motivation   165
    Process Models   165
    Content Models   168
    Common Human Needs   169
    Motivation at Work   171
Morale in Organizations   174
    Major Morale Factors   174
    Morale, Job Satisfaction, and Productivity   175
    Approaches to Studying Morale   175
    The Quality of Work Life   175

Informal Organizations   176
    Informal Leaders   177
    The Effects of Informal Organizations   177
    The Inevitability of Informal Organizations   178
Human Relations Theory in Educational Administration   178
    Democratic Educational Administration   178
    The Human Relations Movement in Education   179
    From Democratic Administration to Human Relations Management   180
    The Effects of the Human Relations Movement on Educational
        Administration   181
    A New Frame of Leadership   181
    A New Paradigm for Educational Leadership   182
    A Motivational Model for Educational Leadership   183
    Contemporary Issues in Human Relations   188
Case Studies   189
References   190

Part III   The Generation and Use of Information in a Learning Organization   195

Chapter 7   The Process of Inquiry and Analysis   197
Inquiry's Prelude   197
Inquiry Unraveled   198
    The Early Beginnings of Inquiry   198
The Historical Development of Inquiry   199
    Paradigms of Inquiry   200
Positivistic and Postpositivistic Theory   201
Critical Theory   202
Interpretivistic Theory   205
Inquiry and Educational Administration   209
Quandaries of Inquiry   210
Inquiry Processes and the Paradigm Debates   214
Case Study   217
References   219

Chapter 8   Evaluation in Education: Theories, Models, and Processes   222
Educational Evaluation: A Brief History   223
    The Early Beginnings of Evaluation   223
    The Modern Development Stages of Evaluation   223
The Basic Aspects of Educational Evaluation   225
    Definition Out of Diversity   225
    Evaluation Modes and Purposes   226
    Evaluation Targets and Processes   228
Evaluation Perspectives and Models   230
The Main Types of Educational Evaluation   231
    Program Evaluation   232
    Teacher Evaluation   238

The Evaluation of Administration   244
    Purposes of Administrative Evaluation   245
    Principles of Administrative Evaluation   245
    Administrative Evaluation Models   246
Standards and Requirements for Educational Evaluation   247
Requirements for Conducting Evaluations   249
The Future   250
Case Study   252
References   252

Part IV   Decision Making and Change   255

Chapter 9   Educational Policy Formulation in a Mixed Economy   257
Education: A Public and Private Good   258
The Influence of the Marketplace on Public Policy   260
    The Free Market   260
    Government and the Market   262
Models of Political Decision Making   264
    Institutionalism   264
    Systems Theory   266
    Incrementalism   269
    Group Theory   269
    Elite Theory   270
    Rationalism   271
Issues Involved in Governmental Intervention   273
    When Should Governments Intervene?   273
    Alternative Methods of Government Intervention   274
    Choosing the Appropriate Level of Government to Intervene   275
Distinctions between Judicial and Legislative Influence on Educational Policy
    Formulation   276
Summary   278
Activities   278
References   279

Chapter 10   Organizational Decision Making   281
Approaches to Decision Making   282
Decision Making and Problem Solving   283
The Historical Underpinnings of Decision Theory   284
Group and Participative Decision Making   287
Frameworks for Classifying Types of Decisions   289
Decision-Making Tools and Techniques   290
Multicriteria Decision Making   291
Decision Support Systems   293
Decision-Making Models   295
    Normative Models   295
    Descriptive Models   297

Idiographic Factors That Influence Decision Making   300
Decision-Making Heuristics and Biases   301
  Availability   302
  Representativeness   302
  Anchoring and Adjustment   304
  Confirmation Bias   305
  Hindsight Bias   305
The Implications of Systems Theory and Decision Making   306
  Decision-Making Implications in Educational Practice   307
Case Studies   308
References   309

Chapter 11   Systemic Change   315
Basic Issues   315
What Is Change?   315
Types of Change   317
Resistance to Change   318
Theoretical Implications of Change   320
Strategies for Change   321
Models for Planned Change and Their Use   324
  Problem-Solving Models   324
  Research–Development–Diffusion–Utilization Models   325
  Social Interaction Models   325
  Linkage Models   325
Organizational Variables within Models   326
Leadership and Change   326
  What Is a Change Agent or Change System?   327
  Characteristics of Effective Change Agents   327
  Functions of Effective Change Agents   327
Managing Planned Change   329
Decision Making   331
Effecting Educational Change   332
  Models for Educational Change   332
  Phases of Educational Change   333
  Effective Change Agents in Schools   334
Planning for a Changing Future in Education   335
  The Fate of Educational Changes   335
  Problematic Features of Change   336
Case Studies   337
References   343

Part V   Strategy Formulation and Implementation   347

Chapter 12   Impact of Universal Principles, Social Expectations, and Personal
             Values on Leadership   349
Philosophical Guides to Leadership   351
  Idealism   352

Liberalism   352
Realism, Logical Positivism, and Postpositivism   355
Pragmatism   356
Existentialism   357
Critical Theory   357
Constructivism   358
Two Views of the World   359
Value and Value Systems   360
Values Defined   360
Archetypes of Leadership   363
Values as Part of Organizational Cultures   366
Organizational Leadership: Values and Vision   369
Values, Democracy, and Followership   370
Values Analysis   371
Metavalues   374
Case Study   376
Activities   378
References   378

Chapter 13   Strategy Formation and Planning at the District and School Levels   381
Strategy Formation   381
Visioning   383
Mission Statements   384
Belief Statements   385
Strategic Policies   386
Planning   387
Intermediate Planning   388
Tactical Planning Including Budgeting   391
School-Based Management: Planning and Budgeting   394
Arguments for Administrative Decentralization   395
Strategy Formation and Planning at the School Level   397
School-Based Budgeting   407
An Application of Strategy Formation and Planning at the District Level   410
Activities   414
References   414

Chapter 14   The Allocation of Resources for Education: Adequacy, Equity, and Efficiency   417
Equity in the Allocation of Resources to Schooling   417
The Extent of Inequities in Resource Allocation   418
Intradistrict Equity Studies   422
Conceptual Considerations   423
Efficiency, Adequacy, and Economic Growth   423
External Efficiency   424
Internal Efficiency   429
Linking Equity, Efficiency, and Adequacy Considerations   443

Summary   444
Activities   445
References   445

Chapter 15   The Role of Information and Technology   450
Informal Information Systems   450
Formal Information Systems   451
Types of Information Systems   451
    Using Information Systems   453
    Data Included in an Educational Information System   454
The Role of Information Technology in Instruction and Learning   456
    Technological Change and Education   456
    Emerging Information Age Schools   458
A Prototype Integrated Information System to Manage Individualized Instruction   461
Summary   464
Activities   465
References   465

Part VI   Leadership for a New Millennium   467

Chapter 16   Educational Leadership for Systemic Change   469
Interlinking Concepts   469
The Traditional Role of Principal   471
Effective Schools and Reform Literature   473
Criticism of Effective Schools Research   474
Emerging Views of Leadership for Schools   477
    Educational Leadership as Transformative Leadership   477
    Moral Leadership   478
    Moral Imagination or Visioning   479
    School Culture and Participatory Democracy   479
    Situational Variations   481
    Critical Theory   481
Leadership at the District Level   483
Reforming Leadership Preparation Programs   486
Looking Ahead: The Educational Leader and the New Millennium   487
References   489

Name Index   491

Subject Index   499

PART I

Leadership in a Period of Dynamic Change

Education in the United States is going through a period of reform and re-structuring. Many of the old certainties have been shaken by the multiplicity of new demands placed upon schools, while new certainties have not yet formed. One thing that is clear is that the educational structure of the twentieth century will not meet the needs of the United States in the twenty-first century.

To guide human organizations effectively, leaders must possess an understanding of the context in which leadership is exercised. Like all other human organizations, educational institutions function in and are shaped by a web of external and internal expectations. It is in the context of complexity and change that the leaders of educational enterprises will have to function now and in the future. Complex systems, embedded in the complexities of the social structure, require leadership that can maneuver skillfully. The potential impact of decisions on the broad scale and on the specific problem at hand must be clearly understood. Traditional linear, cause-and-effect thinking is no longer adequate for the task of leadership.

Educational leaders have to facilitate the development of a vision of the organization's mission and to communicate that vision effectively so that it is shared by all members. Leaders must also act strategically to bring that vision to fruition, shaping new schools and institutions from an amalgam of the useful old and the desirable new. To succeed, they must provide direction for the future while managing within the context of the present systems, ensuring smooth day-to-day operations.

Such leadership springs from understanding the realities of the world as a suprasystem, what it means to be a leader, and when the exercise of leadership is required. In Part I we build a theoretical framework for the study of educational leadership.

Chapter 1: The Context for Leadership.
In this chapter we highlight some of the causes for concern over public education. The failure of the nation's public schools to meet the challenges of Goals 2000 is examined followed by an exploration of the future needs of the educational enterprise and the challenges that they pose for reformers of today's educational environment. The chapter concludes with a presentation of the structure of precollegiate education in the United States and a description of many of the problems that must be corrected.

Chapter 2: The Power of Systems Thinking for Educational Change.
A modified version of systems theory is presented in this chapter as a lens for perceiving the many facets of leadership and as a framework for understanding the interrelationships of those facets. The history of systems theory is traced, including creating significant detail about systems frameworks and properties in general terms. The discussion includes organizational implications of a systems perspective and finally, speaks to issues surrounding the postindustrial paradigm.

Chapter 3: Leadership in a Reform Environment.
In this chapter theories about leadership itself are discussed. The multiple dimensions of leadership are considered. Transformational leadership and other current theoretical models are explored to demonstrate the complexity and variety of components of leadership.

CHAPTER 1

The Context for Leadership

The beginning of the new millennium was the target date set for boys and girls in the United States to exceed the achievement levels of all other nations in the world in mathematics and science and to improve their performance generally in other core subjects. But it didn't happen, at least to the extent anticipated (Hoff, 1999; National Education Goals Panel [NEGP], 1998). The national expectations were expressed in eight goals, six of which were proposed in January 1990 by President George Bush in his State of the Union message and adopted the following month by the National Governors' Association; William Clinton, then governor of Arkansas, was chair of the association. In 1994, as President with bipartisan support, Clinton signed into law the Goals 2000: Educate America Act, making the six goals, and two additional ones, official national policy. The eight goals are presented in Table 1.1.

The goals were intended to provide a focus for the nation's school reform effort, which began in the early 1980s over concerns that weaknesses in the nation's educational systems were placing the nation at risk of losing its ability to compete economically with other nations because of a poorly

Table 1.1
Goals 2000: Eight National Goals for Public Education

Goal 1. By the year 2000, all children in America will start school ready to learn.

Goal 2. By the year 2000, the high school graduation rate will increase to at least 90%.

Goal 3. By the year 2000, all students will leave grades 4, 8, and 12 having demonstrated competency over challenging subject matter, including English, mathematics, science, foreign languages, civics and government, economics, arts, history, and geography, and every school in America will ensure that all students learn to use their minds well, so that they may be prepared for responsible citizenship, further learning, and productive employment in our Nation's modern economy.

Goal 4. By the year 2000, the Nation's teaching force will have access to programs for the continued improvement of their professional skills and the opportunity to acquire the knowledge and skills needed to instruct and prepare all American students for the next century.

Goal 5. By the year 2000, U.S. students will be the first in the world in mathematics and science achievement.

Goal 6. By the year 2000, every adult American will be literate and will possess the skills necessary to compete in a global economy and to exercise the rights and responsibilities of citizenship.

Goal 7. By the year 2000, every school in the United States will be free of drugs, violence, and the unauthorized use of firearms and alcohol and will offer a disciplined environment conducive to learning.

Goal 8. By the year 2000, every school will promote partnerships that will increase parental involvement and participation in promoting the social, emotional, and academic growth of children.

Source: P.L. 103–227, Title I, Section 102 (1994).

prepared workforce (National Commission on Excellence in Education, 1983).[1] Although disappointing, failure to meet the goals was not unexpected. Rather than serving as operational targets, many view the goals as symbols of the continuing need for rigorous academic preparation of the nation's children and youth. The goals are credited with raising national expectations from schools and with inspiring state efforts to improve schools (Johnston & Sandham, 1999).

The National Education Goals Panel (1998) reported that some progress had been made over the decade, however, in that more children are arriving at school ready to learn (Goal 1) and that there had been improvements in student achievement, especially mathematics. Little or no progress had been made toward improving teacher preparation, school safety, and parental participation.

As symbols, the goals reflect a new seriousness about education in the United States that shapes the climate for the foreseeable future in which school professionals are likely to work and schoolchildren are likely to learn (Lazerson, 1999). Forty-nine states (all except Iowa) have or are drafting standards in core subjects. By 1996, all but four states (Colorado, Iowa, Minnesota, and Nebraska) were using minimum-competency testing programs to monitor school progress (National Center for Education Statistics [NCES], 1999, Table 155). Several states are making the results available to the general public through special reports, press releases, and the Internet. Teacher and administrative certification requirements are being strengthened, and both groups are being held accountable for student success or failure. Major changes have, and are, taking place in the way decisions are made about education. More authority is being extended to the school level, and there is more involvement in the process by teachers, by parents, and sometimes, by students.

In looking back at the accomplishments of the public schools during the twentieth century, Graham (1999) saw them concentrating during the first quarter of the century on assimilating the flood of immigrants pouring into the country. The middle years focused on broadening the curriculum, especially at the secondary level, to include vocational subjects and courses in social and personal adjustment that enabled secondary schools to address the educational needs of a majority of the population. In the 1960s and 1970s issues of equity and access among genders and ethnic groups were addressed. During the first three quarters of the century, Graham concluded, the schools were much more successful in enrolling students than in teaching them. Schools have set out to correct that situation during the last two decades of the century by focusing on raising the achievement levels of all students. Graham's (1999) review of the past century identified five continuing issues that schools will need to deal with during the new century:

(1) mandatory academic achievement for all is a revolutionary change in expectations for American students; (2) school is a limited, though important influence in the lives of children, particularly adolescents; (3) fundamental reorganization of schools, particularly high schools, may be necessary; (4) an exclusive focus on academic achievement may prove too narrow a goal for schools; and (5) American schools historically have consistently delivered what the public sought from them, but accomplishment of those goals has taken decades (p. 44).

If there were ever a time when educational institutions required effective leadership, it is now. This is the first time in history that the quality of the education of citizens has been recognized politically as being strategically important to national success and survival. The forces leading to educational reform are not

---

[1]This is not the only time that education has been in a state of perceived crisis. For example, after the Soviet Union launched the first earth satellite in 1957, American education came under close scrutiny. Best-seller lists included books with such provocative titles as *Why Johnny Can't Read, What Ivan Knows That Johnny Doesn't,* and *Death at an Early Age.*

unique to education, however; rather, they reflect worldwide changes in social, economic, political, and technological relationships. Alvin Toffler (1980, 1990) dubbed the forces the "third wave" and subsequently, the "Powershift Era." John Naisbitt (1982) and Naisbitt and Aburdene (1990) identified them as "megatrends." Drucker (1989) has referred to their amalgam as the "post industrial society," the "post business society," and the "information age." Whatever it is called, the age we have entered is quite different from that which preceded it. The magnitude of the shift has been likened to the shift from feudalism to capitalism or from an agriculturally based economy to industrialization. All social institutions must make appropriate adjustments to survive; educational institutions are no exception.

This is a time of shifting paradigms (Kuhn, 1970). Social and economic structures are in a state of flux. Many of the world's totalitarian governments have fallen and, in several instances, have been replaced by more democratic institutions. In other nations, near-anarchy prevails. There has been a decline in overt hostility among the powerful nations of the world, yet there is growing conflict among ethnic groups and violent regional rivalries.

There is both optimism and concern as we enter the new millennium. Naisbitt and Aburdene (1990), optimists, building on Naisbitt's (1982) successful predictions of a decade earlier, see the triumph of the individual and the demise of the collective. With newfound freedom, they predict a global economic boom, a Renaissance in the arts, and a growing interest in things spiritual. According to them, a new free-market socialism will become the dominant socioeconomic structure and the welfare state will be privatized. Women increasingly will assume leadership roles, and global lifestyles and cultural nationalism will emerge. Biology will dominate the sciences, and Pacific-rim nations will dominate economic relationships.

Not everyone is as optimistic about the future as are Naisbitt and Aburdene. Galbraith (1992), for example, sees a growing disparity between the haves and the have-nots in the United States and predicts that eventually the have-nots will rise in rebellion. The disparity is growing, according to Galbraith, because for the first time in U.S. history, the "contented" constitute the majority of the population and are in complete control of government. The contented do not support social legislation that redistributes wealth through higher taxes on the rich and greater services for the poor. Galbraith argues that it was the social legislation engineered by Lloyd George early in the twentieth century that saved British capitalism during the years between the two world wars, and similarly, it was the social legislation of Franklin Roosevelt that saved capitalism in the United States during the Great Depression. In each instance, the legislation was opposed by the contented, who lost; but now that the contented are firmly in the majority, there is little hope of government enacting legislation to bridge the gap between the haves and the have-nots. Galbraith predicts social breakdown as a consequence.

For better or for worse, this is, indeed, a dynamic and exciting period in human history. Because of the fluidity of the situation, it is a period of unparalleled opportunity and potential danger. To capitalize on the opportunities and to minimize the dangers demands extraordinarily wise leadership in all sectors and in all enterprises, including education.

In short, our reality is pervasive social change. Although these changes affect persons in all walks of life, there is bound to be greater impact upon those in positions demanding wide social visibility and concern, such as persons holding administrative and supervisory responsibility for educational institutions and systems. Society has a right to expect competent performance in those positions. Under these circumstances, competent leadership cannot be a matter of copying conventional behavior. To advance education, there is a clear need for educational leaders to have the ability to comprehend the dynamics of human affairs as a basis for relevant action under novel conditions, the need for better understanding of issues and processes in educational institutions, and the need for greater originality and collaboration in designing strategic policies. Their approach to the opportunities and problems confronting them needs to remain hypothetical and open ended so that more may be learned by what is done.

Among other things, leadership is a function of context. In this chapter we highlight some of the causes for concern over public education. Special attention is given to the reported decline in achievement by U.S. students and their relative international standing. Statistics are presented showing that the conditions under which many schools operate are becoming more difficult because the populations they serve are increasing in ethnic diversity, in variation of family structures, and in the proportion of children coming from impoverished homes. We then examine briefly the political and professional responses to the criticisms and step back to look for historical roots of the current dilemmas. The evolution of the tradition of local control of school governance and contemporary challenges to the tradition are summarized. Evidence of the increasing politicization of educational issues is presented. The chapter closes with a capsulated description of the current organization of school governance.

The context for educational leadership today is different from that at any other time in our history. It is essential that contemporary issues and processes be understood if leadership is to result in relevant action.

Causes for Concern

Declining Achievement

Frequently, critics document the decline in the quality of schooling with statistics of falling Scholastic Aptitude Test (SAT) scores, comparisons with the achievement of children in other countries, high dropout rates, violence in the schools, and low achievement of minority children compared with majority children.

SAT scores did decline steadily from an average total score (recentered scale) of 1039 in 1972 to 994 in 1981 (NCES, 1999, Table 132). Scores declined for both verbal and mathematics subtests, although they dropped more dramatically for verbal tests. Since 1981, the total average score and the mathematics test scores have increased modestly, while the verbal test scores have stabilized. The average total score stood at 1017 in 1994.

The Sandia study (Huelskamp, 1993) concluded that "the much-publicized 'decline' in average SAT scores misrepresents the true story of SAT performance." The study attributed the decline to the fact that more students in the bottom halves of their classes are taking the SAT today than in years past. In fact, every ethnic group is performing better today than 15 years ago (Huelskamp, 1993). The reason that each subgroup improved while the overall average declined is that lower-scoring groups represent a larger proportion of those taking the examination today.

Berliner (1993) also challenges the common interpretation of declining SAT scores by pointing out that of the group of current students who match the characteristics of those who took the SATs in 1975, there has been a 30-point increase, more than 10 percentile ranks. More recently, Berliner and Biddle (1995) have consolidated their longitudinal analyses of student performance and have concluded that there never was a rising tide of mediocrity.

Composite American College Testing (ACT) scores have remained stable. Subscores in English have risen slightly while those in mathematics declined slightly. Subscores in social studies and mathematics were relatively stable (NCES, 1999, Table 135).

The National Assessment of Educational Progress (NAEP) has not detected a decline in educational achievement over the past 20 years, although its findings do present cause for concern about the low level of proficiency of some

American youth. Since 1971, virtually all 17-year-olds, regardless of ethnic group, are able to perform at Level 1: follow brief written directions and carry out simple discrete reading tasks; but less than 40 percent of the total age group can perform at Level 4: find, understand, summarize, and explain relatively complicated literary and informational material. Over 80 percent of the total age group are able to perform at Level 3: search for specific information, interrelate ideas, and make generalizations about literature, science, and social studies materials (NCES, 1999, Table 112).

Although average performance of minority groups on NAEP tests has shown improvement, it remains well below that of majority students, whose scores have remained relatively stable over the years (see Table 1.2). From 1975 to 1996, the percent of African-American students performing at Level 4 has increased from 8.1 to 18.0, compared to the white percentage of 45.1. For Hispanics, the percent increased from 12.6 to 20.0. The percent of African-Americans performing at Level 3 has increased from 43.0 to 67.2 and of Hispanics from 52.9 to 64.2. This compares with the white percentage gain from 86.2 to 86.8 at Level 3.

Further evidence of differences in achievement among ethnic groups was provided by an international study of mathematics achievement. Most of the populations of countries participating in the study are homogeneous, whereas the population of the United States is highly diversified. The highest-scoring nations for 13-year-olds were Taiwan (285) and Korea (285), yet American children of Asian descent trained in U.S. schools averaged better (287) (Wainer, 1994). The U.S. average Caucasian score (276) ranked in the upper half of European countries participating in the study. Achievement by Caucasians from the northeastern (279) and central (280) regions of the United States equaled or exceeded that of the top European country. This is both good and bad news. It is good in that it shows that American schools are working relatively well for

Table 1.2

Percent of 17-Year-Old Students At or Above Four Reading Proficiency Levels[a]

Race/Ethnicity and Level	1975	1988	1996
Total group			
Level 1	99.7	100.0	100.0
Level 2	96.4	98.9	97.4
Level 3	80.1	85.7	81.4
Level 4	38.7	40.9	38.6
White			
Level 1	99.9	100.0	100.0
Level 2	98.6	99.3	98.5
Level 3	86.2	88.7	86.8
Level 4	43.9	45.4	45.1
African-American			
Level 1	97.7	100.0	99.8
Level 2	82.0	98.0	94.8
Level 3	43.0	75.8	67.2
Level 4	8.1	24.9	18.0
Hispanic			
Level 1	99.3	99.9	99.9
Level 2	88.7	96.3	94.0
Level 3	52.9	71.5	64.2
Level 4	12.6	23.3	20.0

Source: Data from NCES (1999, Table 112).
[a]As measured by the National Assessment of Educational Progress. Levels: 1, follow brief written directions and carry out simple discrete reading tasks; 2, understand, combine ideas, and make inferences based on short uncomplicated passages without specific or sequentially related information; 3, search for specific information, interrelate ideas, and make generalizations about literature; 4, find, understand, summarize, and explain relatively complicated literary and informational material.

some; it is bad in that it documents how poorly American schools are working for others. The average score for Hispanics was 245 and for African-Americans, 236.

The disparity in performance among ethnic groups is also shown by total average SAT scores, reported in Table 1.3. Although the average score for whites was about the same in 1994–1995 as it was in 1975–1976, and the other ethnic groups had shown substantial gains,

Table 1.3
Scholastic Assessment Test (SAT) Score Averages

Race/Ethnicity	1975–1976	1984–1985	1994–1995
All students	903	906	910
White	944	939	946
African-American	686	722	744
Mexican-American	781	808	802
Puerto Rican	765	777	783
Asian-American	932	922	956
Native American	808	820	850
Other	868	839	918

Source: Data from NCES (1999, Table 128).

white achievement remained well above the other groups except for Asian-Americans, who scored higher than whites in 1994–1995.

Although there is some good news in international comparisons, the news is mostly bad. The results of a 20-nation study published in 1997 found that American fourth-graders ranked tenth in mathematical achievement and fourth in science (Beaton, 1997). At the eighth-grade level, American students ranked twenty-seventh in mathematics achievement and twenty-second in science achievement among 41 nations. By the twelfth grade, American students ranked nineteenth in mathematics achievement and sixteenth in science achievement among 21 nations. The good news is in reading. In a study published in 1992, American 9-year-olds ranked second among 27 nations in reading literacy achievement (NCES, 1999, Table 407); among 14-year-olds, American students ranked ninth out of 31 nations (NCES, 1999, Table 408). The international comparisons suggest that our elementary schools are doing a better job of educating our children than are our secondary schools.

The failure of many American students to complete high school and the linkage between dropping out and unemployment and crime are other concerns of policy analysts. For the first time since such statistics have been collected, the United States has fallen behind most other industrialized nations in the rate at which its students complete secondary school (Langemann, 1999). There is also a racial and ethnic bias on this statistic; nearly 92 percent of white 19-year-olds have completed high school compared with 87 percent of African-American students and 75 percent of Hispanic students (NCES, 1999, Table 105).

Only about one-fourth of minority high school dropouts find employment shortly after leaving school, compared with half of white dropouts. Even the high school graduate has difficulty in finding employment; 75 percent of majority students are successful in finding employment shortly after graduation, compared with barely half of minority students. Some 82 percent of persons in prisons are high school dropouts, costing about $24,000 per person per year in public support (Hodgkinson, 1993b).

The link between education level and employment and income is very strong. Of 25- to 34-year-olds in 1998, 94 percent of males holding a bachelor's degree were employed compared to 79 percent of those with only 9–11 years of education and 87 percent graduating from high school (NCES, 1999). Earnings of male dropouts are only 71 percent that of high school graduates and less than half that of college graduates. The relative earnings disadvantage of the dropout has been growing. Relationships are similar for females and minority groups (NCES, 1999).

There are those who think that the criticisms of public schools in the United States are overblown and unwarranted. "Contrary to the prevailing opinion, the American public schools are remarkably good whenever and wherever they are provided with the human and economic resources to succeed" (Berliner, 1993, p. 36; Berliner & Biddle, 1995). Berliner pointed out, for example, that today's students actually average 14 IQ points higher than their grandparents and 7 points higher than their parents. The number of students scoring in the gifted range today is seven times greater than in the generation now retiring from leadership. The average SAT scores for all ethnic groups has improved since 1970. There is widespread agreement that our higher education system is one of our great strengths (Kirst, 1993) and the envy of the world. Despite falling average SAT scores, scores on the Graduate Record Examination (GRE) have been stable for the verbal section, risen 29 points for the quantitative section, and risen 50 points for the analytical section since 1981, even though the number of test takers has increased by 86 percent and the proportion that GRE takers represent of all bachelor degrees awarded increased from 27 percent to 32 percent. Further, 40 percent of all research articles are written by American scholars; no other nation produces more than 7 percent.

It appears that approximately 20 percent of American elementary and secondary students are well served by the current educational system and that another 40 percent are served acceptably well; but the remaining 40 percent are poorly served, and this is the focus of most concern (Hodgkinson, 1993a; Kirst, 1993). Some analysts, however, place the blame not so much on the schools but on the problems that low-achieving students bring to the school door, particularly poverty, physical and emotional handicaps, lack of health care, difficult family conditions, and violent neighborhoods. Although the achievement statistics may suggest that schools are not doing their job as well as in the past, it is also true that their job may be more difficult now than it was in the past. We address this issue in the next section.

The Making of an Underclass

The United States is facing the real possibility of developing a structural underclass, and many believe that the nature of the public school system is a primary cause and a potential instrument for solving the problem. These fears have been supported by findings of the 1990 U.S. Census. More people were living in poverty than a decade earlier, and the middle class shrank while the number of rich grew. The percentage of households living on less than the equivalent of $25,000 per year in current dollars rose to 42 percent from 31 percent a decade earlier. In 1979, three-fourths of Americans were enjoying middle incomes, compared with two-thirds in 1989. At the same time, the percentage of Americans classified as having high incomes grew from 11 percent to 15 percent of the total population.

Many Americans are experiencing a lower standard of living than that which at one time was taken for granted. The purchasing power of average weekly earnings for U.S. workers has actually dropped by 12 percent since 1969. But the hardship has not been borne equally by all Americans. The top 30 percent of U.S. families with the highest earnings have increased their share of national income from 54 percent in 1967 to 58 percent 20 years later, while the share for the bottom 70 percent dropped from 46 percent to 42 percent. The top 30 percent in income are made up primarily of professional and technical workers, usually graduates of four-year colleges, who are prospering, while frontline workers have seen their real wages shrink year after year. From 1972 to 1987, the relative wage of craft workers dropped from 98 percent of that earned by professional and technical

Figure 1.1
Change in wages for selected occupations relative to each other

Source: Commission on the Skills of the American Workforce (1990).

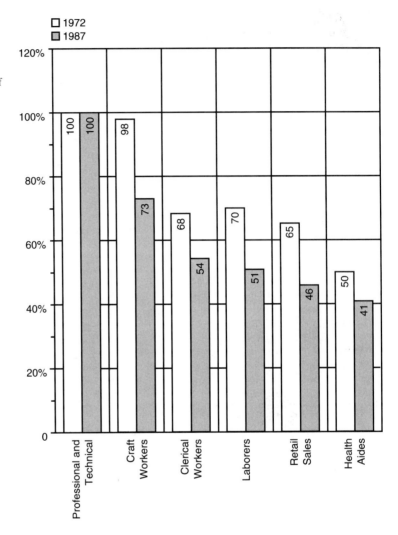

workers to 73 percent; for laborers, the drop was from 70 percent to 51 percent (see Figure 1.1). Despite the robust economy of the latter part of the 1990s, the general pattern prevails.

The problems created by the increasing numbers of children coming from the ranks of poverty is compounded by changes in family structures. During the 1980s and 1990s the characteristics of U.S. families continued to move away from the traditional two-parent two-children configuration; by 1990, barely one-fourth of households were of that variety (Hodgkinson, 1991), fewer in actual number than a decade earlier—the only classification of families to show a decline (see Table 1.4). Households headed by single women increased by 36 percent; those headed by men, by 29 percent, and those of married couples without children, by 17 percent. Sixty percent of all households have no children at all, a fact that makes funding of public schools by locally levied property taxes exceedingly difficult where such levies require voter approval. The 15 million children being raised by single mothers will have about one-third as much family spending on their needs as children being raised by two parents (Hodgkinson, 1991). One-fourth of American children are living in households below

Table 1.4
Numbers of U.S. Households by Characteristics

	1980	1990	Percent Change
All households	80,467,000	93,920,000	+16.7
Family households	59,190,000	66,652,000	+12.4
Married couples	48,990,000	52,837,000	+7.9
Married without children	24,210,000	28,315,000	+17.0
Married with children	24,780,000	24,522,000	−1.0
Single female head	8,205,000	11,130,000	+35.6
Single male head	1,995,000	2,575,000	+29.1
People living alone	18,202,000	22,879,000	+25.7
Living with nonrelatives	3,075,000	4,500,000	+46.3

Source: Data from Hodgkinson (1991).

the poverty level, and 59 percent of all children in poverty belong to households headed by women (NCES, 1991, p. 200).

The proportion of public school enrollment represented by minority groups (those most likely to be ravaged by poverty) is on the rise. In 1976, minorities represented 24 percent of elementary and secondary enrollment. Projections suggest that this proportion will rise to 46 percent by the year 2020 (NCES, 1991). The growth in numbers and proportions of the minority population is due only in part to their higher fertility rates compared with the majority. Another important factor is an upsurge in immigration, especially of persons from Asia and Latin America. Approximately 5 million children of immigrant parents, representing more than 150 languages, enrolled in elementary and secondary schools during the 1990s (Huelskamp, 1993). The trend is expected to continue.

In addition to being three times as likely to be impoverished, minority children are more likely to encounter other "risk" factors, such as coming from a single-parent household, having limited English proficiency, and having a parent or sibling (or both) who has dropped out of school. Minority children are 3.5 times as likely to have two or more of these risk factors as are white children. The effect is also intergenera-

tional; 62 percent of children under age 6 who are below the poverty level have parents who did not complete high school. If one parent completed high school, the rate drops to 26 percent, and it drops to 7 percent if one parent had some schooling beyond high school ("Poverty and Education," 1992).

Family Influences on School Success

School takes up only about 13 percent of the waking hours of a person's first 18 years of life (Walberg, 1984). Children receive their initial instruction in the home and in the community, albeit informally, and those whose parents are well educated usually come to school better prepared to function efficiently in an environment of abstract learning than do children whose parents are less well educated. Schools composed of children who already have developed good learning skills can begin their instruction at a more advanced level than can schools where most of the children enter with poor learning skills. The pervasiveness in U.S. schools of the problem of poor entry-level skills is recognized by the first of the eight national goals for public education, "By the year 2000, all children in America will start school ready to learn."

Research in the United States on the impact of a family's socioeconomic status on the achievement of its children has been clouded by the issue of racial and ethnic group membership. Despite the minority focus, low socioeconomic status has emerged as the dominating detracting factor from achievement, with little, if any, effect being explained independently by minority-group membership. This is not to deny that racial-minority children experience discriminatory situations that have an additional negative impact on the development of self-concept and realistic aspirations and expectations. Some social scientists refer to the treatment of minorities in the United States as functioning more like a caste system than like socioeconomic differentiation (Brown, 1990). As such, minorities quickly learn their castelike status and adopt social habits in order to survive socially and psychologically in schools and elsewhere (Allport, 1958; Myrdal, 1962; Ogbu, 1978; Shade & Edwards, 1987).

Socioeconomic status is only a proxy for *interactions* within a family that *tend* to be related to socioeconomic status. Home environment predicts academic learning twice as well as socioeconomic status of families (Walberg, 1984), but it is much more difficult to measure for research purposes. The "curriculum of the home" includes informed parent–child conversations about everyday events, encouragement and discussion of leisure reading, monitoring and joint analysis of television viewing, expressions of affection and interest in children's academic and personal growth, deferred gratification to accomplish long-range goals, time management, and discipline–reward patterns. In reality, the home environment varies markedly among families with similar financial backgrounds, and many children from families of low socioeconomic status do succeed in school when the home environment is supportive (Clark, 1983; Datcher-Loury, 1989; Lee, 1984; Prom-Jackson, Johnson, & Wallace, 1987; Scott-Jones, 1987; Taylor & Dorsey-Gaines, 1988). Mark (1993), in a study of high-achieving African-American children from low-income, single-parent families, found that the parents who nurtured these children had

high expectations for their children and good communication with them, had high regard for reading, monitored television programs watched by the children, maintained structured households, and established a system of rewards and punishments for the children. The parents were fully aware of their precarious position in society but possessed a sense of conviction in their own abilities and a determination to have their children mature into high-achieving adults.

The W.T. Grant Foundation (1988) study, *The Forgotten Half* (those high school graduates not going on for further education), found that young people want and need adult support. According to their findings, teenagers constantly point to their parents as the most influential adults in their lives. A full 70 percent of high school seniors share their parents' views of what they should do with their lives; and the activity that young people most enjoy sharing with their parents is "just talking." Yet typical American adolescents spend only about 5 minutes per day alone with their fathers and 40 minutes alone with their mothers.

There are other environmental factors that have a direct relationship upon a child's potential success in school. For example, nearly half of all infants are born with one or more factors that mark them for potential school failure later (NEGP, 1993). These include late or no prenatal care, a mother who smoked or drank alcohol during pregnancy, and low maternal weight gain. Nearly 37 percent of all 2-year-olds have not been fully immunized for childhood diseases, and only half of all preschoolers are read to daily by their parents. Further, each year more than 1 million children experience the divorce of their parents; and 60 percent of today's 5-year-olds will live in a single-parent family before they reach the age of 18. Children from single-parent families are less likely to be high achievers; they are consistently more likely to be late to school, truant, and subject to disciplinary action; and they are more than twice as likely to drop out of school (Eitzen, 1992).

Even some privileged families can provide only uneven support for their children's school experiences. Real or perceived economic pressures force most parents to work long hours or at more than one job simply to keep the family's finances on track. Over 50 percent of mothers with children under the age of 6 work outside the home, and about 70 percent of mothers with children between the ages of 6 and 17 do so. As a result, more and more children are being raised in families in which the parents have less and less time for them. This also means that more and more school-age children are spending increasing amounts of time without adult supervision (latchkey children), and more and more preschoolers are being cared for by adults who are not their parents.

Large correlational and status studies are useful in pointing out the overall impact of socioeconomic status on pupil achievement, but they do little to advance our understanding of how the effect is transmitted or what educators can do to intervene. In the latter respect, the work of Basil Bernstein (1971) in England is particularly instructive. He attributed much of the disability of lower-socioeconomic children to differences in language use between lower- and middle-class people. Noting that the general problems involved in teaching children from lower classes are not necessarily derived from a lack of innate capacity to learn, as indicated by intelligence tests, he suggested that the cause is the environment in which they grow up.

Bernstein labeled the communication code typically used by the lower class *restricted*. In the United States, it has been widely recognized that many lower-class African-Americans typically use a different communication code [sometimes referred to as "Black English" or "Ebonics" (Williams, 1975)] from that of the middle-class white majority, but the similarities between this code and communication codes of other lower-class people are not generally recognized. An exception is Foster (1974, p. 118), who noted similarities in patterns of speech between Black English and immigrant groups, although the specific expressions and accents used may vary even from neighborhood to neighborhood within a city, and among cities

and regions. Bernstein (1971, p. 143) suggested that "it is reasonable to argue that the genes of social class may be carried less through a genetic code but far more through a communication code that social class itself promotes."

The middle class also uses a restricted code in its more intimate relationships, but because of the breadth of contact and activities typical of the middle class, it has also developed an "elaborated" code that does not rely on "non-verbal, closely shared, identifications" to serve as a backcloth for understanding (Bernstein, 1961). The elaborated code emphasizes the individual, the abstract, elaboration of process, exploration of motives and intentions, and personalized forms of social control. It is the language of instruction in the school.

Because the language code that typifies the schools is different from the code familiar to lower-class children, the lower-class child is at a severe disadvantage to benefit from school experiences. In commenting on Bernstein's findings, Deutsch (1965) noted that the resulting breakdown in communication between the school and the student is probably a major factor in explaining the generally poor performance of lower-socioeconomic youth in school and their high dropout rate because the student is no longer in communication with anything that is meaningful to him or her in the school.

Heath and McLaughlin (1987) have commented on this phenomenon within an American setting. They pointed out that children who come from families that are strongly oriented toward schooling learn numerous ways to use language in a variety of settings (e.g., dinner conversations, school, ballet classes, tennis and piano lessons, summer camp).

[T]hey [the children] have extensive experience in learning by listening to others tell how to do something, they themselves know how to talk about what they are doing as they do it, and they know how to lay out plans for the future in verbal form. On command, they know how to display in oral or written formats the bits and pieces of knowledge that the school assumes represent academic achievement. (p. 578; also see Heath, 1983)

Children who come from families where the traditional orientation to learning has been through observing and assuming apprenticeship roles beside knowledgeable elders rather than through verbal communication come to school largely untutored in displaying knowledge in verbal form. Heath and McLaughlin have also observed that non–English–speaking parents, even with strong orientations to schooling, often stop speaking the mother tongue to their children, in an effort to speed up the acquisition of English by their children. As a result, such children are denied exposure to sophisticated adult language models and to the wisdom and authority of their parents.

The interrelationships between environment and student achievement are too complex to be explained through the lens of a single discipline. Four main perspectives characterize the literature on school performance of children from lower-socioeconomic status families and racial and cultural minorities: the cultural continuity–discontinuity approach, the secondary cultural continuity approach, cultural reproduction theory, and the culture and cognition approach (Emihovich, 1994). Poor academic achievement by such children is attributed in these theories to a variety of factors, including (1) differences between home and school in interactional, linguistic, and cognitive styles; (2) effects of macroeconomic and social conditions, especially labor market forces and minority groups' beliefs about their access to employment and other social benefits; (3) family values concerning the importance of education, adherence to prevailing social norms, and allegiance to community welfare rather than individual gain; (4) the school's perceived role in reproducing the social order to maintain class and racial barriers to social mobility; (5) student resistance to learning behaviors expected by school authorities which would bestow upon the students identities that are stigmatized among their peers, and (6) individual variations in performance as a function of culturally influenced cognitive capacities.

Several of the foregoing perspectives have been unified through the concept of multiple literacies.

[E]ach literacy is embedded within particular culturally organized settings, shaped by children's early experiences in the home and community environments, and influenced or modified by alternative literacies children encounter daily in schools and other social settings. In short, for children to be successful in school and society, they need to master a broad range of literacy competencies, almost in the sense of being multilingual, to cope with the diversity they can expect to encounter in written and oral formats across a wide array of situations. (Emihovich, 1994, p. 1231)

Research clearly shows that language and cultural differences in students' lives are interwoven with economic and social conditions that facilitate or impede knowledge acquisition. This bonded relationship must be taken into account in designing instructional strategies for children.

In an international review of research on social background and education, Husen (1972) stressed the importance of an action-rich environment in the classroom to assist in developing an elaborated code of language use among those children who come to school without such a code. "The verbalistic feature of the school means a handicap for pupils from homes where the code of communication is 'restricted' rather than 'elaborated.' The more a verbally mediated docility is required, the greater the handicap" (p. 163).

Conversely, the more action-rich a school is, the greater its chances of bringing its linguistically impoverished pupils into the mainstream. A three-way learning process must be established in the classroom among the pupil, the teacher, and the pupil's peers. The peer group should be structured as carefully as the instructional processes used by the teacher (Swanson, 1979); children skilled in using an elaborated code (normally middle class) need to be well represented. The mixing of children alone will not ensure that those not skilled in elaborated codes of communication will acquire such skills; mixing only supports deliberate instructional strategies of the teacher. Without appropriate leadership by the teacher, social class cohesion—and tension among classes—can easily develop within the classroom, reinforcing the pressures of class stratification in the larger society. To preclude this possibility, there needs to be a warm, open, accepting social climate in each classroom and throughout the school. Further, school officials must understand the codes of communication used by the children and deliberately help to develop communication skills using an elaborated code.

Studies of the relationships between home and school show that it is important for parents and educators to work together to develop high-achieving children (Bradley, Rock, Caldwell, Harris, & Hamreck, 1987; Comer, 1980; Durkin, 1984; Reynolds, 1991; Walberg, 1984). Programs that target parent–teacher cooperation and focus on specific achievement goals show the greatest learning effects. The principal plays a key role in establishing and maintaining such relationships.

Heath and McLaughlin (1987) admonished that responses to the generally low achievement of children coming from low-socioeconomic status families can be crafted only if we focus on the total functional requirements of a healthy, curious, productive, and motivated child. This compels us to view the child as an actor in a large social system and to identify the primary networks that make up a child's environment. They suggest that this moves the school from the role of "deliverer" of educational services to the role of "broker" of the multiple services that are available in support of the family and the child.

Peer Influences on Student Achievement

Relationships with peer groups within and outside school also have a strong and direct impact on student achievement (Coleman & Hoffer, 1987). The norms and sanctions generated by fellow students (i.e., youth culture) influence how students respond to the instructional opportunities offered by a school; in designing those experiences, prevailing student attitudes need to be taken into account, especially at the secondary level.

A pupil's achievement is strongly related to the educational backgrounds and aspirations of the other pupils in the school; this is particularly true of at-risk children (Coleman, 1966; Mayeski & Beaton, 1975). Peer groups can provide incentives to high achievement or distractions and disincentives; they determine whether the associations and casual discussions outside the classroom support or undermine the educational mission of the school. Indeed, when parents and educators think of a "good" school, the criterion most frequently used is the nature of the student body, college bound and high achieving being the most preferred.

According to Coleman and Hoffer (1987), in some schools nearly all student social relationships beyond the family revolve around the community of youth in the school. With a high degree of closure, these social relations constitute extensive social capital for the formation of norms and sanctions that can positively shape student behavior. In other schools, students develop most of their social relationships with others the same age outside the school in the neighborhood, in gangs, at work, or elsewhere. In these schools there is little social capital that school personnel can rely on to support their educational mission.

In the 1960s and 1970s, there was a general decline in the strength of the youth communities in schools, a decline manifested in the decreased interest in such school events as interscholastic sports, an increase in the proportion of students holding part-time jobs, and an increase in attention to phenomena that cut across schools, in particular popular music and clothing styles. The reduced focus of students on others within the school reduced the social capital in the youth community of the school and thus reduced the potential of schools to change the students over this period. As a principal might put it, there is "less to work with" (Coleman & Hoffer, 1987, pp. 236–237).

With respect to the nature of the social culture of a school, the norms and sanctions of the peer group may reward athletic prowess, delinquent activities such as drug use and vandalism, social attractiveness, or academic achievement. The effect of the nature of peer values on achievement of educational goals is great when the culture is positive. If the culture supports educational goals, overall academic achievement is enhanced; but if the culture demeans academic achievement, the performance of all pupils is likely to be reduced below potential.

Coleman and Hoffer (1987) drew two implications for school personnel with respect to these possibilities: to develop a student body sufficiently integrated and cohesive that it constitutes social capital that can be a positive force in the lives of students, and to direct that force toward educational objectives. The first goal can best be achieved through collective events in which the entire school is involved, events that compensate for the individualistic nature of the educational process. Interschool competitions are an effective way of doing this, usually taking the form of interscholastic sports. The school cohesion developed around athletics, however, needs to be deliberately and effectively broadened to include other educational objectives.

Pupil–teacher relationships can also be a powerful force in shaping peer values. As cited above, the W.T. Grant Foundation (1988) reported survey evidence that despite popular belief to the contrary, young people want—and need—adult support. A nationwide study of outstanding middle schools reported that students who feel valued by teachers show respect for their schools (George & Oldaker, 1985). A study by Corcoran, Walker, and White (1988) found that many urban teachers want better relations with their students, but their efforts are hampered by disciplinary problems, large class size, lack of time for individual interaction, busing policies, and lack of student participation in

extracurricular activities. Many of these inhibitors can be addressed through school policy and wise leadership.

Thus, past assumptions used by educators in designing school curricula no longer hold across the board. Children are less likely to come from majority backgrounds. They are more likely to be members of nontraditional families, and they are more likely to be poor. Education through high school and beyond is essential if graduates are to be employed in other than menial jobs and to enjoy comfortable standards of living. Well-paying employment opportunities increasingly require sophisticated intellectual skills. Educational leadership is being challenged to design new curricula that recognize the multicultural nature of students, provide institutional support for those at risk, and link schooling and employment. Solving our "educational" crisis will require coordination of schools' efforts with those of other community agencies, including health care, housing, transportation, and social welfare (Dryfoos, 1994; Hodgkinson, 1993a; W.T. Grant Foundation, 1988).

The Education Reform Movement

Waves of Educational Reform

Response to the situation confronting public education has been portrayed as coming in three waves. The first wave, beginning in the mid-1980s, focused on student performance and teacher quality. Structural reform was the focus of the second wave of reform during the early 1990s. The third, and current phase, is *systemic reform,* characterized by two themes: comprehensive change that focuses on many aspects of the system, and policy integration and coordination around a clear set of outcomes (Fuhrman, Elmore, & Massell, 1993). Greater professional discretion is being allowed at the school site under the umbrella of centralized coordination.

To bring focus to the educational reform movement, the state governors joined with

President Bush in 1989 through 1990 and artic- ulated six national goals for public education to be realized by the year 2000 (which became eight with the passage of the Educate America Act in 1994). In 1991, the National Council on Educational Standards and Testing (NCEST) was established by Congress to consider whether and how to develop new standards and tests (Ravitch, 1993). The council recommended the establishment of voluntary national standards in key subject areas and a national system of achievement tests. The work of the National Council of Teachers of Mathematics (NCTM) in developing national standards in mathematics (published in 1989) served as a model for doing this. Following the NCTM model, the federal government funded an effort by the National Academy of Sciences to develop standards in science. Similar arrangements were negotiated with other professional groups to develop stan- dards in history, the arts, civics, geography, English, and foreign languages. Operating un- der the principle that *federalism* does not mean the supremacy of the federal government, but rather a careful balancing of interests of the dif- ferent levels of government, the projects were not to create a national curriculum but to de- scribe what *all* children should know and be able to do in a particular field. In this case it meant steering a course between two extremes: the familiar pattern of complete local control— in which there were no standards or widely dif- ferent standards from district to district—and the imposition of a federal one-size-fits-all pro- gram (Ravitch, 1993, p. 769).

Although there was a change of presidents in 1992, there was little change in overall strategy. It should be recognized that this has been a bi- partisan effort from the beginning and that Pres- ident Clinton was influential in shaping the America 2000 design as the 1989 Chair of the National Governors' Association.

A National Education Goals Panel was au- thorized by the 1994 Educate America Act to monitor progress being made toward those goals and to coordinate efforts of state and na-

tional organizations, but bipartisanism broke down at this point and the panel was never ac- tivated. The issue that divided the two parties was disagreement over the level of government to establish and monitor the standards-setting process. The Republicans felt that such author- ity should remain with the states, whereas the Democrats preferred to have it placed with the federal government. In much the same way, the development of national tests to measure progress in meeting the goals has stalled. The National Assessment Governing Board is au- thorized to draft test questions, but it is not per- mitted to validate them.

Although the reform movement has experi- enced an unusual amount of voluntary coordi- nation to this point at the national level, most of the action is taking place at the state, school dis- trict, and school levels. The best example of sys- temic change is the state of Kentucky, where all elements of the education system have been modified, including its governance and finance (Guskey, 1994). The Chicago school system has undergone a radical form of decentralization, placing policy-making authority in the hands of lay-controlled boards attached to individual schools (Dunn, James-Gross, & Trampe, 1998; G. A. Hess, 1991; J. K. Hess, 1999). Charter schools that are largely independent of school districts have been legalized in several states (Finn, Manno, & Bierlein, 1996; Office of Edu- cational Research and Improvement, 1998), Florida has authorized a statewide system of ed- ucational vouchers, and Minneapolis and Cleve- land have limited programs in operation. Site- based decision making and management are the order of the day, and increasingly, states and school districts are allowing family choice of schooling.

There is also increasing involvement of the private sector in the running and support of public schools. The New American Schools De- velopment Corporation was formed by U.S. business leaders in July 1991 at the request of President Bush. The purpose of the corporation is to underwrite the design and implementation of a new generation of "break the mold" schools. It has raised millions of dollars from private sources to finance the effort. In response to its initial call for proposals, 686 design teams responded, and 11 of them were selected to be supported financially for further development over a five-year period (Olson, 1992). The overriding criteria for selection was the likelihood that a design would enable all students to reach the national education goals and attain "world-class" standards (Kearns, 1993; Mecklenburger, 1992). Several of the resulting models were included in the list of exemplary reform models that schools may emulate to qualify for grants under the bipartisan Comprehensive School Reform Demonstration Program, passed by Congress and signed into law in 1997. Although most partnerships are organized at the local level, in 1996 there was a summit meeting of the National Governors Association and leading business executives focusing exclusively on reform at the state level.

Members of the private sector are also working in other ways to promote and to profit from school reform. Their efforts range from school–business partnerships to creating foundations and trusts to outright entrepreneurial initiatives. The most ambitious of the latter type of initiatives was launched by Tennessee businessman and media magnate Chris Whittle. His Edison Project, which was originally intended to be a network of private schools, has developed a design for a network of publicly chartered and contracted schools to operate in urban areas across the country.

Emerging Patterns of Reform

Obviously, there is much concern over the quality of our educational system and the implications it has for our societal well-being. The concern has generated much debate and experimentation. The issue of national goals, for example, raises a myriad of controversial issues such as national standards, a national curriculum, national assessment, and national teacher certification. There are also issues of balance:

between federal, state, and local governments, between political and professional authorities, and between public and private sectors. Finally, there is the issue of balance between the rights and responsibilities of parents versus those of the public. Structural and financial changes will emerge from the current turmoil. The related issues strike at the heart of American social beliefs and traditions.

Petrie (1990) suggested that the restructuring of the teaching profession initiated by the second wave of reform has profound implications for our concept of educational leadership:

> It seems clear that if teachers are to be viewed as reflective practitioners exercising professional judgment, educational leaders will not tell such professionals what to do. There will not be detailed syllabi imposed. Bureaucratic rules and regulations will be kept to a minimum. Structures will be developed that allow a broad range of discretion and influence, not merely in how to teach the syllabus once the classroom door has been closed, but in the very construction of those syllabi. The leadership will be associated with groups of semi-autonomous professionals rather than the leadership associated with hired help. Relationships will probably look more like the collegial models of higher education or of the associations of professionals in accounting or architectural firms, or like health maintenance organizations rather than like the industrial labor–management arrangements. (p. 22)

Petrie's views are compatible with those of Cuban (1988), who laments that teaching and administering are no longer viewed as one career even though they are anchored in a common history sharing common roles. Cuban views teaching as central to thoughtful administration. According to him, two images dominate teaching and administering schools—the technical and the moral—and they share three common roles: instructional, managerial, and political. Whereas the images and roles are played out in different settings, teaching and administration are inexorably entangled. The instructional role is central to teaching, but there are elements of the political and the managerial. The political role dominates the superintendency, and principalships are likely to experience all three roles in relatively equal proportions.

Cuban also sees the current design of schools and school systems as standing in the way of providing the quality of education that we all desire for our children. In differentiating between leaders and managers, he sees leaders as people who shape the goals, motivations, and actions of others, while managers maintain current organizational arrangements efficiently and effectively. Leaders frequently initiate change to reach existing and new goals; the overall direction of management is toward maintenance. He argues that

> schools as they are presently organized press teachers, principals, and superintendents toward managing rather than leading, toward maintaining what is rather than moving to what can be. The structures of schooling and the incentives buried within them produce a managerial imperative. (Cuban, 1988, p. xxi)

Cuban sees school autonomy as the necessary condition for leadership to arise.

School leaders of the future will not only be working with a student body markedly different from that of the past, but the organizational structures and professional and political relationships are also likely to be quite different. The relationships between teachers and administrators are likely to be collegial rather than authoritarian. Principals and teachers are likely to have greater professional discretion as many decisions formally made at the district, state, and federal levels are left to schools. Local, state, and federal authorities will continue to set certain parameters, however. We can expect states, in particular, to set achievement standards, to design curricula to meet those standards, and to administer examinations to identify schools failing to meet standards. Parents and community representatives are likely to have greater influence on the organization and operation of the schools through membership on school councils or through parental choice of schooling. As a result, acceptable leadership

styles and strategies will be quite different in the future from what they have been in the past.

Having looked at the symptoms of malaise and early efforts made to address them, we need to examine the nature of the educational system that produced the malaise because this is the system within which new leaders must begin their careers. We start by briefly examining the historical origins of the current structure of school governance.

The Scope and Structure of School Governance

The Historical Development of Public Education

Collective concern over formal education of the young dates to the beginning of European settlement of the continental United States. Massachusetts was particularly influential in setting the pattern for public education. It was the Massachusetts Colony that first required parents to train their children in reading and writing, first required towns to establish schools, first appropriated colonial funds to encourage the establishment of schools, and first permitted towns to use revenue from property taxation to support schooling. All of this was accomplished before 1650. These events, however, must be interpreted in light of the interrelationships between the government of the Massachusetts Colony and the Congregational (Puritan) Church. Suffrage and office holding were limited to male church members, a minority of the total population. The property tax that supported the school also supported the church and its clergy. The "meetinghouse" served as the school as well as the church and the town hall (Johnson, 1904). This early pattern of community control of schools in Massachusetts left its imprint on the organization of public education in the United States today, although the connection between church and state has been severed.

Several of the authors of the U.S. Constitution in 1787 had firm beliefs about the importance of an educated citizenry to the success of the new republic. But the Constitution itself is silent on the subject of education; and the Tenth Amendment included in the Bill of Rights assured that the powers not specifically delegated to the federal government were "reserved to the States respectively, or to the people." Founders such as Thomas Jefferson pursued the provision of public education at the state level. In his *Notes on the State of Virginia,* written in 1781–1782, Jefferson (1968) argued: "Every government degenerates when trusted to the rulers of the people alone. The people themselves therefore are its only safe depositories. And to render even them safe, their minds must be improved . . . " (p. 390).

In seeking additional funds for education from the New York State Legislature early in the nineteenth century, Governor DeWitt Clinton (1909) noted the importance of state sponsorship of education in a democracy:

> The first duty of government, and the surest evidence of good government, is the encouragement of education. A general diffusion of knowledge is the precursor and protector of republican institutions; and in it we must confide as the conservative power that will watch over our liberties, and guard against fraud, intrigue, corruption and violence. (p. 114)

In a desperate bid in 1834 to save Pennsylvania's newly enacted common school legislation from the repeal of tax cutters, Thaddeus Stevens (1900), fully aware of the externalities of public education, stated plainly the common benefit to be realized from those tax dollars.

> Many complain of this tax, not so much on account of its amount, as because it is for the benefit of others and not themselves. This is a great mistake; it is for their own benefit, inasmuch as it perpetuates the government and insures the due administration of the laws under which they live, and by which their lives and property are protected (p. 520).

Stevens went on to draw the connection between education and the prevention of crime and argued that it is wiser, less expensive, and more humane to aid "that which goes to support his fellow-being from becoming a criminal,

and to obviate the necessity of those humiliating [penal] institutions." This is a theme that is commonly repeated even today.

Although the importance of education to the general welfare has been recognized traditionally, it should be noted that education was originally promoted for religious, political, and social purposes, not for the economic reasons that it is today. The link between economic productivity and education had been noted by Adam Smith (1776/1993) in his treatise on *The Wealth of Nations* in 1776, but it wasn't until the latter half of the twentieth century that economic theory (human capital theory in particular) became strongly influential in the formulation of public policy on education.

Because of a desire to limit the powers of the federal government and because of the sheer infeasibility in the eighteenth and nineteenth centuries of providing human services nationally, education was made a function of the states. Even at the state level, the dispersion of the population, the primitive means of communication, and the general lack of resources made central control of education impractical. Thus, the states invented the school district as a local form of government to create and oversee schools. Cubberley (1947) commented on the spread of the school district concept nationwide:

> As an administrative and taxing unit it was well suited to the primitive needs and conditions of our early national life. Among a sparse and hard-working rural population, between whom intercourse was limited and intercommunication difficult, and with whom the support of schools was as yet an unsettled question, local control answered a very real need. The simplicity and democracy of the system was one of its chief merits. Communities or neighborhoods which wanted schools and were willing to pay for them could easily meet and organize a school district, vote to levy a school tax on their own property, employ a teacher, and organize and maintain a school. . . . On the other hand, communities which did not desire schools or were unwilling to tax themselves for them could do without them, and let the free-school idea alone. (pp. 212–213)

Cubberley's description points to one of the difficulties of the district system once universal education became the policy of a state. The district system worked well for the willing and able, but for those who were unwilling, there was not the leadership to organize a district, and for those who were not able, there were not the resources. Inequities within the district system became apparent even during the colonial period, but with the increasing concentration of capital wealth through industrialization and urbanization, inequities became much more severe in the nineteenth and twentieth centuries.

Attempts to address these inequities began in the nineteenth century through greater state oversight, the beginning of state aid to school districts, and the encouragement of school district consolidation. Districts that voluntarily came into existence, however, quickly attached loyalty to their achievements and took great pride in them, with the result that they were not responsive to criticism of their endeavors from the state and resented any and all constraints placed on them. Those areas that chose not to operate a common school were equally resistant to external pressure to do so, especially when it involved compulsory taxation.

In an effort to establish order out of chaos, state boards of education were formed and provided with an executive officer. The first state to take such action was New York in 1812. As testimony to the sensitive nature of the position, New York's first superintendent of instruction served only until 1821, when the office was eliminated. A similar office was not created in New York until 1854. Horace Mann, the first secretary to the Board of Education of Massachusetts, ran into similar difficulty; however, attempts to dissolve his office and the board were unsuccessful.

The first school districts to go through the process of consolidation were in cities. Whereas New England cities were coterminous with their school districts from the beginning, this was not typically true of more western cities. Buffalo, the first city to employ a superintendent of schools,

serves as a good illustration. Although it had private schools earlier, the first school supported by taxes was established in 1818. By 1837, the city had 15,000 inhabitants and seven one-teacher school districts. That year, a superintendent of schools was appointed to supervise and to coordinate those seven schools, to establish schools in wards of the city that were without schools, and to provide for a central high school. Detroit, Chicago, and Cleveland followed similar patterns. A few cities continue the practice of multiple school districts within the city limits.

Extensive consolidation of rural school districts had to wait until improved means of transportation became available—well into the twentieth century. The number of school districts did not show a marked decrease until after World War II. In 1930, the number exceeded 127,000 nationwide (NCES, 1999); now, the number has dropped to less than 15,000 districts. Today, the tradition of local control remains strong, but the inequities that are inherent in such a policy are a primary cause of the current system's malaise (Kozol, 1991). Satisfying national and state educational concerns while accommodating unique local needs and priorities remains a dilemma.

The structural, organizational, and curricular changes in the public provision of educational services during the late nineteenth and early twentieth centuries reflected larger social, political, and economic changes experienced by the United States, including industrialization, urbanization, and massive immigration. The net result of these developments was a rapid growth of cities, many having substantial slum sections made up of migrants from the countryside and of immigrants, largely from rural and impoverished sections of Europe. In 1820, there was only one city in the United States that exceeded 100,000 in population; by 1860, there were nine. In 1820, there were only 34 communities with populations over 5000; by 1860, there were 229 (DeYoung, 1989).

With the coming of industrialization, a number of educational advocates became interested in the vocational possibilities of education. The federal government encouraged the development of vocational education with the Morrill Act of 1862, which provided land grants to states, the proceeds from which were to be used to establish colleges wherein agriculture, mechanical arts, and military tactics could be taught. Subsequently, in 1890, the federal government made available money grants for the same purpose. The federal government first made money grants available to secondary education in 1917 for the purpose of encouraging vocational programs at that level.

The early twentieth century saw the formalization of the state's role in the financing of education. At the turn of the century, state involvement was minimal, representing less than 15 percent of total expenditures and distributed primarily in the form of categorical aid. A practical design for equalizing local resources was developed by Strayer and Haig in 1923 in the form of a foundation program that continues to serve as the basis for distributing general aid to schools in most states. Today, state financial support of elementary and secondary education exceeds that provided by local government; federal support represents about 6 percent of total expenditures.

Equity among school districts and among pupils became an increasing concern during the 1950s, 1960s, and 1970s, spurred on by the civil rights movement and litigation in both state and federal courts. At the federal level, the Elementary and Secondary Education Act of 1965 assumed a strategy of compensatory education to meet the special needs of at-risk children; other legislation championed the rights of disabled persons and affirmative action. Legislation similar to that adopted at the federal level was enacted by the states. Tyack, Lowe, and Hansot (1984) described the scope of these programs:

> The redistribution of funds to the needy, increased educational attainment among youth from poor and minority families, new protections of student rights, willingness to address controversial issues, attempts to adapt the school cur-

riculum to a pluralistic population, sensitivity to ethnic and linguistic differences, attempts to remedy bias by gender, efforts to desegregate schools—these were the fruit of a generation of deliberate campaigns to render schools more equal and just. (p. 219)

The schools had reached out to include formerly excluded populations. As schools tried to assist more heterogeneous and needy students, the task of educating all grew harder and the results more ambiguous. In including them, educational costs increased dramatically and average achievement scores dropped, giving the perception of declining standards and less efficiency. The current pressure for "higher" standards is due in part to the recognition that it is not sufficient only to involve formerly excluded populations in the mainstream education system; in addition, these populations must be brought up to the levels of achievement of the majority if they are to be fully participating and contributing members of society.

The Current Organization of School Governance

Governance patterns constitute a network of educational resources available to highly diverse communities with highly diverse sets of interests. Although the particulars vary from state to state, the dominant pattern of educational governance that has evolved provides five levels of influence: the federal government, the state, intermediate districts, school districts, and schools. The authority for making policy is concentrated at two of these levels: the state and the school district.

State Authority.   The primary level of authority is the state, as represented by the legislature, governor, state board of education and superintendent, state education department, and state courts. This level is responsible for establishing basic policy for the system, including its financing, and overseeing and coordinating its components. Structural and financial considerations are usually attended to through formal legislation involving the governor and the legislature.

Oversight of the education law within allowed discretion is delegated to the state board of education and state superintendent of schools. State boards of education are most commonly appointed by the governors, although some are popularly elected. In New York and South Carolina they are elected by the state legislatures, and in Washington, they are elected by local school board members. The chief state school officer (CSSO) serves as head of the state education department and in most cases is the chief executive of the state school board. The CSSO is most commonly a professional educator appointed by the state board of education, although in some states he or she is appointed by the governor and popularly elected in others. State education departments are the administrative agencies that implement the education laws of the states and policies of the state school boards.

States exercise their authority over public education through general statements in their constitutions that give state legislatures authority to establish a system of public schools. For example, the New Jersey Constitution provides that the state legislature shall provide a "thorough and efficient" system of education. For the most part, the detail of school governance (i.e., procedures for establishing, financing, and governing school districts, teacher certification, etc.) is established by statutes enacted by state legislatures or regulations established by state boards of education. This permits states a great deal of flexibility in reforming school governance structures without going through the cumbersome process of constitutional amendment.

School Districts. The second level of authority is the local school district which is charged with implementing state policy. School districts are governed by boards of education that focus on the delivery of educational services. Most school boards are fiscally independent (i.e., have taxing authority), although some are fiscally dependent on another unit of local government, such as the city or county. School board members are typically elected in non-partisan elections, although some board members are appointed, especially in larger cities. One of the board's most important responsibilities is to appoint a superintendent of schools to serve as chief executive officer of the school district and to supervise its professional and support personnel.

Hawaii is the only state to function as a single unit and, with 165,000 students, it is smaller than a number of large city districts. Texas leads the states in the number of school districts with 1052. All are fiscally independent. California has 1002 school districts, including 302 that are unified (provide for pupils in all grades K–12), 593 that operate elementary schools only, and 107 that operate high schools only (Gold, Smith, & Lawton, 1995). Over half of California's school districts enroll fewer than 500 pupils and all are fiscally dependent in that another unit of government provides for their financial support. Of Maine's 284 districts, 211 are fiscally dependent, while the others are fiscally independent.

A much different policy of school district organization than California's, but less common, is illustrated by Maryland. Maryland's school districts are organized by county and the city of Baltimore. It has 24 school districts, all of which are fiscally dependent. The county organization prevails in the southeastern region of the country; Florida, for example, has 67 fiscally independent school districts, and Alabama has 127 fiscally dependent school districts. Some western states also follow a regional pattern of school district organization. Nevada has 17 fiscally independent school districts, and Wyoming has 49 fiscally independent districts (Gold et al., 1995). There is much less inequality among school districts as far as financial and other provisions in states whose districts are organized along county lines than in state's whose districts are organized into subcounty units.

Schools. The school is the basic operating unit; but until recently, this third level is usually permitted little discretion, as it is constrained by policies formulated at higher levels. The range of discretion at the school level is likely to increase in the future as school-site management and governance reforms are implemented. This discretion may not always be placed in professional hands, however. As already noted, in Chicago, policy making has been entrusted to school-level boards that have professional representation but are controlled by laypersons.

Intermediate Units.   The intermediate unit or district is the middle echelon in a state system, serving as an arm of the state while performing services for affiliated school districts of a region. Its organization and governance vary markedly from state to state, and some state systems do not include any intermediate unit, especially in those states where school districts are organized at the county level. It typically has no direct or operational authority over local school districts but may facilitate state regulatory functions. It provides certain administrative and supervisory functions as well as supplementary educational programs and services where substantial economies of scale can be realized, as with occupational education, education of the severely handicapped, staff development, and maintaining information networks and systems.

Federal Authority.   The fifth level of governance is the federal government. Although the U.S. Constitution is silent about education, leaving responsibility for it to the states, from time to time Congress does pass legislation under its authority to provide for "the general Welfare," national defense, and the protection of civil rights. The Office of Education, more recently upgraded to the Department of Education, was created in the Executive Branch to administer federal laws and to keep statistics. The Secretary of Education, who heads the Department of Education, is appointed by the President with congressional approval. The secretary is a member of the President's cabinet.

Federal courts are arbitrators of the U.S. Constitution. Litigation concerning school desegregation and school finance inequities have invoked provisions of the Fifth and Fourteenth Amendments to the Constitution. The Fifth Amendment restrains the federal government from depriving any person of "life, liberty or property without due process of law." In the wake of the Civil War, the Fourteenth Amendment was adopted to extend this restraint to the states. The amendment also restrains states and their agents, including school officials, from denying any person "the equal protection of the laws."

Religious and Other Private Schools.   The right of parents to send their children to private schools has been clearly established by judicial decisions. Approximately 11 percent of school-age children are educated in such schools. Unlike many countries in the world, however, religiously affiliated elementary and secondary schools are not permitted to receive public monies in the United States, although children attending such schools may have access to publicly provided services, especially transportation and some compensatory services. The basis for exclusion of public funds for religiously oriented schools is a narrow interpretation by the courts of the First Amendment of the U.S. Constitution, which states that "Congress shall make no law respecting an establishment of religion, or prohibiting the free exercise thereof." This provision was made applicable to the states by the Fourteenth Amendment; but many state constitutions have provisions of their own which are less ambiguous, clearly stating the prohibition of the use of public funds or credit in support of any activity, including operation of schools, sponsored by religious groups.

Summary

In this chapter we have described the structural context of education in which today's leaders must function. The prevailing pattern of school governance outside our major cities is one of small, self-governing school districts that function within general parameters set by state and federal governments. The economic, ethnic, and social characteristics of school district populations tend to be relatively homogeneous within their boundaries, but very diverse across boundaries. Despite decades of judicial and legislative efforts at all levels to desegregate the schools and make the distribution of resources more equitable, this local control tradition has perpetuated the status quo. At least 40 percent of the clients of the public schools are still achieving at unacceptably low levels. Correcting the inequitable flow of resources while maintaining the vitality and flexibility of decentralized governance is one of the major challenges facing today's educational leadership.

The remedy appears to be systemic reform that involves whole-school reform along with site-based decision making, family choice of schools, and statewide standards, curricula, and assessment. In designing the new schools and their curricula, the nature and influence of family and peer characteristics on behavior and achievement must be accommodated. The climate in which education professionals will practice in the twenty-first century will be quite different from that experienced in the twentieth century demanding a new kind of leadership that is transformational and collegial rather than hierarchical.

Activities for Discussion

1. Collect statistics on the achievement of students in a nearby school or school district. Compare them with those of regional, state, and national norms and with those collected by other members of your class. What are the implications of your findings for school, district, state, and national policy? For schools and districts studied by members of your class, look for relationships between pupil achievement and demographic characteristics, expenditure levels, quality of teaching staffs, and facilities.

2. Select one of the school reform proposals from the following list; study its pros and cons and make a recommendation concerning its acceptance or rejection and under what circumstances.

   a. School site management
   b. Parental choice of schools
   c. Raising high school graduation standards
   d. Year-round schooling and/or longer school day/week
   e. State or national assessment
   f. National teacher certification
   g. State or national curriculum

3. Discuss the "Goals 2000" listed in Table 1.1. Do you believe that they represent the most important challenges to public schools in the United States today? What changes will have to be made in the elementary and secondary schools of the United States if these goals (or goals that you think are more important) are to be realized?

4. Describe possible systems for coordinating the delivery of social services (including educational services) to a child and his or her family. What are the advantages and disadvantages of each design?

5. Describe possible instructional systems for accommodating the diversity of backgrounds found in a school's pupil population. What are the advantages and disadvantages of each design?

6. Discuss the advantages and disadvantages of the following alternative arrangements for expanding diversity in schooling options:

   a. The current arrangement of free publicly financed and operated schools with direct aid to private schools prohibited but allowing supporting services that benefit children attending private schools
   b. Educational vouchers, with options among public and private schools
   c. Tax deductions for tuition and other expenses incurred in public and private education
   d. Tax credits that rebate the cost of tuition up to a specified amount
   e. Direct aid to private schools
   f. Open enrollment among public schools without public aid for private schools

References

Allport, G. (1958). *The nature of prejudice.* Garden City, NY: Doubleday.

Beaton, A. E. (1997). *Mathematics achievement in the primary school years: IEA's 3rd international mathematics and science study, 1997.* Chestnut Hill, MA: Boston College.

Berliner, R. F. (1993). Mythology and the American system of education. In S. Elam (Ed.), *The state of the nation's public schools: A conference report* (pp. 36–54). Bloomington, IN: Phi Delta Kappa.

Berliner, D. C., & Biddle, B. J. (1995). *The manufactured crisis: Myth, fraud, and the attack on America's public schools.* Reading, MA: Addison-Wesley.

Bernstein, B. (1961). Social structure, language and learning. *Educational Research, 3,* 163–176.

Bernstein, B. (1971). *Class codes and control: Vol. I. Theoretical studies towards a sociology of language.* London: Routledge & Kegan Paul.

Bradley, R., Rock, S., Caldwell, B., Harris, P., & Hamreck, H. (1987). Home environment and school performance among black elementary school children. *Journal of Negro Education, 56,* 499–509.

Brown, F. (1990). The language of politics, education and the disadvantaged. In S. L. Jacobson & J. A. Conway (Eds.), *Educational leadership in an age of reform* (pp. 83–100). New York: Longman.

Clark, R. (1983). *Family life and school achievement: Why poor black children succeed or fail.* Chicago: University of Chicago Press.

Clinton, D. (1909). Annual message to the legislature. In C. Z. Lincoln (Ed.), *State of New York: Messages from the governors* (Vol. III, p. 114). Albany, NY: Lyon.

Coleman, J. S. (1966). *Equality of educational opportunity.* Washington, DC: Office of Education, U.S. Department of Health, Education, and Welfare.

Coleman, J. S., & Hoffer, T. (1987). *Public and private high schools: The impact of communities.* New York: Basic Books.

Comer, J. (1980). *School power.* New York: Free Press.

Commission on the Skills of the American Workforce. (1990). *America's choice: High skills or low wages!* Rochester, NY: National Center on Education and the Economy.

Corcoran, T. B., Walker, L. J., & White, J. L. (1988). *Working in urban schools.* Washington, DC: Institute for Educational Leadership.

Cuban, L. (1988). *The managerial imperative and the practice of leadership in schools.* Albany, NY: State University of New York Press.

Cubberley, E. P. (1947). *Public education in the United States.* Cambridge, MA: Riverside Press.

Datcher-Loury, L. (1989). Family background and school achievement among low income blacks. *Journal of Human Resources, 24,* 528–544.

Deutsch, M. (1965). The role of social class in language development and cognition. *American Journal of Orthopsychiatry, 35,* 78–88.

DeYoung, A. J. (1989). *Economics and American education: A historical and critical overview of the impact of economic theories on schooling in the United States.* New York: Longman.

Drucker, P. F. (1989). *The new realities: In government and politics, in economics and business, in society and world view.* New York: Harper & Row.

Dryfoos, J. G. (1994). *Full service schools: A revolution in health and social services for children, youth and families.* San Francisco: Jossey-Bass.

Dunn, R. J., James-Gross, L., & Trampe, C. (1998). Decentralized budgeting: A study in implementation and implications. *The Journal of School Business Management, 10*(1), 22–28.

Durkin, D. (1984). Poor black children who are successful readers. *Urban Education, 18,* 53–76.

Eitzen, D. S. (1992). Problem students: The sociocultural roots. *Phi Delta Kappan, 73,* 584–590.

Emihovich, C. (1994). Cultural continuities and discontinuities in education. In T. Husen & T. N. Postlethwaite (Eds.), *The international encyclopedia of education* (2nd ed., Vol. 3, pp. 1227–1233). Oxford: Pergamon Press.

Finn, C. E., Jr., Manno, B. V., & Bierlein, L. (1996). *Charter schools in action: What have we learned?* Indianapolis, IN: Educational Excellence Network, Hudson Institute.

Foster, H. L. (1974). *Ribbin', jivin', and playin' the dozens: The unrecognized dilemma of inner city schools.* Cambridge, MA: Ballinger.

Fuhrman, S. H., Elmore, R. F., & Massell, D. (1993). School reform in the United States: Putting it into context. In S. L. Jacobson & R. Berne (Eds.), *Reforming education: The emerging systemic approach* (pp. 3–27). Thousand Oaks, CA: Corwin Press.

Galbraith, J. K. (1992). *The culture of contentment.* Boston: Houghton Mifflin.

George, P. S., & Oldaker, L. L. (1985). A national survey of middle school effectiveness. *Educational Leadership, 42,* 81.

Gold, S. D., Smith, D. M., & Lawton, S. B. (1995). *Public school finance programs in the United States and Canada, 1993–94.* Albany, NY: Center for the Study of States.

Graham, P. A. (1999). Delineating the boundaries of a people's aspiration: Our rhetoric of educational access often has belied a contradictory reality. *Education Week, 18,* 20, 44–45, 50.

Guskey, T. R. (1994). *High stakes performance assessment: Perspective on Kentucky's educational reform.* Thousand Oaks, CA: Corwin Press.

Heath, S. B. (1983). *Ways with words: Language, life and work in communities and classrooms.* Cambridge: Cambridge University Press.

Heath, S. B., & McLaughlin, M. W. (1987). A child resource policy: Moving beyond dependence on school and family. *Phi Delta Kappan, 68,* 576–580.

Hess, G. A., Jr. (1991). *School restructuring, Chicago style.* Thousand Oaks, CA: Corwin Press.

Hess, J. K., Jr. (1999). Understanding achievement (and other) changes under Chicago school reform. *Educational Evaluation and Policy Analysis, 21,* 1, 67–83.

Hodgkinson, H. (1991). Reform versus reality. *Phi Delta Kappan, 73,* 9–16.

Hodgkinson, H. (1993a). American education: The good, the bad, and the task. In S. Elam (Ed.), *The state of the nation's public schools: A conference report* (pp. 13–23). Bloomington, IN: Phi Delta Kappa.

Hodgkinson, H. (1993b). Keynote address. In S. Elam (Ed.), *The state of the nation's public schools: A conference report* (pp. 194–208). Bloomington, IN: Phi Delta Kappa.

Hoff, D. J. (1999). With 2000 looming, chances of meeting national goals iffy. *Education Week, 18* (18), 1, 28–30.

Huelskamp, R. M. (1993). Perspectives on education in America. *Phi Delta Kappan, 74,* 718–721.

Husen, T. (1972). *Social background and educational career: Research perspectives on equality of educational opportunity.* Paris: Organization for Economic Cooperation and Development.

Jefferson, T. (1968). Notes on the state of Virginia. In *The annals of America* (Vol. 2, pp. 563–573). Chicago: Encyclopaedia Britannica.

Johnson, C. (1904). *Old-time schools and school books.* New York: Macmillan.

Johnston, R. C., & Sandham, J. L. (1999). States only part of the way toward their goals for 2000. *Education Week, 18* (18), 31.

Kearns, D. T. (1993). Towards a new generation of American schools. *Phi Delta Kappan, 74,* 773–776.

Kirst, M. W. (1993). Strengths and weaknesses of American education. In S. Elam (Ed.), *The state of the nation's public schools: A conference report* (pp. 3–12). Bloomington, IN: Phi Delta Kappa.

Kozol, J. (1991). *Savage inequalities: Children in America's schools.* New York: Crown.

Kuhn, T. S. (1970). *The structure of scientific revolutions* (2nd ed.). Chicago: University of Chicago Press.

Langemann, E. C. (1999). The changing meaning of a continuing challenge: Will the scholarly unraveling of education's "black box" enlarge the concept of access? *Education Week, 18* (20), 47–49.

Lazerson, M. (1999). Access, outcomes, and educational opportunity: Time lines of a historic commitment–and an abrupt about-face. *Education Week, 18* (20), 46, 48–50.

Lee, C. (1984). An investigation of psychosocial variables related to academic success for rural black adolescents. *Journal of Negro Education, 53,* 424–434.

Mark, D. L. H. (1993). *High achieving African-American children in low income single parent families: The home learning environment.* Unpublished doctoral dissertation, State University of New York at Buffalo.

Mayeski, G. W., & Beaton, A. E. (1975). *Special studies of our nation's schools.* Washington, DC: Office of Education, U.S. Department of Health, Education, and Welfare.

Mecklenburger, J. A. (1992). The breaking of the "break-the-mold" express. *Phi Delta Kappan, 74,* 280–289.

Myrdal, G. (1962). *The American dilemma: The Negro problem and modern democracy* (Vols. 1 and 2). New York: Harper & Row.

Naisbitt, J. (1982). *Megatrends: Ten new directions transforming our lives.* New York: Warner Books.

Naisbitt, J., & Aburdene, P. (1990). *Megatrends 2000: Ten new directions for the 1990s*. New York: Morrow.

National Center for Education Statistics. (1991). *The condition of education 1991*. Washington, DC: Office of Education Research and Improvement, U.S. Department of Education.

National Center for Education Statistics. (1999). *The Condition of education 1999*. Washington, DC: Office of Education Research and Improvement, U.S. Department of Education.

National Center for Education Statistics. (1999). *Digest of educational statistics*. Washington, DC: Office of Education Research and Improvement, U.S. Department of Education.

National Commission on Excellence in Education. (1983). *A nation at risk: The imperative for educational reform*. Washington, DC: U.S. Government Printing Office.

National Education Goals Panel. (1993). *National education goals report, Volume One: The national report*. Washington, DC: U.S. Government Printing Office.

National Education Goals Panel. (1998). *National education goals report: Building a nation of learning, 1998*. Washington, DC: U.S. Government Printing Office.

Office of Educational Research and Improvement. (1998). *A national study of charter schools, 1998*. Washington, DC: U.S. Department of Education.

Ogbu, J. (1978). *Minority education and caste*. New York: Academic Press.

Olson, L. (1992). 11 design teams are tapped to pursue their visions of "break the mold" schools. *Education Week, 11*(40), 1, 47.

Petrie, H. G. (1990). Reflections on the second wave of reform: Restructuring the teaching profession. In S. L. Jacobson & J. A. Conway (Eds.), *Educational leadership in an age of reform* (pp. 14–29). White Plains, NY: Longman.

Poverty and education. (1992). *Education Week, 11*(16), 5.

Prom-Jackson, S., Johnson, S., & Wallace, M. (1987). Home environment, talented minority youth and school achievement. *Journal of Negro Education, 56*, 111–121.

Ravitch, D. (1993). Launching a revolution in standards and assessments. *Phi Delta Kappan, 74*, 767–772.

Reynolds, A. (1991). Early schooling of children at risk. *American Educational Research Journal, 28*, 392–422.

Scott-Jones, D. (1987). Mothers-as-teachers in the families of high- and low-achieving low-income black first-graders. *Journal of Negro Education, 56*, 21–34.

Shade, B. J., & Edwards, P. A. (1987). Ecological correlates of the educative style of Afro-American children. *Journal of Negro Education, 86*, 88–99.

Smith, A. (1776/1993). *An inquiry into the nature and causes of the wealth of nations*. Oxford: Oxford University Press.

Stevens, T. (1900). Speech on the common school law repeal to the Pennsylvania House of Representatives, 1834. In *Reports of the Department of the Interior for the fiscal year ended June 30, 1899* (Vol. I, p. 520). Washington, DC: U.S. Government Printing Office.

Strayer, G. D., & Haig, R. M. (1923). *The financing of education in the State of New York (Report of the Educational Finance Inquiry Commission)*. New York: Macmillan.

Swanson, A. D. (1979). An international perspective on social science research and school integration. *Journal of Negro Education, 48*, 57–66.

Taylor, D., & Dorsey-Gaines, C. (1988). *Growing up literate: Learning from inner-city families*. Portsmouth, NH: Heinemann Educational Books.

Toffler, A. (1980). *The third wave*. New York: Bantam Books.

Toffler, A. (1990). *Powershift: Knowledge, wealth, and violence at the edge of the 21st century*. New York: Bantam Books.

Tyack, D., Lowe, R., & Hansot, E. (1984). *Public schools in hard times: The great depression and recent years*. Cambridge, MA: Harvard University Press.

W. T. Grant Foundation Commission on Work, Family and Citizenship. (1988). *The forgotten half: Pathways to success for America's youth and young families*. Washington, DC: The Foundation.

Wainer, H. (1994). On the academic performance of New Jersey's public school children: Fourth and eighth grade mathematics in 1992. *Education Policy Analysis Archives, 2*(10).

Walberg, H. J. (1984). Families as partners in educational productivity. *Phi Delta Kappan, 65*, 397–400.

Williams, R. L. (Ed.). (1975). *The true language of black folks*. St. Louis, MO: Institute of Black Studies.

CHAPTER 2

The Power of Systems Thinking for Educational Change

The current reform efforts in the U.S. school system offer a rich setting for the use of systems theory. In a structural view, schools are composed of critical subsystems such as administration, instruction, finance, and transportation. Additionally, as administrators seek methods to implement multifaceted school improvement programs, a process view utilizing a systems perspective can empower an administrator to emerge as vision setter or more thorough problem solver instead of mere manager. Like managers in the private sector, educational administrators have been using systems analytic administrative methods for more than 30 years. A clearer understanding of systems theory, however, can occur as the practitioner begins to observe and think in terms of system interactivity, interdependence, and integration of critical school systems and subsystems.

Systems thinking in educational administration has proven to be particularly helpful in identifying variables and organizing processes associated with schooling. Understanding the educational environment from a systems perspective enables systems thinkers to capture its holism more thoroughly. Still, it may be time to reflect upon which aspects of the systems paradigm are being enriched through practice and which are being ignored. Definitions of systems are highly visible in popular literature. However, as definitions multiply, clarity about systems views become more complex and can be lost amid the host of approaches available. In the past, the definition and power of popularized versions of Bertalanffy's General System Theory (GST; which we will call *general systems theory*) may have been misconstrued in academic literature as well. As a result, the many versions of "systems thinking" suffered from ill-informed use and therefore had less of an impact. In this chapter we more clearly characterize GST and enable educators to gain a greater understanding about the power of systems thinking. This, in turn, will help practitioners in their quest to develop and practice the "art of educating."

Systems thinking in the last several decades may have been constrained as it coexisted with the industrial age. Applications of systems thinking in schools may currently be too dependent on management science, instructional theories, and systematic applications. As a result, educators may be unaware of the role that GST can play in devising conceptual platforms and practical applications of knowledge about how schools function. Past research on systems concepts (Ashmos & Huber, 1987; Salisbury, 1990) indicated that relatively few systems concepts have been researched and put into operation. These findings may indicate both an untapped potential in the general systems paradigm and a lack of risk taking in the application of general systems concepts.

Despite some evidence earlier that the ore of systems thinking has hardly begun to be mined, systems terms and approaches have proliferated across disciplinary boundaries and slipped quietly past one national boundary after another. The use of systems ideas is now worldwide, attracting large numbers of scientists, theorists, artists, and philosophers. As the globalization of knowledge continues to expand and as systems practices become more commonplace, many persons worldwide may become avid practitioners. As we relate this, for example, global ecological–environmental cooperation and many new business practices can both be traced to general systems theory.

Understanding how any theory and practice interrelate is crucial to all administrators as they attempt to lead school organizations. Offhand practice, sometimes demanded by the constant pressures within a school organization, however, may seem more expedient or practical than reflection about theory that could provide a basis for change. Without a plentiful base of knowledge from which to act, an administrator may be doomed to making immediate decisions that may damage the well-being of the organization. Theorist Jaques (1989) said: "If you dislike theory and seek only 'practical action,' that is unfortunate. Anything you do is founded upon a theory of some sort, and eschewing theory merely means that your decisions are being misdirected by some bad theory which you do not know about" (p. 3). Systems theory has evolved a wide range of concepts to enable the knowledgeable administrator to take appropriate short- and long-term action to promote the overall growth of all elements of the school organization. A thorough understanding of systems theory can empower an administrator to develop as a leader, by helping to identify and define the components comprising organizational life. This process also helps administrators gain greater intellectual and practical capacity about how to think in systems terms and transform education and learning. To avoid misunderstood theory, then, an administrator must become reacquainted with the original and current sources that surround the state of the systems movement and its evolution.

By looking at the history, development, current practice, and future of systems theory, ad-ministrators can understand systems theory and analysis applied to human organizations, in general, and educational systems, in particular. We need to develop systems thinking in relation to the schooling enterprise (i.e., to understand, analyze, and redesign the future of education more systemically). Systems thinking must become commonplace. A thread that must run steadily throughout these explorations is the thread of critical reflection, for to accept ideas uncritically is surely to model "uneducated" behavior. The administrator using GST is asked to be a scholar-practitioner in the discipline. The following explanation of systems theory invites an administrator to consider the value of the theory in light of his or her practice.

Conceptualizing Systems

The Development of Systems Thinking

In this century, the physical sciences dominated scientific endeavor. Scientific minds were engaged almost exclusively in efforts to establish "a predictive system of laws" (Bertalanffy, 1968b, p. 12). On the other hand, other disciplines were uncovering problems that were unsolvable by classical scientific methods. Many of these were problems posed by organized complexity; that is, the entire entity under study could not be broken into discrete elements without losing its organization, and, in fact, its essential character. Bertalanffy, a theoretical biologist, and others called for the development of new conceptual models to facilitate the study of complex biological and social phenomena.

Bertalanffy began incorporating into his own work concepts from physical chemistry, kinetics, and thermodynamics. From this point he says: "I could not stop on the way once taken and so I was led to a still further generalization which I called 'General System Theory' " (1968b, p. 13). He expressed the germ of this theory as early as 1937. As the theory developed, he viewed it as having the character of a basic science. Its correlate, as an applied science, is now known as *systems science*. Systems science has since emerged as operations research, systems engineering, cybernetics, organizational theory, and other sciences that use systems theory, concepts, and methodologies.

In 1954, Bertalanffy and some colleagues agreed to collaborate as cofounders of a society for general systems thinking and research. They agreed upon goals that would seek to encourage the development of theoretical models, to standardize the efforts across disciplines, to promote the unity of science through greater communication, and to investigate the correspondence of concepts, models, and laws in various fields. Over time, they have built a theoretical bridge across scientific disciplines and diminished the fragmentation that once limited cross-disciplinary exchanges and contributions (Emery, 1970). In all, their contributions to the development of a metalanguage and the advancement of the study of holism enabled scientists and practitioners to think about and design new investigative strategies.

Today, these new strategies and other contributions share center stage with other forms of scientific and practical inquiry. These new systems sciences do not abandon the study of variables common in analytical studies but form a partnership to create even more responsible theoretical and practical analysis. These more thorough practices are enhanced by the study of whole entities and the relationships and processes within and among these wholes.

Systems Definitions

Critics comment that the very idea of a "system" loses efficacy because anything and everything can be viewed as a system. In truth, proponents of general systems theory find systems existing in all "shapes and flavors" but also consider this view exclusionary. An aggregate of units does not constitute a system. An often-cited example is an unorganized and inactive pile of marbles (see Figure 2.1). Similarly, a work group of individuals does not possess the same capacities as a self-directed project team. Some form of organizing agent(s) is needed to "motivate" these aggregates to create and further understand system interactivity.

The differentiation between aggregates and systems is important since systems are sometimes treated as if they were aggregates. Practitioners might incorrectly assume that a top-down model of organizational communications implies that each unit or person is insulated from interaction with other units or persons inside or outside the organization (see Figure 2.1). This incomplete view presumes that no other systems (whether interpersonal, organizational, family, or community) are functioning.

Figure 2.1
Aggregate thinking

An aggregate is a collection that does not demonstrate a purpose or relate system activity. Although the diagram at the right demonstrates one view of communication in an organization, it does not exhibit the many other ways that communication takes place. Both demonstrate aggregate thinking that does not thoroughly explain system activity.

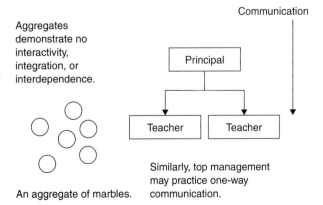

Aggregates demonstrate no interactivity, integration, or interdependence.

An aggregate of marbles.

Communication

Principal

Teacher   Teacher

Similarly, top management may practice one-way communication.

Corporate mergers, acquisitions, or divestitures may also exemplify aggregate rather than systems thinking. If managers perceive people as noninteracting aggregates and imply that other values are more important, they may haphazardly forget to consider the plight of the human components. In a similar light the relocation of teachers from one school to another, or hair-trigger decisions to expel troublesome students regardless of their home situations, are examples of aggregate thinking. The aggregate mentality is additive. It assumes that aggregate units can be added or subtracted at will without damage to the larger aggregate called the company, school, or office. Politically, the aggregate mentality may even encourage the aggression of large nations against small nations, with nearby additions of territory, people, and resources presumed to have no or negligible effect on the social system. In truth, disturbance in one part of a system creates ripple effects that are unsettling for the entire system, often for extraordinarily long periods of time. Systems thinkers can anticipate this, knowing that multisystem interactions are inevitable.

Aggregate nonsystems are closely associated with the idea of system closure. In a closed system all energy is drawn from within the system, all events occur within the system, and all products are used by and within the system. Nothing is imported or exported. This is a recipe for system deterioration and demise, since the closed system exhausts itself in repeated cycles of self-consumption.

The closed system is largely a theoretical construct, as it is unlikely to find an example of a totally closed system. Theorists more commonly speak of relative closure or openness. The relatively closed system is most susceptible to entropy, a physical law of thermodynamics that assumes a condition of deterioration, chaos, and disorganization, or falling into a state of imbalance or disequilibrium that endangers a system's survival. Relatively closed systems need new energy as input. Input is the system

justification for medical or spiritual intervention in the case of human illness or, in the case of organizational disorder, the justification for hiring a consultant or new executive, or seeking additional training or learning. All such interventions are aimed at overcoming entropy in the relatively closed system.

Similarly, the completely open system is a conceptual convenience. When systems theorists speak of open systems, they are actually referring to degrees of openness. The relatively open system remains exposed to many interventions, some of which are deliberately sought and others that are simply not preventable or foreseen. An open system may also reach beyond its boundaries to exert external influence. The notion of permeable boundaries is important in studying relatively open systems. The extent to which any system allows communication and other exchanges in both incoming and outgoing directions determines its degree of boundary permeability. This same principle applies to subunits within systems.

Relative closure of systems appears to be psychologically comforting to many people. In a closed system, unwanted intrusions are guarded against as people prevent or derail efforts to change. On the other hand, excitement and benefit can be enjoyed in relatively open systems. In open systems, self-regulatory devices are established to monitor boundary exchanges and the effects these exchanges have on parts of the system, the entire system, and the environment. The process is somewhat like the regulation of water release from dams: the structure accommodates downstream users and recreational users above the dam, prevents floods and droughts, eases pressure on the dam structure, and adjusts to catastrophic weather conditions. Even the decision to build a dam begins as a multisystem consideration, requiring independent cooperation across political, economic, and social boundaries. Multiple domains must be considered and changed.

For a school administrator, maintaining a relatively open system involves commensurate tasks. Regulating school enrollment, making learning enjoyable for all, monitoring downstream entry of students into work life, anticipating growth in school populations, and more, are each important considerations. Administrators cannot simply turn switches, oblivious to the potential variety and potential value conflicts in the environment. Guided by a thorough knowledge of systems theory, the role of the administrator changes and becomes one of leadership, not mere management.

Once it is clear that systems are not aggregates and are relatively closed or open, other system characteristics become paramount. Every definition of system denotes a connection between parts and wholes. Rapoport (1968), for example, explains, "A whole which functions as a whole by virtue of the interdependence of its parts is called a system" (p. xvii). Although they expanded this definition in several ways, Hall and Fagen (1968) define a system quite simply as "a set of objects together with the relationships between the objects and their attributes" (p. 81). Ackoff's (1974) definition is more complex: "A system is a set of two or more interrelated elements of any kind; for example, concepts (as in the number system), objects (as in a telephone system or human body), or people (as in a social system)" (p. 13). From the beginning of general systems theory, interrelationship, interaction, and interdependence have defined the characteristic elements of systems (Bertalanffy, 1968b).

To be able to identify and relate how and why this trio above is important enables every practitioner broad new ways of viewing education. As onlookers and observers, practitioners become part of the system they observe. It is imperative in complex human systems that individual perceptions are considered part of the system. These onlookers or observers for a school or school district might include various stakeholders, such as the public, industry, political groups, boards, legislators, even participants from other new and evolving educational platforms.

Many of the definitions of systems refer to organization as a condition that enables parts to work together on behalf of the whole. Thus, the ideas of interrelationship and interdependency migrate into the broader concepts of organized complexity and holism (Hodge & Anthony, 1988; Kast & Rosenzweig, 1972). As mentioned earlier, understanding a school must involve more than the comprehension of its internal functioning. Internally, schools may be viewed as being composed of administration, instruction, and learning. These may even form our primary definition. But schools must equally be understood in combination with their external environments including the school districts and state and federal governments. Today, in some venues, views of educational practice are expanding beyond the traditions of the past. As will be related, multiple new views of education are challenging many to look constructively beyond current beliefs and practices—to look at the whole system. As a systems thinker would relate, every venue is important, adds to the complexity, and creates deeper understanding.

Systems Frameworks

Systems literature treats the general characteristics of systems in several ways. Authors may initially discuss the elements of a system and then describe the functions of these elements. They may undertake system model building that seeks to incorporate all pertinent variables and processes, or they may begin with taxonomies that categorize systems and their variables in thought-provoking ways. Most theorists conceptualize a vertical dimension to systems that allows them to speak of hierarchies of systems, hierarchies within systems, or hierarchical levels of abstraction to be used in thinking about systems. In this fashion, the theorist or practitioner can

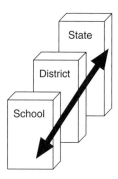

Figure 2.2
Hierarchy of systems

A hierarchy of systems demonstrates level of
embeddedness and potential system activity.

observe a system's embeddedness (see Figure
2.2). A horizontal dimension to systems thinking
and practice is also prevalent. These dimensions
allow researchers to model or map the system of
interest with x and y types of coordinates (i.e.,
intersections of horizontal and vertical dimensions varying according to different assigned values). Yet vertical or horizontal references do not
represent all the dimensions inherent in systems.
Systemic thinking may require a third, z, axis, or
appropriately, a representation that exhibits the
multidimensional aspect or nature of a system or
systems concept over time. Characteristically,
then, a hierarchy of systems demonstrates embeddedness, the vertical dimension captures
system interactivity, and a time dimension may
capture movement or flow.

Banathy (1972) offered another useful set of
ideas with "a map of systems education." On a
continuum of abstraction from low to high, he
speaks of learning about *systems tools* (a technical level of understanding) that are instrumental
to *systems approaches* (a tactical level of understanding). These approaches are derived from
field (systems) models. Banathy is speaking here
about systems models in education, business,
and health care and the need to learn how models are profitably applied at a strategic level. Finally, he lists *general systems models* that

provide frameworks for understanding the constructs and laws of general systems theory at a
level that allows synthesis.

By arranging theoretical systems and systems
constructs in an ascending order of complexity,
Boulding (1968) created what he called "levels
of discourse," or a system for talking about systems. Although he viewed this arrangement as
more systematic than systems actually are, it
yields rich insights about organized complexity.
Education is embedded as a practice within and
across each of these levels. Although it is certainly possible to take issue with any point in
Boulding's formulation, it serves well as an invitation to rethink systems. He proposed that its
value might lie in pointing out the gaps in both
theoretical models and empirical knowledge,
more noticeable at some levels than at others.

Another way of framing systems thinking is
to identify broad categories and then develop
functional classifications. For example, abstract
systems are composed of interrelated symbols,
ideas, concepts, principles, and so on. Concrete
systems are composed of interrelated physical
and material resources. Real systems are observable (i.e., they are "visual–tactile" systems
falling within the compass of human sensory
experience). Human systems add interrelated
organic and psychological dimensions, and embody elements of abstract, concrete, and real
systems. Cybernetic systems steer organizations
through turbulence toward stability. Organizations include all these systems, and each must
be accorded its own importance and value.

The functional behavior of these systems
could be classified as (1) state-maintaining,
(2) goal-seeking, (3) multigoal-seeking, and
(4) purposeful (Hodge & Anthony, 1988). A
state-maintaining system wants to continue in
a customary pattern. A *goal-seeking system*
moves toward a different but highly specified
outcome. A *multigoal-seeking system* pursues
several outcomes that are not mutually exclusive. A *purposeful system* has a clear sense of
mission in a broad, value-laden sense. School

organizations, from the district to the individual classroom units, exhibit qualities of all four system behaviors.

Simon (1970) and Boulding (1968) spoke of a "system of systems" in hierarchical arrangement. Furthermore, some scientists have decided that there are also systems of systems theory—a metasystem. Immegart and Pilecki (1973) constructed five theoretical approaches to understanding these metasystems: (1) comprehensive system theories of wholes and components; (2) subsystem or process theories, with microscopic analysis of input processing; (3) feedback and system control theories, with cybernetics as a prominent contender; (4) theories of system properties that help to formulate longitudinal, evolutionary systems analyses; and (5) output theories and output analysis (i.e., results of system activity). Operations research is a primary example of the latter. Immegart and Pilecki (1973) claim that there is value in multiple approaches to system evaluation and reconsideration. The rate of organizational change in the twentieth century warrants the use of multiple approaches.

To many, systems thinking is a confusing mix of positivistic and naturalistic, or nomothetic and idiographic, points of view (Getzels, 1958; Kimbrough & Nunnery, 1988). For the systems scientist, this is as it should be. By definition, general systems theory organizes and subsumes widely divergent scientific views and methodologies. Systems thinking requires a synthesizing, "both–and" perspective rather than the piecemeal exercise of serial "either–or" judgments.

Because systems are viewed as wholes, their structures and functions are also studied as a dynamic and ongoing process rather than as subsets of analytical interest. A world view founded in holism is not compatible with a reductionist's world view. What is more legitimate is to measure the success of systems science on its own terms. For scientists who have escaped the rigid cause-and-effect line of thought, other criteria of science are not only possible but also

hold more promise. Naturalistic inquiry, for example, has enormous potential for translating observations of systems at work into scientific probabilities and challenging bodies of knowledge. The qualitative research that has resulted and been applied in numerous academic areas has demonstrated new part–whole variables that may prove more valuable.

Systems approaches relying heavily on either all-analytical or all-conceptual modeling are unable to express all of the existing relationships among systems. Presumed causes cannot always account for observed effects in complex systems, and neither quantitative nor qualitative studies provide all the answers that everyone would like. Consequently, whatever approach is used, it still contains the danger of oversimplifying organizational relationships. Using multiple points of view to study organizations may initially yield overwhelming amounts of data, some of which may conflict with other data, but from this muddle, new and testable hypotheses arise. It takes complex science to study complex systems.

System Properties Explored

The simple input–throughput–output model for system activity has been the source of theory building and the metaphoric bane of systems thinkers. It represents an oversimplified version of systems inquiry that can lead to the very rigidity and scaling down of ideas that systems thinking seek to avoid. Graphically, the model overemphasizes analytical, procedural, and directional properties of systems, casting them in a "systematic" stepwise mold. When this model is all that is visible, the systematic approach is taken for the whole of general systems theory. This belies the system's actual, "lived" dynamism and diversity. The simplified input––throughput–output model prevents the systems thinker from observing the system's full energy, interactivity, and interdependence.

Paradoxically, this otherwise regrettable simplicity helps GST newcomers identify important

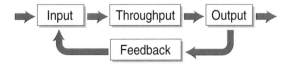

Figure 2.3
Input–throughput–output model

system elements from which more systemic ideas and models are constructed. As an example, management and instructional design models can often be seen as more systematic and procedural than systemic and functional. These models should be understood to be limited accordingly in their explanatory power. In simplest graphic form, Figure 2.3 represents a systematic (procedural) model. Inputs are transformed through system activity to outputs.

By placing an environment around the model and representing boundaries between the system and the environment as permeable, this systematic representation of the system becomes more useful (see Figure 2.4). In this fashion, then, the model begins to represent a holistic nature as it illustrates more thorough knowledge and understanding about the system.

The social, economic, and political milieu that schools and school districts exist within often determines their survival. To ignore the milieu is to ignore the environment that constantly interacts with a system. This interactivity is representative of the new energy, information, material resources, and people from the environment moving into the system as inputs,

providing new "raw materials" for system activity. Other sources of new input activity may include (1) feedback about the input the system has consumed, and (2) feedback about the outputs the system has produced. For example, a more specific input activity could be family impact on the student, community job availability, state and federal mandates, or local or regional economic conditions.

Multiple forms of input are utilized or transformed by the system into output. Transformation processes in the educational context might include instruction, various forms of decision making and problem solving, actual thinking by the student, and so on. Throughput (the transformation) can take many forms.

Outputs may be products, services, energy, damages, or any combination of these. For example, a systems solution to environmental damage might be to capture toxic emissions or substances (outputs) and reuse (input) them in some ecologically sound way. In school systems, capturing dropouts and carefully "recycling" their energies is an appropriate systems solution to educational waste. Outputs can thus become new inputs for the same system as well as inputs for other systems.

As outputs are realized, forms of information are fed back by the system to enable the system to realize its full potential more thoroughly. Instructional content, lesson objectives, and other resources (inputs) are used to instruct the student. The outcome of this process, knowledge acquisition in some form, is evaluated and fed

Figure 2.4
Simplifed systems model

Permeable System Boundary

Input → Throughput → Output

Control System ← Feedback

ENVIRONMENT

back as changes that may or may not provide necessary further control. In this fashion, feedback is utilized to monitor and change the systems activity as further iterations occur.

Installing a cybernetic control device in the feedback loop to show regulation and self-correction of the system completes the basic model. At this point, the organized complexity of systems may be present but can scarcely be inferred from the diagram. Considerable variation is apparent here as the system becomes dynamic. Even in an "assembly-line" transformation, inputs and processes can vary from one "batch" to another. In modern organizations the application of more and more standardization cannot cope with the vast complexity that arises as input continues to vary and grow exponentially. This is particularly evident today in the information age, when system complexity is fueled by greater information availability.

Environment generally refers to the collections of systems that lie outside the system under study. Environments are not controllable by the system but can be selectively responsive to the system's behavior. Environments may be stable, dynamic, or even chaotic. Churchman (1979) suggested that analysis of a system ought to determine whether influences on the system are environmental, systemic, or neither, for such influences are potential growth and survival factors. Strategically, the organization (i.e., the school) must know of the existence of resources, employ managerial talent to import and organize their use, and then call upon organizational intelligence to make sure that the entire system, including its environments, is well served.

Other Properties of Systems

Other system properties are important to the understanding of general systems theory. These additional features help the new practitioner more fully comprehend the full extent of evolving systems beliefs and practices.

1. *Synergy, or the presence of synergism.* Synergy is a process equivalent to structural holism, wherein structural components (e.g., bricks and mortar, classrooms, libraries, offices, gyms) become more than the sum of the parts. Together, these concepts aptly describe part–whole relationships in general systems theory: the whole is structurally, functionally, and synergistically greater than (and other than) the sum of its parts. Team teaching, for example, creates added synergistic features to enhance instruction. Content can be made more relevant as people interact to provide a more profound level of instruction and learning.

2. *Functionalism-system activity.* Similar to synergy, functionalism has implications about system processing. Parsons (1960), an early supporter of the pattern-and-function view of systems, urged a systemic examination of structures, processes, and functions. Just as the openness of a system is perceived to lie somewhere on a continuum between open and closed, so too, the functionality of a system lies on a continuum between optimal functioning and complete dysfunction. The system that functions well has dynamic properties; the system that becomes dysfunctional or "neurotic" suffers from static processes and relationships (Hodge & Anthony, 1988; Kets de Vries & Miller, 1989). Consider individual student differences; for example, the need for standardized control mechanisms coexists with a particular teacher's need for more flexibility in the classroom. These dichotomies exist everywhere but are tilted more often toward higher-level control.

3. *Leading parts* (Hall & Fagen, 1968). Which parts of a system act as its leading parts: the static components or the dynamic components? Administrators may "switch the lineup" or change the dysfunctional components from static to dynamic. In small-group behavior, leading parts may be individuals who emerge when needed or when prepared to do so. Larger organizations display this same flexibility and potential for emergence of unexpected leading parts. The

adoption of a dramatic and new teaching method may raise achievement, shared decision making may allow teachers and administrators to balance standardization and flexibility more effectively, or the school band may unite pride throughout the school. This may be the very pulse of innovation, and systems thinking invites this perception. Leading parts and emergence are interdependent concepts; both are situational rather than positional. School administrators are defined by their positions as leaders, but this neither guarantees that they are leading parts nor excludes them from that status. There may be other leading parts which, at critical times, may emerge to help a school become more functional—for example, an energetic new teacher, lead teacher, student opinion leader, or someone from the external environment. Perhaps the leading part is a new computer system or a new building. System thinkers ought not to assume that the authority figure or the favorite teacher is, or ought to be, the leading part of the organization.

4. *Dynamic homeostasis.* In a cybernetic sense, leading parts help "steer" the organization toward relative equilibrium, a condition that allows the organization to grow and change in a stable way. Thinking of the organization in this systemic way helps to keep system dynamics in perspective. The organization is viewed by more than its positional or status dimensions: in essence, more than a management system and/or instructional system. Systems need the fresh inputs of leading parts as well as the information-communication regulatory systems to magnify helpful forces and minimize destructive ones wherever these leading, regulating components may be found.

5. *Isomorphism.* A system may have structures that show correspondence to structures in another system. This means that, structurally, the parts correspond to each other one-to-one. Obviously, what is learned about one structure (even if it is an abstract structure like a concept) is applicable to its isomorph. Therefore, looking for isomorphism is a way to infer knowledge

from one organization that may hold true in a second organization. For example, can we utilize business practices or knowledge in school settings? One caution is needed: while all isomorphisms are analogies, not all analogies are isomorphisms. The difference is that analogies do not have to meet the condition of one-to-one correspondence (Schoderbek, Schoderbek, & Kefalas, 1990).

6. *Differentiation and specialization in a system.* Most systems contain internal elaboration processes between their subsystems and their influence relationships. This can account for system symbiosis, a situation in which one subsystem becomes so differentiated that it cannot perform certain functions for itself and thus must "live off" another subsystem. If one of the symbiotic pairs is self-sufficient, the relationship is unipolar; if each has something vital to offer the other, the relationship is bipolar. Another type of differentiation occurs in redundant subsystems where design and functioning is duplicated as a backup to other subsystems. An example is central database duplication and access at more than one location of a school. Hodge and Anthony (1988) identified still another kind of subsystem—a decomposable one. This is a "short-run independent" system that has many internal sustaining interactions. A project group might exemplify the decomposable subsystem.

7. *Principle of progressive mechanization.* This principle, postulated by Bertalanffy (1968a), implies that control functions can be decentralized when subsystem routines proceed to the point that regulation is more easily managed at that level. Progressive inclusion and progressive centralization indicate system tendencies to centralize and become more and more integrated and complex. These properties of systems may cyclically emerge and recede, depending on how system variety is managed (Willis, 1977). Progressive segregation refers to the subdivision of systems parts into recognizable, separate subsystems.

8. *Goals and adaptation.* According to Bertalanffy, one cannot talk about organisms, behavior, and society without taking into account the concepts of goals and adaptation toward those goals. Consequently, the property of teleology has a critical role in systems thinking. All systems, living and nonliving, may have directedness or purposiveness, but human systems clearly have purposes (i.e., desired "end states" or teleologies). For example, businesses create profit, schools educate, and students learn. Identifying this property leads naturally to the idea of equifinality, where a system may reach equal-final goals by means of different paths and strategies. Clearly, businesses achieve profit in varying ways, and different schools educate using a variety of different but successful methods.

9. *Negentropy (negative entropy).* Katz and Kahn (1966) reported this property of open systems, the system's defense against decline. Negentropic inputs (feedback) keep a system healthy. The system's dilemma is to determine which of many possible inputs will be most beneficial. Feedback is the mechanism that allows the system to self-correct. Vocal parents demand change, teachers evaluate performance, and administrators review resource utilization. Each of these self-correcting mechanisms changes the system in fundamental ways.

The properties of organized complexity, holism, teleology, emergence, synergy, isomorphism, and leading part activity are often given short shrift when predictive or quasipredictive systems analysis methods are used. When more qualitative approaches are taken, these properties become vital to the analysis. The cybernetic (Weiner, 1968) and adaptive aspects of systems receive much attention from scientists, although some recent writers have suggested that organizational inertia vitiates the notion of adaptability (e.g., Carroll, 1988).

This review of systems theory approaches and concepts serves as a foundation for educational administrators' possible use of systems theory as both a means of understanding the life of a school organization and a means of promoting that life by leadership initiatives.

The Organizational Implications of Systems Thinking

Groundbreaking: Early Organizational Theories

Organizational theory has not totally ignored the impact of systems theory. Educational institutions that prepare school administrators cannot sensibly ignore the impact of systems thinking in other disciplines, nor have they done so. Taking a systems view frees administrators from single-cause analysis, narrow interpretations of what systems are and do, and misunderstandings about the meaning of isolated events. Systems thinking can also add a more thorough cultural perspective to institutional history, to present concerns, and to projections of the future. Numerous opportunities for building new models of whole systems aids our comprehension and analytical understanding in multiple ways. This, in turn, leads to hypothesis generation and research with rich heuristic and scientific value. Chin, Bennis, and Benne (1961) reported that systems approaches were becoming a major operating framework for physical as well as social sciences. Bertalanffy's (1968a) experimental approach to interdisciplinary "parallelism" became everyday reality. Cities now depend on systems thinking to plan urban renewal and transportation; NASA launches spaceships replete with systemic environments; and global economies are understood to be interdependent and synergistic. In place of single-cause thinking of an organization, the systems view promotes (1) multiple perspectives on interdependent phenomena, (2) recognition that the first system interventions are usually made between human and structural subsystems, (3) recognition that change is related to technology and that sociotechnical systems have emerged, (4) understanding that techniques for change need to be selected for appropriateness and feasibility, and (5) realization that continuous diagnosis promotes variety and is needed to protect system viability and growth.

In the following paragraphs, an overview of the research demonstrates the depth and breadth of the systems movement. Barnard (1938) and Simon (1964) were among the first organization theorists to adopt systems thinking in their work. Both recognized that organizational activity could not be modeled in linear forms only but required more thorough techniques.

Homans (1950), an interactionist, believed that activities, interactions, and sentiments were at the very core of social organization. He used systems methods in his study of social groups. Parsons (1960) referred extensively to structures or subsystems in managerial systems. The *technical/production system* is concerned with task performance, research and development, production control, marketing research, and so on, according to his taxonomy. The *organizational/managerial system* coordinates task performance, using materials, information, and energy for its accomplishment. The *institutional/community system* relates the activities of the organization to its surrounding environment.

The managerial system as a whole spans the entire organization and directs technology, people resource utilization, and communication. More simply, these elements are identified as technical, intraorganization interactions, and interorganization relationships. These early precedents with systems show relationships overlapping, functions interacting, and interdependence within organizations. The elements present a more realistic model for understanding how organizations actually function. They set the stage for administrators and managers to explore organization in differing ways.

With new theory, managers can realign system components, reduce uncertainty and ambiguity in the system to tolerable levels, act decisively, and maintain flexibility, all in the service of an organizational balancing act among systems, subsystems, suprasystems, and environments. Managers may be classified as technical, organizational, or institutional—another more systemic view.

Lewin's (1975) concern for human and organizational equilibrium produced force-field analysis, a conceptual device for assessing the relative strength of various organizational "vectors" for or against change. Changing the force of the vectors in either direction results in "unfreezing" the system. This results in a period of change or "moving," after which the new state of the system "re-freezes" and becomes institutionalized. Lippitt, Watson, and Westley (1975) added two steps to Lewin's model: the development of changing relationships and the achievement of a change–process–ending relationship.

Dynamic homeostasis needs to be overcome if the system is to grow, change, and then restabilize. System growth relies heavily on the type and quality of human, technological, and organizational inputs as well as on the social structures and norms that prevail in the system. Huse and Bowditch (1973) mentioned cost control and value adding as strategies for organizational change, human resource accounting propositions, the need for human resource departments to separate into human resource management and human resource development systems, and a topology of personal, interpersonal, and multigroup systems.

In describing the elements of a thriving system, Kimbrough and Nunnery (1988) listed organizational imperatives: (1) the achievement of objectives, (2) internal maintenance, and (3) adaptation to the environment. Individuals in organizations move from immaturity toward maturity, from passive to active, dependent to independent, now-oriented to future-oriented, from external to internal locus of control, and from a limited to a profound sense of commitment.

This brief review illustrates the organizational theories that have enabled development of systems thought and its potential and variety. The addition of these features helps administrators, in turn, to work more effectively.

Changes in Management Roles and Contexts

Systems thinking has brought new capacities to management over time. Boundaries of systems are continually redefined by events in the system or the environment. For example, the series of school district reform and restructuring efforts parlay bureaucratic systems against site-based management systems. An emerging function of management, in addition to combating entropy, is to manage these boundary shifts successfully.

Exploring various management philosophies can readily demonstrate the extent that management beliefs have changed over time. A variety of authors (Hodge & Anthony, 1988; Hodge & Johnson, 1988; Immegart & Pilecki, 1973) all reflect a growing and thoughtful range of changes from traditional hierarchical models, to human relations models, to contingency models, and to those most current models evident today. During these substantive changes, explanatory models related a deepening concern for and understanding of the enlarging systems movement.

Early on, Hodge and Johnson (1988) postulated a taxonomy of six analytical models, including mechanistic/bureaucratic, human relations, individual behavior, technological, economic, and power. To many, these models represent the breadth of activity and are extremely familiar, as they are a product of the recent past.

These models all proceed from several assumptions: (1) the organization exists to satisfy environmental needs; (2) the organization's work system mobilizes to meet objectives that will in turn meet environmental needs; (3) the organization structures itself to facilitate the work system activity; (4) the design of power and authority relationships, system differentiation, and delegation are all dedicated to work facilitation; and (5) renewal and change processes are mandatory for survival and effectiveness. These early models are significant in that they explicitly seek to investigate organizational management from a systemic point of view. The models explore the management of organizations in light of their reality: as open and dynamic systems and subsystems, as interrelated across functional boundaries, as interactive combinations, and as integrative processes. The models specifically demonstrate the necessity for interdependence; one system or subsystem cannot and does not act individually, but always acts in concert with other systems or subsystems. Management then cannot simply justify singular problem solving confined in individual, local, or larger arenas. Analysis must become holistic.

Although literature on the organization of schools borrows from all the foregoing theories, there was initially no specific body of literature that linked systems theory to school organizations. Nevertheless, systems concepts were continually applied in analyses of schools. Today, as will be demonstrated in the following sections, systems theory and practice are more broadly evidenced, understood, and utilized. With more aggressive understanding of management, organizations (in this case, education) also grow and evolve.

Organizational Change

Today, education is remaking itself in many ways. To help assess organizational change across time, Grenier (1972) identified five organizational dimensions: organizational age, size, stage of evolution, stage of revolution, and industry growth rate. In one view, organization growth stages enable the practicing manager to understand related, systemic organizational needs as development continues. At times during a cycle of growth, organizations can be seen as evolutionary, progressive, or striving to change. At other times in the cycle, problematic issues arise as the organization confronts internal crisis and strives to continue its existence. These periods are revolutionary. With organization growth, differing managerial styles are needed. Five different organizational stages and their attributes are explained below.

1. *Evolutionary creativity leading to a leadership crisis.* At this stage, technical and entrepreneurial competence become insufficient. Managers have to be created or imported.

2. *Directed evolutionary growth leading to an autonomy crisis.* Here, communication is often lacking, as people become frustrated and alienated. Management begins to share decision making.

3. *Growth through delegation leading to a control crisis.* Subsystems appear to be too independent. Situations develop that trigger centralization. Other problems emerge as a result.

4. *Growth through coordination, leading to a crisis in bureaucracy.* The organization becomes rigid, inflexible, rule-bound, and inefficient.

5. *Collaboration leading to a crisis of unknown origin.* At this organizational stage, the organization has presumably matured enough to be able to assess its risks and act accordingly.

Contingency theory appropriately links with the model above, since structural forms and managerial characteristics are contingent on the stage the organization is apparently undergoing. Each successive growth stage corresponds to a managerial style. Other aspects of contingency theory are long-range structural adaptation within the system (Darwinian) and within the environment (Singerian). Prerequisite to change is familiarity with the environment, willingness and ability to change, and information acquisition and feedback response (Schoderbek et al., 1990).

Contingency theory also builds on the concept of systems equifinality; there is no one best way to reach systems goals. Initial inputs do not determine the extent of goal achievement, and outputs may vary even when the inputs are consistent (Kimbrough & Nunnery,

1988). The latter feature may be one reason why systems thinking has been overlooked in circles that espouse scientific management models. Yet the concept of equifinality strengthens since it provides answers to problems in organizations. The nonlinear approach can promote a manager's ability to cultivate an environment for creative problem solving and change. Problem solving therefore takes the shape of multifaceted intervention.

Systemic Interventions

Young (1964) proposed a four-way quadrant analysis of systems concepts to guide how we classify and use systemic intervention. The first category is *systemic and descriptive.* This permits discrimination between systems, organizes and analyzes large quantities of data, and helps to conceptualize the fundamental nature of different systems. For example, a state curriculum might begin by describing the totality of the curriculum system to capture all of its essential elements. The second class of concepts, *regulation and maintenance,* provides information on the status of components, the state of feedback systems, negentropic interventions, and communication. In this quadrant numerous processes may be explored. The third category, *dynamics and change,* allows examination of teleology, growth, dynamism, and adaptation. An example could be the development of strategy. The last class, *decline and breakdown,* identifies stress, disturbance, overload, increased entropy, and decay. Problem solving would be an example here. This model allows zeroing in on one quadrant at a time and then moving to other quadrants as necessary. In school systems, for example, budget votes, critiques of instructional systems, constituent demands, teacher–student demands, or technology may all impose regulatory effects on the system and thus signal the need for attention from the regulation and maintenance quadrant.

Marney and Smith (1964) provided another intervention model and cited four major determinants of system change: feedback, organizational memory learning (refined and developed over time), change capacity, and system–environmental relations. For example, a system can choose to change or not. If the decision is to change, resources and energies must be marshaled accordingly. Change is costly, however, and the system needs to balance its immediate fiscal position against long-range survival needs. In other words, the system must utilize its feedback mechanisms. In another example, Selye, in his classic work on stress (1957), showed the effects of stress on individuals and organizations. Although researchers such as Brown (1967) see positive motivation possibilities in stress, others, such as Lasell (1969), report quite the opposite effect. Stress needs monitoring at both individual and organizational levels; individuals experience stress differently and demonstrate varying degrees of success in coping with it. Coping mechanisms provide for maintenance of individuals and organizations and operate on the basis of specific input, output, and feedback structures. Change therefore requires continuous feedback, a capacity to learn from feedback, and knowledge of how to design mechanisms that allow change to occur. In each case the system must be cognizant of its relations with the environment.

Feedback Requirements

Like their counterparts in business and industry, educational administrators need to sense organizational signs of decline and assess the cost of system disruptions. Defenses against decline should be applied in the least costly manner. Rusche (1968) showed that schools receive more negative feedback than positive. It is a challenge to turn perceptions around and alleviate the demoralizing and stressful effects of criticism. A built-in and ongoing feedback system can act against system decline by identifying regulatory and maintenance necessities.

The importance of feedback from within as well as from outside the organization can scarcely be overemphasized. Feedback is an information exchange, often solicited and seldom random or disorderly. Feedback feeds the self-regulatory processes, allows the system to evaluate its viability and contributions, and detects needed changes in the communication system. Purposeful feedback reviews past events, enables present adjustments, and encourages future planning. System functionality and goal achievement depend on feedback. Systems require specific mechanisms, both formal and informal, for receiving, manipulating, and using the data gained from feedback.

In his review of a feedback classification system developed by Carlson and others, Hearn (1958) outlined the various types of feedback. Continuous feedback allows a controlled amount of feedback to be monitored regularly. Mechanized continuous feedback, non-labor-intensive, can provide continuous, valuable self-correction. Security systems are an example. Intermittent feedback arrives at specified intervals or, on some occasions, unexpectedly. Open-door office hours, regular meetings, or regular classroom observations are examples of intermittent feedback mechanisms. Proportional feedback designates feedback that is controlled by the amount and type of information that the system needs. For example, if an administrator is out of touch with faculty, students, staff, or constituents, or unaware of how others perceive him or her, feedback needs tend to be higher. Proportional feedback can also be targeted feedback, as it is capable of prioritizing informational needs. Relay feedback refers to an "on" or "off" flow of information: Feedback is relayed only if and when it is requested. Continuous and intermittent feedback usually incur high costs. Relay feedback loses data or promotes other inefficiencies. Proportional feedback has the most value, but it is time consuming and time bound. A combination of relay and proportional feedback allows timeliness to become less of an issue. In the *informated organization,* however,

feedback may be generated quickly via electronic mail and quickly analyzed by computer
programs designed for that purpose.

Looking Toward the Future

Unrest in Organizations

Systems thinkers have sought and continue to
seek the "law of laws," the "system of systems,"
and the "order of orders," as parallel cognitive
processing occurs across disciplines. Systems
theory does not purport to fill the gaps. General
systems theory does insist on inclusiveness
rather than exclusiveness, more breadth and
depth, and the fullest range of methodologies
that can be brought to bear on the study of systems phenomena. GST promotes far more than
a problem-solving methodology, and it is at its
core far more significant than the innumerable
"approaches" derived from it. It simultaneously
provides a unified concept of the system and a
means for detailed analysis. Those who disclaim
the legitimacy of general systems theory because they doubt it can generate testable hypotheses proceed from the assumptions of
quantifiable science and quasiexperimental designs. For those researchers within positivistic
practice and theory, adopting systems thinking
may appear risky or revolutionary. Kuhn (1962)
articulated how normal science can amount to
paradigm paralysis.

There are many new directions and applications of systems theory to organizational theory
and practice. Some of these new applications
have their roots in earlier work; some seem to
be radically new departures from what has been
done previously. For systems thinkers this is an
exciting time, marked by a convergence of naturalistic inquiry, general systems theory, and
any number of auxiliary paradigms. The research that management systems scientists have
offered is now being recognized as only a pre-
view of what systems science can do. Bertalanffy's (1968a) interdisciplinary energy is being

reinfused to encourage businesspeople, educators, and scientists to read widely outside their
own disciplines. A part of this new energy is being generated by common recognition that old
ways of thinking about and doing things simply
are not responsive to all that is happening in
system environments. This new state of affairs
in organizations has often been described in
such terms as *chaos, turbulence,* and *permanent white water.* Harmon (1989) asserted that
executives all over the world are experimenting
to find a new standard of organization. Before
any such new design can emerge, three dynamic trends must be integrated: (1) technological revolutions in communications; (2) the demand by employees for more complete and
meaningful work; and (3) the rising pressure for
efficiency, fueled by fast-paced and increasingly
global competition. Traditional organizations
everywhere suffer acute stress or even psychological breakdown. The underlying cause is the
struggle to fit these trends into an organizational
design created for a disappearing world. Engdahl (1989) also speaks wistfully of the need for
an improved organization theory net with
which to "catch the world."

Toffler (1990) thinks that the "survival of the
fastest" will be the hallmark of the twenty-first
century. The "fastest" are those with the ability
to shorten development times, to move products and services faster and closer to consumers, and to use information almost instanta-
neously. Toffler envisions a new and
accelerated role of knowledge in the creation of
wealth. Imagination, values, images, and motivation will be components of this knowledge.
Toffler made an interesting system observation
when he suggested that there will be a new economic significance of free expression, "as governments that were closed begin to open the
valves of public discussion."

Schein (1989) has always believed that this
may be the beginning of a major organizational
revolution and mentioned new system forms
being considered: holographic, multigoal, heterarchical, coordinational, informated systems

designed for controlled diversity or for harmonies of dissimilar elements. Organizations need covenantal relationships, according to De-Pree (1989), who views contractual relationships as stifling and having nothing to do with reaching human potential of any kind. In his view, the advantages of covenantal relationships are that they (1) induce freedom, not paralysis; (2) rest on shared commitments; (3) fill deep needs and make work meaningful; (4) reflect unity and poise; (5) enable organizations to be hospitable to the unusual person and unusual ideas; and (6) tolerate risk and forgive errors.

Six themes of recent organizational research have been identified by Weick (1985): (1) rationality is less prevalent, (2) organizations are more segmented than monolithic, (3) organizational segments are small and stable, (4) connections among segments are variable, (5) organizations have a high degree of ambiguity, and (6) the basic task of management is to reduce that ambiguity. Weick notes that ambiguity implies the presence of unregulated variety in the organization. Variety, or lack of it, is a theme that surfaces over and over in contemporary systems and organizational theory.

One way to approach organizational change is to be consciously involved in futuring, Weisbord (1989) believes. Futuring focuses attention away from interpersonal relationships and toward the experiences and values that affect everyone. He considers futuring a purposeful action taken to design a preferred future. Mohr (1989) also prefers conscious, sociotechnical organizational design, a process he says will create high-performance organizations.

At the international level, Ohmae (1990) described an economic system that "follows its own logic and develops its own webs of interest, which rarely duplicate the historical borders between nations" (p. 183). In a borderless world, any small movement in any economy affects all economies. Pluralism is a fact of life, not a generous concession to other nations. Another economist (Carroll, 1988) believes that entire organizations will be selected or replaced in the future, as some organizational forms become obsolete and others become more viable. He views adaptation as severely constrained by existing forms. Carroll insists that organizational ecology demands that organizations and environments move toward isomorphism. There should be an empirical correspondence between environmental change and patterns of organizational founding and mortality.

Change occurs daily in contemporary organizations. Without theory to organize means of coping with change, breakdown can occur within organizations and in their environments. Systems thinking may provide that needed theory. Today, theorists are studying the realities of functioning at the edge of chaotic environments (Brown & Eisenhardt, 1998). As the speed of change heightens, as connectivity broadens information availability, and as intangible features of the contingent environment multiply, educational organizations will need to rethink organizational change (Davis & Meyer, 1998). Reacting to change, even merely adapting to change may not provide adequate methods about how to keep the educational system in tune with cultural, political, and economic environments. System interventions must be rethought.

Systems can certainly adapt utilizing the interventions spoken about previously. In the highly volatile environment that exists today, however, educational administrators and practitioners may need to learn to promote newfound leadership tactics: creating new learning and instructional methods that raise the bar, launching new programs regularly, raising the standards of excellence and performance, redefining learner needs and expectations, and increasing the pace at which all of education ensures its viability (Brown & Eisenhardt, 1998).

Perhaps one of the most profound lessons to be learned is to build our interventions and strategies based on future scenarios. As is often the case, system interventions and strategies are built from events and circumstances relevant to a current and historical environment.

System change, then, is a reflection of values and attitudes from those same environments. Scenario planning and plotting is a new strategic process that holds the potential to revise how educational practitioners create change. Being able to deal with problems associated with some future scenario is wholly different from dealing with existing circumstances from a current or historical frame of reference(s). As a practitioner, the questions associated with future change keeps change agents operating from a differing perspective—a changed belief system. Taking actions, then, is also based on those same new beliefs and leads to broad application of new ideals.

Regulating Variety in Organizations

Conflict emerges in organizations when the need for variety is unappeased. As Ackoff (1974) suggested, "few have tried to redesign education in broad interactive terms. To do so requires recognizing that the current system is a Machine Age product of reductionist, analytic, and mechanistic thinking. We need a system that is the product of expansionist, synthetic, and teleological thinking" (p. 74). How much formal educational systems have learned since then about adaptation and reconfiguration is still to be determined. Ackoff speaks about Wilma Dykeman, who believes that students experience enough control and too little commitment. Students do not dislike discipline; they dislike our inadequate commitment to our own self-discipline. In systems terms, this implies that the regulation of system variety is occurring in the wrong subsystem. In practical terms this suggests that the "products" of our mechanistic schools are not highly adaptable or able to meet the educational needs of our society. A cursory glance at current political and business claims about the ineffectiveness of our schools reflects this same implication.

In circles concerned with performance technology, Nickols (1990) sounded a similar note: "The era of compliance has ended, and with it the dream of engineering individual human performance. The era of individual contribution has just begun, and we do not even have a vocabulary suitable for discussing the issue, let alone formulating decisions and then carrying them out" (p. 196). He saw this as a paradigm problem; the "unengineered" variety that organizations face today freezes paradigms.

Beer (1974) felt that variety engineering is performed in the wrong place with scientifically calculated goals and norms. The system is robbed of the crucial reference point without which it cannot learn, cannot adapt, cannot evolve. Variety regulation is performed at the local level, not at the top of the organization. Referring to Ashby's law of requisite variety, Beer asserted that there are only two ways to provide the requisite variety to keep organizations alive: (1) reduce the variety generated by the system in order to match the available regulatory variety (variety attenuation), or (2) amplify the variety of the system's regulatory part (variety amplification).

Although this may sound complicated, Beer simply means that if administrative variety is insufficient to handle the amount of variety existing in the system, the administrator lessens the variety and everyone follows the rules. That is one way of regulating. The other way is to increase the variety in the regulatory systems. This can be done by deciding how to deal with more information from the system and/or by passing on regulatory responsibility to the lowest levels. The law of requisite variety, an organizing rule for systems, has important implications for educational administrators. Human need for autonomy and internal locus of control is a psychological equivalent of self-regulation in system theory.

Gleick (1987) saw evolution as chaos with feedback. Chaotic variety becomes organized when feedback is available, pertinent, and psychologically usable by the receiver. Feedback, so often depicted as linear, in reality is optimally multidirectional. Those in charge generally have the most intimate knowledge of how decisions made elsewhere affect the rest of the organization. Leaders should be encouraged to organize their feedback for use throughout the organization. The rank-and-file enjoy requisite variety when, acting as feedback senders, they self-select the most important data to be diffused.

Davis and Meyer (1998) believe the added exposure and access that variety breeds adds significant new capacity to learners' and instructional providers' repertoires of abilities. This added capacity increases the likelihood that our educational systems will act in concert with current and future trends that are realized via scenario planning exercises. Indeed, these new leadership tactics support beliefs that are profoundly meshed with change(s) needed for tomorrow's learners.

Metaphor and System Modeling in Educational Administration

Metaphors have been in vogue primarily in natural and social sciences as a means of describing complex phenomena to the lay student. Poets have used metaphors for years as a means of capturing and sharing multidimensional human experiences which are unique and universal simultaneously.

Clancy (1989) stated that in a world of "endemic complexity" metaphors help to sort out and classify phenomena, helping humankind to understand and express one phenomenon in terms of another. Although metaphor is not the thing-in-itself and does not enable users to grasp the entire implied experience, as Clancy argued, a metaphor can shape views of experience. "It is important to recognize that metaphor is an integral part of our thought process. We use metaphor much as we breathe; we cannot avoid its use or its consequences" (p. 13). If this is true, surely the power of metaphor is its ability "to suggest a reality beyond ordinary, discursive thought."

Premodern metaphors have furnished business with its self-perceptions. Since schooling predates business as it is today, it is useful to ask why schooling has not furnished the metaphors for business. The answer is that schooling has, but until recently the competing metaphors of games, wars, machines, and heroic journeys have been dominant. The metaphor of the "learning organization" [i.e., the organization that learns (Kiechel, 1990)] has not received much credence even in educational institutions. The difference is that organizations are not for learners, but *of* and *about* learners. Yet no organizational member should be exempt from universal, systemwide continuous learning (Senge, 1990).

Three metaphors in the premodern era that apply here are the journey, game, and war. The journey elicits images of ships, captains, even ships of fools. The game metaphor is associated with players, playing fields, and winning or losing. The metaphor of war engenders visions of "pinstriped soldiers," receiving and giving marching orders. These are not particularly systemic metaphors; instead, they call up visions of heroic life and heroic death. Educators have always resisted these as images for schooling, even as they adopted some of the philosophical underpinnings.

Another set of metaphors is closer to Boulding's system of system structure (1964): the machine, the organism, and society. The spirit of the machine metaphor remains in organizations in the form of *Taylorism,* the term for unreconstructed "scientific management." The mechanical metaphor implies systems that are ultimately predictable, rational, and deterministic. People are cogs in the machinery, and the leader is an omniscient machine operator. The organism metaphor retains traces of determinism: there is a "genetic" fate in the evolution of the system which must grow and adapt even in the face of complexity and ambiguity. The society metaphor, which educational administration theories have often embraced, is built upon and may overemphasize culture, stakeholders, rituals–myths–symbols, shared values, and meaningful leadership.

Systems thinkers can accept part or all of the organism and society metaphors but still find them insufficient for the future. The metaphors of journey, game, and war can be associated with three paradigms that may have failed: journey, wealth, and the institution. Much of the organizational literature has been concerned with wealth and institutionalization. A new eclectic paradigm needs to be merged with all three metaphors in order to see the problematic future. The paradigm of the moment seems to be the prototype of the "market fair," a medieval convenience that allowed craftspeople, sellers, and clients to conduct their affairs anywhere. The watchword of this paradigm is extreme flexibility; the most important role is that of the "shape changer," a leader whose role and work shifts constantly according to need.

Hopefully, a new paradigm of "invisible powers" will emerge involving a sense of infinite playing out of the unending human spirit. Organizational coactivation must be idiographic (person-oriented) and transactional rather than normative and nomothetic (conformist, controlled). Systems theorists think in terms of the interrelatedness of subsystems rather than "taking sides."

Self-assessment in school organizations typically begins with an analysis of symptoms, but symptoms of what? The answer is typically symptoms of problems as defined by feedback. But feedback is a double-sided coin. The term *negative feedback* is typically used in conjunction with problem solving. In problem identification we typically search for negative feedback (i.e., what went wrong). On the other hand, positive feedback is usually associated with variety. System variety is rarely explored. Systems analysts set out to describe organizational elements, assess environmental demands, discover how congruent the organization is with those demands, predict problem causes, formulate plans, and evaluate plans. This process is certainly embedded in a metaphor more nomothetic than idiographic. The serious question for the new administrator is whether the balance in planning can be shifted at all toward the idiographic, transactional, empowering side.

Benne (1990) believes that "power is to social dynamics what energy is to physicochemical dynamics. One cannot understand or change a human system without taking the uses and distribution of power into account. We desperately need to understand the operation of power if we are to plan democratically" (p. 11). According to him, humans fail to understand that power is not a fixed sum, to be distributed or withheld at will up to some imagined limit. Power is self-amplifying in the positive sense. The empowerment of subsystems is the empowerment of the whole; this is a mutual relationship.

Benne also claimed that students often view the power of school systems over them as naked, illegitimate power, not authority. School resources generally are not perceived as oriented to meeting students' needs for free and responsible learning and growth, but rather to meeting teachers' needs or oriented to meeting the personnel needs of one or another established bureaucracy. Therefore, to the student, power appears to lie everywhere except within himself or herself. Similarly, Benne also noted that organizations everywhere are being forced to bring temporary organizations into being: task forces, advisory groups, project groups. Crossing departmental boundaries and even the boundaries of the system itself can be detected.

Frame (1987) has identified some forms that these projects take. One is the isomorphic team, which is configured to match the structure of the "deliverable" product or service. If the product is a report, different chapters may be allocated to different team members. Another form is the specialty team, where specialists are asked to provide input on two or more of the teams' efforts. Using the report example, one specialist might be working on several different chapters without being solely responsible for them. The egoless team structure is highly interactive; everyone is working on everything, and responsibility for the final product is shared as work flow demands. In the surgical team structure, Frame said that it is the "surgeon" who defines effectiveness. For report writing, this would mean that the chief report writer has the final word and the integrating responsibility. Since this "surgeon" bears the conceptual and skill weight, administrative tasks are carried out by others.

Developing new metaphors and models in any field can be risky since the new forms may elicit commitments to new roles, policies, and an organizational life that change continually. One of the most profound changes notable in society today evolves from the variety of metaphors associated with the information age. Davis and Botkin (1994) have cited numerous examples about how the speed at which educational practitioners change may be directly associated with the speed at which new forms and structures of education develop. Information availability and transfer are readily available to a variety of users, including schooling-at-home users, new organization forms and partners, and more. Added attention is direly needed to realize further how this information age will affect future changes.

Systems Thinking as a Wave of the Future in Education

Throughout this discussion, references have been made to the unrealized potential of systems thinking in all fields, educational administration being no exception. But what can a systems-literate administrator plunged into the district, the school, or the principal's office achieve in practical terms?

He or she can think differently and approach organizational issues, positive or negative, differently. The practice of conceptual modeling should become second nature, allowing the administrator to devise maps and diagrams that help to organize and question data, and enable system members to choose alternatives and enact them. Every case of variety-out-of-control needs this decisive thought: Can this variety producer contain the means of self-regulation, or must regulation be imposed from outside? This mandates an administrators' clear understanding of energy sources and drains in a school system.

Literature on school administration over the past several decades reveals a marked influence of nomothetic biases. Nevertheless, idiographic themes have persisted and seem to be coming into their own in the present state of organizational turmoil. After all, nomothetic planning and evaluation has not yielded what educators or businesspeople seek—the sense of productive, quality, enjoyable work. The place to begin to change the systems of the world is in the minds of the new thinkers in that world. But to change others, the minds of educators need to change. All that may be required is a return to ancient metaphors of what it is to learn. Ironically, these are systems metaphors.

One example of an ancient metaphor in new dress is provided by Engleberg's (1991) discussion of integrative study. He insisted that acute social and political problems cannot be solved by specialists, because resolution of these problems lies at the integrative level. Integrative study takes place in the here and now, among those we live with, and exerts a benign influence on the community in which it takes place. There could hardly be a more cogent belief statement in support of lowering walls between schools and the communities they serve. Engleberg adds that everyone is capable of some level of integrative study. Integration implies participation in schooling by teachers, parents, students, and all other stakeholders. It is intrinsically democratic.

Bredeson (1985), however, found that in only one out of five schools studied were parents highly involved in a formal sense. "In fact, one principal indicated that there were problems in having parents in the schools because they often do not understand many things that are occurring. Therefore, parental involvement was more often viewed as supportive and tangential as opposed to a rich source of expertise and knowledge" (p. 44). Structures for parental involvement were bounded by predetermined roles, much like the roles of all other school stakeholders.

Aside from the implications for less "bounded" schools, the notions of integrative study deserve closer inspection for their systemic version of curriculum. Engleberg believes that since living systems can be understood only by reference to their transformations over time, the objects of integrative study are narratives (histories, case histories, works of literature, etc.). Specialists can function only as long as there is an integrative matrix in which they can find a place. The occupants of the realm of wholes create and maintain these matrices. Engleberg calls for educators to "face away" from their specializations, which have been so powerfully developed and researched by the "realm of parts." He suggests that educators fear facing "nothingness" when they turn away from the disciplines, but instead, they will find themselves *facing life*. The challenge then becomes the difficulty of sharing wisdom without imposing dogma that accentuates fragmentation. This implies a new vision of teachers and administrators as facilitators of learning, not mere sharers of facts.

Engleberg assumed that language exists to facilitate integrative study, carrying learners forward through an integration of differences in which differences are maintained and preserved. While integrative study sessions require a moderator and rules of discourse, their object should be works of art, dense in information, rich in meaning. "Framework statements" (i.e., "a cumulative repository of insights") are the specified outcomes. Correlative outcomes are personal and social integrations. Extending Engleberg's thesis logically, competency-based (specialist) education may be no more than part-sensitive, able to function only if whole-sensitive integrative studies provide the matrices on which the carefully honed parts can hang without fragmentation.

The old metaphors invoked may be "liberal arts," "great books," storytelling, or even myth-making. Speaking of the qualitative uses of mythmaking in organizational development, Boje, Fedor, and Rowland (1982) identify the development of myths with the development of specific organizational situations. When a myth is guiding decision making and strategy successfully, it is a developing myth. When the myth and the organization have become completely intertwined, it is a solid myth. Myth split occurs when some groups in an organization begin to develop competing myths in order to encourage renewal or survival. Myth shift occurs when reformulation and perhaps new leadership of the organization is imminent. Although this is reminiscent of Kuhn's (1962) discussion of paradigm shifts, it is obvious that new metaphors and myths appear with every "scientific revolution" and that sometimes older metaphors and myths are reinstated in contemporary, more acceptable forms.

Bredeson (1985) referred to the influence of studies in general semantics, studies that called attention to the importance of metaphors as a mediator of reality. Bredeson said that the very words or analogies used may limit one's view of phenomena and the world. Aristotelian logic is seen as having drawn researchers in the Western world into a habit of "two-valued" thinking, accompanied by broad sets of fundamental and pervasive silent assumptions and premises. Thus, thought is governed by perceptions of "either–or" rather than "both–and," or even more sensibly, "many and all." On this basis, educators imagine ultravariability in systems with difficulty, if at all. Unchanged semantic traditions may prevent administrators from handling diversity and welcoming the "chaos" of accommodating many simultaneous "truths" and interpretations.

Bredeson cited a number of authors and their uses of prevailing metaphors about the nature or the role of school administrators: the principalship as a "constellation of positions" (Knezevich, 1975) and the principal as consummate manager, organizational change agent, educational/curricular leader, applied philosopher, school manager, behavioral scientist, politician, gamesman, broker, facilitator, missionary, and gardener (Blumberg & Greenfield, 1980; Getzels, 1958; Kmetz & Willower, 1982; Lipham & Hoeh, 1974; Martin & Willower, 1981; Miklos, 1983; Sergiovanni, Burlingame, Coombs, & Thurston, 1980; Small, 1974; Wayson, 1971). Bredeson believed that such topologies are inadequate to represent any school leader and that, instead, a composite imagery is needed. Further, he suggested that metaphors of purpose might be more instructive. If the perceived purpose is to behave like a chief executive officer (CEO), command center behavior will follow and the principal will rarely leave the office. If the perceived purpose is student control (disciplinarian), that will be the principal's modus operandi. If the perceived purpose is to ensure that a school survives in a tight economy, that will engender another set of behaviors. These prevailing metaphors result, systemically, in a maintenance function that occupies more than three-fourths of an administrator's time and energy, overriding any vision or holistic view of the present an administrator might otherwise have.

Bredeson suspects that the expectations of education administration students skew their preparation toward specific skills development that will help them survive immediately in new administrative appointments. This, he says, may help create, foster, and maintain a culturally standardized image of the school principalship that reinforces metaphoric themes and old myths, all of which can stand in the way of change. The obvious solution is to teach skills and theory, with coursework geared toward reflective, theory-based, systemic considerations. Two-valued thinking will not suffice in schools in the twenty-first century.

Conway (1985), for example, called for a rediscovery of values in schools that would parallel current efforts to rediscover values in business organizations. He felt that society asks schools to restructure themselves and their culture, to go through an organizational learning of the most difficult type. Efforts to control time spent on tasks or to extend the school year represent a linear, unitary approach to change that Conway associates with single-loop learning. In contrast, Argyris and Schön (1978), Bateson (1972), and Friedlander (1983) have all envi-sioned a more complex approach called, respectively, double-loop learning, deutero-learning, and reconstructive learning. Conway noted that culture change will not take root without appropriate reconstructive learning. The way beliefs are ordered and linked in a psychological framework can be an analogy of the way organizations believe or disbelieve. In the world map of the organization, what are the structural connections? He asked whether new information can enter to reorganize beliefs, revise ideology, and repattern paradigms. How, also, does the organization view time? If there is a fixation on a given time period, for example, the system tends toward closure. The closure is effected through a "narrowing" process which may include denigration of the past, dissolution of future-oriented functions such as planning, or institutionalizing of a "now" attitude to the exclusion of other time frames. The excluded frames then represent disbelief regions. Conway reported that in his own experience, certain indicators of structural closed-openness conditions have surfaced: knowledge disavowal (it can't be true), belief avoidance (silence), and the relative time perspective that can either expand or truncate organizational memory.

Hoy and Ferguson (1985) attempted to create a model for assessing school effectiveness across such variables as innovation, student achievement, cohesiveness, and organizational commitment. They borrow Steers' (1977) argument that the goal model of school effectiveness and the systems model are complementary. This supports the synthesis of the two models that resulted in the dimensions or variables used in Hoy and Ferguson's study. The researchers chose these dimensions specifically because they addressed Parsons' (1960) imperative for social organizations: adaptation, goal attainment, integration, and latency (creation and maintenance of motivational and value patterns). They sought to draw on the perceptions of different groups in the schools they assessed. Notable for its absence was any effort to sample student perceptions. Although their empirical analysis was considered reasonably successful, the researchers believed that an expanded model could be developed to allow more focused comparative study of schools on both rational systems and subjective dimensions. This would imply the use of various methodologies.

Liberating Systems Theory: The Critical Stance

Earlier in the chapter, the systems paradigm was described as being merely surface-minded and transported far from its origins. Flood (1990) produced a detailed, reasoned argument for a complementarist theoretical position that is open and conciliatory, overcoming the theoretical fortress mentality that has developed in the various streams of systems thinking. Subservience of any of these streams to another, he states, is a distortion of what systems thinking represents. Certainly, such subservience has kept systems thinking from realizing its full potential. Flood felt that those who seriously consider the systems epistemological ideal cannot help but conclude that beyond the positivistic (objectivist) and the interpretivistic (hermeneutic) ideals of science, the emancipatory force of critical self-reflection is necessary. He is concerned that managers tend to hide behind the facade of common interests, claiming to have surveyed opinion and reached consensus when, in fact, only a narrow band of interests are being served. The critical approach has the potential to destroy the facades of rationality and objectivity that allow decision makers to defend their own interests on grounds of rationality.

Further, whereas much of management and systems literature applauds convergence and universality, Flood argues for divergence and multiple truths, reminding us that it is anticritical to expect that we can work toward a view we all feel comfortable with. In the interests of social conservatism, Flood notes, ideological positions are ignored and objectivist research is preferred. However, in the critical inquiry framework, debates over soft versus hard systems research are irrelevant, since the choice is not between nonreflective positivistic and nonreflective interpretivistic research positions, but between nonreflection and critical self-reflection. It is conceptual reflexivity, those self-confirming and self-perpetuating aspects of systems science, that has constrained system thinking, according to Flood. He says that this has ensured that the abstract, paradigmatic richness of the word system is hidden under an avalanche of desolate labels for such things as "hair-replacement systems," "school systems," and "information systems," which have no metatheoretical connection. What Flood demands is antiprovincialism, a thinking between paradigms, a mapping of the intellectual world of systems thinking, in order to embark in new directions. It appears that Boulding's (1968) levels of systems discourse have hit a glass ceiling imposed between biologically based systems and human social systems. Nothing learned or seen above that ceiling can be valued by systems scientists unless it has yielded both positivistic and predictive systems knowledge, because that is the current map of "flat-world" systems thinking. As Columbus had need for a globe, so the adventurers of the future need to be steered by more than positivistic, predictive science.

Greatly oversimplified, Flood's map includes positivistic, interpretivistic, and critical-reflective (complementarist) regions of systems theory. He places Herbert Simon squarely in the positivistic region, with Ackoff (1979), Churchman (1977), and Checkland (1981) belonging to the interpretivistic region. Jackson and Keys (1984) occupy the complementarist region along with Ulrich (1991) and Flood (1990). The first two regions are isolated by their methodologies, whereas those oriented to critical-reflection view all theories and methodologies as complementary. What the complementarists see as necessary is a way to break through the "colonized" territory ruled by traditional management and operations research scientists, and also through the paradigmatic isolation of competing world views, into the openness and "emancipation" of critical systems theory.

This pioneering would allow researchers to deal with such issues as employee empowerment, workplace diversity, cultural anomalies, coercion, ideologies, and ownership of values in a deliberately normative way. Subjective inquiry would be openly acknowledged, not as antithetical to systems science but as part of its legitimate discourse.

Postulating a role for critical systems theory immediately removes most of the "two-value" constraints that have plagued systems literature on educational administration. "Machine" images as metaphors for social systems, those associated with management by objectives, management information systems, accountability, control, efficiency, competencies, and performance objectives (Sergiovanni et al., 1980), can be complemented by contextual analysis and "getting the drama right" (Bolman & Deal, 1991). Surely in an era that speaks incessantly about the need for liberation and empowerment, control must be imagined differently.

Choosing whatever analog inspires, a school's administrator may motivate the school's inhabitants toward that analogue, that inspiration. Images are unlimited and may be used to liberate thought and practice.

Orton and Weick (1990) argued that researchers (and practitioners) must continue to transform methodology to serve theory, and not the other way around. DeGreene (1990) also admitted that the theory and practice of management must change with the dynamic reconfiguration in the environment. Also, the approaches and tools that appeared to be well adapted to more "linear" times may be counterproductive during today's epoch of massive structural change. Robb (1990) noted that "getting a better tailor" to alter organizations will not work, for it is necessary to enter into states of disorder from which new orders can emerge. The future is unknowable. Surprise is the order of the day; strategic imagery and forward planning have no meaning in the traditional systems science sense.

Tomorrow's school administrator need not abandon systems thinking. On the contrary,

systems thinking is needed now more than ever, beyond the ceiling positivistic science has constructed. Analogs and models are also needed more than ever. Hawes (1975) stated that developing analogs should lie at the heart of the social scientist's activity.

Beer (1990) believes that a polyhedron might well be the organizational metaphor of the future. He quotes Buckminster Fuller, creator of the architectural marvel known as the geodesic dome, as having said that all systems are polyhedra. Beer imagines that a management team could be represented, together with its connection to other teams, at one of the nodes of a regular polyhedron. Such a polyhedron is held together by "tensile integrity," for struts between the faces of the geometric figure intensify its structural cohesion. Beer's idea is that an organization might be characterized as a 20-sided, 30-edged icosahedron, gathered together by 12 nodes, each connecting five edges, with each edge representing a person. Each of 30 people would belong to two teams and no two people would belong to the same two teams. Beer calls this "complete democracy" in an "organizational globe" which is "absolutely and regularly cohesive," having only nodal hierarchy. It might be interesting to arrange an imaginary classroom this way.

In a positivistic framework the polyhedron is an image not easily understood as a metaphor for organization. But the school administrator of the future, leaving the cocoon of two-value (either–or) thinking, may embark on even more imaginative journeys in the century ahead. It is not that the nomothetic (i.e., real) world must be left behind but that the idiographic (i.e., subjective) world is ever more insistent and more complex.

If schooling is to flower in the future, if integration is to democratize institutions and nations, systems thinking is, indeed, a wave of the future. The old systems science will be applicable to limited classes of problems, but the leading edge of systems thinking will be made transparent in new metaphors of humanity, its social systems, and the way they organize and act.

The study of systems thinking in this chapter carries implications for the reader's reflection on both organizational life and the research that examines that life. Both avenues for reflection lead to new questions and, furthermore, to a questioning of the conventional established two-dimensional focus of schooling and positivistic research. At no other time in the history of U.S. education has such questioning been more needed than it is today. Perhaps the following questions will stir the reader's understanding of the promise of systems thinking as a theory for the development of effective schools in the twenty-first century.

CASE STUDY

Systems: The Case of Karen Avery

Introduction

Too often classrooms are relatively closed systems. Guided by regulatory bodies, students achieve outcomes that have too little applicability to current need and practice. Similarly, our schools and school districts suffer from this paralysis and tend to be relatively closed.

Consider in the case that follows how we have widened or narrowed the purview of the classroom, the school, and the school district and created a relatively closed or open system. Look for interactions, interdependencies, and interrelationships in the organized complexity of this hypothetical assimilation. The case as developed is derived in part from Reigeluth's (1987) third-wave educational system description.

Convulsions and Vertigo

For many years now, Karen Avery has increasingly been losing the excitement she felt when she first began teaching. Now a department chair, she feels she has even less impact on teaching and governance and over the individual learning of students. She often considered what further limits she would encounter with her next promotion. Her classroom exchanges with students provided fewer insightful moments. Meetings with colleagues were devoted to symptomatic problem solving: discipline, absenteeism, scarcity of time, and relations with school and district administration centered largely on the necessity of meeting growing demands with limited resources.

During the past year Karen participated in a task force created to devise a new strategic agenda for the school district. The national mood to discredit schools, educational practices, and school administration had settled abruptly in her community 14 months ago as a result of national media coverage of a lengthy student-led strike. High visibility at this national level demanded unequivocal action. A variety of subgroups to the task force had met over the last year to study and recommend rigorous improvements, actions, and changes. Each subgroup drew from the latest research, simulations, and actual practices in industry in its efforts to devise solutions to the multitude of student problems. In particular, one subgroup of the task force recommended adoption of total quality management (TQM) to access outcomes on a continuous basis and act on the findings. Another subgroup recommended a service management-based program to include better strategic planning, decentralization of control, more flexibility, and consistency—all designed to release the intrinsic motivation in administrators, teachers, and students alike. A third subgroup recommended "a return to basics": stronger discipline, greater expectations, more definitive rules, and structure. Karen's subgroup was locked in controversy and had not provided its own singular solutions. Other subgroups acted similarly and without much effect. Now, a year later, students again grew restless.

As Karen reflected on the year's events, she realized the limitations of the task force in response to student unrest. Overall the task force accomplished little to foster an understanding of the variety of circumstances existing in their district. It had only offered piecemeal solutions to problems that appeared unmanageable. The multidimensional problems certainly needed methodology beyond that which existed within the task force. Questions raced through her thoughts. "How can we integrate our expertise and our reflections to address the complexity of the tasks we face? Do inquiry methods move squarely to solutions? Do other organizations face similar circumstances? Can we learn from them? Are our problems mutually exclusive? Do our own comfort levels inhibit individual, group, or organizational action?"

Tomorrow Today

During the summer break Karen attended a series of seminars at a national education convention held in her community. By accident she elected to attend several seminars dealing with systems theory and another seminar that sketched a preliminary model for a new school system. During the remaining summer months Karen contemplated the new philosophy and reviewed the model of the new school system over and over. "How can we better understand the systemic nature of our district when all we produce is independent judgments and solutions? Where do we start looking for these so-called interactions, interdependencies, and integration mechanisms? Does the essence of our organizational model really control us at the expense of individuality and concerted action? Are student reactions just a symptomatic expression of more fundamental problems? Has our task force and its subgroups achieved anything of value or consequence? And how do we proceed?"

Early in the fall at the first meeting of the subgroup Karen explained the rudiments of systems thinking and the new school model. Her thoughts had begun to crystalize and she began the process of swaying other group members' paradigmatic stances. Although still somewhat conceptually oriented, her group's progress report follows.

Their model attempts to capture one of the classical meanings of learning, an environment whereby learners achieve their own capacity to act. As devised, the system specifically proposes an integrative framework that exposes the learner to an ever-changing variety of learning methods, learning environments, and outcomes. The learner, the teacher, and the learning system are the research cornerstones. As an individual, each learner brings a variety of abilities, skills, and values to the learning environment. The task of education is to outfit learners with an amalgam of abilities, skills, and values to use and align uniquely with the expectations of the sociocultural environment. At a subgroup meeting one member, quite by accident, coined the phrase, "to earn a living and live a life." The metaphor stayed with the group.

Karen's group first proposed a new structure. In their system teachers would become guides, advisors, motivators, and managers versus content disseminators and disciplinarians. New resources, including interactive computers, videodisks, peer tutors, projects, and learning laboratories would be employed to transfer knowledge to the student. A guide would advise, motivate, and manage students and also coordinate the efforts of other new elements in the system, such as inexpensive assistants, apprentice guides, senior citizens, parents and peer tutors, well-designed projects, discussion groups, learning laboratories, and resource people. Parents, in particular, would help decide instructional goals in conjunction with their guide and the individual student. A student's development in the physical, social, moral, psychological, and intellectual domains would each be considerations. The classroom environment as we know it would disappear. A guide and student or small groups of students would work together to attain agreed-upon developmental goals. A guide would be responsible for a student through one of the four developmental stages within K–12, about four years per student per development stage. Each student's educational goals would be matched to uniquely suited educational resources orchestrated by a guide and other assistants.

A guide would not work independently but would be integrated into a cluster of three to six guides. The guides would participate in decision making and exert control over a particular cluster. In each cluster all guides would be responsible for cluster success. Clusters themselves would create and meet goals. A master guide would also serve in the cluster as an instructional leader. Success of a cluster would depend on parent and student satisfaction. As clusters succeeded in meeting the specified developmental goals, more satisfied parents would elect the very best clusters. Effective clusters survive as a result of incentive–reward and financial support from the school district based on parental choice.

As goal achievement occurs and students pass through developmental stages, new student goals would become more specific. Learning laboratories would provide specialized expertise in traditional, discipline-oriented, and cross-disciplinary areas. Students' progress in their clusters would earn them the privilege of attending a variety of learning labs. These labs would operate independently of the clusters, but also cooperatively.

It is at this point in the case that we join Karen's group. Each of you has undoubtedly raised questions. Your questions and others outlined below, plus several small vignettes, should inspire further discussion.

Questions

1. From a systems perspective, what factors do you believe contributed to the marginal results obtained by the various subgroups within the task force?

2. In the case, identify and discuss instances of an aggregate mentality at work.

3. Would Karen today describe her school or school system as relatively open or relatively closed? Why? Classify the new model as open or closed. Why?

4. Discuss the feedback mechanisms that exist in the new school model.

5. Does the new school model appear to invite chaos or amplify variety? Discuss why.

6. In the case, glimpses of several management philosophies or taxonomies may be apparent to you. Although some tenets within these philosophies may overlap, can you identify and substantiate which actor or group of actors fit the categories below?
   a. Traditionalist view
   b. Human relations view
   c. Situational view
   d. Systems view

7. From the case, as proposed by various subgroups, identify the situations that you view as systematic or systemic.
   a. The TQM model
   b. The service management model
   c. The back-to-basics model
   d. The new school system

8. Use some of the following systems properties to defend your viewpoints determined in Question 7.
   a. Input–throughput–output
   b. Synergy
   c. Leading part and emergence
   d. Dynamic homeostasis
   e. Equifinality
   f. Negentropy

References

Ackoff, R. L. (1974). *Redesigning the future*. New York: Wiley.

Ackoff, R. L. (1979). The future of operational research is past. *Journal of the Operational Research Society, 30*(2), 189–199.

Argyris, C., & Schön, D. A. (1978). *Organizational learning*. Reading, MA: Addison-Wesley.

Ashmos, D. P., & Huber, G. P. (1987). The systems paradigm in organization theory: Correcting the record and suggesting the future. *Academy of Management Review, 12*(4), 607–621.

Banathy, B. H. (1972). A systems analysis of systems education. *Educational Technology, 12*(2), 73–75.

Barnard, C. I. (1938). *Functions of an executive.* Cambridge, MA: Harvard University Press.

Bateson, G. (1972). *Steps to an ecology of mind.* New York: Ballantine Books.

Beer, S. (1974). *Designing freedom.* New York: Wiley.

Beer, S. (1990). On suicidal rabbits: A relativity of systems. *Systems Practice, 3*(2), 115–124.

Benne, K. D. (1990). *The task of post-contemporary education.* New York: Teachers College Press, Columbia University.

Bertalanffy, L. von. (1968a). *General system theory: Foundations, development, applications.* New York: Braziller.

Bertalanffy, L. von. (1968b). General system theory: A critical review. In W. Buckley (Ed.), *Modern systems research for the behavioral scientist.* Chicago: Aldine.

Blumberg, A., & Greenfield, W. (1980*). The effective principal: Perspectives of school leadership.* Boston: Allyn & Bacon.

Boje, D. M., Fedor, D. B., & Rowland, K. M. (1982). Myth-making: A qualitative step in O.D. interventions. *Journal of Applied Behavioral Science, 18*(1), 17–28.

Bolman, L. G., & Deal, T. E. (1991). *Reframing organizations.* San Francisco: Jossey-Bass.

Boulding, K. E. (1964). *The meaning of the 20th century: The great frustration.* New York: Harper & Row.

Boulding, K. E. (1968). General systems theory: The skeleton of science. In W. Buckley (Ed.), *Modern systems research for the behavioral scientist.* Chicago: Aldine.

Bredeson, P. V. (1985, Winter). An analysis of the metaphorical perspectives of school principals. *Educational Administration Quarterly, 21*(1), 29–50.

Brown, A. F. (1967, March). Conflict and stress in administrative relationships. *Administrator's Notebook, 10.*

Brown, S. L., & Eisenhardt, K. M. (1998*). Competing on the edge: Strategy as structured chaos.* Boston: Harvard Business School Press.

Carroll, G. R. (Ed.). (1988). *Ecological models of organizations.* Cambridge, MA: Ballinger.

Checkland, P. B. (1981). *Systems thinking, systems practice.* Chichester, West Sussex, England: Wiley.

Chin, R., Bennis, W. G., & Benne, K. D. (1961). *The planning of change.* New York: Holt, Rinehart and Winston.

Churchman, C. W. (1977). A philosophy for complexity. In H. A. Linstone & W. H. Simmonds (Eds.), *Managing complexity.* Reading, MA: Addison-Wesley.

Churchman, C. W. (1979). *The systems approach.* New York: Dell.

Clancy, J. J. (1989). *The invisible powers:* The language of business. Lexington, MA: D.C. Heath.

Conway, J. A. (1985, Fall). A perspective on organizational cultures and organizational belief structure. *Educational Administration Quarterly, 21*(4), 7–25.

Davis, S., & Botkin, J. (1994*). The monster under the bed: How business is mastering the opportunity of knowledge for profit.* New York: Simon and Schuster.

Davis, S., & Meyer, C. (1998). *Blur: The speed of change in the connected economy.* Reading, MA: Addison-Wesley.

DeGreene, K. B. (1990). Nonlinear management in technologically induced fields. *Systems Research, 7*(3), 159–168.

DePree, M. (1989). *Leadership is an art.* New York: Doubleday.

Emery, F. E. (Ed.). (1970). *Systems thinking.* Harmondsworth, Middlesex, England: Penguin Books.

Engdahl, R. A. (1989, Spring). Thoughts on need for an improved organization theory net with which to "catch the world." *Organization Development Journal, 7*(1), 42–50.

Engleberg, J. (1991). On integrative study. *Systems Research, 9*(1), 5–17.

Flood, R. L. (1990). *Liberating systems theory.* New York: Plenum Press.

Frame, J. D. (1987). *Managing projects in organizations.* San Francisco: Jossey-Bass.

Friedlander, F. (1983). Patterns of individual and organizational learning. In S. Srivasta & Associates (Eds.), *The executive mind.* San Francisco: Jossey-Bass.

Getzels, J. W. (1958). Administration as a social process. In Andrew Halpin (Ed.), *Administrative theory in education.* Chicago: Midwest Administration Center, University of Chicago.

Gleick, J. (1987) *Chaos: Making a new science.* New York: Penguin Books.

Grenier, L. E. (1972, July–August). Evolution and revolution as organization grows. *Harvard Business Review,* 37–46.

Hall, A. D., & Fagen, R. E. (1968). Definition of system. In W. Buckley (Ed.), *Modern systems research for the behavioral scientist.* Chicago: Aldine.

Harmon, F. G. (1989). *The executive odyssey.* New York: Wiley.

Hawes, L. C. (1975). *Pragmatics of analogying: Theory and model construction in communication.* Reading, MA: Addison-Wesley.

Hearn, G. (1958). *Theory building in social work.* Toronto, Ontario, Canada: University of Toronto Press.

Hodge, B. J., & Anthony, W. P. (1988). *Organization theory.* Boston: Allyn & Bacon.

Hodge, B. J., & Johnson, H. J. (1988). Management and organizational behavior. In B. J. Hodge & W. P. Anthony, *Organization theory* (3rd ed.). Boston: Allyn & Bacon.

Homans, G. C. (1950). *The human group.* New York: Harcourt, Brace & World.

Hoy, W. K., & Ferguson, J. (1985, Spring). A theoretical framework and exploration of organizational effectiveness of schools. *Educational Administration Quarterly, 21*(2), 117–134.

Huse, E., & Bowditch, J. (1973). *Behavior in organization: A system approach to managing.* Reading, MA: Addison-Wesley.

Immegart, G. L., & Pilecki, F. J. (1973). *An introduction to systems for the educational administrator.* Reading, MA: Addison-Wesley.

Jackson, M. C., & Keys, P. (1984). Toward a system of system methodologies. *Journal of the Operational Research Society, 35,* 473–486.

Jaques, E. (1989). *Requisite organization: The CEO's guide to creative structure and leadership.* London: Cason Hall.

Kast, F. E., & Rosenzweig, J. E. (1972). The modern view: A systems approach. In J. Beishon & G. Peters (Eds.), *Systems behavior* (pp. 11–28). New York: Harper & Row.

Katz, D., & Kahn, R. L. (1966). *The social psychology of organizations.* New York: Wiley.

Kets de Vries, M. F. R., & Miller, D. (1989). *The neurotic organization.* San Francisco: Jossey-Bass.

Kiechel, W., III. (1990, March 12). The organization that learns. *Fortune, 121*(6), 133–136.

Kimbrough, R. B., & Nunnery, M. Y. (1988). *Educational administration: An introduction* (3rd ed.). New York: Macmillan.

Kmetz, J. T., & Willower, D. J. (1982). Elementary school principals' work behavior. *Educational Administration Quarterly, 18*(4), 62–78.

Knezevich, S. J. (1975). *Administration of public education.* New York: Harper & Row.

Kuhn, T. S. (1962). *The structure of scientific revolutions.* Chicago: University of Chicago Press.

Lasell, W. (1969). *An examination of the interrelationships of stress, dogmatism, and the performance of a stressful task.* Unpublished doctoral dissertation, University of Rochester, Rochester, NY.

Lewin, K. (1975). Field theory in social sciences. In E. F. Huse (Ed.), *Organization development and change.* Boston: West.

Lipham, J. M., & Hoeh, J. A., Jr. (1974). *The principalship: Foundations and functions.* New York: Harper & Row.

Lippitt, R., Watson, J., & Westley, B. (1975). The dynamics of planned change. In E. F. Huse (Ed.), *Organization development and change.* Boston: West.

Marney, M. C., & Smith, N. M. (1964). The domain of adaptive systems: A rudimentary taxonomy. *General Systems, 9,* 113.

Martin, W. J., & Willower, D. J. (1981). The managerial behavior of high school principals. *Educational Administration Quarterly, 17*(1), 69–90.

Miklos, E. (1983). Alternative images of the administrator. *The Canadian Administrator, 27*(7).

Mohr, B. J. (1989). Theory, method, and process: Key dynamics in designing high-performing organizations from an open sociotechnical systems perspective. In W. Sikes, A. B. Drexler, & J. Gant (Eds.), *The emerging practice of organization development.* Alexandria, VA: NTL Institute for Applied Behavioral Science.

Nickols, F. W. (1990, Summer). Human performance technology: The end of an era. *Human Resource Development Quarterly, 1*(2), 187–197.

Ohmae, K. (1990). *The borderless world: Power and strategy in the interlinked economy.* New York: HarperCollins.

Orton, J. D., & Weick, K. E. (1990). Loosely coupled systems: A reconceptualization. *Academy of Management Review, 15*(2), 203–223.

Parsons, T. (1960). *Structure and process in modern societies.* New York: Free Press.

Rapoport, A. (1968). Foreword. In W. Buckley (Ed.), *Modern systems research for the behavioral scientist*. Chicago: Aldine.

Reigeluth, C. (1987). The search for meaningful reform: A third-wave educational system. *Journal of Instructional Management, 10*(4), 3–14.

Robb, F. F. (1990). Morphostasis and morphogenesis: Contexts of design inquiry. *Systems Research, 7*(3), 135–146.

Rusche, P. J. (1968). *A study of selected aspects of the communication flow between a school and a community*. Unpublished doctoral dissertation, University of Rochester, Rochester, NY.

Salisbury, D. F. (1990, February). General systems theory and instructional system design. *Performance and Instruction, 29*(2), 1–10.

Schein, E. (1989, May). Corporate teams and totems. *Across the Board, 26*, 12–17. (reprinted from *Sloan Management Review*, Winter 1989).

Schoderbek, P. P., Schoderbek, C. G., & Kefalas, A. G. (1990). *Management systems: Conceptual considerations*. Boston: BPI/Irwin.

Selye, H. (1957). *The stress of life*. New York: Longmans, Green.

Senge, P. M. (1990). *The fifth discipline: The art and practice of the learning organization*. New York: Doubleday/Currency.

Sergiovanni, J. J., Burlingame, M., Coombs, F. D., & Thurston, P. W. (1980). *Educational governance and administration*. Upper Saddle River, NJ: Prentice Hall.

Simon, H. A. (1964). On the concept of organizational goals. *Administrative Science Quarterly, 9*(9).

Simon, H. A. (1970). *The science of the artificial*. Cambridge, MA: MIT Press.

Small, J. F. (1974). Initiating and responding to social change. In J. A. Culbertson, C. Henson, & R. Morrison (Eds.), *Performance objectives for school principals: Concepts and instruments*. Berkeley, CA: McCutchan.

Steers, R. M. (1977). *Organizational effectiveness: A behavioral view*. Santa Monica, CA: Goodyear.

Toffler, A. (1990, November). Toffler's next shock. *World Monitor, 3*(11), 34–44.

Ulrich, W. (1991). Toward emancipatory systems practice. In R. L. Flood & M. C. Jackson (Eds.), *Creative problem solving: Total systems intervention*. Chichester, West Sussex, England: Wiley.

Wayson, W. W. (1971). A new kind of principal. *National Elementary Principal, 50*(4), 9–19.

Weick, K. C. Sources of order in underlying organizational systems: Themes in recent organizational theory. In Lincoln, Y. E. (Ed.), *Organizational Theory and Inquiry: The Paradigm Revolution*. Beverly Hills: Sage Publishing Co. and in Kimbrough, R.B. & Nunnery, M.Y. (1987). *Educational Administration: An Introduction* (3rd ed). New York: Macmillan.

Weiner, N. (1968). Cybernetics in history. In W. Buckley (Ed.), *Modern systems research for the behavioral scientist*. Chicago: Aldine.

Weisbord, M. R. (1989). Future search: Toward strategic integration. In W. Sikes, A. B. Dresler, & J. Gant (Eds.), *The emerging practice of organization development*. Alexandria, VA: NTL Institute for Applied Behavioral Science.

Willis, V. J. (1977). *Emergent–devolvent synchrony in general systems: Creativity as a special case*. Unpublished doctoral dissertation, State University of New York at Buffalo.

Young, O. R. (1964). A survey of general systems theory. *General Systems, 9*.

CHAPTER 3

Leadership in a Reform Environment

In the 1980s, leadership, or the lack of it, became the named excuse for myriad national problems. According to Rost (1991), leadership in the United States was at fault for our decline in the global economy while being the vehicle needed to restore our lost power and prestige. Bennis and Nanus (1985) asserted that "a chronic crisis of governance—that is, the pervasive incapacity of organizations to cope with the expectations of their constituents—is now an overwhelming factor worldwide" (p. 2). Burns (1978) maintained that "the crisis of leadership today is the mediocrity or irresponsibility of so many men and women in power" (p. 1). Bennis and Nanus claimed that leadership is necessary to develop visions that can move organizations to change from what they are to what they can be. Insightful leadership could help the United States deal with its loss of stature in the world and teach the significance of excellence.

In the 1990s, new and different thinking was emerging about leadership. The world was entering an unprecedented period. Never were so many changes ongoing; the rise of global competition, increased complexity and change, and the demise of hierarchy and position power all were creating broad new challenges (McFarland, Senn, & Childress, 1994). Leaders were needed who could envision differing responses to a changing world. These changes and many others were driving the need for a different quality of education—teaching and learning that could help us transform leadership in businesses, government, and education itself with newer skills, abilities, and values.

Scholarly attempts to analyze leadership have resulted in many diverse definitions, theories, models, and applications. There is still no general consensus about what constitutes leadership or effective leadership within organizations. Apparently, most scholars would agree with Burns's (1978) conclusion that "leadership is one of the most observed and least understood phenomena on earth" (p. 2). Rost (1991) contended that a conceptual framework for leadership cannot be constructed until "a clear, concise, easily understandable, researchable, practical, and persuasive definition of leadership" (p. 8) is formulated. However, most definitions and theories of leadership have served the temporal needs of researchers, organizations, and societies.

Perhaps one of the greatest realizations occurring today involves our single-mindedness. Leadership may simply not be supportable as a set of traits, as intellectual genius or an intelligence quotient, or as a set of behaviors that we can simply understand and make available through research and training. More appropriately, leadership today must be seen in its rich variety—there is probably no single set of standards by which we can judge it, no single, best practice of the art of leadership, and no research agenda capable of capturing it in its entirety. Leadership may be naturally illusive, emergent, and differing within each context and across contexts.

In terms of academic and practical efficacy, definitions of leadership endure for about 20 years. When research uncovers deficiencies in the theories, new perspectives for studying leadership are identified. The complexity of modern organizations, in one sense microcosmically pictured in the changing socioeconomic configurations of the family, suggests that leadership paradigms may change rapidly as we begin the twenty-first century. This condition raises several questions for students who will assume leadership positions in the future. How will leadership paradigms need to change as leaders and followers are observed in new roles and contexts? An examination of leadership reflects the conclusion above, that leadership is not definitive but elusive and constantly changing, reflecting an ever-changing society and world, a new millennium in which collaboration may be a new, serious, and overarching key ingredient. How do and will future organizational contexts affect current theories of leadership and/or lead to new conceptual frameworks about leadership?

Leadership or Management

In this book we examine leaders and managers and the problems they face: most particularly, leadership and management in education. Educational institutions today are in crisis. But is the offender the individual leader or manager? Too often our principals, superintendents, and teachers are the scapegoats for larger institutional, societal, even global problems. Very often the performance of these individuals is labeled inadequate before there is a thorough review of the educational systems and their subsystems or review of the suprasystems where educational practice is conceived. Educators have long believed they can only perform within that system, within its processes, activities, and membership. As we shall observe, however, the face of educational practice, too, is changing, and thus our views about what constitutes leadership.

How does leadership or management occur within this educational environment? Do we have a firm grasp of the meaning of leadership and management? Are leadership and management the same? Can our definitions enhance our understanding of leadership while remaining adaptable in a postindustrial paradigm in a society where leaders and managers help to remodel or redesign our vital institutions, including education?

As the twentieth century closes, we find that leadership and management have been studied extensively. While the study of leadership and management has provided greater understanding for practitioners, and while theories and models of the same have enlightened us, there is no scholarly consensus about what distinguishes leadership from management, what defines each, or how they will change. Leadership and management are different. But the reasons for that difference have not been fully investigated, nor have we arrived at plausible interpretations to explain those differences. At best, Yukl (1989) and others have postulated an expanded conceptual framework of leadership that brings together much of the existing knowledge on leadership. But at the same time, he states: "The terms leader and manager are used interchangeably in this book" (p. 5). Undoubtedly, he might also use leadership and management interchangeably. So what is leadership? What is management? Are leaders and managers really different? Do the definitions coincide? Does it matter in the coming new millennium?

In this book and this chapter we intend to stir learners' thoughts in introductory/preparatory educational administration programs. Its more specific intent is to broaden the scope of our outlook, creating greater understanding and greater subsequent reflective action. Being aware of issues and problems and devising remedies to understanding effective leadership is no longer enough. As we incorporate technological developments and as complexity multiplies exponentially, the need arises for both systematic and systemic understanding within content areas, and more important, across those same areas. Analysis, synthesis, flexibility, and adaptability must cross a variety of venues before evolving into action. Our beliefs about leadership must evolve *with* societal and global change as we empower all our teachers and administrators to new action environments.

The following theories and/or major research approaches to leadership are examined in this chapter: (1) trait studies, which attempt to identify personality traits and intelligence of leaders and the identification of relationships of these to specific skills; (2) behavioral studies, which explore activity patterns and content to identify behavior patterns; (3) power-influence relationships, which investigate how leaders obtain and use power to influence others; (4) contingency/situational studies, which explore how varying situations may influence the relationship of leader behavior to leadership effectiveness; (5) transformative/transactional leadership beliefs, which develop mutual relationships between leaders and followers; and (6) cultural relationships, leader behavior in relation to building an organization's culture. Although many studies focus narrowly on one of the approaches above without examining the possibility of integrating the findings of multiple approaches (Yukl, 1989), our hope is to acquaint the reader with the many dimensions of leadership and to explore each in a systematic and systemic manner. The chapter ends with a brief discussion of leadership in the new millennium.

Leadership Trait Theories

Early studies on leadership were based on the assumption that individuals possessed certain physical characteristics, personality traits, and intellectual abilities that made them natural leaders (Yukl, 1989). Using correlational statistics, these studies compared successful leaders with unsuccessful leaders to see if the possession of specified traits might be a prerequisite for effective leadership. Organizational theorist Stogdill (Bass, 1981), however, contended that leadership cannot only be explained in terms of the individual or group, but must take into account the interaction of leadership traits with situational variables (p. 38). The belief that people possessing leadership traits can be effective regardless of the situation, therefore, is no longer supportable (Gardner, 1990). Smith and Peterson's (1989) review of

trait research also criticized trait studies that provide too little uniformity in design. Bennis and Nanus (1985) discounted the Great Man theory of leadership, which attributes power to character and limits the number of potential leaders based on birthright. Their research also refutes the idea that great events can transform ordinary people into great leaders.

Behavioral Theory

Behavior theorists attempt to determine what effective leaders do by identifying both the behavior of leaders and the effects that leader behavior has on subordinate productivity and work satisfaction. Studies of leader behavior at the University of Iowa (White & Lippitt, 1990) examined the effect on subordinate attitudes and productivity as leadership style is varied. Leaders were trained to demonstrate three leadership styles: democratic, authoritarian, and laissez-faire. Individual leaders demonstrated behavior attributes consistent with each leadership style from complete control to near-complete freedom choice.

White and Lippitt's study (1990) determined that the democratic leadership style was preferred by workers. There was more group-mindedness, friendliness, and efficiency in democratic situations. In sum, workers preferred laissez-faire style over authoritarian style. In other cases, subordinates demonstrated aggressive or apathetic behavior in response to authoritarian leaders. Productivity was also slightly higher with an authoritarian leader than with a democratic leader, and subordinates exhibited more dependence and less individuality with authoritarian leaders. Although the Iowa studies were highly criticized, they are still considered a classic research effort on the effects of leadership styles on subordinates' attitudes and productivity (Lunenburg & Ornstein, 1991).

Leadership studies were also carried out at Ohio State University. Two dimensions of leadership were identified: consideration and the ability to initiate structure (Stogdill & Coons,

Figure 3.1
Two-dimensional leadership model

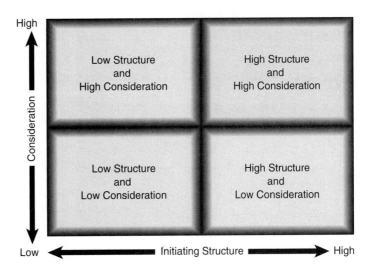

1957). Consideration was defined as the leader's expression of trust, respect, warmth, support, and concern for subordinates' welfare. The capacity to develop initiating structure defined the leader's attention to organizational goals, the organization and assignment of tasks, the delineation of superior–subordinate relationships, and the evaluation of task performance (Lunenburg & Ornstein, 1991). The Ohio State leadership studies formulated a two-dimensional model (see Figure 3.1) identifying four leadership behaviors: low structure, high consideration; high structure, low consideration; low structure, low consideration; and high structure, high consideration. Correlations were established between two items: initiating structures and consideration, and subordinate work satisfaction and performance or productivity as demonstrated by the leaders' behavior. However, causality between leader behavior and subordinate performance could not be substantiated (Yukl, 1989). This behavioral approach to leadership analysis, however, did demonstrate that leadership behaviors may be quantifiable and observable. Subordinate satisfaction and productivity may be improved by leaders who demonstrate high initiating and high consideration behaviors (Lunenburg & Ornstein, 1991).

Leadership studies done at the University of Michigan attempted to identify the relationships among leader behavior, group processes, and group performance. These studies showed three leadership styles: (1) task-oriented behavior similar to initiating structure, (2) relationship-oriented behavior similar to consideration, and (3) participative leadership (Likert, 1961). Preliminary research indicated that productive work groups have leaders who are relationship-oriented rather than task-oriented. Inconsistency in research findings, however, later led researchers to conclude that effective leaders are both task- and relationship-oriented. Group effectiveness is determined by the quality of the leadership present in the group rather than by task differentiation.

Likert's (1961) four leadership styles (see Figure 3.2) are (1) exploitative authoritative, (2) benevolent authoritative, (3) consultative, and (4) participative (democratic). Likert demonstrated that in situations in which leaders used consultative or participative leadership, there was evidence of trust, collaborative goal setting, bottom-up communication, and supportive leader behavior. In organizational situations where exploitative authoritative or benevolent authoritative leadership was utilized, organizations were

Figure 3.2
Likert's four leadership styles

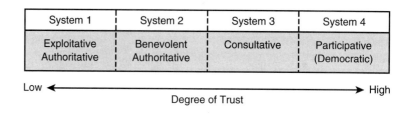

characterized by threats, fear, punishment, top-down communication, and centralized decision making and control. These characteristics were used to elicit subordinate conformity to organizational goals and productivity standards. Likert also suggested that leaders who utilize participative decision procedures are more effective. Likert's continuum is still referred to frequently by leadership analysts because it provides systematic understanding of concepts that can often be applied to cross-organizational studies.

In an attempt to identify one leadership style that is optimal in all circumstances, various studies on theories of universal leadership (Blake & Mouton, 1981; Likert, 1961, 1967) concluded that effective leaders are supportive and task oriented. In these cases the value orientation, rather than the behavior pattern of the leader, becomes the salient theoretical concept. Further studies postulated that leader behavior and trait research should be combined. The contention was that traits and leadership qualities influence leader behavior (Mazzarella & Grundy, 1989).

Current research emphasizes a behavioral approach and seeks to identify the behaviors and skills that could be taught to potential leaders. Ensuing research efforts have attempted to identify elements of leadership, based on social and task behaviors, and to rate them on a continuum to determine leadership effectiveness. Behavior research, however, does not take into consideration the situational factors (i.e., task differentiation, group composition, environmental variables) that influence leadership behavior (Lunenburg & Ornstein, 1991). Behavioral variables cannot be treated but must be examined as interrelating factors (Smith & Pe-

terson, 1989). It is important to note that these studies were first criticized for their leadership research but later resulted in efforts to explain leadership from a more systemic view.

Power Influence

Other studies attempt to understand leadership behavior from a power-influence perspective. This section is more extensive, as power relationships may be one of those more influential components surrounding our understanding of leadership. It may be one of those areas where leadership is changing dramatically, too. Power is "a force that determines behavioral outcomes in an intended direction in a situation involving human interaction" (Abbott and Caracheo, 1988, p. 241). They limited the treatment of power to an organizational context and argued that there are only two bases of power: authority and prestige. Power based on authority is derived from the leader's established position within a social institution's hierarchy and is delegated by the institution. Prestige power is based on the leader's possession of natural (honesty) or acquired (expertise) personal characteristics that are valued by others. This power must be earned by the leader through demonstration of these characteristics. The exercise of "institutional power, the potential to elicit intended behaviors from others . . . takes the form of either coercion or persuasion" (Abbott & Caracheo, 1988, p. 243). They argue that reward and coercive power are not the bases of power, as French and Raven (1968) purported, but ways in which power is exercised in an institutional environment based on either authority or

Table 3.1
Five Bases of Power

Basis of Power	Types of Influence
Reward	• The leader is capable of providing the reward.
	• The follower finds the reward desirable.
	• The follower perceives the leader's offering rewards as legitimate.
Coercive	• The follower perceives that the leader is capable of administering punishment for nonconformity to influence attempts.
Legitimate	• It arises from internalized values or norms in the follower that legitimize the leader's right to influence the follower and obligate the follower to accept this influence.
	• It can be derived from cultural values, acceptance of social structure, and designation by a legitimate agent.
Referent	• The follower perceives oneness and identification with the leader.
Expert	• The follower believes that leader has some superior knowledge or expertise in a specific area and that this power is limited to this area of expertise.

[handwritten: Affiliation • sense of belonging ; association ; positive identity]

prestige or both. Abbott and Caracheo (1988) also stated that legitimate power, derived from followers' conceding legitimacy to those who rule, is based on authority in institutional environments. They view referent and expert power as two of the elements that may comprise prestige power in an institutional setting.

By redefining reward and coercive power as means of exercising power rather than forms of power, and by maintaining that referent and expert power are elements of prestige power, their studies help us understand that authority is also legitimate power. Abbott and Caracheo (1988) postulated that there are only two bases for power. This is clearly more than a semantic finding since it can result in the closer identification of leadership behaviors (see Table 3.1).

Yukl (1989) defined power as an agent's capacity to influence one or more persons. To "influence" in this sense means to have an effect on the target's attitudes, perceptions, and/or behavior. Yukl (1989) claimed that the power to influence, which can be exerted downward, laterally, or upward, stems from three sources: position, personal, and political (or referent) (see Figure 3.3):

1. *Position power.* Followers are motivated to comply with and perceive the legitimacy of the leader and recognize the scope of authority and control over resources, rewards, punishments, and information in the physical environment and organizational subsystems.

2. *Personal power* (expert, referent, and charismatic). Expert power requires followers to recognize and submit to the leader's special skills. Charismatic power uses the leader's ability to identify followers' needs and values and thereby, to motivate commitment.

3. *Referent power.* Power is developed slowly through symbolic actions that demonstrate the leader's consideration of followers and their reciprocity through task compliance and the formation of similar attitudes toward the organization.

A leader's power base may be increased through political power or the means of controlling decision-making processes, coalescing parties to obtain desired results, and increasing the commitment of others to decisions through participation in the decision-making process

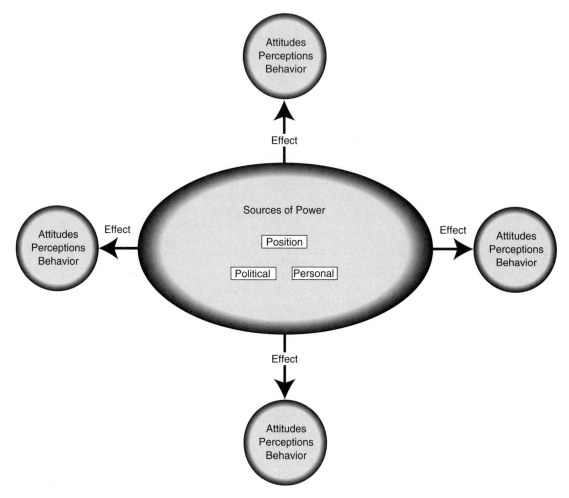

Figure 3.3
Yukl's analysis of power

(cooptation). Alternative ways to view power are summarized in Table 3.2.

Blake and Mouton (1961) defined power relationships using a power spectrum within which social power is distributed to accomplish a task. They identified three areas—competition, collaboration, and powerlessness—and built a power continuum that can be applied to decision making. Competition describes a situation in which each participant attempts to achieve or retain complete decision-making ability. Powerlessness describes a situation in which participants have

no power to influence others or to obtain decisions that permit needed actions. Collaboration describes a situation that allows followers varying degrees of power, ranging from one with little or no power where the leader has complete power in decision making, to one in which the two participants have equal power, and one in which the subordinate has total power.

Blake and Mouton (1961) concluded that as a power relationship becomes balanced, work satisfaction and feelings of responsibility become optimal. Thus, mutual sharing of decision-

Table 3.2
Power-Influence Studies of Leadership

Representatives	Study Concerns
French & Raven (1968)	Reward power, coercive power, legitimate power, referent power, expert power
Abbott & Caracheo (1988)	Authority power, prestige power
Yukl (1989)	*Directions:* downward, lateral, upward
	Sources: position, personal, political
Blake & Mouton (1961)	*Power situations:* competition, collaboration, powerlessness
Hollander (1979)	*Power processes:* gain and loss
Hickson, Hinings, Lee, Schneck, & Pennings (1971)	*Contingent variables:* ability to cope with problems, centrality of function, degree of uniqueness
Salancik & Pfeffer (1977)	*Utilization:* shared power
	Variables: scarcity, criticality, uncertainty
Shetty (1978)	*Situational variables:* managerial, subordinate, organizational
Bennis (1986)	Transformative power
House (1984)	Charisma, authority, expertise, political power
Smith & Peterson (1989), Gardner (1990)	Social- and culture-based power

making responsibilities may lead to the highest balance of satisfaction and responsibility between superiors and subordinates.

The strategic contingencies theory of Hickson et al. (1971) proposes that the use of problem-solving skills in critical situations necessitating unique expertise will lead to increased subunit power and authority over strategic decision making. Hickson et al. (1971) asserted that power is contingent upon specific variables (ability to cope with important problems, centrality of function within the organization, and degree to which expertise is unique). As these variables are altered by changes in the internal and/or external environment, once-critical subunits may lose power to subunits that have newly acquired ability, responsibility, and power to perform critical functions. Their theory does not explain how organizational subunits no longer in critical positions in some instances do maintain their power (Yukl, 1989).

In another strategic contingency model of power, Salancik and Pfeffer (1977) clarified and proposed that the political power of noncritical subunits is used to protect and maintain the subunits' position even though their expertise is no longer required. They maintained that power is shared in organizations not because of a belief in organizational development or participatory democracy but because one person cannot control all the critical activities (p. 7). Three variables that affect the use of political power are scarcity, criticality, and uncertainty. Thus, power becomes institutionalized and protected by the power holder's ability to establish permanent structures and policies that ensure the power holder's position and influence.

Shetty (1978) contended that three situational variables may affect the type of power leaders choose to employ. The variables affecting approaches to power are characteristics of the manager (authoritarian, self-confident, and training), the subordinate's characteristics (professionalism, need, cultural background, and training), and the organizational characteristics (task definition, visibility of task performance, organizational structure, and environmental conditions). These variables determine which characteristics of power may be appropriate in specific situations. Although most managers revert to authority or legitimate power when problems occur, Shetty states that managers might better "broaden their power bases in order to effectively respond to different demands" (p. 185).

According to Bennis (1986), leadership involves managing internal and external relations. As organizations find themselves in an environment where stakeholders, public and organizational, desire a voice in decision making concerning problems that have an impact on diverse, sometimes conflicting societal groups, decision making becomes more complex and ill-defined. Power is diffused over a broad base, creating a new power relationship. Bennis contends that transformative power requires leadership that "knows what it wants, communicates those intentions successfully, empowers others, and knows when and how to stay on course and when to change" (p. 66).

Transformative power is not based on organizational structures or management functions. Its source of power is the leader's ability to raise consciousness, build meanings, and inspire human intent. Vision, purposes, and beliefs embedded in the organization's culture empower participants to excel as meaning is found in routine actions uniting individuals and the organization in a symbiotic relationship (Bennis, 1986, p. 71).

Although the foregoing views of power in organizations are instructive, Smith and Peterson (1989) asserted that there is an "implicit assumption that leaders are valued and constructive members of their organizations" (p. 126). They challenged French and Raven's (1968) five bases of power and House's (1984, 1988) four typologies of power, stating that a "leader's exercise of power resides in the ability to transmit influence by way of a network of meanings which constitutes the organization's culture" (p. 130), not in qualitative descriptions of power bases.

Power is the capacity to bring about certain intended consequences in the behaviors of others, Gardner observed in a 1990 study. He proposed that only the power to accomplish specific objectives, and not a generalized power, functions in a pluralistic society such as the United States. Sources of power can be varied widely (property, position, personality, expertise, persuasiveness, motivational abilities). Possession of one source may provide accessibility to other sources. Within human systems (organizations and institutions), organizational power is given to those possessing key positions; these positions constitute the most common source of power in the modern world. Although a belief system firmly embedded in cultures may significantly legitimize leaders and validate their acts, any belief system usually places constraints on those trying to uphold the belief system. Eventually, this diminishes the leader's power. All of the aforementioned studies of power serve to illustrate important concepts and further our understanding of leadership and leader styles.

Leadership Styles

Leadership style is the pattern of behaviors of a person who assumes or is designated to a position of influence in an organization. The ways that leaders perceive workers and interpret their actions affect the leader's behavior toward the workers (Hall, 1990). Establishing relationships with subordinates is a critical factor in their work as leaders. People react to what they think they see in others. The degree of accuracy of perception determines the appropriateness of those actions taken. This is a mutual leader–follower behavior.

McGregor (1990a, 1990b) presented two perspectives that leaders use in dealing with workers, Theory X and Theory Y. Theory X is based on three assumptions: (1) human beings dislike work inherently and try to avoid it (management must counteract this natural tendency); (2) people must be coerced, controlled, directed, and threatened in order to achieve organizational goals (rewards will not lead to achievement; only external coercion, control, and threats will); and, (3) human beings are irresponsible, want to be controlled, are lazy, and are searching for security.

Theory Y is based on quite different assumptions: (1) people work voluntarily when conditions are appropriate; (2) workers will achieve organizational goals to which they are committed; (3) commitment to organizational goals is based on the rewards of goal achievement; (4) workers will seek responsibility when conditions are appropriate; (5) many workers possess the ability to solve organizational problems; and, (6) human intellectual potential is not fully utilized in organizations.

Theory Y, allegedly founded in human growth, development, and selective adaptation rather than direct control, implies that leaders may create constraints that impede workers from achieving their potential in the organizational setting. Thus, Theory Y challenges many of the routine actions and beliefs of leaders that operate from Theory X assumptions.

The central principle of Theory X, the scalar principle, is based on the belief that followers need direction and control through the exercise of authority (McGregor, 1990a, p. 21). Theory Y's central principle, the integration principle, is based on the belief that workers can achieve their goals best by working toward organizational success. Some pervasive characteristics of many organizations are so firmly ingrained that it is difficult for members to adopt a Theory Y viewpoint. Organizational requirements too often supersede individual needs. However, the principle of integration proposes that organizations can be successful only if they adjust to workers' needs and goals. In this way, the needs of both the organization and the individual are recognized.

Although integration means working together for the success of the organization, "management's implicit assumption is that working together means adjusting to the requirements of the organization as management perceives them" (McGregor, 1990b, p. 24). Integration, however, requires that individuals be encouraged to develop and utilize their capabilities in ways that lead to the success of the organization and the fulfillment of individual needs. Theory Y is based on the assumption that workers will achieve organizational goals they are committed to through self-control and self-direction. McGregor believes that the degree of commitment is influenced by managerial (leadership) policies. Therefore, integration, not authority, is a feasible means for obtaining commitment to organizational objectives. However, he also contends that even in Theory Y, organizations' external control may be an appropriate leadership strategy when genuine commitment cannot be achieved.

Assumptions have a tendency to limit our views and perceptions rather than widen them. The assumptions that inform Theory X and Theory Y define the way that human effort is organized and directed. These theories place limits on the strategies and procedures that leaders choose to direct, plan, control, and organize in the work situation.

A third theory, combining elements of Theory X and Theory Y, has been developed that offers ways to improve relationships between workers and leaders. Ouchi's (1981) Theory Z provides different strategies and perspectives for organizing human effort, focusing on consensual decision making and a team approach to organizational processes and change. Unlike Theory X and Theory Y, Theory Z defines the leader's style according to his ability to create an organizational culture where open communication, trust, and commitment to organizational goals is fostered. Consensual decision making "provides for the broad dissemination of information and of values within the organization, and it also serves the symbolic role of signaling in an unmistakable way the cooperative intent of the firm" (p. 66).

Theory Z views the organization as the development of informal relationships between persons. The development emphasizes the individual person over a narrow role distinction. Theory Z perceptions of organizational members eliminates the dehumanization, authoritarianism, and class distinctiveness found in Theory X and Theory Y organizations that eventually alienate leaders and subordinates. To overcome this alienation, Theory Z advocates maintain that shared goal development undertaken by workers and management can contribute to the development of a consistent organization culture. This process forms a type of insurance for the leader, who hopes that his workers' efforts are aligned closely and constantly with organizational goals and objectives.

Long before Ouchi's Theory Z, in 1961, Likert developed four management systems. These four systems resemble some of the conceptual frameworks that have subsequently emerged in Theories X, Y, and Z. Likert proposed that his four-system management model of participative management approaches an ideal state. Three key factors of this system were supportive relationships, group decision making, and high managerial performance goals. Likert believes that workers perform best when they function as members of effective work groups, not as individuals. The significance of Likert's system is that it acknowledges the important factor of worker behavior as a leadership goal and as a factor in modifying leadership behaviors.

McGregor's Theories X and Y, Ouchi's Theory Z, and Likert's four management systems illustrate that the perspective, or lens, through which leaders view workers' characteristics and the subjective validity system developed for those characteristics determines what leadership style, strategies, and procedures will be employed. Leaders must be able to evaluate objectively and challenge the approaches that they use to be certain that they are viewing their workers through a lens that does not distort their image of workers. Theory Z challenges the traditional assumptions of Theories X and Y and specifically prescribes a new lens through which to view workers, as well as leadership structures and policies. Theory Z sees the organization as a living system demanding constant adaptation on the part of the leader. This adaptation may alter organizational goals and climate due to the leader's response to internal and external forces.

Contingency and Situational Theories and Models

Contingency theories of leadership effectiveness focus on the leader's immediate work environment. Early contingency models focused on leader emergence by studying how the group's tasks and norms (situation) determine the leadership skills and values that would be effective in the group and acceptable to the subordinates (see Table 3.3).

Fiedler's (1967) research represents the first attempt to study leadership by examining the situation, its people, tasks, and organization. Fiedler (Lunenburg & Ornstein, 1991; Rost, 1991; Smith & Peterson, 1989; Yukl, 1989) hypothesized that leaders can improve their effectiveness by modifying situations to fit their leadership styles. Fiedler identified three situational factors that influence leader effectiveness: (1) the quality of leader–subordinate relations, (2) the leader's position power, and (3) the degree of task structure (Smith & Peterson, 1989, p. 17).

As a result of Fiedler's (1967) work, leadership styles are no longer rated as good or bad. Rather, styles are defined according to their effectiveness in specific situations. Fiedler's research recognized that leadership results from the interaction between leadership style and situational variables. This view opened the door to subsequent research that describes leadership behaviors holistically.

During the 1970s, leadership theories reflected this more descriptive flair. For example, House's (House, 1971; House & Dessler, 1974) path–goal theory of leadership is based on the expectancy theory of motivation. House focuses on the leader's ability to analyze the task environment and choose behaviors that maximize subordinates' ability and desire to achieve organizational goals. To accomplish this analysis, leaders examine situational variables such as

Table 3.3
Contingency and Situational Theories and Models

Theory	Situational Variables	Leadership Styles
Fiedler's contingency theory	Quality of leader–subordinates relations Leader's position power Degree of task structure	Task-oriented Relationship-oriented
House's path–goal theory	Subordinates Environment	Directive Supportive Participative Achievement
Hersey and Blanchard's situational leadership theory	Subordinate maturity	Task Relationship
Blake and Mouton's managerial grid	All situations	Participative
Kerr and Jamier's substitute theory	Substitutes Neutralizers	
Vroom and Yetton's decision model	Decision quality importance Leaders' possession of relevant information Degree of structure contained in problem Importance of subordinates' acceptance of the decision Probability that subordinates will accept the leader's decision Importance of shared purpose and goals Amount of conflict among subordinates	Autocratic consultative Group

(1) the subordinates (personal qualities and skills, locus of control, and needs and motives), and (2) the environment (work group, authority system, and task structure), and then select one of four leadership styles (directive, supportive, participative, and achievement oriented) to apply in the situation specified (see Figure 3.4).

Descriptive leadership theories that emerged in the 1980s served to illuminate a range of variables. Hersey and Blanchard's (1982, 1988) situational leadership theory asserted that leader behavior is based on two dimensions of leadership, task behavior and relationship behavior. These dimensions are influenced by one environmental variable, subordinate matu-

rity (Blanchard, Zigarmi, & Zigarmi, 1987; Rost, 1991; Smith & Peterson, 1989; Yukl, 1989). As subordinates develop confidence and ability, leaders vary their behavior by adjusting the amount of task direction and psychological support they give them.

Behavior variables in leaders (directive/supportive) interact with behavior variables in group members (high/low commitment and high/low competence). As the group members pass through various stages of commitment and competence, the leader varies the amount of direction and support given. The leader plays various roles of directing, coaching, supporting, and delegating as the group matures and

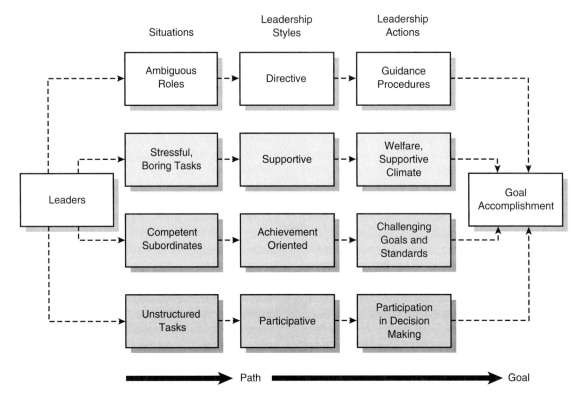

Figure 3.4
House's path–goal theory

becomes able to perform group activities. Group maturity depends on individual maturity.

Examining the validity of Hersey and Blanchard's (1982, 1988) theory, Hambleton and Gumpert (1982) concluded that there is a definite, significant relationship between leadership style in specific situations and a manager's perceptions of subordinate job performance. Their study also suggests that in situations in which situational leadership was applied correctly, subordinate job performance was increased.

Hersey and Blanchard's (1982, 1988) situational leadership theory has not been adequately tested. It contains some broad, ambiguous terms and omits some obvious situational variables. Nevertheless, it does emphasize the effective-

ness of a flexible, adaptive leadership style that varies treatment of subordinates according to maturity levels in the same work environment and in varied work situations (Yukl, 1989).

Blake and Mouton (1978, 1981, 1982a, 1982b, 1990) reexamined leadership theory using a two-factor framework, in which concern for production and concern for people are interdependent but uncorrelated (see Figure 3.5). They believe there is one best leadership style. Their managerial grid provides a schematic behavioral science framework for comparing nine theories of interaction between production and human relationships (Blake & Mouton, 1978). Each variable is delineated on a nine-point scale in which 1 represents minimum concern and 9 represents maximum concern. The model

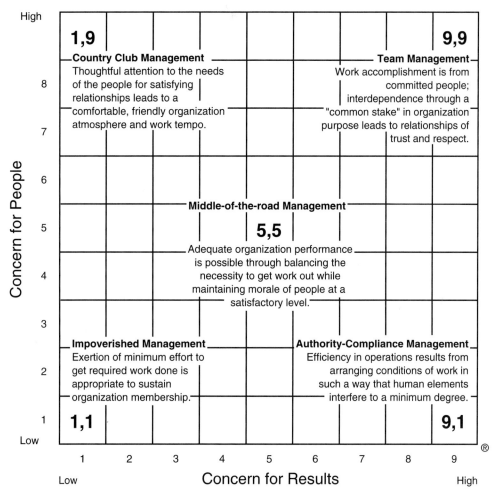

Figure 3.5
Leadership grid

Source: The Leadership Grid® figure for *Leadership Dilemmas—Grid Solutions,* by Robert R. Blake and Anne Adams McCanse (formerly the Managerial Grid figure by Robert R. Blake and Jane S. Mouton). Houston, TX: Gulf Publishing Company, 1991, p. 29. Copyright 1991 by Scientific Methods, Inc. Reproduced by permission of the owners.

develops five management styles and nine theories of how production and people can be integrated to accomplish organizational goals. Based on the belief that concerns for production and relationship are conflictual, Blake and Mouton (1978) posit that three theories evolve: (1) task management (9,1), where the focus is on attainment of production goals and where human beings are viewed as machines; (2) country club management (1,9), where the focus on relationships dominates to the extent of compromising production goals; and (3) impoverished management (1,1), where the focus is on avoidance of conflicts between production and relationships by ignoring or withdrawing from such situations.

The theories of Blake and Mouton (1978, 1981, 1982a, 1982b, 1990) represent a situational approach to leadership. Researchers assume that concerns for production and relationship building will conflict and therefore must be viewed more systemically or risk being compromised. In practice, the systemic nature of this model is accomplished by alternating styles that focus on each concern (1,9 and 9,1), by providing for both concerns through separate organizational structures (management–production, personnel–relationships), or by perceiving each factor as a separate concern that can be dealt with exclusively. Because production and relationship concerns are evident in all management situations, Blake and Mouton contend that the team management theory is the only style that can effectively integrate both production and relationship concerns. All members of the team plan for production and deal with conflict openly.

Vroom and Yetton's (1973) earlier model examines how the decision-making process is affected by the leader, subordinates, and situation to enhance decision quality, decision commitment, and decision satisfaction. The model analyzes decision situations and prescribes feasible decision procedures. Vroom and Yetton evaluate seven questions dealing with power sharing and participation in the decision-making process and their impact on the leadership style or amount of participation prescribed for each decision situation.

Using a decision tree, Vroom and Yetton (1973) analyze problems using seven questions to assess the following: (1) decision quality importance, (2) leader's possession of relevant information, (3) degree of structure contained in the problem, (4) importance of subordinates' acceptance of the decision, (5) probability that subordinates will accept the leader's decision, (6) importance of shared purposes and goals in decision making, and (7) amount of conflict among subordinates that may result from the decision. After the leader moves through the decision tree and answers the seven questions, he or she can identify either one or several feasible alternative ways of dealing with the problem. These alternatives are classified in five leadership styles: two autocratic, two consultative, and one group.

Although its complexity (five leadership styles and seven environmental contingencies) may require computer assistance for data analysis, Vroom and Yetton's (1973) model does provide information that can lead to precise, reliable, and effective decision-making procedures (Smith & Peterson, 1989). Further studies of Vroom and Yetton's model have substantiated its validity and reliability. Its focus on specific behaviors and meaningful intervening variables lends credence to its use as a situational leadership model.

However, Vroom and Yetton's narrow focus on only one situational leadership behavior, decision making, and their assumption that leaders possess the necessary skills and ability to use this skill and diagnose situations weakens the model. As a theory-to-practice model, the Vroom–Yetton (1973) model also has some deficiencies. The model indicates only what a leader should not do instead of what a leader should do, it gives no guidance for choosing alternatives when the process results in multiple alternatives, and it assumes that all seven factors can be delineated by clear "yes" or "no" responses. The model also fails to address such situational variables as the amount of information needed by subordinates in decision making, time constraints for reaching decisions, and the ability of all necessary participants to be present at decision time. Like many models for leadership, the strengths and weaknesses of the Vroom–Yetton model illustrate the complexity of modern organizations and the consequent intensified complexity of the leadership role.

Vroom and Jago (1988) revised the Vroom–Yetton model to address its deficiencies. In addition to the original five decision processes for group problems, two processes (one group and one delegative) were added to address individual problems of decision making. To evaluate problems and decision processes according to decision quality, decision commitment, time, and subordinate development, equations were developed to determine decision effectiveness. These equations also accounted for the trade-offs incurred when the size of a decision-making group varied. Because of the use of mathematical equations and the employment of computers, the Vroom–Jago model is capable of weighing answers to the situational factors (that now include time, geographical, and motivational constraints—expanded from seven to 12) along a five-point continuum instead of using simple "yes" and "no" answers. The new model's use of continuous rather than dichotomous responses, the use of mathematical functions, and expanded situational factor consideration may result in greater validity of the decision-process decisions reached with the model's use. However, until the Vroom–Jago model is tested adequately, its validity is tenuous.

Situational Determinants Theories and Models

Situational determinants theory defines leader behavior as determined by situational characteristics (role expectation, group mission and tasks, and flexible role definition) and leader traits and qualities. Leaders' personalities and values may bias their perceptions of their roles, causing role conflict. The theory suggests that leaders' expectations of behavioral outcomes influence their behavior choice (Nebecker & Mitchell, 1974). Osborn and Hunt's (1975) multiple influence model attempts to explain the complex interactions of the macro-variables organization structure and external environment and the micro-variables task characteristics and subordinate characteristics, and the influence of each in determining leader behavior. The simultaneous interrelationship of multiple variables in leadership and management situations provides a picture of the complexity of the situation. Often, variables cannot be separated into categories of dependent or independent variables that might be validated for causality and/or correlations.

The study of leadership remains complex, as seemingly different situations tax theorists' analysis capabilities. For many decades leadership theorists have attempted to integrate theories under the crush of increasingly complex situations for analysis. Koestenbaum's (1991) leadership model is one attempt to integrate leadership research strategies—traits, behaviors, contingencies, and situational determinants—into one model. The theory looks beyond the individual or traits and immediate work environment or behavior and contingency and examines the interactions of leader traits and behavior with the macro internal and external environment. Leadership is viewed as a mind-set and a pattern of behaviors. Koestenbaum contends that leadership can be learned and taught; therefore, leaders should empower and support subordinates to develop their own leadership potential. He also believes that a majority of a leader's time and energy should be used to facilitate skill development in front-line people in the complex organizational system and in interactions with the external environment. Koestenbaum equates leadership with greatness, however, perpetuating the mistaken belief that leaders are super-human. Effective leaders are people who understand their roles in organizations, can analyze and diagnose task- and human-oriented variables in the environment, can prescribe actions, and can provide vision for goal achievement. Koestenbaum's theory suggests a born-again leader orientation that emphasizes a person's emotional appeal as a qualification for leadership.

Transformational and Transactional Leadership

Burns (1978) examined leadership in a political context by studying distinctions among power, leadership, transactional leadership, and transformative leadership. Burns believed that "power over other persons is exercised when potential power wielders, motivated to achieve certain goals of their own, marshal in their power base resources (economic, military, institutional, or skill) that enable them to influence the behavior of respondents by activating motives of respondents relevant to those resources and to those goals"

Figure 3.6
Transformational versus transactional leadership

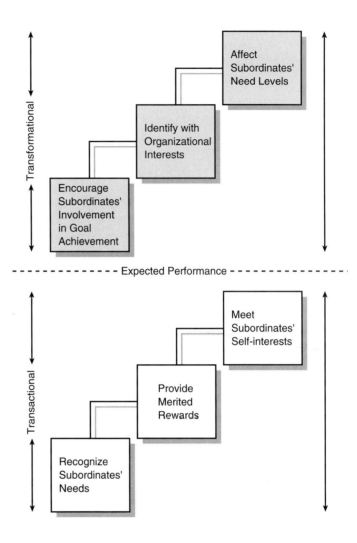

(p. 18). The purpose of such a power wielder is to achieve goals whether or not the followers share in those goals. However, Burns defines leadership as "the reciprocal process of mobilizing, by persons with certain motives and values, various economic, political, and other resources, in a context of competition or conflict, in order to realize goals independently or mutually held by both leaders and followers" (p. 425) (see Figure 3.6).

Burns (1978) differentiated between transactional and transformative leadership. He argued that in transactional leadership, persons engage in a relationship for the purpose of ex-changing valued things. They are conscious of each other's power, usually pursue their own purposes and goals, and form temporary relationships. In transformative leadership, "one or more persons engage with others in such a way that leaders and followers raise one another to higher levels of motivation and morality" (p. 20). In such a relationship purposes are fused, power bases are linked, and leadership becomes moral as leaders and followers unite to achieve higher goals. Burns bases his general theory of leadership on a hierarchy of human needs, structure of values, and stages of moral development (p. 428). The role of the leader is to help followers transcend the levels of need and stages of moral development to achieve mutually held higher purposes.

Burns (1978) further contended that "political leadership, however, can be defined only in terms of purposeful, substantive change in the conditions of people's lives. The ultimate test of practical leadership is the realization of intended, real change that meets people's needs" (p. 461). For Burns, the test of a leader is the ability to achieve significant change that represents the mutual interests of followers and leaders. Burns believes that transformative leadership, with its ability to raise people to higher moral purposes, is the basis for a general theory of leadership that may be applied in all contexts, not just a political context.

Bass's (1985) conceptualization of leadership differs from Burns's (1978) in three areas: (1) Bass includes the idea of expanding subordinates' array of needs and wants in addition to Burns's emphasis on raising subordinates' need levels; (2) Bass eliminates the moral implication of transformational leadership that Burns believes is a requirement (Burns considers all transformative leaders to be good, not evil); and (3) although Burns views transactional and transformative leadership as opposite ends of a continuum, Bass argues that leaders exhibit both types of leadership, depending on the situation.

Bass (1985) contended that transactional leaders work within the organizational culture, the shared values and meanings of organizational members, whereas transformational leaders work to change subordinates' values and beliefs in order to change the organizational culture (p. 24). Thus, for Bass, "the transactional leader induces performance among followers by negotiating an exchange relationship with them of reward for compliance. Transformational leadership arouses transcendental interests in followers and/or elevates their need and aspiration levels" (p. 32).

Bennis and Nanus (1985) argued that transformative leadership is the ability of leaders to shape and elevate followers' motives and goals to achieve significant change through common interests and collective energies (p. 217). Leaders define a vision that is congruent with followers' key values and construct a social architecture, or an organizational culture, that provides shared meanings where followers can pursue tasks and strive for success. To accomplish this, leaders must be able to create a vision, communicate the vision through symbolic actions and shared meanings, exercise integrity through persistent pursuit of that vision, recognize their own strengths and weaknesses, evaluate ability in relation to job requirements, and focus on positive goals.

A key ingredient of transformative leadership for Bennis and Nanus (1985) is empowerment. Empowerment is the ability of leaders through an active and creative exchange of power to encourage followers to achieve a vision and realize goals. Leaders empower followers by bringing significance, competence, community, and enjoyment to leader–follower work relationships, where extraordinary efforts are perceived as the means to realizing vision and achieving goals. Bennis and Nanus focus their interpretation of transformational leadership on the behavior and skills of the leader. Although a key point of Burns' (1978) definition of transformation refers to the ability of leaders and followers to raise each other to higher levels of motivation and morality, Bennis and Nanus's beliefs appear unidirectional, with no reference to the moral implications of the participants' motives and actions.

Leadership within a Culture Context

As shown by the previous discussion, theories about leadership are multidimensional. No one theory has embraced all the necessary variables to define satisfactorily the complexity of the leadership role or to predict best-case leadership scenarios. Some researchers suggest a total reconceptualization of the leadership problem. Among these are Sergiovanni and Corbally (1986), who argued that to change we must move "from a conception of leadership where effectiveness is defined as accomplishing objectives to one of building identity, increasing understanding, and making the work of others more meaningful" (p. 14).

Sergiovanni (1986) defined quality leadership as a balance between tactical leadership (achieving objectives effectively and efficiently) and strategic leadership (obtaining support for policies and purposes and devising long-range plans). Tactical leadership, in which evaluation is quick and success is based on short-term accomplishments, has been the focus of Western societies. Sergiovanni contended that in a cultural perspective of leadership, "cultural aspects of organization are being offered as better able to account for the artificial purposive, and practical aspects of organizational life" (p. 106). Organizations are viewed not as systems but as cultural entities, where meanings derived from actions are more important than the specific actions. "Leadership as cultural expression seeks to build unity and order within an organization by giving attention to purposes, historical and philosophical tradition, and ideals and norms which define the way of life within the organization and which provide the bases for socializing members and obtaining their compliance" (p. 107). Sergiovanni's discussion of Western philosophy highlights the hollowness of some Western theories directed toward assessing effective leadership solely by a measurement of productivity. The inability of theorists to integrate the concerns of culture and productivity surfaces here philosophically just as it surfaces in Theory X and Theory Y practices discussed earlier in this chapter.

As discussed by Sergiovanni (1986), leadership as cultural expression relies on the analysis of the complex interplay of tactical leadership skills (management skills) and strategic antecedents and meanings within a framework of 10 principles that form a cognitive map for quality leadership. To achieve leadership excellence, antecedents and meanings are needed to provide a basis for and direction to leadership skills. Antecedents are defined as perspective, principle, platform (operational framework), and politics (influence others to achieve desired goal) required to guide the leader's decisions, actions, and behavior. Meaning develops in a belief system through purposive reflection (giving meaning to ordinary activities), planning (articulating purpose), persisting (creating climate through attention to issues, goals, or outcomes), and matching people to organizational goals and objectives. From the interaction of these components, Sergiovanni writes that a culture emerges that defines what is important and governs behavior. Organizational patriotism, commitment, and loyalty to a shared set of common beliefs and governing behavior create a strong bond among organizational members and give the organization unique meaning. These actions require leadership behavior (see Figure 3.7).

Sergiovanni's (1986) model appears to represent his interpretation of Burns's (1978) transactional and transformational leadership in one model where quality leadership is achieved by the leader's ability to move beyond the tactical skills component (transactional leadership) to the integration of antecedents and meanings (transformational leadership) , achieving a quality leadership model. The leader here oscillates between the roles of transactional and transformational leader as the situation changes. In this respect, Sergiovanni's perception of leadership is closer to that of Bass than that of Burns.

Smith and Peterson (1989) contended that leadership as an aspect of organizational behavior can best be studied in a social context, not as an influence relationship within the leader–follower dyad. From a global perspective, organizational leadership is seen as comprising two aspects—task and relationship—within a team structure. Assignment of meanings to leadership acts derives from the cultural context of the group or organization. In assimilated cultures, attribution of meaning may be more consensually shared than in Western individualistic, pluralistic societies. Rather than searching for one best type of leadership, this theory implies that there may be one best organizational culture that can be created through a hierarchical structure. The hierarchy can develop shared meanings for organizational activities and events and thus foster shared visions and strategies for achieving organizational

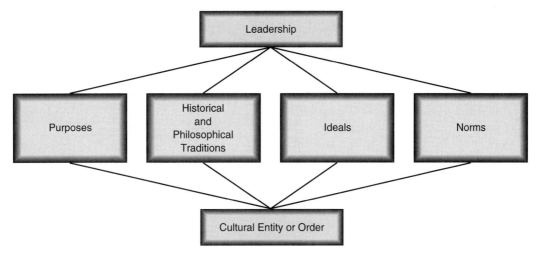

Figure 3.7
Leadership as cultural expression

goals, a cultural form of control. Smith and Peterson state that "a leader's exercise of power resides in the ability to transmit influence by way of the network of meanings which constitute the organization's culture. . . . Such meanings are deeply rooted and amenable only to gradual change" (p. 130). However, within a participative management structure, group members must be able to define participatory mechanisms and purposes through a cultural context. The leader here is a network monitor, creator, and nurturer.

Schein (1985) said that creating, managing, and sometimes restructuring organizational culture may be one of the most decisive functions of leadership (p. 2). Viewing culture as the element that most strongly affects how members of human systems think, feel, and act, Schein refuted the assumption of some leadership theorists that culture can be changed to suit one's purposes. Schein (1985) defined culture as "a pattern of basic assumptions—invented, discovered, or developed by a given group as it learns to cope with its problems of external adaptation and internal integration—that has worked well enough to be considered valid, and therefore, to be taught to new members as the correct way to perceive, think, and feel in relation to those problems" (p. 8).

Because environmental conditions are constantly changing, leadership must be able to manipulate the organizational culture to ensure the system's ability to adapt to and survive in the environment through the evolution of new cultural assumptions. Leadership in practice verbalizes its assumptions and "embeds them gradually and consistently in the mission, goals, structures, and working procedures of the group" (Schein, 1985, p. 317). Leaders need to know how an organization's culture can help or hinder a mission's accomplishment. Leaders need to provide the impetus to implement the intervention strategies necessary to adapt the culture for organizational survival. Although leaders are responsible for replacing or redefining discarded assumptions, organizational members should be involved in the change process to ensure their renewed insight and motivation to achieve the new organizational mission.

Each of these theories sheds some light on the patterns in leadership research since World War II. The uniqueness and complexity of mid-twentieth-century organizations have both increased the demand for effective theories and confounded researchers working at developing those theories. Recently, researchers have quietly begun to abandon tenets of organizational thought, which suggest that leadership may be analyzed or predicted in a linear fashion. New theories are emerging that may shape a new paradigm for thinking about leadership as we move into the twenty-first century.

More recently, significant groups of authors have created and implemented, with varying degrees of success, a new empowerment model of leadership. In this era of rapid change, complexity, and globalness, further pursuits of building anew or remodeling the hierarchical organization have met with considerable resistence (McFarland et al., 1994). There can no longer be rigid hierarchies or leadership in isolation. A more common view today places leadership in the hands of those closest to the situation and nearest to those capable of handling issues. More voices, creativity, innovation, and shared decision making may be akin to stronger organization in these functional systems. Bill Gates believes that "empowering leadership means bringing out the energy and capabilities that people have, and getting them to work together in a way they wouldn't do otherwise." That requires that they see the positive impact they can have and sense the opportunities (in McFarland et al., 1994, p. 68).

Women in Authority

Additional differences in leadership and management styles can be discerned when reviewing the literature on women in positions of authority. With the advent of greater numbers of women in top leadership positions, it is possible to detect some distinctive ways that men and women differ in leadership roles.

Fitzpatrick (1983) described a competent communicator as one who can accurately perceive the environment and create and understand messages based on subsequent interpretation. His goals for communication are (1) getting the job done, (2) avoiding damage to the relationship between sender and receiver of the message, and (3) projecting the desired image while communicating. According to Fitzpatrick, males generally operate from a problem-solving, aggressive, and focused routine and suppress strong emotion. On the other hand, females tend to give and expect to receive rewarding responses and are inclined to emphasize relational goals in interactions.

From this base comparison, Fitzpatrick (1983) conceptualized three models of organizational communicators. The first, or *masculine,* model, focuses on task goals and impression management to the exclusion of relational goals. The second, or *feminine,* model, emphasizes relational goals to the exclusion of task goals. The third, or *androgynous,* model, blends the previous two styles. Androgynous communicators can be assertive and dominant, as is typical of task behaviors, or they can be warm and nurturing, reflecting relational behaviors.

Whereas Gabler (1987) argued that successful women do not necessarily lead differently than successful men, others, such as Carroll (1989), have found that women have a more sharing style of leadership than that of men, and claim that women tend to give more recognition and create an empowering team atmosphere. In replicating a study by men in leadership roles (Mintzberg, 1973), Helgeson (1990) found distinct differences in leadership style. The women in her study worked at the same pace and under similar conditions as the men in Mintzberg's study, but they were less likely to feel controlled by the work schedule, thereby reducing job stress. More time was spent with people, and there was emphasis on sustaining good working relationships. By maintaining a more complex network of relationships both on and off the job, the women were less likely to feel isolated. In Helgeson's view, female leaders were more likely to feel themselves at the center of things instead of viewing themselves at the top, as the men in the study did.

In another context, decision making for men and women also shows distinctiveness. Putnam (1983) identified differences in ways that the two groups deal with conflict. Males are apt to arrive at a settlement using bargaining techniques, logical arguments, and anger in an effort to resolve the conflict. Women tend to work to understand others' feelings, handling conflict by smoothing over and playing down differences and emphasizing similarities. The male focus on independence, competitiveness, and autonomy often creates a win/lose scenario, where the female focus on interdependence produces a win/win scenario where possible.

Shakeshaft (1987) argued that research finding no distinctions between men and women in managing schools is faulty in that conceptually, it is based on the white male model. Under these circumstances, successful women match successful men. However, when the additional motives and approaches of women are factored in, they can be seen to perform not only as well, but differently. She argues that the work of female leaders in schools has five major elements: (1) relationships with others are central to all actions of women administrators, (2) teaching and learning are the major foci of women administrators, (3) building community is an essential part of the female administrator's style, (4) women administrators are constantly made aware of their marginality or status, and (5) the line separating the public and private lives of women administrators is blurred far more than for men.

Although all of the above has been instructive, agendas regarding debate and new research into women in leadership may have effectively run its course. It is certainly past time to avail ourselves of the unique contribution that women bring to the leadership equation. Most assuredly, it is time to see the attributes women bring to organizations—for that matter, to all diverse groups—as appropriate. Caring, collaboration, facilitation, consensus building, networking, and inspiration are all necessary attributes for the new millennium. In true systemic fashion, we will certainly see the blending of attributes, both feminine and masculine, into arenas that produce common ground for all to lead. As a result, our understanding of leadership will certainly improve.

A New Paradigm for Leadership

In criticizing previous leadership studies' emphasis on peripheral aspects (personality, trait, goal attainment) and content (knowledge-possessed leader), Rost (1991) contended that these studies do not address the essential nature of leadership and the process by which leaders and followers relate to each other to achieve purposes. He believed that leadership has not been defined "with precision, accuracy, and conciseness." (p. 6). We still may not be able to label it correctly when we see it happening or when it has been engaged. He further proposed that most theories of leadership reflect an industrial paradigm that is no longer acceptable or applicable to leadership needs for the twenty-first century. According to Rost, a paradigm shift is necessary so that leadership theory and practice can relate to the needs of a postindustrial world.

Rost (1991) defines leadership as "an influence relationship among leaders and followers who intend real changes that reflect their mutual purposes" (p. 102). This is in contrast to management, which he defined as an authority relationship. He maintained that four elements must be present for a relationship to be considered a leadership relationship: (1) a relationship based on influence, (2) leaders and followers who are participants in the relationship, (3) both parties intending that real changes are to take place, and (4) both parties developing mutual purposes. Rost reinterprets transformational leadership as the involvement of "active people, engaging in influence relationships based on persuasion, intending real changes to happen, and insisting that those changes reflect their mutual purposes" (p. 213). Therefore, leadership is seen as a relationship involving multiple followers and multiple leaders who engage in shared or collaborative leadership. The roles, styles, and power influence of leaders and followers are not etched in stone but can shift.

In the new millennium, we will need to proceed further, beyond the myriad of research agendas, beyond the either–or thinking and beyond our tendencies to seek quick fixes to issues that are probably naturally long term in character. The information age is already progressing toward a knowledge age, an age when numerous people will have and need new and stronger leadership abilities. Persons in all walks of life will need to be shown they have the aptitude and potential to direct themselves, to be critical thinkers, and to act, individually and collectively, to enhance their own levels of commitment, vision, and responsibility. Our most important challenge will be to build new leadership capabilities through changes to the way we have educated our future leaders and followers. Higher education will be responsible for these dramatic changes, including:

1. Continuing to establish a world-class education system that is responsive to effective preparation of our future workforce.

2. Broader in-house or intraorganizational capabilities to train one's own.

3. Training new leaders in the art of building learning organizations. Perhaps our most important tasks will revolve around assimilating responses to these questions:

   a. How committed are we to lifelong learning and personal growth?

   b. How is leadership training and education supported in my organization?

   c. Do we collaborate across our communities to enhance our ability to function in the new millennium?

In this chapter we have presented a brief compilation of the important leadership research that has been accomplished to date. It is important to build a framework that can serve as a guide to further reflection about educational and organizational leadership in the future. It is also evident that leadership research has not stood the tests of time well. Numerous authors have commented about leadership theory deficiencies. Theory ought to inform practice, as will be evident throughout the remainder of the book. Although progress is always evident, too little of value has occurred in leadership arenas. We sorely need combinations across disciplines and dimensions of intellectual thought before we can begin to be comfortable with leadership today.

CASE STUDY

Leadership: The Case of the Invisible Principal

John Alvarez was a superior teacher who was known throughout the school district for his intellectual ability; stimulating classes; popularity with students, colleagues, and administrators; and problem-solving techniques. No one was surprised when John was appointed principal of one of the district's secondary schools. What was astounding were the complaints coming from the chair people, faculty, building personnel, and students that nothing was really being accomplished. Department chairs were particularly vocal about John's insistence on knowing every detail of their decisions before permitting them to move forward. They also complained about their inability to arrange meetings with John and his lack of communication. Days would pass without any word from him about decisions. Teachers, building personnel, and students also found it difficult to arrange for personal communication with their principal.

Although acknowledging John's superior teaching ability, successful student management, and creative problem solving, several of the department chairs, faculty, and building personnel questioned whether John would ever be a leader or even understand the difference between classroom responsibilities and those of leadership. John responded that his classroom abilities were the type of leadership that the school needed. He believed that if intelligent people were doing their jobs they did not need close personal contacts with their leaders. John viewed leadership as an extension of his classroom abilities and was amazed that some of his faculty, building personnel, and students were doubtful of his contribution. He could hardly believe that they labeled him their "Invisible Leader."

Questions

1. Is John's perception about leadership appropriate?

2. Are classroom academics and successful student management evidence of the type of leadership that a school principal really needs to provide?

3. Is it possible that both John and the faculty, building personnel, and students need to rethink their beliefs about leadership?

4. How can we define leadership responsibility particular to this situation?

5. Can the definitions that we develop be universally applied? Why or why not?

6. How would you change the leadership scenario above to reflect some of the current thought surrounding leadership today?

References

Abbott, M., & Caracheo, F. (1988). Power, authority and bureaucracy. In N. J. Boyan (Ed.), *Handbook of research on educational administration* (pp. 239–257). New York: Longman.

Bass, B. M. (Ed.). (1981). *Stogdill's handbook of leadership*. New York: Free Press.

Bass, B. M. (1985). *Leadership and performance beyond expectations*. New York: Free Press.

Bennis, W. (1986). Transformative power and leadership. In T. J. Sergiovanni & J. E. Corbally (Eds.), *Leadership and organizational culture* (pp. 64–71). Urbana, IL: University of Illinois Press.

Bennis, W., & Nanus, B. (1985). *Leaders: The strategies for taking charge*. New York: Harper & Row.

Blake, R. R., & Mouton, J. S. (1961). How power affects human behavior. In J. Hall (Ed.), *Models for management: The structure of competence* (2nd ed., pp. 113–120). The Woodlands, TX: Woodstead Press.

Blake, R. R., & Mouton, J. S. (1978). *The new managerial grid*. Houston, TX: Gulf.

Blake, R. R., & Mouton, J. S. (1981). Management by grid principles or situationalism: Which? *Group and Organization Studies, 6*(4), 439–455.

Blake, R. R., & Mouton, J. S. (1982a). How to choose a leadership style. *Training and Development Journal, 36,* 38–47.

Blake, R. R., & Mouton, J. S. (1982b). Theory and research for developing a science of leadership. *Journal of Applied Behavioral Science, 18*(3), 275–291.

Blake, R. R., & Mouton, J. S. (1990). The developing revolution in management practices. In J. Hall (Ed.), *Models for management: The structure of competence* (2nd ed., pp. 422–444). The Woodlands, TX: Woodstead Press.

Blanchard, K., Zigarmi, D., & Zigarmi, P. (1987). Situational leadership: Different strokes for different folks. *Principal, 66,* 12–16.

Burns, J. M. (1978). *Leadership*. New York: Harper & Row.

Carroll, S. (1989, February). Cited in Strategies for women in academe. *Academic Leadership, 5*(2).

Fiedler, F. E. (1967). *A theory of leadership effectiveness*. New York: McGraw-Hill.

Fitzpatrick, M. A. (1983). Effective interpersonal communication for women of the corporation. In J. Pilotta (Ed.), *Women in organizations*. Prospect Heights, IL: Waveland Press.

French, J., & Raven, B. (1968). The bases of social power. In D. Cartwright & A. Zander (Eds.), *Group dynamics: Research and theory* (pp. 259–269). New York: Harper & Row.

Gabler, J. E. (1987). Leadership: A woman's view. In L. T. Shieve & M. B. Schoenheit (Eds.), *Leadership: Examining the elusive*. Alexandria, VA: Association for Supervision and Curriculum Development.

Gardner, J. W. (1990). *On leadership*. New York: Free Press.

Helgeson, S. (1990). *The female advantage: Women's ways of leadership*. New York: Doubleday/Currency.

Hersey, P., & Blanchard, K. H. (1982). Leadership style: Attitudes and behaviors. *Training and Development, 36,* 50–52.

Hersey, P., & Blanchard, K. H. (1988). *Management of organizational behavior* (5th ed.). Upper Saddle River, NJ: Prentice Hall.

Hickson, D., Hinings, C., Lee, C., Schneck, R., & Pennings, J. (1971). A strategic contingencies theory of intra-organizational power. *Administrative Science Quarterly, 16,* 216–229.

Hollander, E. (1997). Leadership and social change process. In K. Gergen, M. Greenberg, & R. Willis (Eds.), *Social exchange: Advances in theory and research*. New York: Winston-Wiley.

House, R. J. (1971). A path–goal theory of leader effectiveness. *Administrative Science Quarterly, 16,* 321–339.

House, R. J. (1984). *Power in organizations: A social psychological perspective.* Unpublished paper, University of Toronto, Faculty of Management, Toronto, Ontario, Canada.

House, R. J., & Dressler, G. (1974). The path–goal theory of leadership: Some post-hoc and a priori tests. In J. Hunt & L. Larson (Eds.), *Contingency approaches to leadership* (pp. 29-55). Carbondale, IL: Southern Illinois University Press.

Kerr, S., & Jermier, J. (1978). Substitutes for leadership: Their meaning and measurements. *Organizational Behavior and Performance, 22,* 375–403.

Koestenbaum, P. (1991). *Leadership: The inner side of greatness.* San Francisco: Jossey-Bass.

Likert, R. (1961). *New patterns of management.* New York: McGraw-Hill.

Likert, R. (1967). *The human organization: Its management and value.* New York: McGraw-Hill.

Lunenburg, F. C., & Ornstein, A. C. (1991). *Educational administration: Concepts and practices.* Belmont, CA: Wadsworth.

Mazzarella, J., & Grundy, T. (1989). Portrait of a leader. In S. Smith & J. Piele (Eds.), *School leadership: Handbook for excellence* (pp. 9–27). Eugene, OR: ERIC Clearinghouse on Educational Management, University of Oregon.

McFarland, L. J., Senn, L. E., & Childress, J. R. (1994). *21st century leadership: Dialogs with 100 top leaders.* New York: Leadership Press.

McGregor, D. (1990a). Theory X: The traditional view of direction and control. In J. Hall (Ed.), *Models for management: The structure of competence* (2nd ed., pp. 11–18). The Woodlands, TX: Woodstead Press.

McGregor, D. (1990b). Theory Y: The integration of individual and organizational goals. In J. Hall (Ed.), *Models of management: The structure of competence* (2nd ed., pp. 19–27). The Woodlands, TX: Woodstead Press.

Mintzberg, J. (1973). *The nature of managerial work.* New York: Harper & Row.

Nebecker, D., & Mitchell, T. (1974). Leader behavior: An expectancy theory approach. *Organizational Behavior and Human Performance, 11,* 355-367.

Osborn, R., & Hunt, J. (1975). An adaptive–reactive theory of leadership: The role of macro variables in leadership research. In J. Hunt & L. Larson (Eds.), *Leadership frontiers.* Kent, OH: Kent State University Press.

Ouchi, W. (1981). *Theory Z: How American business can meet the Japanese challenge.* New York: Avon Books.

Putnam, L. Z. (1983). Lady, you're trapped: Breaking out of conflict cycles. In J. J. Oiletta (Ed.), *Women in organizations.* Prospect Heights, IL: Wareland Press.

Rost, J. C. (1991). *Leadership for the twenty first century.* New York: Praeger.

Salancik, G., & Pfeffer, J. (1977). Who gets power—and how they hold on to it: A strategic contingency model of power. *Organizational Dynamics, 5,* 3–21.

Schein, E. H. (1985). *Organizational culture and leadership: A dynamic view.* San Francisco: Jossey-Bass.

Sergiovanni, T. J. (1986). Leadership as cultural expression. In T. J. Sergiovanni & J. E. Corbally (Eds.), *Leadership and organizational culture* (pp. 105–114). Urbana, IL: University of Illinois Press.

Serviovanni, T. J., & Corbally, J. E. (Eds.). (1986). *Leadership and organizational culture.* Urbana, IL: University of Illinois Press.

Shakeshaft, C. (1987). *Women in educational administration.* Newbury Park, CA: Sage.

Shetty, Y. (1978). Managerial power and organizational effectiveness: A contingency analysis. *Journal of Management Studies, 15,* 176–186.

Smith, P. B., & Peterson, M. F. (1989). *Leadership, organizations and culture: An event management model.* London: Sage.

Stogdill, R., & Coons, A. (Eds.). (1957). *Leader behavior: Its description and measurement.* Columbus, OH: Bureau of Business Research, Ohio State University.

Vroom, V., & Jago, A. (1988). *The new leadership: Managing participation in organizations.* Upper Saddle River, NJ: Prentice Hall.

Vroom, V., & Yetton, P. (1973). *Leadership and decision making.* Pittsburgh, PA: University of Pittsburgh Press.

White, R., & Lippitt, R. (1990). Leader behavior and member reaction in three "social climates." In J. Hall (Ed.), *Models for management: The structure of competence* (2nd ed., pp. 146–172). The Woodlands, TX: Woodstead Press.

Yukl, G. A. (1989). *Leadership in organizations.* Upper Saddle River, NJ: Prentice Hall.

PART II

Schools as Learning Organizations: Communication and Human Interaction

Communication is the flow of ideas and information through the systems of education. From the classroom to the national network, effective communication is the key to the functional life of educational enterprises. Leaders at all levels have to develop the ability to understand and to be understood.

In this part we develop for practitioners communications theories, models, and practices. A broad concept of communication is considered through discussion of schools as organizational systems and the human interactions that take place within them. Effective leadership requires the ability to create social environments that facilitate good communication through the establishment of mutual respect and trust among all members of the organization. Such an environment permits information to flow freely and accurately both within the school system and between the system and its environment. That flow allows messages to be acted on appropriately and in a timely fashion.

Chapter 4: Schools as Organizational Systems.   In Chapter 4 we consider organizational theory and practice that constitute the educational enterprise. Depending on one's view, organizational activity may be linked to values, effectiveness, integration, and more. Metaphors are examined to help the reader envision the broad nature of how we think about, use, and evaluate organizational performance today.

Chapter 5: Communication: The Breath of Organizational Life.

In many disciplines, communication is believed to be a primary building block. In this chapter we explore communication in detail—from educational to societal systems. A key ingredient in effective leadership, communication is the conduit for inquiry that develops understanding within and across environments. As the information age develops, communication will become more important.

Chapter 6: Human Relations: The Base for Educational Leadership.

Human relations is the integration of people that allows them to work together productively and cooperatively. In this chapter we broaden the understanding of teamwork and team learning applications and discuss how mental states affect the human component of educational enterprises. Each person's ability to work harmoniously and understand the educational organization is a key to organizational effectiveness.

CHAPTER 4

Schools as Organizational Systems

Allen (1992) has assessed national educational guidelines as inadequate. He said that they are significantly outdated and in need of drastic reconstruction. Speaking from other points of view, other authors report similar concerns.

Levine (1992) recounted how, as a researcher, he enrolled in high school classes. What he observed and reported was more serious than he had expected: schools then, as today, were facing the decline of the family, rising poverty, changing demographics, a drug explosion, and a lack of parental support. But problematic issues in the economy or the nation are only part of the problem. Hentschke (1992) explained that real school dilemmas are lost in a plethora of overdebated professional issues such as school-based management, shared decision making, performance-based instruction, authentic assessment, accountability, and teacher–parent improvements.

Coombs (1991) cited four reasons underlying his concern for schooling in the United States. They were his perception that there was (1) failure to understand fundamental assumptions about schooling, (2) failure to react to today's realizations spawned by rapid change in a modern world, (3) failure to adapt to new understanding about the nature of the human organism, and (4) failure to construct a system that values and facilitates innovation and true professionalism. Lack of student centeredness, lack of adjustment to changing needs, discouragement of innovation, misunderstanding culture, poor motivational methods, lack of leadership and governance, insufficient funding, and lack of purpose all play their parts as well in Coomb's analysis of the problems of the schools.

There is extensive literature reflecting a seemingly endless list of problems evident in schools. The scope, number, and scale of the problems seem unmanageable. It would seem that changes are needed in organizational climate, organizational development, organizational variance, and organizational adaptability. Quick fixes such as study of school structure, relations with the environment, management, decision making, human behavior, and others abound.

Schools suffer many of the same ills that we find occurring across society. Schools, in fact, may more closely mirror society than we prefer to acknowledge. Schools appear to be locked in extensive red tape, unable to react in a rapidly changing environment. They are seen by many as at risk of wasting resources and suffering from misdirected efforts, inadequate performance, discontented employees, and inadequate leadership. Many, including Coombs (1991), Levine (1992), Sergiovanni (1989), and Solomon and Hughes (1992), believe that our schools, as organizations, are in need of revitalization, even complete renewal—changes across the many contexts of organization.

The complexity of organizational issues driven by the technological knowledge explosion and a variety of changes in societal values, beliefs, and expectations only compounds what must now be apparent. Change is the driving need felt by most critics of education. School systems based on the Weberian model (a model that is defined by control, efficiency, and routinization) have not been able to deal effectively with current needs (Weber, 1947). Other organizational models and theories, such as management science that develops a "science of work" perspective (Fayol, 1949; Taylor, 1947, cited in Pugh & Hickson, 1989), a human sociological or psychological perspective; (Herzberg, 1968, cited in Pugh & Hickson, 1989; Mayo, 1945; McGregor, 1985), or any number of other typologies for thinking about organizations may not have served us well. Further contingency approaches to organization, although encompassing more variables, may also be too narrowly focused.

In all this, however, the purpose of education has not changed significantly. Many view the purpose of schooling to include basic skills development, knowledge of a common heritage, good character development, and preparation for work and/or further study (Allen, 1992; Bennett, 1992; Hentschke, 1992; Hodgkinson, 1991; Levine, 1992; Solomon & Hughes, 1992). At the same time, educational practitioners have molded schools as mirror images of society and organizations in that society. In the latter sense, the purposes of schools, as well as societies, include (1) an aesthetic purpose associated with the fulfillment and enjoyment of life; (2) an economic purpose—making money; and (3) an ideological purpose, as a conveyor of society's cultural, idealistic, and humanistic traits (Hodgkinson, 1991). These myriad purposes of schooling render education more diverse among occupations in society. All organizations exist to achieve similar purposes. Nevertheless, no organization carries with it the degree of totality and uniqueness of purpose that is found in schools. Although the simple marketing slogan "This isn't your parents' Oldsmobile" implies for the year's shopper a desirable product and a narrowly defined purpose for General Motors, the purpose of schooling is infinitely more complex and demonstrates greater scope and scale of action.

For most people, schooling represents a substantial portion of one's lifetime, yet as shown briefly already, ambiguity present in thinking about schools is widespread. As organizations, our schools are not keeping pace with changes in society. Like many other private and public organizations, they are becoming "iron cages" that control and stifle creative action through rigid rules and bureaucracy (Clegg, 1990). Schools consume limited resources and too often house discontented, even apathetic, employees. Perhaps most profound and saddening, they often produce graduates not capable of assuming effective roles in our society. Schools should lead society into the future. As purposeful organizations using an equitable amount of resources, schools should prepare participants for a positive and lifelong adaptation and interaction with society. But schools frequently succumb to the same problems, the same inadequacies, and the same paradoxes as those found in other organizations. They mirror what exists in the larger environment.

In this chapter we explore the enduring parameters of schools as organizations today. Classical, humanistic, and systemic constructs are discussed, and additionally, the integrating elements that unite organizational thought are investigated. Using metaphor, we look at schools as organizations. In addition, current school issues are identified and related to the metaphors discussed. We also discuss schools for tomorrow as grounded in quantum science.

Ways of Thinking about Organizations

Organizations can be conceptualized in a variety of ways: through definition, through one's perception of reality, and through theoretical constructs, even metaphorically, as in such terms as turbulence or chaos. Organizations may be defined as associations of several to many people who are attempting to fulfill a common goal. Etzioni (1964) said that organizations are social units that are deliberately constructed and reconstructed to seek previously defined objectives.

Shafritz and Ott (1992) specified the basic elements of an organization: (1) implicit or explicit purposes, (2) the ability to attract participants, (3) the ability to acquire and allocate resources to accomplish goals, (4) an internal structure that is used to divide and coordinate activities, and (5) reliance on a member or set of members to lead and manage others. Banner and Gagne (1995) developed a parallel list, which included (1) goal direction, (2) relatively identifiable boundaries, (3) social interaction, (4) deliberately structured activities, and (5) a culture common to the members.

Organizations are deliberate creations, according to Sergiovanni (1989), who stated that there must be a reason for the construction of an organization. However, Colapinto (1994) pointed out that any human organization will contain both formal and informal structures. Formal structures are those that are often defined in writing and serve as a frame of reference for interaction among those within the organization and for those interacting with the organization from outside. Informal structures are generally unwritten and are often the more real centers of authority and responsibility.

Some view organizations as having life cycles. Quinn and Cameron (1983) postulated four stages of organizational life, characterized by specific types of behavior: (1) entrepreneurial, (2) collecting, (3) formalized and controlling, and (4) elaborative of structures. Although all four behaviors may exist at the same time within an organization, the issue is the dominant behavior. In the entrepreneurial stage, organizations emphasize innovation and creativity. In the collective stage, emphasis is on informal communication, structure, and development of a sense of family, of "us." In the formalized and controlling stage, emphasis is on efficiency, on production, on observation of rules and procedures. Finally, in the elaboration of structures stage, the emphasis is on monitoring the external environment, self-renewal, and expansion of the organization's domain.

Weber (1947) devised the term *bureaucracy* to represent tightly controlled organizations. Organizations were understood to be well-oiled machines. Specialized parts of the machine were differentiated by function and combined through an authority-based, hierarchial structure. Rules, policy, and procedures enabled the specialized parts to achieve maximum effort. Woodward (1981), on the other hand, described organizations through their technology, a combination of processes or functions that were the result of technological operations. Individuals, in turn, are utilized and identified in relation to a technology component. Thus organizations are conceived through a convergence/divergence lens. The principal effect on specialized organizations is the differentiation of activities so as to integrate the organization with its common purpose(s). This rational deterministic view maintained primacy for many years. Then other theorists began to question the relevance of this "things or events" focus. Today, many visualize organizations as being much more ubiquitous and complex (Barnard, 1938; Drucker, 1987; Mintzberg, 1983; Ouchi, 1981; Peters, 1992). They perceive organizations as instruments to maximize efficiency, a deterministic view that gives greater credence to the "science of work" and management and their applicability to the human component.

Taylor's work concentrated on the area of scientific management. His five principles of work design advocate the following: (1) shift work responsibility to management (managers plan and design work, while workers implement); (2) use scientific analysis to devise precise worker actions; (3) select the best workers for a given job; (4) train workers effectively; and (5) monitor work and worker performance (Morgan, 1986). Frank and Lillian Gilbreth (Spreigel, 1953) tested Taylor's principal contributions studying human motion through work study analysis of performance. In his discussion of management, Fayol (1949) provided a comprehensive explanation of organizations. The functions of management are planning, organizing, directing, coordinating, and controlling. By and large, Fayol's perspective is seen in most discussions of organization today. Although Taylor and Fayol are not viewed as human relations pioneers, their work led to further studies of the human component in organizations. Their scientific analysis, combined with Weberian classical structure, has had a long and profound effect on organizations as they exist today.

Others viewed organizations additionally as systems of interdependent human activities, as human beings were considered another essential resource required to achieve specific organizational purposes. Numerous authors and theorists viewed the human component as special in regard to the organization, not only as a resource for the organization to consume, but as an element whose behavior affects both the structure and the function of an organization. To these writers, people *were* the organization. For Mayo (1945), the major task of management was to organize the people in the organization and to secure the commitment of individuals to achieve ends for the organization. In tightly structured and controlled organizations, workers needed an outlet, an informal mechanism, to combat the ill effects of bureaucracy. Mayo's work, in addition, addresses the importance of communication to successful management as managers succeeded or failed based on their acceptance or disapproval by workers. McGregor (1985) postulated further that managers exhibit beliefs about human behavior in two broad categories of assumptions: (1) theory X, viewing employees as untrustworthy, lazy, and in need of careful controlling; or (2) theory Y, a more positive view of the employee. Similarly, Likert (1987) questioned why units in organizations with low efficiency ratings tended to have job-centered supervisors, whereas supervisors with the best performance records appeared employee-centered. Both Likert and McGregor consider building supportive relationships an ideal supervisory practice. Blake and Mouton (1988) support an analogous approach. "The manager's job is to foster attitudes and behavior which promote efficient performance, stimulate and use creativity, generate enthusiasm for experimentation and innovation, and learn from interaction of others" (Pugh & Hickson, 1989, p. 183). Blake and Mouton's managerial grid identified behaviors they believe can be taught and learned.

Other human behaviorists have examined a variety of aspects of human components in organizations. Herzberg (1968) found distinctively different factors associated with job satisfaction and job dissatisfaction. Theorists who simply maintain that being more supportive is sufficient must recognize further that job enrichment brings about more effective utilization of people in organizations and increases job satisfaction.

As described by Bolman and Deal (1997), the human resource perspective takes the view that organizations can be energizing, productive, and rewarding to their participants. The basic assumptions of the human resource model, they say, are: (1) organizations exist to serve human needs rather than the reverse; (2) people and organizations need each other; (3) when the fit between individual and system is poor, both suffer; and (4) a good fit profits both the individual and the organization. Bolman and Deal (1997) go on to say that an effective human resource model of organization includes specific practices that enhance the fit between the individual and the organization. These practices include (1) hiring right and rewarding well, (2) providing security for employees, (3) promoting from within, (4) providing training and education for employees, and (5) sharing the wealth with the workers.

Schein (1985) extended assumptions about the human aspects of organization beyond the rational, social, and needs-based models. His complex model recognizes that life events and development drive individual motives and that these motives vary across situations and time. Management therefore simply cannot be coordination and control, nor even largely supportive, but must include a diagnostic component whereby managers learn and react to both individual employees and organizational expectations. This added level of understanding of people enables the organization to cope with internal and external realities, adapting to the external and integrating the internal.

Argyris, Putnam, and Smith (1985) developed a strikingly similar diagnostic view. In organizations, people are often confronted with built-in contradictory elements. These contradictory elements cause people to adhere to stability-producing conformance mechanisms and, in the next instant, be penalized for lacking initiative, aggressiveness, or adaptability. Different norms are needed in organizations, norms that decree openness in communication, openness to action, and openness to learning.

For those concerned with the human relations model of organizations, the organizational climate is significant. Cornell (1955) initiated the use of the term *organizational climate,* defining it as a blend of the perceptions of the members of the organization about their roles and the roles of others in the organization. Tagiuri and Litwin (1968) specified that consideration of an organization's climate must distinguish (1) the objective from the subjective environment, (2) persons from situations, (3) the aspects of the organization appropriate to the issue under consideration, and (4) the structures and dynamics of the organization appropriate to the issue under consideration.

To this point, organizations have been viewed as structure, as management, and as human relations. While each of these perspectives provides valuable data to use in understanding organizations, another approach to organizations is provided by systems theorists. Ultimately, in this view, organizations are organic entities or seen as sets of processes that interact with an environment. In the traditional rational/deterministic, scientific, and human relations perspectives, theorists attempt to constrain uncertainty in the organization. With the advent of systems theory, organization study addresses the uncertainty across various boundary conditions. The input–throughput–output–feedback model became the cornerstone of organizational inquiry.

In the earliest studies of organizations using systems methodology, environment, boundaries, variety, feedback, and other elements were treated as another set of scientific variables with which to contend. School systems' environments were thought to include the school, the school district, the state, and the federal government. Others added the community,

parents, businesses, and various professional and educational associations. In the mechanistic organization, problems were resolved in various specialized departments. As change, innovation, and uncertainty continued to grow, the organization became incapable of handling the ensuing variety. In the short term, the organization's communications broke down from the maze of problems that were encountered.

Burns (1966) maintained that this breakdown is inevitable. Organizations function in differing social systems: an authority system, a cooperative system of people, and a political system. In Burns's view, organizational structure was the result of a process whereby the continuous development of these three social systems occurs within and adapts to an ever-changing environment.

Lawrence and Lorsch (1986) maintained that the additional requirement of the organization to interact with its environment complicates organization thinking processes even further. By advocating a contingency approach, they address the issue of integration and differentiation in the organization's internal environment and externally within the organization's suprasystem. In the organization's attempt to integrate and differentiate effectively, conflict resolution founded in compromise and competence balances organizational functioning. Thompson (1967) termed this an *alignment function,* where structure, technology, and environment interact.

Other authors further expand systems thinking as applied to organizations. Understanding organizations in terms of biology and evolution, Hannan and Freeman (1988) proposed a population ecology perspective of organizations. They attempt to explain the replacement of outmoded forms of organization with newer forms. Some organizations prosper and survive, whereas others die out. Emery and Trist (1969) in work at the Travistock Institute conceptualized organizations as *open sociotechnical systems.* In this view, the organization is viewed as being essentially dynamic and having a continual interchange across boundaries with its environment. The work of management is to manage boundary exchanges rather than internal regulation. No longer would traditional redundancy of parts, common in traditional views, suffice. In turn, a redundancy of function in individuals and units would be capable of coping with complexity and change across boundaries. Rather than relying on controls to contain variety, organizations must rely on new, self-regulating mechanisms to achieve effective functioning in a turbulent environment. The true dynamic nature of organizations is exhibited through this new understanding. Silverman (1971) saw all organizational study as inadequate and conceptualized an "action" frame of reference. This approach views organizations as outcomes of the interaction of motivated people who are attempting to resolve their problems and pursue their needs.

The traditional organizational viewpoints focus principally on a series of impersonal elements to explain organizations' functions, while the human relations viewpoint focuses too far into a relationship orientation. To understand organizations further, we need to construct thinking about organizations as they occur in reality. Hypothesizing about either the traditional or human relations focus only serves to limit our true understanding of the reality within and surrounding organizations.

Organizational Learning and Learning Organizations

Brown and Packham (1999) have applied a systems model to the nature and functions of organizations, focusing on critical systems thinking and systemic learning. They defined critical systems thinking as a way of thinking about the world, as constructs rather than objective realities. Such constructs assist in problem solving. The basic themes of critical systems thinking are critical awareness, improvement, and methodological pluralism.

Critical awareness is the examination and re-examination of taken-for-granted assumptions and interpretations of the conditions that gave rise to their creation. Critical awareness helps to maintain awareness of the need to consider a variety of views in defining problems. *Improvement* in the sense of the social constructivist viewpoint is central to critical systems thinking, said Brown and Packham (1999). *Methodological pluralism* implies equifinality, a characteristic of systems theory which indicates that a variety of avenues may be available to reach the same goal. The appropriate avenue may be defined by the current circumstances.

Brown and Packham (1999) defined *systemic learning* as the basis for action research. It embodies both the finding of new information and the taking of action as a result of the discovery. *Organizational learning,* said Brown and Packham (1999), is a social construction through a reflective process that transforms acquired cognition into knowledge. It becomes organizational learning when accountability assigned by the organization is accepted by a person and is acted upon.

When Brown and Packham (1999) considered organizational improvement that comes from critical systems thinking and systemic learning, they identified five possible approaches: (1) action learning, in which improvement is based on disclosure of thoughts to colleagues in group settings and then action is taken; (2) metaphors, in which one or more metaphors are used to gain insights into problems; (3) scenarios, in which models of possible futures are developed to inform strategic planning; (4) storytelling, in which a recounting of the past is used to assist in problem solving and planning; and (5) dialogue, in which conversation is analyzed to determine the thinking that lies beneath it.

Decision Making in Organizations

Another school of thought maintains that decision making is the key to understanding organizational effectiveness. Organizational effectiveness is thought to reside principally in managerial actions. For decision theorists, all managerial action is decision making. In older theories, rationality is thought to be a cornerstone to decision making. The decision maker rationally determines a best course of action from a multitude of variables to maximize organizational functioning. Simon (1977) replaced the rational-economic person, who maximizes decisions, with the administrative person, one who merely satisfices. *Satisficing* is defined as a situation in which the manager does not take the time to seek optimal resolution of a problem, but settles for one that is satisfactory, one that "will do." Organizational action is based individually or organizationally on selection of satisfactory alternatives using a few comparatively relevant factors with which the person is capable of dealing.

In this viewpoint, organizations should necessarily strive to create situations in which unprogrammed decision contexts become programmed. Using these unprogrammed contexts, such as habits, routines, standard procedures, structure, and culture, allows the decision maker and the organization to function effectively. Both March (1988) and Simon (1977) believed the decision maker capable of a *bounded rationality*. The limits of one's knowledge or an organization's knowledge severely limits organizational capability. Cognitive constraints and a scarcity of attention connect with the political aspects of the organization and provide a multitude of action possibilities. Through negotiation and bargaining, the organization progresses to an organizational limit.

Organizations rarely resolve conflict completely because they avoid uncertainty by creating acceptable decision making. Accepting this short-term view results in the need to search for more satisficing alternatives. Over a period of time this process leads to organizational learning based on a reactive stance. March (1988) contended any "garbage can" full of decision rules, and action alternatives will suffice if the organization persists in the short-term action environment. Mintzberg (1989) postulated that individuals as decision makers fall into four patterns: the

entrepreneur, who leads and determines new purpose; the disturbance handler, who resolves others' problems; the resource allocator, who disperses financial resources; and the negotiator, who seeks compromises.

Lindbloom (1980) termed his version of the decision making process *disjointed incrementalism* or the "science of muddling through." It is nearly impossible, according to Lindbloom, to find a rational/deterministic model of decision making in use in most organizations. At best, decision making in organizations may suffer from too much reactiveness, too few long-term horizons, and little effective control.

Tannebaum (1968) held a different view. While many believe that effective control in organizations is and should be concerned primarily with how managers use a particular decision-making model or process, Tannebaum, in contrast, argued that decision making as a process should be shared with a wider variety of players. This provides a greater volume of realistic alternatives from which to satisfice. In Tannebaum's studies, people in organizations aren't interested in exercising more control than others, but simply in exercising more control themselves. Organizations would be wise to consider diminishing the slope of hierarchies to some degree and restricting their attention to who exercises power. Then the organizations should institute processes or models that allow members to increase the volume of decision making. This shared responsibility firmly moves organizational thinking away from its machine connotations to a shared decision-making perspective.

Power in Organizations

Thinking about organizational decision making leads to discussions about power in organizations. Individual, unit, or organizational decisions are based on interests, an orientation to act in one manner or another. Power in organizations relates directly to how these interests are pursued and defined, and the variety of ways in which individuals then position and perceive their interests. Various agendas collide as different players defend their interests. Power in organizations results as systems simultaneously compete and collaborate (Burns, 1966). Up and down the traditional organization, power is a mechanism by which the organization resolves conflict.

Sources of power in organizations are numerous (Morgan, 1986). In the Weberian tradition, power is derived from legitimate authority. The right to rule is a recognized tradition in most organizations, as formal authority is typically associated with position or command structure. Organizations also gain additional sources of power from control of scarce resources. Dependence must be established for this source of power to provide control. Structure and policy or regulation also is a source of power and another form of control in organizations. Bureaucratic regulation, plans, promotion requirements, and other regulatory rules give power potential to various controllers. The ability to influence decision making through these structural mechanisms is most often seen in the control of decision making, whether controlling decision agendas, actual decision making, or organizational objectives. The control of knowledge and information and the determination of what receives attention are also of vital importance. Key actors often resort to information and knowledge control, whether weaving a pattern of dependency via structure, change, gatekeeping, or limiting information or knowledge capability. Boundary management also is a source of power. Control of integrating mechanisms can promote progress, while isolation can limit progress. Other sources of power include networks, control of power relations, alliances, control of technology, coping with uncertainty, managing meaning, and gender management (Morgan, 1986).

Recognizing and understanding these sources of power enables the practitioner to cope with power's many political milieus. In a complex pluralistic society, power is viewed as inevitable. The questions become how to compete, how to collaborate, how to avoid, how to accommodate, or how to compromise (Thomas, 1977). While radical views pit factions against each other, or unitary views integrate interests, in the pluralistic view the nature of the traditional organization is checked by the free interplay of various interest groups that have a stake in the organization.

Culture in Organizations

If power in organizations is as ubiquitous as it seems, it certainly appears that its presence can also become ingrained. In a similar fashion, other elements of the organization can also become habitual. Organizational theorists, sociologists, anthropologists, even managers, have long recognized this trait in organizations. From an anthropologist's perspective, culture is a complex system that includes knowledge, beliefs, arts, morals, laws, customs, and other habits acquired by people in society (Sackmann, 1991). In this respect, a cultural study of organizations has become a means to study the components of an organization. Whether uncovering mainstay principles, realizing hidden mental constructions, or identifying how members' personalities are determined or represented within the organization, cultural study in the organizational context has become the study of the conditions that create the ability of organizations to function and behave more effectively. The study of culture in organizations thus becomes a holistic integration mechanism whereby theorists and consultants study ways of thinking, feeling, and reacting that individuals and organizations have acquired and that somehow have been stored and transmitted through some form of symbolism. As a product of action, a shared system of meaning that incorporates the way people live and work in the organization, culture becomes a method to codify, modify, and control the organization (Sackmann, 1991). Schein (1985) stated that as the culture integrates an organization internally and adapts the organization externally, it defines the valid, correct way to inculcate new members. Phillips (1984) added that these products of action may become so typical that they become tacit.

Numerous authors argue about the value of understanding culture. Problems cited include accurate definition of culture, determining the appropriate dimensions of culture, homogeneity versus heterogeneity, and difficulties with measurement. Despite all this, viewing organizations as culture has stood the test of time and has become part of the vocabulary of organizations (Meyerson, 1991). This view of organizations is promising in that it is neither an oversocialized nor an undersocialized view (Clegg, 1990). The study of organizational culture makes sense of organizations' experiences and behaviors, compiles various norms of action, and results in organizational understanding and new learning (Bolman & Deal, 1991). Culture is probably something that an organization has and is despite rhetoric that argues otherwise.

Leadership in Organizations

In the modern age, theorists, authors, and practitioners alike have sought a connection between leadership and organization. Leadership is often confused with management in this regard. Some authors choose to emphasize similarities, others differences, while still others remain oblivious to these issues (Rost, 1991). Leadership and management are both processes and necessary elements of organizations. In the humanistic frame of reference, the behavior of the leader or manager also becomes a point of relevance. As processes and behaviors that have been discussed over time, however, neither is clearly understood. Mintzberg (in Rost, 1991) lamented that he and his counterparts have yet to understand leadership thoroughly or to define it adequately. Similarly, most authors and theorists have not been able to state leader or manager definitions succinctly (Rost, 1991).

However, much has been uncovered. We know a lot about what constitutes leadership and what doesn't. Leadership in the human context is behavioral and situational (Bass, 1990; Yukl, 1989). Common findings are identifiable. Leadership can also be viewed from a functional orientation: as a set of relationships, as influence, as change, as motivation, as communication, as conflict, or as growth and development (Knezevich, 1989). Similarly, leadership can be a set of personality traits, a particular formal position, or a status. In each regard, leadership has been recognized as an imprecise concept. It can be rooted in values, in action, in power. Above all, it is indeterminate and variable across numerous contexts.

As we continue to attempt to define leadership in this human context, we will undoubtedly continue to find leaders who are "all of the above." In this regard, Rost's (1991) definition seems highly appropriate. "Leadership is an influence relationship among leaders and followers who intend real changes that reflect their mutual purposes" (p. 98). But as we look to larger issues in an organization, leadership takes on a greater focus. In this respect, leadership can be seen better from Davis and Davidson's (1991) perspective. "Leadership is defined in terms which relate a vision of the future to strategies for achieving it, which are capable of coopting support, compliance, and teamwork in its achievement and serve to motivate and sustain commitment to its purpose" (p. 201). Leadership tomorrow takes on an architectural focus (Beckett, 1971).

According to Damme (1995), leadership development falls into several models. These include (1) integrated models, in which actual work problems are reviewed in order to learn from experience; (2) nonintegrated models, in which a link is not made between theory and practice; and (3) individual personal development models, in which an integrated model is applied at several levels: organizational, psychological, and experiential. There is a strong trend toward integrating action and learning, personal and professional development, and leadership and organizational development in order to support organizational change, according to Damme (1995).

Communication in Organizations

A great portion of our communication takes place in organizations, and as Etzioni (1964) said, we spend a great deal of time in different kinds of organizations. Monge and Eisenhart (1987) cited three frames of reference that enable us to view organizations and communication conveniently. In the traditional era, the positional frame of reference viewed communication up, down, and laterally through set positions in the bureaucratic hierarchy. In a more modern era, the relational frame sees communication as occurring naturally among relationships between participants. The organization is shaped and given meaning through these interactions. In another view, the cultural frame stresses the importance of stories, rituals, and work among its members and determines from these how the organization communicates. The real organization in this sense emerges from daily actions of members in their work.

Littlejohn (1989) used the network metaphor to outline how these three different frames of reference enable understanding about organizational communication. In combination with information theory, Littlejohn feels that theorists are able to understand how individual, dyadic, group, and organizational networks function. In the classical organization, management uses formal networks to achieve the purpose of the organization. Power, authority, and legitimacy govern communication in bureaucratic organizations. Informal communication networks flourish in classical organizations as members lower in the hierarchy attempt to gain their own status and power.

Likert's (1987) four systems organizational concept transcends both the positional and relational frames. In the four systems approach, an organization functions along four continuums: (1) exploitative–authoritative, (2) benevolent–authoritative, (3) consultative, and (4) participative. Likert treats communication in organizations as one of many variables. In essence, the more authoritative an organization, the less individual and group loyalty there is to management and the less motivation toward organizational purpose is realized. Conversely, the more participative the organization, the more individuals and groups provide loyalty, performance, and mutual support to the organization. Overall, exploitative systems seem to produce more negative consequences than do participative systems. Tompkins and Cheney (1985) outlined a similar model in their theory of organizational identification. Organizations employ simple control, technological control, bureaucratic control, and concertive control to realize productivity and achieve organizational purpose.

Most recently, communication has been conceptualized through relational and cultural frames. The importance of lines of communication has been set aside as theorists study emergent patterns and interactions among organizational members and how persons really act in organizations. In the traditional perspective on organizations, these frames of reference are an inappropriate parameter with which to study, as the dynamics of ongoing behavior depends on how they are organized. In the social realm peoples' activities create organizations (Weick, 1969). Any act is communication. Interaction serves to develop common meaning among individuals and others in the organization. Uncertainty among members is thus reduced in both internal and external relations through enactment, selection, and retention. Continuous individual, group, or organizational behavior and choice cycles result (Weick, 1969). The theory of structuration (Poole & McPhee, 1983) is similar to Weick's theory of organizing. Organizational structure is created at centers of structuration, implemented into formal codes, and enacted (termed *reception*) in organizational decisions. Organizational climate, an intersubjective phenomenon, arises from the structuration process through member interaction and results in organizational outcomes.

In each theory discussed above, communication develops into organizational networks. The social, structural, and functional channels are the essence of communication in organizations.

Size, Structure, and Complexity in Organizations

The implications of size, structure, and complexity in organizations was best addressed by Mintzberg (1983, 1989). In his detailed analysis of design in organizations, Mintzberg identified five general structural configurations. The key differentiating feature in the design occurs as the result of some predominant part in each. In the simple structure the upper echelon predominates and pulls the organization to centralize, utilizing direct supervision. In the machine bureaucracy the technostructure predominates and causes standardization of work processes. In the professional bureaucracy the *operating core* rules and causes the organization to professionalize through standardization of skills. In the divisionalized form the "middle line" dominates by coordinating and standardizing outputs. Finally, the adhocracy coordinates the *support staff* and causes mutual adjustment in the organization.

The structure of the entrepreneurial organization (a simple structure) is characterized by little or no staff, a loose division of labor, and a small hierarchy. As its size is small, complexity also tends to be negligible. As an organization, the entrepreneurial firm tends to be informal, flexible, responsive, and operates with a sense of distinct purpose. Activities generally revolve around the owner or chief executive. As simple organizations mature, they tend to work toward the machine bureaucracy or professional bureaucracy. In the machine bureaucracy, formal procedures, specialization, differentiation, and extreme hierarchy are common. A powerful support staff and middle management are needed for regulation control complexity through standardization of the work. The organization is stable, consistent, and efficient in relatively stable environments. In unstable environments it tends toward inflexibility and can then change only through long, drawn-out planning processes. As the size of the organization increases, the machine bureaucracy tends to become more and more controlled, to the point of redundancy. Decentralization usually occurs as the organization develops into a divisionalized form. Loosely coupled, autonomous divisions are subjected to performance controls in the form of standardized output, as directed from a central or corporate headquarters. This form is generally also the largest and most mature of the Mintzberg configurations.

The professional bureaucracy is a decentralized form of machine bureaucracy. The organization is characterized by autonomous and democratic professional work groups, typically subject to controls of a profession. A large support staff functions as an administrative arm for the professional core. Complexity becomes extreme in this organization because various autonomous individuals or groups share allegiances to the organization and to a professional external group. As size increases, the professional bureaucracy becomes more and more difficult to operate.

Finally, Mintzberg postulated an *adhocracy:* a fluid, organic, and selectively decentralized organization. As the organization is characterized by autonomy and democracy, it is also the most innovative of the Mintzberg structures. Experts in teams typically work in highly dynamic and complex environments to carry out demanding and rapidly changing requirements. The organization appears to thrive on complexity. Size is a detriment.

More recently, Mintzberg (1989) added a sixth structure, the missionary organization. The organization is characterized by a rich system of values and beliefs, and a strong sense of mission.

This organization thrives due to standardization of norms, reinforced by selection, socialization, and indoctrination. These organizations are typically highly decentralized and complex, as they enact complicated norms steeped in ideology.

In thinking about organization, authors and theorists have had to recapitulate regularly. For example, Blau (1977) defined structure as " . . . the distribution, along various lines, of people among social position that influence role relations among these people" (p. 12). In this example, structure implies a division of labor, position, rules, and behavior. Structure uses power to achieve results. These organizations attempt to maintain a status quo. But as authors and theorists begin thinking beyond Weberian and, more recently, Japanese examples, they note that change may be the essence of organizations today. Thus understanding how structure, size, and complexity affect organizations has been critical in the past, but today our focus must include how organizations change.

Organizational Health and Effectiveness

Organizations are part of a system of interlacing, interacting systems that are in a constant dynamic state, according to Beckhard (1997). They may be construed as existing in various stages of health. Healthy organizations, in Beckhard's view, meet the following criteria:

1. They define themselves as systems. The organization's work is to take in needs and raw materials and transfer them into goods and services.

2. They have strong sensing systems for receiving current information on all parts of the system and its interactions. This is systems dynamic thinking.

3. They have a strong sense of purpose.

4. They operate in a "form follows function" mode. The work to be done defines the structures and mechanisms of the organizations rather than the reverse.

5. They employ team management as the dominant mode.

6. They respect customer service as a basic principle.

7. Their management is information driven.

8. They allow and encourage decisions to be made at the level closest to the customer.

9. They keep communication relatively open within the system.

10. Their reward systems are congruent with the work and support individual development. Managers and work teams are appraised against both performance and improvement goals.

11. They operate in a learning mode.

12. They make explicit recognition of innovation and creativity, and they have a high tolerance for different styles of thinking and ambiguity.

13. Their policies respect the tension between work demands and family demands.

14. They have an explicit social agenda.

15. They give attention to efficiency, quality, and safety in operations, and to identifying and managing change for a better future.

Roufa (1990) argued that organizational health is related to *person–environment fit*, which he defined as congruence in goals between the individual and the organization, which results in the individual meeting the needs of the organization and the organization meeting the needs of the individual. The less congruent the goals, the more stress is generated for both the individual and the organization. Sufficient incongruence can result in ill health for both the individual and the organization.

Ricotta (1992) linked organizational effectiveness to organizational life cycles. Defining organizational effectiveness as the result of the organization's pursuing its goals adequately, she posited that effectiveness would be affected by the organizational life cycles identified by Quinn and Cameron (1983). These are (1) the entrepreneurial stage, where emphasis is on resource acquisition; (2) the collectivity stage, where emphasis is on informal communications and structure; (3) the formalization and control stage, where organizational stability predominates; and (4) the elaboration of structure stage, where the emphasis is on self-renewal and expansion of the organization's domain. These models are competing for preeminence in the organization. As each of these stages predominates, the organization must shift goals, resource allocation, and activities to remain in a state of good health.

Change in Organizations

Over time, organizations of all styles begin, mature, and decline. The life cycle of organizations is thus considered through various maturity—decline and change models. In general, organizations spend a great deal of time in periods of stability punctuated by brief transition periods. Ecologists term this phenomenon *punctuated equilibrium*. Others call it *metamorphosis* or *dynamic equilibrium* (Schön, 1987; Starbach, 1981). These life cycle models usually address formation, development, maturity, and decline. Hannan and Freeman (1988) see a founding and disbanding sequence. Faced with crisis, organizations either tend to move to a next stage of development or develop renewal or revitalization mechanisms. Depending on internal and external environmental factors, organizations may choose strategies of renewal or revitalization. In other contexts, organizations may adopt a particular model of change based on a shift in strategic alignment.

Lewin's (1951) three-stage model of unfreezing, change, and refreezing helps to explain these shifts in vision. *Unfreezing* involves overcoming natural defense mechanisms or discontinuities by scanning the environment for available change parameters. *Change* then demands creating a willingness to step into a new environment, a shift of mind-sets. *Refreezing* involves vigorous

pursuit of the new vision. In this process, people shed old frameworks and understand and implement new ones. In small, simple firms, this can be a relatively easy task, but as organizational size increases, the change process becomes exponentially more difficult to invoke and keep on track.

Empirically based change strategies are structured on a systems management perspective. Setting new goals, monitoring change, and holding individuals accountable reflect a typical methodology. From the organizational development perspective, empirically based change seeks to focus on individual motivations for change. From a power perspective, empirically based change seeks to reduce conflict, to bargain, and to negotiate preference. In contrast, theory-based change seeks to derive change in other ways. The innovation management model focuses on developing factors that improve the probability of successful implementation. The social or cultural model focuses change directly at values held in the organization's domain and seeks change through development of different value sets (Schein, 1985). The organizational learning model focuses change on learning how to learn. Dysfunction and defensiveness are replaced by creating new ways of thinking about future states (Argyris et al., 1985). Finally, the constructionalist model emphasizes social meaning. Change involves creating and realizing new behaviors, symbols, and activities (Deal & Kennedy, 1982).

In any of these models, the various factors that affect the success of organizational change must be considered. Centrality (core competence) emphasizes change that is closely tied to organizational core activities and perceived as significant. Additionally, as the scope and complexity of change lengthens, consideration must be given to a greater period of unfreezing. Change programs must also consider where the change impetus originates from, as improper pressure from the wrong constituencies can have negative effects. Organizational culture also presents roadblocks to change programs. Although some tension is conducive to thoroughness and quality, organizational culture often presents formidable negative pressure. The degree of structural change is also important, as change could also be viewed as just piling on more with fewer available resources. Successful change also involves thinking externally. Very often, crisis creates more willingness to change, but also greater scope. Recognizing the variety of external stakeholders often establishes a more effective and positive change environment. Consideration of broader social values can also bring positive results. Although there is no universal change model or mechanism, these considerations offer a more powerful chance for change mechanisms to work.

Conner (1992) suggested that nine steps were central to effecting successful change: (1) peer group consensus must be recognized as the major influence on willingness to change and acceptance of change, (2) two-way trust related to change is necessary, (3) change should be thought of as skill building developed from training, (4) time must be allowed for the change to take hold, (5) a committed person should be placed in charge of the change, (6) change must be proposed as response to a real threat from outside the organization, (7) transition rituals should be made the pivotal elements of the change, (8) training should be provided in the new values and behaviors, and (9) tangible symbols of the new directions must be provided.

At this point premodern and modern examples of organizations have been shown across the industrial age and through the systems movement, cultural manifestations, and organizational development. In the following section, modern organizations are inspected more thoroughly. Issues that are particularly problematic to education will be highlighted. Finally, several new conceptions of organizations will be developed and discussed. These new constructions will again be explored from an educational perspective.

Early in this chapter, organizations were investigated from traditional perspectives. In the following section, the reader is asked to think about organizations metaphorically. This approach requires readers to remain open and flexible, reserve judgment, and eventually develop a more thorough appreciation and detailed comprehension. The use of metaphor calls for a different way of thinking and seeing organizations. Since organizations are complex and paradoxical, and no one viewpoint is absolutely relevant, metaphors can allow us to see differences not otherwise visible.

Images of Organizations

Morgan (1986) and others (Bergquist, 1993; Clegg, 1990) highlighted the use of metaphor to comprehend organizations and many of their assertions will be discussed. Whether an *iron cage, machine, brain,* or *turbulence,* organizations today are stylized in our thinking by metaphor.

The Machine

Classical management theory emphasized broad-based planning, coordinating, controlling, directing, and organizing (Fayol, 1949; Weber, 1947). Organizations whose major features resemble descriptions from the classical era abound, from the moderately large manufacturing firms or service firms to nearly every educational institution. As the machine metaphor implies, these organizations largely resemble the machine: efficient, hierarchial, highly centralized, planning oriented, highly regulated, highly organized, and tightly controlled (Mintzberg, 1983, 1989). Productivity is, to a large degree, the most vital measure of success and effectiveness. Also, these organizations are deterministic, as demonstrated by the development of simple schedules or plans to larger, more encompassing strategic plans (Mintzberg & Quinn, 1988). Machine organizations move slowly and deliberately.

Machine organizations are highly rational. Tasks are straightforward and precision is usually at a premium. These organizations create consistency and maintain stable environments. They are mass-production oriented. Differentiation of function and specialization of task are primal. There are few strong contemporary counterparts to the machine organization as they existed in times past. As these organizations continued to flourish, limitations began to detract from their functioning both internally and externally. Political conflict between functions occurred. Power was sought to control resources, and an informal mechanism developed whereby those lower in the hierarchy or with less power could also share in the power. In the machine organization, communication was straightforward, or top down. Communication also tended to be slow, as levels of hierarchy needed to be traversed for decision making and problem solving to occur. Most important, the machine organization positioned the human component at two very different extremes. Management controlled and subordinates were controlled.

Early management theorists had somehow managed to believe they had discovered the "one best way," the principle of organizations (Morgan, 1986). However, many, if not all, of these theorists' machine principles form the basis of organizational problems. Understanding organizations from a rational or technical point of view underscores the lack of attention to human components. It also creates organizations that adapt to changing environments slowly, are often mindless and unquestioning, and place organizational and other goals at a premium at the expense of human concerns. In many instances, the humans in the machine organization became complacent, unmotivated, and lost their commitment.

But even more important, a thorough understanding of the writings of classical theorists is also problematic. For example, Clegg (1990) believes that Weberian beliefs run counter to the efficiency developments common in most organizations today. A cornerstone of Weber's work (1947) is not efficiency, but inefficiency (Albrow, 1970; Therborn, 1976). This is readily evident in bureaucratic organizations as inefficiency has prevailed in organization today. Or

consider Taylor's (1947) development of efficiency in organizational settings. In Taylor's four underlying principles of management, several elements are directed at the human component of organizations: high reward for completion of work established through scientific task analysis, selection and development of the worker, and the constant and intimate cooperation between worker and management (Pugh & Hickson, 1989). Emery and Trist (1969) substantiated each of these Taylorisms. Clearly, portions of the machine organization have not been followed as strictly as others. Whether market forces, cultural distinctions, or other variables are at work here, the machine isn't the exact machine many envisioned. As Morgan (1986) illustrated, perhaps instrumental rationality, "fitting people and jobs together in a fixed design" (p. 37) needs to allow for substantial rationality, allowing for more reflection and self-organizing. It is interesting to note here that the lack of reflection and self-organizing is negated by the careerism focus in the machine organization as individuals compete within a closed system. Political issues abound and results often are seen that do not look anything like the organizational purpose originally intended. In the end, the organization may work at divergent purposes, in direct opposition to its organizational goals.

The Organism

The study of organizations as open systems has brought new light to a variety of issues compounded during the machine age. Bertalanffy (1968), the lead theorist and researcher of the systems movement, felt that viewing parts of an organization does not allow us to gain a holistic understanding of that organization. Inquiry into separate functions of an organization cannot realize patterns of interactions, interdependence, or the integration that occurs in the entire organization. Organizational elements are not independent but interdependent as they interact within the organization and with various boundary environments. As with all other living things, constant interaction, interdependence, and integration occurs. General systems theory attempts to explore organizations and their environments to seek explanations that can enhance understanding of the organization.

This image of organization has led to discounting many, if not most, of the ill effects prevalent in the machine image. The movement has largely been maintained in the human resources and organizational development perspectives. In the systems movement manifestations, it has been labeled an "it depends" movement. Regardless of one's philosophical beliefs, however, key organic ingredients do provide a different way of thinking about organizations.

In the organic view, the interaction of subsystems in an organization takes on vital importance. This process largely explores communication links between and within these subsystems and the system environment. The input—throughput–output–feedback model provides the methodology. As a system, an organization is internally connected to its environment through the importation of resources. These resources can be from internal feedback mechanisms or from the larger suprasystem. Each external source, whether it be customers, clients, the community, or the government, has a dramatic bearing on the organization. As the organization realizes and utilizes its true input resources, fundamental change takes place within the organization. No longer can separate functional units act without external consideration as well.

Lawrence and Lorsch (1986) explained that new markets, new technology, and differing societal expectations all affect organizational functioning. Organizations in the machine tradition were conceived largely as closed systems. Eventually they would degenerate and die out. The population ecology and growth–maturity—decline models explore these closed systems.

Equally vital, organizations in response to their new openness must be able to adapt internally. Flexible structure, responsive distribution, self-renewal and revitalization, and cooperation and collaboration are key components of these newer forms. In this fashion, organizations are more likely to be able to respond to change. As a consequence of this internal and external responsiveness, the organization's outputs also change. Customers, clients, and community partners respond to new capabilities within the organization.

The organization also measures this output differently than before, not simply from the production line or through cost/revenue parameters, but through quality, effectiveness, and satisfaction measures. These new measures become part of the organization's feedback systems in the form of new internal inputs. Self-renewal becomes consistent and constant. So, in this new organic organization, the questions become what technology is being used, what kind of people are needed, what the culture of the organization is, and how management philosophies relate to this new configuration (Morgan, 1986). Answers to these questions are the strengths found in the organic organization: openness, a process orientation, needs satisfaction, interactiveness, and a wide range of options both internally and strategically.

A key limitation of this metaphor is its reliance on adaptation. Many organisms in real life can make choices, but this organic model of organizations tends to create a marginal view whereby organizations can only hope to adapt to the environment. This may undermine the ability of the organization to control or change its own destiny. Also, organizations have historically been incapable of promoting harmony within. Although some organizations have created harmonious interaction, others still cannot manage the levels of interaction necessary. Many organizations are still too "tall." Organizational adaptation may thus not be a possibility for many as long as their change mechanisms remain incremental.

The Brain

Another view of organizations is to see them as models of the brain. In actual practice there are few organizations that have the capacity to become systemic. In these organizations the requisite task is the organization's ability to foster self-renewal and self-organization (Morgan, 1986). These models stem from numerous authors (Argyris et al., 1985; Senge, 1990; Weick, 1969). In contrast to the machine and organic views, this image implies almost complete change in the conception of the organization. The organization increases variety through a redundancy of function instead of a redundancy of parts. In this new part–whole schema, the whole is greater than the sum of its parts. For example, as is true of the brain, each activity in the organization is created in a separate part. This reduces the direct need for redundancy of parts in the organization. Second, as opposed to the machine, this new image through redundancy in function encourages all members of the organization to think in congruent terms. The machine organization restricts thinking in this regard as political systems develop to control. As a result, boundaries become more difficult to navigate internally and externally. The brain organization encourages decentralization in structure, and, at the same time increases levels of activity among various agents in a decentralized core. Boundaries between activities and between the organization and the environment become permeable. Third, whereas the machine organization develops structure to maintain accountability, rewards the accountable, and punishes the unaccountable, the brain image of organizations reduces and manages defensive structures, and as a result, approaches new activity from a learning-to-learn emphasis. The brain organization explores differences in individual and organizational theories of action and exposed theories (Argyris et al., 1985). As a result, the organization seeks to face uncertain conditions from a whole organization perspective. The organization self-renews and self-organizes. In the long term, problems and decisions are brought to the forefront of organizational analysis rather than hiding issues, or worse, being unaware of them.

Significant differences also occur between this brain image and the organic image. More accurately, the brain image more fully realizes implications of general systems theory. Whereas the manifestations of the organic organization have gravitated toward systematic implementation in organizations (modeling), brain organizations are more systemic (fluid). The redundancy in function enables self-renewal and self-organization fed by requisite variety and enabled by minimal specification (Morgan, 1986). While the organic form adapts, this newer form learns to learn. While the organic form encourages openness, this form encourages openness coupled with reflectivity. As the organic form maintains structural foundations iterated in the input–output model, this form creates its own organization in an "on the spot" fashion. The organization is configured to action. The organization utilizes the full realm of theory, praxis, and practice in recognition of its norms and values, and at the same time questions these symbols to generate further learning (Hodgkinson, 1991). In this sense, the brain image encourages inquiry and criticism. A broader range of unit and strategic goals is explored, understood, and acted upon. From this systemic format new attitudes and values emerge: activeness over reactiveness, autonomy over dependence, flexibility over rigidity, collaboration over competition, openness or closeness, and democratic versus authoritative. The brain form of organization is extremely difficult to imagine in practice. The questions become how to create this form and how we can penetrate those older-strategic paradigms. These are difficult questions to answer. More problematic than "how?" is the question "what's next?" This is explored in Chapter 16.

Political Systems and Power

In our society numerous organizational forms, each unique, have emerged. Each form must exist in a plethora of pluralistic forces. In one instance, organizations represent the freedom of the individual, in the next equality, in another sense collaboration, or in another competition. Organizations are constantly pulled by these contending concepts and typically yield in a singular direction. As our organizations adapt to a single purpose, power molds a new political system. New images of organization then form: organizations as good management, as quality or excellence, as service, or as information. These new images affect organizational action in various ways, depending on the current political emphasis in the organization. In a structural sense, organization becomes *autocracy:* we do it the way we're supposed to; or *bureaucracy:* we do it this way; or *technocracy:* we do it the best way; or *democracy:* we do it the way we decide. Analyzing its interests, the organization senses and creates an image of itself and proceeds to enlarge and protect its environment. Thus, we can observe how various earlier organizational paradigms can come into existence: the economic focus, the human relations focus, or the organizational development focus. We can also see society viewing its own afflictions more clearly.

This metaphor demonstrates how conflict arises and how organizations as political systems deal with those conflicts. Sources of power are formed, used, and endowed status. In the work unit and functional divisions, these power sources create, sustain, and support values and interests. They become the latest agenda. As the organization adopts these agendas the organization transforms itself to this new value-interest system. Organizational hierarchy breeds formation of new agendas. As career-focused persons become more specialized, the organization loses its ability to function as careerists override new interests in favor of their own developed specialties. The organization tends toward superficiality as it loses its ability to know real necessities. Various power sources continue to act out their own agendas in lieu of pursuing substantive work. Consensus development abounds as individual sources seek support and favor for their interests (Bergquist, 1993). In this light, political forces can become the ideology of organization. In the end, understanding the "political" image of organizations allows us to understand the real limits that exist in the sociopolitical organization.

Organizations as Culture

Although the political metaphor is readily observable in organizations, many have disdain for truly political organizations. The metaphor of organizations as culture, on the other hand, offers an ideological view of the organization. As the organization's values and interests become the norm, they become symbols, rituals, meanings, and interpretations that openly or tacitly govern how the organization interacts internally and externally. No longer is the organization a collection of individuals or agendas but an interdependent collection of shared meanings and circumstances. For example, American culture is one of individualism and separateness, while the Japanese traditional culture is embodied in self-respect through service to a larger system. In an individualist culture, organizations reward individuals for "being first." In Japanese culture, the organization seeks commitment and loyalty to the collective.

Perhaps the greatest reason for studying organizational culture is that such an approach allows us to observe the organization as it truly exists. The integration, fragmentation, and differentiation perspectives are all available to the researcher/observer. This approach offers us a crucial illustration of the organization's *ethos:* its historical purpose, power shaping, motivations, beliefs, informal settings, symbolic expression, visual data, and more. Culture is a part of the organization, and it is the organization. It resides in various subcultures of the organization, whether they be related by gender or occupation or by political, economic, or aesthetic interests. Culture occurs as the human component objectifies reality. These norms, rituals, or symbols are open to scrutiny using various methods of inquiry (Jermier, 1991).

Garfenckel (1967) supported the enactment scenario as an explanation of culture. The questions become what are the shared schemes, where do they come from, and how are they created, communicated, and sustained? Seeking answers to these questions becomes the central task of analysis for the organizational practitioner. The process involves identification of the array of mundane and vivid aspects of the reality construction process (Morgan, 1986). Organizational structure, rules, policies, goals, measures, and job descriptions identify the organizations' shared frames of reference. Upon inspection of the varied and total group of perspectives, practitioners see the "language" of the organization and its derived meanings. New relationships, processes, and functions emerge as the organization communicates with itself. This view is often surprising, as too few organizations are really introspective in this fashion.

Organizations as Psychic Prisons

We have Kuhn (1970) to thank for creating broad acceptance of the metaphor paradigm and Barker (1992) to thank for stretching its use. Morgan (1986) applied the metaphor to organizations. People, even organizations, may become caged by unconscious images, ideas, thoughts, and actions. Examples of this thinking are predominant. Our educational program is so sound that complacency sets in as we come to rely on success factor after success factor; school systems hire administrative specialists to create curriculum rather than face the uncertain probability that those "closest to the action" may know best what and how to teach. Rather than take a risk, we create slack, or we politely, unquestioningly nod our heads in agreement rather than state that we need to explore other venues. These unconscious cognitive traps, once realized, can help us observe and predict the ways we see (culture), but they can also create blindness and eliminate other

views. How long has it taken organizational America to react to the expectations of consumers, or for that matter, quality, or the global organizational environment of today?

More important, understanding our psychic prisons allows us to examine how entrenched our thinking about organizations has become. Have we really explored the complications of regulation of the human component? Why do we continually adopt the belief that we are often inhuman by varying degrees, but then fail to identify action orientations that can produce understanding and change? Have we fully explored our rationale for planning? Doesn't planning, at the same time, set the future and settle it into a possibly inappropriate future? Once we define culture, both its known and hidden elements, what do we do with that knowledge? Are we so locked into "one way" that we cannot fathom diversity, gender difference, or the disabled? Must we constantly rely on a "ruling class" to pronounce acceptable action and then again react against those authority figures?

Instances of side effects of our prisons can be noted across all organizations' functioning. Jacques (1955) showed how in labor management relations we project negative images of those with whom we differ. Chatov (1981) discussed the same phenomenon in relations between government and business. Zalesznik (1970) demonstrated how leaders are inclined to divide and conquer as a result of their inability to build coalitions. As Bion (1959) suggested, organizations regress to patterns of behavior learned previously to protect themselves. That is, they retreat into their psychic prisons.

Determining how organizations and their members explore psychic prisons is a critical aspect of organizational self-renewal. Organizations that study these human patterns and relationships can realize the full extent of ethical behavior, the critical role that power relations play, the barriers to change, and the overrationalization of our actions. Although exploring our psychic prisons may conjure up instances of "organization man," it is not just another approach to controlling organizational functioning. Bringing the "unconscious organization" to the surface can help us further understand our organizations and the limits they impose.

Mirrors of Organizations

Organizations today are combinations of elements developed in the past and new images. "In a typical contemporary organization, one will now find a variety of different (and often contradictory) processes and functions as well as diverse forms and structures of pre-modern, modern, and postmodern origins, some of which are temporary and others permanent" (Bergquist, 1993, p. 177). Over the past several decades, writers have attempted to describe this changing scene: Kanter's (1985) entry into the postentrepreneurial age, O'Toole's (1985) vanguard organization, Deming's (1986) quality revolution, Peters' (1992) liberated-disorganized organization, and Clegg's (1990) de-differentiated organization. Mintzberg (1989) labeled this a trip from convergence, to congruence, to configuration, to contradiction, and to creation. His "life cycle," like Bergquist's, makes the voyage from pre- to postmodern. Organizational thinking dominated by the machine image, creating its rationality through its own irrationality, reduces human systems to impersonal skills and manifests its destruction through its politicization. Clark and Astuto (1991) summarized Weick's earlier work by stating that, in organizations: (1) there is less rationality than meets the eye, (2) there is less simplicity than meets the eye, (3) there is less sequentiality and coupling than meets the eye, (4) there is less causality than meets the eye, (5) there is less orderliness than meets the eye, (6) there is less goal-directed individual behavior than meets the eye, (7) there is less preference-directed individual behavior than meets the eye, (8) there is less planned change and predictability than meets the eye, and (9) there is less hierarchy than meets the eye, (p. 960).

As a consequence, organizational thought may need new life, a generation of broader theoretical perspectives, an acceptance of equifinality and variety, and new tools for inquiry. In this sense, Bergquist (1993) suggested that the future holds many new organizational hybrids.

Mirrors of Education as Organizations

Historically, schools as organizations have been nearly perfect portraits of larger organizations in industrialized society. The influence of scientific management is prevalent throughout all schools and school systems (Owen, 1987). Traces of Taylor, Fayol, Weber, and others are readily perceptible in school organizations. School districts mandate efficiency through standardization of work processes, audit school adherence with control and measurement mechanisms, and certify minimum proficiency of the products. After the 1980 decade of "commissions" that demonstrated repeated and widespread evidence of schools' inadequacies, much more reflection may be required before we fundamentally understand the problems in schools. In too many cases, repeated calls for renewal and revitalization were accomplished by patching the system. Similarly, as the human relations movement garnered attention for the development and use of more favorable human resource models, the revitalization too often became still another set of poorly conceived or enacted sets of one-dimensional spot solutions.

As school achievement and performance ratings continued to decline over the past three decades, there were continued calls for new criteria for excellence: schools need good management, leaders, not just administrators, and schools need to understand and confront their cultures. Some claim that schools need to create their own distinctiveness as they decouple from mainstream organizational thought and become organized anarchies (Cohen, March, & Olsen, 1972). In this context, schools' purposes and definitions become fleeting, fuzzy, even fluid. Or they become reconstituted elements of more highly refined leadership studies, strengthening their core competencies and devising better communication mechanisms. For others, schools are viewed as systems in an effort to capture elements of the systems movement. The administrator or the supervisor at the school level is understood to be an integrative element to upper management, the community, teachers, staff, and students. Getzels and Guba (1957) take the social behavioral view of education, proposing that the entire social system of education comprised of the school, roles and expectations of various members, and various individual personalities and needs, interacts with tools, techniques, and curriculum in a sociotechnical arrangement not unlike what Emery and Trist (1969) posited at the Travistock Institute. During this period, schools were seen as dynamic organisms existing within numerous contexts.

Intertwined with the evolution of education as organization are other integrating elements. Hodgkinson (1991) outlined the historical purpose of schools from Greek liberal educational foundations, to the Roman tradition of administration and governance, to religious and moral reflections of the Protestant ethic. Additionally, he cited the effects of the agrarian and industrialized eras that gave rise to mass education as it generally exists today. Our democratic system of education exists largely to protect the democratic rights of its citizens. As the scientific era spawns productive efficiency, schools find themselves engaged in creating social efficiency (Kowalski & Reitzug, 1993). Schools as well as industries devise methods to control, coordinate, plan, direct, and organize themselves; hence, administration continues its development around scientific and human resource principles. The parade of leadership and management literature crossed boundaries easily as education mirrored industry.

Sergiovanni and Moore (1989) borrowed Burns's (1981) transactional and transformational leadership viewpoints. Leaders in a traditional sense manage the consequences of an exchange process and assure that behaviors of various subordinate actors remain within established norms. In contrast, the transformational leader manages more intrinsic, moral consequences, building shared commitment, distributing and facilitating power, building the capacity in other members, and instigating awareness of self in order to crystalize a more thorough commitment to responsibility and accountability.

In education, teaching professionals mediate conflicting demands across the entire school environment (Sergiovanni & Moore, 1989). While teachers aspire to maintain their own professional responsibilities, the school and school administration ask them to work in a factory environment. The professional role is difficult to maintain in this situation and gives rise to the "informal organization." The autonomous teacher now lives, on one hand, profoundly tied to practice and expertise taught in a profession, and, on the other hand, tied to the realities of a bureaucratic school environment. But success in this political environment is hard to guarantee and requires that leaders and professionals collaborate to tap the strengths evident in both the informal and formal environment.

In the transitional periods of the last several decades, schools have functioned as rational-objective organizations. They examine their training methodologies, strategies for change, and financial controls, and model new curriculums. Structure and audit remain, but front-line teacher and student expectations are often voiced but not heard. Often, empirical reviews present new personnel practices for consideration. But these reviews crumble when confronted with the realities of the school's political structure. Although these transitional periods tout change, new leadership, or revised culture, in practice, they do not have a broad, long-lasting impact. Even with the realization that schools are multicultural, followed by demand for appropriate organizational changes, schools still find themselves mired in the traditional rational-objective structure. School culture and climate are expressed as an environment of learning, but also as restricted, confining, objective-laden, and out of touch with current teacher, student, and societal needs. Educational improvement requires more than a change of pencils and papers; it requires direct change in patterns of human interdependencies, collaboration, and commitment (Schmuck & Runkel, 1985).

In the true transformational sense, schools need to be viewed as living and dynamic. Schools can be natural environments that demonstrate all desirable traits: social justice, freedom, responsibility, and maturing. As the Rand Corporation finds, and as we've alluded to earlier, self-renewal may best be a process of enactment and alignment and accomplished more effectively at the local level (the school or school district). Learning to cope with crisis over the longer term results in a school or school system that shows steady progress and achievement. But those who manage crisis continually only address symptoms (Miles, 1967; Senge, 1990). Through organizational development formulas schools can change if they have direction, show progress, and all players become involved. Administration must learn to command and control less and facilitate and encourage participation more (Hoy & Miskel, 1987). Leadership is more than just management or administration. Leaders in schools today must possess a clear sense of the true and evolving purpose(s) of education and, equally evident, its ambiguities.

Portraits of Contemporary Schooling

Restructuring has become a common theme in education in the United States. The term *restructuring* now emerges any time a discussion of school reform arises (Olsen, 1988). As a label for new strategies, the term has become overused to the extent that we no longer have a clear understanding of its relevance.

Tyack (1990) believes that the term has become synonymous with choice, teacher professionalization, empowerment, decentralization, school site management, parental involvement, national curriculum standards, and a host of other change mechanisms. Chubb and Moe

(1990) think similarly. They equate restructuring to the dysfunction of bureaucracy and the value of autonomy. To perceive the truth, long-term trends must be distinguished from the trendy. What is the true story? Perhaps a brief historic review can help us understand the school as an organization in this discussion.

In earlier parts of the twentieth century, school organization in terms of leadership had become a politicized issue. During the rural and growing urban periods, schools were decentralized as fears of highly centralized government control were widespread. In rural communities trustees, parents, and teachers were deeply involved in a localized structure. In contrast, urban school systems were more highly centralized and controlled. They were the early counterparts of the extreme centralization seen today. A group of highly professional and trained administrators, then called administrative progressives, advocated innovative mechanisms to derive greater efficiency, equity, accountability, and expertise from the schools (Tyack, 1990).

Reorganization took many forms: centralizing districts to include the rural areas, increasing size and scope of district administration, huge staff agencies, and decreasing teacher autonomy. Schools were being driven by a new set of scientific management and educational science principles, perhaps a new ideology. Consolidation occurred from the district through the state and to the federal government. Schools, school districts, and state agencies became models of structure and process. They collected enormous amounts of data to justify their purposes and rationale. Superintendents became power figures, enrollments grew, curriculum expanded, and attempts to reduce costs per person received constant attention.

During the equality reform period in the mid-twentieth century, numerous societal pressures focused on schools and schooling practices. Reformers demanded greater equality for all segments of society. There were calls for more current and applicable curriculum, more teacher responsibility, more equitable funding, and more substantive evaluation of product. In retrospect, Meyer (1980) labeled the era *frag-mented centralization,* as laissez-faire adminis-trators faced contradictory requirements. More *calculative management* resulted as administra-tion attitudes toward schools as school organi-zations fueled more rationalization.

Many recent reports have depicted a nation-wide crisis in education. Back-to-basics school movements ensued. Accountability in teaching was measured in terms of testing results in com-parisons across districts, states, the nation, and the world. The top-down approach beginning at the state level ruled. Learning was measured by scores. Local mandates produced even more centralization in school districts. Greater bu-reaucracy in the divisionalized organizational form intensified and schools refocused on crite-ria for excellence.

Schools and school districts are by and large mirrors of the classical machine style of organi-zation and locked firmly in the "iron cage" (Clegg, 1990; Morgan, 1986). What exactly does society find wrong with schools today? As the 23rd Annual Gallup Poll/Phi Delta Kappan Poll (Elam, Rose, and Gallup, 1991) demonstrated, the variety of issues is extensive. Americans want more report cards from schools. They want accountability. They want more educa-tion, as shown by longer school years. They want education to begin at an earlier age. They generally want more productivity. They want to choose productive schools for their children. They want higher quality and more decentral-ized control. They want equality and an equi-table use of resources, and they want schools and school systems to get in touch with current realities. Although this list may appear incom-plete to some, one can infer that Americans are broadly dissatisfied with teachers, principals, administration, schools, school districts, and state and federal controls.

Today, the educational "machines" grind on. Our educational system is in need of ma-jor overhaul. Problems endemic to the bu-reaucratic organization are reflected in our schools and school systems. The professional bureaucracy (a school), the machine bureau-cracy (a larger school), and the divisionalized configuration (a school district) are all exact replicas of bureaucracy in existence across the country (Mintzberg, 1989). Although it is possible to argue about distinctions between what schools do and how they do it in com-parison to business bureaucracies, these is-sues are largely irrelevant. This distinction looks only at symptoms.

In contrast, the organization of schools and schooling today should be largely organic. But upon closer inspection, we find a mixture of organic and bureaucratic school forms. Magnet schools are a good example of this blending ("Schools That Work," 1991). Conceived during the 1980s, these elite public schools have achieved dramatic results. As schools of excel-lence, they embody significant educational re-forms. Magnet schools thrive on interactive-ness and interdependence, and integrate much of the best that is known about educational practice. They are generally intimate learning environments emphasizing personal contact, teacher designed and controlled, interactive with numerous partners in the community and region, small in size, and have clear purpose. However, they also can resemble the bureau-cratic environment of the past and suffer from similar consequences already discussed. Public reaction has been illustrative of the dissent in the magnet environment raising questions about equity, selection issues, huge costs, and funding support.

Across some of the largest population centers, such as New York City, the standard bureaucratic schools exist next to the magnet schools. For the most part, the magnet schools mirror the realities of quality and excellence, while in the more tra-ditional schools, superintendents and principals struggle with every known societal problem, or-ganizational problem, and educational practice problem (Tyack, 1990). These traditional schools in New York City, Chicago, and Los Angeles stand in stark contrast to Minnesota's Choice schools or Jefferson High School for Science and Technology, Fairfax, County, Virginia (Ayers, 1991; "Schools That Work," 1991; Tyack, 1990).

Across most traditional measurement categories the differences are significant. But even more curious, these "preferred schools" feel different. The sense that education is ongoing is powerful. In response to the organizational differences between them, understanding the organic nature of education and educational administration could be highly useful. Understanding how an organic school organization works in practice can be very instructive. Organic thinking requires seeing beyond aggregates of inspection, development, and implementation to create useful knowledge. Excellence in education is more than an outstanding list of issues (Eisner, 1991), more than steps in a total quality focus (Glasser, 1990), more than relating trends and forecasts (Cetron & Gayle, 1990), and more than a demonstration of how the best of the best perform (Gatto, 1990). Even the professionalization of schools requires more than better teacher preparation, better follow-up, in-service training, and certification. These are only another instance of laying more golden eggs (Sergiovanni, 1989). Still attached to our previous educational paradigms, we view needed variety as complexity, leadership as management, higher test score results and low costs as efficiency, newness as inappropriate change, and autonomy as loss of control. In actuality, these elements are necessary paradoxical components of equifinality, differing ways to arrive at the same goals. Reform in the organic sense demands added variety, creation of more usable products, greater autonomy as a means of control, and structure that reverts to fluid forms. We haven't really adopted the organic view in our thinking and action, only adapted it as a response to the strength of various existing power and political forces, or learned paradigms.

Future Organizations and Schools of the Future

We must focus our thinking about organizations and schools for tomorrow. In this process we must consider whether the Newtonian tools and techniques most familiar to us are appropriate or whether the body of developing knowledge centered in quantum science can affect our understanding of organization. Science in any discipline needs to be grounded in the science of the time. Schrödinger's illustration of the cat in the box can help us define the major distinctions between these two thinking styles (Zohar, 1990). The problem is as follows. Place a live cat in a box with solid walls. No one is able to see into the box. A triggering device at some point is set to release, with equal probability, either poison or food. At some point the cat meets its fate and the box is opened to determine what the cat's fate has been. In the Newtonian world, since our organizations are deterministic, we'll looks for facts, variables, and parts in an attempt to be objective, calculative, and find the truth. Our organizations are built on these same premises as we seek solidarity, identity, distinctiveness, singularity, and rational solutions to issues. We'll measure the box, the food, the poison, or seek environmental clues, and hypothesize about everything. As Davies and Brown (1988) said, we have a theory for everything. In the quantum world, however, the problem in the cat story isn't a problem. Before observation, the fate of the cat is only a set of probabilities, not to be decided until we physically open the box. What we see is what we get.

In this exercise the role of the observer is critical. In organizations we confine humans, students, and others to Schrödinger boxes. Organizations daily make these attempts at objectivity. In the quantum science world, however, objectivity is constructed at the moment of observation. As observers, we may only really be participants in a set of potentials. Herein lies one of the keys to effective quantum thinking about organizations. As participants in today's organizations, we often restrict who gets to "have a say." A senior management official interprets and decides, followed by a reinterpretation by middle management, and then supervisors. But in reality, each member of the organization is part of the potential of the organization. As we restrict who has a say, we lose those potentially critical and important interpretations at the specific moment of observation. Instead, we use the plans, organization, and policy of others. An organization that builds the capacity to utilize all interpretations swims in a sea of rich data which then can be discussed, combined, and built upon. Becoming wiser in this sense and more participative also effects true ownership as the organization builds a capacity to be flexible and responsive to ideas and then promote further action. Participation, ownership, and subjective data enrich relationship construction and further cement ownership.

Exploring further, we find the quantum world in varying degrees all around us. Some continue to try to package these quantum perspectives into the objective world. Key organizational practitioners and theorists, however, are making startling changes across organizations. Leadership study today concentrates on new perspectives: followership, worker empowerment, leader accessibility, and understanding and developing self-identity. Motivation studies explore intrinsic factors. Field theory proposes that we may be able to sense influences of employee behavior not as a future desirable state, but as a way of knowing and then building vision. Organizational studies today concentrate on learning as a self-renewal process. In these views we must constantly fight off our attempts at creating just another "cat in the box" scenario. Our preference for orderliness prescribes limits where disorder may be a key configuration device that drives stability.

Weick (1969) suggested an alternative approach to organizational analysis. Although planning is important, it must be accompanied by action because it is only through action and implementation that we create the organizational environment. In our strategic planning today, we may be accomplishing the opposite. We may be planning as though we are responding to demands from the environment when we should be, as Weick says, creating an environment where strategy should be "just-in-

time. . . supported by more investment in general knowledge, a large skill repertoire, the ability to do quick study, trust in intuitions, and sophistication in cutting losses" (pp. 223, 229). Each of these new thinking methods requires us to view organizational life in new ways: thinking holistically, reducing our reliance on cause-and-effect scenarios, linking with thinking partners and partnerships, and using intuition more and determinism less. In this sense, images of organization again help us.

Morgan (1986) cited three convincing studies to help us further understand organization. The three studies provide insight from biology to help understand how organizations become self-producing, how circular relations may suggest a new logic for change, and how dialectic relations may help to induce change.

Maturana and Varela (1980) argued that organizations may be like closed, autonomous biological systems. This view is obviously in contrast to the organic view, which sees living systems as open and in constant interaction with their environment. In describing organizations as closed and autonomous, the authors aim to illustrate why organizations always attempt to strive toward stability. In this closed system view, internal circular interactions are built, maintained, and renewed in the effort to maintain stability. Any change in the system changes the entire system. Maturana and Varela's view does not represent a closed system view, as the organization still interacts with its environment, but does close itself in order to maintain and regulate its functioning. To study the organization, we need to study the nature of these patterns of circularity, and how this circularity promotes growth for the system and balances the system. Senge (1990) termed these *circles of causality*. These circular systems usually change from within as well as a consequence of random internal disorder that leads to new patterns of order and change. Prigogine and Stengers (1984) termed this change *dissipative structure*. Some believe that human ideas and practices may develop similarly, accomplishing change when "critical mass" is achieved. Thus organizational systems may shape their own futures through self-referential patterns.

This view of organization allows us to see that as individuals and organizations, the interaction that takes place doesn't necessarily have to be flavored with competition or struggle. Organizations can thus become more aware as they self-discover and analyze themselves through understanding their own circles of causality (Maruyama, 1963; Senge, 1990). Organizational elements become more aware of their roles and significance to the whole. They learn and develop patterns of change that allow evolution in a larger system through organizational self-reference.

Circles of causality incorporate positive and negative feedback loops that possess the potential to reveal patterns of relations. These patterns of relations not only reveal relationships but also can be used to leverage change. In the organizational context, we constantly see relationships whose patterns can reveal both the internal and external organizational "ways we do business." The entire dynamic of an organization can be mapped and provide a richer picture of the system. As an example, a representation can be made of how individuals within an organization communicate, and with whom, outside the formal channels.

The development of this reasoning style is in direct opposition to the linear, cause-and-effect manipulation we've grown accustomed to using. Circles of causality allow organizational practitioners to identify principal subsystems or "nests" that unite the whole and then modify existing relations through change. In turn, we learn to appreciate the innate complexity of the organization and to change with change. With the additional realization of new societal influences and changes, we can be poised as detectors and avoid those defensive and destructive tendencies that often aren't noted until they are out of control. A frog will attempt immediately to leap from the hand that threatens a boiling inferno, but may not recognize the gradual temperature increase of a comfortable, cool, but increasingly warmer environment until it is too late.

As mentioned briefly earlier, this is not to imply that circles of causality are the only form of interpretation available to us. We have grown accustomed largely to a view of organization that seeks understanding by looking at opposites, through dialectical analysis. Growth and decline, wealth and poverty, and industrialization and unionization are all dialectic viewpoints that often cause us to take sides. By understanding these dialectic forces, we can learn their importance and determine which of the forces are primary causes versus which are superficial and secondary. By combining self-producing systems, circles of causality, and dialectic analysis, we can better understand the logic of change as it unfolds rather than deal with change in our normal piecemeal fashion.

Self-organizing organizations provide a new view. Instead of viewing the organization through its system structures, contemplation of its system dynamics, its form and function, becomes important. We often incorporate understanding the role of negative feedback as a revitalizing source, but neglect the essence and the importance of positive feedback. Positive feedback can be disruptive if it is taken on blind faith, leading to disorganization and disequilibrium and compromising the integrity of the organization. When considered thoughtfully, positive feedback can be a source of organizational change as well. Positive feedback is merely the variety that already exists in the organization. Disturbance then is a consequence that the organization ultimately responds to, as added neglect builds until the system must respond. In the quantum world this disintegrity system can build a new vital system. Thus disorder creates a new order. Over time, if we view the entropic system long enough, we'd possibly capture its orderly striving to become something new.

Managing this disorder, as De Pree (1987) writes, is in one instance "roving leadership" and points to the emergent qualities of the organization, using its indispensable people, who always seem to make a difference. These indispensable members create *fields of action* in the organization in response to necessities generated on the spot. You can sense this in many organizations: a feeling of good customer service that pervades the organization, or a feeling that "learning is going on here."

Once educated to sense these fields, we then "manage" too often in the Newtonian sense: devising, controlling, and instructing organizational purpose. Wouldn't creating this vision or purpose based on sensing the fields be more advantageous? Prahalad and Hamel (1990) argued that these conceptual controls can be built around an organization's core competencies, self-organizing and self-renewing systems built around flexibility and sensing change versus rigid structure. The organization in its internal disorganization becomes stable and more capable of interacting with its environment. Embedded within the system are actors with the freedom to act autonomously guided by self-referential, conceptual controls. Freedom and order in partnership achieves greater, nearly automatic catalytical action. Organizations built in this fashion need absolute availability of information. Control of information short circuits an organization's ability to create this desired state.

Philosophically, we have described a view of organizational thinking for the future. How does this translate to schools for the future? The forecasts, trends, and the historical record are in place, but enactment must begin (Weick, 1969). Virtual schools must be developed along conceptual versus structural lines. Many ideas are already in place and under consideration.

The virtual school is composed of a partnership among the teacher, student, and learning. As the importance of these new participative relationships is realized and the school organization settles into creating its future, the school can draw new and necessary fields of skills and knowledge. The ongoing administration of the school system would occur within and be self-regulating. Delivery systems could vary according to the needs and expectations created within an organization. Processes to deliver can expand and incorporate new delivery contexts. Partners outside the school, such as parents, the community, and state and federal agencies, become supportive and facilitative.

The virtual description of a school environment postulated by Reigeluth (1987) is given next as an example. Note the highlighted areas that display future organizational contexts.

The new school organization takes on new form and function. In this new system, teachers become guides: advisors, sensors, and managers (self-organization) versus content disseminators and disciplinarians. New resources, including interactive computers, videodisks, peer tutors, projects, and learning laboratories, are employed to help transfer knowledge to the student (variety). Guides advise, sense, and manage students but additionally coordinate the efforts of other partners in education (participation and emergence), including inexpensive assistants (apprentice guides, senior citizens, parents, and peer tutors), well-designed projects, discussion groups, learning laboratories, and resource people (self-organization and renewal). Parents, in particular, help decide instructional goals in conjunction with their guide and the individual student (participation). A student's development (physical, social, moral, psychological, and intellectual) is considered (core competencies). The classroom environment as we know it disappears and a guide and student or small group of students work together to attain agreed upon developmental goals (creating their own vision). A guide takes a student through one of four possible developmental stages (four within K–12), about four years per student per development stage. Developmental stages can be expanded or changed depending on the needs of local constituencies (equifinality). Each student's educational goals are matched to uniquely suited educational resources (equifinality and variety) orchestrated by a guide and other assistants.

Guides do not work independently but are built into a cluster of guides, three to six guides per cluster (form). The guides participate in decision making and control over a particular cluster (function). In each cluster, all guides are responsible for cluster success, with comparable power to meet established goals. A master guide also serves in the cluster to provide instructional "architecture" for the cluster (purpose). The success of a cluster depends on parent and student satisfaction in meeting goals. As clusters succeed, more satisfied parents and students select the particular cluster. Effective clusters survive as a result of financial support from the district based on parental choice (positive and negative feedback).

As goal achievement occurs and students pass through developmental stages, new student goals may become more specific. Learning laboratories (variety) provide specialized expertise in traditional discipline-oriented and cross-disciplinary areas. Students' progress in their clusters advances them to a variety of learning labs. These labs operate independently of clusters, but also cooperatively, as the labs' support depends on students being allowed to participate as determined by a student's guide.

In the last analysis, the degree of change in schooling for tomorrow may become an ethical discussion for society itself to engage in (variety), as the realities of new school concepts are far from familiar to the established paradigms that we hold and value today.

CASE STUDY

School as Organization: The Case of the Future of Education

As changes occur in the global environment, business and society may have to take more responsibility for preparing the future labor force by forming partnerships with educational institutions. Other equally important changes are occurring. For example, the growing numbers of single-parent families will look to schools for more services, beginning in pre-kindergarten, and then throughout the remainder of their children's schooling demand even more. Consider some of the projections for the year 2000:

1. Fewer than 4 percent of families will consist of one spouse working, one at home, and two children.
2. Legal redefinitions of the term *family* are now being made.
3. By the year 2000, both partners in the family will be in the workforce in upward of 75 percent of families.
4. By the year 2000, nearly 75 percent of 3-year-olds will attend day-care centers.
5. Single-parent families will continue to increase due to divorce and parents who choose not to marry.
6. Lifetime employment with the same job or company is becoming a thing of the past.
7. The number of manufacturing and agriculture industries will continue to decline.
8. The advent of the knowledge worker will fill an estimated 43 percent of jobs by the year 2000.
9. The number of people who work at home will increase as office automation becomes more powerful and portable.
10. Shortages in entry-level jobs will continue, followed by increases in those jobs that pay very near minimum wage.
11. The next decade will bring 8 million new highly skilled jobs, mostly in executive, professional, and technical arenas.
12. Small businesses will employ a majority of workers by the year 2000.
13. Overqualified, highly skilled workers unable to find employment will displace lower-skilled workers in some areas.

As these events transpire, so must the shape and scope of education change. Many demand a major restructuring of school organizations.

Major change trends today may not suffice. In the sections below, many of the trends facing education today are identified across several general areas: general trends, students, teachers, curriculum and instruction, higher education, school reform and restructuring, governance and leadership, school law, and school funding. After reading the section below, address the questions posed at the end of the case.

General Trends

Education has been and will remain a major public agenda item for much of the remainder of this century and the beginning of the next. Most will view education as a means to cure economic ills and promote growth. Continued technological advancement and more flexible work environments at home and work will allow for more productive schooling and working. The mismatch in competencies of graduates will continue. Literacy, technological competence, and creative or critical thinking will be at a premium.

Students

The declining enrollments of the 1980s will stop and begin to climb again. But even more problematic will be the large numbers of students who drop out of school each year. Continuing social problems (drug abuse, teenage pregnancy, violence) and increased academic standards will only create further risks for students and probably higher dropout rates than forecast.

Teachers

The demand for qualified teachers will increase. Low pay, difficult working conditions, and too little genuine responsibility will add to shortages, as output will lag behind necessities by upward of 40 percent. In part, teacher shortages will be quelled by implementation of alternative certification routes. The lack of qualified minority teachers will still be viewed as an obstacle to thorough education, as the population of mi-

nority students increases drastically. Universities and schools will combine talents in partnerships and propose new forms of schooling. Teachers' motivation will be explored as formulas for incentives are sought.

Curriculum and Instruction

Lifelong learning will become a principal feature in the development of curriculum and delivery systems. A core curriculum may emerge from the university, teacher, business, school, and parental partnerships that develop. Curriculum will by necessity become more global as more diverse and competent graduates are required by society and business. Vocational education will become paramount as technically literate graduates become more in demand by industry. School reforms will need to consider the demands of highly technical needs in conjunction with academic education.

Higher Education

Fewer college graduates will be required in the workforce, but at the same time, more postsecondary graduates will enter the picture. Colleges and universities will recognize this trend and curriculum changes will cater to students who need education but require less than four years of college. Community colleges will see a great influx of students fulfilling these education requirements and help communities realize their growth potential.

School Reform and Restructuring

A national policy to improve schools still will not have been achieved, and piecemeal efforts will comprise the bulk of activity. No appreciable change to better education will occur. A demand for more learning time will become a norm and result in more flexibility for the school. School-based management may too often still be a top-down approach that creates further conflicts surrounding accountability. Generally, increased accountability will result but not without friction among local, state, and federal agencies.

Governance and Leadership

All stakeholders will demand more involvement in decision-making processes, but too often with too little understanding of the real necessities important to reform or restructuring. Centralized overall control from the higher levels will remain but with more latitude available at local and classroom levels. A shortage of superintendents and principals will occur due to many retirements in the mid-1900s. As a result, new principals will become the major change agents of the new era. Bureaucracy in education will diminish in favor of a shared governance formula but not without fragmentation among the various partners that already erodes traditional schooling.

School Funding

An extreme variety of financial initiatives will be tried ranging from privatization to more centralization. But the real crux of change may involve finding new formulas for funding outside mainstream practice. These new initiatives would probably include using partnerships, as discussed earlier. Regional disparities will undoubtedly increase during the change periods.

As a result of disparities, minority groups will challenge school curriculum, expenditures, methodology, and seek access to education for the less privileged. Equity issues will become major obstacles to growth and change. Both issues of access and expenditure will remain problematic.

Questions

With the limited list of issues and trends identified above, consider your own or your group's beliefs about the future of education.

1. What educational issues are of greatest concern to you or your group?
2. What role should local, state, or the federal government play in educational reform?
3. What changes in the national/world economy dictate or influence the directions you view necessary for education today?
4. What economic factors do you believe affect the future direction of education? Social factors? Other factors?
5. Are there more social factors looming on the horizon in your view?
6. Do you believe schooling is in trouble today? Defend your belief(s).
7. How can we really know the perceptions of the stakeholder in education?
8. Do these stakeholders really have any clout? Defend your belief(s).

References

Albrow, M, (1970). *Bureaucracy.* London: Pall Mall Press.

Allen, D. W. (1992). *Schools for a new century: A conservative approach to radical school reform.* New York: Praeger.

Argyris, C., Putnam, R., & Smith, D. M. (1985). *Action science: Concepts, methods, skills for research and intervention.* San Francisco: Jossey-Bass.

Ayers, W. (1991, May). Perestroika in Chicago schools. *Educational Leadership, 48*(8), 69–71.

Banner, T. K., & Gagne, T. E. (1995). *Designing effective organizations: Traditional and transformational views.* Thousand Oaks, CA: Sage.

Barker, J. (1992). *Future edge: Discovering the new paradigms of success.* New York: Morrow.

Barnard, C. (1938). *The functions of the executive.* Boston: Harvard University Press.

Bass, B. M. (1990). *Bass and Stogdill's handbook of leadership* (3rd ed.). New York: Free Press.

Beckett, J. (1971). *Management dynamics: A new synthesis.* New York: McGraw-Hill.

Beckhard, R. (1997). The healthy organization: A profile. In F. Hesselbein, M. Goldsmith, & R. Beckhard (Eds.), *The organization of the future.* San Francisco: Jossey-Bass.

Bennett, W. J. (1992). What do we want our graduate to be like? In L. C. Solomon & K. N. Hughes (Eds.), *How do we get the graduate we want: A view from the firing lines* (pp. 17–26). New York: Praeger.

Bergquist, W. (1993). *The post modern organization: Mastering the art of irreversible change.* San Francisco: Jossey-Bass.

Bertalanffy, L. von. (1968). *General system theory: Foundations, development, applications.* New York: Braziller.

Bion, W. R. (1959). *Experience in groups.* New York: Basic Books.

Blake, R. R., & Mouton, J. S. (1988). *Executive achievement: Making it at the top.* New York: McGraw-Hill.

Blau, P. M. (1977). *Inequality and homogeneity.* New York: Free Press.

Bolman, G., & Deal, T. (1991). *Reframing organizations: Artistry, choice, and leadership.* San Francisco: Jossey-Bass.

Bolman, G., & Deal, T. (1997). *Reframing organizations: Artistry, choice, and leadership* (2nd ed.). San Francisco: Jossey-Bass.

Brown, M., & Packham, R. (1999). *Organizational learning, critical systems thinking, and systemic learning* (Centre for Systems Studies Research Memorandum 20). Hull, Yorkshire, England: University of Hull.

Burns, T. (1966). On plurality of social systems. In R. J. Lawrence (Ed.), *Operational research and social sciences.* London: Tavistock.

Cetron, M. J., & Gayle, M. E. (1990, September–October). Educational renaissance: 43 trends for U.S. schools. *Futurists,* 33–40.

Chatov, R. (1981). Cooperation between government and business. In P. C. Nystrom & W. H. Starbuck (Eds.), *Handbook on organizational design* (pp. 487–502). New York: Oxford University Press.

Chubb, J. E., & Moe, T. E. (1990, Summer). Choice is a panacea. *Brookings Review,* 4–12.

Clark, D. L., & Astuto, T. A. (1991). Organizational theory. In M. C. Alkin (Ed.), *Encyclopedia of educational research* (6th ed., pp. 955–963). New York: Macmillan.

Clegg, S. R. (1990). *Modern organizations: Organization studies in the postmodern world.* Newbury Park, CA: Sage.

Cohen, M., March, J., & Olsen, J. (1972). A garbage can model of organizational choice. *Administrative Science Quarterly, 17*(1), 1–19.

Colapinto, S. J. (1994). *The impact of organizational structure on implementing change: A comparison of implementation effectiveness in functional and product line health care organizations.* Unpublished dissertation, California School of Professional Psychology, Los Angeles.

Conner, D. R. (1992). *Managing at the speed of change: How resilient managers succeed and prosper where others fail.* New York: Villard Books.

Coombs, A. W. (1991). *The schools we need: New assumptions for educational reform.* Lanham, MD: University Press of America.

Cornell, F. G. (1955, March). Society perceptive administration. *Phi Delta Kappan, 36,* (6).

Damme, S. R. (1995). *Discovering an organization's theories-in-use about leadership and proposal for incorporating action science into leadership development.* Unpublished dissertation, University of Minnesota, Minneapolis.

Davies, P. C. W., & Brown, J. (1988). *Superstrings: A theory of everything?* Cambridge: Cambridge University Press.

Davis, S. M., & Davidson, D. H. (1991). *20–20 vision.* New York: Simon and Schuster.

Deal, T. E., & Kennedy, A. A. (1982). *Corporate culture: The rites and rituals of corporate life.* Reading, MA: Addison-Wesley.

Deming, W. E. (1986). *Out of crisis.* Cambridge, MA: MIT Center for the Advancement of Engineering Study.

De Pree, M. (1987). *Leadership is an art.* East Lansing, MI: Michigan State University Press.

Drucker, P. F. (1987). *The frontiers of management.* New York: Harper & Row.

Eisner, E. (1991, February). What really counts in schools? *Educational Leadership, 48*(5), 10–11, 14–17.

Elam, S. M., Rose, L. C., & Gallup, A. M. (1991, September). The 23rd annual Gallup poll of public's attitudes toward public schools. *Phi Delta Kappan,* 41–56.

Emery, F. F., & Trist, E. L. (1969). Socio-technical systems. In F. E. Emery (Ed.), *Systems thinking.* New York: Penguin Books.

Etzioni, A. (1964). *Modern organizations.* Upper Saddle River, NJ: Prentice Hall.

Fayol, H. (1949). *General and industrial management.* Paris: Pitman.

Garfenckel, H. (1967). *Studies of ethnomethodology.* Upper Saddle River, NJ: Prentice Hall.

Gatto, J. (1990, September–October). Our children are dying in our schools. *New Age Journal,* 62–64.

Getzels, J., & Guba, E. (1957). Social behavior and administrative process. *School Review, 65,* 423–441.

Glasser, W. (1990, February). The quality school. *Phi Delta Kappan,* 424–435.

Hannan, M. T., & Freeman, J. (1988). *Organizational ecology.* Boston: Harvard University Press.

Hentschke, G. C. (1992). How should our schools be structured? A view from the top of the bottom of the heap. In L. C. Solomon & K. N. Hughes (Eds.), *How do we get the graduate we want: A view from the firing lines* (pp. 91–98). New York: Praeger.

Herzberg, F. (1968, November–December). One more time: How do you motivate employees? *Harvard Business Review, 46*(4), 53–62.

Hodgkinson, C. (1991). *Educational leadership: The moral act.* Albany, NY: State University of New York Press.

Hoy, W., & Miskel, C. (1987). *Educational administration: Theory, research and practice* (3rd ed.). New York: Random House.

Jacques, E. (1955). Social systems as a defense against persecutory and depressive anxiety. In M. Klein (Ed.), *New directions in psychoanalysis* (pp. 478–498). London: Tavistock.

Jermier, J. M. (1991). Critical epistemology and the study of organizational culture: Reflections on street corner society. In P. J. Frost, L. F. Moore, M. R. Louis, C. C. Lundberg, & J. Martin (Eds.), *Reframing organizational culture* (pp. 223–233). Newbury Park, CA: Sage.

Kanter, R. (1985). *Changemasters: Corporate entrepreneurs at work.* New York: Touchstone Press.

Knezevich, S. J. (1989). *Administration of public education: A sourcebook for the leadership and management of educational institutions* (4th ed). New York: Harper and Row.

Kowalski, T. J., & Reitzug, U. C. (1993). *Contemporary school administration: An introduction.* New York: Longman.

Kuhn, T. S. (1970). *The structure of scientific revolutions* (2nd ed., enlarged). Chicago: University of Chicago Press.

Lawrence, P. R., & Lorsch, J. W. (1986). *Organization and environment.* Boston: Harvard University Press.

Levine, A. (1992). The graduates we want: Who are they and how do we get them? In L. C. Solomon & K. N. Hughes (Eds.), *How do we get the graduate we want: A view from the firing lines* (pp. 7–16). New York: Praeger.

Lewin, K. (1951). *Field theory in social science.* New York: Harper.

Likert, R. (1987). *New patterns in management.* New York: Garland.

Lindbloom, C. E. (1980). *The policy-making process* (2nd ed.). Upper Saddle River, NJ: Prentice Hall.

Littlejohn, S. W. (1989). *Theories of human communication* (4th ed.). Belmont, CA: Wadsworth.

March, J. G. (1988). *Decisions and organizations.* New York: Blackwell.

Maruyama, M. (1963). The second cybernetics: Deviation amplifying mutual causal processes. *Academy of Management Review, 7,* 612–619.

Maturana, H., & Varela, F. (1980). *Autopoiesis and cognition: The realization of living.* London: Reidl.

Mayo, E. (1945). *The social problems of an industrial civilization.* New York: Ayer.

McGregor, D. (1985). *Human side of enterprise.* New York: McGraw-Hill.

Meyer, J. W. (1980). *The impact of centralization of educational funding and control of state and local educational governance.* Stanford, CA: Institute for Research on Educational Finance and Governance, Stanford University.

Meyerson, D. E. (1991). Acknowledging and uncovering the ambiguities in cultures. In P. J. Frost, L. F. Moore, M. R. Louis, C. C. Lundberg, & J. Martin (Eds.), *Reframing organizational culture* (pp. 254–270). Newbury Park, CA: Sage.

Miles, M. (1967). Some properties of schools as social systems. In G. Watson (Ed.), *Change in school systems.* Washington DC: National Training Laboratories, National Education Association.

Miles, R. E., & Snow, L. L. (1978). *Organizational strategy, structure and process.* New York: McGraw-Hill.

Mintzberg, H. (1983). *Structure in fives: Designing effective organizations.* Upper Saddle River, NJ: Prentice Hall.

Mintzberg, H. (1989). *Mintzberg on management: Inside our strange world of management*. New York: Free Press.

Mintzberg, H., & Quinn, J. B. (1988). *The strategy process: Concepts, contexts, cases*. Upper Saddle River, NJ: Prentice Hall.

Monge, P. R., & Eisenhart, E. M. (1987). Emergent communication networks. In F. M. Jablin, L. L. Putnam, K. H. Roberts, & L. W. Porter (Eds.), *Handbook of organizational communication: An interdisciplinary perspective* (pp. 304–342). Newbury Park, CA: Sage.

Morgan, G. (1986). *Images of organization*. Newbury Park, CA: Sage.

Olsen, L. (1988, November 2). The restructuring puzzle: Ideas for revamping "egg crate" schools abound, but to what ends? *Education Week*, 7.

O'Toole, J. (1985). *Vanguard management*. New York: Berkley.

Ouchi, W. A. (1981). *Theory Z: How American business can meet the Japanese challenge*. Reading, MA: Addison-Wesley.

Owen, R. (1987). *Organizational behavior in education* (3rd ed.). Upper Saddle River, NJ: Prentice Hall.

Peters, T. J. (1992). *Liberation management: Necessary disorganization for the nanosecond nineties*. New York: Knopf.

Phillips, M. E. (1984). *Industry as a cultural grouping*. Unpublished doctoral dissertation. Graduate School of Management, University of California, Los Angeles.

Poole, M. S., & McPhee, R. D. (1983). A structurational analysis of organization climate. In L. L. Putnam, & M. E. Pacanowsky (Eds.), *Communication and organizations: An integrative approach* (pp. 195–220). Beverly Hills, CA: Sage.

Prahalad, C. K., & Hamel, G. (1990, May–June). The core competence of the organization. *Harvard Business Review, 3*, 79–91.

Prigogine, I., & Stengers, I. (1984). *Order out of chaos*. New York: Random House.

Pugh, D. S., & Hickson, D. J. (Eds.). (1989). *Writers on organization*. Newbury Park, CA: Sage.

Quinn, R. E., & Cameron, K. (1983). Organizational life cycles and shifting criteria of effectiveness: Some preliminary evidence. *Management Science, 29*.

Reigeluth, C. (1987). The search for meaningful reform: A third wave educational system. *Journal of Instructional Management, 10*(4), 3–14.

Ricotta, M. C. (1992). *The application of the organizational life cycles and shifting criteria of effectiveness framework to a health professional organization*. Unpublished dissertation., University of Buffalo, Buffalo, NY.

Rost, J. (1991). *Leadership for the twenty-first century*. New York: Praeger.

Roufa, S. A. (1990). *An investigation into the superintendency: The relationships between fit-to-profession and organizational health*. Unpublished dissertation, University of Buffalo, Buffalo, NY.

Sackmann, S. A. (1991). *Cultural knowledge in organizations: Exploring the collective mind*. Newbury Park, CA: Sage.

Schein, E. (1985). *Organizational culture and leadership*. San Francisco: Jossey-Bass.

Schmuck, R. A., & Runkel, P. J. (1985). *The handbook of organizational development in schools* (3rd ed.). Prospect Heights, IL: Waveland Press.

Schön, D., (1987). *Educating the reflective practitioner: Toward a new design for teaching and learning in the profession*. San Francisco: Jossey-Bass.

Schools that work. (1991, May 27). *U.S. News and World Report*, 58–66.

Senge, P. (1990). *The fifth discipline: The art and practice of the learning organization*. New York: Doubleday/Currency.

Sergiovanni, T. J. (1989). The leadership needed for quality schooling. In T. J. Sergiovanni & R. H. Moore (Eds.), *Schooling for tomorrow: Directing reform issues that count*. Boston: Allyn & Bacon.

Sergiovanni, T. J., & Moore (Eds.). (1989). *Schooling for tomorrow: Directing reform issues that count*. Boston: Allyn & Bacon.

Shafritz, J., & Ott, S. (1992). *Classics of organizational theory*. Pacific Grove, CA: Brooks/Cole.

Silverman, D. (1971). *The theory of organizations*. New York: Basic Books.

Simon, H. A. (1977). *The new science of management decision*. New York: Harper & Row.

Solomon, L. C., & Hughes, K. N. (Eds.). (1992). *How do we get the graduates we want: A view from the firing lines*. New York: Praeger.

Spreigel, W. R. (1953). *The writings of the Gilbreths*. Homewood, IL: Irwin.

Starbach, W. H. (1981). A trip to view elephants and rattlesnakes in the garden of Aston. In A. H. de Van & W. F. Joyce (Eds.), *Perspectives on organizational design and behavior* (pp. 167–197). New York: Wiley.

Tagiuri, R., & Litwin, G. H. (Eds.). (1968). *Organizational climate: Explorations of concepts*. Boston: Harvard University Press.

Tannebaum, A. S. (1968). *Control in organizations*. New York: McGraw-Hill.

Taylor, F. W. (1947). *Scientific management*. New York: Harper & Row.

Therborn, G. (1976). *Science, class, and society*. London: New Left Books.

Thomas, K. W. (1977). Toward multi-dimensional values in teaching: The example of conflict behaviors. *Academy of Management Review, 12,* 484–490.

Thompson, J. D. (1967). *Organizations in action*. New York: McGraw-Hill.

Tompkins, P. K. & Cheney, P. K. (1985). Communications and unobtrusive control in contemporary organizations. In R. D. McPhee & P. K. Tompkins (Eds.), *Organizational communication: Traditional themes and new directions* (pp. 179–210). Beverly Hills, CA: Sage.

Tyack, D. (1990, Winter). "Restructuring" in historical perspective: Tinkering towards utopia. *Teachers College Board, 92*(2), 171–191.

Weber, M. (1947). *The theory of social and economic organization*. New York: Free Press.

Weick, K. E. (1969). *The social psychology of organizing*. Reading, MA: Addison-Wesley.

Woodward, J. (1981). *Industrial organization: Theory and practice* (2nd ed.). Oxford: University Press.

Yukl, G. A. (1989). *Leadership in organizations* (2nd ed.). Upper Saddle River, NJ: Prentice Hall.

Zalesznik, A. (1970). Power and politics of organizational life. *Harvard Business Review, 48,* 47–60.

Zohar, D. (1990). *The quantum self: Human nature and consciousness defined by the new physics*. New York: Macmillan.

CHAPTER 5

Communication
The Breath of Organizational Life

Like management in other settings, educational administration stands at a critical juncture in theory and practice. Comprehension and application of various effective communication models are crucial competencies needed by educators during this critical period of educational change. The quality of a school's communication seriously affects the nature of its effectiveness. Systems theory offers educators a means of perceiving the communication processes. The systematic view of both the organization and communication is global, abstract, and less easily codified, but more representative of how organizational communication actually occurs. The traditional understanding of linear communication fails to model the actual webs of communication in which school administration, instruction, and leadership function. To view communication systemically is to see communication acts as relating to and affecting the organizational body. A systemic metaphor for this view is to refer to communication as the "breath of organizational life."

There are over 126 definitions of communication in the literature, but certain elements recur. These elements include the sender of the message, the message, the channel by which the message is sent, the receiver of the message, interference with accurate transmission of the message, and feedback from receiver to sender that allows judgment of the accuracy of the transmission (Allen, 1994).

Conventional wisdom restricts the ways in which the terms *communication* and *information* are defined and used in organizations. Conventionally, communication is thought of as a process in which people are more or less skillfully engaged. Information is something that people do or do not have. Information storage, retrieval, and display have been automated successfully. There is popular agreement that such automation has changed human life. Contrast this with the unconventional idea that, as data have been automated, people have been informed through access to data and electronic ways of manipulating them. It is *informating* rather than *automating* that will fuel social and organizational change in the future. Communication is interactive, interdependent, and integrating, not just a stepwise model or a process that seemingly becomes lifelike as people communicate.

In the informated organization (Schuck, 1985), information is universally accessible. Accessibility to useful information enables the organization to be more responsive, as each actor in the school environment shares equal information access. Combined with shared decision making or problem solving, the school system becomes more flexible as it acts effectively with uniform information. Access is neither controlled nor controllable by people at the top of an organizational hierarchy. The informated are not defined by chronological age or status; anyone can be informated. Given all the new information they have or can easily access, informated students, teachers, and administrators can hardly be expected to understand and enact their roles in organizations in traditional ways. This has vast implications for school thinkers and implementers of the future. In an educational setting of the future, the administrator's communications must logically be derived from the same basic information accessible to all persons in the organization.

Changes in how processes and problems are conceptualized signal not only a shift in paradigms, but also an imperative to rethink and recreate organizational values, processes, and structures. The nation's businesses claim that schools are not meeting market and labor needs, but futurists say that businesses are in many ways as ineffective as the schools they criticize. It may be time for public and private educational organizations to curtail their dependence on traditions founded in principles of management science. It is now necessary to look in unaccustomed places for new insights about their missions and productivity.

For educational administrators, the challenge is to look beyond the fences of their schoolyards and to embrace wider contexts and disciplines as they conceptualize problems in their schools. In many contexts, the global village has already arrived. Diversity and multidisciplinary viewpoints are a fact of informed life. Innovative educational leadership requires a deeper, broader understanding of the future. For this reason, applying the content of this chapter to educational administration practice must be the responsibility of each thoughtful reader.

In this chapter the reader is asked to continue generating new energizing beliefs—in this case to curb the impulse to dismiss this new content as just theory. The reader must be prepared to continue developing more personal insights about what leading means in highly informed organizations, what effective communication requires, how data are gathered and used, and how to ensure that the entire organization is communicating systemically.

Systemic Metaphors of Communication

Communication is a complex, systemic phenomenon of such immense proportions that it defies the explanatory capacity of current communication theories in use. The act of communication is not limited to human beings. With new ecological and information processing awareness, humankind has begun to sense that knowledge has linear, accrual, and goal dimensions. Genetic transmissions in living organisms are communications; so are the information exchanges bused from one smart machine to another. Soon transmission methods will change so drastically that it will be conceivable to stop thinking in terms of classrooms and instead, begin to posit new learning environments with learning groups connected to a provider from a distant place. The occasions and mechanisms for communicating in the near term will proliferate with unprecedented speed and intensity. The old adage that knowledge is power will breed newer meanings as information increases in availability and accessibility. Information will become power. What human beings do or should do with such power is of more than philosophical interest. Information will be seen as nonlinear, instantaneous, and capable of an indeterminate number of interpretations and purposes.

Both living and nonliving entities exchange information. The premise that communication is basic and only conveys information must begin to be enlarged. Communication must be treated as a system with general systems properties. Raising communication to this level of universality sends the message that human organizations can no longer afford to think of themselves solely as independent, self-contained, people-to-people communities. Communication is much more universal, more holistic. Confining communication to a philosophical–cultural, cognitive–behavioral, or social–psychological paradigm inhibits our ability to understand communication fully. The traditional sender–receiver–feedback model in these paradigms cannot explain the necessities we sense in an informated environment. General systems thinking has the theoretical capacity to incorporate all of the prevailing human communication paradigms and to "wire in" all of the communication processes among nonliving systems as well.

To argue for the greatest generality represented by systems thinking is not a specious scholastic exercise. For example, how school administrators perceive and enact communication is a result of the frames of reference used. How the boundaries, processes, and practices of communication evolve depends on individual points of view about human beings and human organizations. At root, communication beliefs and strategies depend on the administrator's personal view of the world and his or her participation in that world view.

If an administrator's view of the world is narrow or static, bounded by narrow past experience and biases of a limited, old paradigm, one type of communication environment will emerge in the school system. This administrator will seek to design and control and even inhibit the process of communication in the organization. If, on the other hand, an administrator's world view takes into account the diversity of evolving systems in the world and the evolution of schooling within those systems, a different communications environment will exist. This administrator will recognize that communication is embodied in a variety and dynamic set of system properties distributed across every part of the school and its environment. Control will be exhibited in every part of the system, not simply as defined by a bureaucratic structure, but in a holographic sense where every part is a whole. This administrator will also recognize the necessity to enlarge the communication arena as additional partners' views add further variability, energy, and variety.

The shift in emphasis from the administrator who values control of communication to the administrator who values the dynamics of communication is a shift from a fixed and proprietary perception of "knowledge" as something gained and owned to a dynamic and open perception of "knowing." Knowing becomes a requisite need for the entire system. It is the personal, intellectual, and behavioral growth imperative for all members of the organization. What schools need are actors who carry within themselves the requisite variety of information and skills to incubate such dynamic and knowing schools as have never existed before. Nothing less will stem the tide of public disillusionment. Clearly, the communication processes in such a dynamic environment will often have to be "made up" to meet a need. There is no one communication formula that may be taught or unilaterally applied.

Thoughtful school administrators are very quickly disabused of the notion that they can walk into a school system and lay claim to being solely in charge. They learn that many other variables are "in charge" in an operational sense, including economic realities, student ennui or enthusiasm, degrees of teacher optimism, energy, and insight, and external "education consumer" perceptions. Much as school administrators would like it to be otherwise, they are not solely in charge of anything except their own thoughts, behaviors, and accountabilities to those they serve. This may be a disquieting picture for those who enjoy command, but it is an unprecedented opportunity for those who view educational administration as educational leadership which is a human service occupation without peer.

Theory Building and Judgment

According to Kovacic (1997), theory may be defined as a form of social knowledge, ranging all the way from the nonfactual to the empirically verifiable. Philipsen and Albrecht (1997) comment that in general, theory building is less systematic a process than it appears after the fact, but that theory building provides a basis for testing and verifying the nature of reality.

Communications theories are based on several assumptions. Cragan and Shields (1995) identify these as (1) human beings possess a natural theory-making and theory-using ability; (2) communications theories focus on the discovery of one or more types of social science facts: material, social, or symbolic; (3) communications theories flow primarily from one of three paradigms: rational, relational, or symbolic; and (4) a theory's true value flows from its utility. According to Kovacic (1997), bases for evaluating the effectiveness of a theory consist of the existence of explicitly developed theoretical components that contain both philosophical elements and empirical or practical elements. Such a theory would contain three structures: (1) mechanisms that would produce observable communications patterns in a number of circumstances, (2) simple or complex models that would specify a precisely verifiable set of relationships among the observed patterns, and (3) important empirical findings that explain the nature of a large number of the communications patterns over time.

Diversity in Communication Theories: A Twenty-First Century Paradox

To insist that systemic (not systematic) epistemology can shed the most light on understanding communication in the twenty-first century is not to discard or disregard all preceding theory. The bases for studying human communication in organizations must be made explicit. If the base of reference is a hierarchical model of organization, then questions of top-down, grass-roots-up linear communication are of interest. If, on the other hand, one assumes a heterarchical or holographic (systemic) model of organization, then communications and other organizational characteristics change dramatically. Such nonhierarchical models are emerging, generated in part by the computer-informed society and in part by the human longing to live and function at work as persons who are not merely cogs in organizational machinery. Schein

(1989) speaks of organizations groping toward new organizational forms even though they are haunted by hierarchies and conditioned by the belief in the "divine rights" of managers. Stephens (1989) cites the creation of what Adler of the Institute of the Future calls virtual companies that exist only by virtue of their computer connections. The creation of Apple's Applelink, a wide-area network, IBM's Learning Initiatives Network, and Internet in schools may be harbingers of the creation of "virtual schools."

The excitement afoot over the creation of new organizational forms, however, also evokes significant new anxiety. How much do self-autonomous work groups need administrators as communicators? In an environment where everything is negotiable by everyone (Kanter, 1989), what role does a manager or administrator play? These are not moot questions. Such organizations already exist in various forms in highly technological, entrepreneurial environments. Considering the growing public demand for school choice and increased achievement and productivity of public schools, it is not too great a stretch for school administrators to imagine themselves in such entrepreneurial environments in the future.

Recognizing that rapid, complex societal changes create the need for new communication theory, past theory becomes a useful building block. Normally, one begins the study of any phenomenon with a definition arrived at by consensus over time. Most researchers agree that communication involves senders, receivers, information transmissions between senders and receivers, and interferences or enablers acting on those transmissions. Nearly everything else about human communication is left to be defined in the situation-specific operational definition of a particular researcher. Dance (1970) found 95 different and sometimes contradictory definitions of communication in use.

Message meaning, provision of feedback, and implications for human action are also attached to most definitions of communication as evidence of the social nature and function of the process. It is generally understood that nonverbal as well as verbal information is "encoded" and "decoded" differently by different participants in the communication process. Some theorists and researchers include extrasensory information, intuition, and unconscious phenomena as part of the communication event. Others are more interested in the overlapping of discontinuous messages from different systems and how that overlap becomes congruent and integrated in the human mind. In educational administration, as in the business world, communication as influence is a pervasive theme in the research literature. The goal of the manager or school administrator is to communicate "vision" and goal imperatives and persuade others to follow the leader to organizational success. Berlo (1960) reported that the meaning of any communication is in the minds of the communicators. Individual experience confirms that communications are often misunderstood. A message may never mean to the receivers exactly what the sender intended it to mean. Why, then, do people continue to struggle so determinedly to share meanings, find common ground, and act in concert? The answer may be simply that humans are social beings. Recent research seems to show through discourse analysis that groups of people who eventually act in concert are not doing so on the basis of full agreement on motivations or rationale but rather because they have agreed on certain mechanisms of communication that allow them to retain their autonomous values and points of view (Donnellon, Gray, & Bougon, 1986). If what these researchers found can be generalized, the goal of communication is not consensus about content or interpretation of the communication but rather, consensus that an equifinal meaning can be reached by each person no matter how idiosyncratic that meaning may be. Stated very simply, participants in an activity do not need to agree on their reasons for taking action or on their perceptions of how they will benefit. They do need to agree on taking collective action. Thus the use of metaphors, logical argument, affect modulation, and linguistic indirec-

tion are simply understood and imply organized action.

The wealth of knowledge and varied disciplinary approaches brought to the field of communication have produced a new profession and a new set of academic specialties. This eclectic field of research comprises components of rhetoric, social psychology, linguistics, mathematics, and many other fields of study. Although there is a need for a more integrative systemic theory, investigating earlier genres is also helpful to educators.

Theory Genres in Communication

Littlejohn (1989) described four basic genres of communication theory, each having characteristics that provide unique ways to understand communication. These are identified as (1) structuralist and functionalist, (2) cognitive and behavioral, (3) interactional and conventional, and (4) interpretive and critical. Each genre contains a broad spectrum of research methodologies and practical applications to the social sciences. Each is associated with certain assumptions that educational administrators may find either closely or loosely aligned with their own belief systems.

Structuralist–functionalist theories are identified by their emphasis on a series of communication exchanges that occur and function almost simultaneously rather than over time, a curiosity about unintended consequences of actions at least as often as about purposeful outcomes, a shared belief in independent and objective reality, and a dualist insistence on the separation of symbols and language from the objects and thoughts being symbolized in communication. The genre borrows from general systems theory as well as from structuralist and functionalist philosophies.

Cognitive–behavioral theories of communication arise from the disciplines of the psychological sciences, employing many of the same assumptions about human knowledge and behavior that one finds in the structuralist–functionalist genre. The difference is that in the cognitive–behavioral paradigm, knowledge is generated through the discovery of psychological "mechanisms." Theories of the cognitive–behavioral nature address communication as a manifestation of individual behavior and thought processes, including the neural basis for these manifestations. According to this genre, major variables having an impact on one's cognitive functioning and its appearances in behavior, including language behavior, are outside the person's control. Still, there are interactional components of the person's behavior that contribute to the particular psychological manifestations studied in this genre.

Interactional–conventional theories of communication are derived largely from sociology, anthropology, and the philosophy of language. The cornerstone concept in this theory is symbolic interaction. Social existence is viewed as a process of continuous interaction that establishes, maintains, and sometimes alters certain social conventions, such as language and symbols. It is interactions, then, that create rules and norms, establish traditions, and on occasion overturn these traditions. Communication is a process of creating social reality and its corresponding culture, norms, and values.

Interpretive–critical theories arise from a variety of investigative traditions, including interpretive sociology, phenomenology and hermeneutics, Marxism and the Frankfurt school, and various text analysis and literary traditions. Common characteristics of interpretive–critical theories include a preeminence of subjectivity and a high value associated with individual experience. In the constructs of the interpretive–critical genre, meaning has great significance. This genre also borrows concepts from general systems theory.

It should be obvious from the differing points of emphasis that each of the genres that Littlejohn described tends to cluster around specific communication contexts. These clusters and contexts provide a hierarchy of research domains that are defined primarily by the size of the groups involved in the communication acts.

From lowest population numbers to highest, these groups include interpersonal, group, organizational, and mass communication areas of research.

Interpersonal theories address communication between individuals, attending primarily to personal and discourse processes and relationships. Group communication theories focus on the interpersonal behaviors and influences that occur in small groups. Therefore, group communication researchers are interested in issues associated with group dynamics, interaction within the group, effectiveness, decision making, and stages of change in both personal and group development. Organizational communication researchers are mindful of interpersonal and group theories, but their primary concern is the role of communication in the achievement of organizational goals (Shockley-Zalabak, 1988). Mass communication carries interpersonal, group, and organizational communication theories into the public realm, generally concerned about the impact of various media on public understanding and resulting public actions.

Although interpersonal, group, and mass communication are of interest to the school administrator, organizational communication constitutes the "breath" of educational organizational life. Without effective communication, an organization is forced to languish in a state of suspended animation, without the nutrients or energy to pursue its collective goals. Understanding what constitutes communication in the organizations in which we live is of vital concern—most of our life is spent in or interacting with organizations (Etzioni, 1964).

Metaphors and Assumptions in Organizational Communication

The assumptions that everyday communicators make about humans and human organizations inevitably create differences in the way that organizational communication phenomena are conceptualized, researched, adjusted, and used. Explicit assumptions are associated with differing metaphors. For example, a theory essentially conceptualized as mechanistic in approach and terminology may be based on the metaphor of the organization-as-machine. However, machines exist to produce wealth in an economic sense, while schools produce educated citizen–workers. In these theories the instrumentality of good communication for getting work done is a constant theme. Theories that emphasize growth and change in organizations may be fundamentally conceptualized in the notion of the organization-as-organism. Here organizational communication is viewed as a crucial element in the organization's survival, akin to a life force that in part drives the entire organization. For the last several decades, the prevalent metaphor that represents the anthropological perspective is the metaphor of organization-as-culture. Communication from this perspective takes on cultural–historical characteristics. Other theorists think of the organization as a complex psychological entity. Organization-as-psychoentity uses metaphors of the mind or psyche to describe organizational communication.

Three emerging metaphors of considerable interest to organization specialists are (1) the metaphor of organization-as-art, implying a continual shaping and reshaping by inner and outer forces or personal agents (e.g., Peters, 1992; Schein, 1989); (2) the metaphor of organization-as-brain (Marsick, 1990; Morgan, 1986), envisioning the organization primarily as an intelligent information-processing center; and (3) the metaphor of the organization-as-learner (Argyris & Schön, 1978), suggesting that organizational learning flow may be as critical for success as cash flow or SAT scores, dropout rates, and numbers of college-bound students. In these newer perspectives, the systemic properties of organizations and organizational communication are dynamic and qualitative. These systems properties require new research methodologies.

The first four of these ruling metaphors—organization-as-machine, organization-as-organism,

organization-as-culture, and organization-as-psychoentity—roughly parallel Littlejohn's theory genres. However, the metaphors of organization-as-art, organization-as-brain, and organization-as-learner are not as clear-cut. These metaphors may be the forerunners of the search for more holistic views of, and metaphors for, organizational communication. Similarly, the literature about school management and supervision, human resource development (HRD), and organizational theory are filled with competing metaphors as writers search for new ways to represent and think about old problems in human organizations. Many attempt to utilize general systems theory (GST) as the foundational thinking system.

Watkins's (1989) discussion of alternative theories for human resource development (HRD) based on five metaphors of practice serve as a prominent example. HRD professionals, including staff developers for educational institutions, typically are concerned with organizational communication. In some ways they may be seen as the "keepers of the metaphors" that characterize organizations. In HRD, skill-building workshops, new-rule communication events, and other instructional leadership efforts are not exempt from inquiry and often use metaphors for their explanatory power. As an example, Watkins names these alternative metaphors for the human resource development role: (1) organizational problem solver, (2) organizational change agent, interventionist, or helper, (3) organizational designer, (4) organizational empowerer or meaning maker, and (5) developer of human capital. If school administrators are performing or guiding the performance of others in light of any one role or any combination of these roles, they are engaged in metaphor-based activity. Watkins may only be associating general systems theory with organizational problem-solving. She links field and intervention theory with the metaphor of the HRD practitioner as organizational change agent, partly on the strength of Kurt Lewin's (1951) field theory contribution to organizational development principles and practices. Watkins found a variety of theories of work as well as theories of design underlying the metaphor of organizational design. In using these new metaphors for organizations, Watkins concomitantly developed new metaphors for leaders in organizations. The organizational empowerer is a metaphor for the believer in critical theory, and the developer of human capital uses human capital theory. The point of making these metaphors and their theoretical origins explicit, Watkins believes, is to enrich and enlarge the understanding of the field of practice.

Other images that educators may profitably reflect upon are Morgan's (1986) pictures of organizations as political systems, psychic prisons, flux and transformation, and/or instruments of domination. Hall (1991) preferred a realistic notion of organizations as actors, and Helgeson (1990) noted that women in charge of organizations often think of them as intricate webs of relationships.

An image that provides a particular insight into the nature of organizations is Pegals's description of a *learning organization* (1998). This he defines as an organization in which (1) there is a climate in which people are encouraged to learn and develop to their full potential, (2) development of the human resources within the organization is a central organizational policy, and (3) continuous organizational transformation takes place. Communication is central to achievement of all three of these characteristics in an organization.

These recent examples do not exhaust the metaphoric possibilities. However, they do verify the fact that single-notioned models of organizations are prevalent and that these differ drastically from the current life of modern organizations.

In the midst of this rich development of metaphors, it is a practical necessity for educators to examine whatever is said about organizational communication with a healthy skepticism and an eye to discovering what metaphors and theories are actually in use in each exchange. It is subsequently imperative to understand the power of metaphor as a means of conceptualizing the school organization as it functions and evolves over time under the stress of constant conflict. For example, although educators in school settings may prefer to think of themselves as the developers of human beings, they often find that role obscured by "control" functions that seem contradictory in purpose or emphasis. What views of the world and what theories are associated with control, what views and theories are associated with development, and what part does communication play as we continue investigating schooling through these metaphors? Such questions should guide school administrators' and teachers' critical reflection about goals, purposes, processes, outcomes, and shareholders in organizational communication.

Distinguishing Features of Organizational Communication

Communication occurs in differing contexts in organizations. Berelson and Steiner (1964) defined four properties of organizations that affect these contexts. First, a typical organization is characterized by formality. Specifically, it has goals, regulations, policies, and procedures that give rise to its form and determine how it will communicate officially. Second, organizations are structured in a hierarchical manner. This structure patterns multidirectional communications. Third, the size of organizations tends to prohibit the development of close personal relationships with all other members and limits the scope of informal organizational communications. Last, organizations most often exist beyond the time frame of a given member's life. Those who work in schools will surely recognize these features as pertaining to educational organizations. They may also recognize that Berelson and Steiner's formulation is several decades old and may represent organizational aspects now in flux. At the same time, the salience of Berelson and Steiner's theory and the current organizational structure of many schools in the United States suggest that schools facing the challenges of the twenty-first century may be out of sync and their old structures and contexts may not fit well with tomorrow's communications needs. Berelson and Steiner's theory serves well, however, as a template for understanding key elements of today's school organizations.

If the feature of organizational communication that separates it from other kinds of communication is its deliberate focus on the achievement of a common or collective goal, then the specific form of any organization can be expected to be mirrored in its forms of organizational communication. According to Berelson and Steiner's premise that form follows goals, communicating organizational goals becomes a "first cause" and shaper of all organizational communication. This is perhaps one impulse behind the first school assembly of each academic year and the traditional goal setting that some school leaders undertake in that forum. Goals are useless if they are not communicated in ways that enlist the cooperative effort of members of the organization. Without the intention to attain goals, organizations would also appear to have no purpose. It is not surprising that those who write about organization see goal attainment and communication systemically intertwined (Hoy & Miskel, 1987). Like Simon (1957), they believe that there can be no organization without communication. This places a clear responsibility on school leaders not only to establish and maintain communication but also to be sure that it is both effective and efficient for goal attainment.

Many studies support the importance of communication in organizational leadership. Hoy and Miskel (1987) stated that "superintendents and principals spend 70 percent or more of their time communicating" (p. 356). Sigband and Bell (1989) reported that chief executive officers in corporations spend 78 percent of their time in oral communication, with lower-level managers spending over 80 percent of their time similarly. Murphy and Peck (1980) cited the ability to communicate as the critical factor in manager promotability. It would appear that competent communication is regarded more highly than such skills as motivating employees, decision making, delegating, flexibility, and educational background. In educational institutions, Striplin (1987) found that the ability of school principals to perform effectively as instructional leaders is contingent on their degree of competence in communication.

Communication's potential contribution to organizational success is present in virtually all organizational activities, from envisioning, to planning, to problem solving and decision making, to coordinating, controlling, accomplishing, evaluating, and reporting organizational results. It is tempting to conclude that effective organizational communication is therefore a panacea for all organizational stresses and difficulties. To the contrary, Hoy and Miskel (1987) pointed out that the diffusion of communication processes throughout an organization makes organizational communication difficult to examine as a separate process. Difficulties in organizational communication that are often reflected in other problems in the school are another construct. Although communication can help resolve problems, it can also obscure other problems not directly under consideration. Finally, communication evokes action even though the quality of the action is questionable and there is no general commitment to the action. Poor leaders can unknowingly use communication to expedite inadequate or irrelevant plans.

To assure effectiveness, the school leader must be fully aware of the intricacy of the school unit or district communication channels on both the formal and informal levels. How the leader facilitates the transmission of a given message can result in a deliberately orchestrated change in staff or student behavior. Given the reality of the constraints that Hoy and Miskel note, the school leader needs to be aware of the power of all communication as a potential force for maintaining or destroying some aspects of the organizational life. Theoretically, this calls for the school administrator to borrow from Yukl's (1989) theory about the role of a "leader" versus that of a "manager" in a school. Yukl suggested that the effective administrator may know when to communicate as a manager and when to communicate as a leader. In the former case the administrator chooses to minimize noise by sending messages, developing channels, and monitoring feedback in settings that are clearly role defined. For example, a school administrator might give his staff a written questionnaire regarding supply requisitions. The staff writes a written response which the administrator subsequently responds to in the format of existing policy. On the other hand, as an administrator seeks staff support on an issue, he or she is best advised to use a variety of communication skills in an effort to gain commitment to an issue. This is a function of leadership and, according to Yukl (1989), requires administrative understanding of communication and a varied repertoire of communication skills. In examining communication processes, the school administrator in a continuous process shifts from the role of manager to that of leader.

Factors Affecting Clarity, Credibility, and Directionality of Organizational Messages

Khandwalla (1987) stated that the primary objectives of communication are to gain attention and to gain understanding and acceptance of a message. Sigband and Bell (1989) contended that the purposes of communication are to be understood exactly as intended, to secure the desired response, and to maintain favorable relations with those with whom one communicates. Reitz (1987) believed that the primary functions of communication are to provide information that makes an organization adaptable to change, to command and instruct employees, and to influence and persuade the organization's

members. The processes involved in accomplishing these purposes are recognized as contributing to the success or failure of a given end. A leader may subscribe to any of these communication objectives either as an expression of commitment to the organization and its goals or as an expression of a personal desire for power and self-aggrandizement. The communicator's world view and personal motivations therefore affect clarity, credibility, directionality, and even the process of communication itself. Modeling communication as a quasimechanical process, a means to an end, leaves out important psychological data. Nevertheless, the linear, mechanical model of information processing, sender–message channel–receiver–feedback, is the usual starting point for talking about communication (see Figure 5.1).

Using a quasimechanical model of communication allows the researcher to examine discrete elements of the communication process without the burden of holistic analysis. Thus, in speaking of the elements sender and receiver, the linear model makes it possible to conceptualize communication as a sharing of messages, ideas, or attitudes that produce a degree of understanding between those elements. The idea of shared meaning permits the study of how well a particular meaning is shared. Shared meaning can be problematic, however, as the receiver's intention may differ from that imagined or meant by the sender.

The linear model provides a starting point not unlike the starting point of behavioral psychology. There is a sender or stimulus source somewhere in the environment that acts on and elicits a response from the receiver. Communication models insert a channel between the sender and the receiver to locate and account for response variations. Recognition of intrapsychic processes within the senders and receivers helps to account for human barriers to communication and for discrepancies in message meaning. The feedback loop overcomes the essential linearity of the early models, looping to revisit any element in the process.

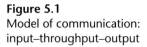

Figure 5.1
Model of communication:
input–throughput–output

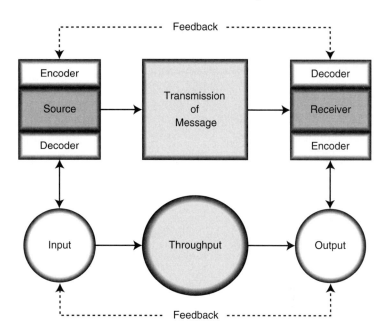

A basic assumption about organizational communication is that if messages are actually sent, and if clarity, frequency, and completeness of those messages are increased, the probability that organization members will be working toward a common or shared goal is also increased. This leads organizational communication specialists to place considerable emphasis on message form and on channels that carry the messages. Their intention is to avoid channels that produce static or distortion, or if those channels must be used, to reduce occurrence of noise, static, or distortion within them. Channels include oral, written, and mediated routing of messages.

Sigband and Bell (1989) identified two communication channels, formal and informal. *Formal channels* of communication include the organizationally sanctioned flows of information, such as electronic mail, scheduled meetings, and other functional necessities. The *informal* ("grapevine") *channels* provide access to information not normally obtained through formal channels. Khandwalla (1987) cited telephone

and face-to-face conversations as the primary means of informal communication. Administrators can monitor the organizational climate by paying attention to messages in the grapevine. They may even intentionally "leak" off-the-record statements to informal channels to monitor communication flow. The advantage of using informal communication is that it transfers information very rapidly. The informal communication network prevents a communication vacuum. If the formal channels do not work, the informal ones will take over. The problem with informal channels is their potential inaccuracy. The lack of official sanction leaves informally conveyed messages at the mercy of unchecked distortions as they travel through the grapevine.

Sigband and Bell (1989) classified the major barriers to communication under two headings: nonverbal and verbal. *Nonverbal barriers* include differences in perception; lack of interest (particularly on the part of the receiver); lack of fundamental knowledge or specific cognitive basis for understanding a message; personal characteristics such as personality, emotions, and prejudices; reactions to the appearance of the communicator; distractions or actual interference; poor organization of the message; poor listening; and competition for attention. Common *verbal barriers* include language, which may result in semantics problems, or inadequate vocabulary, both of which affect comprehension.

Another large category of barriers to communication results from cultural differences. This is particularly evident in the United States, where educators constantly must address the cultural differences of diverse populations in both the student body and the community. Hentges, Yaney, and Shields (1990) noted that because "no two groups ever experience the same cultural history, messages become more dissonant and ambiguous in a more heterogeneous population. To reduce the possibility of misunderstanding or dissonance potential, messages must be repeated many times" (pp. 39–40). Misunderstandings arise out of biases regarding accents and language, culturally defined signs and body language, acceptable degrees of physical proximity, the meanings of a handshake and eye contact, preferences for or against strong authority figures, and class systems brought from other countries. The diversity of cultural references to adversity or joy may seem inexplicable or bizarre to those outside that particular culture. A cultural or privation-induced orientation toward the "here and now" instead of toward the future may be misconstrued as lack of ambition or ability to plan. The roles and significance of particular minority family members may seem unusual to the dominant culture. An Asian student, for example, may not be able to answer a direct question until many older family members are consulted. Choices between being indirect or direct may be culturally determined, and symbolic messages are often unique to the country of origin. Surmounting these communication barriers calls for providing for shared experiences, regularly, often, and in great variety, with an emphasis on valuing rather than judging differences. Future school administrators in the

United States cannot ignore demographic information that mandates multicultural awareness.

Communications problems may spring from a variety of other sources as well as those that have a basis in the individual personality. Some of these as identified by Fredrickson (1991) include personal bias, anxiety and defensiveness, hidden agendas, and participating in groupthink. The sender's credibility is always at stake in organizational communication. Khandwalla (1987) noted that to be credible, the source of information must be perceived as knowledgeable. Thus, a memo about the financial status of a school district needs to come from the district's financial officer rather than the curriculum specialist if it is to carry maximum credibility. However, credibility does not hinge on position alone. Both advance reputation and ongoing experience with a communicator create a track record of credibility or noncredibility. Once credibility is lost, it is difficult, if not impossible, to regain within the organization where the loss occurred.

Message originators can assess the extent to which successful transmission has occurred by encouraging feedback from receivers. This is especially critical in school settings. The concept of feedback is often attributed to Wiener (1954) in his early discussions of cybernetics. In cybernetics, *feedback* refers to the ability of a person and of some machines to detect an error or deviation from that desired in an operation. Feedback identifies deviation and communicates that deviation to a control mechanism that makes a subsequent correction. Expert systems may even suggest alternative new actions. In popular communication practice, feedback refers to the verbal or nonverbal response received from the individual or groups to whom the message is directed. Feedback implies at least a two-way communication. With feedback, the message originator can at least make a rough assessment of whether a message was received as intended (i.e., decoded to yield the same basic meaning as was encoded by the sender). Misunderstandings are detected when feedback is accurate and timely. If delayed or distorted by interpersonal or organizational "noise," feedback may be useless. Feedback is most effective when it is obtained as close to the time of message transmission as possible (Hellriegel, Slocum, & Woodman, 1986; Shockley-Zalabak, 1988; Sigband & Bell, 1989).

Recognizing organizational features that affect the clarity, credibility, and directionality of messages is a function of the school administrator in the role of a leader. As the information above reveals, discovering barriers to effective communication requires the leader to examine an organization's channels through multidimensional lenses. This examination might occur through the school leader's reflection on critical incidents in the communication process. In each of these incidents, the school leader identifies situational variables which elicit a mix of communication approaches. A normative model of leadership is built on the situational exercise of various skills at various times. No single common variable, skill, or approach works with the same degree of efficacy in every leadership situation. This model of leadership is best applied to the practice of communication. Just as clarity, credibility, and directionality are influenced by organizational changes, an administrator's clear perception of the organization and the power of communication as a shaping agent must constantly sharpen. No set formula for monitoring the quality of communication exists for application in a complex school organization. In this context the school administrator bases communication processes on the situational needs that create the communication event. As Smith and Piele (1989) believe, communication choices made by school leaders, like other aspects of their practice, must reflect three abilities: situational sensitivity that enables them to diagnose problems, style flexibility that allows them to match certain practices appropriately to situations, and situational management skills that enable them to alter aspects of a situation to fit work styles. Leadership in

schools is context-bound. Nowhere is this more evident than in communication events, where administrators must act on a constantly changing climate and culture that influences the accuracy and diffusion of messages.

Types of Message Directionality

In hierarchical organizations, communications are directed downward, upward, and horizontally. In most organizations (and certainly in most traditionally designed American schools), vertical top-down communication predominates (Khandwalla, 1987) and filters through successive layers of an organization until it reaches schoolchildren and nonsupervisory personnel. Channels are typically of the formal variety. They direct, instruct, indoctrinate, inspire, or evaluate. Common forms of downward communication include policies and procedures, orders and memoranda, handbooks and reports for various stakeholders, and announcements considered to be of general public interest.

A problem with vertical, top-down communication is that it is premised on the "need to know." The stakeholders farthest away from the executive offices are presumed to need only that amount of information that enables them to perform the tasks assigned to them. Messages become ever more narrow as they move through the organization, often leaving those members of the lowest levels without a sense of connectedness to the organization and its purpose. School administrators, business managers, and supervisors decide how much to communicate in original form and how much to edit, add, interpret, or eliminate at each successive level. In one study, Reitz (1987) demonstrated that by the time a message from top management in business reaches individual workers, 80 percent of the original message has been filtered out. In schools with overlapping formal and informal channels, the filtering is even more prolific.

To overcome message erosion, school organizations need to formulate specific methods for communicating messages. Planning should

minimally address basic issues such as informing all concerned groups of ongoing activities
and/or problems; announcing future plans, directions, and goals; encouraging two-way communication; ensuring timeliness of messages;
and allocating funds for communication purposes. Sigband and Bell (1989) warned that administrative sponsorship of downward communication can forestall the fabrication in the
grapevine of "facts." Establishing good communications from the onset is least costly.

Lateral or horizontal communication occurs
between individuals at the same authority level
in the hierarchy. Organizational peers spend a
significant amount of time communicating with
each other, more time than they spend communicating with their superiors (Reitz, 1987). Sigband and Bell (1989) question the efficiency of
lateral communication, considering how little
pressure there is in organizations to use it productively. Problem solving and coordination are
clearly enhanced by lateral communication, and
duplication of effort is often avoided by means
of this fast, direct exchange of messages apart
from the chain of command. However, potential
disadvantages of lateral communication might
include overuse, a burying of peers in inconse-
quential memos, or an increase in "activity" that
carries with it a false impression of productivity.
There may also be an unequal exchange, with
some peers withholding information as an exercise of power. Since usually, no system of accountability is involved in lateral communication, the arbitrary bartering for power that
occurs in these settings can be dangerous to an
organization.

The efficacy and volume of upward communication depends on the degree of trust that
lower-level stakeholders have in their superiors.
Upward communication serves to alert upper
levels of school management to the climate, activities, and performance declines or improvements that are of concern at the grass-roots level
of the organization. As is the case with downward communication, selective filtering occurs.
Filtering occurs because lower-level employees

often tell their superiors what they think those
supervisors want to hear, thus introducing a
positive bias toward themselves through the information they pass upward (Krivonos, 1982).
Personnel at the bottom of the organizational
pyramid rarely, of their own accord, take the
risk of initiating upward communication. Mechanisms are often put into place to encourage
such communication. These mechanisms might
include the use of employee suggestion boxes,
the creation of quality circles or employee (or
student) councils, and the use of various employee and client–customer survey techniques.
Anonymity is always an issue in data gathering
at all levels of an organization.

Educational organizations are generally alert
to the need to communicate with the community at large, as well as the need to enlist participation from that external environment. It is
incumbent on school administrations to maintain open-system perspectives, so that information coming in and going out is useful to all concerned. Kefalas (1977) considered careful
monitoring and response to incoming communication an identifying characteristic of an effective organization. Reitz (1987) underscored
the importance of external communication by
citing a study of small businesses that showed a
direct positive relationship between time spent
in outward communications and business financial success. Communication with the community at large requires a definite leadership
role for a school administrator. The possibility
for organizational noise increases as the size of
the receiver group increases because of cultural
and psychological interference. Increasingly,
schools must learn to rely on the support of local communities. The administrator should use
communication to influence that support. In this
sense, the administrator, like his or her counterparts in other organizations, must project a vision and seek to implement that vision through
partnerships with the community. However, vision is not enough. Schools must utilize the "human agency," whether it be school board meetings, newsletters, or public appearances, to

mobilize community members to share the values of the vision. This requires selective and direct communication. The creation of new communication channels can operationalize shared values with the community. The community and school become active partners in the larger system, society.

Communication networks are a special case of directionality, involving vertical and horizontal (or lateral) communication. Much of the early research on communication networks was conducted in a laboratory setting and focused on the comparative effects of centralized and decentralized networks on the quality of communication. Although variations and elaborations exist, two basic patterns can be used to represent centralized and decentralized networks: the wheel and the circle. In the *centralized network,* or *wheel pattern,* persons at the periphery of the wheel send their communications to the hub person, who has control over the distribution of information. The structure of this network imposes its own brand of hierarchy, with the hub person becoming the executive figure. In the *decentralized network,* or *circle pattern,* all members communicate with those on either side of them, and the network avoids the hierarchical structure. Helgeson's (1990) *web* image of organizations combines wheel and circle networks, with communication nodes at each intersection of the web. Miller (1978) also refers to the intersection of communication channels in living systems as nodes of a net.

Using success in problem solving as the criterion of efficiency, Hall (1991) contended that repeated investigations have found the wheel pattern to be superior to the circle pattern. Khandwalla (1987) qualified that position and suggested that the effectiveness of the differing patterns depends on the nature of the task. He found that centralized patterns are faster and more error-free for simple tasks, whereas decentralized networks perform better if the problems are complex and unexpected. Fisher (1978) noted that although the wheel can be an effective form of network, its effectiveness is largely contingent upon the encoding and decoding skills of the person occupying the "hub" position.

Other Factors Affecting Organizational Communication

Reitz (1987) listed other major variables that affect direction, frequency, and participant satisfaction with communication. These include the availability of opportunities to interact, the degree of coherence of groups, the status of individuals or groups, and two-direction communication flow. Each are of considerable importance in school environments.

Communication among individuals and groups can be fostered by arranging physical and psychological distance so that common facilities are shared and interaction is a natural occurrence. Campbell and Campbell (1988) showed in the study of physical environment and interaction that the location of lounges is a strong predictor of lounge use and that an effect on informal types of communication can therefore be inferred. A variety of business studies have shown that managers interact most often with subordinates who are located in offices closest to them. The resulting inequities in organizational communications are obvious. Altering spatial relationships can occur through the leadership of a school administrator. Modeling new spatial arrangements may improve communication and shape relationships.

Cohesiveness and communication are mutually reinforcing. As the level of one rises, so does the level of the other. Status affects both the frequency and the direction of communication because people tend to direct their communication to those of similar or higher status. Reitz (1987) attributed this to perceptions of common interests, to shared experiences, or to mutual reinforcement. The desired outcome of interaction with a person of higher status may be to move closer to the person who controls the organizational reward structures.

The two-step communication flow refers to a process that depends on personal contacts with "opinion leaders," who in turn are influenced by mediated information from inside and outside the organization. Information transmitted to opinion leaders is disseminated to large numbers of people, who turn to the opinion leaders for "news" and for "reality testing" of their own points of view. This is an important process for educational administrators, who depend on such contacts for successful interface with the local community. Aside from effects that are triggered by status or distance, preference and perception also affect comprehension and overall effectiveness of a communication environment. Reitz (1987) reports that face-to-face communication tends to be more effective than written communication (i.e., if the verbal and nonverbal cues are compatible) but admits that written communication tends to yield greater comprehension. If the receiver typically relies on external guidance and is predisposed to act on information provided by others, the message will be more likely to have the desired effect. If, on the other hand, the receiver is independent, confident, and self-directed, the message may not have the same effect. In general, nonverbal cues can influence communication effectiveness either by corroborating or contradicting a given verbal message or by conveying a message that is independent of verbal material—for example, wearing a business suit or engaging in impatient pencil tapping.

A Sampling of Approaches to Organizational Communication

Structural and Functional Approaches

Productivity and task accomplishment are outputs (goals) of major concern to proponents of structural/functional approaches to communication. Shockley-Zalabak (1988) asserted that this results from adopting the principles of scientific management, following the lead of such writers as Max Weber, Henry Fayol, and Frederick Taylor. This approach stems from a bureaucratic management theoretical basis and results in communication style that is top-down, formal, of moderate load, and subject to minimal distortion.

This utilitarian model underpins most public schools in the United States today. Examining the structural–functional approach, along with the emerging concerns of general systems theorists, provides a clearer understanding of the organizational structure embedded in our current school systems. By understanding these models, an administrator will more clearly recognize the differences in the roles of the administrator-as-manager and the administrator-as-leader. As persistent calls for school reform result in the restructuring of schools, it is natural for conflict of roles to occur. Variables affecting school climate and culture, the knowledge explosion, the advance of technology, the rapidly changing family, and the increase in national poverty and political pressures are forcing changes in school organizations. These changes will force changes in school administrators' roles. Emerging successful administrators will undoubtedly be leaders who have a full understanding of organizational history and structure. Also, these leaders will be unrestrained in envisioning new models for both understanding and reshaping their school districts for success through careful use of communication.

More recently, structural–functional theories of organizational communication have been dominated by the systems approach (Kefalas, 1977; Littlejohn, 1989; Shockley-Zalabak, 1988). These researchers view information processing as the primary function of organizational communication systems. The organization is defined as a system made up of interrelated units or subsystems. The system as a whole can be distinguished from other systems or organizations because it maintains organizational boundaries. If, however, the system is open (i.e., accepting and using environmental information and also communicating outward to the environment), its chances of success are greater than if it maintains closed boundaries and subsists only on internally generated, more bounded information. Because schools are so sensitive to their environments, the systems approach appeals to school administrators as a model for studying internal and external communication.

In the open communication system, incoming information is called *input*. The process by which input is transformed into a form usable by the system is known as *throughput*. Information transmitted from the system outward to its environment, whether intentionally or unintentionally, is referred to as *output*. Figure 5.1 demonstrates an input–output model of communication. Many general systems theorists warn that the model is too simplistic; it lacks the ability to model the complex elements and dynamics of the actual communication process. System theorists find such a figure too linear and much more systematic than systemic, since the models obscure the richness and holistic orientation of the system paradigm.

Barnard (1938) is credited by many authors as being a pioneer in the application of system concepts to the study of organizations and organizational communication. Farace, Monge, and Russell (1977) defined an organization as a system composed of members who are characteristically interdependent; who process input, throughput, and output; and who treat information as a critical resource for reducing uncertainty. Within this framework, communication depends on the use of common symbolic forms that have widely understood referents. Here information is subdivided into two types: (1) *absolute information,* which refers collectively to all the information within the system, and (2) *distributed information,* which resides in different places throughout the system. Distributed information is often neglected by school administrators and other managers.

Farace et al. (1977) indicated that conceptualization promotes discussion of communication at three levels: the system level, the functional level, and the structural level. At the system level three hierarchical interchanges occur: Individuals communicate in dyads, the dyads cluster into groups, and the interconnected groups form the organization or macronetwork. At the functional level there is evidence of three organizational operations: production, innovation, and maintenance. At the structural level, communication elements of the frequency, regularity, and patterns of communication are plotted.

At the individual communication level, load is an important concept. *Load* refers to the quantity, volume, rate, and complexity of messages (Shockley-Zalabak, 1988). Major problems related to load include the extremes of underload, which is evident when the flow of messages falls below a person's capacity to process them; and overload, which represents a flow of messages that exceeds the person's information processing capacity. Technological advances enabling the transmission of vast quantities of messages at extremely high rates have been the source of chronic overload for many people, resulting in impaired decision making. *Chronic overload* is a term that resonates with teachers and administrators alike. It is imperative that an administrator understand technology and its impact on communication.

At the dyad level of organizational communication, the key concept is *rules,* explicit and implicit norms or axioms for communications within an organization. Generally, rules are either thematic or tactical. *Thematic rules* are behavioral norms that reflect organizational values and beliefs, and *tactical rules* prescribe behaviors relevant to more general themes, such as referring analogically to the organization as a "family." A person who is socialized into an organization and who learns to identify with it will generally comply with both thematic and tactical rules.

Littlejohn (1989) considered three structures within the group setting: (1) the micronetwork, the pattern of group interactions, (2) the power structure, (3) and the leadership structure, including interpersonal influence roles of group members. The various members and their links constitute the communication network. Links have five properties: (1) symmetry, the extent to which linked members interact on an equal basis; (2) strength, the frequency of interaction; (3) reciprocity, the extent to which people concur about the links; (4) the content of the interactions; and (5) mode, the vehicle that carries the interaction (e.g., verbal or written communication). Within the micronetwork, people have distinct roles: acting as liaisons with other groups, becoming isolated and in essence "unlinked," or performing as gatekeepers who control information coming into or released by the group. Using the systems approach to organizational communication, large numbers of variables can be addressed. Littlejohn (1989) contended, however, that such approaches do not adequately account for situational variables that are not systemlike.

No single approach can serve to explain or identify all the variables in the communication process; therefore, no single method of communication will suffice for all situations that a school administrator encounters. Again, the concern for situational leadership (Yukl, 1989) emerges. The more complex an organization is, the more complex communication will be. The constant flow of communication in a school necessitates a constant practice of a variety of skills by the administrator, who decides to get tasks done to manage or to influence commitment to lead. In both these roles the administrator must have clear knowledge of organizational structure in practice and in the ideal.

Behavioral Approaches

As management theories change to accommodate a more humanistic view, complementary changes occur in the way that organizational communication is viewed. The *Hawthorne effect* demonstrates that giving management attention to human relations factors has a favorable impact on organizational success. This is an early example of many subsequent studies that reached the same conclusion. When communication theorists felt that the complexity of human behavior was misrepresented in the structuralist–functionalist approach as a handmaiden of scientific management, they sought other approaches.

Human relations theorists believe that messages should move in all directions, through both formal and informal networks. They emphasize oral over written channels and suggest a moderate communication load with predictable levels of distortion. One theoretical model representing this position is Likert's four systems. Likert (1967) suggests that organizations operate along a continuum of high-to-low-control leadership styles, which have correlates in organizational communication styles.

The first style, *exploitative–authoritative,* is associated with top-down management. This style rarely accommodates feedback and therefore limits both the direction and frequency of communication. The second style, *benevolent–authoritative,* is also identified with top-down management, but the communication patterns here tend to give at least the appearance of management sensitivity to employee needs. The third style, *consultative,* accommodates vertical communication interchanges both upward and downward in the organization. The fourth style, *participative management,* accommodates the greatest amount of multidirectional communication, with employees expected to participate fully in organizational decision making. Critics of Likert's model suspect that participative management is also constrained by hierarchical assumptions and suggest that there may be yet another, structurally different power-sharing style (Schein, 1989). These styles are discussed in more detail in Chapter 3.

Human relations approaches are often criticized because of the implied notion that high morale leads, without exception, to high productivity. Other critics see a failure to address important structural and functional variables. In this regard the human relations perspective may be suffering from the same misapprehensions and "turf wars" that system thinkers experience. Regardless of this academic criticism, in reality, organizations function on the basis of morale and missions of productivity at some echelons. How organizations are modeled for an understanding of the shaping and life-giving effects of communication may not be determined solely by viewing the organization through one of the less-structured approaches. Nevertheless, these approaches provide important elements for consideration by school administrators, whose very job it is to promote the delivery of a human service and to enable teachers, students, and staff to achieve. The school administrator cannot ignore the inevitable "humanness" of the school's character, especially in attempting to understand communication needs and responses.

Approaches Related to the Process of Organizing

Weick's (1969) theory of organizing appears systemic, with an ethnographic or cultural accent. As characterized, it is considered to be one of the few "truly organizational communication theories" (Littlejohn, 1989). Weick believes that organizational environments do not preexist but are enacted. Organizational members continually enact and reenact the environment as warranted by attitudes, values, and experience. Organizing is therefore evolutionary and is contingent not only on enactment but also on information selection and retention processes. Enactment incorporates an acknowledgment of equivocality, but selection enables a group to admit certain relevant information and reject other data as irrelevant to the enactment. Retention entails decisions about which information should be saved for future use. In Weick's theory, assembly rules and interlocking behavior cycles are viewed as the basic mechanisms for organizing. Assembly rules guide the choice of routines that are used for enactment, selection, and retention. Interlocking behavior cycles are sets of interrelated behaviors that enable a group to agree on which meanings should be included and which rejected. After retention occurs, organizational members must decide whether to reenact the environment in some manner or to modify their behavior to achieve consistency with the information they hold. The flexibility implied by these evolving decisions

may be of particular interest to school administrators. This flexibility implies ways in which change can be orchestrated on the basis of understanding communication.

Poole and McPhee (1983) extended the principle of structuration (organizing) into the realm of organizational communication. Interactions create norms and rules relative to the achievement of organizational goals and markedly affect both structure and climate. Poole and McPhee believe that organizational structure is a representation and a product of organizational communication. Structure is also an indirect way of informing employees and others about an organization. Structure becomes a form of metacommunication by which an organization can address its needs and patterns.

Structuration can occur at three sites: (1) the site of conception, any site where individual or group decisions are made about what will happen in an organization; (2) the site of implementation, locations from which formal codification and dissemination of decisions about what will happen in the organization are proceeding; and (3) the site of reception, those points at which organizational members act in accordance with the decisions made. Although anyone in the organization can participate in communication at any of the three sites, structuration tends to be specialized. For example, administrators are involved primarily at the site of conception. At this site administrators have the most opportunities to serve as leaders by establishing the means to influence the commitment of staff and students. Through the deliberate creation of channels (i.e., committees, forums, jobs, etc.), administrators may lead their organizations to build efficient communication systems. These systems can promote the general health of an organization. An administrator may simply be getting staff to commit to using channels. In this way the administrator has led them to follow an example of life-giving, multi-directional communication.

Equally important, Poole and McPhee (1983) defined the organizational members' collective attitude as *climate,* an attitude that is constantly affected by organizational interactions. Climate is viewed as both a medium and an outcome of interactions, influenced not only by the structure but also by such climate-modifying strategies as publication of newsletters or holding contests. Climate is also affected by the composite of individual attributes, such as the possession or lack of knowledge and skills.

In contrast to organizational climate, the term *organizational culture* commonly refers to the shared realities that are played out in "performances" displayed during interchanges (Pacanowsky & O'Donnell-Trujillo, 1982). These performances can be classified as (1) rituals (personal, task, or social in nature), performances that are regularly repeated; (2) passions, including storytelling or passionate repartee exchanged in dramatic and lively interactions; (3) sociality, including social performances dedicated to the creation of a group sense of identity, such as joking, talking shop, or sharing personal experiences; (4) organizational politics, creating and reinforcing notions of power and influence and perhaps involving activities such as bargaining; and (5) enculturation, including performances aimed at initiating new members into the accepted organizational culture. Most school-based educators easily accept the notion that schools are cultural entities.

As cultural entities, schools present myriad communication opportunities. The administrator must choose, in the context of a shared mission, how to emphasize positive school-cultural traits at each opportunity. In an increasingly multicultural context, the role of the school administrator must be defined by communication that is reflective of school values and a school culture that is open to all stakeholders.

Sociopsychological Perspective on Individual Communication in Organizations

Elements of other theories and approaches to organizational communication are incorporated in sociopsychological theories. Paramount in this genre of communications theory are the effects on or created by individual communication acts. Here we revisit elements and processes associated with basic, quasimechanistic communication models in order to add psychological perspectives.

Psychological perspectives conceptualize organizational communication as a loop in which a sender initiates a message and a receiver obtains it and then considers possible courses of action. If the receiver responds or provides feedback, the roles of sender and receiver reverse. This looping behavior occurs in an organization's bureaucratic structure, which is subject to noise from the informal structure. It is this extraneous noise that often interferes with message understanding. The meaning of a message depends not only on the content but also on the organizational context. O'Reilly and Pondy (1979) utilized the formula

$$meaning = information + context$$

to depict this process.

The message source may be a person or an intermediary medium, such as a newspaper, a memorandum, or a visual image. Credibility of the sender is critical in sociopsychological theory. Receivers may ignore noncredible messengers at will, regardless of message content. Not only are there psychological interpretations of the right of the sender to comment, but there are also psychological demands regarding a particular sender's choice of media. The encoding and decoding processes both allow "mental sets" to detract from or enhance message communication. According to psychological theorists, personality variables, values, gender or cultural differences, and personal interest ensure that a filtering process occurs at all points in the flow of communication.

Because the message form is often contingent on the channel or medium selected for message transmission, individual preferences can either override a communication system or be overridden by it. The channels or media selected determine, in large part, the routing pattern the message will follow (i.e., whether the message will be conveyed vertically or horizontally, formally or informally). Formatting the message also has psychological implications because people do not perceive or process information in identical ways. Business executives are increasingly concerned that the medium selected may determine the richness and the impact of the information processed by receivers (Daft & Lengel, 1984; Lengel & Daft, 1988). Richness of medium is determined by the overall reception of a message. School administrators are also beginning to be selective about the medium they use. Face-to-face verbal communication is preferred, with telephone communications and "written personal" next in order. "Written formal" and "numeric formal" complete the low end of the richness continuum. Face-to-face, filmed, or televised speech is considered "primary oral" communication, and all forms of written communication are considered "secondary verbal."

Communicators in educational settings place some reliance on the relationships between the message chosen and the medium selected. Message comprehension tends to be higher when it is in written form, but opinion change is greater when face-to-face communication is employed. Media redundancy (i.e., a combination of written and oral) increases both message richness and accuracy of reception. Written communication tends to be effective when the message contains general information or requires future action. Oral communication tends to be effective in situations demanding immediate feedback. Examples of such situations are offering praise, giving procedural directions, settling disputes, issuing reprimands, and even saying "good morning" to other organizational members.

Nonverbal, as well as verbal, signals have meaning, and this meaning may conflict with or reinforce verbal message sending. Even nonword sound expressions, such as grunts or laughter, complicate the problem of message accuracy. Sociopsychological theorists seem to believe that the best to hope for is that the message received will be functionally comparable to the message sent.

Because the range of message-sending options and the range of responses are both subject to individual differences, feedback itself becomes a psychosocial phenomenon. Feedback varies even in its degrees of purposefulness, especially in its nonverbal aspects. For example, an unintended yawn can convey entirely the wrong feedback message. The concept of feedback implies that constant adjustments in the communication process can and should be made on the basis of clues the communicators get from feedback. Feedback can improve task performance and positively influence organizational climate.

On the other hand, feedback can either reflect or create situational noise. If physical, social, or psychological barriers are in place, feedback can either strengthen or reduce those barriers. Telling a communication partner that a freight train is passing can help that partner understand your communication situation. Telling a partner that your boss is in the office helps the partner understand a reluctance to stay on the phone, and telling a partner that a particular phrase or mannerism is upsetting helps that person either adjust or decide not to adjust behavior according to his or her intent. Feedback is a powerful tool for educational administrators who can set the tone and examples for the entire school system. Feedback can therefore be verbal or nonverbal; however, in any form, it must be situationally appropriate.

Nonverbal communication has been researched extensively in a variety of settings. For educators, two nonverbal modes are of particular interest: the impact of facial expressions and the use of spatial cues. Lipham and Francke (1966) studied nonverbal behavior of school principals as influencing promotability or nonpromotability. The variables they examined were (1) the structuring of self (i.e., self-maintenance, clothing, physical movement and posture); (2) the structuring of interaction, including interaction initiation, interaction distance, and interaction termination behaviors; and (3) the structuring of environment, including such matters as office decor, spatial arrangements, neatness, and status symbols. The researchers cited above found significant differences in interaction and environmental structuring. Promotable principals tended to keep less distance in their interpersonal encounters. They also tended to use status symbols more casually, for example, using a desk nameplate as a paperweight versus using it as a psychological fence.

Communication satisfaction suggests that a real or perceived lack of two-way communication is a critical variable in educational institutions. Situational noise also poses a considerable threat to the success of organizational communication. Interpersonal communication seems always to be more effective than organizational communication because face-to-face situations rule out many sources of distortion, permit immediate feedback, and encourage message reframing.

Bureaucratic models of organization, described by Barnard (1938), require that the channels of communication reach every organizational member, take the shortest and most direct route, remain available for constant use, and be authenticated by position power that tells receivers that the sender has the required authority to be a sender. The model assumes that such formality ensures message accuracy because it is "in writing," is from competent superiors, and is contextually the same for everyone. Although context may change to coordinating activities, providing information, influencing or directing, or simply telling organizational stories, formality is prominent. School bureaucracies display the dimensions above to the extent that they are centralized, hierarchically shaped, and either more or less dependent on information technology.

Formal communication channels can carry both instrumental and expressive content (i.e., to help the organization reach its goals and to affect attitudes, norms, and values). Informal channels are complementary in the sense that they typically reflect the impact of content carried in the formal channels. Informal communication also serves to gratify social needs of busy people by helping them to express themselves personally and socially.

To understand formal and informal communication, researchers have used content analysis, sociometry, interaction analysis, participant observation, continuous observation, communication sampling, and general survey or network survey techniques. In educational institutions, general and network survey techniques are widely used. Surveys are designed to assess communication accuracy, openness, and frequency. Surveys provide useful representations of informal communication patterns and structures and often identify attractions, resistance, or lack of opportunity to communicate. Communication problems identified sociometrically can be deliberately brought into the networks so that information and social meanings are not lost. Communications typically form along task-focused lines, so that members of some groups are not members of others and therefore communicate less often. This can prevent formal authority and social networks from overlapping, especially when school administrators wish to introduce new information or practices. In other cases, overlapping may be deliberately planned to increase the accuracy of message reception.

Pathways to the Future

People in leadership positions spend the majority of their working days communicating; however, at the same time, communication skills are an acknowledged weakness of such leaders (Baeshen, 1987). In the United States, millions of dollars are spent every year on efforts to develop the leadership, communication, and interpersonal skills of business, industry, and government leaders (Carnevale & Gainer, 1989). Middle managers are especially targeted for such training, with close to one-fourth of Fortune 500 training and development budgets allocated for these purposes. School administrators do not have access to comparable developmental resources and, after professional education, are expected to attend to their own development.

Although school personnel may already be alert to interpersonal and organizational communication issues, business organizations more clearly understand the impact of communication processes on the organizational "bottom line" (i.e., understanding how communication processes affect survivability). Schools do not have the same clear, generally agreed-upon standards of productivity, although the current efforts for national achievement standards and the high emphasis placed on test scores suggest that some stakeholders want more identifiable, unilateral outcomes. In the new millennium, more public pressure will plague schools. The public, especially political and business/industry leaders, indicate that schools should be producing literate, law-abiding citizens who are well prepared to enter the workforce. At the same time, school-based administrators and staff struggle to maintain safe, effective, future-oriented environments. With varied perceptions of productivity and varied goals of stakeholders, communication becomes even more important as diverse actors seek to agree upon reform and restructuring efforts.

Employees' satisfaction is contingent upon the degree of autonomy they experience in doing their jobs; yet organizations are so oriented toward hierarchy that other social and work arrangements have not been considered. The challenge for school administrators is to examine all organizational arrangements for their critical effect on communication processes and for their ultimate effect on schoolchildren, communities, and the future labor force. School administrators are called upon to imagine the unimaginable: new forms of schooling, new visions, new plans, new procedures, and new assessments to measure success.

Earlier in this chapter, historical roots of organizational communication theory were noted, and several authors were cited extensively for their comprehensive coverage of communication phenomena, theory, and research, especially in relation to school organizations. These are retrospective summaries, and while much of what is discussed is still operative in today's organizations, the future of organizational communication still can advance dramatically. Organizations and organizational leaders need to create that future consciously, not by tradition or default.

Educators are particularly interested in long-term goals and often view the short, hectic cycles of business planning, particularly in regard to demands for trained personnel, with some alarm. At the same time, the positivistic, linear, cause-and-effect thinking of business organizations may be attractive to school administrators who must also find or create order in the midst of organizational chaos. Possibly neither private- nor public-sector paradigms and practices will suffice in the turbulent future. There is a growing discomfort in all sectors with "the way things are presently done." This discomfort may also refer to the way "things" are conceptualized. Nowhere is there a more important necessity than to understand fully how communication affects our organizations. Both internal and external communication helps to shape "realities." If school administrators wish to emphasize achievement scores at the cost of emphasizing an understanding of learning styles and paces, they may report achievement test scores to their staff as a motivation or evaluation measure. If school administrators focus on these scores in their district newsletter, they have communicated their emphasis externally. External feedback may begin to pressure and shape internal realities: curriculum, scheduling, and methodology.

Able administrators need to analyze and interpret their personal frames of reference, their metaphors, beliefs, and biases about organizations and organizational communication. Are they finite, firmly bounded scientific management systems using finite control mechanisms? Are they open, dynamic, holographic, reenacting systems using multiple variety stimulation/regulation strategies? Whichever the case, administrators and teachers alike must be able to understand their own preferences and how their beliefs affect practice.

Synthesizing Known Principles of Organizational Communication

As discussed above, there is general agreement that communication is (1) purposive, (2) sociopsychological, (3) carried in both formal and informal channels, and (4) incomplete without feedback. There is still disagreement, however, about the importance of information theory in sociopsychological approaches. In essence, all the approaches to organizational communication can make valid claims to definitions of communication because multiple perspectives and frames of reference are inevitable. By the same token, all of the approaches described can be challenged because they do not incorporate all possible perspectives or account for all possible communication variables. A more comprehensive understanding and use of general systems theory may help to integrate multiple perspectives and accommodate richer mixes of variables. This integrative theory building seems to be a task for the future.

Message sending and receiving skills are so important (Haugland, 1987) that procedural models have been devised to help the communicator. Khandwalla's (1987) model suggests a front-end analysis to include (1) determining the objective of the message, and (2) analyzing the situational variables, including available channels, best media, time constraints, and the nature of recipients. In this model, the communicator seeks to anticipate potential communication difficulties and devise strategies for overcoming them. At a minimum, words and phrases that are likely to be emotional triggers are avoided, and calls to action are crafted and understood as a collective enterprise rather than like military commands. The message sender thinks about potential miscommunication ef-

fects, even though there is no guarantee that negative effects will not occur. The school administrator will find that messages encouraging participation are generally well received, but that, by tradition, some organization members will expect and even welcome the military command. Steering through the mine fields of individual differences is never easy and is always a situational judgment call. From the perspective of a knowledgeable administrator whose primary communication goals are to maintain organizational status quo, the ever-active balancing of forces in an organization can prevent poor judgments from destroying positive organizational climate.

Employees and client groups want straight answers, straight information, and candid talk from their leaders (Ragan, 1990), even though there is often no agreement about what exactly ought to be communicated. Constituents reflect both a fear of communication and a fear of candor, but a fear of the unknown is far more unsettling (Wartenberg, 1990). The atmosphere of "waiting to find out" is an atmosphere of skepticism, insecurity, and cynicism. This leads lower-level stakeholders to engage in counterproductive speculations or self-preservation tactics. On such occasions, messages in informal communication channels can be organizationally destabilizing. The old adage that some news, however unpleasant, is better than no news remains true in organizational communication. Using "leaks," opinion leaders, and increased face-to-face communication can help educational administrators relieve the tension in such a situation. By openly accepting feedback from all parts of the organization, the administrator can build the unity and health of the organization. Some of the imperatives for effective communication are discussed next.

The amount of redundancy and feedback, along with the amount of face-to-face communication needed, is situationally dependent. Giving short, concise messages or addressing problems of organizational climate are occasions for face-to-face communication, whereas delivering messages that require an understanding of background or context may best be accomplished in writing. There may be considerable value in communicating in both ways at the same time.

Personal skill and planning are essential for giving and receiving useful feedback. For positive effect, feedback should be helpful. It should be very specific and descriptive, accompanied by examples if possible. It should be given by someone who is perceived as trustworthy, should be timely, and should be presented in such a way that the receiver feels confident to do something about the situation. However, it should be noted that feedback is not automatic and often not voluntary; it may need to be pursued. Feedback consists of verbal and nonverbal messages that may or may not be congruent. It may even consist of misleading information that is meant to be tactful. Misleading information may also be used as a manipulative strategy by a person who fears for survival in a given organization.

The filtering of messages in all directions remains a serious problem in the communication process. If open and complete honesty is a threatening condition for either school leaders or followers, the filtering process can close down cooperation and yield erroneous messages. If open communication can prevail, subordinates can use it to get their work done with satisfaction, and leaders will have reliable sources of information to enable them to avert organizational problems. A positive organizational climate is the outcome of open communication. Miller (1978) cautioned, however, that even in the preferred channel-and-network arrangement of organizational communication, the relay nodes are also potential bottlenecks. He also notes the obvious: the longer the channels, the slower the flow of information.

Educational administrators serve organizational and personal interests well if they can devise a number of different ways to encourage upward and horizontal communication.

One successful method has been the use of "linchpin" or liaison structures, where a person who communicates in two or more separate communication networks is deliberately charged with transferring information upward, downward, and horizontally across groups. Such linchpins can transcend a number of hierarchical levels. Another linking method is the formation of communications matrices where each educational staff member participates in at least two formal subsystems (e.g., instructional and schoolwide). One should be warned, however, that these communication strategies are effective only as long as trusting relationships are maintained. Any serious breach of trust can take years to repair since many layers of the communication network are damaged simultaneously when trust is breached in one area of the network.

Boundary spanning roles, either formal or informal, can be established to help individuals or groups to form communication links with their environments. The triangulation principle applies here: Multiple and independent sources of information provide data about matters that may not be researchable in any direct fashion. Creating overlapping and redundant information systems can be a means to overcome the possibility that some gatekeepers, liaisons, or isolates may misuse the power inherent in their position. In this connection even isolates have power, for either by their voluntary withdrawal or by their involuntary job demands they may block projects on which they are genuinely needed. Assigning isolates to task groups and altering job assignments to allow them to participate may enable the organization to draw on their skills and experience effectively. Leadership is a social act. Understanding the roles of groups and isolates and altering their roles via selective communication modes is the responsibility of the school leader. Schools are social by nature and mission. Whether tasks need to be performed or commitment won, school leaders are necessarily bound to act on their awareness of the effects of social interaction.

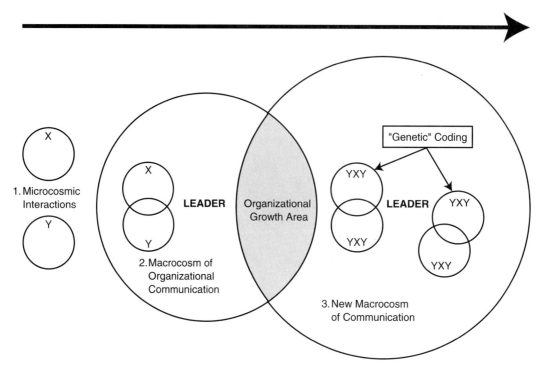

Figure 5.2
Organic migration and enlargement of microcosmic interactions in organizational communication

Combining the Metaphors

Returning to the sets of metaphors and assumptions cited earlier in this chapter, it becomes clear that some metaphors are more helpful than others for exploring new forms of organization and new requirements for organizational communication. The machine metaphor has already been labeled problematic. Therefore, the heavy burden for productivity also moves from the shoulders of humankind to the electronic databases that support human thinking and information processing. The organization possesses machine-based components of organizational communication but is not itself a machine.

The organization-as-organism model is still feasible and supports the idea that human be-

ings and their interactions are microcosms of the organizations that they create around themselves. The holographic metaphor extends this idea. "Common cultural assumptions in an organization could be thought of as genetic codes that permit reconstruction of the whole from any part" (Schein, 1989, p. 12). The reference to genes as cellular reproductive microcosms of whole organizations is both biological in functioning and holographic in image. Organizational communication can be depicted similarly, as shown in Figure 5.2.

The organic model overlaps with the cultural–anthropological model but moves the focus from individual organism or organization to the organization as a culture embedded in a larger culture. The communication emphasis shifts accordingly, with cultural transmission be-

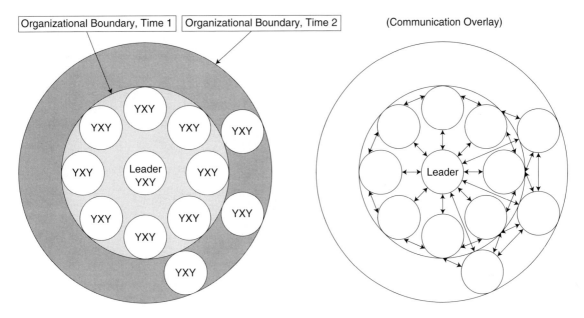

Figure 5.3
Culture-coded (YXY) organizational parts in systemic relationship, with organizational communication overlay

coming its primary rationale. This perspective supports the mores of particular organizations and may even legitimize leaders as organizational gurus even though a culture may be expected to change over time (see Figure 5.3).

Psychological metaphors remind organizational communication specialists that no two human beings send, receive, perceive, or interpret data—even sensory data—in exactly the same way. Human psychological uniqueness intrudes on every formulation of organizational communication. These claims cannot be denied and must be taken into account in modeling (see Figure 5.4).

The metaphor of the organization as brain permits analogies of computerlike information processing, much less dependent on structures and organizational layering for productive activity. It also allows for continuous research, action, and research. The difficulty some have with this metaphor is that it is easily confused with leader

as brain of the organization. No such idea is intended. Rather, the brain metaphor is meant to convey a broader, more holistic, more versatile picture of organizational thought and activity.

Organization as art easily allows the interpretation of organizational communication as a selective repertoire of plastic arts and media. Communication then becomes drama, painting and drawing, sculpting, prose or poetry, oration, conversation, or any other art form that conveys meaning throughout the organization. Art that is hung throughout corporate and other executive offices may be a minor acknowledgment of this point of view.

The metaphor of organization as learner shares many elements with the metaphor of organization as organism, brain, or art form. This metaphor optimistically represents a human organization acting as a cooperative learning community that thinks, feels, performs, values, and adjudicates its own work and its relation to

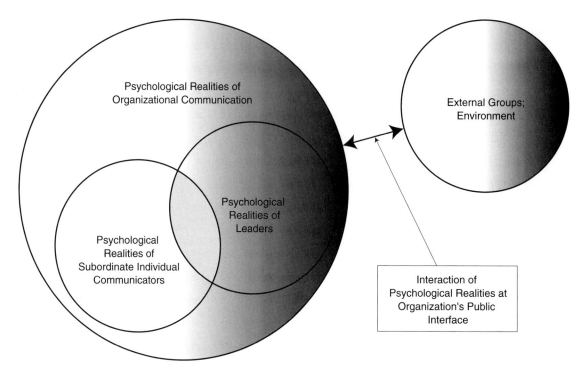

Figure 5.4
Psychological impacts of organizational communication

human life at every level of the organization. In many ways, it requires that informed systems erase the image of people as production machines and insists on a restored image of people as perpetually learning, growing, exchanging, and caring about those exchanges in both the personal and organizational sense. Communication modeling for such holographic, artistic, learning–growing models can be only rudimentary at this time (see Figure 5.5).

People need to breathe to live. So do organizations composed of living human beings. Metaphorically, communication becomes the "breath" of the organization, enabling its electronic and human systems to work in concert, to reach outside the organization, and, perhaps, to work with a new sense of craftsmanship. In an ailing organization, an administrator with a clear understanding of the stakeholders' mission

can provide the life-support system to sustain the breath of the organization. That life support needs attentive monitoring, constant updating, and vision changing. This life-support role may be the opportunity for an administrator to exercise a leadership role.

Moving Forward: Potential New Directions

Greenfield (1987) states that the top-down leadership style is characteristic of educational institutions. This style reduces distortion but also strangles organizational communication in the participative sense and drains creative energy away from the system. The limitations this style imposes on upward communication are resented by self-confident, self-directed professionals, and in school systems, even resented by

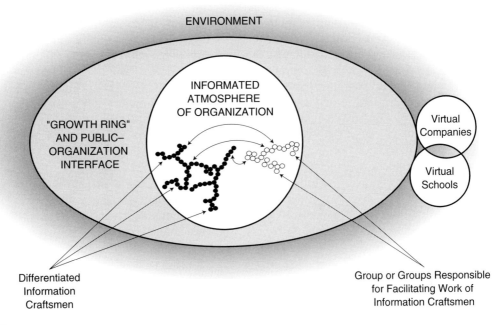

Figure 5.5
Informed atmosphere of organizational communication: the breath of organizational life

students, who receive the most filtered information of all. Fortunately, educational leadership styles appear to be shifting in the direction of greater openness, with greater sharing of information and problem solving occurring between levels.

Educational administrators have the opportunity to set a cooperative tone for the entire organization and can deliberately model the behaviors that they want to see in others. They can identify and correct chronic blocks and distortions in communication networks and, if pertinent, establish new channels and networks as well. As open-door administrators, they should be willing to listen thoughtfully and be ready to go the "extra mile" to value others as persons and as senders and receivers of messages. Instructor involvement in the organization itself—and not just in the classrooms—is crucial to organizational success. The annals of educational administration are strewn with the wreckage

caused by lack of such involvement. It should be acknowledged that it is a great deal to ask of both teachers and administrators to be involved organizationally in addition to their heavy work schedules; however, such involvement is an enabler for positive change and greater work satisfaction.

To be an instructional leader means to be concerned at least as much about instruction and learning as about organizational policies, rules, and regulations. If instructors do not see evidence of this concern, whatever else an administrator may say or do will be received skeptically. The administrator is immediately relegated to the role of a mundane manager. A powerful and probably unintended message has been communicated.

If it seems that the role of educational administrator is becoming too enormous to be embraced by a single person, this may have occurred because new roles are adopted without eliminating older ones. Since many schools operate structurally as they did in the early twentieth century, restructuring efforts that clarify the administrator's leadership role may diminish the conflict between roles. The current enormity of the school administrator's role is a result of administrators trying to manage and lead at the same time. In each role, mixed messages are sent within and outside the organization; it is no wonder that communication becomes muddled. Informated stakeholders may need translators for their twenty-first century counterparts who seek organizations the "way they were" at the turn of the century. In a book based on 10 years of intensive academic and field research, Zuboff (1988) suggested that leaders tend to rejustify their "right to rule" whenever sweeping social changes call previous justifications into question. In the informated society (Schuck, 1985; Zuboff, 1988), organizations cannot rely on twentieth-century justifications. They must not only respond effectively to changes in their image, or symbolic environment (Krippendorff & Eleey, 1986), but also alter their views about how information and work are distributed.

Those who interact with information on a real-time basis (e.g., those who are "in the trenches" of teaching or those who work with core databases) use intellectual skills that are not different from those required elsewhere in the organization. It is the contexts that vary. In this model the justifications for hierarchy begin to erode and the emphasis shifts from "acting for" or "acting on" to "acting with." All members of the organization are engaged in data interpretation, since there are more data than can be gathered from or consigned to any one area or any one cadre of leaders. Therefore, it follows logically that communication becomes multidirectional. Some communication events are task-oriented and linear. Some are global/vision-oriented and definitely nonlinear.

Zuboff (1988) noted that organizational emphasis on wholeness causes leaders and many employees to feel disoriented initially. Changes in the distribution of authority are frightening.

The level of involvement and commitment required in a new, flexible organization is daunting. There are implications for social integration that many fear are a precursor to the loss of individual rights. The fact is that while top-down regimes allow for little creativity, they also protect members from ambiguity. Different people have different thresholds for enjoying, tolerating, or breaking apart under conditions of ambiguity. This is not a slight concern to new organization planners.

New divisions of learning based on the premise that learning is the new work of organizations are at the heart of the posthierarchical organization. In such organizations, the new leadership role that Zuboff (1988) described is facilitative, teacherlike, and very vulnerable. The new risk is needing constantly to admit that one does not have all the answers and that the answers where they exist at all may be found only by cooperative action. The new leaders in schools, as in other organizations, will need to be concerned about intellectual skill development, technology development, strategy formulation, and social system development. However, they cannot actually control any of these in the old sense of giving orders and being sure of specific action. The new leaders can only orchestrate opportunities to promote community and to develop communication skills throughout the organization.

Playing this different role imposes new communication imperatives. Optimal communication in the formal bureaucracies have been regarded as two-way, but in an informated organization, two ways are not enough. In the informated organization an explosion of information is available to everyone. The communication questions become how to share, interpret, and feed back information at specific points and times to specific places in the organization when it is needed. Communication in this sense becomes interdependent and fluid. At least some measure of skill homogeneity is implied. Another implication is that a higher baseline of entry-level communication skills may be required of the leader. Communication in the informated organization changes the internal functioning of the organization itself and so changes the environmental expectations of the organization.

Educational administrators may personally either reject or accept the possibilities and challenges of inviting new forms of organization and new requirements for communication. The initial stages of new paradigms have always been ignored. Many are already thinking and writing seriously about such organizational changes and can scarcely be ignored. At present, school leaders are already trying to manage complexity, perhaps with old ideas and tools, and quite possibly, with less than perfect success. Life has changed dramatically in the last few decades; schools have not. The lack of change has trapped administrators in structures that were designed to be successful in another age. The popular image of a successful "little red schoolhouse" is equally inadequate today considering emerging circumstances. Only risktakers who are willing to envision and create new school structures have an opportunity to develop a successful model appropriate for the future.

CASE STUDY

Communication Paralysis

The day after a community forum, Superintendent John Shapiro immediately scheduled an emergency meeting with his most trusted staff. He felt that his ongoing promotion of a revitalized school environment was being derailed. He feared that community leaders were upset with the distinct lack of progress. Parents continued to be confrontational, complaining about calls for higher teacher pay and school district needs. Student achievement scores were, at best, barely average in the community. Lately, even his own teachers had begun to organize. They objected to the added expectations and responsibilities assigned to them and complained that they received too little freedom of action, too many unidirectional policy decisions, and little incentive to change.

At the staff meeting, Superintendent Shapiro expressed his concerns. "Thank you for making room in your schedules for this meeting. This morning, I want to open new lines of dialogue. It appears we've reached an impasse. Last night's forum meeting was a disaster, as everyone here can attest, and I'm not going to sit still and watch this happen." His voice became distraught.

"I certainly don't understand the massively negative reactions to the reform effort. At last month's forum meeting, I thought that we had made dramatic inroads and that the new third-wave school program was really taking shape. Last night, parents were relentless in their opposition to the new district budget. I also heard rumors that a small group of teachers are becoming vocal dissenters to the program. They'll probably raise union issues again. Worse than that, after the meeting, I was approached by the mayor." At this point his voice rose an octave. He even got up and began pacing as he spoke. "The mayor said that he was considering removing his support for the whole project until we get the teachers aligned. He was adamant! He said I'd better get our teachers on board now or the funding for the project would dry up permanently. For all I know, they've probably got the funds earmarked for his reelection campaign."

Superintendent Shapiro paused, returned to his seat, and spoke again more calmly. "I thought the project was really taking shape. We need to set a course and patch this up. I'm sure many of you felt some of this resistance too. Any thoughts?"

Assistant Superintendent Michelle Glazer said, "John, I didn't read last night's meeting like that at all. I talked with several parents. They were all upbeat. Even Paul Tracy, the city controller, stopped by to talk. He and I had a long discussion about funding possibilities for the project. We discussed a couple of new and really promising avenues that he said he would call me about. He wanted to form a small discussion group to explore them more fully. In all, I found the whole agenda and reaction last evening very open and enlightening. Don't let the mayor or those more vocal teachers dampen your spirit. Listen to their reaction as a means to learn from them and keep going."

"I also spoke with Paul and he did have some interesting ideas about budgeting for the project," the superintendent replied. "Charlie, how did you assess the meeting?"

"I wasn't at all concerned, John," said Charlie Frantz, the human resources director, in a matter-of-fact tone. "As we all know, there are numerous variables that surround this project, and I didn't see that the meeting was any different from past meetings. We'll always be confronting issues like this and even more in the third-wave system. I did hear a similar rumor. The mayor is running scared. How about you, Diane, did you read this any differently?"

Diane Hall, a training consultant working with the district, said to the superintendent in a conciliatory tone, "I think Charlie is on the right track, John. You all know that this project has been controversial from the start. Everyone has an opinion about this project and is operating from his or her own beliefs. Overcoming that diversity is difficult. Do you remember a month or so ago when I suggested we consider developing in-service training of our teachers? Perhaps this is an important opportunity for us. They're on the firing line constantly and, at the same time, they're the most important asset we've got. We need to communicate and share our beliefs about the program with them and improve our overall communication patterns."

"I've thought about this for some time now." Diane became more intent. "Perhaps we could develop some additional seminars for the upcoming district retreat in the fall. These seminars could improve our overall organizational communication. After all, how we communicate is our life's breath. What do you think? I could outline rough drafts of

seminar work over the next month and pass around copies for each of you to look at."

The meeting went on for another hour. Diane obtained approval to develop the in-service training objectives more fully. Over the next several weeks while preparing drafts, she began thinking more critically about the aims of the seminars. She had done a fair amount of research in her doctoral studies about communication. She knew that the seminars would be explosive if the teachers perceived the new training to be just another quick fix for the school district's problems. She knew that the teachers needed an active voice in the district's affairs.

What could she include in the training seminars beyond the idea of communication as problem solving, as focused on change, or as empowerment? How could new communications methods reshape and unite the district's teachers? What other internal and external strengths and constraints were important?

Perplexed

Over a month had passed and Diane found herself more confused. After an extensive literature review, she had not been able to address the important gaps that existed between theory and practice at the school district. She knew more about organizational communication and had defined the district's needs. However, she still was not able to devise an in-service training program that would address the needs of the group and also serve the school district well into the new third-wave implementation. The two seemed diametrically opposed.

Discussion

Setup: Describe possible characteristics for the school district discussed above. Then identify a possible change project for the district that you have described.

Tasks:

1. Given the setup that you have established, develop a set of objectives for the communi-

cations training program for teachers and principals in this district. Plan for a year's training.

2. In what ways will your training program help the district to implement its change project? In what ways will it not be helpful?

3. Develop a plan to communicate the district's change plan and its rationale:

   a. To the staff

   b. To the community

4. In your communication plan, what parts are to be played by:

   a. The superintendent

   b. Middle managers and principals

   c. Teachers

   d. Community members

   Why?

5. Assume that you are presenting your proposals for the communications training plan and publicity plan to the district supervisory board for funding. What information is available in this chapter to help you to explain your intent? To help convince the board to fund your proposals?

References

Allen, D. (1994). *Training directors in communication for the rehearsal process:* A pilot study. Unpublished dissertation, Texas Tech University, Lubbock.

Argyris, C., & Schön, D. A. (1978). *Organizational learning: A theory of action perspective.* Reading, MA: Addison-Wesley.

Baeshen, N. (1987). *The effect of organizational communication on the middle and lower-level managers' participation in the decision-making process in Saudi Arabia.* Unpublished doctoral dissertation, University of Arizona, Tucson.

Barnard, C. (1938). *The function of the executive.* Cambridge, MA: Harvard University Press.

Berelson, B., & Steiner, G. (1964). *Human behavior: An inventory of scientific findings.* New York: Harcourt & Brace.

Berlo, D. K. (1960). *The process of communications.* New York: Holt, Rinehart & Winston.

Campbell, D. E., & Campbell, T. A. (1988, March). A new look at informal communication: The role of the physical environment. *Environment and Behavior, 20*(2), 211.

Carnevale, A. P., & Gainer, L. J. (1989). *The learning enterprise.* Alexandria, VA: American Society for Training and Development and U.S. Department of Labor.

Cragan, J. F., and Shields, D. C. (1995). *Symbolic theories in applied communication research.* Cresskill, NJ: Hampton Press.

Daft, R. L., & Lengel, R. H. (1984). Information richness: A new approach to managerial behavior and organizational design. *Research in Organizational Behavior, 6,* 195–198.

Dance, F. E. X. (1970). The "concept" of communication. *Journal of Communication, 20,* 201–210.

Donellon, A. G., Gray, B., & Bougon, M. G. (1986, March). Communication, meaning, and organized action. *Administrative Science Quarterly, 31*(1), 43–55.

Etzioni, A. (1964). *Modern organizations.* Upper Saddle River, NJ: Prentice Hall.

Farace, R. V., Monge, P. R., & Russell, H. (1977). *Communicating and organizing.* Reading, MA: Addison-Wesley.

Fisher, A. (1978). *Perspectives of human communication.* New York: Macmillan.

Fredrickson, M. P. (1991). *Design juries: A study in lines of communication.* Unpublished dissertation, University of California, Los Angeles.

Hall, R. H. (1991). *Organizations: Structure, processes and outcomes* (5th ed.). Upper Saddle River, NJ: Prentice Hall.

Haugland, M. (1987, Fall). Professional competencies needed by school superintendents, as perceived by school board members in South Dakota. *Spectrum, 5*(4), 40–42.

Helgeson, S. (1990). *The female advantage: Women's ways of leadership.* New York: Doubleday/Currency.

Hellriegel, D., Slocum, J., & Woodman, R. (1986). Interpersonal communication. In *Organizational behavior* (4th ed.) New York: West.

Hentges, K., Yaney, J., & Shields, C. (1990). Training and motivating the new labor force: The impact of ethnicity. *Performance Improvement Quarterly, 3*(3), 36–44.

Hoy, W., & Miskel, C. (1987). Communication. In *Educational administration: Theory, research, and practice* (3rd ed., pp. 356–381). New York: Random House.

Kanter, R. M. (1989, November–December). The managerial work. *Harvard Business Review* (Reprint 85-92).

Kefalas, A. (1977). Organizational communications: A systems viewpoint. In R. Huseman, C. Logue, & D. Freshley (Eds.), *Readings in interpersonal and organizational communication* (3rd ed., pp. 25–43). Boston: Allyn & Bacon.

Khandwalla, P. (1987). Communication processes. In *The design of organizations*. New York: Harcourt Brace.

Kovacic, B. (Ed.). (1997). *Emerging theories of human communication*. Albany, NY: State University of New York Press.

Krippendorff, K., & Eleey, M. F. (1986, Spring). Monitoring a group's symbolic environment. *Public Relations Review, 12*(1), 13–36.

Krivonos, P. (1982). Distortion of subordinate to superior communication in organizational settings. *Central States Speech Journal, 33*(1), 335–352.

Lengel, R. H., & Daft, R. L. (1988, August). The selection of communication media as an executive skill. *Academy of Management Executive, 2*(3), 225–232.

Lewin, K. (1951). *Field theory in social science*. New York: Harper.

Likert, R. (1967). *The human organization*. New York: McGraw-Hill.

Lipham, J. M., & Francke, D. C. (1966). Nonverbal behavior of administrators. *Educational Administration Quarterly, 2,* 101–109.

Littlejohn, S. W. (1989). *Theories of human communication* (3rd ed.). Belmont, CA: Wadsworth.

Marsick, V. J. (1990, Spring). Altering the paradigm for theory building and research. *Human Resource Development Quarterly, 1*(1), 5–23, 29–34.

Miller, J. G. (1978). *Living systems*. New York, McGraw-Hill.

Morgan, G. (1986). *Images of organization*. Beverly Hills, CA: Sage.

Murphy, H., & Peck, C. (1980). *Effective business communication*. New York: McGraw-Hill.

O'Reilly, C. A., & Pondy, L. R. (1979). Organizational communication. In S. Kerr (Ed.), *Organizational behavior*. Columbus, OH: Grid.

Pegals, C. C. (1998). *Handbook of strategies and tools for the learning company*. Portland, OR: Productivity Press.

Pacanowsky, M., & O'Donnell-Trujillo. (1982). Organizational communication as cultural performance. *Communication Monographs, 50,* 126–147.

Peters, T. (1992). *Liberation management: Necessary disorganization for the nanosecond nineties*. New York: Knopf.

Philipsen, G., & Albrecht, T. L. (1997). *Developing communications theories*. Albany, NY: State University of New York Press.

Poole, M. S., & McPhee, R. D. (1983). A structurational theory of organizational climate. In L. Putnam & M. Pacanowsky (Eds.), *Organizational communication: An interpretive approach*. Beverly Hills, CA: Sage.

Ragan, L. (1990, May–June). The great debate. *Communication World, 7*(6), 85–87.

Reitz, H. J. (1987). Communications. In *Behavior in organizations* (3rd ed., pp. 301–330). Homewood, IL: Irwin.

Schein, E. (1989, May). Corporate teams and totems. *Across the Board, 26,* 12–17. (reprinted from *Sloan Management Review,* Winter 1989).

Schuck, G. (1985, Autumn). Intelligent technology, intelligent workers: A new pedagogy for the high-tech workplace. *Organizational Dynamics, 14*(2), 66–79.

Shockley-Zalabak, P. (1988). *Fundamentals of organizational communication*. New York: Longman.

Sigband, N., & Bell, A. (1989). Communication in organizations. In *Communication for management and business* (5th ed., pp. 23–51). Glenview, IL: Scott, Foresman.

Simon, H. A. (1957). *Administrative behavior* (2nd ed.). New York: Free Press.

Smith, S. C., & Piele, P. K. (Eds.). (1989). *School leadership: Handbook for excellence*. Eugene, OR: ERIC University of Oregon.

Stephens, M. (1989, March 27). Wired: How PC networks are changing the way we work. *Infoworld, 11*(13), 41–46.

Striplin, P. (1987). An exploratory study of teachers' opinions to important competencies needed by principals to perform effectively as instructional leaders (Doctoral dissertation, Florida State University, 1987). *Dissertation Abstracts International, 48,* 12A.

Wartenberg, M. R. (1990, June). How to merge—and survive. *Management Review, 79*(6), 64.

Watkins, K. (1989). Five metaphors: Alternative theories for human resource development. In D. Gradous (Ed.), *Systems theory applied to human resource development* (Theory to Practice Monograph). Minneapolis, MN: University of Minnesota Training and Development Research Center and American Society for Training and Development Research Committee.

Weick, K. (1969). *The social psychology of organizing.* Reading, MA: Addison-Wesley.

Wiener, N. (1954). *The human use of human beings: Cybernetics and society.* Garden City, NY: Doubleday/Anchor.

Yukl, G. A. (1989). *Leadership in organizations* (2nd ed.). Upper Saddle River, NJ: Prentice Hall.

Zuboff, S. (1988). *In the age of the smart machine.* New York: Basic Books.

CHAPTER 6

Human Relations

The Base for Educational Leadership

Concerns about educational leadership have increased in recent years. This attention is, in part, related to the role that principals and superintendents play in achieving excellence in education. In its 1987 report *Leaders for America's Schools,* the National Commission on Excellence in Educational Administration (Griffiths, Stout, & Forsyth, 1988) claimed that efforts to achieve excellence in education "cannot be successful without strong, well-reasoned leadership from principals and superintendents" (p. 6). Other recent reviews of school effectiveness reveal that principals and superintendents can and must help schools achieve excellence (Mangieri, 1985; Sergiovanni, 1991).

Calls for strong leadership in the search for educational excellence in public schools have been argued frequently (Berney & Ayers, 1990; Duignan & Macpherson, 1992; Guthrie & Reed, 1991; Kouzes & Posner, 1987; Maxcy, 1991; Reavis & Griffith, 1992; Schlechty, 1990; Sergiovanni & Moore, 1989). Schlechty states: "Educators and citizens who value the American system of education, and who believe, as I do, that excellence in public education is directly linked to excellence in all other areas of social life in a democracy, have a special interest in ensuring that the leaders of American education, unlike the leaders of the railroad industry, get their business right before it is too late" (p. 151).

In addition, the search for strong educational leadership has been echoed simultaneously by public expectations for schools. With increasing global competition, our expectations of public

schools are rising. Schools are perceived as places where human potential can be increased by raising levels of thought, knowledge, skills, and socialization. These expectations for schools require that educational leaders provide strong leadership to improve the quality of schooling and raise student achievement to new levels. Thus, as the 1980s and 1990s have become the era of reform, leadership correspondingly has been summoned to fulfill the new expectations—excellence.

This faith in the power of leadership and in its potential to make a difference in schools underlies much of the literature on leadership for educational excellence. The literature reveals that leaders in competent schools are skilled in managerial, instructional, and interpersonal tasks. In this era of excellence, more demands exist; school leaders must shape values, develop vision, create meanings, and develop unique culture based on their moral values (Sergiovanni, 1984, 1991, 1992). Like other organizational domains, school leadership must not only "do the things right" but also "do the right things." In goal-driven organizations, complex human interactions necessitate that educational constituencies, superintendents, principals, teachers, students, and community partners alike have a clear understanding of human nature and human behavior patterns—hence the necessity to understand human relations.

Excellence must also be matched by a broad social and technical appreciation of the educational environment. Individual leaders and followers interact across a wide variety of roles and activities. In this interactive and interdependent environment it is imperative that the study of human relations be investigated in a more open framework. As opposed to traditional inquiry, inquirers today must explore these larger contexts. Exploration of these larger contexts acknowledges the importance of reality and the variety in reality that leads to further understanding. Similarly, as other authors posit, the study of educational leadership should incorporate an action perspective in which sources of meaning for all members of the educational unit are viewed from a thinking–acting perspective and a theory–practice foundation (Argyris, 1985; Silverman, 1971).

The Development of Human Relations Concepts

Although human relationships have existed since the beginning of time, the art and science of trying to deal with them in the work setting is relatively new. It was not until the second half of the nineteenth century that researchers turned their attention to workers' needs. The evolution of the main concepts of human relations occurred in six stages: (1) classical thinking, (2) systematic development, (3) teaching and practice, (4) refinement, (5) decline, and (6) revolving (Davis, 1967; Sanford, 1977).

The Stage of Classical Thinking (pre-1930s).
This stage is characterized by classical economic theory and the scientific management movement. The proponents of the theory of economic man believe that human behavior is determined by economic needs and economic goals. Human relations is a matter of establishing an incentive that contributes to the necessities of life and replenishment of the workforce. The scientific management movement focuses on increasing efficiency and productivity while drawing attention to the importance of people in the work situation. Taylor (1911), the father of scientific management, was one of the first to

call attention to people in the work situation as an important factor in the quest for efficiency in production. In his view, human problems are what stand in the way of greater productivity. Taylor himself calls for the scientific selection and development of the worker.

Although some scholars (Dennison, 1931; Frankel & Fleisher, 1920; Gantt, 1916; Ure, 1835) emphasize individual human psychological and social needs, their ideas have been accepted slowly or not at all. In contrast, the dominant ideas of classical human relations research tend to view persons employed as a means or as specialized resources. Attempts were made to design bureaucratic structures to overcome the shortcomings of human factors. Practitioners and theorists recognized the importance of people in industries but did not include this more holistic view of humankind. Effective and efficient organizations were characterized as if they were machines. Workers were perceived from an efficiency perspective or as productivity resources.

The Stage of Systematic Development (1930–1950).
Most of the foundation of modern human relations theory and practice developed during this stage. As an early reaction to mechanistic interpretation of organization, Follett (1930) spoke out on the dignity and value of satisfied workers. The works of Mayo (1933) and Roethlisberger and Dickson (1939) at the Hawthorne plant also sparked an early interest in human relations. Findings from the Hawthorne studies indicated that productivity had something to do with social and psychological interactions among human resources. Further studies showed that workers in continuous and close contact create informal social structures that may influence their productive behavior. Various iterations of the Hawthorne studies marked the beginning of the end of reliance on economic concepts as the primary explanation of work motivation and behavior. The study of organizations as social systems in which social needs are the most important motivator of workers became a focus.

To Taylor and his contemporaries, human problems stood in the way of production. However, little attention was paid to this viewpoint. In contrast to Mayo and his colleagues, human problems became a new field of study and an opportunity for progress. While Taylorism increased production by rationalizing it, Mayo and his colleagues sought to increase production by humanizing it.

Another proponent of human relations, Barnard (1938), viewed the organization as a system composed of human beings working cooperatively to reach goals rather than a formally structured impersonal mechanism. Barnard asserted that within every complex organization there are small operating groups interacting that often lead to the creation of informal working relationships and standards within the formal organization. Barnard was clearly ahead of his time, as many years passed before his concepts were taken seriously or practiced.

The Stage of Teaching and Practice (1950–1960).

After the conclusions of the Hawthorne research were disseminated, human relations concepts began to be applied on a significant scale. As a result of the Hawthorne studies, the focus of human relations practice shifted from an economic emphasis to a sociopsychological emphasis. Worker need satisfaction was seen to lead to greater productivity, and the social and psychological needs of the worker were seen as significant determinants of behavior. The expectation was that worker productivity would increase if human relations activity in the organization was attended to and manipulated. Workers would derive greater social and psychological satisfaction as a result.

It was also believed that social satisfaction demands freedom to socialize on the job. Psychological satisfaction could be fulfilled by allowing workers to participate in managerial decisions. This, in turn, would result in greater need satisfaction, resulting in increased performance and higher productivity. Morale, a related concept, also became an interesting research topic. All these concepts reflected an optimistic view of human nature.

Research and theory development in this stage continued. Argyris (1964), Blake and Mouton (1964), Fiedler (1967), Herzberg, Mausner, and Snyderman (1959), Likert (1961), Maslow (1954), McGregor (1960), Porter and Lawler (1968), Tannebaum and Schmidt (1958), and Vroom (1964) were among the most important scholars. They elaborated on human aspects of organization as well as individual needs and motivation.

The Stage of Refinement (1960–1970).

Efforts continued in several arenas, including the development of better theory and improvement in the practice, resulting in a synthesis of human relations theories. Three major theory modifications include Miles's (1975) human resources model, Likert's (1967) supportive model, and Tosi and Hamner's (1974) contingency model.

Miles's human resource model assumes that work is not inherently distasteful and that people want to contribute to meaningful goals. For Miles, the most important matter in organizations is how to make use of untapped human resources. Likert's supportive model emphasizes the supportive climate of the organizational life. A supportive climate ensures that members in an organization will feel a sense of personal worth and importance in all their interactions and relationships with the organization.

Tosi and Hamner's contingency model requires that we explore the organization as a system or unit of behavior composed of subsystems or subunits that have identified boundaries within the system. The behavior of one unit is dependent on its environmental relationship to other subunits and has some control over the consequences desired by the subunit. Individual and group behavior are contingent on four related elements: psychological determinants, organizational determinants, internal organizational characteristics, and environmental characteristics.

The Stage of Decline (1970–1980).

Research in human relations declined after the 1970s as

researchers became interested in other factors. A majority of the theoretical studies in this period focused on leadership roles with reference to leaders rather than on the workers themselves. These studies explored functions, procedures, and the outcomes of human relations activities. A more detailed review of literature reveals that most of the studies and models developed in this period limited themselves to studies of various parts of the leadership process (e.g., communication, planning, decision making, evaluation). No significant attempts were made to construct an integrative framework of human relations.

The Stage of Revolving (1980–Present).   Today it seems apropos to study the phases of successful Japanese management performance and "evolve" through the various applications of Japanese human relations concepts. This period looks critically at the human side of organizations. Ouchi's (1981) Theory Z, which includes quality of work life, collective decision making and responsibility, lifetime employment, implicit control, and quality circles, currently reflects the concepts being explored in the human relations paradigm (Kossen, 1987). Ouchi is credited with having drawn substantial attention during the 1980s to the differences between Japanese and North American styles of management. His models conceptualize organizations that maintain formal and explicit control mechanisms and believe in formal planning, management by objectives, and sophisticated information and accounting systems. Quality circles, groups consisting of rank-and-file workers who exchange information for mutual improvement, began the revival of managerial concern back to workers.

Conceptualizing Human Relations Theories

While the stages above help us to trace the human relations movement, it is also important to understand the conceptual underpinnings of the movement. The human relations movement emphasizes the important roles of human factors in organizations. Researchers define human relations based on the following concepts: optimistic assumptions of human nature, the clinical and ethical dimensions, human needs, human motivation and its roles in human performance, morale, and informal organizations.

Definitions of Human Relations

Efforts have been made to conceptualize human relations from different perspectives. Saltonstall (1959) viewed human relations as the "study of people in action" (p. 3). Saltonstall also saw human relations as the study of people at work, "not only people as individuals but people as members of informal work groups, people as executives in management, people as union members, and people as members of organizations with economic goals" (p. 4).

From the management perspective, Scott (1962) defined human relations operationally as processes of effective motivation of individuals in a given situation to achieve a balanced objective that yields greater satisfaction and helps accomplish organization goals. Concern with human relations promises higher productivity, greater organizational effectiveness, and satisfied employees.

Like Scott, Halloran (1978) defined the term *human relations* as all the interactions that can occur among people, whether they occur in conflict situations or cooperative behaviors. The study of human relations in organizations is the study of how people can work effectively in groups to satisfy both organizational goals and personal needs.

Realizing the complexity of human organizations, Davis (1977) gave a broad explanation of the concept of human relations. Davis explained that the term *human relations* applies broadly to the interaction of people in all types of endeavor, in business, government, social clubs, schools, and homes. Much of this interaction is in work organizations, where people have bonded together in some sort of formal structure to achieve an objective. The human interactions developed are called *employee human relations* or *organizational human relations*. Therefore, human relations is the study of human behavior at work and an effort to take action in operating situations in order to produce better results. Human relations is perceived as the integration of people into a work situation that motivates them to work together productively, cooperatively, and with economic, psychological, and social satisfactions. Human relations has the potential to motivate people in organizations and develop the teamwork that effectively fulfills their needs and achieves organizational objectives.

Optimistic Assumptions of Human Nature

The perceptions of basic human nature vary with the experiences of those addressing this controversial topic. Classical studies tend to adopt the pessimistic view of human nature. Human beings are portrayed as rebellious, greedy, aggressive, and uncooperative. In contrast, human relations embraces an optimistic view. Proponents of this view believe that it is natural for human beings to be self-motivated and self-controlled, although behavioral reactions are influenced by the treatment received from others (Knezevich, 1984).

The optimistic view of human nature emphasizes four aspects: individual differences, the whole person, caused behavior, and human dignity (Davis, 1967, 1977). Davis and others hold that although people have much in common, each person in the world is also individually different. Individual differences require therefore that justice and rightness be determined on a case-by-case basis and not statistically. Davis also maintains that a person's various traits may be studied separately, but in the final analysis, they are all part of one system making up a whole. Similarly, a person's emotional condition is not separate from one's physical condition. Each affects the other.

Psychological studies of human relations indicate that most human behavior is caused by a person's need structure. Behavior is influenced by motivating people to fulfill their needs as they see them. However, people are not motivated by what others think ought to motivate them, but by what they themselves want. More important, human relations emphasizes human dignity. The people in an organization deserve to be treated differently than the other aspects of production. A person's humanness demands that he or she be treated with respect and dignity.

Clinical and Ethical Dimensions

The study of human relations can also be viewed from two other dimensions: a clinical dimension and an ethical dimension. From the clinical dimension, human relations uses tools and data to solve concrete human problems in situations where they occur. Human relations can also be studied from an ethical dimension, on a continuum from an individualistic to a sociological perspective. The former is a conglomeration of ideas pertaining to personal freedom and the preeminence of individual action. The latter is an affirmation of the value of human collaboration and solidarity (Scott, 1962).

The Importance of Human Needs

Human relations theory spotlights the needs of human beings. Human relationists maintain that all people have needs. As classical management study has determined, people cannot survive for long without the primary needs, such as food, drink, sleep, and air to breathe. Yet classical management thought also demonstrates that secondary needs are equally important, especially in daily organizational life. Therefore, we are eager to feel secure, to be with other people, to be respected, and to fulfill our potential. Since these human needs arise from the biological and sociopsychological makeup of individuals, they are significant

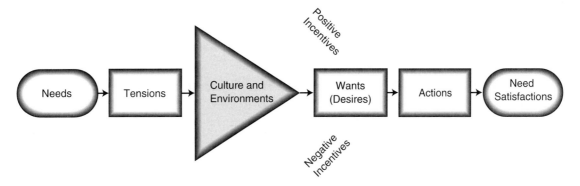

Figure 6.1
Motivation and behavior

elements of human behavior. In practice, most human behaviors are influenced or motivated by human needs.

Human Motivation and Human Behavior

Motivation is a central concept used by human relations thinkers in the explanation of human behavior. They see the terms *motivation* and *behavior* as closely related because human behavior occurs as a result of motivation. However, they also recognize that motivation and behavior are not as synonymous as they may appear. Motivation is only one but probably the most important class of determinants of behavior.

Motivation and behavior are connected through needs and wants (desires) (see Figure 6.1). Needs create tensions that are modified by one's culture or situations to cause certain wants (desires). These wants are interpreted in terms of positive and negative incentives to produce a certain response or action. The action is directed toward the accomplishment or the satisfaction of the needs (Davis, 1967; Halloran, 1978; Sanford, 1977).

Not all needs create tension and result in behavior. At any given point in time people have some needs that are relatively well satisfied, or

at least partially well satisfied, as well as some unsatisfied needs. The satisfied needs do not motivate; the unsatisfied needs are the ones that create tension and motivate behavior.

The Role of Motivation in Performance

In organizational life, the human relations school perceives motivation as one of two major factors that a person contributes to task performance. The other factor is the ability to perform the task. Ability includes the physical and mental skills and the knowledge and experience that a person applies to a task. Motivation is the effort with which ability is applied to a task. Performance is viewed as a function of ability in interaction with motivation (Reitz, 1987):

$$\text{performance} = f(\text{ability} \times \text{motivation})$$

Generally speaking, when people of both low ability and high ability are unwilling to put effort into their performances, the differences in the performances will be minimized. Changes in level of effort make more of a difference in the performance of high-ability people than in low-ability people (Reitz, 1987). Motivation is therefore a vital constituent in terms of organizational behavior.

Morale and Productivity

Morale is one of the important concepts of the human relations school. Morale, a concept closely related to motivation and satisfaction, refers to the atmosphere created by the attitudes of the members of an organization (Reitz, 1987). The human relations school believes that there is a relationship between productivity and morale. Under conditions of poor morale, favorable output is difficult to sustain for long periods. However, good morale does not necessarily cause high productivity. Although it may be an important factor, it is merely one influence on total productivity. For high morale to affect productivity favorably, it must be accompanied by reasonable direction and control. Although morale is not a factor that can be bought or ordered, human relations theorists have warned against underestimating its power.

The Significance of Informal Organizations

One of the most significant and far-reaching conclusions of the Hawthorne studies relates the importance of the informal organization and its relation to the total work situation. The informal organization is a network of personal and social relations not established or required by formal authority but arising spontaneously as people associate with one another. In the formal organization, authority coincides with a position in the structure. Power in the informal organization resides with a person. Since informal organizations exist within formal organizations, the behavior of people in organizations is influenced by the informal as well as formal organization.

Theorists also indicate that informal organizations sometimes create problems for organizations. They transmit false information through the grapevine, resist changes, cause excessive conformity to group norms, and even develop goals that conflict with those of the formal organization. The informal organization, however, also performs a variety of positive and useful functions. It provides most members with the opportunity to satisfy their psychological and social needs. Many of these needs go unsatisfied in the larger formal organization framework.

The Application of Human Relations Concepts

It is worth noting that it is not true that dissatisfied workers will adversely affect productivity. Nor is it true that participation necessarily leads to job satisfaction and productivity.

Human relations management does not imply simply liking people. It is not a belief that workers adversely affect productivity, or that participation leads to job satisfaction and greater productivity. Its major emphasis should be on ways to make workers feel like contributors to worthwhile task accomplishment, and that they are doing something constructive and meaningful about working relationships within the organization. Human relations theorists are not a group of "do-gooders," but work to reduce discrepancies between individuals and their organizations and to channel the remaining discrepancies into constructive results. Human relations does not focus simply on a specific group but on all people within an organization (Argyris, 1957; Davis, 1967; Sanford, 1977).

Theoretical Perspectives of Human Relations

As seen above, research from various disciplines has contributed to the development of numerous usable human relations concepts. Nevertheless, most human relations concepts result from findings in industrial experiments and organizational psychology. Relevant human relations studies and their relation to leadership are summarized into four categories—(1) human nature, (2) human motivation, (3) morale in organizations, and (4) informal organizations—and are examined in the following sections. It should be noted that these studies use the terms *management* (managers) and *leadership* (leaders) interchangeably.

Human Nature

Theory X and Theory Y.   Psychological studies indicate that for the most part, our perception of others determines how we will treat others and respond to them. Our perception is the lens by which we judge and see others (Hall, 1980; Hammond, 1966). McGregor (1960) categorized two distinct lenses that managers use: Theory X and Theory Y. Actually, Theory X and Theory Y contrast the perceptions that classical managerial and human relations thinkers espouse.

Theory X, representing the traditional mechanistic view, assumes the following: (1) the average human being has an inherent dislike of work and will avoid it if he can; (2) because of this human characteristic, most people must be coerced, controlled, directed, and threatened with punishment to get them to put forth adequate effort to achieve organizational objectives; and (3) the average human being prefers to be directed, wishes to avoid responsibility, has relatively little ambition, and wants security above all. McGregor argued that although Theory X provides an explanation of some human behavior in organizations, there are many readily observable phenomena that are not consistent with this view of human nature.

Theory Y, representing the human relations view, provides a distinctly different assumption regarding human nature. It maintains the following: (1) the expenditure of physical and mental effort in work is as natural as play or rest; (2) external control and the threat of punishment are not the only means for bringing about effort toward organizational objectives (people will exercise self-direction and self-control in the service of objectives to which they are committed); (3) commitment to objectives is a function of the rewards associated with their achievement; (4) the average person learns, under proper conditions, not only to accept but to seek responsibility; (5) the capacity to exercise a relatively high degree of imagination, ingenuity, and creativity in the solution of organizational problems is widely, not narrowly, distributed in

the population; and (6) under the conditions of modern industrial life, the intellectual potential of the average person is only partially utilized.

Theory X offers a rationalization for ineffective organizational performance and the nature of the human resource. In contrast, Theory Y suggests that the ineffectiveness of organizational behavior lies in different organizational contexts and processes. The central principle of organization evident in Theory X is direction and control. The principle derived from Theory Y demands that the needs of both the organization and the individual be recognized. McGregor (1960) stated that since external control and direction are appropriate means under certain circumstances, assumptions in Theory Y do not deny the appropriateness of those of Theory X. Theory Y simply shows that Theory X does not apply in all cases.

Pygmalion Leadership.   Research has shown that the selection of an appropriate style of management is a crucial task for managers. The perspective of a lens that filters our perceptions of reality and provides the basis for interpreting our own experiences exerts a powerful influence, as workers may be caught in a self-fulfilling prophecy or Pygmalion effect (Berlew & Hall, 1966; Merton, 1948; Rosenthal, 1974; Rosenthal & Jacobson, 1968). Thus, when managers treat their subordinates as creative, committed, competent people, as in McGregor's Theory Y, and manage accordingly, both the manager and the subordinates will reap the rewards of the self-fulfilling prophecy. When managers vacillate and treat their subordinates as incapable people, subordinates are less likely to perform at their full potential (Duchon, Green, & Taber, 1986; Eden, 1990a; Scandura, Graen, & Novak, 1986). In this scenario, the self-fulfilling prophecy has detrimental effects. Four factors that mediate the Pygmalion effect are socioemotional climate, feedback, input, and output (Brophy, 1985; Rosenthal, 1981). These factors reveal that providing greater warmth, acceptance, and approval, as well as opportunities for challenge on the part of

Figure 6.2
Pygmalion leadership

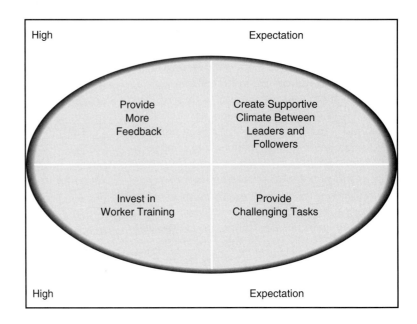

managers, will result in better subordinate performance. The same "magic" is not to be expected, however, if subordinates are treated impersonally with less feedback and challenge.

Leadership plays an important role in mediating the effects of self-fulfilling prophecy in organizations (see Figure 6.2). Pygmalion leadership is the consistent encouragement, support, and reinforcement of high expectations of followers. Pygmalion leadership, according to Eden (1990b), is an approach that leaders may adopt in order to lead their followers toward excellence. Pygmalion leadership can create a supportive climate between leaders and followers through such behaviors as looking the followers in the eye, nodding affirmatively and approvingly, smiling, voicing warmth, and speaking supportively. These behaviors are also the foundational factors of Likert's (1961) principle of supportive relations.

Pygmalion leadership can also provide more feedback. Evaluating followers' performances and letting them know where they stand are leadership acts that make followers aware that someone is observing and monitoring activities. The Pygmalion leader can use many opportuni-

ties in day-to-day interactions to comment on followers' performances, either as compliments or as corrections. Positive feedback maintains good work performances, while negative feedback encourages performance improvement (Komaki, 1986). Pygmalion leadership entails increased investment in workers. Training at every opportunity is thought to foster workers' growth and propel them to higher levels of achievement. Followers are provided with ample opportunity to tackle challenging assignments. Although this leadership style is risky, leaders must determine the real capabilities of their followers. Giving workers opportunities to show what they can do fosters high performance both by expressing high expectations and by allowing excellence to occur (Eden, 1990b).

Pygmalion leadership is effective only when it functions in all four interrelated dimensions, as shown in Figure 6.2. A leader providing continuous feedback to followers will guide them in the right direction with confidence. A leader showing enthusiasm in worker training will find that workers progress well. Thus, increases in expectations become possible. The result of a supportive climate in the organization will be

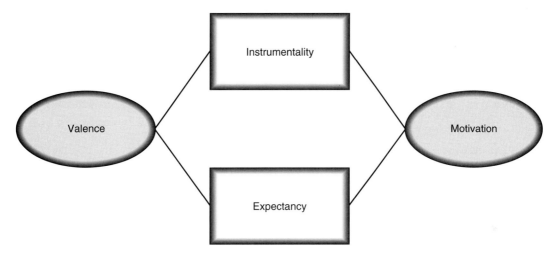

Figure 6.3
Vroom's expectancy model
Source: V. H. Vroom, *Work and motivation,* New York: John Wiley & Sons, Inc., 1964.

mutual respect between leader and followers. This mutual respect enables the followers to put more effort into the job. A leader wishing to provide more challenging tasks can examine the potential of the workers, which is often not fully realized. Challenging tasks upgrade workers' performances and facilitate high expectations.

Human Motivation

Students of human behavior and human motivation have identified two basic types of theoretical models that deal with human motivation in organizations: process models and content models (J. D. Campbell & Pritchard, 1983). Process models explore how and why motivation generally works. Content models deal with what specifically motivates people.

Process Models

Among the several different process models of motivation are the expectancy model, the behaviorist model, and the social learning model.

Expectancy Models.   Expectancy models are derived principally from Tolman's (1932) cognitive theory and Lewin's (1938) field theory. Expectancy models suggest that the motivation to perform a task is a function of a person's expectations or beliefs about effort, performance, and outcomes. Vroom's expectancy model and the Porter and Lawler model are two widely used expectancy models that explain human motivation.

Vroom (1964) contended that motivation is a function of three factors: (1) the strength or desirability of the goal, (2) the perceived ability to exhibit the required behavior, and (3) the perceived probability that the behavior will result in goal achievement (see Figure 6.3).

Motivation is the product of how strongly one desires something and one's perception of the probability that certain strategies or instrumentalities are likely to fulfill those desires. Vroom called the intensity of the personal desire *valence,* and the achievement probability by pursuing a given strategy, *expectancy.*

Vroom's expectancy model has been replicated and refined numerous times (Dachler & Mobley, 1973; Feldman, Reitz, & Hiterman,

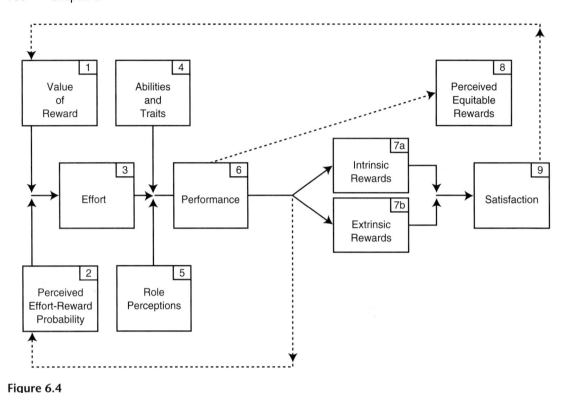

Figure 6.4
Porter–Lawler model of motivation

Source: L. W. Porter, and E. E. Lawler, *Managerial attitudes and performance* (p. 165). Homewood, IL: Irwin, 1968. Copyright 1968 by Richard D. Irwin. Reprinted by permission.

1976; Porter & Lawler, 1968). Porter and Lawler developed a more complete and complex expectancy model by investigating the relationship between satisfaction and productivity. They suggested that the effort a person puts into work depends on (1) the value one places on the expected reward, and (2) the likelihood that the reward actually will be received if the effort is made.

This process is completed in three steps (see Figure 6.4). First, the worker assigns some value to the possible reward for performing work. Based on this performance, the person expects to receive a fair reward and is then rewarded either intrinsically or extrinsically. Finally, this process is completed with two feedback loops. One results from the person's perception of the likelihood that effort will actually yield the expected reward. The other feedback loop results from the person's judgment as to the value of the rewards obtained. The Porter and Lawler model suggests that performance leads to satisfaction and that the level of satisfaction obtained shapes future effort to perform (Owens, 1987).

Path–goal theory is a leadership theory that utilizes the expectancy model. Path–goal theory, as developed, includes four differing behavioral styles to influence employee satisfaction, the employees' acceptance of the leader, and employee beliefs that effort can result in performance and that performance will result in deserved rewards (House & Mitchell, 1974).

The four styles of leadership derived from expectancy theory are directive, supportive, participative, and achievement oriented. Path–goal theory assumes that leaders are capable of exhibiting more than one of those styles, depending on the circumstances. In whatever situation, the exhibition of the leadership style should (1) recognize and arouse employee needs and attempt to increase the payoff to employees for successful performance when it occurs, (2) attempt to influence subordinates' expectancy beliefs by assisting with the accomplishment of difficult tasks and clarifying vague task assignments, and (3) make the distribution of rewards contingent on the successful accomplishment of work.

Behaviorist Models.   Origins of the behaviorist model can be traced back to 1910 and the behavioral approach advocated by Watson. Watson (1930) limited the behaviorist approach to acts that can reliably be observed, what a person says or does. The model, elaborated by Skinner (1953, 1971, 1974), in use today follows that tradition. The behaviorist model is based on two simple assumptions. First, behavior is essentially determined by the environment through basic reinforcement processes: environmental stimuli, behavioral responses, and outcomes (S-R-O). Second, human behavior, like the behavior of physical and chemical elements, is subject to certain laws. Human behavior can be modified through reinforcement.

Behaviorist models question the concept of internal motivation that implies internal causal force that cannot be observed directly (Luthans & Otteman, 1977). Instead, according to behaviorists, people are motivated by external events called *reinforcers,* and through positive and negative reinforcement processes (Skinner, 1974). Both positive and negative reinforcements strengthen the probability that a behavior is likely to occur. Positive reinforcement increases behavior frequency by the application of some circumstances, while negative reinforcement decreases behavior frequency by the removal of some circumstances that were previously part of the environmental context. By definition, negative reinforcement is not punishment. It aims at decreasing, not increasing, behavior occurrence. Behaviorist models indicate that the timing of rewards is often more important than their magnitude. Immediate rewards can affect performance more effectively than larger delayed rewards, while variable reinforcement can maintain high levels of effort more effectively than can mixed rewards (Reitz, 1987; Skinner, 1974).

The application of behaviorist models by management assumes that employees' desires for the rewards of positive reinforcement and recognition will, in large measure, motivate them to perform satisfactorily in anticipation of such rewards. Leadership in this model then requires the leader to (1) inform subordinates concerning which behaviors are desirable and are rewarded and which behaviors are not rewarded; (2) provide continuous feedback to employees regarding the nature and quality of their work; (3) recognize employees for good work; (4) ensure that employees receive immediate, unscheduled reinforcement during or immediately after strong performance; and (5) reward differently depending on the performance level (Hamner & Hamner, 1976).

Social Learning Models.   A third process model of human behavior in organizations is the social learning model. Developed by Bandura (1968, 1976, 1977), Mahoney (1974), Mischell (1973), and Staats (1975), it combines features of the cognitive and reinforcement approaches to help explain human behavior. It places emphasis on learning from other people (i.e., social learning).

Social learning is based on the principles of behaviorism and stresses the importance of reinforcement in explaining behavior. However, the social model maintains that the role of the environment in shaping behavior is mediated by cognitive processes. These processes are depicted in social learning models by adding one element to the basic S-R-O reinforcement model: cognitive processes (C) mediate the effects of environmental stimuli (S) on behavioral responses (R), which then are followed by outcomes (O). The social learning model is then S-C-R-O (Bandura, 1977).

Modeling and self-control are two types of behaviors that exemplify the social learning process. *Modeling* refers to the process by which a person learns a behavior by imitating an observed model. Self-controlled behavior is exhibited by the person's recognition of the external limits. Research in social learning reveals that people tend to reproduce the actions, attitudes, and emotional responses exhibited by models in modeling behavior (Bandura, 1969; Bandura & Walters, 1963; Flanders, 1968). Whether events or circumstances become reinforcing depends partly on observing or modeling the reinforcing or punishing outcomes of other people's behavior. People are motivated not only by their direct experience of response outcomes but also by observing the consequences of other people's behavior. Social learning models also indicate that people are motivated not only by the external consequences of their behavior, but by the consequences they create for themselves (Bandura, 1968; Kanfer & Karoly, 1974). When their own self-created consequences are not fulfilled, people are motivated to keep working until expected outcomes are accomplished.

One of the most important implications of social learning is that leaders need to be especially aware of their own behavior. Leaders who have one set of expectations for their followers but then behave differently themselves may be setting themselves up for disappointment. It may be true that most effective leaders lead by example. A second implication of social learning is also instructive. As illustrated earlier, both formal and informal organizational structures are of vital importance to leadership. Although it is important for leaders to understand this informal agenda and monitor informal leaders' rhetoric, leaders may find that the best insights into greater understanding of the informal organization result from observing actions.

The behavioral and social learning models provide a means to further develop leadership skills. Leaders who are prepared to serve as mentors, or persons who wish to prepare themselves for future leadership opportunities can seek positive ways to achieve these opportunities. The efficacy of this approach has been demonstrated directly over the past few decades by women and minorities who have sought leadership roles. As more women and members of minority groups have ascended to leadership ranks, they have provided increasing opportunities for mentoring and role modeling. This has steadily increased access to leadership positions for these groups.

Motivation Approaches at Work. Two concepts implied by process models deserve leadership consideration. These two concepts are (1) motivation to work harder versus motivation to work smarter, and (2) positive motivation versus negative motivation. Motivating people to work harder means encouraging them to apply more physical energy to their work. Motivating people to work smarter means encouraging them to think and work creatively and to develop better ways of doing things. The first approach offers only limited increase in output and probably a decrease in satisfaction. The second approach is likely to offer greater reward without the necessity of harder work, because new and better ways of work can be developed to replace the old ones. In addition, leaders can use positive and negative reinforcement at their disposal. Positive motivation involves the cultivation of a cooperative attitude among followers so that organizational goals can be accepted and achieved. Stimulating action through fear is the foundation of negative motivation. Negative motivation forces a person to select between undesirable alternatives. Most leaders use both. In light of the trend toward better employee education and greater independence, leaders need to reduce negative leadership and increase the positive. Followers need to cultivate working smarter.

Content Models

Process models describe how motivation works in general terms. In application, managers need to know more about how models work and what specifically rewards or reinforces human behavior.

Content models help to understand human be-havior further. Content models of motivation can be classified into two schools based on their re-search concerns. The first school focuses on common human needs, while the second school concentrates on human motivation at work.

Common Human Needs

Psychologists working on content models of motivation have identified scores of different re-wards and reinforcers and have arranged them into categories to aid understanding. Cognitive psychologists and psychoanalysts have further refined these categories into classes of needs and motives.

Maslow's Need Hierarchy.   The most widely known classification of needs was compiled by Maslow, who described human motivation as arising from five categories of needs. Maslow (1954) conjectured that while different cultures satisfy these needs in different ways, the needs themselves remain the same. He identified five categories of needs:

1. *Physiological needs:* needs basic to the sur-vival of the human species, such as hunger, thirst, respiration, and sex.
2. *Safety needs:* needs basic to the physical and psychological protection of the individual, such as shelter, orderliness, consistency, pro-tection from threat and danger, and pre-dictability in one's environment.
3. *Social needs:* needs basic to one's association with and acceptance by other human beings, such as needs for friendship, love, and affili-ation.
4. *Esteem needs:* needs related to respect, in-cluding two subsets: self-esteem and esteem from others. Need of self-esteem is the desire for achievement, adequacy, confidence, in-dependence, and freedom; need of esteem from others is the desire for reputation, pres-tige, recognition, attention, importance, or appreciation.

5. *Self-actualization:* the need to fulfill one's potential, to test one's limits, and to become whatever one can become.

According to Maslow (1954), these five cate-gories of needs form a hierarchy. Each level of need has to be gratified to some extent before the next level in order assumes importance. Lower-order needs do not become unimpor-tant, but higher-order needs achieve greater sig-nificance for the person as basic needs become satisfied.

The first two levels of needs (lower-order needs) are satisfied primarily through economic behavior; the other three (higher-order needs) are satisfied primarily through symbolic behavior of psychic and social content. In light of these five basic needs, the classical economic-man concept can be considered incomplete in that it applies largely to lower-order needs. Self-actualization needs are the highest order of needs and may rarely be satisfied by most peo-ple. An important feature of self-actualization needs is that they express themselves through different behaviors in different people. More-over, unlike other levels of needs, the satisfaction of self-actualization needs tends to increase their importance rather than reduce it (Maslow, 1962).

In practice, behavior by any given person during any given time probably is the result of more than one need or class of needs. Most acts are influenced by all five classes of needs, with one of the levels having a greater effect in the specific case.

Porter's Need Hierarchy.   Porter (1961) refor-mulated Maslow's original needs hierarchy slightly. He assumed that few people are moti-vated by such basic physical needs as thirst and hunger, and instead, after self-esteem, have a need for autonomy. *Autonomy* refers to individ-uals' needs to participate in making decisions that affect them, to exert influence in controlling the work situation, to have a voice in setting job-related goals, and to have authority to make de-cisions and latitude to work independently.

Alderfer's Three Categories of Needs. In an attempt to reconcile Maslow's theory with research on human needs in work settings, Alderfer (1969, 1972) proposed three categories of needs: (1) existence, (2) relatedness, and (3) growth. Alderfer argued that these three categories of needs are primary, and that they are innate to human nature rather than learned.

Existence refers to basic needs for survival, similar to Maslow's physiological and security needs. For Alderfer, Maslow's physiological and security needs are equal in importance to the existence of the person. Typically, subordinates attempt to satisfy existence needs that are more concrete in nature. In addition, these needs often relate to scarce resources. More satisfaction for one person will tend to result in lower potential satisfaction for others. Pay and fringe benefits are two examples of existence needs in the work setting.

According to Alderfer, Maslow's concept of social needs, love, self-esteem, and belonging are equally important. All people require interaction with others and the development of meaningful relationships with others. Alderfer refers to this category of needs as *relatedness*. Relatedness needs encompass social and interpersonal concerns, similar to Maslow's social and esteem-from-others needs. Unlike the zero-sum aspects of existence needs, satisfying relatedness needs for one person tends to be positively associated with the same satisfaction for others.

Growth needs suggest that people need to develop their own skills, abilities, and self-esteem. This is similar to Maslow's need for self-esteem and self-actualization. While Maslow saw self-actualization as consisting of the fulfillment of an innate potential, Alderfer's growth needs consist of desires to interact successfully with one's environment. As the person's environment changes, so will the expression of growth needs.

Although Alderfer's three categories cover roughly the same domains as Maslow's, he did not maintain that preceding needs have to be fulfilled before others can influence behavior.

Instead, he proposed that cultural background or experience may make certain needs more important than others, and some needs may be insatiable.

McClelland's Social Motives. Another explanation and description of common human needs is provided by McClelland and Atkinson. Extending Murray's (1938) manifest need theory, McClelland and Atkinson (Atkinson, 1964; McClelland, Atkinson, Clark, & Lowell, 1953) maintained that only two needs are inherent: the need for pleasure and the need to avoid pain. All others are learned. However, since many of life's problem-solving experiences are almost universal, people tend to learn the same types of needs, called *social motives,* but in different degrees.

McClelland (1955, 1975) identified three important social motives: (1) achievement, (2) power, and (3) affiliation. The *achievement* motive is the strongest common human need. Achievement refers to the desire of people to compete against a standard of excellence. The need for achievement is perceived as an important motive in organizations. For a worker with a high need for achievement, challenging work serves to cue the achievement motive. This, in turn, activates achievement-oriented behavior. When high-need achievers are placed in routine or nonchallenging jobs, the achievement motive will probably not be activated (McClelland, 1961, 1987; Steers & Spencer, 1977). Realizing this characteristic, leaders can promote excellence.

A second strong common need is the need for *power* or *dominance.* Power motives represent a desire to influence others and to control one's environment. For leaders, power motives can take two forms: personalized power and socialized power. People who seek personalized power attempt to dominate others without regard to greater objectives. On the other hand, those who have a socialized need use their power to work with and through others to accomplish objectives. To them, power is important, but as a means to an end rather than as an end in itself.

Affiliation is the need for positive relationships with other people. A major aspect of the affiliation motive is the need for communication. People with a high need for affiliation tend to take jobs characterized by a high amount of interpersonal contact. They tend to perform better when given supportive feedback. In this regard, leadership attempts to create a cooperative, supportive work environment where positive feedback is tied to task performance.

According to McClelland (1975, 1976), those managers with a high need for socialized power are often excellent leaders. On the other hand, a high need for achievement can be detrimental. Similarly, a high need for affiliation leads to indecisiveness. Instead, McClelland (1976) found that power-oriented managers, when truly concerned about the organization as a whole, provide the structure, drive, and support necessary to facilitate goal-oriented group behavior.

Ardrey's Territorial Theory.   Another description of common human needs is derived from cultural anthropologists. According to Ardrey (1966), people have three types of basic needs: (1) identity, (2) security, and (3) stimulation. People strive for identity, not anonymity; stimulation, not boredom; security, not anxiety. Ardrey believed that property or territory is one of the prime concepts that satisfies these needs; therefore, much individual behavior is directed toward acquiring property or defending territory. Property and territory refer to a range of things, running from real property to a favorite and customary seat in the classroom.

Leadership Consideration.   Although theorists propose a variety of need components or hierarchies, the question remains, is the hierarchy of needs plausible? There is evidence that different needs do exist and that they can be measured. There is also less empirical support that these needs vary so consistently in relative importance among different people (Mitchell & Moudgill, 1976). To believe so seems to ignore substantial

differences at various stages in people's lives and careers (Katz, 1980; Pinder, 1984).

Despite the criticisms, some implications suggested by theories and models of common human needs are significant for leadership. Study of common human needs reveals that it is unrealistic for leaders to think that they can satisfy all needs through entitlement. This economic-man concept may apply only to lower-order needs. Higher-order needs are satisfied primarily through symbolic behavior of psychic, social, and cultural content. It is also necessary for leaders to recognize that normally gratified needs are no longer highly motivating. Employees are more enthusiastically motivated by their own achievements than by needs that normally would have been satisfied.

Motivation at Work

There are almost as many theories of work motivation as there are writers on the subject of motivation. Their works commonly focus on the connection between motivation and work-related behavior. Two significant models are presented here: Herzberg's motivator–hygiene theory and Shamir's collectivistic motivation.

Studies in collectivistic motivation represent a new trend in work motivation. Although the models described earlier help us understand worker motivation to perform, their usefulness in everyday organizational contexts is limited. Leaders become confused when they try to apply these theories to workers in practice. If all people have changing needs, how can leaders or managers attempt to motivate an entire workforce? What the practicing leader or manager needs is an answer to the question: What will motivate most of the people most of the time? Herzberg and Shamir sought to provide practical representations to answer the question.

Herzberg's Motivator–Hygiene Theory.   Herzberg's motivator–hygiene theory is one of the most recognized and most practical models. Herzberg and his associates aimed to determine what

affects worker motivation and productivity in organizations (Herzberg, 1966, 1968; Herzberg, et
al., 1959). From their research, Herzberg and his
colleagues developed the motivator-hygiene theory of work motivation. The theory assumes that
employees are motivated to produce at high levels to the extent that they perceive satisfactory results. In his theory, Herzberg proposes that the
opposite of satisfaction and motivation is not dissatisfaction, but simply no job satisfaction. The
opposite of dissatisfaction, in turn, is not job satisfaction but simply the absence of dissatisfaction. The distinction between job satisfaction and
dissatisfaction becomes clear when the two are
related to levels of performance. There is a neu-
tral point in performance levels where employees are not dissatisfied with their jobs, but neither
are they experiencing job satisfaction. At this
point, employees simply perform at the minimum acceptable level necessary to maintain their
jobs and employment. Eliminating sources of dissatisfaction does not mean that the reduction is
motivating to the worker or will lead to job satisfaction. Rather, job satisfaction and dissatisfaction are affected by different sets of factors and
have different effects on employee motivation
and performance. One set of factors, *hygiene,*
tends to affect dissatisfaction and performance
below acceptable levels, while a second set of
factors, *motivator,* tends to affect job satisfaction,
motivation, and performance above acceptable
levels.

Herzberg (1968, 1981) found that hygiene
factors such as company policy, types of supervision, status, job security, salary, working conditions, and interpersonal relations keep employees from being dissatisfied, although they
do not necessarily motivate employees. Motivating factors such as achievement, recognition,
the work itself, responsibility, growth, and advancement appear to motivate people and are
associated with job satisfaction. Although
Herzberg posited that motivation is composed
of two separate, independent factors, the theory
appears to be highly compatible with Maslow's
and Porter's hierarchy models.

To motivate an employee, Herzberg claimed
that those factors originally identified as motivators must be built into an employee's job. The
content of the work rather than the setting in
which it is conducted is the important factor. The
work must be enriched in such a way that it allows a person opportunities to feel achievement
and recognition and provides for advancement
and meaningful responsibility. When jobs are
designed in this way, motivation should be
forthcoming. When these factors are missing, no
dissatisfaction results. Satisfaction is simply not
present (Herzberg, 1966). Enriching jobs to motivate workers has broad support among theorists and practitioners (Aldag, Barr, & Brief, 1981;
Griffin, 1982; Hackman & Oldham, 1980). The
two-factor aspect of the theory may not be a
necessary element in the use of the theory for
designing jobs. Although the two factors may assist in clarifying and increasing understanding,
there is no need to assume that failure to provide these factors will not lead to job satisfaction, or that the provision of certain hygiene factors in the workplace cannot also be motivating
in the true sense of the word (Pinder, 1984).

Shamir's Collectivistic Work Motivation. All
models of motivation to this point are individually and rationally oriented, due to their deriva-
tion from psychological and economic paradigms. These assumptions assume that people
are motivated to satisfy their own personal
needs. Recent studies, however, have shown
that not all human motivations can be explained
on the basis of individualistic or hedonistic considerations (Shamir, 1990). This is particularly
evident given the individual contributions to collective work efforts in most organizational life.

In his study, Shamir (1990) pointed out that
many collective entities in such organizations as
government agencies, schools, and hospitals
cannot be explained on purely individualistic
and economic grounds, termed *calculative* by
Etzioni (1961). Shamir maintained that "in order
to understand individuals' contributions to such
collective actions we have to consider both the

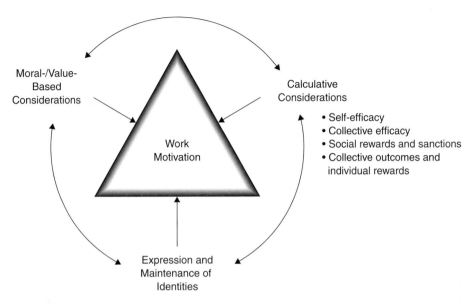

Figure 6.5
Shamir's collectivistic work motivation

calculative and the normal dimensions of the person's motivation simultaneously" (p. 314). Shamir proposed that understanding individual contributions to collective work efforts should be approached from three aspects simultaneously: calculative considerations, moral or value-based considerations, and expression and maintenance of identities (see Figure 6.5).

A person's motivation to contribute to collective efforts can be explained, in part, by calculative considerations in terms of self-efficacy, collective efficacy, social rewards and sanctions, and social linkage between collective outcomes and individual rewards. *Self-efficacy* (i.e., expectancy) refers to the likelihood that a person's contribution will increase group performance. Expectancy models have addressed how self-efficacy affects people's motivation to perform. In contrast, *collective efficacy* refers to a person's subjective probability that collective efforts will result in collective accomplishment. Like self-efficacy, collective efficacy affects a person's effort to perform. In discussions of col-

lective motivation, social rewards and sanctions are those employed to control a member's behavior. Obviously, social reward, such as social acceptance and social recognition or status, and social sanctions, such as pressure to conform, social rejection, and loss of status, influence a person's effort at collectivistic work motivation.

The relationship between collective outcomes and individual rewards is twofold. On the one hand, collective outcomes can be translated into individual rewards in terms of profits consumed by individuals. On the other hand, many outcomes of collective work efforts constitute a common good, such as improved equipment or a better technology, which cannot be consumed individually. The two dimensions have equally important impacts on individuals' efforts at collective work motivation. Second, norms and values exert motivational influence through their association with expected social rewards and sanctions. When norms and values become internalized by an individual, the person may be motivated by the expected internal reactions to his or her actions. Finally, an element other than norms and values is the expression and maintenance of individuals' identities. Etzioni (1988) referred to this element as a *sense of affirmation*. A person will seek out opportunities to maintain self-identity in a perceived social situation. People may be motivated to contribute to a collective effort, because by doing so they will maintain and affirm relevant identities. Shamir (1990) emphasized that the concept of identity is important in that it provides an obvious linkage between the individual and the collectivity. Japanese workers' strong tendency toward organizational identity is a typical example.

Shamir proposed (1990) that in order to increase collective cohesiveness (members' attraction to the collectivity and their identification with the collectivity), leaders should try to establish the symbolic environment in ways that emphasize the unique identity of the organization or suborganization and increase organizational identity salience in members' self-concepts. Leaders need to instill norms of cooperation and contribution in an organization. Leaders also need to engage frequently in attempts to show organizational members the link between organizational actions and members' cherished values.

Morale in Organizations

Morale is an emotional attribute, providing energy, acceptance of leadership, and cooperation among members of an organization. Morale has been conceptualized from three perspectives: physiological, psychological, and social. From the physiological point of view, satisfaction of the basic human need of survival is the prime morale factor. From the psychological perspective, morale is determined by a continual satisfaction of higher-order needs. From the social approach, morale can be considered a social phenomenon caused by people's strong desire to be associated with their peers.

In reality, morale is better described by the combination of the three perspectives. Morale is the atmosphere created by the attitudes of the members of an organization. Morale is more likely to be revealed by groups than by individuals (Benge & Hickley, 1984). Morale is influenced by how employees perceive the organization and its goals in relation to themselves, in terms of their physical, psychological, social, and cultural background.

Major Morale Factors

The attitudes of employees are influenced significantly by the ways in which they perceive a number of important factors: the organization itself, their own activities, their self-concept, the nature of their work, their peers, the satisfaction of their needs, and leadership (Kossen, 1987). The organization significantly influences employees' attitudes toward their jobs. Higher employee morale results when an organization has a favorable reputation. An employee of a public agency encountering reduced public financial support might experience poor morale. Employees' personal lives may also affect their attitudes on the job. Relationships with families and friends, as part of their total environment, influence employees' morale in their working environment. Employees' self-concepts also tend to influence their attitudes toward organizational environments. Therefore, individuals who lack self-confidence or suffer from poor physical or mental health frequently develop morale problems. In addition, employees' current values and education lead them to expect considerably more from their work than just material prosperity. However, many types of jobs seem to lead to boredom and obsessive thinking, such as uniform pacing, repetition, large impersonal organizational structures, and vague as well as unattainable goals. These characteristics are likely to lower employee morale without appropriate design.

The informal system and actions of leaders in an organization also affect morale significantly.

As a member of a group, an employee's attitude toward a working condition could be swayed by the collective attitudes of his or her cohorts. High rates of turnover often indicate ineffective leadership.

How employees' personal needs are satisfied can influence their morale. Salary and employee benefits are two examples that help to satisfy personal needs. While increases in pay do not necessarily motivate employees to increase productivity, poor pay can be a source for poor morale, especially when compared to the pay of employees doing similar work (Kossen, 1987; Reitz, 1987).

Morale, Job Satisfaction, and Productivity

Morale is closely connected with the satisfaction that a person hopes to derive from work. Whereas work satisfaction is the result of various attitudes by an individual employee at a given time, morale is the result of the total satisfaction of the employees in an organization. As noted earlier, job satisfaction does not have to be apparent immediately, but it has to be anticipated by the employee. Low morale often accompanies high rates of absenteeism, tardiness, and high turnover.

Morale is also related to productivity. Some feel that there tends to be a direct relationship between high productivity and high morale. However, the nature of the relationship between morale and productivity is inconclusive. Others see an inverse relationship, circular, or even reciprocal relationship between productivity and morale. The morale–productivity relationship can therefore be perceived as situational.

Approaches to Studying Morale

At least three approaches have been developed to study employee morale. The first approach involves analyzing organizational records for changes in resignations, tardiness, absenteeism, productivity, and complaints. The second approach is to interview employees using prepared questions or allowing employees to respond in an unstructured format. The third approach is to administer unsigned questionnaires and then report morale indices (Benge & Hickley, 1984). The three approaches are complementary and can be conducted simultaneously. To be effective, studies of morale should be conducted periodically, not just once.

The Quality of Work Life

Regardless of the real relationship between productivity and morale, high morale remains an important organizational goal. However, morale frequently is not noticed unless it is poor. Far too often, leaders do not recognize how badly morale has deteriorated until they are faced with serious crises. Leaders must continually be alert to clues revealing the state of morale. Leaders need to be sensitive to the warning signs of low morale in their employees, such as absenteeism, tardiness, high turnover, strikes and sabotages, and lack of pride in work. They also need to secure actively all available information through statistical data (e.g., absenteeism and turnover records), employee counselors, observation and listening, or surveys. Studies on morale reveal that leaders should be concerned with the quality of employee work life. The more affluent and better educated workforces of today expect a higher quality of work life (O'Toole, 1981). To satisfy employees today, leadership is expected to improve the quality of work life.

Quality of work life (QWL) refers to how effectively the job environment meets the personal needs and values of employees. QWL consists of seven components: (1) adequate and fair compensation, (2) safe and healthy work conditions, (3) opportunity for continued growth and security, (4) a feeling of belonging, (5) employee rights, (6) work and total life span, and (7) social relevance of work life (Greenberg & Glaser, 1983; Walton, 1975).

Several recent methods have been developed to improve the quality of work life, including job rotation, job enlargement, job enrichment, and sociotechnical systems (Aldag & Brief, 1979; Champagne & McAfee, 1989; Hackman, 1983; Hellriegel & Slocum, 1976; Lawler, 1992; Pinder, 1984; Plous, 1987; Reitz, 1987).

Job rotation is the practice of training a worker in several different tasks and rotating that worker through those tasks in a given time period. Job rotation attempts to reduce the boredom and fatigue from endless repetitions of a task and increase job satisfaction, primarily by increasing task variety. Workers can also acquire a broader set of skills and knowledge, which increases efficiency during periods of absenteeism.

Like job rotation, job enlargement increases the scope of a job. It intends to reduce boredom and fatigue and increase satisfaction by increasing the number of tasks a worker performs within a given job. It emphasizes the performance of a greater number and variety of skills. It also allows for more decision making about work methods and more responsibility.

Job enrichment is an attempt to involve the worker in more than just the performance of a task. In job enrichment, employees are provided with greater work content that requires advanced skills and new knowledge. The worker is more autonomous and responsible for planning, organizing, and evaluating the work as well as carrying it out. This autonomy and responsibility provides the opportunity for personal growth and meaningful work experience.

It is important to note that job enlargement and job enrichment do not merely call for adding more low-level tasks to a worker's job. This may be demotivating. There are four criteria in deciding whether or not a job can be enlarged or enriched. Any addition to the job should (1) increase responsibility, (2) increase worker autonomy, (3) permit the worker to do the complete task, and (4) provide feedback to the worker.

Sociotechnical systems design jobs around groups of workers rather than individuals. In this approach, the leader defines a complete unit of work and assigns responsibility for that unit to a group. The workers in the group share responsibility for determining what each of them will do, for deciding how they will accomplish it, and for scheduling and completing the work. The group itself assumes the responsibility for supervising its work.

Informal Organizations

Informal worker networks emerge spontaneously in organizations from the needs of the worker. They are not planned but occur as individual social interactions within the formal organization. These informal networks have their own leaders, unwritten policy, hidden agendas, communication channels, and even their own goals. Informal networks can play a significant part in organizational life. Informal organizations arise and persist as a means of compensating for the inadequacy of formal organizations in providing individual need satisfactions and/or as a means of adding to the need satisfaction provided by membership in formal organizations (Bales, 1953, Davis, 1977; Kossen, 1987; Roethlisberger & Dickson, 1939). Workers enter into organizations with individually shaped expectations, and bring with them differing values, interests, and abilities. Informal activities emerge when some particular need is not being fulfilled by the formal organization. Informal organizations help members of formal organizations satisfy needs by performing three important functions: social interaction, social control, and communication.

One of the most important functions provided by informal organizations is the provision of social interaction. Individuals have social needs that they attempt to satisfy at work in formal organizations; however, the social satisfaction provided by the formal organizations is limited. Informal organizations arise to help individuals satisfy these social needs, thus giving a person recognition, status, and further opportunity to relate to others.

The second major function provided by informal organizations is social control. This function helps preserve and maintain the existence, identity, and values of the informal organizations. Social control is maintained and enforced over informal organization membership through norms and standards of behavior. Norms are enforced through social pressure. Informal organizations also attempt to exert control over people outside their group but within the formal organization (e.g., by influencing the leadership or staff personnel). Much of this external control is exerted indirectly by regulating the behavior of members of the informal organizations.

A third informal organization function is communication. To keep its members informed of what is taking place and how it may affect them, the informal organization develops a system of communication to supplement the information provided by the formal organization. This communication system is known as the *grapevine*. Grapevines are inevitable, as it is practically impossible for formal organizations to keep everyone well informed. It is worthwhile to examine informal organizations because they have a tremendous capacity for carrying and disseminating important information quickly.

Informal Leaders

The leaders of informal organizations arise for various reasons and under slightly different circumstances. There are typically several informal leaders of varying importance in an informal organization, but one primary leader usually has the most influence. The general role of informal leaders is to help the informal organization achieve its goals and to maintain and enhance informal organizational life. In return for their services, informal leaders usually enjoy certain rewards and privileges, such as esteem and power (Davis, 1977; Wolman, 1956). As a result, these people's informal roles may take on more importance than their formal work roles. The informal organization may be a desirable source of potential leaders for the formal organization. However, caution is necessary here, as the agendas of informal leaders often may not coincide with organizational agendas. The dynamics of informal organizations and their in-

formal leaders can be studied using sociometric techniques (Moreno, 1947) and interaction-process analysis techniques (Bales, 1950).

The Effects of Informal Organizations

The existence of informal organizations always affects the operation of formal organizations. In most cases, informal organizations have both detrimental and beneficial effects (Davis, 1977; Kossen, 1987; Ruben, 1988; Sanford, 1977; Scott, 1981). Four potential disadvantages exist in informal organizations. They may (1) transmit false information, (2) resist changes, (3) cause excessive conformity to group norms, and (4) develop goals that conflict with formal organizational goals. Transmitting false information is one of the most troublesome problems attributed to the communications systems of informal organization. Rumors are efficiently and effectively transmitted through the grapevine. Since rumors often are inaccurate, they create problems in organizations. It should be noted that informal organizations do not necessarily cause rumors; however, they do transmit rumors. In trying to preserve and maintain their values and status, informal organizations tend to resist change, especially changes that will have detrimental effects on the organization. They resist changes through members' conformity enforced by social control. The quest for social satisfaction in informal organizations may lead their members away from organizational goals. What is good for the workers is not always good for the organization. Role conflicts occur and often lead to limited productivity.

The existence of informal organizations can also benefit the formal organization. Informal organizations satisfy employees' social needs, provide a useful employee communication network, provide employees with emotional escape valves, and complement the formal organization. A significant benefit of informal organizations is that they provide satisfaction and stability to employees and the formal organization. The existence of informal organizations provides employees with a sense of belonging, acceptance, and security. The satisfaction provided by informal organizations compensates for some of the inevitable undesirable aspects associated with formal organizational membership. Thus, informal organizations help the formal organization reduce turnover and may increase employee motivation. An additional benefit of informal organizations is that they provide a means for people to keep in touch, to learn more about their work, and to understand what is happening in their environment. Informal organizations serve as safety valves for employee frustrations and even other emotional problems. They provide an escape valve where negative feelings caused by the formal organization can be aired.

Overall, the existence of informal organizations tends to facilitate the functioning of a formal organization in certain important respects. They fill gaps in the formal organization's management, can promote more efficiency in the formal system, often supplement authority and responsibility mechanisms within the formal organization, and provide additional channels of communication.

The Inevitability of Informal Organizations

Informal organizations are inevitable for at least two reasons. First, they supplement need satisfaction provided by formal organizations. Second, membership in formal organizations tends to stimulate people's needs for more information than formal organizations can provide. Informal organizations therefore will always be present and cannot be eliminated.

Realizing the inevitability of the informal organization, leaders must consider the possible effects their actions have on informal systems in order to integrate as far as possible the interests of informal organizations with those of the formal organizations and to keep formal activities from unnecessarily threatening informal organizations in general. The most desirable informal/formal organization relationship seems to be one in which the two systems maintain unity toward goals. Leaders of the formal organization would be wise to consider the value of the informal organization and work to maintain and enhance overall group cohesiveness and teamwork through it (Davis, 1977; Scott, 1981).

Human Relations Theory in Educational Administration

The human relations view of educational administration incorporates two distinctive bodies of thought. The first school is democratic administration, a philosophy of administration originating shortly after 1900 in John Dewey's work. The second arose after 1945, when notions about democratizing school organizations combined with humanistic studies drawn from behavioral science and the industrial studies discussed earlier. The fusion of these two bodies of thought in the 1940s was described first as democratic human relations and later as simply the human relations approach to educational administration (R. F. Campbell, Fleming, Newell, & Bennion, 1987).

Democratic Educational Administration

Unlike the human relations approach that originated in industrial and social science research, the democratic view of educational administration first evolved among educators in the early years of the twentieth century in response to several factors. These included new social changes in the character of school organizations and reactions on the part of some to autocratic and authoritarian supervisory practices in schools. One of the earliest promoters of democratic administration in education, John Dewey (1946), argued against the increasing popularity of scientific management techniques among school leaders and emphasized the need for educational managers to secure the consent of those they governed. Scientific management's preoccupation with efficiency did little to foster what he described as a well-balanced social interest. Dewey argued this as contrary to the proper ends of education. Giving teachers opportunities for greater participation changes both the character of the school organization and the quality and kind of relationships between teachers and administrators. For the educational leader, a cooperative approach to school management would necessitate that leadership provide intellectual stimulation and direction through give and take with others. A cooperative approach would not produce an aloof, official, imposing, or authoritarian environment. Others who supported democratic leadership include educational scholars, social reconstructionists, and social and philosophical scholars.

According to its supporters there are three significant bases of democratic administration: (1) a widely shared belief exists that if teachers were treated in an autocratic manner by principals and superintendents, they would treat pupils accordingly; (2) the enormous growth in size and specialization of schools demanded that structural changes occur within school systems, which compels superintendents and other administrators to rely on the expertise of teachers and other staff members; (3) democratic leadership promises to help school administrators secure the cooperation of their staffs by making them members of the team.

The democratic administration that originated in educational settings and the human relations movement of the industrial era bear close resemblances. On the surface, both approaches react against autocratic administrative practices associated with scientific management. More important, human relations research seems to confirm empirically what supporters of democratic administration have believed for some time: that organizational morale and productivity could be enhanced by humanistic leadership practices.

The Human Relations Movement in Education

The educational interest in applying human relations ideas to problems of school administration has been spurred by several developments taking place inside and outside schools. Outside the school, the growing urban character, as well as improvements in transportation, have narrowed the distance between home and school. More and more, schools are being located in suburban areas to accommodate the educational needs of the nation's middle class, who are increasingly abandoning the cities (Link & Catton, 1967). This trend facilitates community involvement in educational affairs. Parent–teacher associations and interactions between school staff and the public have increased. The changing environment around the schools and the need for better public relations provide sound reasons for educators to adopt a view of management that promises to enhance their social and interpersonal skills. Conditions inside school organizations also cause administrators to look to human relations. Staffing difficulties, which began after 1941 when teachers left the classroom to join the armed forces or work in wartime industry, became an acute administration problem by the end of the war (Link & Catton, 1967). Teacher shortages and the general high rate of attrition within the profession were aggravated by economic factors that made teaching an unattractive occupation (Hill, 1947). To address such problems, school managers needed to gain public understanding and support and improve morale among school staff.

The changing character of school populations in the late 1940s and early 1950s was another factor that encouraged educators to develop human relations skills. More students from different backgrounds were enrolled in public schools than ever before (Moehlman, 1940). In addition, the increasing mobility of postwar society, the quickening pace of events, and the loosening of long-held values and traditions posed new and different problems, especially in the decades after the Supreme Court's landmark *Brown v. Board of Education* decision. Others condemned public schooling for its alleged anti-intellectual tone, its dominance by professional educators, and its undemocratic methods in preparing and selecting pupils for careers. In light of such criticisms, it is not surprising that professors of education recommended a form of management that suggested strategies for cooperation borrowed from industrial research.

Ralph Tyler was one of the first educators to appreciate the changing view of administration that human relations research espoused. Tyler (1941) noted the relevance of recent human relations research to school administrators and suggested that future research in educational management be guided by the Hawthorne studies. Wilbur Yauch's and Daniel Griffiths's studies were two other important milestones that applied concepts of human relations to education. Yauch (1949) provided one of the first complete educational studies that combined ethical generalizations from democratic administration with human relations research drawn from industry. He brought together the prescriptive approach to school management advanced by educators throughout the 1920s and 1930s with a more objective appreciation of administrative problems. He advocated teacher involvement in all areas of administration, including staff participation in decisions concerning supervision, budget allocation, curriculum, general policy making, and clerical duties associated with operating a school.

Griffiths's (1956) study synthesized more than a quarter century of educational and social science thought about administration. Griffiths believed that staff morale was related to the kind of leadership operating within schools. He saw the school leader as someone whose chief responsibility is to facilitate the actions of others: an initiator, a coordinator, a helper, and a resource person. The school leader is a social person, sensitive to the human needs of all concerned. Griffiths's study was not intended as a handbook containing lists of human relations rules and techniques that can be applied to various situations, but rather, it sought to provide an intellectual basis for the study of schools drawn from research in other social sciences and from other fields of professional study. As such, it signaled the beginning of a shift in educational interest from a practical application of human relations research to a concern with theoretically grounded understanding of human behavior derived from the social sciences, a change later characterized as one in which educators begin to conceive administration as a domain of study rather than a domain of action (Getzels, 1977).

From Democratic Administration to Human Relations Management

Teacher performance in school affairs or democratic administration, as discussed by Dewey and others, represents a way of bringing organizational practices in schools in line with long-standing political and social values, thereby endowing teachers with rights of organizational citizenship. The most critical functions of schools may be their ability to serve as laboratories for democracy and agencies of national regeneration. Schools must therefore develop better human resource mechanisms to achieve these primary goals.

Human relations research stems from industrial experiments designed to improve worker performance and generally to assist the cause of management. Early scholars embraced human relations ideas because they promised to assist the cause of democratic leadership. Adoption of these early ideas, however, eventually helped in solving administrative problems and tasks more than in restructuring or democratizing schools.

By midcentury, students of educational administration cast aside the focus on democracy in schools and teacher participation in favor of other issues related to understanding the roles and responsibilities of school leaders. Human relations writers on school management generally were more concerned with understanding how group dynamic skills could assist administrators in dealing with problems related to public relations and staff morale. Their writings therefore addressed issues related more to managing and administering schools than notions about what enlightened leadership should accomplish (R. F. Campbell et al., 1987).

After midcentury, concepts of school leadership were no longer defended on philosophical worthiness but shifted to how well school executives understood human behavior and the dynamics of interpersonal relations. In human relations writings, development of skills in nondirective counseling and psychological testing were viewed as essentials for effective administrators (R. F. Campbell et al., 1987).

The Effects of the Human Relations Movement on Educational Administration

The human relations movement had relatively little impact on school district administrators compared to its substantial impact on supervisors (Owens, 1987). Superintendents today continue to emphasize organization, while supervisors emphasize such human relations concepts as morale, group cohesiveness, collaboration, and the dynamics of informal organizations.

Those who see their roles as educational administrators tend to emphasize budgets, politics, control, and asymmetrical exercise of power from the top down, whereas those concerned with instruction and curriculum place much more emphasis on participation and communication. Status–power relationships have been deemphasized. This difference in emphasis persisted into the 1980s. Additionally, motivation, the core concept of the human relations movement, was not implemented well in schools or the school environment. There was no good fit between teachers who tried to achieve excellence and at the same time demanded more entitlement.

A New Frame of Leadership

In ordinary times, people look to managers for predictable, smooth-running, and cost-effective operations. Managers help supply the clarity, certainty, and efficiency required to get the job done right. In times of crisis, however, good management is not enough. People facing uncertainty turn to leaders for direction, confidence, and hope. Leaders encourage long-range planning, spirit, and cohesion when doubts about the future of the organization occur. Leadership must consistently sense its history and, at the same time, look ahead to discover or rediscover why the new organization exists, what it stands for, and where it might be headed. As external circumstances shift and sway, organizations waver between their need for management and their need for leadership. The issue is not which is better but what balance is best in view of contemporary challenges.

Several years ago, a national commission formally announced a nation at risk, a time of crisis in educational systems. Since that time there has been little success in reshaping schools. New structures, strengthened curriculum, less money, and greater diversity create formidable new administrative obstacles. Coupled with these issues is a strong belief that our nation's schools can never be as they once were. Moreover, this new call for leadership is not confined to education (Deal, 1992).

Volumes of literature have reinforced leadership as a crucial ingredient in all collective endeavors. But despite the attention, the essence of leadership remains mysteriously elusive. Modern concepts view leadership as a complex interaction among members of an organization, in which context rather than position usually determines who will take the lead. However, it is still possible to distill some essential attributes of leadership.

Bolman and Deal (1991) synthesized the organizational literature into four distinct frames, each emphasizing a different aspect of cooperative ventures. Each frame is explained by a corresponding arena of emphasis as shown in Table 6.1.

Recent studies of administrators in business, higher education, and schools suggest that most administrators operate primarily from either a structural or a human resource orientation (Bolman & Deal, 1991). Both orientations are linked significantly to their administrator's effectiveness as a

Table 6.1
Frames of Leadership

Frame	Emphasis
Human resources	Human needs and cares
Structural	Organizational goals and costs
Political	Power and competition
Symbolic	Symbols and cultures

manager and their effectiveness as perceived by subordinates. Today, however, symbolic and political orientations play much more dominant roles. Attention to symbols appears to be a very significant factor in effective leadership. Leaders operate more as negotiators and poets than as servants, catalysts, or social architects. In terms of crisis, effective leaders barter and build coalitions and shape and reshape symbolic forms that influence organizational purpose and meaning.

The issue of the frame of reference of a leader becomes particularly significant when viewed in the context of the actions that a leader may take. As examples, a leader seeking to develop strategic planning within the human resources framework may gather groups together to promote participation, as opposed to working in isolation. Decision making in the human resources frame of reference implies an open process involving others and intended to secure the commitment of others to the decisions to be made. Evaluation of organizational activities in the human resources framework is a process for helping people to grow rather than an opportunity for the leader to confirm and exercise power. Conflict management in the human resources context is preventive rather than remedial. It involves developing relationships that will minimize future conflicts. Communication in the human relations frame of reference is informal as well as formal; up, down, and lateral rather than one-way. Its function is exchanging information, needs, and feelings rather than simply influencing and manipulating others (Bolman & Deal, 1997).

A New Paradigm for Educational Leadership

As predicted by national and international forces influencing the educational system, the leadership role in education is assuming new dimensions. The public expects educational leaders to improve the quality of schooling significantly. These expectations require leaders first to clarify educational outcomes and assessment strategies. They also require leaders to be proficient in staff development practices and experiments in labor relations. In another leadership role, school leaders are expected to develop new political, social, and business connections within the broader community (Wallace, 1992).

Student achievement in the United States compares unfavorably with achievement outcomes in Asia and Europe (Stevenson & Stigler, 1992). These results raise questions about the economic model and the human resources models used so pervasively in educational systems throughout the nation. Unless future generations are more effectively educated, serious deficiencies will continue to mount as achievement continues to wane further. For example, changing demographics suggest that schools must be more effective in educating an expanding population of poor and minority students. Reports today indicate that these pupils are underserved by the public schools. It is likely that in the future these students will form a major portion of the workforce (Edmonds, 1979; Little, 1981). With these realizations, school leaders will be required to exhibit a higher level of educational, civic, and political leadership. Citizens must be better prepared to participate effectively in societies of the twenty-first century.

Perhaps the most significant recent change in educational administration is the demand for aggressive and effective leadership at the building and district levels. More than ever, the general public expects school administrators to be active leaders of the instructional program. Educational leaders must envision strengthened schools and be able to bring about conditions that will ensure a high-quality education. They must also be capable of conveying symbolic meaning to nourish aspirations and achieve these goals. They must articulate a coherent vision as well as define the components of quality education for students. More important, they must motivate professionals at the school and district levels to implement these new visions. In a word, schools need to become more collegial and less bureaucratic.

A Motivational Model for Educational Leadership

As discussed earlier, motivation is generally considered to be rooted in human needs. People respond to their needs by attempting to fulfill them. Therefore, the basis for understanding motivation in organizations lies in understanding the needs that motivate the behavior of people in these organizations. These views of motivation, however, have not been well implemented in schools.

Research indicates that recognition, achievement, advancement, and responsibility are major forces in motivating educators to lift their performances to their maximum potentials (Savage, 1967; Schmidt, 1976; Wickstrom, 1971). Sergiovanni and Carver (1973) also found that routine housekeeping, such as taking attendance, paperwork, lunch duty, insensitive or inappropriate supervision, irritating administrative policies, and poor relationships with colleagues and/or parents are major sources of job dissatisfaction among educators. Sergiovanni and Carver argued that teaching offers little opportunity for advancement. These general dissatisfactions cause teachers to consider other, more satisfying professions in the educational realm.

In the past, there were two focal points in educational leadership. The first emphasized such things as planning, organizing, coordinating, commanding, and controlling. This approach long defined leadership as task structure and initiating structure. On the job, this means attending to scheduling, organizing, supervising, and monitoring, all of which are absolutely essential to running schools well. The second focal point of educational leadership is consideration based and develops concern for subordinates, morale, motivation, group process, conflict management, and decision making, in essence a participative and human resource orientation.

However, there is more to educational leadership. For example, exemplary educational leaders have long been known to be skilled instructional leaders; that is, they are adept at diagnosing educational problems, counseling teachers, developing curriculum, developing staff, evaluating, and remediating the educational work of teachers. Sergiovanni (1984) defined the three types of leadership as technical, human, and educational. He maintained that these three types of leadership are essential for competent schools. However, to move from competence to excellence in schools, two other forms of leadership, symbolic leadership and culture-building leadership, are also necessary.

Symbolic leadership signals and demonstrates to others what is important, what is valued, what is wanted, and what goals override others. Symbolic leaders create and communicate a vision for followers; they describe a desired state of affairs to which followers commit themselves. They seek to make clear to subordinates the connections between, on the one hand, what they do, and what, on the other hand, they can do toward the achievement of excellence. In other words, symbolic leaders organize their personal time and energies so as to provide a unified vision of the school to students and teachers alike.

However, research suggests that even symbolic leadership alone is incapable of achieving excellence in schools (Sergiovanni, 1984). Excellent schools are characterized by a distinctive organizational character that seems to set such schools apart from others. Equally important, excellent schools must be managed so that teachers feel that they belong to effective work groups, feel good about the work they do, and believe that their achievements are worthwhile.

Leaders of excellent schools must take care, not only to preserve inherited traditions but also to set about building new higher-order traditions.

Leadership and the development of an organizational culture means building behavioral norms that exemplify the best that a school stands for. It means building an institution in which people believe strongly, with which they identify personally, and to which they gladly render their loyalty. All of this gives meaning to the work that they do and additionally builds greater significance into the school environment. In total, the work environment becomes more motivating as commitment develops further.

Leaders who attempt to build strong organizational cultures in schools spend time articulating the purposes and the mission of the school. They bring others together to accept these values as the uniqueness of the school is constantly redefined. These schools are characterized by the bonding that occurs between people and organizations in which they have faith and toward which they have commitment. Under such leadership, students and teachers alike come to understand that they are part of an important and worthwhile larger mission.

Other profound effects on the human relations movement stem from more recent studies of leadership in organizations. For example, Burns (1978) and Bass (1985) conceptualized leadership as transactional and transformational. *Transactional leadership* is an exchange process or problem intervention relationship and correlates with the traditional command and control styles of management. In *transformational leadership,* leaders attribute their own power to better interpersonal skills, hard work, networking, and inspiration. In this view, leadership is individual consideration and intellectual stimulation, and inspires followers to raise their own levels of self-awareness.

Sergiovanni (1992) proposed that transformative leadership be capable of enhancing the ability of members in social organizations to realize their visions and achieve goals. Sergiovanni added a moral dimension to leadership that allows for the creation of a covenant

of shared values, commitment, and vision that can move members to develop an effective, successful organization. However, he also asserted that transactional leadership has a role to fill within organizations. This can be seen in the expanded needs for instructional and interpersonal leadership. Burns (1978) and Greenfield (1987) also called for a moral aspect to leadership. Burns translated this as the ability to raise followers to higher levels of motivation and morality. Greenfield referred to the leader's ability to see things as they are and as they might be within a moral context.

Bass (1981) identified transactional leadership with first-order change based on expected performance. Transactional leaders provide rewards when merited, encourage individual self-interests, and attempt to align self-interests with organizational goals. He identified transformational leadership as second-order changes in attitudes, beliefs, and values, based on performance beyond expectations. Both Bass and Sergiovanni asserted that the practice of transformational leadership can result in organizational members achieving beyond expectations because of the intrinsic self-motivation. Organizational members become committed to a shared set of values and beliefs that become a professional covenant embodied in their thoughts and actions.

The New York State Department of Education's initiative for educational reform, *A New Compact for Learning* (1991), is transformational. In the new compact, the school superintendent is responsible for coordinating the creation of a shared vision for the school district, both symbolic and practical. Elements of this transformation include establishing means to achieve desired outcomes, nurturing community involvement, sharing planning and decision making, and developing and sharing vision of the district with both schools and the community.

This type of leadership is not exercised solely at the district level, but rather, is diffused throughout the entire school environment to include the district, schools, and community. In the normally loosely structured district environ-

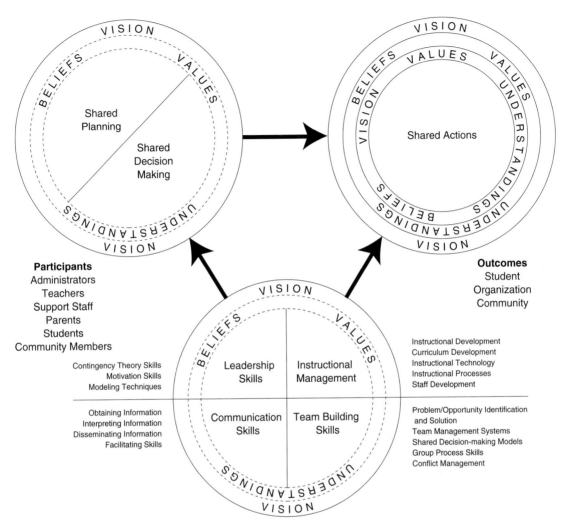

Figure 6.6
Conceptualization of transformative leadership

ment, development of a united subculture provides an opportunity for members to work collaboratively and collegially toward common goals. With the district, members of new coalitions share leadership as individual expertise and roles match with goals.

Sergiovanni's leadership concept is illustrated in Figure 6.6. Each circle is enveloped by a shared vision that drives all beliefs and actions within the district. This vision originates from the chief supervisor and is developed through

meanings attached to that supervisor's actions, decisions, and behaviors. Congruent with this vision are the shared values, beliefs, and understandings that are developed by other organizational partners. The chief supervisor works with this constituency to develop means for shared planning and decision making.

From these actions a compact forms that fuels the activities of each school or department. Shared actions result in the school or departments as a culture forms to build shared commitment to action and enhance student success as outlined in the vision. In this budding environment, leaders in these settings must be adept at communication, team building, and instructional management. Equally important, a third arena represents the tactical leadership skills needed by the chief supervisor of the district. Newly formed teams will each need to learn to rely on each other's expertise, develop collaboration mechanisms, become reflective, and together, formulate plans, make decisions, and act. Supervisors must be adept at instituting an environment that builds the capabilities for all concerned.

More recently, Rosner (1990) studied this transactional–transformational continuum in relation to women's leadership roles and developed a style of leadership she termed *interactive*. Specifically, women encourage participation, share power and information, enhance other people's self-worth, and inspire excitement about work and the work environment. Rosner's views indicate that data support a new view of the way that women lead and contribute an added level of knowledge and understanding for human resource authors, theorists, and users. Other writers have given credence to other views of leadership. Leaders manage attention, meaning, trust, and self (Bennis & Nanus, 1985). Leaders are teachers, designers, and stewards (Senge, 1991). As further research continues to contribute to our understanding, leadership and human resource management will continue to evolve.

The study of human relations is concerned with human potential in organizations. In the future, supportive climates, more feedback, and increased investment in workers must somehow bring excellence to organizations. People work because they are motivated to do so. Studies of people in the work environment are extensive. Process models of motivation focus on how and why motivation works. Content models of motivation discuss what specifically motivates people. Expectancy models, behaviorist models, and social learning models are categorized as process models. Studies on content models fall into two areas: common human needs and motivation at work.

Although theorists have proposed a variety of needs components operating in human beings, they all assume that people are motivated in pursuit of the fulfillment of their own needs. The major tasks of leadership are to provide opportunities for workers to satisfy these needs. As Herzberg claims, people are motivated by factors that he termed *motivators*. To motivate employees, leaders should consider building motivators into employees' jobs, giving them a sense of achievement and formal responsibility.

Morale reflects how members feel about their organizations. Morale is influenced by public perception of the organization, the employee's personal life, the nature of the work, interpersonal relationships, the employee's self-concept and needs, and leadership. Leaders need to observe the morale of the organization and develop a sensitivity to employees' needs. Leaders also need to improve the quality of employee worklife by using such techniques as job rotation, job enlargement, job enrichment, and sociotechnical systems.

Informal organizations emerge from individuals' social contacts within a formal organization. Informal organizations provide people with alternatives for achieving satisfaction not provided by the formal organization: social interactions, social control, informal communication, and alternatives for achieving satisfaction not provided by the formal organization. Informal organizations have four potential disadvantages. They tend to transmit false information, resist changes, cause excessive conformity to group norms, and even develop goals that conflict with formal organizational goals. However, informal organizations do provide some benefits for the formal organization. They satisfy employee social satisfactions, provide a useful employee communication network, and provide employees with an emotional escape valve. Faced with the inevitability of the existence of informal organizations, the job of leadership is to accept and understand them, to take into account the possible effects on informal organiza-

- Influence Expectancy Beliefs
- Timely and Sound Rewards
- Behavior Models
- Existence of Variable Needs
- Opportunities for Needs Satisfactions
- Job Enrichment
- Develop Collective Identity

- Supportive Climate
- More Feedback
- Training
  - Growth
  - Achievement
- Opportunities to Tackle Challenges

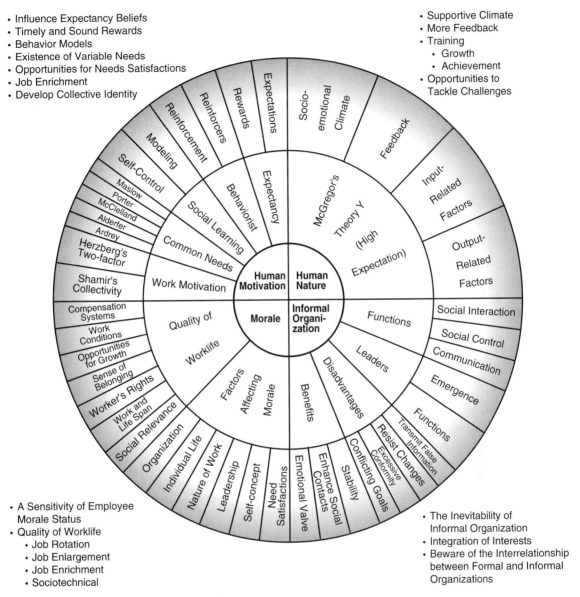

Figure 6.7
Taxonomy of theoretical works of human relations

- A Sensitivity of Employee Morale Status
- Quality of Worklife
  - Job Rotation
  - Job Enlargement
  - Job Enrichment
  - Sociotechnical

- The Inevitability of Informal Organization
- Integration of Interests
- Beware of the Interrelationship between Formal and Informal Organizations

tions when taking actions, to integrate the interests of informal organizations into the formal organizational activities, and to avoid unnecessary threats to informal organizations.

Human relations is not a prescription to make people happy. Instead, the true essence of human relations management is an attempt to make people's contributions to organizational life more meaningful. The focus on provision of meaningful organizational life is evident in light of the theoretical works of human relations study, as pictured in Figure 6.7.

In large part, human relations thinkers have adopted McGregor's Theory Y viewpoint,

in which human beings are viewed as full of potential. This potential can be tapped by holding
and encouraging high expectations. To develop
human potential in organizations, leaders need
to provide workers with a supportive climate,
more feedback, training programs for professional growth, and challenging opportunities.

Contemporary Issues in Human Relations

Discrimination is a continuing problem in all organizational environments. It may be particularly critical in the educational environment as
educators become more accountable for developmental responsibilities that once were largely
family centered. Although much progress has
been made in recent decades, considerable
prejudicial and discriminatory practices remain.
Too often, this prejudice and discrimination are
directed at ethnic minorities and other special
employment groups. Prejudice stems from internal judgments based on insufficient evidence. A prejudiced person often tends to think
in stereotypical terms without considering individual differences. Prejudice becomes a serious
human relations problem when actions become
discriminatory. Too often in our organizational
activities, time constraints and prejudgments
about others and situations create undue pressure to act. Our actions become inappropriate
as we inadvertently fail to withhold judgment
until issues are investigated fully.

In our attempts to build a just working environment, we must somehow learn to create a
fair and equal working climate. Leaders and
managers alike must balance objectivity and
sensitivity. Kossen (1987) identifies some typical problems that contribute further to discrimination in the workplace. For example, some
managers stereotype ethnic minorities and
other special employment groups as being less
capable than white males. As a result, managers
tend to expect less from these groups, and poor
work results. In reality, these managers may be
eliciting the exact poor behavior they expect.

Their insensitivity to their own prejudices
causes discrimination as they view these
groups from an inappropriate perspective. In
other cases, in attempts to avoid prejudice,
managers may assign more difficult projects to
these special groups to create an appearance of
equal treatment. Managers' inabilities to understand their own prejudice contribute to further
discrimination.

Racial discrimination is an emotional issue. A
review of the research demonstrates that society is moving slowly to overcome racial discrimination (Wildstrom, 1986). Many events in
the recent past have aroused greater public interest and protest. African-Americans were the
first to recognize that protests and demonstra-
tions play a significant part in forcing public
recognition of racial injustice (Coulmad, 1992;
Kossen, 1987). Their demands for new laws,
better education, and government action have
brought change. Strong self-pride has helped
the African-American cause in the search for
equal job opportunity and a better place in society. Equally important, discrimination against
Hispanics, Native Americans, and Oriental
Americans are as problematic for our society
and educational institutions.

There has been great progress in women's
rights in recent decades. One of the major concerns of women in the workplace has been
equal pay for equal work. This issue asserts that
women should be paid equally for performing
tasks requiring the same skills, training, responsibility, and effort as men. Other issues are
equally significant: calls for more and better
quality child care, better promotion potential,
better legal protection against sexual harass-
ment, broader maternity benefits, and equal political power. Although much action in these areas is evident today, more needs to be done.

Much still needs to be accomplished in the human resource realm, as noted by the numerous
commissions exploring reform and restructuring
in the educational environment. Most problematic will be how to assure that educational leadership pinpoints action strategies that deal effec-

tively with broad human resource activities. Most important, practitioners today must become adept at understanding human relations and devising visionary practices that elicit the best of human potential. As much literature has shown, the best outcomes generally occur in an environment where concern for the individual worker or administrator is responsible and accountable in a team atmosphere, where individual need achievement transcends entitlement, and where people strive for and have the opportunity to achieve excellence in their own terms.

CASE STUDIES

Human Relations: The Case of the New Hires

Valerie Rizzo has just been appointed the new principal of the East Ruxton Middle School. East Ruxton is a city of approximately 20,000 persons serving as a marketing and light manufacturing center for the two adjacent rural counties. The city school district at one time had been one of the outstanding programs in the state for a community of its size. However, over the past decade, that reputation began to slip as changes in the economy caused reductions in the tax base and thus cutbacks in the schools' budgets and services. The superintendent and current administration have all held their positions for a number of years, with the junior administrator having seven years of service. The teaching staff also have tended to stay in place. In the middle school, only two of the teaching faculty have less than five years' tenure.

When she was hired, Valerie was told by the superintendent that the most recent school board election had brought in three new persons, and that the balance of voting power on the new board lies with them. The new members ran on a platform of reform and upgrading for the schools, and they are looking to Valerie as the new administrator to spearhead change in her school. The new members are hoping that changes in the middle school will provide an example that will influence the rest of the district.

Questions

1. If you were Valerie Rizzo, what steps would you take in the first 30 days of your incumbency as the middle school principal to introduce the change-related issues discussed above while establishing effective human relations with your building staff?

2. How will you approach the issues discussed above with your administrative peers across the district?

3. What model(s) of human needs and leadership discussed in this chapter will you use to guide you in your new role? Why?

4. Prepare an action plan for yourself for the first half-year that will allow you to begin the job, operate your school, and initiate appropriate changes. Be prepared to discuss the means by which you will motivate your staff to meet the challenges to come, and explain why you are selecting those particular means.

The Case of the Rumor Mill

Rumors are rampant at Schoolville. At recent school board meetings, the superintendent has been confronted on several occasions by irate parents and the local press. Somehow these groups have gained access to privileged state budget documents. The new budget has granted a sizable pay increase to teachers. However, the community is not satisfied with recent student achievement scores. In addition, the student scores have been poor for several years running. In light of these circumstances, discuss the following:

1. How to deflect attention away from the apparent informal network that seems to have more information than the school board and the superintendent

2. How to address the schools' fundamental problem, poor student achievement

The Case of the Reality Check

The Schoolville superintendent has prided himself on the high-quality graduates his district has been able to recruit from excellent teaching colleges over the past several years. Recently, these graduates have raised complaints about the bureaucratic nature of the district and schools, and have united an even larger group of dissatisfied tenured teachers. The new teachers bring with them high expectations. It seems that the educational excellence movement has passed Schoolville by, and the dissenters are demanding more than the district can offer. Discuss this scenario in light of the following:

1. How to achieve more flexibility for teachers, while maintaining control
2. How to maintain current levels of efficiency
3. How to "fast forward" into the era of excellence

The Case of Professionalizing

The Miller Middle School principal has kept up to date with recent educational literature. But she is perplexed by some recent school-based management principles. Although she is an advocate of professionalization of the school environment, during discussions with teachers, she has become skeptical. For example, while she believes in the tenets of shared decision making, she also realizes that this approach has not been effective in other schools. What steps can the principal take to bring school-based management to her school?

References

Aldag, R. J., Barr, S. H., & Brief, A. P. (1981). Measurement of perceived task characteristics. *Psychological Bulletin, 90,* 415–431.

Aldag, R. J., & Brief, A. P. (1979). *Task design and employee motivation.* Glenview IL: Scott, Foresman.

Alderfer, C. P. (1969). An empirical test of a new theory of needs. *Organizational Behavior and Human Performance, 4,* 143–175.

Alderfer, C. (1972). *Existence, relatedness, and growth: Human needs in organizational settings.* New York: Free Press.

Ardrey, R. (1966). *The territorial imperative.* New York: Atheneum.

Argyris, C. (1957). *Personality and organization.* New York: Harper & Row.

Argyris, C. (1964). *Integrating the individual and the organization.* New York: Wiley.

Argyris, C. (1985). *Action science.* San Francisco: Jossey-Bass.

Atkinson, J. W. (1964). *An introduction to motivation.* Princeton, NJ: Van Nostrand.

Bales, R. F. (1950). *Interaction-process analysis: A method for the study of small groups.* Reading, MA: Addison-Wesley.

Bales, R. F. (1953). The equilibrium problem in school groups. In T. Parsons, R. F. Bales, & E. A. Shils (Eds.), *Working papers in the theory of action.* Glencoe, IL: Free Press.

Bandura, A. (1968). A social learning of interpretation of psychological dysfunctions. In P. London & D. Rosenhan (Eds.), *Foundations of abnormal psychology* (pp. 293–344). New York: Holt, Rinehart & Winston.

Bandura, A. (1969). *Principles of behavior modification.* New York: Holt, Rinehart & Winston.

Bandura, A. (1976). Social learning theory. In J. T. Spence, R. C. Carson, & J. W. Thibait (Eds.), *Behavioral approaches to therapy* (pp. 1–46). Morristown, NJ: General Learning.

Bandura, A. (1977). *Social learning theory.* Upper Saddle River, NJ: Prentice Hall.

Bandura, A., & Walters, R. H. (1963). *Social learning and personality development.* New York: Holt, Rinehart & Winston.

Barnard, C. I. (1938). *The functions of the executive.* Cambridge, MA: Harvard University Press.

Bass, B. M. (1981). *Stogdill's handbook of leadership: A survey of theory and research* (revised and expanded edition). New York: Free Press.

Bass, B. M. (1985). *Leadership and performance beyond expectation.* New York: Free Press.

Benge, E., & Hickley, J. (1984). *Morale and motivation: How to measure morale and increase productivity.* New York: Franklin Watts.

Bennis, W. G., & Nanus, B. (1985). *Leaders: The strategies for taking charge.* New York: Harper & Row.

Berlew, D. E., & Hall, D. T. (1966, September). The socialization of managers: Effects of expectations on performance. *Administrative Science Quarterly, 11*(11), 207–223.

Berney, M. F., & Ayers, J. B. (1990). *Evaluating preparation programs for school leaders and teachers in specialty areas.* Boston: Kluwer Academic.

Blake, R. R., & Mouton, J. S. (1964). *The managerial grid.* Houston, TX: Gulf.

Bolman, L. G., & Deal, T. E. (1991). *Reframing organizations: Artistry and choice in management.* San Francisco: Jossey-Bass.

Bolman, L. G., & Deal, T. E. (1997). *Reframing organizations: Artistry, choice and leadership* (2nd ed). San Francisco: Jossey-Bass.

Brophy, J. E. (1985). Teacher–student interaction. In J. B. Dusek, V. C. Hall, & W. J. Meyer (Eds.), *Teacher expectancies* (pp. 303–328). Hillsdale, NJ: Erlbaum.

Burns, J. M. (1978). *Leadership.* New York: Harper & Row.

Campbell, J. D., & Pritchard, R. D. (1983). Motivation theory in industrial and organizational psychology. In M. D. Dunnette (Ed.*), Handbook of industrial and organizational psychology* (pp. 63–130). New York: Wiley.

Campbell, R. F., Fleming, T., Newell, L. J., & Bennion, J. W. (1987). *A history of thought and practice in educational administration.* New York: Teachers College Publication, Columbia University.

Champagne, P. J., & McAfee, R. B. (1989). *Motivating strategies for performance and productivity: A guide to human resources development.* New York: Quorum Books.

Coulmad, F. (Ed.). (1992). *Attitudes and accommodation in multilingual societies.* New York: Mouton de Gruyter.

Dachler, H. P., & Mobley, W. (1973). Construct validation of an instrumentality–expectancy–task–goal model of work motivation: Some theoretical boundary conditions. *Journal of Applied Psychology, 58,* 397–418.

Davis, K. (1967). *Human relations at work* (3rd ed.). New York: McGraw-Hill.

Davis, K. D. (1977). *Human behavior at work: Organizational behavior* (5th ed.). New York: McGraw-Hill.

Deal, T. E. (1992). Leadership in a world of change. In S. D. Thomson (Ed.), *School leadership: A blueprint for change* (pp. 1–7). Newbury Park, CA: Corwin Press.

Dennison, H. (1931). *Organizational engineering.* New York: Macmillan.

Dewey, J. (1946). *Problems of men.* New York: Philosophical Library.

Duchon, D., Green, S. G., & Taber, T. D. (1986). Vertical dyad linkage: A longitudinal assessment of antecedents and gender label. *Journal of Personality and Social Psychology, 46,* 991–1004.

Duignan, D. A., & Macpherson, R. J. S. (1992). *Educative leadership: A practical theory for new administrators and managers.* Washington, DC: Falmer Press.

Eden, D. (1990a). Pygmalion without interpersonal contrast effect: Whole groups gain from training manager expectations. *Journal of Applied Psychology, 75,* 394–398.

Eden, D. (1990b). *Pygmalion in management: Production as a self-fulfilling prophecy.* Lexington, MA: Lexington Books.

Edmonds, R. (1979). Effective schools for the urban poor. *Educational Leadership, 37,* 15–24.

Etzioni, A. (1961). *The moral dimension: Toward a new economics.* New York: Free Press.

Etzioni, A. (1988). *A comparative analysis of complex organizations.* New York: Free Press.

Feldman, J. M., Reitz, H. J., & Hiterman, R. J. (1976). Alternatives to optimization in expectancy theory. *Journal of Applied Psychology, 61,* 712–720.

Fiedler, F. E. (1967). *A theory of leadership effectiveness.* New York: McGraw-Hill.

Flanders, J. P. (1968). A review of research on imitative behavior. *Psychological Bulletin, 69,* 316–337.

Follett, M. P. (1930). *Creative experience.* London: Longmans, Green.

Frankel, L. K., & Fleisher, A. (1920). *The human factor in industry.* New York: Macmillan.

Gantt, H. L. (1916). *Industrial leadership.* New Haven, CT: Yale University Press.

Getzels, J. W. (1977). Educational administration twenty years later, 1954–1974. In L. L. Cunningham, W. G. Weck, & R. O. Nystrand (Eds.), *Educational administration: The developing decades.* Berkeley, CA: McCutchan.

Greenberg, P. D., & Glaser, E. M. (1983). Viewpoints of labor leaders regarding quality of worklife improvement programs. In R. M. Steers & L. W. Porter (Eds.), *Motivation and work behavior* (3rd ed. pp. 547–561). New York: McGraw-Hill.

Greenfield, W. (1987). *Instructional leadership: Concepts, issues, and controversies.* Newton, MA: Allyn & Bacon.

Griffin, R. W. (1982). *Task design: An integrative approach.* Glenview, IL: Scott, Foresman.

Griffiths, D. E. (1956). Human relations in school administration. In 63rd *Yearbook of the National Society for the Study of Education,* Part II. Chicago: University of Chicago Press.

Griffiths, D. E., Stout, R. T., & Forsyth, P. B. (Eds.). (1988). *Leaders for America's schools: The report and papers of the National Commission on Excellence in Educational Administration.* Berkeley, CA: McCutchan.

Guthrie, J. W., & Reed, R. J. (1991). *Educational administration and policy: Effective leadership for American education* (2nd ed.). Boston: Allyn & Bacon.

Hackman, J. R. (1983). Work design. In R. M. Steers & L. W. Porter (Eds.), *Motivation and work behavior* (3rd ed., pp. 490–516). New York: McGraw-Hill.

Hackman, J. R., & Oldham, G. R. (1980). *Work redesign.* Reading, MA: Addison-Wesley.

Hall, J. (1980). The managerial lens: What you see is what you get! In J. A. Shtogren (Ed.), *Models for management: The structure of competence* (pp. 4–10). The Woodlands, TX: Teleometrics International.

Halloran, J. (1978). *Applied human relations: An organizational approach.* Upper Saddle River, NJ: Prentice Hall.

Hammond, K. R. (1966). *The psychology of Egon Brunswick.* New York: Holt, Rinehart & Winston.

Hamner, W. C., & Hamner, E. P. (1976). Behavior modification on the bottom line. *Organizational Dynamics, 4*(4), 3–21.

Hellriegel, D., & Slocum, J. W., Jr. (1976). *Organizational behavior: Contingency views.* St. Paul, MN: West.

Herzberg, F. (1966). *Working and the nature of man.* New York: Crowell.

Herzberg, F. (1968). One more time: How do you motivate employees? *Harvard Business Review, 46,* 56–57.

Herzberg, F. (1981). Motivating people. In P. Mali (Ed.), *Management handbook.* New York: Wiley.

Herzberg, F., Mausner, B., & Snyderman, B. B. (1959). *The motivation to work.* New York: Wiley.

Hill, H. (1947). Personal problems in American education. In American Association of School Administration official report (1946). Washington DC: National Educational Association.

House, R. J., & Mitchell, T. R. (1974). Path–goal theory of leadership. *Journal of Contemporary Business, 3,* 81–98.

Kanfer, F. H., & Karoly, P. (1974). Self-control: A behavioristic excursion into the lion's den. In M. J. Mahoney & C. E. Thoresa (Eds.), *Self-control: Power to the person* (pp. 200–217). Monterey, CA: Brooks/Cole.

Katz, R. (1980). Time and work: Toward a integrative perspective. In B. M. Staw & L. L. Cummings (Eds.), *Research in organizational behavior* (Vol. 2). Greenwich, CT: JAI Press.

Knezevich, S. (1984). *Administration of public education: A sourcebook for the leadership and management of educational institutions.* New York: Harper & Row.

Komaki, J. I. (1986). Toward effective supervision. *Journal of Applied Psychology, 71,* 270–279.

Kossen, S. (1987). *The human side of organization (4th ed.).* New York: Harper & Row.

Kouzes, J. M., & Posner, B. Z. (1987). *The leadership challenge: How to get extraordinary things done in organizations.* San Francisco: Jossey-Bass.

Lawler, E. E., III. (1992). *Ultimate advantage: Creating the high involvement organization.* San Francisco: Jossey-Bass.

Lewin, K. (1938). The conceptual representation and the measurement of psychological forces. *Contributions to psychological theory* (Vol.1, No. 4). Durham, NC: Duke University Press.

Likert, R. (1961). *New patterns of management.* New York: McGraw-Hill.

Likert, R. (1967). *The human organization.* New York: McGraw-Hill.

Link, A. S., & Catton, W. B. (1967). *American epoch: A history of the United States since the 1890s.* New York: Knopf.

Little, J. W. (1981). *School success and staff development in desegregation schools.* Boulder, CO: Center for Action Research.

Luthans, F., & Otteman, R. (1977). Motivation vs. learning approaches to organizational behavior. In F. Luthans (Ed.), *Contemporary readings in organizational behavior* (2nd ed.). New York: McGraw-Hill.

Mahoney, M. J. (1974). *Cognition and behavior modification.* Cambridge, MA: Ballinger.

Mangieri, J. N. (1985). *Excellence in education.* Fort Worth, TX: Texas Christian University.

Maslow, A. H. (1954). *Motivation and personality.* New York: Harper & Row.

Maslow, A. H. (1962). *Toward a psychology of being*. New York: Van Nostrand.

Maxcy, S. J. (1991). *Educational leadership: A critical pragmatic perspective*. New York: Bregin & Garvey.

Mayo, E. (1933). *The human problems of an industrial civilization*. Cambridge, MA: Harvard University Press.

McClelland, D. C. (1955). *Power: The inner experience*. New York: Irvington.

McClelland, D. C. (1961). *The achieving society*. Princeton, NJ: Van Nostrand.

McClelland, D. C. (1975). *Power: The inner experience*. New York: Irvington.

McClelland, D. C. (1976). Power is the great motivation. *Harvard Business Review, 54*(2), 100–110.

McClelland, D. C. (1987). Characteristics of successful entrepreneurs. *Journal of Creative Behavior, 3,* 219–233.

McClelland, D. C., Atkinson, J. W., Clark, R. A., & Lowell, E. L. (1953). *The achievement motivation*. New York: Appleton-Century-Crofts.

McGregor, D. (1960). *The human side of enterprise*. New York: McGraw-Hill.

Merton, R. K. (1948). The self-fulfilling prophecy. *Antioch Review, 8,* 193–210.

Miles, R. E. (1975). *Theories of management*. New York: McGraw-Hill.

Mischell, W. (1973). Toward a cognitive reconceptualization of personality. *Psychological Review, 80,* 284–302.

Mitchell, V. F., & Moudgill, P. (1976). Measurement of Maslow's need hierarchy. *Organizational Behavior and Human Performance, 16,* 334–349.

Moehlman, A. B. (1940). *School administration*. Boston: Houghton Mifflin.

Moreno, J. L. (1947). Contributions of sociometry to research methodology in Sociology. *American Sociological Review, 12,* 287–292.

Murray, H. A. (1938). *Exploration in personality*. New York: Oxford.

New York State Education Department. (1991, March). *A new compact for learning: Improving public elementary, middle, and secondary education results in the 1990s*. Albany, NY: State University of New York.

O'Toole, J. (1981). *Making America work*. New York: Continuum.

Ouchi, W. G. (1981). *Theory Z: How American business can meet the Japanese challenge*. Reading, MA: Addison-Wesley.

Owens, R. G. (1987). *Organizational behavior in education* (3rd ed.). Upper Saddle River, NJ: Prentice Hall.

Pinder, C. C. (1984). *Work motivation: Theory, issues, and applications*. Glenview, IL: Scott, Foresman.

Plous, F. K. (1987, March). Redesigning work. *Personnel Administrator, 99.*

Porter, L. W. (1961). A study of perceived need satisfaction in bottom and middle-management jobs. *Journal of Applied Psychology, 45,* 1–10.

Porter, L. W., & Lawler, E. E. (1968). *Managerial attitudes and performance*. Homewood, IL: Irwin.

Reavis, C. A., & Griffith, H. (1992). *Restructuring schools: Theory and practice*. Lancaster, PA: Technomic.

Reitz, H. J. (1987). *Behavior in organizations* (3rd ed.). Homewood, IL: Irwin.

Roethlisberger, F. J., & Dickson, W. J. (1939). *Management and the worker*. Cambridge, MA: Harvard University Press.

Rosenthal, R. (1974). *On the social psychology of the self-fulfilling prophecy*. New York: MSS Modular.

Rosenthal, R. (1981). Pavlov's mice, Pfungst's horse, and Pygmalion's PONS: Some models for the study of interpersonal expectancy effects. In T. A. Sebok & R. Rosenthal (Eds.), *The clever Hans phenomenon*. Annals of the New York Academy of Science, No. 364.

Rosenthal, R., & Jacobson, L. (1968). *Pygmalion in the classroom*. New York: Holt, Rinehart & Winston.

Rosner, M. (1990). *The second generation: Continuity and change in the kibbutz*. New York: Greenwood Press.

Ruben, B. D. (1988). *Communication and human behavior* (2nd ed.). New York: Macmillan.

Saltonstall, R. (1959). *Human relations in administration: Text and cases*. New York: McGraw-Hill.

Sanford, A. C. (1977). *Human relations: The theory and practice of organizational behavior* (2nd ed.). New York: Macmillan.

Savage, P. M. (1967). *A study of teacher satisfaction and attitudes: Causes and effects*. Unpublished doctoral dissertation, Auburn University, Auburn, AL.

Scandura, T. A., Graen, G. B., & Novak, M. A. (1986). When managers decide not to decide autocratically: An investigation of leader–member exchange and decision influence. *Journal of Applied Psychology, 71,* 579–584.

Schlechty, P. C. (1990). *Schools for the twenty-first century: Leadership imperatives for educational reform.* San Francisco: Jossey-Bass.

Schmidt, G. L. (1976). Job satisfaction and secondary school administrators. *Educational Administration Quarterly, 12,* 81.

Scott, W. G. (1962). *Human relations in management: A behavioral approach.* Upper Saddle River, NJ: Prentice Hall.

Scott, W. R. (1981). *Organizations: Rational, natural and open systems.* Upper Saddle River, NJ: Prentice Hall.

Senge, P. (1991). *The fifth discipline: The art and practice of the learning organization.* New York: Doubleday.

Sergiovanni, T. J. (1984). Leadership and excellence in schooling. *Educational Leadership, 41*(5), 4–13.

Sergiovanni, T. J. (1991). *The principalship: A reflective practice* (2nd ed.). Boston: Allyn & Bacon.

Sergiovanni, T. J. (1992). *Moral leadership: Getting to the heart of school improvement.* San Francisco: Jossey-Bass.

Sergiovanni, T. J., & Carver, F. D. (1973). *The new school executives: A theory of administration.* New York: Dodd, Mead.

Sergiovanni, T. J., & Moore, J. H. (1989). *Schooling for tomorrow: Directing reforms to issues that count.* Boston: Allyn & Bacon.

Shamir, B. (1990). Calculations, values, and identities: The sources of collectivistic work motivation. *Human Relations, 43,* 313–332.

Silverman, D. (1971). *The theory of organizations: A sociological framework.* New York: Basic Books.

Skinner, B. F. (1953). *Science and human behavior.* New York: Macmillan.

Skinner, B. F. (1971). *Beyond freedom and dignity.* New York: Knopf.

Skinner, B. F. (1974). *About behaviorism.* New York: Knopf.

Staats, A. W. (1975). *Social behaviorism.* Homewood, IL: Dorsey.

Steers, R. M., & Spencer, D. G. (1977). The role of achievement motivation in job design. *Journal of Applied Psychology, 4,* 472–479.

Stevenson, H. W., & Steigler, J. W. (1992). *The learning job.* New York: Summit Books.

Tannebaum, R., & Schmidt, W. H. (1958). How to choose a leadership pattern. *Harvard Business Review, 36,* 95–101.

Taylor, F. W. (1911). *The principles of scientific management.* New York: Harper & Brothers.

Tolman, E. C. (1932). *Purposive behavior in animals and men.* New York: Century.

Tosi, H. L., & Hamner, W. C. (1974). *Organizational behavior: A contingency approach.* Chicago: St. Clair.

Tyler, R. T. (1941). Educational adjustments necessitated by changing ideological concepts. In W. C. Reavis (Ed.), *Administrative adjustments required by socio-economic change: Proceedings of the 10th annual conference of administrative officers of public and private schools.* Chicago: University of Chicago Press.

Ure, A. (1835). *The philosophy of manufacturers.* London: Knight.

Vroom, V. H. (1964). *Work and motivation.* New York: Wiley.

Wallace, R. C., Jr. (1992). Leadership in school. In S. D. Thomson (Ed.), *School leadership: A blueprint for change* (pp. 8–9). Newbury Park, CA: Corwin Press.

Walton, R. E. (1975). Criteria for quality of working life. In L. E. Davis & A. B. Cherns (Eds.), *The quality of working life* (Vol. 1). New York: Free Press.

Watson, J. B. (1930). *Behaviorism.* Chicago: University of Chicago Press.

Wickstrom, R. A. (1971). *An investigation into job satisfaction among teachers.* Unpublished doctoral dissertation, University of Oregon, Eugene, OR.

Wildstrom, S. H. (1986, January 27). Affirmative action: A deal to patch up the Brock–Meese feud. *Business Week,* 51.

Wolman, B. (1956). Leadership and group dynamics. *Journal of Social Psychology, 43,* 11–25.

Yauch, W. (1949). *Improving human relations in school administration.* New York: Harper & Brothers.

PART III

The Generation and Use of Information in a Learning Organization

Inquiry is the close examination of a phenomenon in order to understand it. It is the process of knowing, of puzzle solving, of finding truth. Inquiry into any subject is shaped by one's view of reality, which is a philosophical issue. In this part we discuss the philosophy of administration of systems and the related issues of values, ethics, and morality. There is in-depth discussion of inquiry frameworks, including value generation and understanding, evaluation and assessment, and applicability for practitioners. Inquiry is considered as a basis for creation of learning organizations.

Chapter 7: The Process of Inquiry and Analysis. This chapter emphasizes the importance of human inquiry. We discuss common errors made in inquiry and the development of safeguards to ensure that fundamental issues are addressed and observed. Theory-based quantitative and naturalistic approaches are shown as being important for the inquirer. Theory is developed with emphasis on practical applications intended to provide a strong connection to effective functioning of organizations.

Chapter 8: Evaluation in Education: Theories, Models, and Processes. Mobilizing resources to enable organizations to function effectively is a critical aspect of educational leadership. Judgments of effective functioning are based on monitoring outcomes and measuring them against established goals and objectives. In this chapter we discuss means by which leaders pursue this process. The quality movement and its relation to program evaluation, student achievement, and staff evaluation are considered. There is also discussion of national and state standards and assessment activities.

CHAPTER 7

The Process of Inquiry and Analysis

Inquiry's Prelude

Educational research has been labeled in the recent past as "at best, inconclusive, at worst, barren" (Tom, 1984, p. 2). In classroom research, for example, Barrow (1984) contends that we know little of importance that would make us feel more secure. The scientific method as espoused by such educational proponents as Thorndike, Barr, and Ryan, although rigorous and seemingly thorough, may have met the same fate as the Weberian bureaucratic system. Correlational studies in educational research investigating limited variables, some even combined with observational studies, are, in large part, not persuasive.

As we embark on the study of educational inquiry, cognizant of increased complexity and ambiguity in education today, many may already have arrived at the commonsense conclusion that scientific methods will never realize the truths they claim to discover. We might ask the question: Aren't teaching and learning intimately tied to the intentions, goals, and purposes of education—from which its meaning is derived? How can we claim that one best way exists or that causal links exist everywhere, knowing that in reality we perceive and act differently? Perhaps we can only approach research in this manner because our scholarly forebears conditioned us to this methodology through the process of normal science (Kuhn, 1970).

We're beginning to see many people questioning the efficacy of the most recent renditions of the structure of knowledge brought to bear by so-called interpretivistic and critical theory paradigms. Despite some scholars' attempts, others sense only modest progress from previous eras as scholars try to replace the problematic features of past inquiry paradigms with newer models. Melding old and new paradigms provides incremental and adaptive movement as a next step. But at the same time, others are demanding that new tenets replace the old and outmoded. Interpretivists, for example, reject the underlying assumptions about a uniformity in nature and reject linear-causal sequencing. Interpretivists instead seek to understand behavior from a phenomenological perspective as a result of a social construction process (Erickson, 1985). From this perspective people's actions create the world that exists, not the reverse. In the interpretivistic paradigm, causation is determined from interpreted symbols, which then provide meaningful understanding.

The critical theorist movement provides a further example. Displeased with the technical-, rational-, efficient-, and objective-oriented approaches of the past, this paradigm supports methods that investigate relationships: for instance, relationships among schools, teaching, and society and their political and economic foundations. Unwittingly, educational scholars today and in the recent past may simply be reproducing the inequities prevalent in the most observed social class structures. Educational researchers must, instead, raise our awareness of these inequities and not replicate them. Educational research should seek to move society or the educational environment toward greater social justice, not simply mirror the current status. A transformation of the entire structure of schooling in systemic terms should be the intent of effective research (Gage, 1989).

Gage's (1989) article pinpoints the problems we face in the future. The questions below and others construct the context for this chapter on inquiry. How does a theory of knowledge inform our inquiry practices? What are the paradigms of inquiry, their nature, their relationship with the knower, and the methodology that informs them? What critiques exist for each of these paradigms? What are the strengths and weaknesses? What is the necessity behind the paradigm wars, or is this simply a case of intellectuals arguing about those same philosophical questions that they have for ages? Will older paradigms live on with newer ones? Which will survive? Will the debate merely continue? Perhaps you'll recognize your own inquiry paradigm in the discussion that follows.

Inquiry Unraveled

The Early Beginnings of Inquiry

Inquiry has been described as the process of knowing, of solving puzzles, of probing, and of finding truth (Eisner, 1981; Guba, 1990; Kuhn, 1970). With varying degrees of success, scholars have attempted to characterize the nature of inquiry, to answer the question: What is going on here? Dewey defined inquiry as "the controlled or directed transformation of an indeterminate situation into one that is so determinate in its constituent distinctions and relations as to convert the elements of the original situation into a unified whole" (Dewey, 1938, p. 104). Kuhn (1970) referred to normal science as puzzle solving. Babbie (1989) simply defined inquiry as a search for regularity. More recently, Guba and Lincoln (1989) and others asserted that inquiry is embraced in and reflected through the belief system of the inquirer.

Littlejohn (1992) believes that inquiry is the "systematic, disciplined ordering of experience that leads to the development of understanding and knowledge" (p. 8). In this regard, inquiry is a focused and planned means, process, or method to arrive at an outcome. In a cyclical process of questioning, observation, and generalization, scholars stage the continued development of knowledge creation and discovery. The process is structured and ordered by a community of scholars who ensure that scientific experience is "true" or adequate to meet the demands of a culture, time, or person. Thus, the normative force of logic is applied by the community of scholars in an ever-unfolding process termed *inquiry* (Dewey, 1938). Inquiry, then, as defined by the community of scholars, can only be understood within the context of a culture. Dewey also maintains that the logic of theory is subservient to the metaphysical and epistemological preconceptions of the inquirer. The process of inquiry, then, arises from a historical and cultural environment. While the creation of knowledge in and of itself may seem like a mundane task, scholars see the development of knowledge from differing circumstances. What is knowable and how knowledge arises are not as apparent as a cursory view may indicate.

Although many inquiry paradigms exist, knowledge creation is generally thought to evolve from the three distinctive approaches identified earlier. Littlejohn (1992) labeled them knowledge of discovery, knowledge of interpretation, and knowledge of criticism. In Littlejohn's view, the discovery approach seeks to achieve objective observations which, when refined, produce instances of structural reality. In contrast, the interpretive approach seeks to construct a picture of reality through the eyes of both the participant and the observer. Knowledge is then reconstructed as the next instance(s) of reality. The critical approach seeks to define knowledge through critical judgments which then lead to social improvement and change.

From another vantage point, Eisner (1991) clarified building and defining the origins of inquiry further. Objectivity is surely among the world's most cherished beliefs. Objectivity seeks to see things the way they are. To see is to know. In this context, then, the aim of inquiry is to achieve truth and certain knowledge. In addition, understanding is derived from the community of believers. What inquirers say, therefore, is of equal importance. Just as important is the understanding that knowledge is used and developed via certain methodology. In part, knowledge is freed from personal judgment as a result of choice of method.

Representation, too, is problematic. Any account that furthers knowledge is offered via a symbol system (Eisner, 1991). Representations of knowledge are revealing and at the same time concealing, depending on the constraints of the symbol system. In this respect we can begin to sense how the subjective view gains its stature. Subjective knowledge becomes an important distinctive view. But similarly, as we have developed the objective view above, so can we erode the premier stations that comprise subjectivity. Eisner (1991) summarized the disparities herein as he explained that ontological subjectivity is possible if we accept the idea that truth exceeds belief. That is a belief in itself. Active minds in commerce with the world are the product of an active mind. To seek more than what ultimately is referenced in our own beliefs after using appropriate criteria for holding them is to retreat to a higher authority or to seek a dominant view that bypasses the mind's observation of nature (p. 51).

Eisner concluded that a different belief structure is needed to avoid the dichotomy between objectivity and subjectivity. What may be needed is a process by which we can enlist the strength of objectivity and subjectivity from their separate consequences and move to a unification of understanding and principle. Since what we know of the world is a product of the arbitration of our subjective life and an axiomatic objective world, life and worlds cannot be separated. To separate them would require that we engage the mind, and since the mind would need to be employed to make the separation, anything separated as a result of its use would reflect a mind as well as what was separated from it (Eisner, 1991, p. 52). Inquiry in the absence of reality is simply a picture. We can already sense that inquiry has become a difficult and controversial subject. How were these developments shaped from the past, and how are they exhibited today?

The Historical Development of Inquiry

Today's version of inquiry can be traced back to Greek times. The Greek culture viewed the world in wholes. Inquiry, as a developing science, involved "maneuvering to get a better view" of something already there (Dewey, 1938, p. 88). All knowledge was seen as part of the whole, a larger good. Anything quantifiable was subject to change and, therefore, not worthy of sustained study. The Greeks looked for order and structure in the universe, based on philosophical and religious foundations, a teleological view. The aim of science in this regard was to differentiate knowledge from belief. Whatever we know is true. If it were not true, we didn't know it (Eisner, 1981). Scientists, therefore, were the discoverers of laws that rule the universe. Scientific practice was to uncover the facts.

During the Middle Ages, changes to empiricism included the teleological view of the Greeks. The "new scientist" replaced the philosopher and cleric. Descartes and the Cartesian philosophy of certainty have since dominated the search for knowledge. Newton, Bacon, Galileo, and others stressed the need to discover the order within nature through experimental confirmation (Polkinghorne, 1983). To discover the order in the universe, measurement and quantification became essential. Positivism and the development of the scientific method as a way to discover unchanging truths ushered in the physical sciences and the technological advances of the nineteenth century.

In the nineteenth century a development parallel to positivism as it applied to human behavior occurred. Compte, writing between 1830 and 1850, proposed that the study of human beings conform to methods used in the study of natural science (Polkinghorne, 1983). John Stuart Mill's system of logic (1843) supports the positivistic approach in his study of human behavior, stating that the "backward state of moral sciences can only be remedied by applying to them the methods of physical science, duly extended and generalized" (Polkinghorne, 1983). Dewey supported this positivistic stance, stating that the inability of social sciences and natural sciences to "act in accord with logical conditions which have been pointed out [positivism] throws light on its retarded state" (1938, p. 487). This positivistic approach proposes that human problems would finally be solved using the one correct approach to inquiry, positivism.

The view that social sciences should adopt the methodology of the physical sciences developed throughout the twentieth century. Polkinghorne (1983) identified five phases of the current "received view" of science (postpositivism). The first phase proposes that science should describe only the observable. The second phase expands this theory to include nonobservable entities and searches for axioms based on universal statements. The third phase consists of the critique of positivism, which allows the inclusion of alternative systems of science based on the history of science in the fourth phase. The fifth phase is based on pragmatic reason and inclusion of the contextual considerations of inquiry.

The current positivist approach has broadened its methodologies and its definition of truth. However, science is still viewed as the search for ever closer approximations of truth through the stringent application of scientific methods. Although frequently denied by the current positivists, science still aspires to the Cartesian ideal of certainty, even though positivists might say "I'm relatively sure" rather than "I'm certain." Methodologically, this view generates more latitude.

At the same time that Mill proposed use of the positivistic methods for the study of behavior, the antipositivist movement arose. The movement argued that people are part of a complex structure made up of historical and social reality. It was believed that life could be ordered into laws or broken into analyzable parts. The term *life* denotes what is to everyone the most familiar and intimate, and at the same time, darkest, even most unthinkable. One can delineate its peculiar and characteristic traits. One can even inquire about its tone, rhythm, and melody. But one cannot totally analyze it into all its factors, for it is not totally resolvable in this manner. It cannot be verbalized in a simple formula or explanation. Thought is an expression of life, but it does not supersede life. Polkinghorne's (1983) writings contained the seeds for interpretivistic inquiry. They discussed a holistic approach to inquiry, viewing the individual as part of the whole of culture in a search for meaning. All are basic to naturalism but were largely ignored until recently.

Although generally supportive of the views described above, Weber did not accept the differences others created between the physical and social sciences (Smith & Hesusius, 1986). Weber believed that the two sciences needed to think in terms of integration (Aron, 1967; Benton, 1977; Outhwaite, 1983; Simey, 1969; Smith & Hesusius, 1986). Weber further believed that explanation and understanding are two essential parts of social research. Both are essential to understanding the two strata of human beings: the animal and mechanistic level, and the level of rational evaluation of subjective meanings. Although he realized that the science of human beings was vulnerable to bias, he believed that the two approaches could be synthesized.

Paradigms of Inquiry

Currently, methods of scientific inquiry can be described as suffering an identity crisis. Each of the three methods described earlier have avid disciples and equally avid critics. The general patterns of inquiry, more recently termed *paradigms,* have received special attention over the past 30 years. Kuhn, in *The Structure of Scientific Revolutions* (1970), challenged the traditional view of science as developing knowledge by accumulation or the knowledge of piecemeal facts. He suggested that the growth of knowledge also occurs through scientific revolution and enables thinkers to move from current assumptions to new paradigms of understanding. Normal science, according to Kuhn, was the building of existing knowledge in a developmental fashion. The growth of knowledge, he surmised, is bounded, restricted by the world view of scholars and educators in the community. Within a paradigm, then, science accumulates knowledge related to that particular world view, using its own paradigm symbols, tools, and values learned from its own narrow existing scientific community. However, for progress or change to occur, science must undergo a revolution. Science (normal science in Kuhn's view) proceeds from anomaly in a current context, to preparadigm struggles, to crisis, and finally, to revolution. During the crisis period, existing paradigm symbols, tools, and values are discarded in exchange for new ones. The revolution frees the community from the restrictiveness of the old paradigm to allow new questions to be asked.

Inquiry paradigms form the basis of how we as theorists and practitioners see the world. As we internalize our paradigms, they take on great power and determine how we interact with the world. Like inquiry in general, educational inquiry revolves around numerous paradigms. Our inquiry paradigms become so powerful that more concern is given to methods of inquiry than to determining what has really happened. Practitioners of the positivistic paradigm often refer to it as scientific, experimental, or behavioral, or, very loosely, as simply quantitative. The second mode of inquiry, interpretivistic, is dominated by ethnographic research and is often termed qualitative or constructivistic inquiry. Finally, the critical theorist inquiry paradigm, sometimes termed conflict theory, explores power, dominance, and conflict in society.

One of the difficulties in defining inquiry is the paradigm community's reliance on the means–ends argument to substantiate its various viewpoints. Although the scientific model of inquiry is extremely valid in the proper context, inquiry in this model is more than an outcome driven by a series or set of means. Inquiry as a process implies a system of inquiry with component parts, outcomes, methods to change, and a philosophical base around which the process itself is built. To enable further discussion and thought about this identity crisis, each of the three, often considered competing, paradigms is described and clarified further.

Positivistic and Postpositivistic Theory

Since Descartes, inquiry has been firmly entrenched in the positivistic and postpositivistic paradigms. Both are foundational paradigms and rooted in a realist ontology, a belief system that a reality exists out there. The true nature of science is to discover truth, and thereby, enable prediction and control. As a consequence of this ontology, researcher practices are objective. As inquirers, the realists separate their values from reality. Only then can experimentation or manipulation result in an independence necessary for nature to truly expose itself. Such scientific inquiry seeks to uncover natural laws which are then summarized in the form of generalizations or cause-and-effect laws (Guba, 1990).

Postpositivism evolved as a result of the problematic tenets of positivism. Critics of positivism have therefore forced positivistic theorists to revamp and soften their ontological stance. Although a real world exists, it is impossible for the realist to truly perceive it outside his own values and judgments. As a result, the postpositivist is a critical realist, recognizing that objectivity on the part of the observer can

never truly be achieved. In this more critical tradition, postpositivistic inquiry must be more
consistent as determined by scholarly tradition
within a research paradigm. All inquiry is subjected to the community's critical review.
Methodologically, the postpositivist also moves
away from previous objectivity requirements
and posits development of findings that have
been exposed to as many methodological
sources as possible. Inquiry in this research
arena then attempts to isolate objective knowledge and apply the new knowledge to practice
or policy. Emphasis is placed on creating
knowledge that allows further prediction and
control of educational processes and products
(Soltis, 1984). Methodology is statistical and experimental and relies on creating validity
through objective testing, mathematical rigor,
and reliable observation instruments.

Postpositivistic science has maneuvered,
some would say migrated, far from many of the
original positivistic precepts. Although critics
have been relentless, postpositivists have
worked diligently to address imbalances that
prevailed from their new postures surrounding
objectivity. Guba (1990) cited four imbalances:
those between (1) rigor and relevance, (2) precision and richness, (3) elegance and applicability, and (4) discovery and verification. For example, a shift can be noted to more naturalistic
inquiry in regard to rigor and relevance differences. As rigor is relaxed to gain greater external validity, generalizability increases; relevance
is assumed to increase at the expense of internal validity.

In the most recent developments, positivism
has become more untenable and postpositivism
more thorough about its own tenets. In midcentury, Hempel (1966) and other theorists acknowledged that operational science must begin to remove itself from notions that concepts
can each be reducible to a string of observation
statements. More appropriately, the concepts of
science are like the bindings in a network of
systematic interrelationships: The more inclusive the convergence of bindings, or that issue

from a conceptual binding, the stronger the orderliness of the system (p. 94).

Instances of changing views of theorists as
demonstrated above cause some to distance
themselves from positivistic research. Although
some researchers may never depart from the
older views, others view the newest directions
of postpositivistic science as illustrative of its re-
silience. Firestone (1990) confirmed the views
of Phillips (1990) and contended that scientists,
like any workers, are in the business of providing reasonable justifications for their assertions.
Dewey (1938) attempted to explain this same
principle in his preference for the term *warranted assertibility in lieu of truth*. A warrant is
not forever and thus assertions are never safe
from criticism and may even be proven false. In
this sense, objectivity only comes closest to the
firmest warrants. Adequacy is judged through
an internal competitive process that rules out error. In total, postpositivism is no longer held up
as a "queen science" (Firestone, 1990) but firmly
entrenched and still possibly useful in practice.
In fact, most would claim that disparities between these paradigms erode as we move far-
ther from philosophical debate forums. As
noted in later discussions, accommodation between paradigms is more prevalent than some
would acknowledge.

Critical Theory

Critical theory developed in the middle of the
nineteenth century. More recently, it has been
formulated by the Frankfurt School (Marcuse,
Adorno, Horkheimer, and others) and most recently revived by Habermas (1970, 1987). Critical theory focuses on educational problems and
their role in relation to social, political, cultural,
and economic patterns that result. In this regard, critical theory is the systematic inquiry
into contradictions that exist in educational
practice. Agger (1991) contended, however, that
critical theory must today be rejuvenated for it
to remain adaptable. Critical theory may have

lost much of its power to analyze the social problems of modernity and postmodernity in society and, in particular, in the educational realm. Critical theory may need to be fortified with additional currency, from the poststructural, postmodern, and feminist perspective.

Critical theory has demonstrated convoluted beginnings as authors' translations and applications were in need of further clarification due to their extreme variability (Agger, 1991). As developed by the Frankfurt School, early critical theories attempted to explain the failure of Marx's socialist revolution. In their revisitation, the theorists attempted to link economic, cultural, and ideological analyses to explain the revolution's failure. In these early versions of critical theory, the Frankfurt School believes that Marxism failed to recognize the ability of the capitalist economic system to exploit the working class. Capitalism, it is postulated, deepens the false consciousness of the working class by developing its own coping mechanisms that forestall social revolution. This is termed *domination* by the Frankfurt School. Workers adopt new shared values and beliefs that are seemingly rational; at the same time the capitalistic system exploits sociopolitical and economic liberties in exchange for freedom of consumer choice. Positivism, they argued, is just another coping mechanism. Positivism, a descendant of the Age of Enlightenment, also becomes the shared problem-solving methodology. People are taught and assume that the "world as it is" is the prominent reality. The positivistic system therefore perpetuates itself. With these convictions, one experiences the world as rational and necessary and thus sees little that needs to, or can, be done to change it.

Critical theory, however, breaks from the rational-reality viewpoints (positivism) and develops into a mode of consciousness and thinking that views social facts as history that can be changed (Jay, 1973). Critical theory looks beyond the appearance of social fact finding and seeks ways to achieve new social understanding. More precisely, critical theory attunes re-

searchers to their own underlying empirical beliefs through rigorous self-reflection and self-criticism (Horkheimer & Adorno, 1972).

Guba (1990) briefly outlines the basic beliefs of critical theory. Although the label *critical theory* seemingly narrows the philosophical landscape comprising this expansive view, all beliefs about critical theory converge in light of a rejection of "value freedom." Our values are inevitably reflected in numerous ways: in selecting the problem to study, in the choice of tools for analysis, and in the interpretations, conclusions, and recommendations created. Given these possible value premises, inquiry becomes a political act, as participants are either empowered or disempowered through the inquirer's choice of a value system. The burden of inquiry is, by definition, to raise oppressed people to a level of true consciousness (Guba, 1990). Once they acknowledge how oppressed they are, they can act to revolutionize the world (Guba, 1990, p. 24). This transformation extends beyond the typically manipulative-interventionist methodology, as critical theorists seek to establish a commonness through a dialogic/hermeneutic approach. Features of the real world are scrutinized and judgments created which then alter reality and energize and facilitate future action. So critical theory has also evolved.

In recent times critical theory can be seen to exist under different banners. *Poststructuralism* is a theory of textuality and knowledge. Within this framework, Derrida (1981; cited in Culler, 1982) posited a process termed *deconstruction:* Text conceals conflicts between differing voices (text and subtext). What appears to be said must be understood in conjunction with references that are concealed; meaning is more than it appears to be on the surface. People often make important assumptions about this concealed meaning, and their assumptions are suppressed or even become tacit. This diverts a reader's/listener's attention, making text undecipherable. Derrida termed this *deference,* the ability to produce meaning only with reference to other meaning. Thus, to the poststructuralist, meaning is held in the constitutive practices of language. Deconstruction demystifies by revealing suppressed values and interests. Poststructuralists believe that ". . . every rhetorical gesture of text contributes to its overall meaning" (Agger, 1991, p. 30): how we arrange a plan, title a section of a paper, describe a decision process, and more, contribute to the sense that exists in the text.

Postmodernism, another translation of critical theory, requires the investigation of society, culture, and history. In this tradition, the social world is examined from the multiple perspectives of class, race, gender, and other constituencies. Additionally, the postmodernists rely on heterogeneous "subject positions" to explain social phenomena (Agger, 1991). As a result, ". . . knowledge is traced through discourse/practices that frame the knowledge formulated from within them" (Foucault, 1976, 1980; cited in Agger, 1991, p. 32). From "subject positions" the experiences of the world are framed against their own perspectives. In this realm, social science becomes an accounting of multiple perspectives rather than a universal truth. Social science in the educational realm becomes a discourse, suggesting that by "reading" a school, we can "do" social science (Agger, 1991).

In educational practice, *critical science* involves finding the conditions that produce selectivity in the process of teaching and the organization of schooling (Popkewitz, 1990). In this regard, Popkewitz attached critical science to inquiry of the commonplace and socially accepted contradictions that may result in various struggles in the educational environment. Exploration of the constraints produced in school affairs occurs through understanding how boundaries and structures limit our active potential. Debates about the constructions of schooling give rise to differing structural representations, around such issues as ethnicity, class, and gender, for example. Thus, deference creates sensitivity to potentially new concepts and builds a relationship between knowledge and identity.

Popkewitz (1990) further argued that a commitment to critical methods requires greater responsibility on the part of researchers to reflect on proper rules and standards of the work of science. A critical stance reconstructs education by providing relevance to history as it relates to methodology and accommodates the influence of questioning, conceptual development, and strategies to social values, struggles, and interests. He further asserted that six themes should frame any discussion of practices of a critical science of education.

1. Institutional practices support the contention that educational inquiry is comprised fully in procedural practice. In actual practice we may be inappropriately separating social movements, historical issues, or political interests from the strategies of research. As a philosophy of science, intellectual traditions and institutional conditions are of equal importance. Rules of inquiry are bounded in both traditions. Methodology is in constant flux as it is reworked through its relationship with questions, concepts, and procedures directed at empirical phenomena. Methodology emerges from inquiry in this sense, not the other way around.

2. Popkewitz (1990) also claimed, despite conventional beliefs about logic as a process of continued clarification, that the logic of science must also be a problem of social epistemology. The concepts, rules, or procedures of inquiry are not inevitable but are made real within institutions and through social construction. Critical science deals with questions that are a part of a field of science, including its ontology and epistemology, what is known and the means of knowing.

3. In another sense, Popkewitz (1990) admonished us and our willingness to simplify the context of inquiry in an objective and subjective dichotomy. "Objectivity has nothing to do with external laws or a 'nature' to be discovered or verified" (p. 56). Objectivity rules when it is unquestioned, but most important, detracts when it fails to recognize dynamic and changing patterns. Paralleling this, subjectivity directs our focus into the minds of people. By themselves,

neither can confront the complexity that exists in social relations, but in combination they may be able to provide the inquirer with greater ability to confront interrelations of objective and subjective conditions. Inquiry must not relegate itself to individual schema formed by unforeseen or unacknowledged rules acting as a horizon for individual reason (p. 57).

4. The foregoing rejection of a singular prescription with which to evaluate the products of science is accompanied by the belief that the scientist is a disinterested observer. In its most profound form, disinterest can imply relativity, but Popkewitz contends not without paradigmatic boundaries formulated in the practice or beliefs of one's own paradigm. But this cannot mean that ". . . a lack of commitment or ideas that have no social location or consequence . . ." exists (p. 59). Today, educational research must investigate more than teaching, learning, or organization and seek more than an understanding of the conflict of values across these considerations.

5. The multiplicity of values must be seen as multiples of knowledge. Knowledge creation and value creation are ideological. When we separate the creation of knowledge from its value contexts, we create poverty in understanding. Methodologically, when values are separated to control or identify bias we lose the interactiveness within all of science. In this view, then, critical theory posits an added systemic panorama.

6. Finally, Popkewitz contrasted the ability of science in its present form as a method for understanding boundaries that exist or have existed with the generalizability of science to enable a future condition. Although science can predict and control by sensitizing us to issues, critical theory more appropriately recognizes that science is an ongoing construction that challenges us to find our relation to it.

Critical theory makes a sociological contribution in two different manners: methodologically, in the ways that researchers write and read, and substantively, in the contributions to the studies of state, ideology, culture, discourse, and social movements (Agger, 1991). Agger's implications are that (1) critical theory forces interrogation of the unquestioned reliance on value freedom, (2) critical theory establishes a new science capable of recognizing its own grounded interests, (3) poststructuralism can deconstruct most rhetoric by examining hidden meanings, (4) poststructuralism reveals how language can constitute reality, and (5) postmodernism rejects one best way. Substantively, Agger contends that critical theory may suggest new ways of theorizing about the role of the state and culture, offer valuable contributions through the study of discourses, suggest empirical studies of the ways that discourses are structured by gender themes, and offer new social movement theories displaying insights that explain historical meaning and display impact.

Critical theory posits a view that is antifoundational, reflective, and recognizes the perspective of the knower. In this sense, inquiry can be recast between the object of study and a conditioned observer. In another sense, this establishes critical inquiry as engagement. Its main emphasis may be more thorough than we hoped as we realize that knowledge is born from being open to multiple dimensions of reality. The task for the future may be to move beyond these strict distinctions contained within paradigmatic definitions through discourse and to reunite schooling with democracy and justice (Skrtic, 1990).

Interpretivistic Theory

Most interpretivistic theorists believe that the positivistic and critical theorist viewpoints are flawed. For example, let's look at Guba's (1990) contentions.

1. Reality exists only as a mental framework for thinking about reality. In this view, the major premise of the interpretivistic approach can be noted. Reality is constructed on a

moment-by-moment basis, not on a cultural or historical basis as the realists or critical realists surmise.

2. There are no unequivocal explanations for one best way, nor is there, as so often stated, one best way to pursue inquiry and discover truth. In this view, the interpretivistic framework posits a multitude of possible theories that could each possibly provide a reasonable explanation of fact. Reality, then, becomes the window of theory "seen only as it occurs."

3. As many differing constructions of theory are possible, it also follows that inquiry must be value laden, tied to the values of the researcher.

4. Since theory is value laden, inquiry is shaped by the interaction of the inquirer and those issues of study. Even today, the physical sciences have disproved their own stance on objectivity.

With these critiques in mind, the full panorama of the interpretivistic framework can be completed. The *interpretivistic approach* is antifoundational and relativistic. Reality is found in multiple constructions of, and entails the continued search for, more informed reconstructions of people's own reality. Equally, the interpretivistic position relies on the social constructions of the researcher and referent agent(s). In this regard, the interpretivistic epistemology is subjective, as social interaction cannot be possible without the inquirer/inquired dyad. Finally, the interpretivist seeks to understand by identifying the variety of possible constructions of knowledge. This variety is investigated with the sole purpose of bringing consensus to understanding. Methodologically, hermeneutic reasoning of the interpretivist seeks to depict individual constructions as accurately as possible, while ongoing dialectic compares and contrasts individual constructions to enable the inquirer and the client to come to grips with their constructions. More informed choice results as the methodological process

enables continuously deeper communication to ensue. In this sense, the interpretivist seeks to derive more thorough understanding via an ongoing reconstruction process (Guba, 1990).

Like critical theory, interpretivistic inquiry, has had a complex history. Often termed *naturalistic inquiry,* the interpretivist position lies in direct contrast to the realist posture found in the positivistic or postpositivistic inquiry framework. While the axioms of positivism are generated in value-free "environments," the axioms of the interpretivistic framework are created and shaped in the social processes of interacting minds. Reality is, therefore, the product of the collective cognition of value-laden inquiry (Levine, 1985, 1992). Research cannot be thorough without due consideration to the values, beliefs, and preconceptions of inquiry's set of actors. This interpretive process, termed *verstehen,* acknowledges and utilizes the constant flux inherent in human activity and thereby incorporates behavior in its natural settings.

The naturalistic research paradigm is new to educational circles and, more important, is still at odds with the existing positivistic paradigm ingrained through time. Many educational researchers are still largely tied to their old paradigms. For example, Babbie (1989) offered a full text on sociological research based largely on realist methodology. Borg and Gall (1989) offered scant explanations of the most current sociological research methods. Clearly, those interested in developing, adapting, or changing their inquiry beliefs and methodology cannot fully internalize an interpretivistic epistemology. Their basic beliefs are still informed largely by earlier value traditions, research methodologies, and theories (Smith & Hesusius, 1986). Many prefer to remain adamant about and continue to operate within their earlier paradigms. They also continue to critique the research methods of the interpretivist position with fervor. Their critique would include a lack of parallel validity and reliability constructs (Guba, 1978; Miles & Huberman, 1984), a lack of tools to provide ethnographic description and comparison, codification of the role of the researcher, role management within the research context, observational strategies, and more. But progress has been accomplished as those adopting newer views struggle with a generation of newer methods. More generally today, researchers are clarifying field techniques, outlining participant–observer–agent traditions, enhancing mechanisms that derail outsider–insider constraints, developing better criteria about what to observe versus what to infer, and becoming more attuned to the inherent flux in the social interaction process.

Early authors and philosophers have become disconcerted by measurement research methodology that relies on measurement and quantification perspectives in which ". . . the indices of a phenomenon seemingly were more important than the phenomenon itself" (Giorgi, 1970, p. 291). In their earliest works, Guba and Lincoln (1981, 1982, 1985) grappled with conventional assumptions associated with older paradigms. More precisely, Guba and Lincoln (1989) outlined problematic features of the positivistic paradigm. In their terms, the *Standards for Evaluation Practice* (Rossi, 1982), as developed by the Evaluation Research Society, are unacceptable from the standpoint of a new generation of evaluators. Speaking strictly about evaluative practice, Guba and Lincoln critiqued the society's views and outlined the rationale behind their inability to accept its compatibility stance. Their positions include the following:

1. They disagree about the interactive role of the evaluator in relation to the client. Whereas traditional methodology postulates a formulation and negotiation role, researchers today see research activities as a cyclic and iterative process.

2. Equally important, Guba and Lincoln do not see the standards for practice enlightening the methodological tenets of the interpretivistic approach, as the standards do not directly identify or specify criteria appropriate to constructivist evaluation efforts. Most often, treatments relating to quantitative methodology are prevalent, embodied in such terms as *sampling, reli-*

ability, generalizability, and more. Lacking are interpretivistic terms that Guba and Lincoln (1989) see as equal or more applicable: such terms as *authenticity, trustworthiness, credibility,* and so on.

3. Like interpretivistic philosophy since its inception, the older positivistic standards still rely almost exclusively on the cause-and-effect relationship that Guba and Lincoln contend blinds evaluators and clients from discerning more powerful social forces operating in individual situations. In their view, social construction is at least as important as possible cause-and-effect relationships.

4. Guba and Lincoln (1989) additionally cite the constant unfolding of ethical dilemmas, as client and researcher in the traditional model of inquiry typically leave information availability, decision making, and power relationships in the hands of the client. But newer models of inquiry necessitate removing this leverage from the client–sponsor to more fully enable a broad spectrum of decision making to arise from more readily available information and subsequent interaction with other stakeholders.

5. Guba and Lincoln (1989) make a plea in defense of the mounting body of evidence that posits a value-bound approach to evaluation: "In retrospect, the possibility of acting to 'value' a project (program, curriculum, and so on) while acting as though values were unimportant or corrupting to the valuing (evaluation) effort should have struck us long ago as bizarre, if not contradictory, behavior" (p. 233). In light of these numerous problematic features, Guba and Lincoln (1989) and Lincoln and Guba (1986) continued in their quest to create criteria for judging the adequacy of evaluation and more suitable to the interpretivistic paradigm.

A brief review of their thinking in this regard can be helpful. Their beliefs can be summarized into three broad categories: (1) trustworthiness criteria, (2) the nature of the hermeneutic process, and (3) authenticity criteria.

Trustworthiness Criteria. Trustworthiness criteria are intended to parallel the standards for rigorous research within the positivistic framework (i.e., validity, reliability, and objectivity). Although each of these is grounded firmly in positivistic frameworks and is very familiar, there are no direct translations of these criteria to the interpretivistic realm. A realist ontology cannot pretend that there is a concurrence between findings and a real world, nor can findings within the interpretivistic tradition then be generalizable. Too many other constructions are possible. Lincoln and Guba (1986) posit that establishing credibility, transferability, dependability, and confirmability are criteria more appropriate to the interpretivistic framework.

They submit that establishing a parallel concept of credibility establishes a more appropriate likeness, matching constructed realities of respondents to the reality of the evaluator. Techniques that enhance the possibility of greater credibility are more prolonged engagement enabling greater rapport, persistent observation allowing greater scope, peer debriefing as a disinterested quality control, negative case testing assuring subjective confidence, progressive subjectivity to capture the privileged view of other contributing others, and member checks to enlist the construction of stakeholders.

Equally critical, transferability is foundational to the interpretivistic paradigm. It parallels generalizability criteria of the positivistic paradigm. Generalizability in the positivistic framework stems from adherence to random sampling techniques. The burden of proof lies with the inquirer. But this cannot be the case with the interpretivistic approach, as the burden of proof lies with the agent and client(s) and therefore is always relative. The consequences of transferability are not considered relevant to confidence limitations prevalent in a positivistic sense. Rather, degrees of transferability are established by providing as complete a database as possible (thick descriptions) to facilitate traversing to other contexts.

Another criterion of the interpretivistic paradigm is reliability, the stability of data over time.

Design alterations and shifts in hypotheses would render research studies unstable in the traditional research paradigm but are considered normal in the interpretivistic framework. This ability to change or redesign purpose is commonplace considering the emergent characteristic that defines naturalism. In deference to the importance of reliability, interpretivists need to guarantee a sense of tractability. This method of inquiry needs to be scrutinized continuously as others attempt to recreate for their edification the decisions and interpretations of the inquirer. For example, can others track the inquirer's logic of process?

Finally, Lincoln and Guba (1986) submit that inquiry must maintain a sense of objectivity to assure that data, interpretations, and products of the inquiry are affixed in contexts and persons different and separable from the inquirers. But unlike objectivity from previous traditions, interpretivistic inquiry relies on confirmability of the data itself. In this sense, integrity is maintained by assuring that data can be tracked to various sources and that coherent interpretations are both distinctive and implied.

The Hermeneutic Process. Within the hermeneutic or dialectic process, data input are immediately available for feedback, elaboration, correction, revision, or expansion. As such, inputs are another form of assuring quality in the inquiry process. As data originate and are revisited, they immediately become accessible to emergent and joint reconstruction efforts. This alliance of information and elaboration mechanisms allows data to be challenged continuously by a variety of clients, which, in turn, sustains credibility in outcomes. This partitioning of inspection requirements prevents impoverishment of information.

Authenticity Criteria. Although the foregoing approaches to the maintenance of "health" in the interpretive process are worthwhile, they also typically originate from and parallel positivist methodological assumptions about goodness. Interpretivistic inquiry needs its own explicit set of criteria based on constructivist assumptions (Lincoln & Guba, 1986). These authenticity criteria would need to include fairness, ontological authenticity, educative authenticity, catalytic authenticity, and tactical authenticity. Fairness arises from the requirement to provide equal "voice" and balance to the value pluralism that arises from varying constructions. In this sense, the inquirer's role is one of mediation, as conflicting constructions must each have their "day in court." Fairness also requires that the inquirer conduct what Lincoln and Guba term an *appellate mechanism,* whereby stakeholders can arbitrate process procedures and policy. The remaining derivatives of authenticity build the power of this process. Any inquiry process must be able to be improved upon and matured. Ontological authenticity seeks continuously to enhance the sophistication of both stakeholders and inquirers. Educative authenticity requires that inquirers fulfill their moral responsibility to stakeholders by assuring that a variety in design viewpoints is present. Catalytic authenticity demands that the inquiry process not rest solely as a experiential exercise, but that the process agitates decision making and action outcomes. Theory must evolve through praxis (commitment and understanding) to practice. Finally, tactical authenticity requires the competition of a complete process that additionally includes granting stakeholders the power to act. Having explored the three major paradigms in some depth, a more thorough look at inquiry in educational practice is appropriate.

Inquiry and Educational Administration

Evers and Lakomski (1991) provide a vehicle for us to relate to educational practice the philosophical underpinnings described above. The three major areas addressed by Evers and Lakomski correspond to those previously discussed: the theory movement, the paradigm approach, and coherence. The theory movement in educational administration flourished in the 1980s. During these years educational researchers

looked to the "hypothetical-deductive structure with laws at the top and facts at the bottom" (Evers & Lakomski, 1991, p. 3). The purpose of research was to provide educational administrators with findings that would allow them more accurately to predict events and to better control those events. Organizational elements were identified, operationalized, and measured in an attempt to increase efficiency and effectiveness within the educational environment.

In this classical paradigm, educational organizations were viewed as simple, hierarchical, and mechanical. Predictions of events were considered and research faithfully followed foundational scientific practice. Inquiry's goal was unchanged: break down the object of inquiry into discrete parts, examine them, and arrive at generalizations to extend to other domains. In keeping with changing practices in other organizational arenas, however, educational administration also began a shift. Literature is replete with examples of ongoing attempts to change the way that organizations function and create new knowledge. Certainly, the extreme tenets of the positivistic paradigm in organizational inquiry are no longer an acceptable archetype (Cziko, 1989; Howe & Eisenhart, 1990). But although postpositivism was more palatable to youthful research participants, the old empiricism remained entrenched (Howe & Eisenhart, 1990).

Guba and Lincoln (1989) provide other illustrations of inquiry's coming of age in educational administration. While each generation concentrated on its own particular methods to accomplish inquiry and their research represented an advance, pervasive problems remained. Collection of data for measurement was fundamental. For example, in educational circles, the measurement of the attributes of school children was primary. The purpose of schooling was to teach what was known to be true of the basics and to assure that students were then able to demonstrate their knowledge on standardized tests. As the humanistic movement became more prominent, findings that individual differences in reaction times were typical of human subjects and led to suggestions that measurement was, indeed, a proper new inquiry trail. Business and industry also contributed to the era of measurement as researchers prospected for efficiency and effectiveness criteria. Although this first generation of educational administration researchers provided valuable data, the limited scope of the findings has garnered calls for greater breadth.

In a second generation, researchers began to utilize other methods to increase the influence of their scholarly activity. Descriptions of programs, material, teaching strategies, and organizational patterns attempted to broaden the scope of inquiry results, but retained much of the measurement era's almost religious reliance on quantification. This research almost certainly resulted in beneficial change as more broad-based curricula resulted, deeper understanding of students occurred, and testing revealed whether students learned what teachers had intended. However, more change was needed. Value determination became the area of study for the next generation of inquirers.

In this new period, researchers became seasoned adjudicators of differing research methods in addition to masters of measurement and description. In this arena, not only was performance a matter of concern to the inquirer, but goals and objectives became the subject of inquiry. Researchers now were required to deal with merit, both inside and outside the school educational research perspective. Researchers, although not competent in this venue, suddenly entered the "political realm." In the section that follows we address the problematic features of this area of research more fully.

Quandaries of Inquiry

Earlier in the chapter we discussed the emergence of various inquiry paradigms. Understanding the series of practical problems that emerge in research approaches is now necessary. Eisner (1981), Agger (1991), and Guba and Lincoln (1989) each provide thoughtful discussions of the limitations of research, in general, and more specifically, educational research.

Eisner (1981) postulated several points of concern. Given the reliance on interpretivistic inquiry found today, exploitations of the inquirer's own unique strengths are paramount. Whereas some see this as a singular political problem, others point to broader ethical concerns. Researchers in classrooms or schools or from universities must address the privilege of both the agent and the client. In this light, thoroughness of research training, individual researcher's attributes, and contractual arrangements each reflect a necessary concern that inquiry be more thorough. Another consideration involves the timeliness of research outcomes. Thorough research in the interpretivistic frame is often kin to the "action science" orientation of Argyris (1985), taking weeks, months, even years before closure in a study is available, if ever. Thus research often gravitates to procedural preoccupations, which disempowers—the effect of inquiry becomes too short term and loses its applicability over time. To maintain the inherent flexibility of interpretive methods, the complete realm of the inquiry, from aims to findings, must be available for adjustment. In light of the above, Eisner submits that qualitative research is frequently viewed as less deterministic and final than previous methodologies may suppose. Clients may become discouraged, as results cannot generate immediate and effective change as assumed in the positivistic eras.

From another frame of reference Guba and Lincoln (1989) contended that three major defects have dominated administrative inquiry in education: a tendency toward managerialism, the failure to accommodate value pluralism, and overcommitment to scientific inquiry (p. 32). In the first case, Lincoln argues that managerialism yields a number of faults: in effect, disempowering the participant stakeholders, disenfranchising evaluators' findings, and lacking the ability to assert accountability. In aggregate, managerialism combines several distasteful features that can compromise an entire research scenario.

Also important is the realization that value pluralism is paramount in all research efforts. Research that disregards value tenets sets aside differing heritages of students in schools, differing learning rates, and disassociates researcher bias possibly due to monetary necessities, among other problems. Finally, as Guba and Lincoln contended, educational inquiry is still largely committed to the scientific approach. From textbook issues brought to light earlier to graduate programs that still resonate with methodological courses that are largely quantitatively focused, the scientific method is firmly entrenched. In education administration and across management science, the scientific method is viewed as the right way to do things. This reliance often strips evaluations from their context and renders research results of questionable value. Only recently has the scientific method been questioned. Guba and Lincoln (1985) argued for responsive constructivism, beyond the initial views of the constructivistic approach.

Agger (1991), a critical theorist, contended that applications of postmodernism and critical theory that we see today are resolved by commodifying popular culture. Although it may be important to transform society's structures, this cannot be accomplished simply by remembering the collective experience of events. It must develop by identifying the meaning and identity of events—both their text and texture. Concentration on the events of popular experience creates the possibility that as events become more common, they will tend to be idealized and become the norm of behavior. Our investigation in a sense stops and does not critically examine those events further except from superficial points of view. Postmodernism, replacing substance with style, can be seen in numerous instances: in quick-fix adjustments such as empowerment, school choice, or school-based management. All seem intent on gaining access to the bandwagon to define their own unique versions of needed change.

Guba and Lincoln (1985) outlined the parallel movement of inquiry paradigms as a result of ongoing change in organizations. Seven contrasting concepts provide the basis for an in-depth exploration of the impact of ongoing change in the way we construct knowledge. Understanding this parallelism can further substantively help to counteract some of the problem areas previously cited.

Simple to Complex. This change implies and is largely a result of an organization's inability to change and its tendency to continue to view the world simplistically. In previous eras our ability to identify, comprehend, and quantify the entirety of a problem was assumed. For example, it is unlikely that we would fully comprehend the impact of high dropout rates only by surveying those who left, or by including a sequence of other variables in search of correspondence. A more complex question demands a more complex approach to science, one that includes, in this case, a systemic panorama of the school, the family, the teaching environment, and more. Even more important, this situation demands an exploration of the relationships among other variables identified above. Most important may be the realization that there may be no objectivity in the example above. Identifying poor teaching or any other single or multiple condition as being causal excludes relationships and conceals more appropriate findings.

In educational research, strong reminders of simplistic accommodation to problems exist everywhere. Rationality as demanded by the realists' postures is still problematic. Even today we find university teaching institutions focused on older, possibly largely irrelevant research practices that have lived past their time. Complexity necessitates dramatic change. In the future, those who teach research methods must acknowledge that meaningful inquiry must account for "history and detail rather than permanence and generality" (Guba & Lincoln, 1985, p. 89). Huff explains that in order to ". . . understand the complex . . . aspects of the world, one must have complex sources of information" (Huff, 1985, p. 165).

Hierarchical to Heterarchical. If we look at organizations today, we find many examples of unusual organizational structures. Clusters, networks, upside-down pyramids, interlocking links, and more are representations of changes in organizational structure necessitated by other forces. Similarly, in educational circles, further revision of organizational structure has emerged in such examples as school-based management, team-based structures and combinations, and more decision-making interaction between learner and teacher. Even schools without principals are not hard to find. Pluralism or multiplism is replacing "pecking order" organizations that have constrained knowledge creation. In the new world view, any set of factors can become a controlling phenomenon, depending on the context.

In the traditional view, educational systems were organized top down, from the federal level all the way to the teacher. Hoy and Miskel (1987) described administrative theory as "a set of interrelated concepts, assumptions, and generalizations that systematically describe and explain regularities in behavior in educational organizations" (p. 2). Literature is laden with organizational charts reflecting a top-down organization, full of sequential-linear-systematic curriculum development charts and saturated with stepwise models of instructional practice. In times past, inquiry validated the hierarchical nature of school organizations and schooling.

The newer paradigm views educational organizations as heterarchical, oriented to pluralism and a heteracity of guiding principles (Guba & Lincoln, 1985). For example, the realization that language is descriptive, or that visual arts depict, opens new knowledge, creating venues that cannot be subsumed as singular, as top down, or stepwise. Latitude must be available to researchers who insist on newer interactional research methods, latitude that allows a variety of approaches to reconstitute our understanding.

Mechanical to Holographic. In chapters to come, school organization will be described as an "iron cage" or as machinelike. Metaphors connect mental images with reality. Schools are machinelike: classes are 45 to 50 minutes long, five or six classes per day is common, the school year is 180-plus days long, and it takes 12 years to complete schooling; unless, of course, your standardized tests reflect greater ability and you plan to apply to college, at which time you can then increase the number of years of schooling to 16. Even teachers are like robots. The agenda of inquiry in this environment is no different. Are there not enough studies of class length in journals already? Need we say more?

Holograms are dimensional images from reflected light, but more important, they possess unique properties. Conceptualizing the school organization as a hologram is difficult and attempts to visualize a holographic school often result in chaos and confusion. In a hologram, every part contains enough information to reconstitute the whole. "the part is in the whole and the whole is in the part . . . Parts have access to the whole" (Wilbur, 1985, p. 2). When light is shown on the holographic image, the image can be reconstituted from any portion or part. Consider then, the holographic school organization, an organization in which compartmentalization is absent, where teachers share information broadly, or where students are colleagues. Learning is the issue in this school, as the whole school is built to facilitate learning. In the holographic sense, as you walk into a school can you sense the learning going on, or did you sense those iron cages? Similarly, educational inquiry has just begun to consider the relevance of organizing features that inspire holistic knowledge creation.

Determinacy to Indeterminacy. Is it possible to predict and control; or is everything relative? These disparate views evolve from distinctly different organizational theory and inquiry paradigms and have far-reaching implications. If, as the traditionalists believe, there is one right way to organize and administer education, hypotheticodeductive inquiry will result in a body of knowledge about that "right way." Weber thought that the bureaucratic system was "superior in precision, in stability, in the stringency of its discipline, and its reliability" (Parson, 1947, p. 337). Time studies and efficiency models served to validate a determinate approach to administration.

The emerging research paradigm, however, provides a critique of logical empiricism and assumes an indeterminate universe where prediction is not possible. The goal of organizational inquiry would have to be to "realize an interpretive understanding of the meanings people give to their own situations and their interactions with others" (Smith & Blase, 1991, p. 11). Lawlike generalizations are not possible because the social world is not determinate. Therefore, the best that an inquirer can hope for is to describe the complexity of organizations in the context of their history, people, and environment. Matters of human significance will render interpretive understanding possible (Smith & Blase, 1991).

Linear Causality to Mutual Causality.

Instances of singular cause-and-effect scenarios in real life, if we reflect, are hard to imagine. But traditional research establishes just such causality as foundational. Assuredly, if our purpose is to reduce the origin of events to finite causal variables, we may find them, perhaps even find proper ones. But generalizing from these finite circumstances back to issues more complex must be done with extreme care. If–then relationships are established in normative inquiry and represent a specific set of variables for the relationship to hold true. Stepping outside the confidence of the relationship leads to error.

Naturalistic inquiry, on the other hand, assumes mutual causality, nonlinear, and growth-oriented relationships between variables. As an inquiry methodology, case studies are built purposely as a historical–cultural sketch of, for example, a school or classroom environment. In this sense, the case study is a living example from which actions are connected to their total environment. Once actions are understood to

occur within, an interpretive discourse can reconstitute the school or classroom environment, but from the view of the inquirer. A deeper understanding of the total environment can result.

Assembly to Morphogenesis.

In the inquiry paradigms, assembly implies construction from simple to complex. In the reductionist view, wholes are separated into smaller and smaller segments as a method to control/manipulate experimental parameters and arrive at truth. Experimental findings then generalized are attached to larger and larger wholes. An aggregate of findings must not, however, substitute for license to apply across greater and greater range. Poor mathematics scores in New York inner-city schools may not be related to poor mathematics scores in Los Angeles or anywhere else. Generalizations can transfer only when we can confidently relate across those environments.

Morphogenesis is a mutual change that occurs across parts and the whole of a structure. It can be considered the combined use of objectivity and subjectivity, a balance of rigor and relevance, or other paradoxical features of inquiry. Although a rigorous school-based experiment may serve to address a local issue, relevance of broader issues to the whole issue is then lacking. Proper balance of these two validity concerns creates a different whole. Thus, disparate measures combine to recreate a greater whole. Similarly, school organization was long thought to revolve around building the proper functions into the environment and operationalizing them—adding functions, operationalizing, adding-operating. In this sense the school was never truly able to adapt itself and create those new organizing relationships necessary as a result of growth or any other measure. Without this process–relationship orientation, the large school becomes cumbersome, inflexible, procedural, and bureaucratic. If our previous decision making and problem solving had related concern for form and function, perhaps flexibility mechanisms could have co-developed, or procedures could have adapted to encompass newer relationships. In this sense, schooling could become self-organizing and self-renewing.

Objective to Perspectival.   As a corollary to the change discussed above, newer inquiry paradigms seek to expose multiple perspectives through inquiry and enable multiple findings. If we continually reduce the variety of issues that can affect a research effort, we also reduce the ability of the inquirer to pursue the most informed effort. Inquiry needs requisite variety to function effectively.

These axioms as Guba and Lincoln (1985) describe them develop a new view of knowledge creation in educational organizations—as an ongoing process. Traditional methodologies continue to have a strong impact on administrative inquiry (Smith & Blase, 1991). However, there has been a steadily growing body of research based on the interpretivistic perspective and the above "new" axioms as described by Schwartz and Olgivy (1979) and Guba and Lincoln (1985). We must be familiar with both the traditional and the newer views of organizational inquiry. As Gage (1989) pointed out, we may still be in the midst of a battle for paradigm supremacy or, alternatively, cooperation. Educators in the future must heed these multiple approaches to educational administrative research.

Inquiry Processes and the Paradigm Debates

The process of inquiry is not merely philosophical debate, but instead, is intended to answer specific questions and thereby, result in specific knowledge. To illustrate the process of inquiry, several examples are developed in an effort to observe inquiry processes in action.

Salomon (1991) analyzed several sets of studies in his thought-provoking argument for analytic and systemic inquiry. In his first study, a controlled experiment, he and his colleagues tested the hypothesis that interaction with an interactive computer tool, the writing partner, would improve writing ability. Students were required to test a variety of variables: internalization, expenditure of effort, quality of writing, and transfer after subsequent use of the writing tool. Essay writing pre- and posttests were developed. Students were randomly assigned to two groups. The results supported their hypothesis. A new era of computer use was born. In a separate test, in experiments using a similar design, reading skills were also enhanced. Finally, a third study in geography using a computer database yielded similar results. Inspired by all the results noted above, a fourth test introduced the database format to studying the U.S. Constitution. It became apparent that the limited scope of the experimental model would not suffice for a project of this magnitude. Instead, a new series of social science classroom activities would need to be developed: team events, a constitutional convention, and more. As the project progressed, new events demanded other on-the-spot changes. With this plethora of differing activities came the need for the use of different tools of measurement: interviews, self-reports, questionnaires, and other unobtrusive measures. Teachers' roles changed, too, as they hovered around students: directing them, guiding them, and suggesting and advising new avenues of exploration. Clearly, normative inquiry parameters were not useful. This obviously suggests the utilization of differing inquiry paradigms. But before we specifically explore these differences, a few additional anecdotes will assist the reader to grasp the nature of the inquiry process in practice.

For decades the study of leadership has unfolded in two different research domains: the empirical and the hermeneutic (Smith & Blase, 1991). In the empirical tradition, the educational leader is seen as a decision maker, a controller, and a manager of resources. Instructional leaders accomplish similar tasks that revolve around instructional demands. These views of leadership as technical expertise are equated with effectiveness and seen to be efficiency oriented.

In these scenarios, leaders seek to choose rationally from among competing options. The leader seeks to study properly organized organizations and learning processes in order to arrive at lawlike generalizations, theory, and so on. The laws, generalizable then, allow them to predict further alternative programs and policy. Others, however, contest this approach, citing multiple instances for which generalization is not possible. What is missing is the discovery of enduring causal connections between and among events and processes. In this new paradigm, there is no lawlike, bottom-line world out there. Hence, the set of rational choices cannot be available to the educational leader.

In contrast, the hermeneutic view describes leadership in terms of the leader acting in various situations. In the previous representation, leadership emphasizes the calculation of means and ends, while a significance view seeks interpretive understanding of matters of human significance. Leadership, then, is an openness to issues of human significance. Decisions about what and how to teach are not a matter of technical development but are grounded in reasoned discourse, sharing of personal experience, and taking into account the experience of others. Leadership is not a controlled phenomenon, ordering, or orderliness, but is tied to who we are and how we lead our lives. Leadership in the dialogic tradition seeks deeper understanding so we can live our educational lives more fruitfully. What is to be done, and why we must do it, takes on added significance in this discourse. These two views, seemingly at odds with each other, have a dramatic effect on inquiry.

In one last narrative, a further audit of how inquiry processes unfold is explained. Stevenson (1993) addressed the problem of educating administrative and teaching professionals and develops for the reader the more typical approaches to administrator development. In the craft orientation (a metaphor), prospective professionals are treated like novices and participate in a kind of apprenticeship. In a traditional scientific approach, the developing professional is seen to be an agent outside the curriculum development process whose only responsibility is empirically tested knowledge assigned by an appropriately research-oriented teaching staff. Finally, Stevenson outlined a reflective approach whereby budding professionals develop the ability to make informed, reflective, and self-critical judgments about their practice. Even more important, these professionals are readily exposed to other systemic means of analysis as they interact with real-life cultural and structural conditions in schools. It is in this last tradition that a preparation program becomes critically reflective. Preparation takes on an action orientation as professionals' critical reflection includes the "articulation and reasoned justification of educational intentions (to create more defensible reasons for action) and the examination of the relationship between those intentions and the consequence of one's actions" (Stevenson, 1993, p. 107). This newer convention demands that professional preparation programs, while properly maintaining a strong research tradition, must also begin to develop the means for new professionals to engage knowledge as part of their instructional program. Some would only require total commitment to this venue. Stevenson (1993) suggested that colleges and universities need to learn to do both collaboratively.

These previous anecdotes suggest the multitude of methods through which people address inquiry problems. As Stevenson (1993) implied, theory and practice are both of concern. Perhaps we can also shed some valuable light on the paradigm debate issues at the same time. Although the issues addressed in the anecdotes above were complex ones, complexity had little to do with researchers' decisions on how to proceed. Salomon (1991) and his colleagues were not particularly interested in selecting a process of inquiry. Process selection seemingly results from their traditional mode of researching problems, as defined by a series of questions that the researcher sought to answer. Although these researchers were presumably familiar with a multitude of research methodologies, they were most adept at scientific research.

In each case discussed above, however, researchers moved beyond the paradigm problems within scientific inquiry to consider the applicability of their research approach to a community. Debating philosophical points of view may be worthwhile, but at the practical level, debate must end, as researchers and stakeholders need to address questions of importance to a community in need of action outcomes. Our anecdotes demonstrate important constructs which if explored have immediate relevance to professionals and students alike. Debates aside, an outcome orientation subsumes from acceptance of a "logic in use" (Firestone, 1987) and its own necessary localness. As Goodman (1978) implied, the world in its multiplicity has as many ways to describe it. Salomon (1991) contended that this encourages a multiplicity of methods—we would add, a multiplicity of venues, too.

Methodological practice often concerns itself with validity. In specific cases this may range from extreme concern for validity to little concern. Even qualitative approaches need to portray some sense of validity, some adherence to validity, or as Guba and Lincoln (1989) labeled it, authenticity. In the use of the scientific method, validity was a "planned for" event. Discrete events lend themselves to traditional measures so the results seemed highly appropriate. But in other cases, we begin to sense the real necessity for authenticity measures, as systemic events and contexts must utilize a more ecological approach to believability. Correspondingly, how do we also assure trustworthiness or transferability of findings? Although standards are a concern and must be considered, they are not as important as the generation of reflective and critical outcomes of value as judged by the community of users. Authenticity and trustworthiness and other measures are not created for a community of scholarly auditors, but are more valid criteria for qualitative

research when applications of research derive satisfactory outcomes for stakeholders.

If we listen to many proponents of soft educational science, we might hear them implying that research should only be used to describe, appreciate, interpret, or explain socially constructed phenomena. In other instances, positivists proclaim that universality is foundational. Cziko (1989) apparently takes both sides of the issue as he suggests an interpretive stance, followed by a desire to see research "lead to the implementation and dissemination of innovative educational practices" (p. 23). Proponents of no accommodation argue that both are not possible together, but a review of dissimilar research projects shows the semblance of both. There are attempts to arrive at an accommodation of differing paradigms within a larger framework of complementarity. In the larger sense, as inquiry occurs from a larger ecological viewpoint, it can only provide usefulness and applicability. In the discrete sense, combinations of variables can be shown to have broader usefulness and hence, possibly, generalizability.

Proceeding to more process-oriented concerns also helps us further to understand. Although we have already critiqued validity concerns prevalent to basic and applied research, and experimental versus natural distinctions, other important considerations must be at work in our application of inquiry. Bertalanffy (1968) long ago argued that biological systems presumed a formidably different approach to discovery. The rational-reductionist heritage does have applicability, but as Bertalanffy would assert today, not before we have investigated the dynamics of the whole. As they extended their research model to a larger experimental project, in the computer examples above, Salomon (1991) and his colleagues found that their proclivity for seeking discrete variables in the material studied could not be sustained. In Stevenson's discussion of professional education requirements, developing formidable structure or investigating individual processes cannot alone support a critically reflective inquiry program. It is not that these studies pose problematic variables (statistical methods have aspired to overcome this), but that, as our earlier discussion of holography suggests, form and function studied separately lose vital interactiveness—their essence in conjunction with the operation of the whole. Mechanical separation for the convenience of methodological concerns is effective only when we fully consider and understand the effects of form and function. Our inquiry may be more appropriately termed *systemic* in these ecological cases.

In considering the above further, we see the consequences of Bartlett's (1932; cited in Iran-Nejad, Mckeachie, and Berliner, 1990) simplification by isolation versus simplification by integration (see also Bertalanffy, 1968). For example, in leadership studies, authors today are only beginning to realize the necessity for studying leadership from a systemic perspective in its multiple contexts and roles (Smith & Blase, 1991; see also Hunt, 1991; Rost, 1991; Senge, 1991; Senge, Kleiner, Roberts, Ross, and Smith, 1994). To help the researcher pursue systemic inquiry, Salomon (1991) suggests a mapping process, Senge (1991) and Senge et al. (1994) develop archetypes, and others develop similar mapping models. Working with these differing "maps," one soon realizes that although inquiry can be contrived, it is also humanmade, full of variety, and still applicable in its own localness.

As Salomon (1991) contended, four considerations are important when selecting a process of inquiry: the paradigmatic assumptions one adopts, the perceived nature of the phenomenon studied, the question analyzed, and the research methodology employed. Each differing selection, regardless of where one starts the process, yields separate kinds of knowledge. Epistemologically, the system chosen justifies the "terms" of the entire process. In this light, differing inquiry systems are expected to yield different results with their own unique set of methodological requirements. As Lakatos (1978) also said, each separate inquiry system builds on the other. Theoretically based inquiry

leads to empirical progress through testing of hypotheses, and theory evolves from a more systemic approach.

For researchers and those who study inquiry, it may be time to realize that no one paradigm can fulfill all the needs of sociological research. But to arrive at this conclusion by assuming that various forms of inquiry are then fragmentary is ill-advised. Inquiry is not just hit or miss. This type of belief structure leads to the same limited view posited throughout the history of positivism.

What may be clear from the preceding discussion is the necessity for theorists to stop debating and begin a valid search for the form and function of inquiry. We have seen examples of many who would choose to remain strapped in their own expertise, and others who have begun to shake off their paradigm paralysis in hopes of riding the crest of those newest successful developing paradigms. Perhaps as philosophers we need to look to many of those practitioners who live in the real world and adapt to the future. "The systemic study of complex learning environments cannot be fruitful, and certainly cannot yield any generalizable [applicable] findings and conclusions in the absence of carefully controlled analytic studies of selected aspects in which internal validity is maximized" (Salomon, 1991, p. 16). As Salomon also contends, if we do not look to the real world more often, we may end up researching the least educationally significant aspects of that reality.

CASE STUDY

Inquiry: How Do You Know?

In the fall of 1985, then–Secretary of Education William Bennett visited a high school near Washington, DC, to teach a lesson on James Madison's *Federalist Papers*. Although his primary intention was to show a Secretary of Education coming into contact with the U.S. education system, Bennett also saw his visit as a demonstration of how substantive teaching can be valuable to America's youth. Eisner (1991) was one of four educational analysts asked to study Bennett's performance. He provides a unique look into the Secretary of Education through a narrative analysis of the proceedings. Eisner's analysis has been adapted for this study. After reading the adaptation, consider the exercise provided at the end of his study.

Adaptation of Eisner's "A Secretary in the Classroom"

Secretary Bennett prepares to deliver a lesson on the *Federalist Papers* to a class of high school students. The secretary, at one time a professor of philosophy, enters the classroom at the beginning of the new school year to teach a class of multiracial students. No secretary has ever taught like this in the past. How will he do? Can this man teach adolescents? How will teachers in the school react?

From the start, one gets a sense of Bennett's purpose and intensity. Adjusting the electronic equipment provided to televise and record the event nationally, Bennett opens by acknowledging sarcastically, "This is no typical day here," and then tells the class, "If you want to, turn around and say hi." "Hi mom!" he says, and the class of students do likewise. As an icebreaker, this works and helps to release the tension that has developed.

"All right, let's get to work. I'm putting my name on the board so you can write me if I make any mistakes." Neither Bennett nor the students laugh. With the preliminaries over, Bennett hangs his coat on the chair next to the desk and rolls up his sleeves as he begins pacing back and forth in the front of the room. "Why read the Federalist 10—Why bother? Why not catch the Georgia–Alabama game?" He leaves no doubt that this is a serious encounter. "Let's get to work." Today's lesson will be no once-over-lightly, no open-ended superficial discussion of anything on anyone's mind, but a serious examination of ideas about which the secretary cares deeply.

The task the secretary has set for the students is to read and understand the *Federalist Papers,* specifically, paper 10. The aims of the lesson are twofold. He wishes to convey to the students the idea that assumptions about government are built upon a conception of human nature, in particular, Madison's view of human nature and his beliefs about how government should be formed. Second, Bennett is interested in developing the students' analytic and critical thinking abilities. He has planned teaching tactics that are typically a teaching strategy employed in teaching the humanities. He is interested in sharing his ideas about the nature of a just government and the joy of helping the young slowly discover what he has already learned. Bennett is no stranger to the material as he has taught the *Federalist Papers* many times before. The book he uses, he tells the class, is "properly dogeared." "What is a faction?" he asks, "and why is it a problem in a society like ours? Why does liberty cause the problem of factions?" Liberty, faction, and self-interest were problems in Madison's time and still exist now.

"Liberty provides the opportunity to hold different opinions," one student responds. "If you get liberty and give it to people, people will have different views about liberty. There will be factions."

"How do we solve the problem of faction?" Bennett asks. "Remove liberty," he responds and then quickly follows with a question: "Why not remove liberty?"

"This problem of faction has at least two solutions. The first is to remove liberty. But do that and our country as we know it disappears. That cure, to quote Madison, is worse than the disease. Second, give everybody the same opinion. But that is not probable either. How, then, does one keep a self-interested majority from exploiting the interest of a minority while maintaining liberty that all wish to have?"

The pattern of repartee on these issues is predictable. Bennett asks an open-ended question, one that requires recollection of material read and an interpretive understanding of it.

Students respond by asking for elaboration and clarification. After a period of bantering, Bennett expands upon the students' elaboration in a context that none of the students are able to comprehend.

Bennett's responses are usually about 10 times longer than his students' responses. Bennett uses two pedagogical moves that are often acknowledged but seldom employed. He summarizes main points the class has discussed at various intervals and he teaches for explanation. His intensity is fierce, he paces, sometimes clenches his fists, his eyes dart from side to side. He is on camera, but one senses that this is more than just a show for the camera. Bennett seems to truly care about what he is teaching. The ideas he expresses are part of him. His earnestness takes the whole affair beyond the media event; he is intent on helping the students understand just how important this subject is.

"I get so frustrated when I hear people talk about special-interest groups as though they were a new thing. Madison had to deal with them in his own time. Pick up your newspaper—you read the newspaper every day, don't you?" He jibes the class, implying that they should be reading it. "Pick up any newspaper and you'll find special-interest groups pleading their case." He demonstrates his point with a newspaper he brought to class for that purpose. He illustrates his point about the self-interested nature of human beings by describing a situation in which a crowd of 150 people are trying to buy 25 tickets to a Bruce Springsteen concert. He illustrates complex and abstract notions from the *Federalist Papers* with an example from today that these youths can understand.

Not only does Bennett try to link the past to the present, but also relates the problem of self-interest and violence to his own college days. He brings credibility to himself and at the same time shows his own humanness. Bennett also uses the makeup of the class to his advantage, as he fine-tunes examples to particular students. "Was the union saved?" he asks. He talks about Lincoln's desire to save the union and the tension between two goods, the liberty of the slaves and the maintenance of the union. At least five times during his lesson, such connections are made. "Madison was intent on observing that the latent causes of faction are sown in the nature of man." Human nature, therefore, breeds potential conflict and violence. Government is a means through which self-interest can be reconciled to the public good. Bennett addresses government and the virtues of our view of people and government. Bennett has a mission and a message and shares them both readily with the students. He relishes the fight, cultivates questions, probes, and challenges the students continuously. Questions are asked intensely, and each makes a point, designed to lead the students through the main ideas and to a deeper understanding of the material.

Questions

1. What is your inquiry paradigm?

2. Based on your paradigm, how would you analyze the teaching environment described above?

3. What are the major tenets of your inquiry paradigm that would help us to teach more effectively?

4. As a result of the research that you would carry out under your inquiry paradigm, what further generalizations could we make?

5. Could you make any generalizations after viewing the original tapes of this event? What is your hypothesis?

References

Agger, B. (1991). *A critical theory of public life: Knowledge, discourse, and politics in an age of decline*. New York: Falmer Press.

Argyris, C. (1985). *Action science*. San Francisco: Jossey-Bass.

Aron, R. (1967). *Main currents in sociological thought* (R. Howard & H. Weaver, Trans.). New York: Penguin Books.

Babbie, E. (1989). *The practice of social research* (5th ed.). Belmont, CA: Wadsworth.

Barrow, R. (1984). *Giving teaching back to teachers: A critical introduction to curriculum theory.* Totowa, NJ: Barnes & Noble.

Bartlett, F. C. (1932). *Remembering: A study in experimental and social psychology.* Cambridge: Cambridge University Press.

Bebe, E. (1989). *The practice of social research.* Belmont, CA: Wadsworth.

Benton, T. (1977). *Philosophical foundations of the three sociologies.* London: Routledge & Kegan Paul.

Bertalanffy, L. von. (1968). *General system theory: Foundations, development, applications.* New York: Braziller.

Borg, W. R., & Gall, M. D. (1989). *Educational research: An introduction* (5th ed.). New York: Longman.

Culler, J. (1982). *On deconstruction: Theory and criticism after structuralism.* Ithaca, NY: Cornell University Press.

Cziko, G. (1989). Unpredictability and indeterminism in human behavior: Arguments and implications for educational research. *Educational Researcher, 18*(3), 17–25.

Derrida, J. (1981). *On grammatology.* Baltimore: Johns Hopkins University Press.

Dewey, J. (1938). *Logic: The theory of inquiry.* New York: Holt, Rinehart & Winston.

Eisner, E. W. (1981, April). On the differences between scientific and artistic approaches to qualitative research. *Educational Researcher,* 5–9.

Eisner, E. W. (1991). *The enlightened eye: Qualitative inquiry and the enhancement of educational practice.* New York: Macmillan.

Erickson, F. (1985). Qualitative methods in research on teaching. In M. C. Wittrock (Ed.), *Handbook of research on teaching* (3rd ed., pp. 119–161). New York: Macmillan.

Evers, C. W., & Lakomski, G. (1991). *Knowing educational administration: Contemporary methodological controversies in educational administration research.* Oxford: Pergamon Press.

Firestone, W. A. (1987). Meaning and method: The rhetoric of quantitative and qualitative research. *Educational Researcher, 16*(7), 16–21.

Firestone, W. A. (1990). Accommodation: Toward a paradigm-praxis dialectic. In E. Guba (Ed.), *The paradigm dialog* (pp. 105–124). Newbury Park, CA: Sage.

Foucault, M. (1976). *The archaeology of knowledge.* New York: Harper & Row.

Foucault, M. (1980). *Power/knowledge.* New York: Pantheon Books.

Gage, N. L. (1989, October). The paradigm wars and their aftermath: A historical sketch of the research on teaching since 1989. *Educational Researcher, 18*(7), 4–10.

Giorgi, A. (1970). *Psychology as a human science: A phenomenologically based approach.* New York: Harper & Row.

Goodman, N. (1978). *Ways of worldmaking.* Indianapolis, IN: Hackett.

Guba, E. G. (1978). *Toward a methodology of naturalistic inquiry in educational evaluation.* Los Angeles: Center for Studies of Evaluation, University of California.

Guba, E. G., (1990). *The paradigm dialog.* Newbury Park, CA: Sage.

Guba, E. G., & Lincoln, Y. S. (1981). *Effective evaluation.* San Francisco: Jossey-Bass.

Guba, E. G., & Lincoln, Y. S. (1982). Epistemological and methodological bases of naturalistic inquiry. *Educational Communication Journal, 30,* 233–252.

Guba, E. G., & Lincoln, Y. S. (1985). *Types of inquiry.* Unpublished paper, Indiana University, Bloomington.

Guba, E. G., & Lincoln, Y. S. (1989). *Fourth generation evaluation.* Newbury Park, CA: Sage.

Habermas, J. (1970). Technology and science as ideology. In *Toward a rational society.* Boston: Beacon Press.

Habermas, J. (1987). *The philosophical discourse of modernity.* Cambridge, MA: MIT Press.

Hempel, C. (1966). *Philosophy of natural science.* Upper Saddle River, NJ: Prentice Hall.

Horkheimer, M., & Adorno, T. W. (1972). *Dialectic of enlightenment.* New York: Herder and Herder.

Howe, K., & Eisenhart, M. (1990). Standards for qualitative (and quantitative) research: A prolegomenon. *Educational Researcher, 16*(1), 5–13.

Hoy, W., & Miskel, C. (1987). *Educational administration: Theory, research, and practice.* New York: Random House.

Huff, A. S. (1985). Managerial implications of the emerging paradigm. In Y. S. Lincoln (Ed.), *Organizational theory and inquiry: The paradigm revolution* (pp. 161–184). Newbury Park, CA: Sage.

Hunt, J. G. (1991). *Leadership: A new synthesis.* Newbury Park, CA: Sage.

Iran-Nejad, A., Mckeachie, W., & Berliner, D. (1990). The multisource nature of learning. *Review of Educational Research, 60,* 509–515.

Jay, M. (1973). *The dialectical imagination.* Boston: Little, Brown.

Kuhn, T. S. (1970). *The structure of scientific revolutions* (2nd ed., enlarged). Chicago: University of Chicago Press.

Lakatos, I. (1978). *The methodology of scientific research programs.* Cambridge, MA: Cambridge University Press.

Levine, H. G. (1985). Scientists and culture heroes in the classroom. *Reviews in Anthropology, 12,* 338–345.

Levine, H. G. (1992). Types of naturalistic inquiry. *Encyclopedia of educational research* (6th ed., Vol. 2, pp. 889–892). New York: Free Press.

Lincoln, Y. S., & Guba, E. G. (1986). But is it rigorous? Trustworthiness and authenticity in naturalistic evaluation. In D. Williams (Ed.), *Naturalistic evaluation: New directions for program evaluation* (Vol. 30, pp. 73–84). San Francisco: Jossey-Bass.

Littlejohn, S. W. (1992). *Theories of human communication* (4th ed.). Belmont, CA: Wadsworth.

Miles, J. K., & Huberman, A. M. (1984). *Qualitative data analysis: A sourcebook of new methods.* Beverly Hills, CA: Sage.

Outhwaite, W. (1983). *Concept formation in social science.* London: Routledge & Kegan Paul.

Parson, T. (Ed.). (1947). *Max Weber: The theory of social and economic organization* (A. Henderson & T. Parsons, Trans.). New York: Free Press.

Phillips, D. C. (1990). Postpositivistic science: Myths and realities. In E. Guba (Ed.), *The paradigm dialog* (pp. 31–45). Newbury Park, CA: Sage.

Polkinghorne, D. (1983). *Methodology for the human sciences: systems of inquiry.* Albany, NY: State University of New York Press.

Popkewitz, T. S. (1990). Whose future? Whose past? Notes on critical theory and methodology. In E. Guba (Ed.), *The paradigm dialog* (pp. 46–66). Newbury Park, CA: Sage.

Rossi, P. H. (1982). Standards for evaluation practice. In *New directions for program evaluation* (Vol. 15). San Francisco: Jossey-Bass.

Rost, J. (1991). *Leadership for the twenty-first century.* New York: Praeger.

Salomon, G. (1991, August–September). Transcending the qualitative–quantitative debate: The analytic and systemic approaches to educational research. *Educational Researcher, 20*(6), 10–18.

Schwartz, P., & Olgivy, J. (1979). *Emergent paradigm: Changing patterns of thought and beliefs* (Analytical Report: Values and Lifestyles Program). Menlo Park, CA: SRI International.

Senge, P. (1991). *The fifth discipline: The art and practice of the learning organization.* New York: Doubleday.

Senge, P., Kleiner, A., Roberts, C., Ross, R., & Smith, B. (1994). *The fifth discipline fieldbook: Strategies and tools for building a learning organization.* New York: Doubleday/Currency.

Shulman, L. (1986). Paradigms and research programs in the study of teaching: A contemporary perspective. In M. C. Wittrock (Ed.), *Handbook of research on teaching* (3rd ed., pp. 3–36). New York: Macmillan.

Simey, T. (1969). *Social science and social purpose* (E. Shils & H. Finch, Eds. and Trans.). Glencoe, IL: Free Press.

Skrtic, T. M. (1990). Social accommodation: Toward a dialogical discourse in educational inquiry. In E. Guba (Ed.), *The paradigm dialog* (pp. 125–135). Newbury Park, CA: Sage.

Smith, J., & Hesusius, L. (1986, January). Closing down the conversation: The end of the qualitative–quantitative debate among educational inquirers. *Educational Researcher,* 5–10.

Smith, J. K., & Blase, J. (1991). From empiricism to hermeneutics: Educational leadership as a practical and moral activity. *Journal of Educational Administration, 29*(1), 6–21.

Soltis, J. (1984, December). On the nature of educational research. *Educational Researcher,* 5–10.

Stevenson, R. B. (1993, March). Critically reflective inquiry and administrator preparation: Problems and possibilities. *Educational Policy, 7*(1), 96–113.

Tom, A. (1984). *Teaching as a moral craft.* New York: Longman.

Wilbur, K. (1985). *The holographic paradigm and other paradoxes.* Boulder, CO: Shambala Press.

CHAPTER 8

Evaluation in Education
Theories, Models, and Processes

Evaluation is a necessary, critical dimension of educational administration and leadership. In broad terms, educational evaluation can be thought of as a deliberate and desirable monitoring and adjustment process that educators engage in for the sake of assuring or improving educational quality. Evaluation reveals how well educational programs are working and provides insight into how they can be improved.

As a general rule, evaluation activities that are sensibly conceived and carried out competently can only add to the quality and viability of schools, curricula, personnel, facilities, and institutional support systems. Conversely, the inability or unwillingness to undertake evaluation or conduct evaluation exercises inevitably detracts from educational quality. Effective self-managing organizations engage in data collection and create feedback-rich environments.

To a large extent, educational evaluation today has evolved into a distinct professional field, represented by a variety of specialists and experts. For example, it is common to find state and district education offices, particularly in large districts, as well as offices within education associations and funding agencies, that are specifically organized to conduct evaluation functions. Typically, these offices are staffed by people who do specialized work as evaluators, researchers, analysts, statisticians, planners, economists, or accreditation experts. Even with this trend toward professionalism, however, it should be noted that the field of educational evaluation is still growing and changing and that evaluation systems and methods are based more on enlightened practice than on theory. Currently , a great deal of debate centers on methodology, values, and uses of evaluation processes. The use of qualitative methods has become increasingly effective as a means of lending flesh and bones to the skeletal pictures presented by empirical data alone.

Much of the work that falls into the category of educational evaluation remains in the hands of educational administrators, teachers, and other personnel who, for the most part, are nonspecialists. This is particularly true in smaller districts and institutions. This approach helps to keep evaluation grounded to educational realities at the practitioner's level, where educational delivery occurs. However, the middle and upper echelons of education systems often escape evaluation entirely. This may contribute to stagnation. The limited amount of evaluation of administrators is reflected in educational administration literature. To the research community this may suggest that researchers and practitioners may still be attempting to define the effective school administrator in light of the complex tasks they perform in school organizations. Unless a process, role, or task is clearly defined, it is not possible to establish validity and/or reliability of the evaluation. Equally, as seen in other organizations, evaluation by a superior of a subordinate may be problematic. Other types of personnel evaluation mechanisms, for example, peer evaluation and self-evaluation, may be more appropriate and advantageous. Educational organizations have become more and more dominated by the processes of assessment and evaluation In total, all evaluation may need to become more systemic, as we show in this chapter.

Educational evaluation can be employed creatively to focus on numerous practical problems and issues, both simple and complex, that crop up in educational settings. It can focus on different institutional functions, including instruction, curriculum change, testing, facilities improvement, program funding, planning, and community relations. Evaluation can occur formatively as an ongoing process, or it can be interposed summatively as a periodic or special event. In addition, it may involve almost any combination of subjects and participants, including students, teachers, administrators, parents, community groups, and government agencies.

While recognizing that educational evaluation is very individualistic and uniquely problem-solving oriented, it is also important to note within the field the existence of some basic divisions and conflicts. Educational evaluation is characterized by the coexistence of various philosophical and theoretical perspectives. There is an assortment of models and methodologies that guide evaluation practices. These different evaluation perspectives and approaches (quantitative versus qualitative methods, behavioral versus humanistic) tend to provide a basis for both renewal and greater sophistication. At the same time, the assortment of evaluation models available makes it difficult for the practitioner to absorb and utilize competing models effectively. There are differences related to professional and political issues: conflicts, for example, over who controls evaluation and who decides the purposes and priorities for evaluation.

In this chapter we present a general overview of assessment. It considers the historical development and contemporary nature of evaluation in education, including a consideration of the most prevalent models. We discuss program, teacher, and administrative evaluations, as well as need assessment, and point out a number of

practical evaluation aspects that are of particular concern to educational administrators.

Educational Evaluation: A Brief History

The Early Beginnings of Evaluation

The concept and practice of evaluation are hardly new. As Popham (1975) stated: "Through the centuries, most capable scholars have recommended that human beings engage in evaluative operations; that is, the evaluation of their own actions, . . . of other people's acts . . . [and] of myriad aspects of their environment" (p. 1).

Equivalent terms for *evaluation* can be found in ancient languages and texts, and the use of evaluation for educational purposes, to assess learning, knowledge, and skill, was also known in early times. Teachers in ancient Greece, such as Socrates, engaged in verbally mediated evaluations as part of the dialogic learning process, and emperors in China, as early as 200 B.C., made use of regular exams and proficiency tests to evaluate candidates for government service positions (Tyler, 1970; Worthen, 1973).

Despite its ancient roots, however, educational evaluation did not begin to take shape as a distinct field of endeavor until the advent of the industrial revolution. Evaluation issues emerged with the development of modern education systems in Europe and North America. As a general pattern, many early developments in the evaluation field, between 1800 and 1930, revolved around early psychological measurement and testing. However, around 1900 the field gradually began to expand its scope to include the formal evaluation of teachers, programs, and institutions, in addition to students.

The Modern Development Stages of Evaluation

A helpful outline of the modern history of educational evaluation is provided by Madaus, Scriven, and Stufflebeam (1983). They trace the development of educational evaluation in the

United States through six periods or ages, from 1800 to the present time.

1. The *Age of Reform* (1800–1900) was characterized by the development of the first mental tests and the application of psychological and behavioral measurements to educational problems. This age also saw the rise of experimental pedagogy and the use of external school inspectors to evaluate and promote schooling standards.

2. The *Age of Efficiency and Testing* (1900–1930) saw evaluation efforts that were largely dedicated to the development and use of standardized achievement tests and test batteries. Publication of *The Principles of Scientific Management* by Frederick Taylor in 1911 marked the influence of the ideas of systematization, standardization, and scientific method on industry and provided a methodology for the administration of education along progressive lines (Taylor, 1911). During this time, leaders in the educational evaluation movement, such as Robert Thorndike, sought to make testing more scientific and to make test scores a key factor in educational decision making, in student placement and pass–fail standards, and in comparative evaluation of programs via analyses of subject achievement scores.

3. The *Tylerian Age* (1930–1945) is associated with the work and thinking of Ralph W. Tyler, who is often considered the father and founder of educational evaluation. Tyler was initially concerned with educational measurement, but he also stressed the importance of considering the goals and objectives of educational programs when evaluating student learning and program outcomes. Tyler's emphasis on goal identification and goal achievement had the effect of widening the field of educational evaluation, both theoretically and practically. These goal orientations allowed learning evaluation measurements to be criterion referenced (as opposed to being norm referenced). Tyler's work gave evaluators an analytical framework for comparing a program's intended effects and its actual outcomes.

4. The *Age of Innocence* (1946–1957) saw the proliferation of Tylerian-style evaluation, especially its application in local school programs. Educational evaluation and measurement courses became commonplace at teachers colleges. Many refinements of tests and testing methodologies developed throughout this period. Leading educators praised evaluation as a major foundation element for building new systems of schooling, curriculum, and program delivery. Evaluation also became a major issue in teacher employment and in-school supervision.

5. The *Age of Expansion* (1958–1972) is most notable for an increased emphasis on personnel evaluation and the development of improved, multifactor evaluation models. During this period in the United States, numerous Title I programs were established that required the development of evaluation programs for continuation of funding (Berk, 1981). The implications of required evaluation drew researchers' attention to the limitations of rigorous experimental designs. Evaluators were charged with assessing new programs and intervening in practical situations. Also, goal-attainment evaluation models of the Tylerian type were expanded and refined to account adequately for adverse or unique program operating conditions. These requirements led to the acceptance and use of new qualitative evaluation models and systems models by expert practitioners. The new generation of evaluation models tacitly allowed evaluations of educational programs and systems to go far beyond the assessments of goal attainment.

6. During the current *Age of Professionalism* (from 1973 to the present), educational evaluation emerged as a distinct realm of professional specialization. This period is marked by a recognition that useful evaluation must draw upon a number of different models and methods, both quantitative and qualitative, and a more general acceptance of the fundamental philosophical positions that tend to divide the profession (Cronbach, 1982). Also, widespread calls for educational reform during the 1970s and 1980s tended to enhance the role of evaluation in planning and monitoring significant projects and programs intended to create educational change, including policy change.

From this chronological sketch, it is apparent that the field of educational evaluation has become progressively larger and more sophisticated, especially since the 1930s. Today, educational evaluation is a diversified field, involving educational specialists and generalists alike. Evaluation fulfills an essential role in educational development and change.

The Basic Aspects of Educational Evaluation

Definition Out of Diversity

As suggested already, educational evaluation is individualistic, more an applied art than a science. Evaluation approaches and designs are influenced by a variety of theories and models; evaluation practices can vary to suit different purposes (Shadish, Cook, & Leviton, 1991). In this regard, educational evaluation may be seen as lacking any single overriding theory or "best" method. There is a growing consensus that the existence of multiple evaluation approaches and methods presents no great problem for evaluation specialists and professionals. Rather, most problems seem to arise only when evaluation models are used inconclusively or inappropriately for purposes that are inconsistent with their inherent properties (Glasman & Nevo, 1988; Wolf, 1984).

Furthermore, the apparent diversity within the field of educational evaluation need not prevent the recognition of several major principles and conceptual features that give shape to the field as a whole. Despite its essential diversity, educational evaluation does have certain patterns associated with its usual functions and purposes. This awareness of commonalities, in fact, has stimulated recent attempts to develop integrated theoretical frameworks for the field (Shadish et al., 1991). In a similar vein, as we survey the wider field we will note that many of the better definitions of educational evaluation have been constructed around a few major viewpoints and common notions.

In keeping with the historical development of the field, formal definitions of *educational evaluation* tend to emphasize three prevalent viewpoints. Some definitions emphasize a mode of evaluation that is concerned primarily with the achievement of specified norms or goals (e.g., Tyler, 1970). Other definitions emphasize a type of evaluation that is qualitative, open-ended, or goal-free, and dedicated primarily to insightful descriptions and judgments of educational realities (e.g., Guba & Lincoln, 1989; Patton, 1984; Scriven, 1980a). There are also definitions that emphasize the pragmatic aspects of the evaluation process: information gathering, followed by analysis and judgmental assessment, followed by decision making. The pragmatic, process-based definitions of educational evaluation appear to be the most serviceable ones for administrators. These methods also reflect current thinking in the field.

Examples of process-based definitions can be seen in the writings of Cronbach (1982), and Stufflebeam (1990). Their definitions all highlight two process elements: the collection and use of information and the purpose of making decisions and taking actions related to educational matters.

Evaluation may be defined as a systematic collection and interpretation of evidence leading to a judgment of value with a view to action." This definition is particularly nonrestrictive, as it does not limit the evaluation process to any prescribed target or methodological approach. Yet it does serve to emphasize the essential, purposeful connections among information, evaluation (i.e., judgment), and action. Evaluation, in other words, forms the rational center of a wider educational management process.

Investigating definitions further, we frequently find that evaluation becomes confused with two other terms, measurement and research. *Measurement* simply identifies the act of measuring, which is essentially a value-free technical exercise for collecting and arraying data. *Research* is a process that attempts to generate new knowledge for the sake of theory testing and theory building. The results of research are often compared and generalized. But evaluation, by definition, is more valuative than measurement and more decision and action oriented than research (Kowalski, 1988, p. 151).

Norris (1990) identified a variety of differences between evaluation and research, including the following:

- *Motivation of the inquirer.* Research is generally pursued to satisfy curiosity; evaluation is generally pursued to solve a problem.
- *Objectives of the search.* Research seeks conclusions; evaluation leads to decisions.
- *Social utility.* Research results may or may not be directly socially useful; evaluation results are intended for social utility.
- *Criteria for assessing the activity.* Adequacy of research is judged by internal and external validity; adequacy of evaluation is judged by utility and credibility.
- *Discipline base.* Research generally focuses on a single discipline; evaluation often crosses disciplinary lines.

Some definitions of evaluation tend to get bogged down in attempts to establish hard semantic distinctions between kindred terms, for example, *testing* versus *measurement,* or *appraisal* versus *assessment* versus *evaluation* (Berk, 1981; Mehrens, 1973). Such terms often carry overlapping meanings and people tend to use the terms almost interchangeably in common parlance. Even experts use the terms differently, depending on the evaluation situation and focus. Global definitions of evaluation that dwell on such semantic distinctions actually do very little in the way of promoting a better or more realistic understanding of evaluation. A student of educational administration, however, does need to understand the variety of philosophical definitions of evaluation. This allows the practitioner to use evaluation processes for the right reason at the right time.

Evaluation Modes and Purposes

Educational evaluation is generally understood to fall into two primary categories: summative evaluation and formative evaluation. When most people contemplate evaluation, they typically are thinking about *summative evaluation,* evaluation that occurs at (or near) some identifiable endpoint of a project, program, or course. For example, comprehensive final exams and course grades for students, annual performance and merit reviews for teachers, and program assessments all represent different forms of summative evaluation applied to education.

As the term implies, summative evaluation, is usually conducted with the intent of making summary judgments about the overall worth of educational endeavors, activities, and programs. Data collection and analysis usually aim at measuring outcomes and achievement levels with reference to formally stated or well-understood goals and standards. The value judgments made via this process become the formal bases for making official decisions. Examples are decisions regarding the continuation or noncontinuation of programs, school activities, teacher assignments, student placement, and grade promotion. Decisions can also stem from comparative value judgments, replacing old curricula with new curricula based on the results of pilot trials and multifaceted comparisons (Scriven, 1980a, 1980b).

The term *formative evaluation,* on the other hand, refers to evaluation that occurs while processes or products are being designed. Formative evaluation is used principally to foster improvement, and it can be thought of as ongoing evaluation that accompanies some larger development effort or change process.

Formative evaluation is highly desirable, for instance, when implementing new programs or instructional delivery systems. Through formative measures, teachers and administrators can monitor the progress of implementation efforts. These measures give practitioners the means to detect and solve problems before they become unwieldy. Formative evaluation methods are also very useful in conjunction with programs aimed at staff development and organizational change. For obvious reasons, formative evaluation techniques also nurture effective teaching and educational testing, the normal concerns related to "student development."

In addition to summative and formative evaluation, Tuckman (1985) suggests a third mode of evaluation: *ex post facto evaluation*. These after-the-fact review processes study events and data in a longitudinal manner to determine the factors that contributed to educational success or failure. This evaluation is usually done to obtain information and review assessments needed for educational planning, to note outcomes, trends, and problem factors. However, summative and formative modes of evaluation still command the most attention among evaluation researchers and school practitioners.

Several authors have commented on some of the essential distinctions and relationships between the summative and formative evaluation functions. Glasman and Nevo (1988) reinforced the point that summative evaluation emphasizes accountability in education, whereas formative evaluation emphasizes improvement. Walberg and Haertel (1990) contended that summative evaluations are conducted with greater formality, primarily to serve the needs of external audiences. Formative evaluations tend to be informal, limited, and intended primarily for internal use by participants. Additionally, Lewy (1990) noted that summative evaluation is perceived as having more methodological rigor than formative evaluation.

Worthen, Sanders, and Fitzpatrick (1997) summarized the relationships of formative and summative program evaluation as follows:

- *Purpose.* Both determine the value or quality of the program.
- *Use.* Formative: to improve the program; summative: to make decisions about the future of the program.
- *Audience.* Formative: program personnel; summative: program personnel and prospective consumers or funding agencies.
- *By whom.* Formative: primarily internal evaluators; summative: often external evaluators.

- *Design constraints.* Formative asks what information is needed and when; summative asks what evidence is needed for major decisions.
- *Measures.* Formative: sometimes informal; summative: require validity and reliability.
- *Questions asked.* Formative: What is working? What needs improvement? How can it be improved? Summative: What results occurred? Under what conditions? At what costs?

It is possible to have methodological integrity at both levels, and as often as not, summative and formative evaluation functions can be regarded as complementary. Often, the same evaluation study can be viewed by one client as summative and by another client as formative (Borich, 1974; Lewy, 1990; Scriven, 1980b). Much depends on when and where the mechanisms are utilized and by whom. Indeed, many experts suggest that evaluation designs ought to include related plans for summative and formative evaluation (e.g., Edwards, Guttentag, & Snapper, 1975; Lewy, 1990; Mark & Cook, 1984).

It is also possible to identify other end functions or purposes of educational evaluation that occur as formative or summative activities are used. These parallel purposes for evaluation reveal, more or less, the basic reasons for conducting evaluations in the first place. For example, Glasman and Nevo (1988) mention that educational evaluation may be undertaken for sociopolitical and psychological purposes, such as gaining public support and professional commitments. Evaluation may also be carried out for authoritative and administrative purposes, such as demonstrating administrative control and authority over educational systems and processes.

Programs of instruction are commonly measured in terms of student performance. A. H. Miller, Imrie, and Cox (1998) categorized these measures of student performance as measures of potential, most commonly diagnostic tests used to place students appropriately, and measures of achievement, most commonly intended to measure student mastery of concepts or skills that have been taught. Measures of achievement may

Table 8.1

Evaluation Modes, Functions, and Purposes

Mode	*Functions and Purposes*	
	Motivational	**Corrective**
Formative	• Improve individual performance • Improve efficiency • Determine future goals	• Modify poor performance • Determine operative problems in a new program
Summative	• Reward outstanding performance • Determine degree of goal achievement • Grant tenure	• Dismiss deficiencies in a program • Determine deficiencies in a program • Establish institutional needs and priorities

be criterion referenced (performance matched to an absolute standard) or norm referenced (performance matched to the performance of others in a specified group).

Hopkins, Jackson, West, and Terrell (1997) categorized evaluation of school improvement (and by extension evaluation of programs) as three types: evaluation for school improvement, evaluation of school improvement, and evaluation as school improvement. In the first case, evaluation is intended to produce results that may be used to improve the quality of the school and its programs. In the second case, evaluation is intended to determine the success of attempted improvements. In the third case, evaluation is built into the operation of the school and its programs as a regular process intended to provide ongoing feedback and improvement of performance.

From the viewpoint of educational administrators, it appears that evaluation, whether formative or summative in nature, can be carried out for *motivational purposes,* on the one hand, and for *corrective purposes,* on the other hand. This general viewpoint and combination of purposes is illustrated by Table 8.1.

Evaluation Targets and Processes

As suggested earlier, educational evaluation may focus on a variety of targets or objects of interest. In general, evaluation targets tend to

fall into five main categories or areas of visible concern.

1. *Evaluations of learning:* measurements, assessments, and inquiries regarding student learning gains, learning rates, and performance

2. *Evaluations of instruction:* measurements, assessments, and appraisals of instructional quality, competence, and success in relation to instructional standards, goals, and norms

3. *Evaluations of courses:* evaluations of course design and content, of instructional support, and of testing and remediation systems

4. *Evaluations of programs:* evaluations of program curricula and course combinations; evaluation of program design, efficiency, and effectiveness, including assessments of administration, institutional fit, social impact, and cost benefits

5. *Evaluations of institutions and wider education systems:* evaluations of multiprogram or multisite education systems, including institutional and sectoral evaluations of national (or even international) education systems.

These target categories are interlinked, and when taken together, they represent an integrated continuum selection of specific evaluation targets. Evaluation of targets in any one category of primary concern can easily lead to consideration of targets in other categories. Evaluations of learning (target level 1), for example, are not simply restricted to a consideration of student behaviors or test scores; learning evaluations can include related assessments of instruction and course content. Similarly, course evaluations (at target level 3) can include assessments of instructional methods and materials (target level 2) in one direction, and of program design and institutional support (at target levels 4 and 5) in the other direction.

In practice, educational evaluation may focus on as few or as many targets as the specific evaluation situation dictates and allows. In this regard, evaluation becomes *situational*, as targets of any given evaluation will depend on the immediate concerns of the evaluators, participants, and audiences involved in the process and the commitment of resources and time.

Evaluation processes permit great *flexibility* with regard to the choice of procedures, methods, and participants. Fink (1995) provided a list of processes, including (1) posing questions, (2) setting standards, (3) designing the study, (4) selecting participants, (5) collecting information, (6) analyzing data, and (7) reporting the results.

McGee (1993) expressed these issues as " . . . political decisions such as who will conduct the evaluation, what is to be evaluated, and to whom . . . the results of the evaluation [will] be disseminated" (p. 32). She went on to include in the same category procedures for conducting evaluation and the analysis and interpretation of results.

Palomba and Banta (1999) specified a set of strategies that they felt were so pervasive that they could be called assessment essentials (p. 6). These include (1) agreeing on goals and objectives; (2) designing and implementing a thoughtful approach to the project; (3) involving a wide range of interested persons; (4) carefully selecting or designing data collection processes; (5) examining, sharing, and acting on the results; and (6) regularly reexamining the process.

This list reflects some of the commonalities that help define the general evaluation process. Glasman and Nevo (1988, p. 45) explained that all evaluation processes are characterized by three essential activities: (1) focus on a particular evaluation problem; (2) collection and analysis of empirical data, and (3) communication of findings and recommendation to evaluation audiences. The administrative, process-based definitions of evaluation offered by Popham (1988) and Wolf (1984) add two additional elements: (4) interaction between evaluators and people being evaluated, and (5) decisions and actions resulting from evaluation. Finally, it is also important to conclude with (6) an overall assessment of the entire evaluation project and its results. Edwards (1990) held that needs assessment as one of the elements of an evaluation process would help to focus the evaluation appropriately in terms of changing social or client needs.

A composite list of the core processes of educational evaluation from the viewpoint of educational administrators and leaders would include the following elements:

1. Problem setting
   a. Determine the situation to be evaluated.
   b. Determine the objects and people involved in the situation of interest.
   c. Determine the purpose(s) of the evaluation.
2. Problem specification
   a. Determine relevant elements for examination in the evaluation problem.
   b. Select appropriate evaluation mode and method(s) of inquiry.
   c. Select participants and sample groups; identify likely data sources, informants, etc.
3. Data collection and analysis
4. Communication of findings and recommendations
5. Decision making
6. Action derived from decision making
7. Assessment of the evaluation:
   a. In relation to the initial purpose.
   b. In relation to the process used.
   c. In relation to the expected results.

Throughout these evaluation stages, interaction among participants, evaluators, evaluation subjects, and evaluation audiences is necessary and especially advantageous. Interaction can occur at any stage of the evaluation process, but it is especially beneficial in the problem setting, communication, and evaluation review stages (Cronbach, 1982; Glasman & Nevo, 1988; Holloway, 1988).

As a final point, the last stage of the prototype evaluation process, overall assessment, has an impact apart from the evaluation reviewed. Assessments of any given evaluation ought to serve a corrective function. Problems and inadequacies noticed in the evaluation process are addressed to improve *future* evaluation efforts. Unless problems encountered in evaluation projects are thoroughly aired and examined, improvements in the process probably will not occur. Without corrective mechanisms in place, participants may come to regard evaluations as frustrating exercises devoid of worth.

Evaluation Perspectives and Models

In addition to recognizing the practical flexibility and situational adaptability of typical evaluation processes, it is necessary to recognize that educational evaluation also encompasses a wide range of theoretical perspectives and approaches. There is a plethora of models that have emerged in the field of educational evaluation. The array of models includes both descriptive and prescriptive models in various categories: research models, quantitative versus qualitative models, goal-attainment versus goal-free models, specialized limited-purpose models (such as cost-effectiveness) versus comprehensive systems models, and more.

Some models are highly theoretical, and other models are more pragmatic and oriented toward field use by nonspecialists. Nevo (1995) contends that the term *model* is used inappropriately in the realm of educational evaluation

because a large number of so-called models lack completeness and complexity. Many models appear to be single-use designs, created on the spot to meet the particular or peculiar need in a specific evaluation project(s). Research synthesis of these models-in-use into more generalized models is lacking. Nevertheless, practitioners need to be aware of the different theoretical bases reflected in various evaluation models, to better enable rational choice among the differing approaches and methods (Davis, 1986, p. 10).

In this regard, a number of different classification schemes for the various models have been developed for educational evaluation. One classification, presented by Popham (1988), grouped evaluation models into five basic categories (p. 23). Table 8.2 includes Popham's five model categories: goal attainment, judgmental, decision-facilitation, naturalistic, and self-evaluation. The fifth category for self-evaluation models was added to make the table reflect other current methods, including approaches suggested by Clift, Nutall, and McCormick (1988), Holt (1981), Wilson (1988).

Given the numerous models, some experts suggest that an eclectic approach is both possible and desirable in coming to grips with the multifaceted evaluation problems facing educators today (Glasman & Nevo, 1988; Popham, 1988; Wilson, 1988). Indeed, Brandt (1981) showed how different methods and techniques can be used by professionals to address identical evaluation problems. However, if an eclectic blend of approaches and methods is recommended, the blend can be effective only to the degree that practitioners know about different approaches and feel confident about their worth. Additionally, this implies that educators must become more knowledgeable, competent, and experienced with respect to educational evaluation.

Finally, House (1996) made the point that to develop an effective evaluation in an educational context, one must "conceive of students, teachers, and administrators as normal, rational

Table 8.2
Categories of Educational Evaluation Models

Category/Model Type	Method/Terms	Proponents
Goal-attainment models: The degree to which predetermined goals are reached is the sole criterion for evaluation	• Goal sources and goal screens • Five-step model • Eight-step model	Tyler Hammond Metfessel and Michael
Judgmental models: Major attention is given to the evaluator's professional judgment. The evaluator concentrates on inputs or outputs of the system being evaluated and determines their value.	• Accreditation model • Comparative evaluation • Countenance model • Payoff evaluation • Goal-free evaluation	School associations Cronbach Stake Scriven Scriven
Decision-facilitation models: Evaluation is viewed as the recollection of data to service decision makers. Models center on obtaining relevant information.	• CIPP model • "Evaluator as teacher" • Discrepancy model	Stufflebeam Cronbach Provus
Naturalistic models: The main instrument for data collection is the human being, and constraints imposed on the evaluation situation and evaluation activities are held to a minimum.	• Human instruments • Responsive evaluation • Connoisseurship mode • Ethnographic evaluation	Guba and Lincoln Stake Eisner LeCompte and Goetz
Self-evaluation models: The main source of data collection *and* analysis are the subjects being evaluated. The evaluator is more a facilitator who helps the group evaluate itself.	• LEA schemes • Curriculum reviews • School-initiated and/or teacher-initiated evaluation • GRIDS	Turner McCormick and James Elliot McMahon

people who have ambitions and motivations of their own, like everyone else" (p. 8). To idealize or demonize members of the system to be evaluated risks skewing the process, achieving inaccurate results, and ultimately failing in fulfilling the purposes of the evaluation.

The Main Types of Educational Evaluation

Scriven (1980a, 1980b) introduced the term *evaluand* to refer to the entity or set of targets being evaluated; he noted that virtually anything can serve as an evaluand. However, several authors

(Glasman & Nevo, 1988; Walberg & Haertel, 1990) suggest that outside the popular realm of assessing student learning, the most common foci of educational evaluations are program and teacher evaluations. As educational administrators reflect, these do seem to be the most prominent. Both of these, program and teacher evaluation, warrant further discussion.

Additionally, however, evaluation of educational administrators is also becoming an issue. R. I. Miller (1979) noted that in 1973 there was so little material available on this topic that he placed three announcements in *The Chronicle of Higher Education* hoping to get some leads, and even then he had limited success. More recently, however, literature on this topic has expanded.

Program Evaluation

Fink (1995) defined program evaluation as a "diligent investigation of a program's characteristics and merits [intended to] optimize outcomes, efficiency, and quality" (p. 2). Cronbach (1982) justified the need for eclectic methods in program evaluation. He explained that varied educational situations, epistemological perspectives, methodologies, and political concerns that characterize the field each demand unique consideration. Given this tendency toward diversity, no single model or methodology for educational program evaluation can hope to prevail. Thus, as a general prescription for program evaluation, eclecticism provides the most realistic and efficient approach. Cronbach's eclectic view also focuses the evaluation process distinctly in the political realm, as it is considered natural for people involved in the program evaluation to structure the evaluation activities in ways that coincide with their own priorities, preferences, and abilities. In this way, program evaluation methods inevitably reflect the values and perspectives of participants who control the evaluation process, seemingly to the exclusion of others. In any case, it is evident that the content and dynamics of any program evaluation will be determined by evaluators and other participants according to their motivation, intellectual outlooks, and expectations with reference to the evaluation problems and situations.

As an example, in the Texas Gifted and Evaluation Program Evaluation, the Texas Education Association, the sponsoring state board, specified the following principles: (1) evaluation of the program will be both continuous and comprehensive, (2) evaluation of the program will measure student progress and performance, and (3) evaluation of the program will determine the effectiveness of the program administration. Criteria specific to each of these broad principles shaped the full program evaluation.

Perspectives on Program Evaluation.   Theoretical and philosophical assumptions obviously help to shape any program evaluation. Historically, the scientific method of inquiry, which is based on hypothetic and deductive principles, has had a strong influence over the social sciences and disciplines such as education. Not surprisingly, then, educational program evaluations in earlier eras demonstrated a distinctive slant toward hypothesis testing via the collection and analysis of "hard" or quantitative data, preferably obtained via experimental or quasi-experimental studies. However, with the proliferation of education programs during the 1960s and 1970s, it became obvious that rigorous study designs and strict insistence on quantitative methods was insufficient to meet the needs of educators, administrators, and policy makers. This led to an expanded use of qualitative methods and of less rigid, more interpretive evaluation models.

Ultimately, program evaluation involves a judgment of the value of a given program endeavor (Wolf, 1984). However, the values to be addressed by evaluation must be clarified prior to the determination of an appropriate strategy and methodology. Mitzel, Best, and Rabinowitz (1982) cited five questions that help to clarify the values inherent in a given program evaluation: (1) is this thing any good? (an intrinsic value question); (2) what is it good for? (an instrumental value question); (3) is it better than something else? (a comparative value question); (4) can I make it better? (an idealization value question); (5) is this the right thing to do? (a decision question).

There are many purposes for conducting a program evaluation within a school or school district. Commonly identified purposes include understanding how students are doing in the educational system, identifying problems, understanding cost-effectiveness, and assessing the impact of attempts to improve the program.

The manner in which the foregoing value issues affect program evaluation are instructive. For example, addressing an optimization value would be best served by both formative and summative methodologies and would usually require a comparison against a standard. However, a decision question such as developing a new program may not entail any existing standard. In that case, no comparative judgment could be made.

Value assumptions, seen as having worth by interested parties and stakeholders, are often determined by the external perspectives used. In many cases, programs that have federal or private funding bases may require some form of stricter accountability, to demonstrate effective utilization of funding. Along these lines, Mitzel et al. (1982) contended that the political-economic and cost-benefit perspectives are most commonly used to determine the worth of a given program.

The political-economic perspective focuses on the principle of utilitarianism and implies that program value can be determined by the benefits, the greatest worth or utility (House, 1978). This principle has influenced the assessment of value in programs. However, social interventionists have questioned the utilitarian perspective by noting that occasionally, concern should be focused on subgroups within the population. Subsequently, the principle of utility was expanded using five criteria that address the distribution of benefits: (1) *equity,* emphasis on the equalization of outcomes or the minimization of individual differences; (2) *Pareto optimality,* achieving outcomes for all, regardless of individual gains; (3) *majority,* majority distribution of gain, even if those gains are minimal; (4) *minimax,* addressing those at the bottom or in the most need, regardless of the status of the ma-

jority; and (5) *dominance,* comparisons across competing groups in terms of outcome measures and implying that those evidencing better concluding measures experience better programs (Mitzel et. al., 1982).

Another common method to determine the worth of a given program is with a cost-benefit approach. This approach transcends the outcomes for a given group, as evidenced in Shapiro's focus on the criteria of distribution, and explores the consequences of such distributions. The field of economics has derived a variety of methods that accommodate the conversion of values to costs and benefits. But given the diverse thinking of multiple parties typically involved in most programs, consensus as to the costs and benefits corresponding to a specific value can be problematic (House, 1978). Debates over the worth of a program occasionally result in an examination of intrinsic versus pragmatic values, as shown through classical, organizational, or bureaucratic decisions (Mitzel et al., 1982).

Program Evaluation Approaches and Models. Mitzel et al. (1982) contended that the field of educational program evaluation is dominated by four major evaluation viewpoints: experimental, eclectic, descriptive, and cost-benefit. Table 8.3 compares the characteristics of these four orientations along 10 dimensions noted in the left-hand column. Distinctive features of these four orientations may help us understand program evaluation more thoroughly.

An experimentalist attempts to discover causal links between a program and its outcomes. The eclectics draw upon experimental or quasiexperimental designs that accommodate intervening variables such as contextual constraints and search for multiple causality to generate probable explanations of reality. The describers reject experimental designs, contending that meaningful data can be obtained only through in-depth, contextual descriptions of the program and through personal

Table 8.3
Four Methodological Approaches to Program Evaluation

	Experimentalists	Eclectics	Describers	Benefit–Cost Analyzers
Proponents	Cook and Campbell Riecken and Borich Rivlin and Timpane	Bryk Cronbach and Associates R. S. Weiss and Rein	Parlett and Hamilton Patton Stake	Haller Levin Thompson
Philosophical base	Positivist	Modified positivist to pragmatic	Phenomenological	Logical/analytical
Discrepancy base	Psychology	Psychology; sociology; political science	Sociology; anthropology	Economics; accounting
Focus of methodology	Identify causal links	Augment search for causal links with process and contextual data	Describe program holistically and from perspective of the participants	Judge worth of program in terms of costs and benefits
Methodology	Experimental and quasiexperimental designs	Quasiexperimental designs; case studies; descriptions	Ethnography; case studies; participant observation; triangulation	Benefit–cost analysis
Variables	Predetermined as input–output	Predetermined plus emerging	Emerging in course of evaluation	Predetermined
Control or comparison group	Yes	Where possible	Not necessary	Yes
Participants' role in carrying out evaluation	None	None to interactive	Varies (may react to field notes)	None
Evaluator's role	Independent of	Cooperative	Interactive	Independent of program
Political pressures (internal–external)	Controlled in design; or ignored	Accommodated	Describe	Ignore
Focus of evaluation report	Render "go/no go" decision	Interpret and recommend for program improvement	Present holistic portrayal program in process	Render judgment

Source: Adapted from H. E Mitzel, (Ed.), *Encyclopedia of educational research* (5th ed. Vol. 2, p. 600). New York: Free Press, 1982.

testimony. The cost-benefit analyzer attempts to gauge a program's economic worth. However, rather than adopt any single generic approach and attempt to adapt it to the needs of specific applications, evaluators may want to utilize a mixed evaluation approach, one that is suitable for the program environment and its sociopolitical context (Berk, 1981).

There is no single generalizable model for conducting program evaluations (Mitzel et al., 1982), as already stated. Yet it is important to note that there is a basic typology of the numerous program evaluation models that are currently in use. Regardless of the debate over what can be classified as a model, a model gives direction to evaluation design and provides a mechanism for explicitly or implicitly conveying the evaluation assumptions and evaluand relationships. For this reason, model building for program evaluation is extensive, and most evaluations are planned with one model or another in mind.

Like the educational evaluation models discussed earlier, models for program evaluation take various forms. The most comprehensive classification scheme for program evaluation models is provided by House (1978) in his taxonomy of major evaluation models. This taxonomy, shown in Table 8.4, includes eight basic model types that are applicable to program assessment and evaluations.

The limitations and complications regarding general evaluation discussed earlier exist for program evaluation models. Program evaluations must therefore be designed with reference to certain external factors and constraints in addition to the primary evaluands. In education, program evaluations include instructional effectiveness information gained through teacher evaluation. As noted by Stufflebeam (1990, p. 104), it is "fundamentally impossible to remove personnel evaluation from sound program evaluation." In the educational environment, that directs attention to teacher evaluation.

Examples of Program Evaluation Models.

Without attempting an expansive presentation of program evaluation models, it is at least possible to consider briefly a few of the more prominent all-purpose models that educational administrators might find most useful.

One type of total evaluation model is the *CIPP model,* developed a number of years ago by Daniel Stufflebeam and others (Stufflebeam, 1990; Worthen, 1973). The CIPP model for educational program evaluation is billed as a total model for several reasons. First, it compels evaluators to consider four integral areas of concern, indicated by the letters C-I-P-P: context evaluation, focused on the program context and evaluation situation; input evaluation, focused on the resources and human energies pertaining to the evaluation problem(s); process evaluation, focused on the internal program dynamics and interactions related to the evaluation problem; and product evaluation, focused on program products and accomplishments. Figure 8.1 illustrates the main conceptual aspects of the CIPP model, including the relationships among program decisions, program activities, and program evaluation influences. The CIPP model and its nearest cousins can be used for both formative and summative evaluations. It is best regarded as a decision-making model, strongest when used in a formative mode to plan and implement change.

A similar type of model, though more succinct, is the *Provus model,* represented in Figure 8.2. Like the CIPP model, the Provus model can be regarded as a planning and decision-making model, useful for monitoring program innovations. Evaluation is both formative and summative in the Provus model, so that it can be viewed as an ongoing event that produces information needed for decision making from the beginning to the end of a project or change attempt.

Figures 8.3 and 8.4 illustrate the principles of another type of program evaluation model: *Stake's congruence-contingency model* for evaluation. Like the two preceding models, Stake's model seeks to provide a rather complete understanding of program contexts and problems. It gathers information from as many sources as

Table 8.4
Taxonomy of Major Program Evaluation Models

Model	Proponents	Major Audiences	Assumes Consensus on:	Methodology	Outcome	Typical Questions
Systems analysis	Rivlin	Economists, managers	Goals; known cause and effect; quantified variables	PPBS: linear programming; planned variation; cost-benefit analysis	Efficiency	Are the expected effects achieved? Can the effects be achieved more economically? What are the most efficient programs?
Behavioral objectives	Tyler, Popnam	Managers, psychologists	Prespecified; objectives; quantified outcome variables	Behavioral objectives; achievement tests	Productivity; accountability	Are the students achieving the objectives? Is the teacher producing?
Decision making	Stufflebeam, Alkin	Decision makers, especially administrators	General goals: criteria	Surveys, questionnaires, interviews; natural variation	Effectiveness; quality control	Is the program effective? What parts are effective?
Goal-free	Scriven	Consumers	Consequences: criteria	Bias control; logical analysis; modus operandi	Consumer choice, social utility	What are all the effects?
Art criticism	Eisner, Kelly	Connoisseurs, consumers	Critics, standards	Critical review	Improved standards	Would a critic approve this program?
Accreditation	North Central Association	Teacher, public	Criteria, panel, procedures	Review by panel; self study	Professional acceptance	How would professionals rate this program?
Adversary	Owens, Levine, Wolf	Jury	Procedures and judges	Quasilegal procedures	Resolution	What are the arguments for and against the program?
Transaction	Stake, Smith, MacDonald, Parlett-Hamilton	Client, practitioners	Negotiation; activities	Case studies, interviews, observations	Understanding, diversity	What does the program look like to different people?

Source: Adapted from E. House, Assumptions underlying evaluation models, *Educational Researcher*, 7(3), 12, 1978.

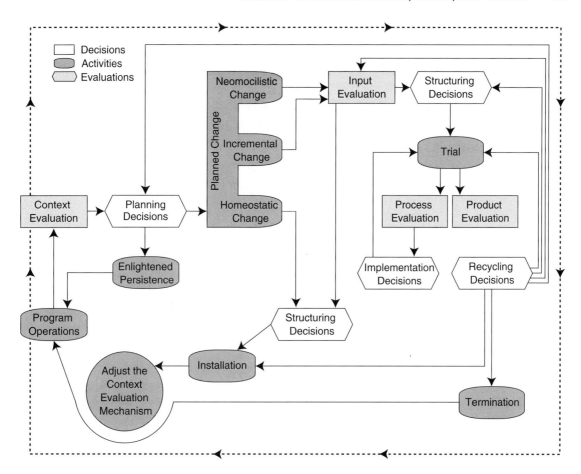

Figure 8.1
Total evaluation model: CIPP

Source: B. R. Worthen, *Educational evaluation, theory, and practice* (p. 41). Worthington, OH: Chas. A. Jones Publishing, 1973.

possible. As illustrated in Figure 8.3, multiple program features listed in the left column are examined in relation to a program's performance (i.e., with reference to data about intents, standards, and judgments) shown across the top of the figure. Data collection using the Stake model tends to be naturalistic because it relies on in-depth interviews and status reviews.

The analysis framework of Stake's model, represented in Figure 8.4, seeks to compare intended program conditions or logical contin-

gencies to program conditions that are actually found to exist (empirical contingencies). If congruence is lacking between what is intended and what actually exists within a program, the "gap" or problem indicated can become the focus of corrective action.

The three program evaluation models discussed in this section may help educational administrators appreciate some of the theoretical and practical implications of model building that have taken place in the research field.

Stage	Content		
	Input	Process	Output
Design	Design Adequacy		
Installation	Installation Fidelity		
Process	Process Adjustments		
Product	Product Assessment		
Program Comparison	Cost–Benefit Analysis		

Figure 8.2
The five stages of the Provus model and steps of evaluation associated with them

Source: J. G. Saylor and W. M. Alexander, *Curriculum planning for better teaching and learning* (4th ed.). New York: Holt, Rinehart & Winston, 1981.

Teacher Evaluation

Teacher evaluation has received increasing attention. As evidenced by a 1979 Gallup Poll, emphasis on improving teacher quality was a high concern (Gallup, 1979). The quality emphasis has continued to this day, as shown by a 1991 Gallup Poll; nearly 70 percent of respondents favored effective teaching (Elam, Rose, & Gallup, 1991). However, like program evaluation, teacher evaluation is not characterized by a single best or universal method. For example, both the theory and practice of teacher evaluation reflect disagreements as to whether instructor evaluations should detect incompetencies, prevent incompetence, or correct deficiencies, all of which suggest different methodologies and approaches. Additionally, different characterizations of the act of teaching mandate a variety of ways for collecting information and making evaluative judgments about the worth of instructional abilities and quality.

In this regard, even the bare essentials above are not holistic enough. As shown earlier with program evaluation, teacher evaluation may be accomplished for a variety of reasons, none of which are or can be explicitly measured in isolation. In this sense, teacher evaluation, in fact all evaluation, remains problematic.

Perspectives on Teaching and Teacher Evaluation. Darling-Hammond, Wise, and Pease (1983) contended that the work of teaching is variously perceived as a labor, a craft, a profession, or an art. Each viewpoint suggests a theoretical framework for teacher evaluation. When teaching is viewed as labor, teaching activities are characterized by standard operating procedures, and evaluation involves direct inspection of the teacher's work (e.g., monitoring lesson plans and classroom performance). If teaching is conceptualized as a craft, it requires a repertoire of specialized techniques, and the corresponding evaluation is indirect in ascertaining whether a teacher has the requisite skills to practice the craft. As a profession, teaching requires a repertoire of specialized techniques, similar to the craft perspective. But evaluation here calls for judgment about when those techniques should be applied. Thus, some evaluation standards are developed by peers, and evaluation focuses on the degree to which teachers are competent at professional problem solving. When teaching is perceived as an art, it calls primarily for intuition, creativity, and expressiveness. Corresponding evaluation methods that address holistic qualities and involve both self-assessment and critical assessment by others are applicable.

In practice, these four perspectives on teaching will not be found in their pure form. People will have mixed or overlapping opinions about what teaching entails or ought to emphasize. Such overlapping of teaching perspectives is natural given the fact that instructional behaviors that are effective in moderation can produce negative effects when they are overutilized or

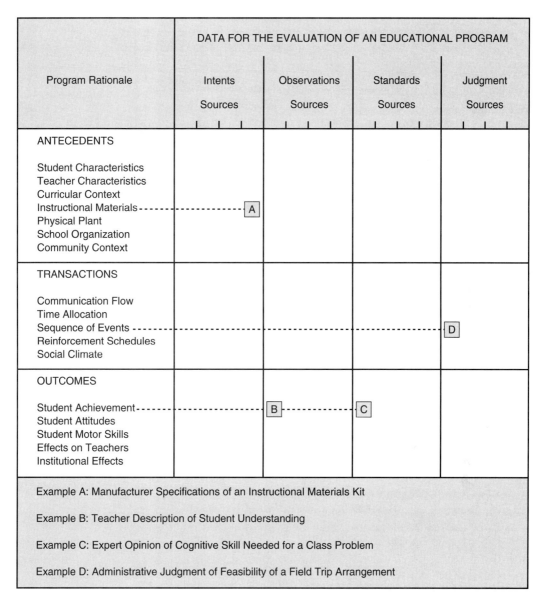

Figure 8.3
Elements of Stake's congruence-contingency model for educational evaluation

Source: R. E. Stake, in W. H. Beatty (Ed.), *Improving educational assessment and an inventory of measures of affective behavior.* Washington, DC: Association of Curriculum Development, 1969.

applied in inappropriate circumstances. The very nature and dynamics of teaching make it impossible to define a single perspective or set of behaviors that are globally successful (Coker, Medley, & Soar, 1980). Yet, as noted by numerous authors (e.g., Darling-Hammond et al., 1983; Millman, 1981; Shavelson & Stern, 1981), these perspectives on teaching undeniably

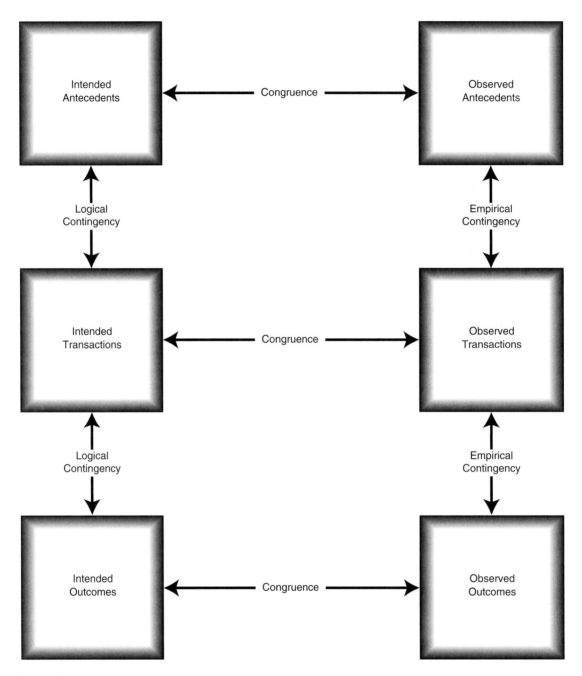

Figure 8.4
Analysis framework for Stake's congruence-contingency model for educational evaluation

Source: R. E. Stake, in W. H. Beatty (Ed.), *Improving educational assessment and an inventory of measures of affective behavior.* Washington, DC: Association of Curriculum Development, 1969.

determine varying definitions of success as well as corresponding values that are evident in different teacher evaluation systems.

Purposes of Teacher Evaluation.

Teacher evaluation generally addresses four purposes: (1) individual improvement, (2) school improvement, (3) individual accountability, and (4) organizational accountability (Darling-Hammond et al., 1983). Individual and organizational improvement needs are addressed primarily via formative evaluation. Accountability needs are typically satisfied by summative evaluation, with evaluation results subsequently used for personnel decisions and school status decisions (Darling-Hammond et al., 1983). However, some purposes, such as teacher promotion or tenure, are most frequently served by focusing the assessment on teacher competence, performance, or effectiveness (Millman, 1981).

Teacher Evaluation Methods.

Teacher evaluations tend to utilize quantitative or qualitative methodologies, depending on whether the evaluation is used to determine competence, performance, or effectiveness. Darling-Hammond et al. (1983) reported that eight evaluation methods are most commonly mentioned in current literature on teacher evaluation: teacher interviews, competency tests, indirect measures, classroom observation, student ratings, peer review, student achievement, and faculty self-evaluations.

Darling-Hammond et al. (1983) also noted that in the past, teacher appraisal interviews and classroom observation constituted the instructor evaluation process. Currently, the interview is used as just one element of the broader evaluation procedure. The two common uses of the teacher interview are to facilitate employment or promotion decisions and to communicate performance appraisals to practicing instructors. Moreover, the interview process has evolved from a primarily unstructured activity into a more formal one that employs standardized methodologies, such as teacher–perceiver interviews (Haefele, 1981).

Teacher competency tests represent a growing trend in response to the public's demand for institutional and professional accountability. Although there are also numerous state and locally developed examinations, the most widely used professional test is the National Teacher Examination (NTE). Competency tests are most commonly used for initial certification and hiring. These instruments offer the advantages of eliminating interviewer bias and verifying minimum standards of knowledge. The tests are usually legally defensible as screening mechanisms (Darling-Hammond et al., 1983). However, critics contend that the tests cannot assess actual performance or higher levels of knowledge, and success on the tests does not necessarily guarantee effective teaching, which is reflected by data showing that only 11 percent of teachers believe that NTE scores are valid measures of effectiveness (Haefele, 1981). As noted here, teacher competency as measured by the NTE may be a minimal necessity and must be combined with other evaluation mechanisms.

Traditionally, indirect measures, such as work experience and educational level, have been linked to teacher promotion opportunities. However, "no single set of skills, attitudes, interests or abilities" have been identified as capable of distinguishing between ineffective and effective instructors, although some research suggests a correlation between flexibility and effectiveness (King, 1981). Subsequently, less indirect measures connected to career and job performance, such as indications of professional advancement and commitment, seem appropriate as supplementary sources of evaluation data.

Classroom observation is a central aspect of most instructor evaluations and is typically used as a formative technique to address performance improvement (Mitzel et al., 1982). Classroom observations may include a preliminary interview. However, observation protocols reflect a range of structures and methodologies, from observations that entail standardized observation forms to those that address items agreed upon by both the instructor and the evaluator (Darling-Hammond et al., 1983). Observations are often conducted internally by an administrator, and this offers the advantage of including information as to the instructional climate and performance that is not available to outsiders. However, the numerous limitations of this method include observer bias, insufficient sampling of performance to provide reliable data, and measurement instruments that frequently lack appropriate focus (Darling-Hammond et al., 1983; Mitzel et al., 1982).

In actuality, student ratings are simply another form of classroom observation. These ratings provide a different perspective from that of an independent evaluator or administrator. Although this form of evaluation is most typically utilized at the higher education level, several authors (e.g. Haefele, 1981; Peterson & Kauchak, 1982) contend that student ratings could be effectively applied at the secondary level or, in some cases, even at the elementary level. This method of evaluation has several inherent advantages: for example, the proven correlation between student ratings and student academic achievement (i.e., minimally 0.8). Even so, some authors have debated the validity and utility of this form of evaluation (Darling-Hammond et al., 1983).

Mitzel et al. (1982) noted that despite the potential benefits of teachers evaluating their colleagues, peer review is rarely used and is not desired by teachers themselves. This form of evaluation usually entails peer examination of lesson plans, examinations, and other instructor-designed materials and documents, plus classroom observation. Peer review is based on the assumption that peers are in the best position to assess competence and performance because of their familiarity with classroom conditions and subject matter. In addition, peers are in a position to render specific and practical suggestions for improvement. However, many authors (Darling-Hammond et al., 1983; Haefele, 1980; Mitzel et al., 1982) concur that this form of evaluation should serve a formative function and not be used for personnel decisions or summative purposes.

Although evidence of student achievement should be included as part of the overall evaluation system, specifically for formative purposes, teacher evaluation based on student achievement has inherent limitations. For example, research has indicated that the connection between student test scores and teacher effectiveness is quite low, so the connection between appropriate teaching behaviors and resultant learning appears to be situational (Darling-Hammond et al., 1983). Also, the use of student test results to measure teacher effectiveness often leads to putting instructors' teaching to the test (Centra & Potter, 1980). However, when student scores are used as a formative evaluation methodology as part of a larger evaluation system, students' scores provide a mechanism of addressing the overall goal of the teaching endeavor, student outcomes (Darling-Hammond et al., 1983).

Faculty self-evaluations are an important source of information and evaluation in a broader evaluation program. Two of the most widely discussed teacher evaluation models, Manatt's mutual benefit evaluation model and Redfern's management by objectives evaluation model include faculty self-evaluation components. Typically, this methodology allows an instructor to use data derived from any technique (such as peer ratings, student ratings, or student achievement) to assess his or her own strengths and weaknesses. Although this methodology should not be considered an evaluation method in itself, self-evaluation is becoming a more popular technique in teacher evaluation systems. When combined with individual goal setting, self-evaluation may lead to self-reflection and motivation promoting professional change and growth (Darling-Hammond et al., 1983).

However, problems with teacher evaluation include the facts that evaluation systems are developed for reasons of accountability external to teachers and are not used to improve teaching practice, the multiplicity of relevant factors to be evaluated can make results difficult to interpret, and it is difficult to find consistent factors that work in most situations (House, 1996).

Overall, the low levels of reliability, generalizability, and validity attributed to teacher evaluation methods suggest that one-dimensional approaches to assessing effectiveness, competence, or performance are unlikely to capture adequate data about teaching attributes to completely satisfy any of the purposes of the evaluation process. Numerous authors (Millman, 1981; Peterson & Kauchak, 1982) note that additional research is needed in this area to determine and develop instructor evaluation systems that rise above the limitations already noted. Mitzel et al. (1982) suggested that despite the questions raised regarding the efficacy of feedback, the most useful outcome of current teacher evaluation efforts is that it provides instructors with accurate information, whether developed from administrators or students.

Teacher Evaluation Models. The configurations of methodologies and processes used for teaching evaluation are often classified as models. Although Nevo (1995) noted that the term *model* is applied inappropriately to many evaluation methodologies, certain approaches appear consistently in the literature and warrant mention. Borich (1977) contended that teaching models, including teaching evaluation models, are a combination of iconic, analogue, and symbolic typologies, and generally can be divided into two major categories: planning models and quantitative models. One basic planning model that serves as a basis for many others is Knezevich's systems evaluation model. This model, which is formative in nature, addressing personnel and organizational improvement, includes four phases: (1) determination of the purpose and effectiveness of the system, (2) development of monitoring procedures, (3) data collection, and (4) decision making and actions (Borich, 1977). Although Knezevich's model is not specific, precise, and verifiable, it does include all the steps necessary to develop an appraisal system.

The planning model by Coleman (cited in Borich, 1977) offers advantages over Knezevich's model in that it is more precise. Coleman's model specifies a number of teacher behaviors (i.e., warmth, indirectness, cognitive organization, and enthusiasm) and suggests corresponding measurement methods. This model is intended to address both formative and summative data. However, a limitation of the model is that research fails to support the assumption that Coleman's four teaching behaviors have wide application as effective instructional behaviors; rather, the behaviors may only have relative, situational merit (Darling-Hammond et al., 1983).

Two common quantitative models that have served as the basis for other models of this genre are Klein and Aikin's model and Dyer's model. Klein and Aikin's model uses an objective-based approach that excludes all subjective judgments of teachers. This model uses a regression analysis to measure the performances of one teacher's pupils against those of all teachers being appraised, to weigh only those variables under a teacher's control, and to adjust for variables considered as contaminating influences, such as differing pretest score levels (Borich, 1977). Dyer's model is also quantitative in nature, addressing four groups of variables: input variables of the students, output of the students, educational process variables of the school, and surrounding conditions. However, Dyer's model has diagnostic advantages not inherent in Klein and Aikin's model. Using Dyer's model, it is possible to adjust pupil outcome measures and those variables beyond the teacher's control and to focus on teacher behaviors that are "easy to change" (Borich, 1977).

Whereas quantitative models tend to be underrepresented in teacher evaluation systems, the planning approach is strongly reflected in two of the most widely discussed evaluation models: *Manatt's mutual benefit evaluation model* and *Redfern's management by objectives evaluation model* (Darling-Hammond et al., 1983). Both models have been implemented in numerous schools and are characterized by centralized teaching standards and criteria and by goal setting and teacher involvement in the evaluation process. Essentially, both models are designed to address teacher improvement by promoting professional growth and by integrating individual performance objectives with school policies. Both models straddle the competency- and outcomes-based evaluation philosophies, and both models are results oriented while they accommodate the numerous perspectives of "results." Manatt's model includes four major steps: (1) the administrative establishment of minimum teaching standards, (2) diagnostic evaluation to determine instructors' status as compared to standards via a multimethod approach, (3) cooperative establishment of measurable objectives for teacher improvement, and (4) reevaluation leading to the establishment of new job targets.

The steps in this model are basically similar to those included in Redfern's model; that is, they are based on the management by objectives (MBO) approach, borrowed from the field of business. However, in Redfern's model the teacher is involved in the development of mutually established objectives and standards prior to any evaluation. In this model, self-evaluation is more integral to the process (Darling-Hammond et al., 1983).

The models for teacher evaluation discussed above are the seminal models on which most other models are based (House, 1978; Mitzel et al., 1982). These key models assume that teacher effectiveness should be evaluated in an environment in which teaching occurs in order to address stable, consensual programmatic, and instructional goals. However, Knapp (1982) contended that in actual practice, most teacher evaluation systems are based on other multiple organizational demands. Evaluations must simultaneously strive to be legally "defensible" and address the needs to rate teachers, maintain staff morale and collegiality, and maintain organizational distance from environmental demands. Moreover, despite idealistic claims, most teacher evaluation schemes tend to call for improvements that require only modest, incremental change.

The Evaluation of Administration

Although the literature on formal evaluation of educational administrators has been limited until quite recently, as noted above by R. I. Miller (1979), this is an area of growing activity. As Farmer (1979) stated, there is no question that informally, administrators are evaluated continuously. The real issue is to determine when and why formal evaluation should take place.

Farmer (1979) enumerated the arguments for and against formal evaluation of administrators. Arguments against include (1) diversity, including program diversity, role diversity, and evaluation participant diversity, all of which make it difficult to get a consistent evaluation system for persons with similar titles; (2) lack of technique, which argues that no valid, reliable means of evaluating educational administrators has been devised; and (3) politics, which argues that evaluation is used simply to bolster subjective impressions and political agendas when dealing with educational administrators. Farmer countered these arguments by noting that (1) diversity may be a problem, but it is a fact of academic life and must be coped with by devising a flexible system and attending to the problem of inappropriate data; (2) the lack of technique argument is based more on perception than reality, and there are techniques that have been tested and validated over time; and (3) although politics is a real issue, establishing clear criteria for evaluation and developing good descriptive data can minimize the impact.

According to several authors (including Dressel, 1976; Hoyt, 1982), the basis of effective administrative evaluation, is to define clearly the role of the person being evaluated. Then the procedure, including appropriate instruments, should be designed to match the circumstances.

In any event, in any educational setting there is a clear relationship between the effectiveness of instruction and programs and the effectiveness of those assigned responsibility for management of those activities. Evaluation of a system without evaluating the performance of an important leading part would not be rational behavior.

Purposes of Administrative Evaluation

"Given the time-consuming and complex nature of administrator evaluation, the single most important step for any institution is to make sure that there are compelling reasons for starting a formal program of administrator evaluation" (Genova, Madoff, Chin, & Thomas, 1976). Arguing that the primary function of an administrative evaluation is to form a basis for establishing and attaining institutional goals, Genova et al. (1976) went on to enumerate the reasons for such an evaluation. These include (1) establishing and attaining institutional goals; (2) helping individual administrators to improve their performance; (3) making decisions on retention, salary, or promotion; (4) increasing the effectiveness and efficiency of the administration as a team; (5) keeping an inventory of personnel resources for reassignment or retraining; (6) informing the governing body of the degree of congruence between institutional policy and institutional action; (7) sharing governance; (8) informing internal and external audiences on administrative effectiveness and worth; or (9) conducting research on factors related to administrator effectiveness.

Farmer (1979) used the Genova listing to establish three major functions of administrative evaluation: formative, summative, and institutional. Formative functions are to (1) serve as a basis for administrative development; (2) help administrators compare their perceptions of performance with those of superiors, peers, and faculty; (3) provide a vehicle for team building; and (4) determine factors that influence effectiveness by analyzing evaluation data. Summative functions are to (1) determine retention, promotion, and salary decisions; and

(2) formulate and measure an administrator's specific program objectives. Institutional functions are to (1) explicitly define desired administrative roles and relationships; (2) assess strengths and weaknesses of administrative staff in order to assign them to appropriate tasks; (3) determine the congruence between instructional policy and administrative action; (4) extend participation in decision making by permitting staff input in the personnel process; (5) serve as a model and inducement for other evaluative processes; and (6) increase awareness of administrative efforts and achievements with external audiences, such as legislators and funding agencies.

Principles of Administrative Evaluation

Based on a review of the literature of administrative evaluation, Hoyt (1982) discussed the basic principles of an effective evaluative program. According to Hoyt, two basic principles underlie all effective evaluation: (1) uniqueness, in that there needs to be mutual understanding of the unique set of job expectations under which the administrator works, and (2) contextual interpretation, in that evaluation should be done within the context of the resources available to work with, the personal and situational obstacles encountered, and other factors beyond the administrator's control. Further criteria for effective evaluation, Hoyt (1982) noted, are the principles of credibility, validity, and fairness.

Credibility.   Concerned parties must have confidence that the procedures are appropriate and will yield meaningful results. To be credible, an evaluation needs to be developed with input from all parties affected. Also, there needs to be a clear understanding that the evaluation has potential for producing positive results.

Validity.   Validity of evaluations is based on their comprehensiveness and accuracy. To accomplish this, a description of relevant outcomes for each major activity of the evaluated person needs to be developed. Based on these criteria, the evaluation should measure meaningful change in persons or situations that resulted from the administrator's efforts. Further, any evidence used in the evaluation must have a direct relationship to the criteria identified. Face value of the evidence is vital. Finally, there should be a representative sampling of respondents to the evaluation, from as wide a variety of sources as is feasible.

Fairness.   The evaluation must be open, even though it may create some problems in validity. Participants in the evaluation, both the evaluee and the respondents, should know what they are doing, why they are doing it, and how the results will be used. Further, the person being evaluated should not be held responsible for events or conditions beyond his or her control. If this person does not establish salary scales or assign levels of pay, that is not a reasonable area to include in the evaluation.

Administrative Evaluation Models

Evaluation of an administrator must be tied to the context of the person's work, as noted above. Lists of the tasks and responsibilities of an administrator abound in the literature. Goodwin and Smith (1981) provided a representative example: (1) accomplishment of goals and objectives, (2) implementation of policy, (3) organizing skills, (4) position knowledge, (5) quality of work, (6) quantity of work, (7) innovating or taking the initiative, (8) professional development, (9) judgment, (10) facilities management, (11) planning, (12) budgeting, (13) delegating, (14) staffing, (15) communications, (16) decision making, (17) evaluating, (18) supervising, (19) professionalism/integrity, (20) reliability/dependability, (21) personal qualities, (22) attitude, (23) fairness, (24) human relations, (25) public/internal relations, (26) conflict management, (27) recognition of performance, and (28) producing reports. Not all of these items are of equal value, nor is their

relative value fixed. It is the breadth of this list and its fluidity that makes definition of the role in the specific case such a vital initial step.

Once the role is defined and the areas to be evaluated selected, the standards against which the person being evaluated is to be measured must be identified. Farmer (1979) cited the person's past performance, stated performance goals, and the performance expectations of others as workable standards. The performance of predecessors, the performance of others in similar positions, and an ideal standard are all unsatisfactory from his point of view, since conditions may have changed. Similarly named positions may be quite different, and no one has yet identified a valid theoretical standard for this work.

Participants in the evaluation process should include as broad a representation as possible of those directly affected by the administrator's performance. These might include faculty, peers, supervisors (both upper-level administrators and boards), students, alumni, clerical staff, and members of the public, depending on the situation.

With these elements determined, the means of evaluation must be determined. Farmer (1979) identified four general models: (1) rating scales, (2) growth contracting, (3) ad hoc committee, and (4) management by objectives.

Rating Scales. Rating instruments include forms, scales, and questionnaires. They may be of closed form, with a limited number of preset answers, or of open form. Although seemingly the least complicated of the models to use, they are considered the most abused because of the skill needed for valid construction and proper interpretation of results. Rating scales allow the user to classify information from various sources rapidly and efficiently. They are relatively easy to make confidential, allow for classification of responses, and allow for longitudinal study when the same questions are used from year to year. However, professionally produced rating scales do not generally include institutional expectations for specific administrators, nor do they match the administrator's performance to institutional goals. Rating scales are often low in validity, subject to the biases of the respondents, and may seek the simplest and most quantifiable aspects of the evaluee's performance. Because they tend to fragment responses, they do not generally give an effective overall picture of the person being evaluated. To be effective, rating scales need to be developed for each person in his or her specific situation, with the attendant difficulty of producing a valid and reliable instrument.

Growth Contracting.

Growth contracts are evaluation plans that allow the evaluee to think through and write out goals and objectives for the future. These goals and objectives are generally job related, but often will include personal as well as professional development issues. Growth contracts are generally considered an acceptable means of demonstrating professional competence. They can lead to improved satisfaction with personal and professional growth. They have the advantage of specificity in setting goals when they are done properly.

Growth contracts generally contain four elements: (1) self-evaluation, including a statement of past performance and a perception of strengths and weaknesses; (2) areas for improvement, selected from those areas of difficulty discussed in the self-evaluation; (3) plan for improvement, based on the areas selected for improvement and phrased as clearly defined objectives; and (4) long-range goals, which allow the person to place the improvement plan into a larger context.

Ad Hoc Committee.

The ad hoc committee is an extension of the screening committee concept, according to Farmer (1979). Ad hoc committees are appointed for a specific evaluation. They should be broadly representative of the constituency served by the administrator, but should not be so large as to be ungainly. They should operate within stated rules and guidelines that are recorded in writing and open to all. Parameters for effective ad hoc committee

evaluations, according to Farmer, include (1) assurance of confidentiality and dignity, (2) understanding that criticism as well as recognition is inherent in evaluation, (3) open disclosure of the evaluative processes and criteria, (4) understanding of the complexity of a valid evaluation, and (5) understanding of the specifics of time and place, expectations at the time of appointment, and issues at the time the administrator was hired as they impinge on the administrator's work and evaluation.

Management by Objectives.

Management by objectives (MBO) is a systems planning and management process that includes evaluation as a component. Evaluation (as performance review) follows naturally upon the process steps of goal clarification, establishment of measurable objectives, unit and individual self-analysis, action planning, and implementation. Following implementation, evaluation, feedback, and renewed planning and implementation complete the system.

According to Farmer (1979), the premise of MBO is that one person cannot direct all the activities of a complex organization. Under the MBO model, various administrators assume responsibility for a defined set of institutional outcomes for a defined period of time. At the end of that period, the results are matched to previously stated measurable objectives and performance evaluation results.

MBO is discussed at length elsewhere in the literature. For the purposes of this discussion, we simply note that its strengths and weaknesses stem from the same source: the people involved. If the participants are committed, clearly definable and measurable progress can be made toward specific individual and organizational goals. If the participants are not committed, MBO deteriorates to ineffectiveness.

Standards and Requirements for Educational Evaluation

During the past 30 years, there have been substantial efforts in the United States to control and ensure the quality of evaluation endeavors, a trend that has accompanied the emergence and growth of educational evaluation as a distinct discipline. One result of these efforts was the document produced by the Joint Committee on Standards for Educational Evaluation entitled "Standards for Evaluations of Educational Programs, Projects and Materials" issued in 1981. The document sets forth program evaluation standards in four major areas: (1) utility standards, (2) feasibility standards, (3) propriety standards, and (4) accuracy standards. Moreover, the document promotes the view that evaluation itself should be subject to quality assurance efforts (Stufflebeam, 1990).

The *utility standards* are intended to guide the evaluation process so that it will be timely, informative, and influential, and address the needs of the audiences to be served by the process. Essentially, the utility standards focus on eight areas: (1) audience identification, or specifying the group to be served so that their needs can be addressed; (2) assuring evaluator credibility, which requires that the person conducting the evaluation be both competent and ethical; (3) adequate information scope and selection, which suggests that the evaluation information gathered should sufficiently address pertinent questions about the person or activities being evaluated and be responsive to the needs of the audiences served; (4) evaluation interpretation, which requires adequate description of the perspectives, procedures, and rationale used for data interpretation so that the reasons for corresponding judgments are clear; (5) report clarity, which specifies that the evaluation report should explicitly describe the evaluand and its context, the evaluation process, procedures, and rationale, and any resultant conclusions and recommendations; (6) report dissemination to appropriate audiences; (7) report timeliness, which is important to the usefulness of the data; and (8) evaluation impact, which suggests that evaluations should be planned and conducted in a manner that fosters appropriate follow-through by the audiences served by the process (Stufflebeam, 1990). These utility standards require that evaluators give priority to the interests of clients and stakeholders and that evaluators satisfy the intended purposes of evaluations, even if it requires that they supersede their own interests or methodologies.

The *feasibility standards* are designed to ensure that program evaluations are cost-effective and practical, particularly since such assessment efforts occur in a political environment in that constituent interests are inherent. Basically, the feasibility standards advocate (1) practical procedures, to ensure that the evaluation process is not overly disruptive and can be managed in a real-world setting; (2) political feasibility, to ensure that the process is planned and conducted in a manner that promotes cooperation among the various constituencies while inhibiting the misuse of the results; and (3) cost effectiveness, to ensure that resource expenditures are justified, given the value and adequacy of the information generated by the process (Stufflebeam, 1990).

Propriety standards reflect the American value system. They address the areas of formal obligations (e.g., contracting); conflict of interest issues; full and frank disclosure; the public's right to know, balanced against the limits and statutes dealing with the right to privacy and public safety; human subjects considerations; human interactions, or assuring participants' dignity; balanced reporting that includes notation of an evaluation's strengths and limitations (such as the limits of certain methods or the generalizability of results); and fiscal responsibility, which addresses ethics, accountability, and prudence (Stufflebeam, 1990). Some of these areas are guided by regulations, such as standards promulgated for the protection of human subjects. In addition, Worthen, Worthen, and Sanders (1987) suggest that one of the most useful means of addressing evaluation propriety is through an evaluation contract, which can protect the evaluator against arbitrary or unethical actions by a client while protecting the client from an unscrupulous evaluator.

Accuracy standards address whether an evaluation has produced sound information. In fact, Stufflebeam (1990) contends that the rating of an evaluation against these standards provides a good indication of the evaluation's overall "truth value." Basically, the accuracy standards address 10 issues: object identification; context evaluation; description of purposes and procedures so they can be assessed; defensible information sources; valid measurement; reliable measurement; systematic data control; analysis of qualitative information; justified conclusions; and objective reporting. These accuracy standards are of great importance; without accurate results, the usefulness of the entire educational evaluation process is suspect.

In 1981, when *Standards for Evaluations of Educational Programs, Projects and Materials,* was released, the Joint Committee on Standards for Educational Evaluation knew that standards for personnel evaluation were also needed, as these could not be logically separated from other forms of evaluation (Stufflebeam, 1990, p. 104). However, because of concerns over support from teachers' organizations, the *Personnel Evaluation Standards* document was not released until 1990. The personnel evaluation standards are classified into similar categories used for presentation of the program evaluation standards (i.e., utility, feasibility, propriety, and accuracy); but some of the topics, out of necessity, differ between the two sets of standards. For example, the program evaluation propriety standard of full and frank disclosure is not included in the personnel standards because of confidentiality requirements; similarly, service orientation (i.e., requiring that evaluators show concern for the rights of students to be taught well), a key entry in personnel evaluation standards, is not included in the program standards.

It is also noteworthy that neither of the two reports on evaluation standards promote or endorse any single approach to evaluation. However, they do encourage the sound use of a variety of methods and approaches to meet the needs of the evaluation project and client. Overall, the pervasive message in both of these important documents on standards is that all evaluators should strive to make their evaluations useful, feasible, ethical, and accurate, regardless of the evaluation situation or targets. In essence, these standards may be most beneficial when examined a priori and used as guidelines for designing evaluations.

Requirements for Conducting Evaluations

Administrators of education systems must exert a leading role if the program and teacher evaluation standards mentioned above are to be attained in actual evaluation situations. Whether evaluation is summative or formative, motivational or corrective, primarily external or internal, administrators are bound to play a leading role in organizing and implementing the evaluation process. Therefore, it is incumbent upon educational administrators to be knowledgeable and competent with respect to evaluation functions and to have a thorough understanding of evaluation requirements.

As suggested earlier, the evaluation requirement can be regarded as "an evaluation problem with an evaluation context" (Glasman & Nevo, 1988). The administrator needs to understand the evaluation problem as it exists within the particular educational situation, with the aim of determining efficient evaluation methods that will result in better analyses to aid decision making. However, in addition to the need to understand key aspects of the evaluation problem, it is necessary for the administrator involved in any evaluation to understand the operational context in which the evaluation will occur. In this regard, the administrator must consider time and resource factors and must also take into account the values, routines, and perceptions of others directly or indirectly involved in the evaluation process.

Figure 8.5
Understanding the evaluation requirement

Source: N. Glasman and D. Nevo, *Evaluation in decision making: The case of school administration.* Boston: Kluwer Academic Publishers, 1988.

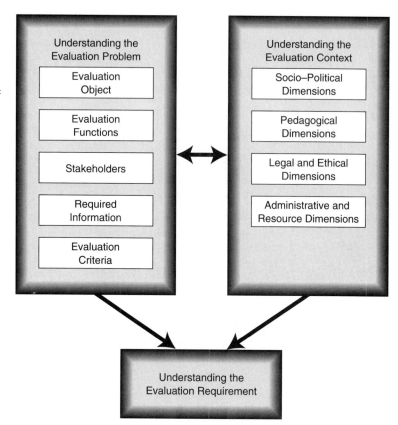

Once the evaluation problem and evaluation context are examined and weighed together, an administrator can get a fair understanding of the overall evaluation requirement. This, in turn, will allow the administrator to organize and support the evaluation at hand more effectively, so that evaluation activities can proceed with efficiency and produce the information and judgments needed. A conceptual illustration of understanding the evaluation requirement is presented in Figure 8.5.

The Future

Predicting the future of educational evaluation is as risky as predicting the future of the educational effort in general. However, some things seem reasonably clear. As long as education remains a human process, it will remain imperfect and open to improvement. As long as education remains a broad public concern, it will continue to be subject to scrutiny from multiple constituencies. As long as education remains a complex system, it will need to consider evaluation and feedback as legitimate components of that system.

During the past two decades there has been an increasing move toward assessment of the performance of educational institutions. This has taken clear form in the student outcomes assessment movement in colleges and universities [see Gray (1989), and Banta (1988), as examples of discussion of the movement]. Developed in part as an extension of management by objectives, outcomes assessment has drawn widespread public and professional attention. In one form or another, its emphasis on defining prospective outcomes and then looking closely at the results can be expected to figure strongly in the future design of the overall educational enterprise. Equally important, if we use earlier discussions as a reference point, we must realize that to date, evaluation mechanisms have been highly systematic. They lack the critical systemic emphasis and action orientation that ties evaluation to its other subsystems. Evaluation systems will need to be rethought, for example, as the era of the knowledge worker unfolds (Drucker, 1993) and as society becomes more global and as we recognize the interdependence of seemingly disconnected systems and subsystems. The era of postpositivistic thought may be dying or dead. That points to the necessity for more usable evaluation orientations for the future. To date, evaluation hasn't approached this crossroad.

With increasing emphasis on accountability, Worthen et al. (1997) foresee a series of trends that they anticipate will have an impact on the future of program evaluation, including (1) increasing emphasis on internal evaluation, (2) expanded use of combined quantitative and qualitative methods, (3) preference for multiple-method models, (4) introduction and development of theory-based models, and (5) increasing concern over ethical issues in conducting program evaluations.

Evaluation is, and will continue to be, pervasive in the field of education. At its best, evaluation serves to aid in improvement of the overall enterprise (i.e., personnel performance, student and program outcomes, and school and systemwide success). Even so, the benefits of evaluation must be considered in light of the corresponding limitations. As a general rule, evaluations do not yield generalizable results; they are time dependent in that most objects of the evaluation are not static; and although they may be useful in the diagnosis of problems, they may not be helpful in elucidating appropriate solutions (Wolf, 1984). Additionally, both evaluators and their clients must be sensitive to relevant ethical issues (e.g., informed participation) and be able to weigh and make use of evaluation results in arriving at educational judgments and decisions.

Problems are inherent in both program and personnel evaluation applications. For example, program evaluations often do not involve curricula appraisal; there is little empirical evidence regarding the efficacy of alternative evaluation plans, techniques, or components common in most models; evaluators rarely call in outside expertise, even when warranted; and discipline-prone evaluators sometimes tend to cluster around their respective evaluation banners like "vassals in a form of provincial bondage" (Worthen, 1990, p. 47). Many of these faults apply to teacher and administrative evaluations, but major problems in these areas occur for other reasons, too. There is no definitive agreement about effective teaching competencies, behaviors, and skills. There is a wide diversity of administrative tasks and responsibilities, even under the same job titles. Also, most personnel evaluations are conducted by administrators or supervisors who have little or no training in evaluation, and they may lack the knowledge needed to make informed, eclectic decisions in planning and carrying out the evaluation process (Walberg & Haertel, 1990).

In view of the problems that exist in the realm of applied evaluation, there is a significant need for empirical research, particularly with regard to instructor applications. This need is supported by an observation by Worthen et al. (1987) that the literature regarding educational systems shows large deficits on topics concerning effective educational evaluation.

Models of evaluation used in reviewing programs, teachers, and administrators have been discussed, with a review of their respective strengths and weaknesses. Means of establishing validity and reliability have been considered in each case.

In the future, evaluation of the educational system and its various components can be expected to continue to be a significant issue for all, professional educators and public alike.

CASE STUDY

Assessment Problem

Background

You have just completed your second year as assistant principal at Washington High School. As a teacher in this building for five years prior to your current assignment, you noticed a number of problem areas: teachers appeared to be growing more complacent, student achievement and progress had steadily declined, coursework often had little to do with job skills needed for the community workforce, school administrators seemed to lack the know-how to effect change, and the school seemed to lack the resources to combat even the simplest of these problems. This morning you were called in to meet with the building principal, who was appointed three months ago. During the discussion it was clear that the principal shared your view of the school. The principal is developing a long-range plan to attack the problems as described above. The principal expects to present the plan to the faculty and staff and to the superintendent of schools in 60 days. As part of that plan, you have been asked to develop an evaluation model for the school.

Your Task

Design an evaluation model for Washington High School. Draw on the information provided in this book; on your own experience as a student, teacher, administrator, parent, and/or taxpayer; and on other relevant reading and experience. Your overall model should include subsystems that evaluate programs, teaching, and administration. Be sure to consider issues of responsibility for follow-up and continued assessment of results. When you have completed designing the model, be prepared to discuss the implications of putting the plan into effect in a real school in the real world.

References

Banta, R. W. (Ed.). (1988, Fall). Implementing outcomes assessment: Promises and perils. *New Directions for Higher Education,* No. 59. San Francisco: Jossey-Bass.

Berk, R. A. (Ed.). (1981). *Educational evaluation methodology: The state of the art.* Baltimore: Johns Hopkins University Press.

Borich, G. D. (Ed.). (1974). *Evaluating educational programs and products.* Upper Saddle River, NJ: Educational Technology.

Borich, G. D. (1977). *The appraisal of teaching: Concepts and process.* Reading, MA: Addison-Wesley.

Brandt, R. S. (Ed.). (1981). *Applied strategies for curriculum evaluation.* Washington, DC: Association for Supervision and Curriculum Development.

Centra, J. A., & Potter, D. A. (1980). School and teacher effects: An interrelational model. *Review of Educational Research, 50*(2), 273–291.

Clift, P., Nutall, D., & McCormick, R. (Eds.). (1988). *Studies in school self-evaluation.* New York: Falmer Press.

Coker, H., Medley, D., & Soar, R. (1980). How valid are expert opinions about effective teaching? *Phi Delta Kappan, 62*(2), 141–144, 149.

Coleman P. (1977) In G. D. Borich, (Ed.) *The improvement of aggregate teaching effectiveness in a school district: The appraisal of teaching: Concepts and process.* Reading, MA: Addison-Wesley. pp. 216–230.

Cronbach, L. J. (1982). *Designing evaluations of educational and social programs.* San Francisco: Jossey-Bass.

Darling-Hammond, L., Wise, A. E., & Pease, S. R. (1983, Fall). Teacher evaluation in the organizational context: A review of the literature. *Review of Educational Research, 53*(3), 285–328.

Davis, B. G. (Ed.). (1986). *Teaching of evaluation across the disciplines.* San Francisco: Jossey-Bass.

Dressel, P. L. (1976). *Handbook of academic evaluation.* San Francisco: Jossey-Bass.

Drucker, P.(1993). *Post capitalist society.* New York: Harper Business.

Edwards, W. (1990). *Staff development of student services practices through participation in the programs of professional organizations.* Unpublished dissertation, University of South Dakota, Vermillion.

Edwards, W., Guttentag, M., & Snapper, K. (1975). A decision-theoretic approach to evaluation research. In E. L. Strevening & M. Guttentag (Eds.), *Handbook of evaluation research* (Vol. 1 pp. 139–181). Beverly Hills, CA: Sage.

Elam, S. M., Rose, L. C., & Gallup, A. M. (1991, September). The 23rd annual Gallup poll of the public's attitude toward public schools. *Phi Delta Kappan*, 41–56.

Farmer, C. H. (1979). *Why evaluate administrators?* In R. C. Nordvall (Ed.), *Evaluation and development of administrators* (AAHE-ERIC/Higher Education Research Report 6). Washington, DC: American Association for Higher Education.

Fink, A. (1995). *Evaluation for education and psychology.* London: Sage.

Gallup, G. H. (1979). The eleventh annual Gallup poll of the public's attitudes toward the public schools. *Phi Delta Kappan, 60,* 33–45.

Genova, W. J., Madoff, M. K., Chin, R., & Thomas, G. B. (1976). *Mutual benefit evaluation of faculty and administrators in higher education.* Cambridge, MA: Ballinger.

Glasman, N. S., & Nevo, D. (1988). Evaluation in education. In *Evaluation in decision making: The case of school administration* (pp. 31–45). Boston: Kluwer Academic.

Goodwin, H. I., & Smith, E. R. (1981). *Faculty and administrator evaluation: Constructing the instruments.* Morgantown, WV: West Virginia University.

Gray, P. (Ed.). (1989, Fall). *Achieving assessment goals using evaluation techniques* (New Directions for Higher Education, No. 67). San Francisco: Jossey-Bass.

Guba, E. G., & Lincoln, Y. S. (1989). *Fourth generation evaluation.* Newbury Park, CA: Sage.

Haefele, D. L. (1981). Teacher interviews. In J. Millman (Ed.), *Handbook of teacher evaluations.* Beverly Hills, CA: Sage.

Holloway, M. L. (1988). Performance appraisal. In R. Middler & E. Holzapel Jr. (Eds.), *Issues in personnel management.* San Francisco: Jossey-Bass.

Holt, M. (1981). *Evaluating the evaluators.* London: Hodder & Stoughton.

Hopkins, D., Jackson, D., West, W., & Terrell, I. (1997). Evaluation: Trinkets for the natives or cultural change? In C. Cullingford (Ed.), *Assessment versus evaluation.* London: Cassel.

House, E. R. (1978, March). Assumptions underlying evaluation models. *Educational Researcher, 7*(3), 4–12.

House, E. R. (1996, October). A framework for appraising educational reforms. *Educational Researcher,* 6–14.

Hoyt, D. P. (1982, March). Evaluating administrators. In R. F. Wilson (Ed.), *Designing academic program reviews* (New Directions for Higher Education, No. 37). San Francisco: Jossey-Bass.

King, J. A. (1981). Beyond classroom walls: Indirect measures of teacher competence. In J. Millman (Ed.), *Handbook of teacher evaluation.* Beverly Hills, CA: Sage.

Knapp, M. S. (1982). *Toward the study of teacher evaluation as an organizational process: A review of current research and practice.* Menlo Park, CA: SRI International.

Kowalski, T. T. (1988). Program evaluation. In *The organization and planning of adult education* (Chap. 11). Albany, NY: State University of New York Press.

Lewy, A. (1990). Formative and summative evaluation. In H. J. Walberg & G. D. Haertel (Eds.), *The international encyclopedia of educational evaluation* (pp. 26–27). New York: Pergamon Press.

Madaus, G. F., Scriven, M. S., & Stufflebeam, D. L. (1983). *Evaluation models: Viewpoints on educational and human services evaluation.* Boston: Kluwer-Nijhoff.

Mark, M. M., & Cook, T. D. (1984). Design of randomized experiments and quasi-experiments. In L. Rutman (Ed.), *Evaluation research methods: A basic guide* (2nd ed., pp. 65–120). Beverly Hills, CA: Sage.

McGee, V. H. (1993). *An analysis of the inservice training practices of the centers for economic education in Alabama.* Unpublished dissertation, Auburn University, Auburn, AL.

Mehrens, W. A. (1973). *Measurement and evaluation in education and psychology.* New York: Holt, Rinehart & Winston.

Miller, A. H., Imrie, B. W., & Cox, K. (1998). *Student assessment in higher education: A handbook for assessing performance.* London: Kogan Page.

Miller, R. I. (1979). *The assessment of college performance.* San Francisco: Jossey-Bass.

Millman, J. (Ed.). (1981). *Handbook of teacher evaluation*. Beverly Hills, CA: Sage.

Mitzel, H. E., Best, J. H., & Rabinowitz, W. (1982). *Encyclopedia of educational research* (5th ed., Vol. 2). New York: Free Press.

Nevo, D. (1995). The conceptualization of educational evaluation: An analytical review of the literature. In *School-based evaluation: A dialogue for school improvement*. Tarrytown, NY: Pergamon Press.

Norris, N. (1990). *Understanding educational evaluation*. London: Kogan Page.

Palomba, C. A., & Banta, T. W. (1999). *Assessment essentials: Planning, implementing, and improving assessment in higher education*. San Francisco: Jossey-Bass.

Patton, M. Q. (1984). Data collection: Options, strategies, and cautions. In L. Rutman (Ed.), *Evaluation research methods: A basic guide* (2nd ed., pp. 39–63). Beverly Hills, CA: Sage.

Peterson, K., & Kauchak, D. (1982). *Teacher evaluation: Perspectives, practices and promises*. Salt Lake City, UT: Center for Educational Practice, University of Utah.

Popham, J. W. (1975). *Evaluation in education*. Upper Saddle River, NJ: Prentice Hall.

Popham, J. W. (1988). *Educational evaluation* (2nd ed.). Upper Saddle River, NJ: Prentice Hall.

Saylor, J. G., & W. M. Alexander. (1981). *Curriculum planning for better teaching and learning* (4th ed.) New York: Holt, Rinehart & Winston.

Scriven, M. (1980a). *Evaluation thesaurus* (2nd ed.). Inverness, CA: Edgepress.

Scriven, M. (1980b). *The logic of evaluation*. Inverness, CA: Edgepress.

Seller, M. S. (1988). *To seek America: A history of ethnic life in the United States*. Englewood Cliffs, NJ: Ozer.

Shadish, W. R., Cook, T. D., & Leviton, L. C. (1991). *Foundations of program evaluation: Theories of practice*. Newbury Park, CA: Sage.

Shavelson, R., & Stern, P. (1981). Research on teachers' pedagogical thoughts, judgments, decisions and behavior. *Review of Educational Research, 51*(4), 455–498.

Stake, R. E. (1969). In W. H. Beatty (Ed.). *Improving educational assessment and an inventory of measures of affective behavior*. Washington, DC: Association of Curriculum Development.

Stufflebeam, D. L. (1990). Professional standards for educational evaluation. In H. J. Walberg & G. D. Haertel (Eds.), *The international encyclopedia of educational evaluation* (pp. 94–105). New York: Pergamon Press.

Taylor, F. W. (1911). *The principles of scientific management*. New York: Harper & Brothers.

Tuckman, B. (1985). *Evaluating instructional programs* (2nd ed.). Boston: Allyn & Bacon.

Tyler, R. W. (1970). *Educational evaluation: New roles, new means*. Chicago: University of Chicago Press.

Walberg, J. J., & Haertel, G. D. (Eds.). (1990). *The international encyclopedia of educational evaluation*. New York: Pergamon Press.

Wilson, J. D. (1988). *Appraising teacher quality*. London: Hodder & Stoughton.

Wolf, R. M. (1984). *Evaluation in education* (2nd ed.). New York: Praeger.

Worthen, B. R. (1973). *Educational evaluation: theory and practice*. Worthington, OH: Jones.

Worthen, B. R. (1990). Program evaluation. In H. J. Walberg & G. D. Haertel (Eds.), *The international encyclopedia of educational evaluation* (pp. 42–47). New York: Pergamon Press.

Worthen, B. R., Sanders, J. R., & Fitzpatrick, J. L. (1997). *Program evaluation: Alternative approaches and practical guidelines* (2nd ed.). New York: Longman.

Worthen, B., Worthen, B. R., & Sanders, J. R. (1987). *Educational evaluation: Alternative approaches and practical guidelines*. New York: Longman.

PART IV

Decision Making and Change

All that has gone before—understanding education as a complex network of systems; grasping the nature of leadership; developing the skills of observation, inquiry, evaluation, human relations, and communication; and mastering the practicalities of planning, resource allocation, and evaluation—is a prelude to the ultimate task of the educational leader: decision making. Without decision making, all the other activities are academic exercises. It is only when translated into action that their potential for good becomes reality.

Educational decision making assumes many forms. Formally, it is practiced in the political context of educational policy development at the school, district, regional, state, and national levels. The resulting policies affect the daily operation of all educational enterprises: public and private schools, colleges, universities, and vocational/technical training programs.

Chapter 9: Educational Policy Formulation in a Mixed Economy.
Policies are sets of rules for guiding the operation of an organization that have been formally adopted through a prescribed process. In this chapter we focus on policy formulation as collective decision making through the market (economics) and through governments (politics). A number of public policy models are described and critiqued. Special attention is given to assessing the impact of current proposals for decentralizing decision making in education, placing more authority at the school level and involving teachers, parents, and students.

Chapter 10: Organizational Decision Making.
Decisions are also made in school organizations, as discussed in this chapter. Decision making, the process of choosing among alternatives, is one of the most crucial skills

needed by an effective educational leader. We criticize the common practice of viewing decision making as a linear process (identifying a problem, defining the problem, weighing alternative solutions, and making a choice). Instead, we propose a circular process that is more compatible with the inherent dynamics of the educational environment.

Chapter 11: Systemic Change.

The ultimate objective of educational organizations (or any organization, for that matter) is to maintain internal stability. To maintain stability while existing within turbulent environments requires constant change—the focus of this chapter. Change is not a product to be pursued in and of itself; it is a process by which other ends may be reached. Those organizations that are able to maintain flexibility and react appropriately to new environmental conditions survive and prosper; those that do not become less and less able to serve society.

It is one of the great paradoxes of educational systems that they are simultaneously conservators of knowledge and social values and direct instruments of change, both for the people with whom they react and for society at large. For the educational leader, this means that he or she must be attuned to the complexities of selecting courses of action in a changing environment for a system that values stability while in a state of flux and serving those who are in the process of change themselves.

Educational leaders of the new millenium must be prepared to develop, articulate, and bring to fruition new educational systems, and to do so in such a way that the new systems meet societal demands for flexibility and quality. This is the great challenge that is discussed in this portion of the book.

CHAPTER 9

Educational Policy Formulation in a Mixed Economy

Any organization, whether it is the U.S. government, a state government, a business or industry, a voluntary or charitable association, a local school district, or a school, needs to agree on a set of rules under which it will operate. These rules are called *policies*—or *laws* in the case of government when formally adopted through a prescribed legislative process. Rules and regulations generated by a government bureau or agency under authorization of a law are also considered policy.

Policies establish the parameters within which an organization will function. They specify the activities that the organization will or will not carry out. Policies act to guide coherent action by channeling the thinking of employees and other members of the organization. They set constraints within which discretion can be exercised. They are necessary so that all partners in an endeavor have the same "marching orders," visions, and intentions (Kaufman & Herman, 1991).

The state and federal constitutions specify the formal procedures to be followed in adopting laws. But laws are usually written in quite broad terms and must be interpreted in order to be implemented. The interpretation begins with the bureau within the executive branch of government given the responsibility for administering the law (e.g., state education departments and the U.S. Education Department). Decisions made by bureaucrats to guide actions at lower levels of authority, and written in the form of regulations, are as much policy as the laws themselves. State law specifies general procedures to be followed by local school districts in formulating policy, although variation is permitted in specific practices. School districts may specify procedures to be followed by schools in setting policy or they may let schools establish their own procedures subject to district review and approval. Private organizations may go through formal incorporation that specifies a corporate procedure to be followed in making decisions, or they may informally agree upon a constitution or a set of bylaws to guide corporate decision making. In the public sector, policies are usually (and preferably) written. Policies may, however, be informal, unwritten, and unstated agreements by which members of an organization bind their actions.

Although constitutions, laws, charters, bylaws, and so on, spell out the formal steps to be followed in arriving at group decisions (i.e., policy), the human interactions in carrying out those steps are not specified. Often, these interactions involve elaborate strategies, power plays, and intrigue employed by individuals and subgroups bonded by common interests to shape an organization's (or government's) decisions. These interactions, whether simple or elaborate, can be referred to as *politics*. Indeed, Hodgkinson (1983) has referred to politics as "administration by another name." The nature of both the structure of the policy-making process and the politics employed within the structure are believed to influence policy outcomes (Dye, 1987).

In the United States, about 90 percent of the boys and girls enrolled in elementary and secondary schools are in schools operated by government (i.e., public schools). The other

10 percent are in schools operated independently or by religious or other not-for-profit organizations, but even these schools are monitored to varying degrees by governmental agencies and are formally chartered or incorporated by a governmental unit. Public schools, on the other hand, are strongly influenced by what goes on in the nongovernment sector, through their dealings in "the market" and through formal and informal pressures placed on governmental decision-making processes by individuals and private interest groups.

It is not possible to understand why public schools have acquired the nature they possess or how to change that nature without understanding how decisions about schooling are made and how public and private resources are transformed into the realization of societal and individual aspirations for education. In this chapter we describe the functioning of the economic and political arenas in which those decisions are made and implemented. We also address issues of when and how governments should become involved in the process.

We begin this chapter by examining the basic arguments for providing elementary and secondary education through the public sector (i.e., government) and the social tension this creates in attempting to accommodate personal preferences. Then we turn our attention to describing the political and economic processes that determine how many and what kind of resources will be used for educational purposes, how those resources will be used, and who the beneficiaries will be. Criteria are established for determining when government involvement is warranted and the range of possible involvement strategies are discussed. Attention is given to the placement of authority to make public policy within our federated governmental structure, and the tensions between centralization and decentralization forces. Special attention is given to the role of the courts in policy formulation.

Education: A Public and Private Good

Education brings important benefits to both the individual and society. If public benefits were simply the sum of individual benefits, there would be no problem, but this is not the case. Frequently, there are substantial differences between societal and individual interests (Labaree, 1997). Full public interest would not be realized if provision of education were left solely to private vendors and to people's ability to pay for education; and it is unlikely that the full private or individual interest would be satisfied if education were left solely to public provision. Thus, education is considered to be both a public and a private *good*.

Private goods are divisible and their benefits are left primarily to their owners. If a person desires a particular item or service, he or she can legally obtain the item by negotiating an agreed-upon price with the current owner. The new owner can enjoy the item or service, whereas those unable or unwilling to pay the price cannot. A good is private if someone who does not pay for it can be excluded from its use and enjoyment. This is known as the *exclusion principle*. Such goods are readily provided through the market system (i.e., the private sector).

The private (or individual) benefits of education, whether gained through public or private institutions, include the ability to earn more money and to enjoy a higher standard of living and a better quality of life. As part of this, educated persons are likely to be employed at more interesting jobs than are less educated persons. Schooling opens up the possibility of more schooling, which in turn leads to even better employment possibilities; long-term unemployment is much less likely. Similarly, educated persons, through knowledge and understanding of the arts and other manifestations of culture, and with greater resources at their disposal, are likely to have more options for the use of leisure time and are likely to use such time in more interesting ways. As informed consumers, they are likely to get more mileage out of their resources. Finally, better educated persons are likely to enjoy a better diet and have better health practices. This results in less sickness and a longer productive life.

Educational opportunities can be excluded from those unwilling or unable to pay for them; thus schooling could be provided exclusively through the private sector as it was prior to the organization of public schools during the nineteenth century. But if this were the case, there would be a number of socially undesirable external effects because the public (or societal) benefits of publicly provided education would be lost or at least severely diminished. These benefits include enlightened citizenship among the general population, which is particularly important to a democratic form of government. Also, in projecting a common set of values and knowledge, schools can foster a sense of community and national identity and loyalty among a diverse population. A public school system can provide an effective network for talent identification and development, spurring the creation of both cultural and technological innovations and providing the skilled workforce required for the efficient functioning of society. This is believed to contribute to economic growth and to a generally more vital and pleasant quality of life for everyone.

These benefits are considered to be of such social importance that public funds are used to provide for the schooling of approximately 90 percent of the school-age population in the United States. At the same time, parents of at least 10 percent of the school-age population hold private preferences so strong that they are willing to pay tuition to private schools as well as taxes in support of the public schools. Pure private provision would probably mean that education services would be less available than is socially desirable. Public provision by taxation is called for when social benefits exceed private benefits. When private benefits predominate, user fees or full-cost tuition becomes appropriate.

Structuring the decision-making process for education is particularly complex because education provides both social and private benefits. Procuring educational services incurs costs and produces benefits that accrue to individuals independently while incurring social costs and producing benefits that accrue to society collectively. Levin (1987) concluded that there is a potential dilemma when schools are expected to provide both public and private benefits:

> Public education stands at the intersection of two legitimate rights: the right of a democratic society to assure its reproduction and continuous democratic functioning through providing a common set of values and knowledge and the right of families to decide the ways in which their children will be molded and the types of influences to which their children will be exposed. To the degree that families have different political, social, and religious beliefs and values, there may be a basic incompatibility between their private concerns and the public functions of schooling. (p. 629)

To ensure that both individual and societal demands for schooling are met, decisions about the provision of education are made in both the public and private sectors. Decisions in the public sector are made through political processes by governments, whereas decisions in the private sector are made by individuals using market mechanisms. Easton (1965) described politics as the process by which *values* are allocated within society. Economics, on the other hand, is the study of the allocation of *scarce resources* within society. Economics is concerned with production, distribution, and consumption of commodities. Efficiency in the use of resources is the objective of economics. Politics is powered by collective (societal) concerns, whereas economics is powered by individual or private concerns.

Obviously, one's value priorities strongly influence one's judgment as to what are efficient and equitable allocations of material resources. Thus, there is continuing interaction between economics and politics. Decisions about the nature of education for a society's youth, how it will be provided, and how it will be financed are prime points of interaction. Decisions about public involvement in education are made in

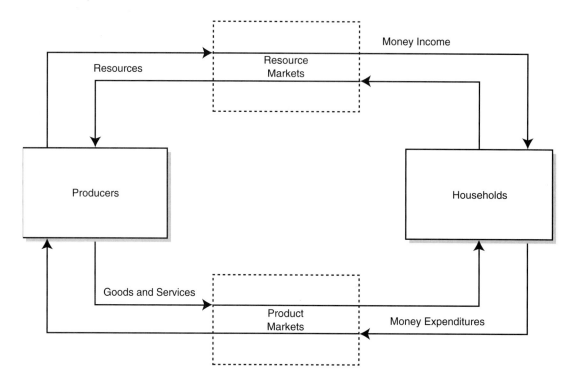

Figure 9.1
Circular flow of resources in a monetary economy

political arenas; but the decisions made in those arenas will have strong economic implications for individuals and for private businesses as well as for communities, states, and the nation. Individuals and businesses will respond independently to political decisions by deciding whether or not to participate in government programs or to supplement or substitute for government programs by purchasing services provided through the private sector.

The Influence of the Marketplace on Public Policy

The Free Market

Any society has to make certain fundamental economic decisions: *What* shall be produced? *How* shall it be produced? *For whom* shall it be produced? (Samuelson, 1980, p. 16).

In a capitalistic economy, people prefer to make such decisions for private goods through unrestrained or self-regulating markets. Figure 9.1 illustrates the circular flow of a monetary economy between two sets of actors, households and producers. It is assumed that households own all resources (capital) and that producers (or enterprises) have the capacity of converting resources into finished goods and services.

Resources are traditionally grouped into three categories called *factors of production:* (1) land, (2) labor, and (3) physical capital. *Land* refers not only to the dry surface area of the earth, but also to its vegetation, wildlife, and mineral content. *Labor* represents the human resources that go into production. Originally, economic analysts defined labor in quantitative terms only as the number of workers and the time they worked. With the advent

of human capital theory (T. W. Schultz, 1963), the quality of labor has also been considered to be an important economic characteristic of labor. Formal education is, of course, an important means of improving the quality of the workforce. A primary motivating force of the current school reform movement is the fear that the United States is not improving the quality of its workforce as rapidly as its international competitors and more sophisticated technologies demand. *Physical capital* refers to the produced means of production, such as machinery, factory buildings, and computers. Households may own land and capital outright or as shareholders in a corporation, and they also control the availability of their individual labor. The education level of the workforce correlates directly with the level of sophistication of capital that may reasonably be used in the production process.

The households (e.g., teachers and their families) and the producers (e.g., schools and school districts, colleges, and universities) each have something the other wants and needs. Producers need the resources controlled by households in order to produce finished goods and services. Households need the goods and services provided by the producers: for survival in the case of food and shelter and for improved quality of life in the case of many other goods. To facilitate the exchange, markets provide a means of communication. Producers acquire the resources they need through resource markets by making money income available to households in the form of wages, rents, interest, and profits. Households in turn use the money acquired through the sale of resources to purchase finished goods and services in product markets (e.g., private schooling). It is these sales that provide producers with money to purchase resources from the households. And so the cycle continues.

Through markets, households and producers negotiate prices to be paid for resources and finished goods and services. The outcomes of these negotiations ultimately determine the answers to the three economic questions raised previously. Resources are scarce and un-

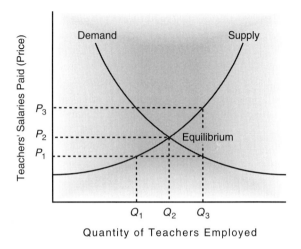

Figure 9.2
Supply and demand curves

evenly distributed among households, while household wants are unlimited. This means that each household must prioritize its wants and satisfy as many of them as possible within the constraints of the resources it controls and the cost of those resources. The value, or price, of resources depends on supply and demand.

Figure 9.2 illustrates the interaction between supply and demand as related to the number of teachers that schools employ and the amount they pay for their services. The demand curve shows that there is an inverse relationship between the level of teacher salaries and the number of teachers that school districts are willing to employ. Conversely, the supply curve shows that the number of persons willing to take jobs as teachers is high when salaries are high and low when salaries are low. Thus, if salaries are at P_1 as illustrated in Figure 9.2, there is a gap (Q_1 to Q_3) between the number of persons willing to work at that wage and the number of teachers desired to be employed by school districts. To close the gap, school districts must raise salaries to P_3 in order to attract the desired number of teachers (Q_3), or strike a compromise whereby the number of teachers to be employed is reduced to Q_2, for example, and

raising salaries it is willing to pay to P_2. With fewer teachers than the number originally desired, a shift in strategy is required for organizing schools in the district. One strategy is to substitute technology for teachers. As teacher salaries increase, technological substitutes become relatively less expensive; thus, fewer teachers in large classes using sophisticated instructional technology may produce similar results to more teachers in small classes using little instructional technology. Alternatively, rather than purchase instructional technology, a district may provide low-cost teacher aides to assist teachers in managing their large classes.

Producers in the private sector will produce only that which will incur reasonable profits. Profit depends on the amount of a good or a service that is sold, the price, and the cost of production. If the demand for a product is not sufficient to sell all units produced at a price above the cost of production, no profit can be made. Under such circumstances, the producer has three options: reduce the cost of production by adopting more efficient means of production, shift production to another product that can be sold for a profit, or go out of business. When conditions permit an above-average profit for producing a given good or service, more producers are attracted into the field. The number of units produced increases and the price drops to the point at which supply equals demand and the rate of profit returns to a normal range.

Each dollar controlled by each consuming household is a potential vote to be cast in favor of the production of one good or service over another or the product of one producer over the product of a competitor. The influence of a household over producers is approximately proportional to the value of the resources controlled by the household. This poses ethical dilemmas. The rich make expenditures for improving the quality of life while the poor lack basic necessities. Also, development of highly efficient low-cost technologies leads to a reduction in the demand for labor, causing reductions in wages and/or widespread unemployment.

The design and operation of highly sophisticated instruments and techniques is usually done by well-educated persons; thus the burden of unemployment and low wages is likely to fall disproportionately on those with little formal education. The issue of equity with respect to allocation of resources for education is discussed in Chapter 14.

Government and the Market

We do not rely solely on market mechanisms to make economic decisions, however, because society has many needs that cannot be met through the market. Over 40 percent of our gross domestic product (GDP) is distributed according to political decisions made by governments (e.g., municipalities and school districts). Important differences distinguish governmental units from households and producers in the ways they answer economic questions and the criteria they use. Downs (1957, p. 282) identified government as that agency in the division of labor which has as its *proper* function the maximization of social welfare. When results generated by free markets are ethically or economically unsatisfactory from a societal perspective, government can be used as a tool of intervention to set things right (p. 292). Governments have the unique power to extract involuntary payments, called *taxes,* from households and producers alike, and the federal government controls the money supply, upon which both public and private sectors depend. Governmental programs and agencies are not profit oriented and they rarely "go out of business." When they do, it is the result of political decisions and not market forces, although conditions in the market may influence political decisions. Efficiency has not traditionally been an overriding objective of the public sector, but growing numbers of persons think that it should be. Thus, efficiency of educational operations has become an important criterion in evaluating the progress of school reform.

Figure 9.3 inserts government (the public sector) into the center of the circular flow of a

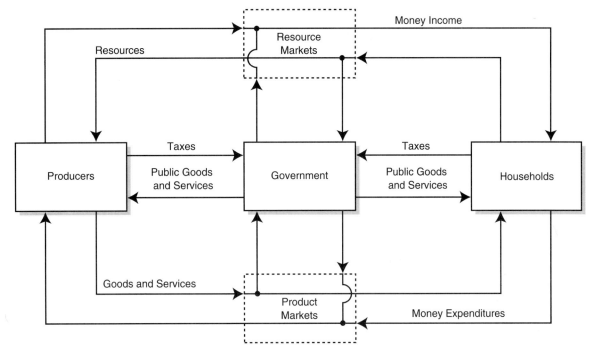

Figure 9.3
Circular flow of resources, including government (the public sector)

monetary economy. As noted, government obtains money for its operations through taxes on producers and households. With this money, government acquires resources through resource markets and goods and services through product markets. There are no separate markets for the private and public sectors; government demands are factored into the resource and product markets in establishing prices. Thus, there is not a unique market for school personnel, for example; school districts compete with businesses, professions, and other governmental units for desired human services. When the federal government borrows heavily from the financial market, interest rates go up for everyone alike—for the school district borrowing to build a schoolhouse as well as for a person borrowing to buy an automobile or a home.

Governments produce some goods and services that are desired by households and producers. These include public schooling, national

defense, fire and police protection, airports, harbor facilities, and roads. Typically, such services are neither distributed through the market nor priced through the market. Decisions concerning supply and efficiency of production become political decisions; thus, the "price" of such goods and services is equivalent to their "cost." Efficiency of public schools, for example, becomes an issue only when the electorate makes it an issue since public schools will not go out of business due to market forces because of high costs or poor performance. By serving 90 percent of the potential clientele and having access to the power of taxation to meet their revenue needs, public schools take on the characteristics of a monopoly.

Because public-sector decisions are political and, ideally, political power is distributed evenly among the electorate (i.e., one person, one vote), there are marked differences in the answers given to the three economic questions cited earlier than if the decisions were made through the private sector (market), where influence is distributed in proportion to the amount of resources controlled (i.e., the rich have much influence and the poor have little). The greater relative power of the poor in the public sector compared with the private sector leads to an equalitarian bias in decisions made in the public sector. The private sector has a bias toward efficient use of resources as well as a libertarian bias to permit the exercise of individual preferences within the limits of resources available to each person.

Thus, in making decisions about education, natural tensions exist among households, members of the teaching profession, and society. To the extent that decisions are made in the private sector, individuals and families can maximize their personal aspirations within the limits of their economic resources and according to individual value preferences. Professionals are free to provide or to withhold services and to determine the nature of those services. But when decisions are made through the political process, individuals and groups of varying value orientations must negotiate a single solution and their value preferences may be compromised in the process.

Proponents of decentralizing and privatizing the public educational bureaucracy, school-based decision-making, and family choice of schooling share the view that too many educational decisions are being made by government. Some proponents believe that this has led to an unwarranted emphasis on social values such as equity, making difficult the realization of a variety of privately held values through public education. Others believe that governmental operation of public schools has resulted in the inefficient use of resources, resulting in high costs and poor performance. In contrast, supporters of governmental operation of schools fear that educational services will be even more inequitably distributed than they are now if schooling enterprises are privatized, and that the sense of community that binds us together as a people would be weakened.

Models of Political Decision Making

There is no overarching general theory of political decision making, but there is a "grab bag" of heuristic theories and contrasting methods (Wirt & Kirst, 1982). *Heuristic theory* is a method of analytically separating and categorizing items in experience. Among the most useful for understanding policy relating to schools are: (1) institutionalism, (2) systems theory, (3) incrementalism, (4) group theory, (5) elite theory, and (6) rationalism. These theories and models complement one another. Each emphasizes a particular aspect of the policy-making process. Taken together, they provide a rather complete picture of the total process. Although these theories were developed primarily to describe policy formulation at the national level, they are fully applicable at the state level and can provide much insight to understanding the policy-making process at the school district and school levels as well.

Institutionalism

Institutionalism focuses on the structure of the policymaking process (Elazar, 1972; Grodzins, 1966; Walker, 1981) and is highly relevant to our earlier discussion of the allocation of authority within that process. Unlike most of the rest of the world, where education is a function of the national government, educational governance in the United States is characterized by the primacy of state governments, with power delegated to school districts. On the positive side, this arrangement has produced educational systems that are quite diverse, dynamic, and responsive to local conditions. On the negative side, the structure has resulted in gross financial and curricular inequities. Some school districts spend several times as much per pupil as do other districts. Some districts operate schools that are unequaled in quality throughout the world, whereas others operate schools that are an embarrassment to the profession and to the nation.

The devolved nature of school governance impeded state and federal efforts during the 1960s, 1970s, and 1980s to equalize educational opportunities in terms of finance, curricular provision, and the integration of students and staff with respect to race, ethnicity, and national origin.

But the structure of educational governance has changed over the years and it continues to change. The change is reflected in Table 9.1, which shows the trends in school revenue provided by each level of government in the United States since 1920. During the early part of the twentieth century, state governments on average paid less than 20 percent of the cost of elementary and secondary education; the rest was provided by school districts and/or local governments. The state share grew steadily after 1930. By 1980, total aggregate state aid of the 50 states exceeded revenue raised from local sources for the first time. Federal participation grew from virtually nothing at the beginning of the century to nearly 10 percent in 1980. Federal aid has since declined to 6.6 percent of all revenues for public schools (National Center for Education Statistics, 1999, p. 50).

The growing participation by state and federal governments in the financing of schools parallels their growing interest in and influence over educational policy in general. While state education departments and the U.S. Education Department have increased in size and influence, state governments have become particularly active in the prescription of basic curricula, monitoring student progress through mandatory testing programs, and the certification of teachers.

According to Wirt and Kirst, (1982, p. v), "the 1970s will be remembered as an era when the previous hallmark of American education—local control—became fully a myth." The local superintendent has lost his or her once preeminent position in setting the school district agenda and controlling decision outcomes. The discretionary range of superintendents and school boards has been narrowed at the top by federal and state action and at the bottom through collective bargaining with employee unions. The more recent trend toward school-based management is narrowing the range even further. Nevertheless, local school districts

Table 9.1
Revenue Sources for Public Elementary and Secondary Schools, 1920–1996

Year	Total Revenue (millions)[a]	Sources (Percentage of total)		
		Local	State	Federal
1920	$ 970	83.2	16.5	0.3
1930	2,089	82.7	16.9	0.4
1940	2,261	68.0	30.3	1.8
1950	5,437	57.3	39.8	2.9
1960	14,747	56.5	39.1	4.4
1970	40,267	52.1	39.9	8.0
1980	96,881	43.4	46.8	9.8
1990	207,753	46.8	47.1	6.1
1996	287,703	45.9	47.5	6.6

Source: National Center for Education Statistics, *Digest of education statistics, 1998*. Washington, DC: U.S. Department of Education, 1999.
[a]Current dollars.

continue to exert a considerable, though declining amount of influence on educational policy (Odden & Marsh, 1989).

Other structural changes of political institutions are taking place that will have an impact on the decision-making process and the ultimate nature of decisions made. Small districts have consolidated and large districts have decentralized. Progress is being made toward the professionalization of teaching and parental choice of schools. The practice of letting parents choose the schools their children attend is gaining in popularity, as are educational vouchers, charter schools, and tax credits, all of which have greatly changed the face of educational governance. The recent changes in school governance structures in Chicago (Hess, 1991, 1999) and Kentucky (Guskey, 1994) are dramatic examples of the contemporary belief that the nature of the decision-making structure of educational institutions influences the quality of the decisions they make and the efficiency of their operations.

Systems Theory

The most comprehensive of the models represents an application of systems theory to the political process. As explained in Chapter 2, a system is made up of a number of interrelated elements. An open system, which is characteristic of political systems, draws resources from its environment, processes them in some fashion, and returns the processed resources to the envi-

ronment. All systems tend toward entropy or disorganization and they must consciously combat this tendency in order to maintain equilibrium. A key function for combating entropy is feedback (i.e., continual monitoring of a system's internal operations and its relationship with its environment). Accurate feedback is particularly critical to a system's health in that the system depends on the environment for resources, without which the system would shrink and die. Equilibrium is maintained by modifying or adapting system structures and processes based on analysis of feedback (cybernetics). Maintaining equilibrium is a dynamic process leading to growth and evolution of a system in harmony with its environment.

Easton (1965) adapted general systems theory to political systems. His model, illustrated in Figure 9.4, conceptualizes public policy as a response by a political system to forces from the environment. Environmental pressures or inputs come in the form of (1) demands for public action through interest groups, and (2) support of government by individuals and groups through obeying laws, paying taxes, and accepting outcomes of elections. The inputs are processed through the political system and transformed into policy outputs. Political systems consist of sets of identifiable and interrelated institutions and activities at all levels, such as those associated with the U.S. Congress, state and county legislatures, common councils, town councils, village boards, school boards, commissions,

Figure 9.4
Simplified model of a political system

Source: D. Easton. *A systems analysis of political life* (p. 32). Chicago: University of Chicago Press, 1965. Copyright 1965 by University of Chicago Press. Reprinted by permission.

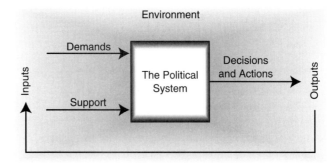

authorities, and courts. Feedback in a political system is both formal and informal. Formal feedback is provided through elections, referenda, hearings, and policy analyses. Informal feedback occurs through personal interactions with constituents and others.

Figure 9.5 is an adaptation to education of Easton's (1965) simplified model of a political system. Social values and goals (of multiple interest groups) are treated as demand inputs to the policymaking process in the new model. Other demand inputs include existing knowledge (e.g., the professional expertise of teachers and administrators) and requirements for a qualified workforce. The latter requirement is, at the same time, a support input in that trained

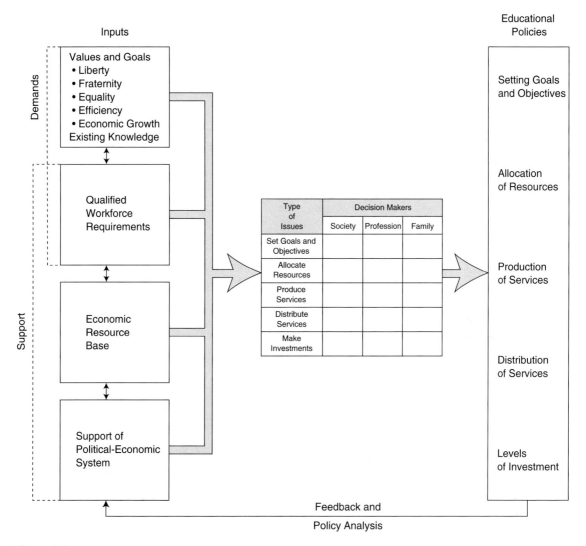

Figure 9.5
Model of the political–economic system of educational policy development

Source: A. D. Swanson and R. A. King. *School finance: Its economics and politics.* New York: Longman, 1991. Copyright 1991 by Longman Publishers USA. Reprinted with permission.

personnel (teachers and administrators) are required to implement any educational policies that are made and, indeed, the qualifications of available labor will strongly influence which educational policy alternatives are feasible and which are not. Other support inputs are the economic base from which resources must be drawn to finance implementation, and the behavior of citizens in general that sustain the political–economic system (Swanson & King, 1997).

The political system is represented by a grid composed of issues to be decided and the interests and expertise of potential decision makers [i.e., individuals (or families), the teaching profession, and society]. Regardless of who makes the decisions, there are five broad areas in which educational policy must be formulated (Benson, 1978): (1) setting goals and objectives for the educational enterprise, (2) determining for whom educational services are to be provided, (3) determining the level of investment in population quality (e.g., education) to promote economic growth and the general welfare, (4) allocating resources to and among educational services, and (5) determining the means by which educational services are to be provided. These five policy areas represent an elaboration of the three fundamental economic decisions presented earlier in the chapter.

The potential concern of each group of decision makers extends to each issue although the actual level of interest and expertise of a given group will vary from issue to issue. Societal concerns are expressed by individuals and interest groups and moderated through the political process of government, including school boards, and through the formation of coalitions such as those now negotiating a national curriculum and standards and procedures for national certification of teachers. Societal concerns take precedence over family and professional concerns for those issues in education in which there is significant spillover of benefits (i.e., collective or public goods) and in which there are redistributive considerations (shifting of wealth and benefits from one group to another).

The teaching profession holds the technical expertise about schooling and has a vested interest in the conditions of employment. Teachers, along with other members of the polity, participate in general elections and referenda and the related political activities accompanying them. Professional educators also have a very strong impact on public policy through the lobbying activities of their unions and professional associations. Lobbyists for the National Education Association (NEA) and the American Federation of Teachers (AFT) are particularly effective at the state and national levels. At the local level, in addition to serving on advisory committees and the like, teachers and administrators have had a great impact on educational policy through the collective bargaining process (Bacharach & Shedd, 1989; Mitchell, 1989).

Parents are the guardians of the interests and needs of individual children. In most instances, the family holds intimate knowledge about and caring concern for the child. It is through the family that the child's voice is heard (Bridge, 1976; Coons & Sugarman, 1978). In addition to participating in school board elections and referenda, individual parents may approach school board members or school administrators directly to express their concerns. They may also align themselves with other parents holding similar concerns, forming such associations as the National Congress of Parents and Teachers (PTA) and the Council for Basic Education (CBE), which direct their activities largely at influencing state and federal policy. Other parent groups focus on the needs of special children, such as the emotionally disturbed, physically disabled, or intellectually gifted.

Organizations such as the League of Women Voters and the American Association of University Women embrace educational issues as a continuing secondary concern. Other organizations attempt to influence educational policy as a means of accomplishing ends that transcend the school. These might include taxpayer groups or groups with a specific political agenda, such as civil rights, affirmative action, pro-choice and antiabortion, environmental protection, the promotion of patriotism, religious fundamentalism, and so on.

The outcomes of the process are educational policies, categorized in the figure according to the five types of issues addressed through the political process. The policies are a composite of decisions made by society, the profession, and the family.

Incrementalism

Lindblom (1959) described the public policy process in the United States as a continuation of past government activities, with only incremental modifications. He insightfully labeled the process as "muddling through." Although some deplore his exaltation of the process, one of his most ardent critics credits him with presenting "a well considered theory fully geared to the actual experience of practicing administrators" (Dror, 1964, p. 153).

Lindblom (1968, p. 32) took issue with the popular view that politics is a process of conflict resolution. He argued that "governments are instruments for vast tasks of social cooperation" and that "conflicts are largely those that spring from the opportunities for cooperation that have evolved once political life becomes orderly." Within this context, he described the play of power as a process of cooperation among specialists. It is gamelike, normally proceeding according to implicitly accepted rules. "Policy analysis is incorporated as an instrument or weapon into the play of power, changing the character of analysis as a result" (Lindblom, 1968, p. 30).

The focus of the play of power is on means (policy), not ends (goals or objectives). This, according to Lindblom, is what permits the political system to work. Because of the overlap in value systems among interested groups, and the uncertainty of the outcomes of any course of action, partisans across the value spectrum are able to come to agreement on means where agreement on ends would be impossible.

Since according to Lindblom (1968, p. 33), agreement on goal priorities is impossible in a pluralistic society, the type of analysis appropriate to the political process is termed *partisan analysis*. It is analysis conducted by advocates (organized interest groups) of a relatively limited set of values and/or ends, such as teacher associations, taxpayer groups, and religious and patriotic organizations. Comprehensiveness is provided by the variety of partisans participating in the political process. The responsibility for promoting specific values thus lies in the hands of advocates of those values (pressure groups and lobbyists) and not in the hands of an "impartial" analyst (as is the case with rationalism, discussed later).

The net result of this advocacy process is incremental rather than revolutionary policy change. In light of our grand state of ignorance about the relationships between public policy and human behavior, Lindblom viewed incremental policy decisions as being well justified. Incrementalism permits the expansion of policies that prove successful while limiting the harm caused by unsuccessful policies. Within the context of strategic planning, incrementalism can assure that each increment leads toward desired goals while minimizing organizational disruption. Incrementalism preserves the system while changing it.

In the next two sections we discuss group theory and elite theory. Both provide explanations of how incrementalism works in practice.

Group Theory

Truman (1951), a leading proponent of group theory, saw politics as the interaction among groups (as opposed to individuals) in the formulation of public policy. Individuals band together into formal or informal groups, similar to Lindblom's partisans, to confront government with their demands. The group is the vehicle through which individuals can influence government action. Even political parties are viewed as coalitions of interest groups. Elected and appointed officials are seen as being involved continually in bargaining and negotiating with relevant groups to work out compromises that balance interests.

Group theory, as portrayed by Dye (1987), is illustrated in Figure 9.6. Public policy at any point in time represents the equilibrium of the balance of power among groups. Because the power alignment is continually shifting (e.g., in Figure 9.6, toward group B as it gains supporters or partners in coalition on a particular issue), the fulcrum of equilibrium also shifts, leading to incremental changes in policy (in the direction desired by group B, as illustrated).

Stability in the system is attributed to a number of factors. First, most members of the electorate are latent supporters of the political system and share in its inherent values. This latent group is generally inactive but can be aroused to defend the system against any group that attacks it. Second, there is a great deal of overlap in the membership of groups; a given person is likely to be a member of several groups. This tends to have a dampening effect with respect to any group taking extreme positions, because although the group may be focused on a single issue, its membership is much more broadly oriented. The third factor promoting system stability results from group competition. No single group constitutes a majority in American society. Coalitions are easily formed to counter the influence of any group appearing to gain undue influence. As a result, the political process is characterized by evolution as in incrementalism, rather than revolution.

Elite Theory

Elite theory focuses on actions by a select group of influential citizens. Elite theory (Dye & Zeigler, 1981) characterizes the general public as apathetic, ill-informed, and uninterested where public policy is concerned, not unlike the characterization of the latent group in group theory. This leaves a power vacuum that is readily filled by an elite group. Elites do more to shape the opinion of the masses on public issues than the general public does to shape the opinions of elites, although influence is reciprocal [e.g., civil rights legislation (Dye, 1987, Chap. 3)]. According to this theory, policy is developed by elites within the trappings of democratic government.

Elites tend to be drawn from upper socioeconomic levels. They are not necessarily against the general welfare of the masses, as in the case of civil rights legislation, but approach their welfare through a sense of *noblesse oblige*. Although not agreeing on all issues, the elite share a consensus as to basic social values and the importance of preserving the system. The masses give superficial support to this consensus, which provides a basis for elite rule. When events occur that threaten the system, elites move to take corrective action. According to

Figure 9.6
Group theory model
Source: T. R. Dye. *Understanding public policy* (6th ed., p. 27). Englewood Cliffs, NJ: Prentice Hall, 1987.

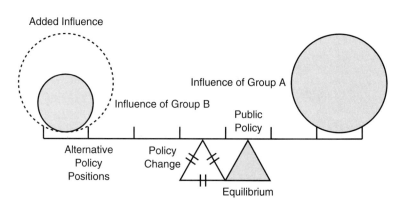

elite theory, changes in public policy come about as the result of elites redefining their own positions, although this redefinition may be a function of external pressures. Because of the elite's conservative posture with respect to preserving the system, policy changes tend to be incremental.

Rationalism

Adherents of rationalism seek to shape the policymaking process in such a fashion as to assure the enactment of policies that maximize social gain. According to Dror (1964, p. 132), the assumptions of pure rationality are deeply rooted in modern civilization and culture and are the basis of certain economic theories of the free market and political theories of democracy. Rationalism is derived from the postpositivist philosophy described in Chapter 12. Dror characterized the pure rationality model as having six

phases: (1) establishing a complete set of operational goals, with relative weights allocated to the various degrees to which each may be achieved; (2) establishing a complete inventory of other values and resources, with relative weights; (3) preparing a complete set of alternative policies open to the policy maker; (4) preparing a complete set of valid predictions of the costs and benefits of each alternative, including the extent to which each will achieve the various operational goals, consume resources, and realize or impair other values; (5) calculating the net expectation of each alternative by multiplying the probability of each benefit and cost for each alternative by the utility of each, and calculating the net benefit (or cost) in utility units; and (6) comparing the net expectations and identifying the alternative (or alternatives, if two or more are equally good) with the highest net expectation (p. 132). These phases are organized sequentially in Figure 9.7.

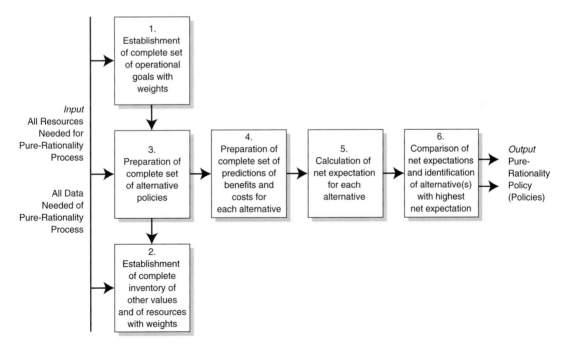

Figure 9.7
Phases of pure-rationality policy making

In theory, rationalism involves all individual, social, political, and economic values, not just those that can be converted to dollars and cents. In reality, the measurement difficulties make inclusion of other than economic values unlikely. Thus, this model elevates economic efficiency above other potential societal objectives, such as equity and liberty.

To "know" all that would be required to select a policy "rationally" (i.e., all of society's value preferences and relative weights, all available policy alternatives, and the consequences of each alternative) is what Lindblom (1959, p. 88) termed *superhuman comprehensiveness* and Wise (1979), *hyperrationality*. In essence, rationalism attempts the impossible by quantifying all elements of the political process and human behavior and expressing the decision-making function in mathematical terms (Lavoie, 1985). Although imperfect, the representative legislature (e.g., school boards and Congress) is a political mechanism for approximating "all of society's value preferences and relative weights."

Rational techniques that are based on economic principles and procedures should be an important factor in budget development. However, Cibulka (1987) acknowledged that even budgetary decisions are not actually made on the basis of rationality. Wildavsky (1964) also argued that pure rationality is an illusion. Political realists argue that decisions in the public sector, including public education, are made on the basis of political rationality rather than economic rationality. To them, rationalism is at best irrelevant and can be downright dysfunctional to the political process (C. L. Schultz, 1968).

Rationalism was a key principle behind the comprehensive centralized planning schemes of socialist and communist countries. With the collapse of many of the latter, and with the routine failure of five-year plans in socialist—mostly developing—countries, rationalism has lost much of its credibility (Agarawala, 1984; Weiler, 1980).

Nevertheless, rationalistic philosophy has had an important impact on policy analysis and an indirect effect on policy decision making. Its bias of economic efficiency is a value that is all too frequently neglected in the traditional political process. The philosophy of rationalism has fostered such management devices as planning programming budgeting systems (PPBS), zero-based budgeting (ZBB), management by objectives (MBO), and operations research (OR), as well as cost-benefit and cost-effectiveness analysis. The terms *accountability* and *assessment* are now a part of the schooling vernacular, and teacher, pupil, and program evaluations are accepted procedures. Local school boards and state and federal governments are adding to their long-standing concerns over the quantity and quality of school inputs, a similar concern over school outputs through mandatory evaluation and testing programs and achievement standards.

Whereas tools of rational analysis have had some effect on the educational decision-making process, rationalistic approaches have fallen short of the expectations of their supporters and have met with strong opposition from some segments of the traditional educational decision-making process. A major source of resistance to the use of analysis in schools is the teaching profession itself. In addition to their vested interests as employees, teachers are acutely aware of the almost impossible task of quantitatively measuring the complex variables associated with educational inputs and outputs and with the learning process.

The most ardent supporters of rational analysis are economic purists who seek economic efficiency in the public sector. Within the private sector, the market provides powerful mechanisms to weed out inefficiencies. Indeed, one of the roles of government is to police the marketplace, keeping in check those forces that would impede the functioning of these mechanisms. Few, if any, similar mechanisms operate in the public sector.

Unlike incrementalism, which focuses on means, rationalism requires agreement on outcomes, which is unlikely in pluralistic organizations (e.g., state and federal governments and large urban school districts). Because of the reduced number of conflicting interest groups at the school level (which may also be the case with small, homogeneous school districts), such agreement is frequently obtained, and rationalism can become functional at that level.

Issues Involved in Governmental Intervention

To this point we have sketched the functioning of the economic and political systems separately and have indicated probable differences in decisions made in the two sectors. Each sector is capable of answering the policy issues posed, but as already noted, as individuals and as a society, we would probably be quite unhappy with the results if *all* decisions were made through either sector acting alone. Given the general preference of a capitalistic society for the private sector as a venue for making decisions, we now address the matter of when governments should intervene in private-sector decision making and how they should intervene.

When Should Governments Intervene?

Eckstein (1967) identified four situations in which market mechanisms fail and government intervention is necessary: (1) collective goods, (2) external economies (i.e., divergence between private and social costs or benefits), (3) extraordinary risks, and (4) natural monopolies. Education as a collective or public good was discussed earlier.

External Economies. The market works well when the prices charged reflect the total costs involved in producing goods or services. There are instances, however, in which a producer can escape paying the full cost of production, with the consumer benefiting in terms of lower prices, or a producer cannot charge the full value of that which is produced. These are known as *external economies* or *diseconomies*. When external economies occur, the good or service is not fully provided by the private sector; education is a case in point. Whereas there

are profit incentives to provide for educational programs with a specific focus such as occupational education and college preparation, there are few profit incentives to provide for universal education in the private sector, especially to the poor and the disabled.

External economies are illustrated by paper manufacturing. Without environmental protection legislation, paper manufacturers were likely to dump highly toxic waste generated by the manufacturing process into adjacent rivers and streams, killing wildlife and fouling the air. Requiring the detoxification of waste prior to returning it to the environment increased the cost of production and raised the cost of paper to the consumer. Prior to protective legislation, manufacturers were able to escape paying a portion of the true costs of production. Part of the price was paid by those living in the environs of the mill in the form of low quality of life and low property values because of the pollution.

Similarly, when pupils drop out or are forced out of school, there is a high probability that they will become wards of society in one form or another. They are much less likely to be regularly employed than are persons completing their schooling and are more likely to receive governmental assistance in the form of unemployment insurance payments, welfare, and Medicaid. School dropouts are also more likely to turn to lives of crime and be incarcerated in penal institutions. The resources saved by some school districts by not fully educating such persons are lost many times over by society at large in providing social services later in life, financed largely at the federal and state levels.

Until intervention by federal and state governments, many persons with severe mental and physical disabilities were denied access to schooling because of the high cost of special education. This meant that they were institutionalized their entire lives. Now, having access to schooling, many are able to work and live independently or with minimal supervision. The increased expenditures for education are paying dividends in terms of lower costs for social services and a better quality of life for persons with disabling conditions.

Extraordinary Risks. Extraordinary risks refer to situations for which the probable payoff on investment is low. The development of atomic energy, space exploration, and cancer research are examples. Investments in research on learning, teaching, and curriculum may also fall into this category. The growing global economy requires investment in retraining low-skilled workers to prevent the development of a permanent underclass as a result of free trade agreements: a social, but not necessarily economic, problem.

Natural Monopolies. A natural monopoly is an enterprise enjoying a continually falling cost curve. In other words, the cost to produce a unit becomes less and less as the number of units produced or served increases. Thus, because of economies of scale, the largest firm has a distinct competitive advantage, eventually driving smaller firms out of business. Electricity, gas, and water utilities are examples. The technology governing most businesses and industries is such, however, that economies of scale are realized only up to a point when diseconomies of scale set in, that is, the cost per unit increases as the number of units produced or serviced increases. This produces a U-shaped cost curve, nullifying any advantage of large firms over small ones and preserving competition.

There is a general misperception that there are substantial economies of scale in providing educational services; such misperception is a primary motivation of school consolidation policies. But in reality, economies of scale affect only the very smallest of schools and school districts (as demonstrated in Chapter 14), and there are, in fact, severe diseconomies in scale for them. Despite this, schooling has been organized as a near-public monopoly.

Other Reasons for Intervention. Governmental intervention also takes place for other reasons. The federal government has assumed responsibility for controlling business cycles

and inflation, and to a limited extent, the redistribution of wealth. Schooling and training frequently become means through which such control is exercised. All governments use the power of eminent domain, through which they can force the sale of private property for public use, as in the construction of interstate highways or schools.

Alternative Methods of Government Intervention

Once the decision to intervene is made, there are numerous modes of intervention. Public schools are currently owned and operated by government. So are police and fire departments and the U.S. armed forces. Ownership is not the typical type of governmental intervention, however. Governments may also oversee the public interest through regulation, licensure, taxation, subsidies, transfer payments, and contracts.

Most communication systems, utilities, and intercity transportation enterprises in the United States are privately owned, yet they are carefully monitored and regulated by government. Restaurants are regularly inspected for health code violations. The licensing of professionals is done by governments, although most professionals, an important exception being teachers, work in the private sector. Private schools and home schooling are regulated by state government.

Governments can attempt to influence human behavior by changing the price paid for specific items through subsidies or taxation. Consumption of cigarettes, alcoholic beverages, and gasoline is discouraged through excise taxes that increase the cost to consumers, with the intent of reducing demand. On the other hand, the government may pay subsidies to farmers to encourage them to increase (or decrease) production of specific products, or to businesses to enable them to remain in operation in the face of foreign competition. Similarly, subsidies and scholarships that reduce the cost of higher education encourage families and individuals to pursue education beyond high school. Complete subsidization makes universal elementary and secondary education possible.

Governments also contract for services from private companies. Federal, state, and local governments rely on contractors to build their buildings, highways, and parks. While the federal government coordinates space exploration, privately contracted vendors conduct research and development and manufacture space vehicles. During periods of rapid enrollment increases, school districts may rent or lease space from private vendors. Instead of providing their own services, many school districts contract with private vendors for transportation, cleaning, and cafeteria operations. Recently, some school districts have contracted for the operation of individual schools, for specific administrative services, and in a couple of cases, for the administration of the entire business of the district.

Many governmental responsibilities are met through transfer payments to individuals. Social Security, Aid for Dependent Children (i.e., welfare), unemployment insurance, food stamps, and educational vouchers are examples. Through transfer payments, the government can equalize the distribution of resources while permitting the individual maximum discretion as to how the payments are used. For example, prior to Social Security, elderly indigents were institutionalized in facilities owned and operated by local government as are schools. Now, with monthly payments through the Social Security system, recipients have many options open to them, such as living in their own homes, in smaller apartments, in retirement communities, in residences for the elderly, in nursing homes, as well as living with relatives. The public policy of providing senior citizens with at least a subsistence living standard is realized without prescribing their lifestyles. The G.I. Bill, which paid the tuition of World War II and Korean War veterans to public and private post secondary institutions is an example of education vouchers. A few states are beginning to make limited use of vouchers at the elementary and secondary levels.

Choosing the Appropriate Level of Government to Intervene

Within any given context, significantly different patterns of allocation of authority among levels of government and potential decision makers can be structured depending on the relative priorities given to policy objectives (Kirst, 1988). Extreme centralization of authority is characterized by making all decisions collectively and by administering them through public institutions. Extreme decentralization of authority is characterized by having no public schools and no subsidies, leaving the production and distribution of educational services to be determined solely by market forces. This position enhances the potential for realizing values of efficiency and personal freedom, but it has severe negative implications for the realization of other societal values, such as equity.

Increasing centralization of authority has been used in the post–World War II years as a vehicle for promoting equity considerations, but judging from the flood of national criticism over the past decade, the efficiency of the education system may have suffered. To promote values of efficiency and liberty while retaining considerable control over equity, some school districts have taken modest steps in decentralizing decision making by adopting policies that create magnet schools and/or permit open enrollment among schools (Raywid, 1985). Other districts have devolved substantial policymaking authority to schools and teachers (i.e., school-based decision making and teacher empowerment). Recent centralizing policy proposals aimed at improving efficiency in the educational system include setting state standards for student academic performance and raising state standards for entering the teaching profession.

Wirt and Kirst (1982) diagnosed centralization/decentralization tensions as a function of the inherent conflict between individualism and majoritarianism. They saw the political stress in today's society stemming from the emphasis that we, as a society, place on translating private preference and need into public policy. In acknowledging that all persons are regarded as important, government, if it is to survive, must mediate conflicts arising out of diverse individual desires so that the conflicts remain at tolerable levels. Majority rule is an integral part of democratic governance. Individualism, on the other hand, is reflected in our economic system and in the bills of rights in our national and state constitutions designed to protect individuals from the "tyranny of the majority."

McGinn and Street (1986) characterized centralization and decentralization as a dyad.

> Decentralization is not primarily an issue of control by government of individual citizens. Instead it is a question of the distribution of power among various groups in society. A highly participatory society—one in which all citizens actually do participate—is likely to require a competent and powerful state that actively and continuously seeks to redistribute power among groups and individuals in the society. The location of authority in local government does not protect the local citizen from tyranny, and the redistribution of power through the market mechanism in a society that currently is highly inequitable is a guarantee that inequities will persist and worsen. On the other hand, competition and markets can contribute to social justice in circumstances where there is a relatively equitable balance of powers among the participants in the competition or market. . . . A strong state must first achieve some minimal degree of social equity so that decentralization can lead to genuine participation. (pp. 489–490)

Friedman (1962) analyzed the situation as follows:

> The widespread use of the market reduces the strain on the social fabric by rendering conformity unnecessary with respect to any activities it encompasses. The wider the range of activities covered by the market, the fewer are the issues on which explicit political decisions are required and hence on which it is necessary to achieve agreement. In turn, the fewer issues on which agreement is necessary, the greater the likelihood of getting agreement while maintaining a free society. (p. 24)

With respect to education, driven by a priority concern for equity, the trend during the 1960s and 1970s was toward centralizing decisions at the state and federal levels. In seeking higher educational standards, the first wave of reform in the early 1980s produced further centralization; the second wave, however, was directed toward greater decentralization. These may appear to be contradictory developments, but they are happening throughout the Western world and in the private as well as the public sector (Beare, Caldwell, & Millikan, 1989; Iannaccone, 1988; Lawton, 1992; Whitty, 1992). Peters and Waterman (1982) referred to the phenomenon in the private sector as *loose/tight structures*. In the organizational literature it has been referred to as *loose coupling*.

It appears that some decisions about education may best be made by central authorities, particularly those involving equity, but others are best left to those with professional expertise at the school level or to those having a personal stake in the happiness and welfare of a specific child—the family (Coleman & Hoffer, 1987; Coons & Sugarman, 1978; Cremin, 1976; McNeil, 1986; Wise, 1979, 1988). Determining the optimal allocation of authority in education is a complex and unending process.

Thus, centralization and decentralization of authority should be viewed as means toward desired ends, not ends in themselves (Hanson, 1986). The same is true of state power, teacher power, and people power. There are legitimate concerns about education at all levels of the sociopolitical hierarchy; the critical issue is achieving the best balance among legitimate interests. The best balance will vary from society to society and over time within a society as contexts, value definitions, and priorities change (Wirt, 1986).

Distinctions between Judicial and Legislative Influence on Educational Policy Formulation

Federal and state courts are having an increasing influence on the formulation of school policy. In this section we examine that influence and how judicial procedures and influence differ from those of the legislative branch of government.

Judicial and legislative branches of government perform different functions in the formation of policy. State and federal education programs can only be enacted through the legislative process, but the judiciary may be asked to test whether or not these policies satisfy societal expectations as expressed in federal and state constitutions. This external review provides a check on legislative actions, and judicial reviews often stimulate (even force) legislatures to alter legislated policies. The courts do not, however, initiate the subjects of judicial review; they react to conflicts and problems posed to them by members of society (i.e., plaintiffs).

In Chapter 12 we discuss in detail inherent conflicts among the metavalues of equality and liberty (or individual freedom). Suffice it to say at this point that equality is a value that can best be championed at the societal level (by state or federal governments, i.e., centralization of authority). The value of liberty, on the other hand, is best realized through an unregulated market (i.e., decentralization of authority) that is anathema to equality. Adherents of each value battle incessantly in both courts and legislatures. Federal courts made equality a national concern through numerous decisions affecting education, starting with the Supreme Court's decision in *Brown v. Board of Education* (347 U.S. 483 1954). In the mid-1960s Congress responded with such legislation as Title VI of the Civil Rights Act, to ease inequities in children's educational opportunities.

Despite strong national pressures from a variety of sources to improve educational opportunities for poor and minority students, state legislatures were slow to respond. The nature of the legislative process, characterized by "give-and-take, negotiation, and compromise" (Fuhrman, 1978, p. 160), inhibited reform by the states. Even when states responded to pressure brought by impending and actual court reviews, the equality thrust raised at the national level and by both state and federal courts deferred to consensus-building processes that shape the actual content of reforms adopted through state legislatures.

Unlike judicial decision making, which is narrowly focused on constitutional principles, policy development in legislatures is broadly influenced by their representative nature, the distributive nature of education policy, and the ongoing nature of the decision-making process (Brown & Elmore, 1982). First, legislators, as representatives of school districts to be affected by proposed reforms, are frequently more concerned with protecting their school districts' interests (subdivisions of state government) than with equalizing opportunities for poor children. Second, the distributive nature of educational policy requires at least a majority of the population to perceive that the reforms benefit them. In the process of finding solutions, equity goals are frequently bargained away. Major consideration in the bargaining and compromise process is given to which districts gain and which lose. Finally, the resolution of issues is not isolated from other concerns placed before legislators. Rather than concentrating solely on the specific merits of the proposal at hand, lining up votes on an education issue may depend on positions taken by legislators on prior and subsequent policy issues that are likely to have no relation to education whatsoever.

While the legislative process gives attention to school districts' interests and to consensus building, challenges to states' educational policies heard in the courts are more likely to consider inequities in the treatment of pupils. The plan that results from negotiations through the legislative process may or may not reflect the equity concerns of the courts or the original proponents of reform. "The closer one gets to the process of reform in specific states, the more elusive equity seems and the more complex are the values and objectives operating on reform proposals" (Brown & Elmore, 1982, p. 113).

On the whole, the evidence leaves little room for optimism about substantial and long-term improvements in educational equity through either the legislative or judicial process (Swanson & King, 1997). The conflict among values of equity, personal freedom, and efficiency is ongoing; the policy result is an ebb and flow of emphasis from one to the other.

Summary

In this chapter we have described how formal educational policy decisions are made. Because education provides benefits that are highly valued by individuals and society, often in different ways, the process is particularly complex and involves both government and the market. Allocation of scarce resources through markets was described and several models of political decision making were presented.

Five education issues were identified that any society must answer either through the political process of government or through market transactions. Since the political process is biased toward the metavalue of equity and the market holds biases toward metavalues of personal freedom and efficiency, preferences for the resolution of the issues is quite different, depending on sector. Guides were provided for determining when issues should be resolved by government and when they should be left to individual initiatives through the market. The range of ways for structuring governmental involvement and the implications for placement of authority with local, state, and federal authorities were presented. The chapter concluded with a discussion of the differences between the roles of the legislative and judicial branches of government in developing and evaluating educational policy.

Activities

1. *Political decision making*
   a. Interview your superintendent of schools and/or members of your board of trustees about how educational policy is developed in your school district.
   b. On the basis of the information gathered from these interviews, describe situations that illustrate each policymaking model discussed in this chapter.
2. *Restructuring education:* Numerous proposals have been put forth for reforming education. Discuss each proposal listed below in reference to Figure 9.5. For each, describe the change from the status quo in the allocation of decision-making authority.
   a. Family choice of public schools
   b. Unregulated educational vouchers
   c. Tax credits for private school tuition
   d. Professional control over admission to the teaching profession
   e. Career ladders for teachers
   f. School-based decision making
   g. Full state financing of public schools
   h. State achievement testing to determine successful completion of high school
3. *School governing boards:* Imagine a policy board for each public school made up of the principal, serving as the chief executive officer, and representatives of teachers, parents, and students.
   a. What are the advantages and disadvantages of such an arrangement?
   b. Would you add representation from any other group?
   c. Would you eliminate representation of any group?
   d. Assuming that each representative has one vote, how many representatives should there be from each group?
   e. What constraints, if any, would you place on the decision-making powers of the board?
   f. Provide the rationale for each of your answers.
4. *Allocation of decision-making authority:* Within the context of the decision-making matrix presented in Figure 9.5, what educational decisions are best placed at the school level? What safeguards need to be implemented to protect family and societal interests? Give the rationales for your responses.

References

Agarawala, R. (1984). *Planning in developing countries: Lessons of experience* (World Bank Staff Working Papers, No. 576). Washington, DC: World Bank.

Bacharach, S. B., & Shedd, J. B. (1989). Power and empowerment: The constraining myths and emerging structures of teacher unionism. In J. Hannaway & R. Crowson (Eds.), *The politics of reforming school administration* (pp. 139–160). New York: Falmer Press.

Beare, H., Caldwell, B. J., & Millikan, R. H. (1989). *Creating an excellent school: Some new management techniques.* London: Routledge.

Benson, C. S. (1978). *The economics of public education* (3rd ed.). Boston: Houghton Mifflin.

Bridge, R. G. (1976). Parent participation in school innovations. *Teachers College Record, 77,* 366–384.

Brown, P. R., & Elmore, R. F. (1982). Analyzing the impact of school finance reform. In N. H. Cambron-McCabe & A. Odden (Eds.), *The changing politics of school finance* (pp. 107–138). Cambridge, MA: Ballinger.

Cibulka, J. G. (1987). Theories of education budgeting: Lessons from the management of decline. *Educational Administration Quarterly, 23,* 7–40.

Coleman, J. S., & Hoffer, T. (1987). *Public and private high schools: The impact of communities.* New York: Basic Books.

Coons, J. E., & Sugarman, S. D. (1978). *Education by choice: The case for family control.* Berkeley, CA: University of California Press.

Cremin, L. A. (1976). *Public education.* New York: Basic Books.

Downs, A. (1957). *An economic theory of democracy.* New York: Harper & Row.

Dror, Y. (1964). Muddling through—"science" or inertia? *Public Administration Review, 24,* 153–157.

Dye, T. R. (1987). *Understanding public policy* (6th ed.). Upper Saddle River, NJ: Prentice Hall.

Dye, T. R., & Zeigler, H. (1981). *The irony of democracy.* Monterey, CA: Brooks/Cole.

Easton, D. A. (1965). *A systems analysis of political life.* New York: Wiley.

Eckstein, O. (1967). *Public finance* (2nd ed.). Upper Saddle River, NJ: Prentice Hall.

Elazar, D. J. (1972). *American federalism.* New York: Harper & Row.

Friedman, M. (1962). *Capitalism and freedom.* Chicago: University of Chicago Press.

Fuhrman, S. (1978). The politics and process of school finance reform. *Journal of Education Finance, 4,* 158–178.

Grodzins, M. (1966). *The American system.* Chicago: Rand McNally.

Guskey, T. R. (Ed.). (1994). *High stakes performance assessment: Perspectives on Kentucky educational reform.* Thousand Oaks, CA: Corwin Press.

Hanson, E. M. (1986). *Educational reform and administrative development: The cases of Colombia and Venezuela.* Stanford, CA: Hoover Institution Press.

Hess, G. A., Jr. (1991). *School restructuring, Chicago style.* Newbury Park, CA: Corwin Press.

Hess, G. A., Jr. (1999). Understanding achievement (and other) changes under Chicago school reform. *Educational Evaluation and Policy Analysis, 21,* 1, 67–83.

Hodgkinson, C. (1983). *The philosophy of leadership.* Oxford: Blackwell.

Iannaccone, L. (1988). From equity to excellence: Political context and dynamics. In W. L. Boyd & C. T. Kerchner (Eds.), *The politics of excellence and choice in education* (pp. 49–65). New York: Falmer Press.

Kaufman, R., & Herman, J. (1991). *Strategic planning in education: Rethinking, restructuring, revitalizing.* Lancaster, PA: Technomic.

Kirst, M. W. (1988). Recent educational reform in the United States: Looking backward and forward. *Educational Administration Quarterly, 24.* 319–328.

Labaree, D. F. (1997). Public goods, private goods: The American struggle over educational goals. *American Educational Research Journal, 34,* 1, 39–81.

Lavoie, D. (1985). *National economic planning: What is left?* Cambridge, MA: Ballinger.

Lawton, D. (1992). *Education and politics in the 1990s: Conflict or consensus?* London: Falmer Press.

Levin, H. M. (1987). Education as public and private good. *Journal of Policy Analysis and Management, 6,* 628–641.

Lindblom, C. E. (1959). The science of muddling through. *Public Administration Review, 19,* 79–88.

Lindblom, C. E. (1968). *The policy-making process.* Upper Saddle River, NJ: Prentice Hall.

McGinn, N., & Street, S. (1986). Educational decentralization: Weak state or strong state? *Comparative Education Review, 30,* 471–490.

McNeil, L. M. (1986). *Contradictions of control: School structure and school knowledge.* New York: Routledge & K. Paul.

Mitchell, D. E. (1989). Alternative approaches to labor–management relations for public school teachers and administrators. In J. Hannaway & R. Crowson (Eds.), *The politics of reforming school administration* (pp. 161–181). New York: Falmer Press.

National Center for Education Statistics. (1999). *Digest of education statistics, 1998.* Washington, DC: U.S. Department of Education.

Odden, A., & Marsh, D. (1989). State education reform implementation: A framework for analysis. In J. Hannaway & R. Crowson (Eds.), *The politics of reforming school administration* (pp. 41–59). New York: Falmer Press.

Peters, T. J., & Waterman, R. H. (1982). *In search of excellence: Lessons from America's best-run companies.* New York: Warner Books.

Raywid, M. A. (1985). Family choice arrangements in public schools: A review of the literature. *Review of Educational Research, 55,* 435–467.

Samuelson, P. A. (1980). *Economics* (11th ed.). New York: McGraw-Hill.

Schultz, C. L. (1968). *The politics and economics of public spending.* Washington, DC: Brookings Institution.

Schultz, T. W. (1963). *The economic value of education.* Berkeley, CA: University of California Press.

Swanson, A. D., & King, R. A. (1997). *School finance: Its economics and politics* (2nd ed.). New York: Longman.

Truman, D. B. (1951). *The governmental process.* New York: Knopf.

Walker, D. B. (1981). *Toward a functioning federalism.* Cambridge, MA: Winthrop Press.

Weiler, H. N. (1980). *Educational planning and social change.* Paris: UNESCO.

Whitty, G. (1992). Urban education in England and Wales. In D. Cowlby, C. Jones, & D. Harris (Eds.), *World yearbook of education: Urban education* (pp. 39–53). London: Kogan Page.

Wildavsky, A. (1964). *The politics of the budgetary process.* Boston: Little, Brown.

Wirt, F. M. (1986). *Multiple paths for understanding the role of values in state policy.* Paper presented at the Annual Meeting of the American Education Research Association, San Francisco, CA (ERIC Document Reproduction Service ED-278086).

Wirt, F. M., & Kirst, M. W. (1982). *School in conflict: The politics of education.* Berkeley, CA: McCutchan.

Wise, A. E. (1979). *Legislated learning: The bureaucratization of the American classroom.* Berkeley, CA: University of California Press.

Wise, A. E. (1988). Two conflicting trends in school reform: Legislated learning revisited. *Phi Delta Kappan, 69,* 328–332.

CHAPTER 10

Organizational Decision Making

In the traditional view of organizations, including educational institutions, power was thought to reside solely in a top-down structure. As a consequence, principals, deans, and directors possessed wide latitudes, while those lower in the hierarchy shared limited power. Decision making in this tradition was thought to be the domain of those in charge. Today, these traditional views of organizations have changed, and shared power and worker empowerment is advocated. The prevailing thinking is that power, decision making, and responsibilities in educational settings should be shared among principals, teachers, students, and parents (Scott, 1991). Although we can all relate instances of highly productive teachers who have shared their decision making in the classroom with students or even parents, and of principals who share substantial responsibility, these instances are not the norm.

Weick (1976) was undoubtedly correct in stating that our theories of how organizations function can rarely be generalized and that we would be hard-pressed to find instances of ideally rational decision making in organizations. Textbook decision making would be hard to find. "No example of a general theory of decision proper exists that is even modestly developed, although dimensions have been developed quite far" (Hooker, Leach, & McClennen, 1978, p. viii). In truth, practitioners may construct for us a fully different view of organizational decision making. It is the purpose of this chapter to explore the realm of organizational decision making from theory to practice and beyond.

In the neoclassical economic theory it was assumed that the goal of an enterprise was to maximize profit. This view was attacked and has been changed over the years. Managerial and behavioral theories indicated that decision making in an organization is characterized by a number of objectives, which may be conflicting, and often these cannot be all optimized. Cyert and March (1963) and March and Simon (1958) are among the behavioral scientists who have tried to formalize some theory of the decision-making process. They postulate that organizations do not have goals but the people who are in them do. There is bargaining among the people, and the organization's goals represent some result of this bargaining.

Decision making is the process of choosing among alternatives (Baron, 1985; Conway, 1984; White, 1969). Numerous authors (Cornell, 1980; Hoy & Miskel, 1978; Krepel, 1987; Steers, 1977) concur that decision making is among the most crucial skills for an effective educational administrator. Furthermore, Baird (1989) contends that the "primary output of all administration is decisions" (p. 4) and that "most executives are evaluated by superiors, peers, and subordinates in terms of their last few decisions" (p. 5), regardless of their prior decision-making performance. This is a general perception of those studying the field. The decision process is at the core of administration, and all administrative action is dependent on making a decision. Decision making may be seen as the process whereby organizations choose among alternative courses of action with the goal of maximizing the outcomes resulting from the choices made. Despite the importance of skills in this area, research suggests that individuals tend to make decisions that do not reflect optimal or "rational" choices (Bazerman, 1991; McNeil, Pauker, & Tversky, 1988; Tversky & Kahneman, 1988).

Herbert Simon (1977) says that decisions may be considered to lie on a continuum, with programmed decisions at one end and nonprogrammed decisions at the other. The former tend to be repetitive and routine, while the latter are often uncommon, unstructured, and of greater importance. Due to their unstructured and unusual nature, nonprogrammed decisions are more difficult to handle and are often more complex than programmed decisions. Simon further emphasizes that these are two ends of a continuum, with an entire gray area of semistructured decisions in between.

Approaches to Decision Making

There are two basic approaches to decision making: the normative approach and the descriptive approach. The rational/idealized *normative approach* explores how the process should occur, while the *descriptive approach* describes how the process actually occurs, accommodating cognitive constraints, idiographic traits, and other factors that impose limitations on idealized, rational decision making (Baird, 1989; MacPhail-Wilcox & Bryant, 1988; Reitz, 1987). Normative literature explores how decisions should be made to achieve a particular standard or outcome. These standards or outcomes are typically explicit or objective. Descriptive literature relates how decision making occurs in empirical terms. Decision styles, decision process maps, and devising mathematical models are often used in descriptive typologies. Some authors (Baron, 1985; Keeny & Raiffa, 1976) use a trichotomy that includes a prescriptive category. The *prescriptive approach* essentially extends the normative approach to describe how individuals' decision-making skills can be improved. Authors who use the prescriptive classification as an extension of the normative approach concede that it "may not be necessary . . . if we were to clarify further the normative category" (Bell, Raiffa, & Tversky, 1988, p. 2).

The literature on decision making ranges from discussions of highly quantitative approaches to how decisions should be made and situations analyzed, to elaborate discussions of the cognitive limitations and implications of information processing relative to choice strategies.

Historically, normative decision making has been associated with decision theory and quantitative methods such as Bayesian statistics, probability, and inference. Normative decision making was first expressed formally in the theoretical works of social economists of the industrial revolution. These economists, most notably John Stuart Mill and Jeremy Bentham, explained that choices are made on the basis of utility. Mill claimed that individuals choose alternatives according to the maximum return that the alternative will produce. This is the original economic theory used by entrepreneurs and industrial planners, who were fascinated with the possibility of creating a great deal of capital through mechanized labor in the nineteenth century. As the division of labor in organizations became more complex in the twentieth century, theorists in economics and behavioral science attempted to construct models of decision making. These early theorists were, by and large, dealing with rational decision making and conditions of certainty.

One of the seminal contributions to descriptive decision making was provided by Simon (1955, 1956), who proposed a *behavioral model* of rational choice. This model is founded on the premise that because of psychological constraints and other limiting factors, such as time, a decision maker's behavior could be described in terms of *bounded rationality*. Individuals tend to operate from a simplified or approximate model of an actual decision situation and *satisfice,* or make decisions that are satisfactory rather than optimal. Simon's work is credited with directing researchers to "examine the psychological processes by which decision problems are represented and information is used in action selection" (Slovic, Lichtenstein, & Fischhoff, 1988, p. 674). As a result of this focus, empirical evidence on the psychological factors that influence decision making has raised serious issues regarding the feasibility of existing theories and "poses a challenge to the decision-aiding technologies that have been derived from these theories" (Slovic, Lichtenstein & Fischhoff, 1988, p. 674).

The administrative or management training components of some professions have traditionally addressed decision-making skills as a distinct component of their training programs. Some research suggests that certain types of training, such as formal statistical training, can facilitate the avoidance of common reasoning errors (Fong, Krantz, & Nisbett, 1989). Other studies suggest that training in statistics and decision making does not necessarily reduce the incidence of basic decision-making errors (Eddy, 1982; Elstein & Bordage, 1979; McNeil et al., 1988) and that decision making may be domain specific (McGuire, 1985).

Decision Making and Problem Solving

Decision making, which includes the "mental activities that recognize and structure decision situations and then evaluate preferences to produce judgments and choices" (Carroll & Johnson, 1990, p. 21), must also be distinguished from the broader process of problem solving. Problem solving is considered a series of related decisions (Tallman & Gray, 1990). Huber (1980) noted the importance of making this distinction because the terms, along with associated theories and research and their respective applications, are differentiated in the literature of various fields, including education, management, and psychology (Atkinson, Herrnstein, Lindzey, & Luce, 1988; Bittel & Bittel, 1978; Dejnozka & Kapel, 1991)). However, Alkin (1991) does not specifically attend to the distinctions between these two processes and uses problem-solving terminology (ill-structured and well-structured problems) in discussions of decision making. Others include theories under decision making

when another classification might be more appropriate. For example, Janis and Mann's conflict decision theory "comes closer to approximating problem solving" (Tallman & Gray, 1990, p. 424).

Bell et al. (1988) contended that the lack of cohesion in the area of decision making is partially attributable to the differing approaches to the process: normative, or quantitative and ideally rational, versus descriptive, or how the process actually occurs. Assumptions that an individual's decision making can be idealized, rational, and maximized are strongly reflected in early normative approaches to the decision-making process. However, within the past several decades the feasibility of these assumptions has been questioned. Empirical evidence that decision makers do not necessarily make choices in an ideally rational or maximizing fashion (Einhorn & Hogarth, 1978; Fischhoff, 1982; Kahneman, Slovic, & Tversky, 1982; McNeil et al., 1988) has served as a catalyst for the development of descriptive decision making with an emphasis in two areas: explaining behaviors that violate the tenets of rationality and determining ways to improve individuals' choice behavior.

A number of authors (Baron, 1985; Cornell, 1980) have suggested that decisions should be evaluated by the strategy used rather than the outcome because ideally, rational decision making occasionally yields unfavorable or undesirable outcomes. This contention suggests that the strategy employed should be consistent with the normative approach, although numerous researchers (Chapman & Chapman, 1967; Kahneman et al., 1982; Tversky & Kahneman, 1988) have identified several commonly used heuristics and biases that although economical and often effective, also lead to serious decision-making errors in violation of normative principles. For example, a bias associated with the representativeness heuristic, the failure to recognize base rates, may lead to serious outcome errors (Tversky & Kahneman, 1982a). In other instances, biases associated with decision-making heuristics may be compounded, in that choice behavior can be externally influenced by the ways in which decision options are presented or framed (Bazerman, 1991; Tversky & Kahneman, 1974). The phenomenon has been observed in individuals with training in the domain in which the decision task is posed (McNeil et al., 1988).

Normative, descriptive, and prescriptive decision-making research has too often treated the elements of decision making as discrete when, in fact, much evidence suggests that more complex and interactive models aid understanding and description of decision processes and outcomes. Differences of opinion are numerous about the exact stages or subroutines within stages. Even proper ordering of stages may not be clear (Hogarth, 1980; Mintzberg, 1979; Simon, 1957). MacPhail-Wilcox and Bryant (1988) suggested at least three stages that appear with frequency in the literature: perception and information gathering, information manipulation and processing, and choice strategies.

Fragmentation in the decision-making literature transpires frequently due to the evolution of the area. Decision making had its roots in game theory, probability, and inference, and was developed under the premise that the process should ideally be rational. Decision making in this context was amenable to quantification via axioms that could define the appropriate approach to choice behavior. However, within the past several decades, empirical research has demonstrated that people do not always make choices in a manner consistent with the traditional tenets of rationality. This has fostered a reexamination of existing theories and considerable development, both normatively and descriptively (Slovic et al., 1988). Although this fragmentation has led to useful efforts to unify work from the various disciplines (Bell et al., 1988; Hooker et al., 1978), decision making remains a fertile area for empirical work, particularly for those interested in advancing applied decision making.

An understanding of the current fragmentation in the area of decision making can be gained by examining several fundamental components of choice behaviors. In the remainder of this chapter we explore decision theory, normative and descriptive processes, system theory applications, idiographic factors, and decision-making heuristics and biases. We close the chapter with a look at implications for educational administration.

The Historical Underpinnings of Decision Theory

The origins of decision theory lie in both statistical decision theory and game theory. Game theory provided the basis for probability theory, which initially was applied to games in the middle of the sixteenth century (Tallman & Gray, 1990). Probability theory provided the mathematical basis for classical statistical inference, which was developed at the onset of the nineteenth century (Baird, 1989). In the mid-twentieth century, in deference to classical and Bayesian inference, radical new approaches to decision theory were developed as decision makers' judgments were allowed into analysis (Baird, 1989).

As practiced currently, decision theory is a discipline for dealing with alternative courses of action by a critical analysis of all possible alternative courses and their outcomes. Although there is some variation in the specific methodology, all decision-theoretic analyses share a common structure and some basic elements (Holloway, 1979). The basic components of decision theory include the *acts,* or strategies, available as decision choices; the *states of nature,* or outcomes, to which probability of occurrence may be assigned; the *payoff,* or consequences, of a given decision; and the *criteria* for selecting the optimal alternative (Cornell, 1980). Some expand this framework, others reduce it.

Although the term *decision theory* is used to describe choices when probabilities are unknown and unpredictable, as currently used it assumes that the decision maker enters a situation with judgments about relative probabilities for uncertain events and with preferences for decision outcomes or consequences (Baird, 1989). Thus, theory combines these preferences and judgments along with objective data in a systematic, structured, and quantitative analysis of the problem that permits the decision maker to evaluate potential outcomes and, subsequently, identify the best decision (Baird, 1989). Traditional decision theory is primarily normative in that it is most useful in describing how decisions should be reached in a given situation rather than explaining how a decision maker actually behaves, although it has been used for both purposes (Bell et al., 1988).

Original economic theories tied to utilitarian ideals were not focused on explaining how decisions are made in conditions of uncertainty. According to Hicks (1939), these theories could not account for the predicted utility of decisions made in situations for which risks could not be calculated. In economics, this gap in theory was addressed in 1947 by von Neumann and Morgenstern in *Theory of Games and Economic Behavior*. They asserted that all decision making assumes that there are hidden costs in any choice and theorize that decision making is not purely linear and a process-product event. As precursors of cost-accounting theorists, economic theorists suggest that the decision-making models must include scales for assessing the utility and the total costs of any decision. Von Neumann and Morgenstern (1947) proposed denser models for economic decision making. They acknowledged the effects of uncertainty or rational, utilitarian decision-making processes, but explained that all risks and utility can be measured. Thus, their model, rooted in mathematical game theory, is normative. The fact that von Neumann and Morgenstern appealed for the application of less linear decision models in economics, however, later served to inform the construction of descriptive models for decision making in the behavioral sciences.

Influenced by the work of von Neumann and Morgenstern, economists developed game theories as normative models for decision making. Al-

though these theories may have limited application in the social sciences, they have been used as reservoirs from which single ideas have been extrapolated for the construction of descriptive theories. The use of the term *game* in no way connotes that these theories are constructed for recreation. Instead, they have been defined as theories that represent decision-making situations, wherein the decision maker has some type of opponent and a strategy must be employed to overcome that opponent (D.W. Taylor, 1965). Game theory deals with those situations for which there is a definite risk factor since there is uncertainty. The uncertainty is generated when the decision maker is not able to estimate exactly the impact of his or her decision on other player(s) in the situation. The degree of uncertainty is limited in game theory because each player knows the objectives of the other.

Over time, game theorists expanded the work of von Neumann and Morgenstern in several ways. McKinsey (1952) commented that mathematicians might find the theory faulty when applied to situations with more than two players because coalition building could result in greater, incalculable uncertainty. Coalition building is called *regret payoffs* in game theory. In a field of several players with several decisions to be made, the decision maker may select from a range of choices that will maximize utility or minimize regret (loss/risk). In another theory, the concept of weighed choice was proposed. Using a mathematical matrix, this concept implied that choices could be weighted, using common sense, to offer some rendition of an equation.

Overall, others have concluded, as did von Neumann and Morgenstern (1947), that game theory can be used only for determining optimal strategies and decisions when there are two players in a given situation. Game theory may not be flexible enough to use as a predictor of behavior when a mixed strategy emerges as the result of the varied interests of several players. The development of coalitions confuses the clarity of game theory when more than two players confront the decision-making situation.

Luce and Raiffa (1967) explained that game theory might form the conceptual construction of decision-making theories in the social sciences. They advised caution, however, in using the theory and its five key assumptions or behaviors in the decision-making situation. The assumptions are: (1) all the possible outcomes of a specific decision must be clearly specified; (2) each player has a constant pattern of preferential behavior in reference to the outcomes; (3) each player will make his decisions in order to maximize the utility of the choice; (4) each player knows fully the utility that is preferred by the other players in the situation; and (5) all the variables in the situation that affect the outcomes are clearly specified in numerical or value statements. Clearly, game theory and its rigid assumptions were becoming troublesome.

Shubick (1964) saw the criteria above as essential in the purely normative models of game theory. However, he warned that these key characteristics do not account for the wide range of conflict-of-interest situations that many decision makers in complex social organizations are forced to confront. Shubick suggested that decision makers usually have some control over the game. They may simply be able to see more alternatives. This may help the decision makers understand the influence of situational variables. Shubick modified game theory to include more flexible concepts, reflecting what he considered to be the nature of human behavior in organizations. He addressed the issues of conflict and cooperation in his model and outlined four conditions that must be present in a decision-making setting if his model is to be used: (1) each decision maker must be autonomous and in control of resources, (2) the rules of game theory must specify how the resources will be utilized, (3) the outcomes will depend on the strategies selected by the players, and (4) for every outcome of the game each player will have an evaluation. In Shubick's model, the game theory is applied to situations with certainty. In other words, the model may be more aptly applied to situations that do not occur in dense social organizations.

Game theory can also be expanded to include the concept of bargaining as an essential component of the decision-making process. In social organizations, decision makers are part of an interactive process in which (1) there is no interpersonal comparison of utilities; (2) the solution condition requires that neither party will accept, as a resolution to their negotiations, any outcome for which another alternative outcome is better for both; (3) the solution is independent of irrelevant alternatives; and (4) symmetric bargaining will give both players the same payoff. This view simultaneously acknowledges the interactive nature of the decision-making process and chooses to ignore the effects of the interdependence of decision makers within an organization.

Negotiation as a concept of game theory was introduced by Schelling in *The Strategy of Conflict* (1970). Schelling used the language of game theory to explain the variables of conflict and cooperation in the decision-making process. He saw conflict as a bargaining opportunity where one participant's ability to achieve a specific end is dependent on the decisions that another participant makes. Schelling recognized that this theory does not offer a decision-making model that may be applied to complex social organizations for which there may be more than two decision centers. He acknowledged that normative models must provide some flexibility to include the factors of bargaining among players, coalitions, or constituencies.

Other theories featured negotiation and bargaining as key concepts. Game theory was viewed as too simple to explain human behavior. Layers of concepts needed to be added to the theory to explain the factors that stabilize conditions in a decision-making process. In these theories, continual oscillation in the bargaining process occurs as initial decisions and preferences are aligned and realigned by decision makers.

Bargaining is a prerequisite condition related to resource allocation in a given decision-making situation. Game theory could only inform normative models in the utility of decisions that could be articulated in definite negotiable utility.

Few of the economic-normative models, however, have been applied as normative models in the behavioral sciences. In economics and mathematics the models have been questioned because of the exhaustive number of conditions under which they would have to be tested for validity. As D.W. Taylor (1965) concluded, "no normative model for decision making under uncertainty has been found."

Group and Participative Decision Making

Decision making as discussed to this point has been confined to individual choice behavior. Vroom and Yetton (1973) have investigated the role of managers as decision makers and the characteristics of leaders and styles of leadership. Vroom and Jago (1988) emphasized the increasing importance of development of participative decision-making styles, with need for managers to encourage involvement in the decision-making process. The decision-making stages employed by individuals and groups may essentially be the same. However, in decision-making tasks involving several people, the process used to reach consensus is influenced by other factors, such as leadership, group pressures, status differentials, intergroup competition, and group size (Reitz, 1987). Some authors (MacPhail-Wilcox & Bryant, 1988) suggest that participative decision making may balance out the idiographic traits inherent in an individual and, in this respect, yield better decisions.

Reitz (1987) claimed that group decision making may not be more effective than individual choice when the "situation requires a sequence of multiple stages, when the problem is not easily divisible into separate parts, and when the correctness of the solution is not easily demonstrated" (p. 346). Group decisions (1) can be more accurate, particularly when a member or members of a group have experience with the problem being addressed; (2) tend to be com-

patible with widely held beliefs; and (3) can result in greater member understanding and commitment. However, Conway (1984) suggested that participative decision making does not necessarily yield heightened support or other benefits commonly associated with the process, and labels several of these claims "myths."

Although group judgment and problem-solving skills tend to exceed those of the average group member, they are frequently inferior to those of the best group member, who in a group forum, is influenced toward mediocrity (Reitz, 1987). There is no group technique capable of enabling groups to yield more numerous or creative ideas than the same number of individuals working alone (Hill, 1982). Furthermore, group decision making promotes the likelihood of problems specific to a collective process, such as "group-think," which results in premature consensus and failure to examine realistic decision options (Janis, 1989). Decisions involving risk and uncertainty can polarize a group toward prevailing cautions or a risk-taking stance. Group polarization hampers examination of decision options (Myers & Lamm, 1976).

Rice and Schneider (1994) have made an empirical assessment of changes in teachers' perceptions of their decision-making involvement from 1980 to 1991. They found that while there were significant increases in involvement in decision making, the educators desired further increase in their roles in decision making. The study also found increases in interest in the decision-making process and in job satisfaction.

In reviewing the literature on decision making, Carroll and Johnson (1990) found that many authors failed to extend the elements of individual decision concepts to groups by noting a lack of ease in applying the same concepts to inherently more complex groups. However, "studies that have directly compared groups and individuals on the same problems find that groups fall prey to the same errors and biases as do individuals" (Carroll & Johnson, 1990, p. 28). Furthermore, individual decision making reflects the choice processes at an elemental level.

Robert Carson (1965) studied teacher participation in decision making in education and other local community activities in three communities in Oregon. In this early study Carson found that teacher involvement in decision making was limited to decisions related to their own classrooms and curriculum matters. The teachers felt that they should be involved in educational decision making to a greater extent than they had been in the past. In areas outside education, elementary teachers consistently desired a lower level of involvement than did the secondary teachers and were more interested in recreation in the community than in issues related to business or local government. Although teachers may not have involved themselves in community matters because in many cases they did not want to, in matters related to decisions regarding education, they desired a stronger voice in the decision making. Carson's research is one example of several studies over the decades that indicate the desire and need for participative and group decision making in educational institutions and also in other institutions and organizations unrelated to education.

In the recent past, decision making has moved beyond individual choice discussions to also include the analysis of participation in the decision-making process. The data on participative decision making did not appear to support a participative decision-making model. But with the advent of productivity increases readily apparent in Japanese education and management, renewed interest has stirred.

Participative decision making has widespread applications. Inherent in participation are questions about how subordinates respond to shared decision making. Subordinates may have been motivated to participate for various reasons: to meet needs of achievement, for financial incentives, and to bring meaning to work. Management may see other advantages: improved quality, increased worker commitment, increased productivity, and peer pressure. But studies to replicate these beliefs have not demonstrated accurate understanding about

participation and decision making. It is possible to point to ambiguities. Participation may be a result of stronger training or differences within groups, better goal setting may be a more effective rationale, and distribution of control may advance participative effects more readily than needs, incentives, or other issues.

The impact of diversity in council membership on decision making in the school-based leadership councils has been researched by Robertson and Kwong (1994) who found that moving the decision-making authority from central administration to the local school level enhanced value-driven organizations that are more responsive to their local markets and environment. Norrel London (1994) investigated the decision-making process that led to delays in the establishment of an education project in a developing country. The project required negotiations with and participation of several government agencies, the World Bank, and other private institutions, and political considerations had an impact on the entire process. John Thomas Scott (1991) conducted a case study of a school district that engaged in a change from a top-down to a participative model of decision making in their budgeting process. They found that the education institution was politicized. This was consistent with other literature related to budgeting, which indicates a dichotomy between politicization and economic rationality. Scott notes that "since budgets are political documents, their formulation may be explained not through economic rationality alone, but through models of group processes, and through an understanding of participative decision making." Thus political considerations play an important role in group and participative decision making.

Conway (1984) provided a summary of the literature on participation. According to him, participation does not demonstrate a higher level of quality decisions, although it does increase feelings of self-worth. Participation may influence decision making more due to stronger goal setting among participants, and although this does seem to increase satisfaction, the satisfaction varies largely by type of organization. Much surrounding participative decision making is still not clear.

Frameworks for Classifying Types of Decisions

Decision theory generally considers decisions against nature. In this context a common system of classifying decision situations is based on the amount of prior information known about the consequence of the choices. Specifically, decision situations are classified based on whether outcomes associated with the decision options involve certainty, risk, or uncertainty (Baird, 1989; Eppen, Gould, Schmidt, Moore, & Weatherford, 1998; Roberts, 1979).

Krepel (1987) and Reitz (1987) add other decision situations, such as those involving competition or novelty. In these situations one assumes that an active, intelligent entity or competitor is working against you and the decisions are not just against nature. These types of situations abound in real life where we have any form of competition: for example, decisions that are needed when there is competition for resources within a school or a school district, or competition among individuals for promotions or better positions.

Certainty is used to describe a situation in which the outcome is known if a particular decision option is selected (Baird, 1989; Roberts, 1979). Although this decision-making situation under certainty appears to be straightforward, as the number of options increases, so does the complexity of the decision. In addition, there may be a number of constraints and interrelationships among various components in the system, which do not allow an obvious solution or choice.

In situations for which there is certainty, deterministic models may be used to aid decision makers. The deterministic models assume that all data and relationships within a system are known and the outcomes can be determined by appropriate calculations using a well-defined algorithm. The formulation of an appropriate, good deterministic model for decision making is considered the biggest challenge today. Once a deterministic (quantitative) model has been formulated, the optimal choice among options involving certainty can often be determined quickly by using computers, which can compensate for human cognitive limitations. A large part of the field of management science or operations research (also called quantitative analysis) includes a study of approaches to help decision making under certainty, where all the data are assumed to be available and the outcomes are deterministic (Bodily, Carraway, Frey, & Pfeifer, 1998; Eppen et al., 1998; Hillier & Lieberman, 1995; Render & Stair, 2000; B.W. Taylor, 1999; Wagner, 1975). Examples of these deterministic approaches include use of all the mathematical programming techniques (linear, integer, and nonlinear programming) and economic order quantity models for inventory management. These deterministic models are all derived and operate under well-defined assumptions that may not be satisfied in a given decision-making situation, and this makes application of those approaches in such instances questionable. "Even in routine situations, there is a need to be aware of the assumptions that are being made and the degree of congruity between those assumptions and reality. Small amounts of dissonance can require a review of the routine decision-making process" (Bodily et al., 1998).

Risk is used to describe situations in which "for each act there is a set of possible consequences, none of which occurs with certainty, but each of which occurs with a known probability" (Roberts, 1979, p. 6). Thus "decision-making under risk is a probabilistic situation. Several states of nature may occur, each with a given probability" (Render & Stair, 2000, p. 85). "In this context, the term *risk* has a restrictive and well-defined meaning. When we speak of decisions under risk, we are referring to a class of decision models for which there is more than one state of nature and for which we make the assumption that *the decision maker can arrive at a probability estimate for the occurrence for each of the various states of nature"* (Eppen et al., 1998, p. 445).

Uncertainty applies to situations "when a manager *cannot* assess the outcome probability with confidence or when virtually no probability data are available . . ." (Render & Stair, 2000, p. 90). The term *uncertainty* is applied specifically to decision situations where, as under *risk,* there is more than one state of nature; however, in this situation, the probability of occurrence of the outcomes is unknown. "There is a long-standing debate as to whether such a situation should exist; that is, should the decision maker always be willing to at least subjectively specify the probabilities when he or she does not know very much (anything) about what state of nature is apt to occur?" (Eppen et al., 1998, p. 451). Although there are some who consider risk and uncertainty as dimensions of the same continuum and consider them both together as *stochastic* processes, most differentiate between the two decision-making situations as we have in this discussion.

Feinstein (1990) has reported the application of decision analysis to the question of whether to test student athletes for drug use and implement a drug-testing program for intercollegiate athletes at the Santa Clara University. Decision analysis indicated that the probabilities for misleading results, the costs and other problems associated with such a program were significant. The athletic governing board decided against implementing a drug-testing program based on the analysis.

In the educational environment, it is apparent that decision situations vary dramatically. Although conditions involving certainty are identifiable, for example, budgeting and scheduling, it is also apparent that situations involving risk and uncertainty are much more prevalent. Today, this realization has become more pronounced as the availability of information explodes. The simple availability of extensive information and new knowledge has compounded decision making to the point that most models of decision making must deal with complex situations involving risk and uncertainty. Simply understanding the apparent cause and effect of illiteracy or dropping out cannot and has not produced decisions, which then solve the illiteracy or dropout problems. Equally evident, the typologies of certainty, risk, and uncertainty do not deal effectively with the interpretivistic or critical theorists' perspective. Decision theorists and practitioners will naturally be prone in this environment to explore heuristics and biases that explain the limitations of decision-making models and explicitly demonstrate relevance.

At best, decision situations under conditions of risk and uncertainty, particularly those with multiple attributes, can be facilitated with the aid of decision-making tools and techniques, even when they yield only probable optimal choices.

Decision-Making Tools and Techniques

The tools and techniques that can facilitate decision making are numerous, often quantitatively oriented, and require that the user can meet many associated assumptions, such as the ability to quantify the usefulness or probability associated with a particular choice. Operations research/management science (OR/MS) is the study of quantitative approaches or models used as aids to decision making. An overview of the operations research/management science models at a basic level is provided in any one of several introductory texts (e.g., Bodily et al., 1998; Eppen et al., 1998; Hillier & Lieberman, 1995; Render & Stair, 2000; B.W. Taylor, 1999; Wagner, 1975). Each one of the models discussed in introductory texts is in a class by itself and the subject of entire texts devoted to a detailed exposition of that one type of model.

The quantitative models of OR/MS may be classified in a manner similar to decision-making situations, according to the type of decision situation in which they are used. Models that assume certainty include mathematical programming, inventory, scheduling, transportation, and assignment techniques. Stochastic models (those assuming risk or uncertainty) include queuing, simulation, decision trees, and stochastic program evaluation and review technique/critical path methods. Other quantitative models include forecasting techniques such as regression and time-series analyses, Bayesian decision theory, Markov decision models, topology, and network theory models. Selection of a particular technique requires that the decision maker understand the characteristics, assumptions, and technical details of each tool or technique or model being considered.

The beginnings of operations research (OR) as a field are often traced to World War II, when there was a pressing need to allocate scarce resources in the military operations in an efficient and effective manner. A number of scientists were recruited to apply scientific approaches for military strategic and tactical decisions (Hillier & Lieberman, 1995 p. 2). The success of OR in the war operations led to applications in industry, business organizations, and government agencies. The introduction of computers with their ability to handle complex and lengthy computations with ease (and absence of human errors in doing numerical calculations) greatly facilitated the applications of OR for decision making. In terms of computational capacity and speed, the power of a desktop computer today far exceeds that of mainframe computers of a few decades ago. The tremendous advances in computer technology have made even computing power-hungry applications of OR/MS techniques such as simulation readily available for use. This has spurred the development of numerous software tools that facilitate applications and make them available to managers who may have very limited training in the technical aspects of the specific techniques used in the applications software packages.

Ralph Keeney (1993) has suggested that decision makers should use *value-focused thinking* in place of the traditional *alternative-focused thinking*. He states that value-focused thinking differs from alternative-focused thinking in its purpose and thought processes. Alternative-focused thinking is used to solve decision problems. Value-focused thinking is a way to identify desirable decision situations and then reap the benefits of these situations by solving them. Keeney (1992) provides a framework and suggests procedures that a decision maker may use for creating better alternatives for choice in a decision situation.

The tools and techniques employed by a decision maker are often influenced by the number of attributes associated with a decision, such as single- versus multiple-attribute decisions, as well as the corresponding level of risk or uncertainty. For example, Reitz (1987) claimed that people facing higher levels of risk tend to prefer tools and techniques that provide substantial quantitative data to indicate the optimal alternative, regardless of the fact that effective decisions are more than information quantity (Zeleny, 1981). Although many tools and techniques are routinely employed quite effectively, in practice those actually used by decision makers may not yield optimal choices, as evidenced by the polarization of decision-making models between the normative (ideal, rational) models and those that describe actual choices.

Multicriteria Decision Making

The traditional approaches in operations research/management science considered a single goal or objective to be optimized. Many decisions in real situations have multiple criteria, and there are multiple objectives to be optimized. For example, a school may desire to provide a sound academic preparation, have good educational facilities and equipment, have small class sizes, have a good athletic program, cater to an increasing student body, and reduce the cost of operations. As a second example, consider a community that needs to build a new school. The cost to acquire land would vary depending on location, and if cost were the sole criterion, the decision would be to choose the least expensive land location. However, there would be other considerations: The school should be in a location that is easily accessible from all points in the community, operating costs may differ at different locations, and aesthetic criteria and even political considerations may be necessary. No available location may be the best based on all the criteria.

Thus in a number of cases it may not be possible to optimize all of several objectives simultaneously, and one or more of the objectives may conflict with others and compromises become necessary. Decision making in such a situation is often referred to as *multicriteria decision making* (MCDM) or alternatively, *multi-attribute decision making* (MADM), and this has been an area of growing interest over the past several decades (Zeleny, 1982; Zionts, 1979). "MCDM is decision making in a situation where there exist a number of objectives that are to be optimized. The objectives may be inherently conflicting and/or it may not be feasible to have a solution to the problem with optimum values for all objectives. It may then be necessary to reach a compromise over the different criteria" (Khairullah, 1982). The field of MCDM is an off-shoot of management science/operations research, with parallel developments in other fields, such as psychology and marketing. It provides a number of approaches for decision making and choosing a preferred alternative in situations with multiple criteria. Multicriteria approaches have been applied to a number of actual situations in education: for example, Reeves and Hickman (1992) formulated and implemented a multicriteria mixed-integer linear programming model for decisions regarding assignments of their MBA program students to summer field study projects at the University of South Carolina. Benjamin, Ehie, and Omurtag (1992) have reported the use of a combination of two multicriteria techniques (goal programming and analytical hierarchy process) for facilities planning for the engineering department at the University of Missouri–Rolla.

The general framework of the OR/MS approach of linear programming was extended to develop a technique known as *goal programming,* which minimizes a composite objective function that consists of deviations from a set of multiple goals. If there is a hierarchy among the goals, preemptive priorities may be assigned to goals ensuring that the attainment of a higher-level goal cannot be traded for the satisfaction of a lower-level goal (Anderson, Sweeney, & Williams, 2000, pp. 697–711; Render & Stair, 2000, pp. 491–501). Charnes and Cooper (1961, 1975) developed and applied the goal programming approach in the context of personnel planning. Other early contributors to this approach included Ignizio (1976), Ijiri (1965) and Lee (1972).

Lee and Clayton (1972) applied the goal programming model for decisions related to academic resource allocation. Later, Kwak and Diminnie (1987) used goal programming for budget allocations among academic units in educational institutions.

The *analytic hierarchy process* (AHP), developed by Thomas L. Saaty (1994), is another established multicriteria decision approach. The approach uses pairwise comparisons to determine weights of the various criteria in a multicriteria decision environment of choosing among alternatives. The criteria weights provide the relative importance among the different criteria (Anderson et al., 2000, pp. 715–726; Render & Stair, 2000, pp. 520–530; Taylor, 1999, pp. 348–359). Liberatore, Nydick, and Sanchez (1992) have reported their successful application of AHP in the evaluation of research papers for the annual research awards program at the college of Commerce and Finance at Villanova University. C. Carlson and Walden (1995) employed the AHP to help decide the location of a new ice-hockey arena in Finland. While AHP helped decide the best location for the arena, the political groups agreed on the third-ranked site. As noted earlier (Scott, 1991), in group and participative decision making, politics play an important role. Carlson and Walden state that in such cases the political processes involved rarely recognize optimal decisions, and at times inconsistent decisions are made for political convenience. Golden, Wasil, and Harker (1989) have edited a book that provides a collection of articles covering the basics of AHP and presenting a wide variety of applications.

In addition to goal programming and the analytic hierarchy process discussed above, a number of other multicriteria/multiattribute approaches have been developed and applied to decision making in situations where multiple objectives are present. For example, an approach of choosing among alternatives based on pairwise comparisons has been developed by Khairullah and Zionts (1987). Yu and Zeleny (1976), Zionts (1981), and Zionts and Wallenius (1976) have proposed linear programming based multicriteria approaches. Mollaghasemi and Pet-Edwards (1997) have provided a classification and an overview of a number of multicriteria decision-making methods and their practical applications. Yoon and Hwang (1995) have provided a review of a number of multiattribute approaches and provided numerical examples, including real applications. They have suggested a *decision support system* that would help a decision maker select an appropriate multiattribute decision-making approach based on the choice strategy to be employed. A growing number of applications of MCDM/MADM approaches are incorporated as part of decision support systems (DSS), which are applied today in education and noneducational institutions.

Decision Support Systems

According to Watson, Houdeshel, and Rainer (1997),"a decision support system is an interactive system that provides the user with easy access to decision models and data in order to support semistructered and unstructured decision-making tasks." The term *decision support systems* (DSS) was coined by Gorry and Scott Morton (1971). While the idea of DSS existed since the late 1960s, these Massachusetts Institute of Technology professors developed the Gorry and Scott Morton grid based on Simon's concept of programmed and nonprogrammed decisions and Robert Anthony's concept of management levels. Steven Alter (1976, 1980) extended the framework of DSS further by developing a taxonomy of six types of DSS based on the level of problem-solving support: from enabling managers just to retrieve data and information, to proposing decisions, and finally, to making decisions in given situations. Keen and Scott Morton (1978) suggested that a DSS should accomplish three objectives: assist in making decisions in semistructured situations, support a manager's decision choice, and improve the effectiveness of decision making. Holsapple and Whinston (1996), Sauter (1997), and Watson et al. (1997) have effectively discussed the concepts, applications, and development of DSS. Joey George (1991–1992) addressed the development of decision support systems in organizations. Leonard Adelman (1992) states that DSS "improves the judgments and decisions inherent in system development." Adelman emphasizes the importance of evaluating DSS and suggests that evaluations should be based on system development efficiency, system decisions, user's beliefs about the system, and finally, user–system interactions.

Eom and Lee (1990) have surveyed DSS applications from 1971 through 1988. Their survey indicated development of a wide variety of DSS applications in a number of different areas, including education; however, they failed to find implementation of DSS that integrated organizational decision making vertically among strategic, tactical, and operational levels, and horizontally among functional areas at the same level. Such vertically and horizontally integrated applications of DSS still do not appear to be prevalent. Sprague and Watson have researched and written extensively (Sprague & Watson, 1996) on the subject and effectively introduce the principles and concepts of DSS and provide a variety of concrete cases of applications.

Traditionally, it was assumed that managers make decisions and solve problems on their own, as individuals. The trend today is to encourage a more participative mode of decision making. Educational institutions and companies emphasize task forces, committees, and project teams in the decision-making process. *Group decision support systems* (GDSSs) are computer-based systems that facilitate this process (Jessup & Valacich, 1993). A key contribution of GDSS is to enhance communication and support cooperation among the group engaged in problem solving and decision making. A growing amount of computer software called *groupware* is now available for this purpose. Lancione and Coleman (1995) advocate an orientation session for the team before embarking on a GDSS journey. Barrett (1996), Lancione and Coleman (1995), and Nosek and Shephard (1995) have provided an overview and offered guidelines for the use of groupware. Satzinger and Olfman (1995) have grouped the GDSS into four classes: software that facilitates brainstorming, alternative rating and ranking, consensus building, and group authoring and outlining. Obviously, much of the GDSS and related software does not relate directly to decision making, but many of these resources definitely affect decision making with the increasing use of technology today, and therefore it is important to be informed about them.

Ferland and Fleurent (1994) report the use of a DSS they call SAPHIR that incorporates optimization procedures with an interactive interface, which aids in course scheduling decisions at the University of Montreal and the Sherbrooke University in Canada. The approach uses both quantitative modeling and human factors in assisting with the demanding task of scheduling at the two academic institutions. Graves, Schrage, and Sankaran (1993) have described the use of a computerized course registration system that allocates limited classroom and faculty resources while satisfy-ing course-offering preferences of students. The OR/MS-based optimization model has worked successfully with human systems input to assign about 18,000 seats in about 475 course sections each year at the University of Chicago Graduate School of Business. Sexton, Sleeper, and Taggart (1994) provide an application of *data envelopment analysis* (DEA) to produce a pupil transportation funding process that improves operational efficiency and reduces cost in North Carolina. DEA is an OR/MS linear programming–based technique that calculates relative efficiency scores for several decision- making groups. The DEA approach has been employed successfully in a number of different situations by many researchers. Carter, Laporte and Chinneck (1994) have described a personal computer–based system developed jointly by the University of Toronto and Carleton University for scheduling examinations, which includes objectives such as avoiding conflicts, availability of rooms, times, and proximity of examination times for the students. The authors report successful implementation and use in deciding examination schedules. Awad and Chinneck (1998) successfully applied a system of problem-specific heuristics, a genetic algorithm framework, and a user interface to help meet the need for proctors for final examination periods at Carlton University. The computer-based system was found to be superior to the manual system it replaced, freeing up staff and overload schedules at the university.

In his Nobel prize–winning theory, Herbert Simon has suggested that decision makers often do not optimize their decisions; rather, they satisfice and settle for a decision that is good enough and not necessarily the best decision. DSS are not intended to replace managers. They apply computer models to the structured portion of the problem, with the manager being responsible for the unstructured portion, using judgment, experience, and intuition. The DSS support and aid managers in making better decisions.

Decision-Making Models

As described earlier, there are two major classifications of decision-making models within conventional dogma: normative and descriptive models (Bell et al., 1988; Grandori, 1984). Normative models are primarily quantitative and suggest how decision making should be conducted to be consistent with rational behavior. While descriptive models address how the process actually occurs, accommodating cognitive limitations and idiographic influences inherent in the decision maker, normative models are based on the assumption that the decision maker recognizes all possible alternatives and their corresponding congruences, can evaluate the consequences against some value system, and can rank and ultimately select the best alternative. In the normative realm, the economic model reflects the essence of this approach. The expected utility model is also fundamental to the traditional tenets of rational decision making. D.W. Taylor (1965) reported that the use of highly complex social organizations as test examples has been difficult for researchers, who hope to use the pure, normative models as a means of offering fruitful descriptions of how decision making may occur. Nevertheless, these normative models have fueled the debate.

Conversely, descriptive models accommodate the psychological constraints that establish as unlikely the probability that a person will operate in a consistent and highly rational manner (Reitz, 1987; Watson & Buede, 1987). Although the distinction between the two classes of decision-making models appears unambiguous, debate over the differences between these two classifications and their appropriate definitions continues. Models that are constructed as descriptive by one group occasionally are perceived as normative by another (Baird, 1989; Grandori, 1984). The confusion is compounded further when a model such as subjective expected utility is treated descriptively but used to characterize normative applications (Bell et al., 1988).

Descriptive methods of the decision-making process continue to emerge as social scientists attempt to apply theoretical constructs as a lens to understand or predict individual human or organizational behavior. The models are built on the assumption that decisions in organizations are made via complex processes.

The most prominent developer of these theories was Herbert Simon, who in his work *Administrative Behavior* (1976) defined the decision maker in an organization as a "rational administrative man" (p. 9). Borrowing from the earlier work of C. I. Barnard (1938), Simon suggested that decisions are actually a composite of rational choices and refuted the theory of the purely economic man as a theory that can legitimately describe the behavior of decision makers in real-life organizations. He called for the construction of new models that attend to the rational processes involved in human choices. In contrast, he rejected the economic rational models which assume that a decision maker can be completely informed when making a decision and able to maximize something through a decision.

Normative Models

Elemental to normative decision-making models are the concepts of maximization and rationality (Einhorn & Hogarth, 1988). Traditionally, these models have reflected the assumptions that every possible outcome may be assigned a utility or subjective value as well as a subjective probability or expectation and that such a decision should reflect the outcome with the greatest utility and probability (Neel, 1977). According to Neel, five principles serve as the bases for rational, normative decisions: (1) transitivity, (2) comparability, (3) dominance, (4) irrelevance, and (5) independence. *Transitivity* refers to a phenomenon in which a person prefers A to B and B to C, when in reality he or she could also prefer A to C. *Comparability* implies a willingness to compare options and determine a preferred outcome or a lack of preference, such as indifference. *Dominance,* or the sure-thing principle, suggests that the alternative that is not worse than the others on any attribute and is better on at least one should always be selected (Montgomery, 1983). *Irrelevance* refers to a situation in which two choices may yield the same outcome. Under these circumstances the selection should not matter. *Independence* suggests that a person's wishes for a particular outcome should not influence his or her "expectation about the outcome" (Neel, 1977, p. 547).

Although the essence of the normative principles of decision making are reflected in the axioms of the benchmark expected utility model, various other models, particularly some of the newer ones, omit some of these axioms to accommodate empirical evidence demonstrating that people often violate them (e.g., people occasionally display intransitive preferences or violate stochastic dominance). The model that is often used to exemplify the normative approach to decision making is the economic model.

The Economic Model.   The economic person is assumed to be a maximizer; that is, he or she will make decisions that will provide the highest return. In keeping with this notion, the economic model assumes that the decision maker recognizes all possible decision alternatives, is aware of all consequences of each alternative, evaluates the consequences against a value system, ranks the alternatives by the order in which they are likely to meet the decision objective, and makes a choice that maximizes the objectives (Reitz, 1987; Watson & Buede, 1987).

Although this model represents idealized, rational decision making, its application is questionable given its limited ability to indicate the best choice in some situations. Bell et al. (1988) provided the example of a person in a gambling scenario who bluffs more than is profitable, to maximize his or her personal monetary gain, and suggests that psychological baggage may make

the notion of maximization subject to loose interpretation. As the economic model exhibits limitations in actual application due to its inability to accommodate violations because of psychological factors, so too does the fundamental normative model. The expected utility model, a normative model, is the "most extensively applied and most often maligned" (Bell et al., 1988, p. 20).

The Expected Utility Model.   Bell et al. (1988) stated that although expected utility has been used as a descriptive model of economic behavior, it serves primarily as one form of idealized rational behavior and addresses normative applications. With the evaluation of probability theory came the concept that the best choice was the one that maximizes the expected value of the decision, a major premise of this model. In 1738, Bernoulli proposed the concept of expected utility, rather than expected value, to explain the decision maker's violation of expected profit maximization (e.g., the more money a person possesses, the less he or she values additional increments of the same amount of money). This concept was discussed further by Atkinson et al. (1988), who developed axioms to accommodate the "simultaneous measurement of utility and subjective probability" (p. 692).

The current assumptions underlying expected utility assume that a decision maker is capable of (1) assessing probability for the state of the world, (2) designating a utility value for each consequence, (3) determining the expected utility value associated with each "lottery" corresponding to each alternative, and (4) comparing the alternatives based on their utilities (Bell et al., 1988, p. 21). Baron (1985) provided a useful explanation of the quantitative substance of expected utility, stating that ". . . the relative attractiveness of behavioral choices should be determined by the expected utility of each of the (objective) probabilities of each outcome times its (subjective) utility, given the decision maker's goals" (p. 9).

Four axioms that serve as the foundation of expected utility include (1) *cancellation,* the elimination of any state of the world that regardless of choice yields the same outcome, a property encompassed in other formal properties, such as von Neumann and Morgenstern's substitution; (2) *transitivity,* the assignment of an option value that does not depend upon the value assigned to other options; (3) *dominance,* which suggests that an option should be selected if it is better in one state of the world and at least as good in all other states; and (4) *invariance,* which suggests that differing representations of the same option should yield the same choice (Tversky & Kahneman, 1988). However, empirical studies (e.g., McNeil et al., 1988; Tversky & Kahneman, 1988) have demonstrated that many of the axioms of expected utility theory are "systematically and consciously violated" (Slovic et al., 1988, p. 697), leading to the development of models and theories that weaken or eliminate axioms. For example, the cancellation axiom has been eliminated by many authors to address the violations noted in the alias paradox (cited in Slovic & Lichtenstein, 1983). Others have maintained invariance and dominance but relinquished transitivity. Some have eliminated invariance and dominance (Tversky & Kahneman, 1988).

Violations of expected utility theory have led to modifications and new developments in both normative and descriptive theories of decision making (Fishburn, 1988). The limitations of utility theory do not suggest that the model is not valid in some situations, as it "still forms the basis for the analysis of many applied decision problems . . . and provides an excellent approximation to many judgments and decisions" (Slovic et al., 1988, p. 674). One reason for continuing to use this theory is that it provides good approximations, even though it may be wrong in principle, so it is going to be used until a more useful theory comes along (Slovic et al., 1988, p. 704). Although noted violations of expected utility theory have led to questions regarding previously held tenets of rationality, the controversy has facilitated useful developments in descriptive decision making.

Descriptive Models

Unlike normative models, descriptive models recognize that people do not always make ideally rational decisions; their preferences for consequences "are often ill-formed, labile, shifting and endogenous to the problem" (Bell et al., 1988, p. 20). Like normative models, descriptive models also run the continuum as to the level of complexity of decisions they address, from single attribute to multiattribute choice. "Even the most elaborate descriptive theories . . . are viewed by their creators as useful approximations, but incomplete and not fully adequate" (Slovic et al., 1988, p. 710). Furthermore, some descriptive models are modifications of the expected utility model, although not all are necessarily intended as such (Neel, 1977). As the economic model is frequently used to embody the normative approach, the administrative model is frequently employed as the model that embodies the vistas of the descriptive approach in educational practice.

The Administrative Model. The administrative model holds that the decision-making process is guided by the principle of *bounded rationality.* Due to computational limitations, decision makers use simplified decision procedures or satisfice, accepting the first simplified decision procedure rather than pursuing an optimal or perfectly rational solution (Bell et al., 1988; Simon, 1955, 1956; Watson & Buede, 1987). In developing the model, Simon (1955) conceded that although perfectly rational decisions are ideal, they are unlikely because of the time and cost involved in attempting to undertake the normative model. There are several subsets of the administrative model.

Affiliative Decision Rules. Janis (1989) noted that in a crisis, decision makers seek solutions that will not endanger their relationships with those to whom they are accountable and will not be opposed by subordinates expected to implement the decision. To cope with the demands of such affiliative constraints, decision makers use a corresponding set of rules. Tetlock (1985) referred to the *acceptability heuristic,* whose central theme is to avoid blame. It is applied by finding out whether other powerful persons in the organization already favor a particular action, then supporting that action without consideration of alternative choices. Janis called attention to the subtle effects of *groupthink,* an affiliative rule whose underlying motivation is the strong desire to avoid spoiling the harmonious atmosphere of a group from which members are dependent for maintaining self-esteem and for coping with the stress of decision making. The rule calls for preserving group harmony by going along with whatever consensus seems to be emerging (Janis, 1989, p. 57).

Emotive Rules (Conflict Theory).   Simon (1976) noted that emotions interfere with cognitive processes in decision making. He postulated that anxiety and stress are aroused when decision makers realize that whichever course of action they choose could turn out badly and that they will be held accountable. Mann and Janis (1977) specified conditions that determine whether the stress of decisional conflict facilitates or interferes with decision making. According to their conflict theory, extremely low and extremely intense stress produce defective coping patterns, whereas intermediate levels are associated with analytic decision making. Whenever decision makers deal with unconflicted adherence or unconflicted change, they are so unaroused by the risks that they resort to "lazy" or routine ways of making judgments because of lack of motivation to engage in the analytic process.

The Vigilant or Reflective Approach.   When the stakes are high, Janis (1989) observed that many executives do not stick to the seat-of-the-pants approach they ordinarily use in daily decision making. They adopt what he refers to as a vigilant decision-making approach, in which they do not ignore the various constraints but take full account of them and go out of their way to obtain more information about them. The state of vigilant, or reflective, problem solving requires the decision maker to ask and answer a variety of questions that can be conceptualized as a complex set of decision rules that put heavy emphasis on eliciting and critically evaluating information feedback. In contrast to giving one of the constraints top priority and resorting to one or two simple decision rules to cope with it, decision makers treat the constraints they are aware of as requirements to be met in their search for a solution.

Prospect Theory.   In developing the administrative model, Simon (1955) conceded that although perfectly rational decisions are ideal, they are unlikely because of the psychological constraints of the decision maker as well as the time and cost involved in attempting to undertake the idealized version of the decision-making process. The premise forwarded by Simon has served as a catalyst for the development of other descriptive models that accommodate noted violations of normative theory. For example, regret theory holds that choices are influenced by the potential regret and/or rejoicing associated with option selection (Loomes & Sugden, 1982).

Prospect theory (Kahneman & Tversky, 1979) holds that people are averse to risk in the positive or gains domain and risk seeking in the area of losses. One component of the theory, framing effects, refers to the way a decision option is presented or framed, specifically such as a loss or a gain, and has been shown to influence choice selection (Kahneman & Tversky, 1979). Staw and Ross (1991) contended that this phenomenon explains behavior in escalation situations in which people appear to continue commitment to a losing course of action. Prospect theory has been used as the basis of numerous other efforts in the area (Fiegenbaum & Thomas, 1988; Fischhoff, 1983; Schurr, 1987), with many researchers attending to a particular aspect of this model.

Kahneman and Tversky's (1979) prospect theory, an algebraic model, addressed people's tendency to violate the implications of utility theory, specifically the axioms of dominance and invariance. The development of this theory demonstrated three pervasive phenomena: (1) the *certainty effect,* the tendency to overweigh outcomes considered certain and conversely underweigh those considered as merely probable; (2) the *reflection effect,* which addresses people's tendency to demonstrate risk aversion in the positive domain as compared to losses and gains determined by the reference point adopted by the decision maker; and (3) the *isolation effect,* which reflects a tendency to discount characteristics common to alternatives and focus on those that differentiate them and lead to inconsistent preferences if the same option is presented in another form (Slovic et al., 1988).

Prospect theory includes two distinct steps in the choice process, a framing and editing phase and an evaluation phase (Kahneman & Tversky, 1979). One of the major contributions of this model is the notion of *framing,* a phenomenon by which the choice process is influenced by the manner in which the choice problem is viewed relative to an adopted negative or positive reference point. This poses an interesting dilemma since many decisions can be viewed as either gains or losses.

Numerous authors (Kahneman & Tversky, 1979; McNeil et al., 1988; Slovic, Fischhoff, & Lichtenstein, 1982) noted that manipulation of the decision frames presented to a decision maker can influence his or her preferences for options and that these effects are sizable. The effects sometimes include preference reversals and violate the tenets of rationality.

A well-known example of a framing problem is the following Asian disease question provided by Tversky and Kahneman (1981):

Imagine that the U.S. is preparing for the outbreak of an unusual Asian disease, which is expected to kill 600 people. Two alternative programs to combat the disease have been proposed. Assume that the exact scientific estimate of the consequences of the programs are as follows:

- If Program A is adopted, 200 people will be saved.

- If Program B is adopted, there is ⅓ probability that 600 people will be saved and ⅔ probability that no people will be saved.

Which of the two programs would you favor?

Tversky and Kahneman found that 72 percent of the people given this frame preferred to save 200 lives for sure rather than gamble on saving a larger number of lives. Next, the authors changed the description of the consequences and posed the following options to another set of subjects:

- If Program C is adopted, 400 people will die.
- If Program D is adopted, there is ⅓ probability that nobody will die, and ⅔ probability that 600 people will die.

In this case 78 percent of the subjects preferred to gamble rather than accept a sure loss of 400 lives. The outcomes in the first choice between the programs A and B and in the second choice between programs C and D were mathematically equivalent; however, the way the questions were framed caused a reversal of preferences.

Similar results of preference reversals due to framing effects have been observed and published by other researchers. Concern for framing effects has been noted in the medical and legal literature with respect to their influence on patients' preferences in informed consent (Eraker & Sox, 1981; Meisel & Roth, 1983) as well as in discussions of the presentation of information to the users of computer decision support systems (Holtzman, 1989). Other studies have noted differences in framing effects by gender, although gender differences in response consistency may be an artifact of other underlying characteristics, such as quantitative skills. Slovic et al. (1988) discussed the example of an insurance policy that actually provides only partial coverage. For example, one that provides insurance protection against fire and theft but not flood appears more attractive if framed as offering unconditional protection against a set of risks. This provides an illusionary sense of certainty.

When given decision tasks, decision makers appear to utilize only displayed information in problem formulation, which places significant responsibility on those charged with presenting decision makers with information (Slovic et al., 1982). Ewell (1989) suggested that institutional researchers should know those for whom they provide data and either organize information to address their preferences or explain why various formats are used. He failed to elaborate on the associated framing effects if this approach is adopted. Some authors (Bell et al., 1988; McNeil et al., 1988) suggested that the potential to influence a decision maker by intentionally or unintentionally framing decision options warrants further exploration as an ethical issue, particularly in cases such as framing information presented on informed consent forms. To some extent that leaves a person to his or her own devices in problem formulation and places significant responsibility on those charged with information presentation and use. However, framing is also influenced by the decision maker's inherent characteristics (Tversky & Kahneman, 1988). The knowledge of framing effects can therefore help decision makers to consciously examine the choices before them from different frames.

Idiographic Factors That Influence Decision Making

Various idiographic factors, personality (e.g., confidence and dogmatism), and status (e.g., age and gender) influence decision making (Johnson, 1990; MacPhail-Wilcox & Bryant, 1988). Hogarth (1980) identified 13 idiographic factors, including ego strength, autonomy, and tolerance for cognitive ambiguity, that he contended affect decision making and are associated with productive scientists. However, the generalizations that can be made from Hogarth's work, as well as other studies of idiographic factors that influence decision making, are limited.

Many studies explore single variables (Johnson, 1990) or a limited combination of idiographic factors (e.g., Hogarth, 1980). Others compare a study variable to only one aspect of the decision-making process, such as information search, thus limiting the generalizations that can be made from the research. For example, in her study of age as a factor in decision making, Johnson (1990) found differences in the information search and use techniques but not in the time spent to reach a decision. In her study, younger subjects used more information but spent less time examining the information than did older subjects addressing the same decision tasks. Although Johnson's study demonstrated that the older subjects used noncompensatory decision rules that have lower cognitive processing demands, the quality of the decision outcome was not evaluated. The study did not indicate whether a particular strategy was detrimental to the decision outcome. Johnson (1990) conceded that other factors, such as vocabulary skills, which were higher in the older subjects, and intelligence, may have affected the information search and use patterns. However, other research suggests that it is difficult to generalize about age-related differences in intellectual functioning, particularly in older subjects (Bloom & Lazerson, 1988). However important the factors, generalizations are still limited.

In another interesting observation, Reitz (1987) noted that "there is little clear-cut evidence to directly relate intelligence and decision making ability" (p. 137). He suggested that if intelligence does affect decision-making success, it is not a major factor. Tversky and Kahneman (1974) contended that intelligence is not associated with any particular heuristic processing or information search pattern; even people with specialized training, for example in areas such as statistics and medicine, make the same decision-making errors as others. Reitz (1987) stated that the apparent lack of correlation between intelligence and decision making may be attributed to the complexities of intelligence, as well as the fact that decision making requires various types of skills, a contention supported by McGuire (1985). She noted that a physician's problem-solving and decision-making skills in the professional domain do not necessarily carry over into other areas.

Although single and dualistic approaches to decision-making research have not enlightened the study of choice behavior fully and significantly, four quadrant combinations have proven somewhat more thorough despite concerns about the validity of formats. The Myers–Briggs type indicator (Myers & Lamm, 1976) attempts to classify people by preferred modes of information gathering and processing. On one continuum, information gathering ranges from sensation to intuition. In another continuum, information processing is classified from feeling to thinking. The four measures combine to yield four decision styles: (1) interpersonal, (2) pragmatic, (3) verbal expressive, and (4) occupational. Decision makers may be classified as convergers, divergers, assimilators, and accommodators. The most current and popular four quadrant typology is based on hemispheric specialization. In this view, qualitative and quantitative differences are seen between the functions of the right and left hemispheres of the brain. The left side of the brain maintains responsibility for verbal expression and linear, analytical, and deductive processing. The right side of the brain functions as a synthesizer, processing information more holistically, creatively, intuitively, and inductively. Similarities have been found between hemispheric specialization and classes of decision behavior, right- and left-hemispheric and logical and nonlogical decisions, right- and left-hemispheric and rational and intuitive decisions, and so on. Tacit and explicit knowledge produce a type of knowing critical to management performance. Numerous other inferences have been drawn from hemispheric studies: women function more integratively than men, planners are more left-hemispheric, managers more right, analysts left, and executives right. In combination, these studies propose important ways of understanding choice behavior more completely, particularly in information-processing functions. Al-

though decision styles and dispositional variables influence decision-making processes and outcomes as developed from two- and four-quadrant research, more research needs to be accomplished from a unifying perspective. A fully systemic approach exploration of decision style and dispositional variables as they interact in decision processes and result in outcomes is needed (MacPhail-Wilcox & Bryant, 1988).

Without knowing how one or several variables interact with other factors that influence the decision-making process (e.g., one factor may negate another or several others), the usefulness of information about discrete or several idiographic factors is limited at best. Even MacPhail-Wilcox and Bryant (1988), who developed a descriptive decision-making model in which decision styles (e.g., hemispheric dominance and intelligence) and dispositional variables (e.g., age, race, and gender) affect choice behavior, conceded that the relations between the variables have not been studied adequately. Existing research does not specify whether idiographic and other personal factors affect "decision outcome directly or indirectly" (p. 18).

Current research on idiographic factors that affect decision making is still limited in its ability to explain or improve individual choice behavior. Other useful insights and improved individual choice behavior have been noted in decision-making literature, resulting from the study of heuristics and biases.

Decision-Making Heuristics and Biases

People often use heuristics to simplify the decision-making process. Although heuristics processes can be economical, by reducing cognitive load, as well as effective, they occasionally result in serious decision-making errors. Tversky and Kahneman (1982a) claim that people "rely on a limited number of heuristic principles which reduce complex tasks of assessing probabilities and predicting values to simpler judgmental operations" (p. 3). Some authors have identified errors specific to applications, such as those that Nisbett, Krantz, Jepson, and Kunda (1983) refer to as *statistical heuristics* (i.e., intuitive, abbreviated, and abstract versions of statistical principles). However, a broader perspective on heuristics may be obtained by examining the major biases associated with the commonly used heuristics noted by Tversky and Kahneman (1974): (1) the availability heuristic, (2) the representativeness heuristic, and (3) anchoring and adjustment.

Availability

Occasionally, people assess the probability or frequency of an event by other instances of the same event that can be recalled or are available in memory. Tversky and Kahneman (1973) refer to this heuristic as *availability* and note that it can be very useful in addressing complex tasks that involve assessing probability or frequency "because instances of large classes are usually reached better and faster than instances of less frequent classes" (Tversky & Kahneman, 1982a, p. 11).

Bazerman (1991) noted three biases commonly associated with the availability heuristic: the ease of recall, retrievability, and illusionary correlation. The ease of recall bias is evidenced when people assign higher probabilities to events than are warranted. Based on their ability to recall easily more recent or vivid occurrences, use of these probabilities often overestimates unlikely events. This assumption is erroneous. For example, because plane crashes are spectacular, some people assume that they should be associated with a higher mortality rate than car accidents, which are often less spectacular.

As decision makers recall information, retrievability may influence their perceptions. Essentially, instances that are readily available in memory will seem more numerous than those that are less retrievable, even if they occur with equal or lower frequency (Tversky & Kahneman, 1982b). Tversky and Kahneman (1973) illustrated this bias by asking subjects which was more prevalent, words that began with the letter

"r" or those that had an "r" in the third position, hypothesizing that people tend to alphabetize words by the letter in the first position. Most subjects erroneously answered that there were more words beginning with an "r" and could readily list examples for their reasoning.

Presumed associations, or illusory connections, refer to a bias in which individuals assume higher probabilities of phenomena co-occurrence than actually exist. These paired associations take precedence, whether or not the pairing is warranted (Bazerman, 1991). Paired associations are commonly evidenced in stereotypes, such as the "smart kid with glasses," or folklore. For example, Chapman and Chapman (1967) demonstrated the phenomena in clinical psychologists, who overestimated the correlation between patients' diagnoses and features in their drawings. Social lore dictated that certain types of eyes on patients' drawings implied suspiciousness, for instance.

Tversky and Kahneman (1974) noted another bias associated with the availability heuristic: the bias of imaginability. They pointed out that this bias may be exemplified by the risks imagined to be associated with a trip, even though the imaginable risks may exaggerate or underestimate the actual situations that could be encountered.

Although the availability heuristic may be useful in assessing probabilities, it can lead to biases that are predictable and cause decision makers to overestimate the probability of event occurrence because of their experiences and learned associations (Tversky & Kahneman, 1974). When decision makers are provided with contradictory information that demonstrates their erroneous and inaccurate assumptions, they tend to resist changing their conclusions (Chapman & Chapman, 1967).

Representativeness

People often assess the probability of a relationship by evaluating the extent to which one item or phenomenon is representative of, or similar to, another. The representativeness heuristic (Kahneman & Tversky, 1972) is often used in making intuitive predictions regarding outcomes. However, "this approach to the judgment of probability leads to serious errors, because similarity, or representativeness, is not influenced by several factors that should affect judgments of probability" (Tversky & Kahneman, 1982b). Use of this heuristic leads to decision-making errors when people attend to "normatively irrelevant" characteristics or ignore those that are "normatively important" (Slovic et al., 1988). Studies have shown that this heuristic is used by both naive and sophisticated subjects (Kahneman & Tversky, 1973).

Biases associated with the representativeness heuristic include a failure to recognize base rates, insensitivity to sample size, misconceptions of chance, insensitivity to predictability, the illusion of validity, and misconceptions of regression (Bazerman, 1991; Tversky & Kahneman, 1974). Although people can use base rates correctly, they tend to overlook them in assessing probabilities when descriptive information is provided, even if it is irrelevant (Kahneman & Tversky, 1972, 1973). An example of how base-rate information is ignored can be elicited by asking subjects about a description that suggests a stereotype, such as whether a male Asian-American student is likely to be an engineering or education major. More often than not, responses are based on the provided physical characteristics rather than the base-rate of people actually engaged in the occupation (Tversky & Kahneman, 1982a).

People frequently demonstrate an insensitivity to sample size, a fundamental issue in statistical generalizability, by assigning probabilities based on a sample of limited representativeness. As noted by Tversky and Kahneman (1974), "intuitive judgments are dominated by the sample proportion and are essentially unaffected by the size of the sample, which plays a crucial role in the determination of the actual posterior odds" (p. 1125). This bias is evidenced by a study of theirs in which subjects, provided

with information that approximately 50 percent of all babies are boys, projected that an instance in which the birth of male babies exceeded 60 percent was likely to be the same for two different-sized hospitals, one with 15 births per day and another with 45. This phenomenon is more likely in the smaller hospital, the one with 15 births per day, because a larger sample is less likely to deviate from the mean, they noted. Frequently, this bias unknowingly influences a person's decisions regarding the probability of events. However, it is occasionally used intentionally, as seen in Bazerman's (1991) example of the advertising slogan: "Four out of five dentists surveyed recommended sugarless gum for their patients who chew gum" (p. 461). Who would question this claim? The advertiser benefits from the fact that most consumers will not question whether the data cited in this claim is representative of all dentists.

The misconceptions of chance bias occur with the gambler's fallacy. For example, after observing a long streak of black on a roulette wheel, a person may unwittingly assume that red would be the next occurrence, even though events do not necessarily occur in a manner likened to "equilibrium." This equilibrium dilutes the distribution as more observations are made (Kahneman et al., 1982; Tversky & Kahneman, 1974). Citing assumptions regarding hitting streaks in baseball is another area in which this bias occurs. McKean (1985) reported that people often overlook the idea that streaks are sometimes contained in random sequence simply due to probability, and repeated exposure to chance incidents does not necessarily lead people to "recognize them as such" (p. 29). Bazerman (1991) summarized this bias by noting that people expect a series of random events to look "random," even when a series of observations is too limited to be "statistically valid." Tversky and Kahneman (1971) demonstrated that succumbing to this bias extends beyond the lay public to research psychologists and is frequently evidenced in research communities, where decisions are based on the assumption that results can be replicated. For example, drug trials conducted prior to the use of some new medication for human therapeutic purposes often use limited samples. Too often, these studies include only young to middle-aged male subjects to determine drug efficacy and safety for the general population.

Tversky and Kahneman (1974) noted two biases emanating from the representativeness heuristic not included in Bazerman's (1991) corresponding listing: insensitivity to predictability and the illusion of validity. Insensitivity to predictability reflects a tendency to violate normative statistical theory by making predictions based on "representativeness," regardless of the reliability or accuracy of the observation on which the conjecture is made. The illusion of validity refers to the overconfidence often placed in the correlation between an input observation or data used to predict a corresponding outcome (Tversky & Kahneman, 1974). This bias has been documented in experts and nonexperts and may be particularly problematic when used by people entrusted as expert decision makers. Einhorn and Hogarth (1978) claimed that research suggests that "neither the extent of professional training and experience nor the amount of information available to clinicians necessarily increases accuracy" (p. 395). People may persist in their overconfidence because they fail to learn from experience and selectively forget their incorrect judgment. Overconfidence and conjecture increase. Operating in conjunction, these biases can lead to an erroneous prediction based on the representativeness of evidence and overconfidence in the accuracy of the conjecture.

People tend to be cognizant that observations regress toward the mean in extreme cases but are less likely to acknowledge its occurrence in unusual circumstances and may develop spurious explanations for the phenomenon when it is noted. For example, McKean (1985) reported that flight instructors claimed that pilots' performances diminished after positive feedback and improved after reprimand. This change in performance was spuriously attributed to the feedback, even though "by regression alone, behavior is most likely to improve after punishment and to deteriorate after reward" (p. 25). This bias has implications for the usefulness of reward and punishment in promoting changes in performance. However, the evaluator's judgment of a performance level may be affected by another heuristic: anchoring and adjustment.

Anchoring and Adjustment

Anchoring refers to a process in which people develop estimates. In the process, people with a specific value or reference point adjust the point up or down to yield a final value. However, adjustments are typically insufficient to negate the influence of the initial anchor, as final answers tend to be biased toward the anchor, even when it is irrelevant (Slovic & Lichtenstein, 1971). The biases emanating from anchoring and adjustment include insufficient anchor adjustment, biases in the evaluation of conjunctive and disjunctive events, and overconfidence in judgments (Bazerman, 1991; Kahneman et al., 1982; Tversky & Kahneman, 1974).

Insufficient anchor adjustments are reflected in people's failure to alter their initial values in establishing a final or estimated value. Anchoring occurs when people are given or have a starting value or when they have their final value estimate on incomplete computation (Tversky & Kahneman, 1974). This bias includes assessments of clinical pathology, risk assessments, projections as to the probability of nuclear war, and conjunctive and disjunctive events (B. W. Carlson, 1990). Bazerman (1991) cited a study in which real estate brokers and undergraduates who were provided with various listing prices for a house were asked to estimate the true value of the house. The study demonstrated that even experts are prone to the anchoring bias, although they "are less likely to realize their use of this bias" in decision making (p. 467). Anchoring biases occurred in both groups. Furthermore, this bias may be detrimental to efforts to improve individuals' decision-making skills.

Nisbett and Ross (1980) contended that the anchoring bias impedes efforts to improve individuals' decision strategies because existing heuristics and biases serve as cognitive anchors and are inherent in the corresponding judgment process.

Bias in evaluating conjunctive and disjunctive events is reflected in people's tendency to overestimate the probability of chain-like conjunctive events and underestimate the probability of chain-like disjunctive events. Tversky and Kahneman (1974) contended that occasionally the anchoring bias direction can be inferred from the event structure. They noted that overestimating " . . . the probability of conjunctive events leads to unwarranted optimism in the evaluation of the likelihood that a plan will proceed or that a project will be completed on time and underestimating the probability of disjunctive events can lead to an underestimation of the probability of failure in complex systems, composed of multiple components, each with its own associated error or probable failure rate" (p. 112).

Bazerman (1991) stated that most people tend to demonstrate overconfidence in their estimation abilities, fail to acknowledge the appropriate level of uncertainty associated with their assessments, and are likely to evidence a confidence level inversely correlated to their knowledge level in a given subject area. This bias affects not only laymen in their everyday decision making, but researchers have demonstrated that this bias is also evidenced by experts in decision-making tasks within their own specialty area. This bias was shown in clinical psychologists (Oskamp, 1982), physicians (Elstein and Bordage, 1979), and the United States Nuclear Regulatory Commission (cited in Slovic et al., 1982). Some of the overconfidence people place in their judgments may be due to the confirmation bias.

Confirmation Bias

Confirmation bias occurs in the process individuals adapt to seek confirmatory data in the searching, recollection, and assimilation of information and exclude or overlook disconfirming evidence in this process (Bazerman, 1991; Einhorn and Hogarth, 1978). As a consequence of the confirmation trap, evidence tends to bolster an initial hypothesis or belief and sustain it. This is true even in the face of empirical rejection or attacks on the original evidence, a phenomenon evidenced by numerous researchers (Ross, Lepper, Strack, & Steinmetz, 1977). In educational forums this bias is demonstrated through the *Pygmalion studies* (Ross and Anderson, 1982, p. 150). Although this bias may help circumvent cognitive dissonance, Einhorn and Hogarth (1978) suggested that it may impede individuals' abilities to learn from experience as the failure to attempt to disconfirm initially held beliefs precludes gathering new insight. Another bias that has been associated with impeding learning is the hindsight bias.

Hindsight Bias

The common axiom that "hindsight is 20–20" inadvertently reflects a decision-making bias. The hindsight bias refers to people's tendency, once given the results of a decision, to overestimate the degree of accuracy to which they would have predicted the correct outcome (Bazerman, 1991). Once people are given information about an occurrence, this information is integrated into their existing knowledge about the subject and reinterpreted to seem logical. The result is a "tendency to view reported outcomes as having been relatively inevitable," an inclination that has also been called *creeping determinism* (Fischhoff, 1982, p. 342). Staw and Ross (1991) noted that other authors, such as Tversky and Kahneman and Slovic and Fischhoff, suggested that the hindsight effect may be influenced by other heuristics, such as anchoring, representativeness, or availability. They also suggest that the major effect of this bias may be an impairment of the ability to judge past events adequately and learn from them.

The Implications of Systems Theory and Decision Making

While the literature explored in this chapter investigated different decision-making approaches, further attention needs to be given to the implications of decision making and the systems movement. Decision-making theorists have, by and large, viewed decision making from within their own reductionist paradigms. An all-analytical approach or an all-conceptual or descriptive approach cannot extend to the dynamic relationship that exists in systems. Oversimplification in decision making implies submitting to a cause-and-effect relation that cannot account for the existing variety present in educational systems or their interrelations. However, a multitude of new points of view are available from systems theorists. This has only recently become useful to decision theorists and decision makers. A systems view of decision making recognizes the complexity of the decision-making process. Decision making, like inquiry, requires complex science.

Decision-making models may also deteriorate from the same systematic tendencies of the more traditional systems approach, the input–throughput–output model. Decision making can never simply be an aggregate phenomenon. Simply creating another decision-making model to explain a particular new phenomenon only creates another snapshot. The decision maker cannot just add variety or another combination of inputs, as complexity can still overwhelm the process and the decision maker. In this sense, decision making must begin to incorporate a thinking or reflective component (Argyris, 1985). This thinking or reflective component allows a decision-making model to become dynamic, to enable its own continuing relevance and growth. To be effective, this "living" quality can be enabled repeatedly through leveraging mechanisms, thus allowing the decision maker or the decision process to be continually generative (Senge, 1990).

Decision making could also benefit from a more interdisciplinary focus. Decision making

and inquiry may be isomorphic. Although many developers of models of inquiry stumble as a result of their positivistic tendencies, other inquiry researchers have proposed models that are systemic. Argyris (1985), for example, proposed an interpretive inquiry model that at the same time demonstrates generative capabilities. In his inquiry model, significant research questions must be explored in their totality and exposed to the whole of its system: problem definition, problem study, problem identification, intervention, and redefinition. Only when inquiry reinvents itself or recycles itself can it be useful from a systems perspective. Similarly, decision making can be renewed from this viewpoint. In devising and using any decision process, one must explore alternatives thoroughly and invent a variety of action strategies which then create the next need for a new decision. As decision makers become accustomed to using new systemic approaches, perhaps decision making will then become truly iterative. Decision making as a process with a beginning and an end breeds decision makers who are ineffective in a constantly changing and evolving environment.

Feedback is also critical. The dynamic nature of systems requires that mechanisms be available for renewal. As the inquiry process and the decision-making process are utilized, additional internal and external inputs open the processes. This "openness" allows the existing variety of the system to emerge and is a requisite need for the system. Closing the process to input typically assures less than complete action and future action. Feedback is a primary ingredient.

This connection between systems thinking and decision making is by no means complete. Decision-making theory has long been viewed from the narrow confines of the normative and descriptive approaches of the past. Decision making must be explored from a more informed and enlightened arena, systems thinking. Prospect theory and the descriptive agenda discussed earlier and proposed by MacPhail-Wilcox and Bryant (1988) are steps in this direction.

Decision-Making Implications in Educational Practice

A number of applications of decision-making approaches have been mentioned in this chapter, including applications in academe. As stated earlier in this chapter, decision making is a central responsibility for many educational administrators. Knowledge about decision-making idiographic factors, decision processes, and choice outcomes are requisite skills necessary to arrive at successful accomplishment of educational objectives. But how does all this theory convert to practical use? In other words, how does a general theory of educational administration and decision theory unite in organizational principles that ensure effective action?

Although the classical model of decision making is an ideal, a more realistic approach to decision making has evolved from satisficing strategies (Simon, 1957). In practical use, satisficing strategies have evolved to be viewed as a dynamic process or cycles of decision events that include development, initiation, and appraisal sequences. It is the administrator's responsibility to assure that the organization perpetuates itself and survives, maintains stability, and progresses and grows. In this context the administrator becomes a maximizer acting on behalf of the organization to maintain internal and external integrity and preserve and enhance all educational practice. Although these ideals are admirable, educational administrators most often operate in arenas filled with incomplete information. Administrators may never maximize, as they lack the knowledge to do so. In situations in which specific goals drive action, maximizing may only be partially accommodated. As complexity continues to increase, options expand beyond what can feasibly be utilized, and prediction becomes less likely, due to expanding consequences contained within alternatives. People are not capable of making completely rational decisions when dealing with complex matters. As a result, satisficing strategies or good enough solutions replace optimizing strategies. To accomplish this, administrators limit the scope of decisions to approach rationality as closely as possible. Limits are, in turn, confined to comfortable functional areas: policy, resources, and execution. Policy is derived from goals that guide action across the school organization, and execution occurs as integration and synthesizing of resources unite to create a purpose-bound organization. Administrators seek choices that serve to "quantify" curriculum and instruction, physical facilities, finance and business, evaluation, recruitment and selection, public relations, and more (Hoy & Miskel, 1978).

In situations where administrators find undefinable alternatives and greater unpredictability, Hoy and Miskel (1978) propose substituting satisficing strategy with an incremental model, a process of successive limited comparisons (Lindbloom, 1965). In this decision-making process, goal setting and generation of alternatives become intertwined. Feasible actions are identified as limited consequences and their alternatives are explored in turn. In this sense, incremental steps are achieved and progress observed in comparison with a previous stage.

Within these implications, deficiencies can be noted in educational decision making. In the classical sense, decision making is a means–ends analysis, an optimizing strategy. It engages all alternatives and relies heavily on theoretical constructs. From the satisficing point of view, a means–ends analysis is typical, but ends are changeable as a result of analysis. Satisficing achieves results that fall within established boundaries, alternatives result from a problemistic search, and theory and experience guide the total process. Incremental strategies investigate goals and alternatives concomitantly. Choice is a matter of agreement between successive comparisons made by the various decision makers, and practical application replaces the need for theory.

Decision making has been considered in a systems-like context by various educational authors. In these models decision making is still a linear process (identify problem, define problem, weigh alternatives, and make choice), but in addition, these models come replete with feedback loops, environmental factors, subsystems, and boundaries. As discussed earlier, systems thinking is more than additive thinking. To truly move beyond the limiting boundaries of aggregate thinking, school leadership must learn to address decision-making scenarios from a more dynamic viewpoint. Senge (1990) suggests that organizational management, including school administration, must learn to deal with circles of influence, those patterning actions that display and describe the inherent dynamics of the educational environment. Administrators who continually remain committed to linear, satisficing, or incremental decision-making methodologies may arrive at choices that seem fitting (symptomatic), but eventually suffer again from inadequate understanding of the dynamic nature of the school and its environment (fundamental). A constant struggle ensues as principals, deans, and directors exchange snapshots.

Like any other thinking system in the educational environment, decision making must continue to observe those traditions that have molded educational thought to date. Various instances of satisficing and incremental decision-making strategies can produce worthy results. But future administrators must also become cognizant of the power of thinking and acting in a dynamic fashion. Only then will leadership truly occur in our educational institutions.

CASE STUDIES

Teaching Versus Research

For half a century your college has been known for its teaching excellence. However, over the last decade a number of faculty have begun important technological research. Others have proposed and obtained funding through government and industry grant programs. During the last three years enrollment and retention has declined modestly. Apply decision-making techniques and strategies to arrive at one of the options listed below.

1. Increase technological research.
2. Recapture the status of an excellent teaching college.
3. Apply a combination of the two spheres of interests described in options 1 and 2.

Budget Reductions and More

As superintendent of schools, you have reduced the budget to your schools this year by 20 percent each. One principal, in order to "live within budget," proposed that the following changes will need to be considered: (a) increased class size, (b) a 5 percent reduction in teaching staff, (c) a 2 percent reduction in support staff, and (d) more efficient control of heating and air conditioning. Consider these in light of the additional constraints listed below. Apply decision-making techniques and strategies to arrive at a workable solution.

1. A large citizens group opposes all options.
2. The state board is considering school choice.
3. You can expect litigation from the teachers union if class size increases.

Math and Science and Dropouts

The school dropout rate reached 22 percent last year, an all-time high. A combination of reasons exists for the high rate. Additionally, the math chairman advised that the state has mandated a number of new requirements in the math curriculum. The math faculty agrees with the changes. However, you know math and science are significant factors in the dropout problem. Apply decision-making techniques and strategies to arrive at workable solutions for the problems listed below.

1. Implement the new math requirements from the state.
2. Decrease the dropout problem.
3. Staff the math department.

Do More with Less

As a classroom teacher, you have arrived at a difficult crossroad in your own lesson planning. Year after year, district requirements seem to keep adding "essential" new knowledge components with little regard to how they fit into the total schema of an individual teacher's plans. You realize that some of your most effective learning devices will not be practical when more "essentials" are added. Devise decision-making strategies to arrive at optimal use of instructional time, use of existing instructional materials and delivery systems, and integration of newly identified, producible instructional materials.

Confirmation Bias

Confirmation bias occurs in the process that people adapt to seek confirmatory data in their information searching, recollection, and assimilation, and exclude or overlook disconfirming evidence in this process (Bazerman, 1991; Einhorn & Hogarth, 1978). As a consequence of the confirmation trap, evidence tends to bolster an initial hypothesis or belief and sustain it. This is true even in the face of empirical rejection or attacks on the original evidence, a phenomenon evidenced by numerous researchers (Ross, Lepper, Strack, & Steinmetz, 1977). In educational forums this bias is demonstrated through Pygmalion studies (Ross & Anderson, 1982, p. 150). Although this bias may help circumvent cognitive dissonance, Einhorn and Hogarth (1978) suggested that it may impede people's ability to learn from experience, as the failure to attempt to disconfirm initially held beliefs precludes gathering new insight. Another bias that has been associated with impeding learning is the hindsight bias.

Who's to Blame?

Illiteracy exists in segments of the population in which your school district is located. As superintendent of schools, you have heard community and business leaders constantly lay the blame upon the education process. In contrast, administrators and teachers indicate illiteracy rates have increased because of dropout rates, increased state requirements, and lack of adequate resources. Devise a holistic problem-solving strategy to address the problem of illiteracy in your school district.

References

Adelman, L. (1992). *Evaluating decision support and expert systems.* New York: Wiley.

Ahlbrecht, M., and M. Were. (1997, June). An empirical study on intertemporal decision making under risk. *Management Science, 43(6), 813–882.*

Alkin, M. D. (Ed.). (1991). *Encyclopedia of educational research* (6th ed.), (Vol. 3). New York: Macmillan.

Alter, S. L. (1976, November–December). How effective managers use information systems. *Harvard Business Review, 54,* 97–104.

Alter, S. L. (1980). *Decision support systems: current practice and continuing challenges.* Reading, MA: Addison-Wesley.

Anderson, D. R., Sweeney, D. J., & Williams, T. A. (2000). *An introduction to management science: Quantitative approaches to decision making* (9th ed.). Cincinnati, OH: South-Western.

Argyris, C. (1985). *Action science.* New York: Jossey-Bass.

Atkinson, R. C., Herrnstein, R. J., Lindzey, G., & Luce, R. D. (Eds.). (1988). *Steven's handbook of experimental psychology* (Vol. 2). New York: Wiley.

Awad, R. M., & Chinneck, J. W. (1998, March–April). Proctor assignment at Carlton University. *Interfaces, 28(2),* 58–71.

Baird, B. F. (1989). *Managerial decisions under uncertainty.* New York: Wiley.

Barnard, C. I. (1938). *The functions of the executive.* Cambridge, MA: Harvard University Press.

Baron, J. (1985). *Rationality and intelligence.* Cambridge: Cambridge University Press.

Barrett, R. (1996, June). Will groupware become the ultimate user interface?. *Enterprise Reengineering, 3.*

Bazerman, M. H. (1991). Foundations of decision processes. In B. M. Staw (Ed.), *Psychological dimensions of organizational behavior* (pp. 451–478). New York: Macmillan.

Bell, D. E., Raiffa, H., & Tversky, A. (Eds.). (1988). *Decision making: Descriptive, normative and prescriptive interactions*. Cambridge: Cambridge University Press.

Benjamin. C. O., Ehie, I. C., & Omurtag, Y. (1992, July–August). Planning facilities at the University of Missouri-Rolla. *Interfaces, 22* (4).

Bittel, L. R., & Bittel, M. A. (1978). *Encyclopedia of professional management*. New York: McGraw-Hill.

Bloom, F. E., & Lazerson, A. (1988). *Brain, mind, and behavior* (2nd ed.). New York: W. H. Freeman.

Bodily, S. E., Carraway, R. L., Frey, S. C., & Pfeifer, P. E. (1998). *Quantitative business analysis: Text and cases*. Boston: Irwin McGraw-Hill.

Carlson, B. W. (1990). Anchoring and adjustment in judgments under risk. *Journal of Experimental Psychology: Learning, Memory and Cognition, 16*(4), 665–676.

Carlson, C. & Walden P. (1995, July–August) AHP in political group decisions: A study in the art of possibilities. *Interfaces, 25*(4).

Carroll, J. S., & Johnson, E. J. (1990). *Decision research: A field guide*. Newbury Park, CA: Sage.

Carson, B. R. (1965). *Teacher participation in decision making and other local community activities in three Oregon communities*. Doctoral dissertation, University of Oregon.

Carter, M. W., Laporte, G., & Chinneck, J. W. (1994, May–June). A general examination scheduling system. *Interfaces 24*(3), 109–120.

Chapman, L. J., & Chapman, J. P. (1967). Genesis of popular but erroneous diagnostic observations. *Journal of Abnormal Psychology, 72*, 193–204.

Charnes, A., & Cooper, W. W. (1961). *Management models and industrial applications of linear programming*. New York: Wiley.

Charnes, A., & Cooper, W. W. (1975). Goal programming and multiple objective optimizations, part 1. *Management Sciences Research Report 381,* Carnegie Mellon University. Paper presented at the joint ORSA-TIMS meeting in Las Vegas, NV.

Conway, J. A. (1984). The myth, mystery, and mastery of participative decision making in education. *Educational Administration Quarterly, 20*(3), 11–40.

Cornell, A. H. (1980). *The decision-makers handbook*. Upper Saddle River, NJ: Prentice Hall.

Cyert, R., and March, F. (1963). *A behavioral theory of the firm*. Upper Saddle River, NJ: Prentice Hall.

Dejnozka, E. L., & Kapel, D. E. (1991). *American educators' encyclopedia*. New York: Greenwood Press.

Eddy, D. M. (1982). Probabilistic reasoning in clinical medicine: Problems and opportunities. In D. Kahneman, P. Slovic, and A. Tversky (Eds.), *Judgment under uncertainty: Heuristics and biases* (pp. 249–267). Cambridge: Cambridge University Press.

Einhorn, H. J., & Hogarth, R. M. (1978). Confidence in judgment: Persistence of the illusion of validity. *Psychological Review, 85*(5), 395–416.

Einhorn, H. J., & Hogarth, R. M. (1988). Behavioral decision theory: Processes of judgment and choice. In D. Bell, H. Raiffa, & A. Tversky (Eds.), *Decision making: Descriptive, normative, and prescriptive interactions* (pp. 113–151). Cambridge: Cambridge University Press.

Elstein, A. S., & Bordage, G. (1979). Psychology of clinical reasoning. In G. Stone, F. Cohen, & N. Alder (Eds.), *Health psychology* (pp. 333–368). San Francisco: Jossey-Bass.

Eom, H. B. & Lee, S. M. (1990, May–June). A survey of decision support system applications (1971–1988). *Interfaces, 20*(3), 65–79.

Eppen, G. D., Gould, F. J., Schmidt, C. P., Moore, J. H., & Weatherford, L. R. (1998). *Introductory management science,* (5th Ed.). Upper Saddle River, NJ: Prentice Hall.

Eraker, S. A., & Sox, H. C. (1981). Assessment of patients' preferences for therapeutic outcomes. *Medical Decision Making, 1*(1), 29–39.

Ewell, P. T. (1989). *Enhancing information use in decision making*. San Francisco: Jossey-Bass.

Feinstein, C. D. (1990, May–June). Deciding whether to test student athletes for drug use. *Interfaces, 20*(3), 80–87.

Ferland, J., & Fleurent, C. (1994). SAPHIR: A decision support system for course scheduling. *Interfaces, 24*(2), 105–115.

Fiegenbaum, A. & Thomas, H. (1988). Attitudes toward risk and risk-return paradox: Prospect theory explanations. *Academy of Management Journal, 31*(1), 288–299.

Fischhoff, B. (1982). For those condemned to study the past: Heuristics and biases in hindsight. In D. Kahneman, P. Slovic, & A. Tversky (Eds.), *Judgment under uncertainty: Heuristics and biases* (pp. 335–351). Cambridge: Cambridge University Press.

Fischhoff, B. (1983). Predicting frames. *Journal of Experimental Psychology: Learning, Memory and Cognition, 9*(1), 103–116.

Fishburn, P. C. (1988). Normative theories of decision making under risk and under uncertainty. In D. Bell, H. Raiffa, & A. Tversky (Eds.), *Decision making: Descriptive, normative, and prescriptive interactions* (pp. 78–98). Cambridge: Cambridge University Press.

Fong, G. T., Krantz, D. H., & Nisbett, R. E. (1989). The effects of statistical training on thinking about everyday problems. In D. Bell, H. Raiffa, & A. Tversky (Eds.), *Decision making: Descriptive, normative, and prescriptive interactions* (pp. 299–340). Cambridge: Cambridge University Press.

George, J. F. (1991–1992, Winter). The conceptualization and development of organizational decision support systems. *Journal of Management Information Systems, 8,* 109–125.

Golden, B. L., Wasil, E. A., & Harker P. T., (Eds.). (1989). *The analytic hierarchy process: Applications and studies.* New York: Springer-Verlag.

Gorry, G. A., & Scott Morton, M. S. (1971, Fall). A framework for management information systems. *Sloan Management Review, 13,* 55–70.

Grandori, A. (1984). A prescriptive contingency view of organizational decision making. *Administrative Science Quarterly, 29,* 192–209.

Graves, R. L., Schrage, L., & Sankaran, J. (1993, September-October). An auction method for course registration. *Interfaces, 23*(5), 81–92.

Hicks, J. R. (1939). *Value and capital: An inquiry into some fundamental principles of economic theory.* Oxford: Clarendon Press.

Hill, G. W. (1982). Group versus individual performance: Are $N + 1$ heads better than one? *Psychological Bulletin, 91,* 517–539.

Hillier, F. S., & Lieberman, G. J. (1995). *Introduction to operations research* (6th ed.). New York: McGraw-Hill.

Hogarth, R. (1980). *Judgment and choice: The psychology of decision.* New York: Wiley.

Holloway, C. A. (1979). *Decision making under uncertainty: Models and choices.* Upper Saddle River, NJ: Prentice Hall.

Holsapple, C. W., & Whinston, A. B. (1996). *Decision support systems: A knowledge-based approach.* St. Paul, MN: West.

Holtzman, S. (1989). *Intelligent decision systems.* Reading, MA: Addison-Wesley.

Hooker, C. A., Leach, J. J., & McClennen, E. F. (Eds.). (1978). *Foundations and applications of decision theory* (Vol. 1). Boston: D. Reidel.

Hoy, W. K., & Miskel, C. G. (1978). *Educational administration: Theory, research, and practice.* New York: Random House.

Huber, G. P. (1980). *Managerial decision making.* Glenview, IL: Scott, Foresman.

Ignizio, J. P. (1976). *Goal programming and extensions.* Lexington, MA: Lexington Books.

Ijiri, Y. (1965). *Management goals and accounting for control.* Chicago: Rand McNally.

Janis, I. L. (1989). *Crucial decisions: Leadership in policymaking and crisis management.* New York: Free Press.

Jessup, L. M., & Valacich, J. S. (1993). *Group support systems: New perspectives.* New York: Macmillan.

Johnson, M. S. (1990). Age differences in decision making: A process methodology for examining strategic information processing. *Journal of Gerontology, 45*(2), 75–78.

Kahneman, D., Slovic, P., & Tversky, A. (Eds.). (1982). *Judgment under uncertainty: Heuristics and biases.* Cambridge: Cambridge University Press.

Kahneman, D., & Tversky, A. (1972). Subjective probability: A judgment of representativeness. *Cognitive Psychology, 3,* 430–454.

Kahneman, D., & Tversky, A. (1973). On the psychology of prediction. *Psychological Review, 80,* 237–251.

Kahneman, D., & Tversky, A. (1979). Prospect theory: An analysis of decision under risk. *Econometrica, 4*(2), 263–291.

Keen, P. G. W., & Scott Morton, M. S. (1978). *Decision support systems: An organizational perspective.* Reading, MA: Addison-Wesley.

Keeney, R. L. (1992). *Value-focused thinking: A path to creative decision making.* Cambridge, MA: Harvard University Press.

Keeney, R. L. (1993, May–June). Creativity in MS/OR: Value-focused thinking—creativity directed toward decision making. *Interfaces, 23*(3), 62–67.

Keeney, R. L., & Raiffa, H. (1976). *Decisions with multiple objectives: Preferences and value tradeoffs.* New York: Wiley.

Khairullah, Z. Y. (1982). *A study of algorithms for multicriteria decision making.* Unpublished doctoral dissertation, State University of New York at Buffalo.

Khairullah, Z. Y., and Zionts, S. (1987). An approach for preference ranking of alternatives. *European Journal of Operational Research, 28*(3).

Krepel, T. L. (1987). Contemporary decision theory and educational leadership. *Educational Research Quarterly, 11*(4), 37–44.

Kwak, N. K., & Diminnie, C. B. (1987). A goal programming model for locating operating budget of academic units. *Socio-Economic Planning Sciences, 21*(5), 333–339.

Lancione, F., & Coleman, D. (1995, August). Groupware tools for business process reengineering. *Enterprise Reengineering, 2.*

Lee, S. M. (1972). *Goal programming for decision analysis.* Phaladelphia: Auerbach.

Lee, S. M., & Clayton, E. R. (1972). A goal programming model for academic resource allocation. *Management Science, 18*(8), 395–408.

Liberatore, M. J., Nydick, R. L. & Sanchez, P. M. (1992, March–April). The evaluation of research papers (or how to get an academic committee to agree on something). *Interfaces, 22*(2).

Lindbloom, C. E. (1965). *The intelligence of democracy decision making through mutual adjustments.* New York: Free Press.

London, N. A. (1994). Interorganizational decision making in the establishment of an education project in a third world country. *Journal of Educational Administration, 32*(2), 54–67.

Loomes, G., & Sugden, R. (1982). Regret theory: An alternative theory of rational choice under uncertainty. *Economic Journal, 92*(368), 805–824.

Luce, R. D., & Raiffa, H. (1967). *Games and decision, introduction and critical survey: A study of the behavioral models project, Bureau of Applied Social Research, Columbia University.* New York: Wiley.

MacPhail-Wilcox, B., & Bryant, H. D. (1988, Fall). A descriptive model of decision making: Review of idiographic influences. *Journal of Research and Development in Education, 22*(1), 7–22.

Mann, L., & Janis, I. (1977). *Decision making: A psychological analysis of conflict, choice, and commitment.* New York: The Free Press.

March, J. G., & Simon, H. A. (Eds.). (1958). *Organizations.* New York: Wiley.

McGuire, C. H. (1985). Medical problem solving: A critique of the literature. *Journal of Medical Education, 60*(8), 587–595.

McKean, K. (1985, June). Decisions, decisions. *Discover,* 22–31.

McKinsey, J. C. (1952). *An introduction to the theory of games.* New York: McGraw-Hill.

McNeil, B., Pauker, S., & Tversky, A. (1988). On the framing of medical decisions. In D. Bell, H. Raiffa, & A. Tversky (Eds.), *Decision making: Descriptive, normative, and prescriptive interactions* (pp. 562–568). Cambridge: Cambridge University Press.

Meisel, A., & Roth, L. H. (1983). Toward an informed discussion of informed consent: A review and critique of the empirical studies. *Arizona Law Review, 25,* 265–346.

Mintzberg, H. (1979). *The structuring of organizations.* Upper Saddle River, NJ: Prentice Hall.

Mollaghasemi, M. & Pet-Edwards, J. (1997). *Technical briefing: Making multiple objective decisions.* Los Angeles, CA: Computer Society Publications.

Montgomery, H. (1983). Decision rules and the search for a dominance structure: Towards a process model of decision making. In P. Humphreys, O. Svenson, & A. Vari (Eds.), *Analyzing and aiding decision making processes* (pp. 343–369). New York: Elsevier.

Myers, D. G., & Lamm, H. (1976). The group polarization phenomenon. *Psychological Bulletin, 83,* 602–627.

Neel, A. (1977). *Theories of psychology: A handbook.* New York: Schenkman.

Nisbett, R. E., Krantz, D. H., Jepson, C., & Kunda, Z. (1983). The use of statistical heuristics in everyday inductive reasoning. *Psychological Review, 90,* 339–363.

Nisbett, R., & Ross, L. (1980). *Human inference: Strategies and shortcomings of social judgment.* Upper Saddle River, NJ: Prentice Hall.

Nosek, J. & Shephard, G. (1995, June). Making groupware payoff: The British model. *Communications of the ACM, 38,* 11–13.

Oscamp, S. (1982). Overconfidence in case-study judgments. In D. Kahneman, P. Slovic, & A. Tversky, A. (Eds.), *Judgment under uncertainty: Heuristics and biases* (pp. 287–293). Cambridge: Cambridge University Press.

Reeves, G. R., & Hickman, E. P. (1992, September–October). Assigning MBA students to field study project teams: A multi-criteria approach. *Interfaces, 22*(5).

Reitz, H. J. (1987). *Behavior in organizations* (3rd ed.). Homewood, IL: Irwin.

Render, B., & Stair, R. M., Jr. (2000). *Quantitative analysis for management* (7th ed). Upper Saddle River, NJ: Prentice Hall.

Rice, E. M., & Schneider, G. T. (1994). A decade of teacher empowerment: An empirical analysis of teacher involvement in decision making, 1980-1991. *Journal of Educational Administration, 32*(1), 43–58.

Roberts, F. S. (1979). *Measurement theory with applications to decision making, utility, and the social sciences.* Reading, MA: Addison-Wesley.

Robertson, P. J. & Kwong, S. S. (1994). Decision making in school-based management leadership councils: The impact of council membership diversity. *Urban Review, 26*(1), 41–54.

Ross, L., & Anderson, C. A. (1982). Shortcomings in the attribution process: On the origins and maintenance of erroneous social assessments. In D. Kahneman, P. Slovic, & A. Tversky (Eds.), *Judgment under uncertainty: Heuristics and biases* (pp. 129–152). Cambridge: Cambridge University Press.

Ross, L., Lepper, M. R., Strack, F., & Steinmetz, J. L. (1977). Social explanation and social expectation: The effects of real and hypothetical explanations upon subjective likelihood. *Journal of Personality and Social Psychology, 35,* 817–829.

Saaty, T. (1994, November–December). How to make a decision: The analytic hierarchy process. *Interfaces, 24*(16).

Satzinger, J. W., & Olfman, L. (1995, Spring). Computer support for group work: Perceptions of the usefulness of support scenarios and end-user tools. *Journal of Management Information Systems, 11.*

Sauter, V. (1997). *Decision support systems.* New York: Wiley.

Schelling, T. C. (1970). *The strategy of conflict.* Cambridge, MA: Harvard University Press.

Schurr, P. H. (1987). Effects of gain and loss decision frames on risky purchase negotiations. *Journal of Applied Psychology, 72*(3), 351–358.

Scott, J. T. (1991). *Case study of a school district undergoing change from a top-down to a participative decision-making budget planning process.* Unpublished doctoral dissertation, State University of New York at Buffalo.

Senge, P. (1990). *The fifth discipline: The art and practice of the learning organization.* New York: Wiley.

Sexton, T. R., Sleeper, S., & Taggart, R. E. (1994, January-February). Improving pupil transportation in North Carolina. *Interfaces, 24*(1), 87–103.

Shubick, M. (Ed.). (1964). *Game theory and related approaches to social behavior.* New York: Wiley.

Simon, H. A. (1955). A behavioral model of rational choice. *Quarterly Journal of Economics, 69,* 99–118.

Simon, H. A. (1956). Rational choice and the structure of the environment. *Psychological Review, 63,* 129–138.

Simon, H. A. (1957). *The new science of management decisions* (rev. ed.). Upper Saddle River, NJ: Prentice Hall.

Simon, H. A. (1976). *Administrative behavior: A study of decision-making processes in administrative organizations* (3rd ed.). New York: Free Press.

Simon, H. A. (1977). *The new science of management decisions,* (rev. ed.) Upper Saddle River, NJ: Prentice Hall.

Slovic, P., Fischhoff, B., & Lichtenstein, S. (1982). Response mode framing and information-processing effects in risk assessment. In R. Hogarth (Ed.), *New directions for methodology of social and behavioral s cience: Question framing and response consistency* (pp. 21–36). San Francisco: Jossey-Bass.

Slovic, P., & Lichtenstein, S. (1971). Comparison of Bayesian and regression approaches in the study of information processing and judgment. *Organizational Behavior and Human Performance, 6,* 649–744.

Slovic, P., & Lichtenstein, S. (1983). Preference reversals: A broader perspective. *American Economic Review, 73,* 596–605.

Slovic, P., Lichtenstein, S., & Fischhoff, B. (1988). Decision making. In R. Atkinson, R. Herrnstein, G. Lindzey, & R. D. Luce (Eds.), *Stevens' handbook of experimental psychology* (Vol. 2, pp. 673–738). New York: Wiley.

Sprague, R. H., Jr., & Watson, H. G., (Eds.). (1996). *Decision support for management.* Upper Saddle River, NJ: Prentice Hall.

Staw, B. M., & Ross, J. (1991). Understanding behavior in escalation situations. In B. Staw (Ed.), *Psychological dimensions of organizational behavior.* New York: Macmillan.

Steers, R. M. (1977). *Organizational effectiveness: A behavioral view.* Santa Monica, CA: Goodyear.

Tallman, I., & Gray, L. N. (1990). Choices, decisions and problem-solving. In W. R. Schoo & J. Blake (Eds.), *Annual Review of Sociology* (Vol. 16, pp. 405–433). Palo Alto, CA: Annual Reviews.

Taylor, B. W., III. (1999). *Introduction to management science,* (6th ed). Upper Saddle River, NJ: Prentice Hall.

Taylor, D. W. (1965). Decision making and problem solving. In J. G. March (Ed.), *Handbook of organizations.* Chicago: Rand McNally.

Tetlock, P. (1985). Acccountability: The neglected social context of judgment and choice. In B. M. Staco & L. Cummings (Eds.), *Research in organizational behavior* (Vol.1). New York: Oxford University Press.

Tversky, A., & Kahneman, D. (1971). The belief in the "law of small numbers." *Psychological Bulletin, 76,* 105–110.

Tversky, A., & Kahneman, D. (1973). Availability: A heuristic for judging frequency and probability. *Cognitive Psychology, 4,* 207–232.

Tversky, A., & Kahneman, D. (1974). Judgment under uncertainty: Heuristics and biases. *Science, 185,* 1124–1131.

Tversky, A., & Kahneman, D. (1981). The framing of decisions and the psychology of choice. *Science, 211,* 453–458.

Tversky, A., & Kahneman, D. (1982a). Evidential impact of base rates. In D. Kahneman, P. Slovic, & A. Tversky (Eds.), *Judgment under uncertainty: Heuristics and biases* (pp. 153–160). Cambridge: Cambridge University Press.

Tversky, A., & Kahneman, D. (1982b). Judgment under uncertainty: Heuristics and biases. In D. Kahneman, P. Slovic, & A. Tversky (Eds.), *Judgment under uncertainty: Heuristics and biases* (pp. 3–20). Cambridge: Cambridge University Press.

Tversky, A., & Kahneman, D. (1988). Rational choice and the framing of decisions. In D. Bell, H. Raiffa, & A. Tversky (Eds.), *Decision making:*

Descriptive, normative, and prescriptive interactions (pp. 167–192). Cambridge: Cambridge University Press.

Von Neumann, J., & Morgenstern, O. (1947). *Theory of games and economic behavior.* Princeton, NJ: Princeton University Press.

Vroom, V. & Jago, A. (1988). *The new leadership: managing participation in organizations.* Upper Saddle River, NJ: Prentice Hall.

Vroom, V. & Yetton, P. (1973). *Leadership and decision making.* Pittsburgh, PA: Pittsburgh University Press.

Wagner, H. M. (1975). *Principles of operations research with applications to managerial decisions.* Upper Saddle River, NJ: Prentice Hall.

Watson, S. R., & Buede, D. M. (1987). *Decision synthesis: The principles and practice of decision analysis.* Cambridge: Cambridge University Press.

Watson, H. J., Houdeshel, G., & Rainer, R. K., Jr. (1997). *Building executive information systems and other decision support applications.* New York: Wiley.

Weick, C. (1976). *Applied electronics.* New York: McGraw-Hill.

White, D. J. (1969). *Decision theory.* Chicago: Aldine.

Yoon, K. P., & Hwang, C. L. (1995). *Multiple attribute decision making: An introduction.* Thousand Oaks, CA: Sage.

Yu, P. L., & Zeleny, M. (1976). Linear multiparametric programming by multicriteria simplex method. *Management Science, 23*(2), 159–170.

Zeleny, M. (1981). Descriptive decision making and its applications. *Applications of Management Science, 1,* 327–388.

Zionts, S. (1979). MCDM—If not a roman numeral, then what?" *Interfaces, 9,* 94–101.

Zionts, S. (1981). A multiple-criteria method for choosing among discrete alternatives. *European Journal of Operational Research, 7,* 143–147.

Zionts, S., & Wallenius, J. (1976). An interactive programming method for solving the multiple-criteria problem. *Management Science, 22*(6), 652–663.

CHAPTER 11

Systemic Change

Basic Issues

In the popular imagination of educational leaders over the past few years, images of themselves as change masters, pathfinders, gamesmen, entrepreneurs, visionaries, and transformational leaders have been widely evident. The spirit of the educational leader has been founded in novelty, chaos, innovation, and change. Educational administrators everywhere have been called on to envision alternatives, to inflame the collective human spirit in renewal, to capture the turbulent environment, and to break the barriers of conventional practice. Change may be about to take on a value of its own (Bell, 1976). For organizations, it may be a foregone conclusion that change is ubiquitous; it is and will remain the norm. Winners will be managed by those who love change and battle bureaucracy. Although change resides as a cure-all, numerous examples of change programs fail as a result of their disruptiveness and from the confusion and threats they pose to participants who must change (Beer, Eisenstat, & Spector, 1990). Tried and true practices, already established personal investments, and already aligned commitments are devalued in favor of innovations that lack continuity (Srivastva, Fry, & Associates, 1992).

Schooling today is confronted with numerous pressures. The ideological, political, and economic environment, as viewed by the American public, is vastly different today than it was in the past. The public demands a more significant connection between effective schooling and national development in the light of dramatic changes in demographics and economic circumstances. A more learning-oriented literate workforce will be in high demand. Continuous improvement will be in high demand, while changes in schooling that have been judged as fundamentally inadequate during the 1980s will fade (Cetron & Gayle, 1991). Change, as the never-ending task, will necessitate an understanding of what change is, what change scenarios are available or can be developed, and how and why change is necessary. In the early stages of professional development, educators and administrators must become familiar with the interactive and interdependent nature of these contexts. With all this understood, change will remain a difficult process to handle, as leaders of change must learn to resolve several basic conflicts: change versus tradition, self-fulfillment versus participation, and decentralization versus integration (Hahn, 1991). The tasks will seem overwhelming.

What Is Change?

Change in organizations is defined by Hanson (1985) as the altering of " . . . behavior, structures, procedures, purposes, or outputs of some unit within an organization" (p. 286). Some describe change as innovation, others as adaptability, even novelty. Thompson (1965) viewed innovation as "the generation, acceptance, and implementation of new ideas, processes, products, or services" (pp. 1–20). Mort (1962) preferred adaptability and simply labeled change as the capacity to respond to various roles in society.

Extensive organizational change is defined by Simsek and Louis (1994) as a paradigm shift. "Organizations are defined by their paradigms, that is, the prevalent view of reality. . . . [S]tructure, strategy, culture, leadership, and individual role accomplishments are defined by this prevailing world view. . . . [R]adical change in organizations may be construed as a discontinuous shift in this socially constructed reality" (p. 2).

Change is a process rather than a single adjustment. Kanter, Stein, and Jick (1992) saw organizations as fluid entities that are constantly in motion. Managing change in this context is a matter of "grabbing hold of some aspect of the motion and steering it in a particular direction. . . " (p. 10).

The literature of change process offers a number of step-based models. Typical are Caldwell's four-step model (1968): (1) identification and priority ranking of needs, (2) development of broad strategies and specific plans, (3) implementation of selected approaches, and (4) assessment of outcomes; Kohl's five-step model (1968): (1) awareness, (2) interest, (3) evaluation, (4) trial, and (5) adoption; and Bushnell's six-step model (1971): (1) diagnosing the problem, (2) formulating objectives, (3) identifying constraints, (4) selecting potential solutions, (5) evaluating alternatives, and (6) implementing the selected alternative. Sheive (1981) described developmental organizational change, that is, periods in the life of an organization when it is significantly different. Basing her discussion on the work of Perrow (1961), Pfeffer and Salancik (1978), and Chin (1976) among others, she proposed a recurring-cycle model of organizational life in which change takes place as a consequence of the influence of new situations and environmental factors encountered during the pursuit of organizational goals.

Change is not a product to be pursued in and of itself for its own value. It is a process by which other ends may be reached. It is the primary means by which any organization or system remains fit, healthy, and able to cope with new and differing demands. The adaptations produced by change in an organization constitute an evolution of the organization. Those organizations that are able to maintain flexibility and react appropriately to new environmental

conditions survive and prosper. Those organizations that cannot become less and less able to serve society.

Change is important to schools. Whether change occurs as a result of self-renewal or continuous improvement programs, or as a result of adjustment to new and different environmental conditions, change must be viewed as an extension of administration and normative action. The primary function of a school system is service, in the broadest sense, to its students, its community, and its political state. It is the responsibility of the school system to prepare our youth to function in an adult world. To do this, the school system must remain constantly aware of the nature and requirements of that environment. As the environment changes and as new technology, new social structures, and new values develop, schools must be aware of those changes and be prepared to adjust curriculum, instruction, and organization to remain viable.

Although it is necessary for schools to remain sensitive to changes in the nature and expectations of their environments, there are also countervailing expectations that schools be conservators of culture, transmitting values and an understanding of the cultural history from one generation to the next. With these new cultural "tools" they can become the initiators of their own self-renewal and continuous improvement. School systems must remain constantly aware of the nature and lessons of the past, must constantly work to fit them into the current world, and must seek to create their own new futures. The task is formidable, but any less may be insufficient.

These expectations, that schools continuously monitor the environment, initiate self-renewal, and adjust to change while remaining conservators of the past, mean that change in school systems will be fraught with complexity. Educational systems are in a constant state of dynamic tension, drawn between the natural responsiveness to change necessary in a dynamic system and the natural stability of a conservator. This tension generates resistance to change within the system and is a hallmark characteristic of educational systems in general. In the past, schools have therefore changed incrementally with too little consideration given to self-renewal or continuous improvement.

In any system, including educational systems, there is a built-in inertia that tends to maintain the stability of the organization. Kowalski and Reitzug (1993) noted that educational systems, as all social systems, develop a character that moves them toward resistance to change. A function of all such organizations is to provide a framework for values, beliefs, and practices that allow people to function effectively. In schools, policy, regulation, and curricula provide a meaningful environment for the work of teachers, students, and staff. Change may threaten this framework of meaning and produce anxiety and resistance.

Kowalski and Reitzug (1993) summarized the extensive discussion of the nature of change by noting that change occurs along a variety of continua. Such a continuum includes the source of change, the type of change, and the time orientation. "One change may be externally generated, unplanned, and spontaneous, whereas another may be internal, evolutionary, and planned" (Kowalski & Reitzug, 1993, p. 306). Internal variances by source might include curriculum committee actions and administrative initiatives. Pressure groups and court decisions would be considered external sources. Types of change include planned and unplanned. For example, an unexpected drop in funding that calls for budget cutbacks would be considered unplanned change, whereas the use of long-range goals and objectives would be considered planned change. The time span can vary from spontaneous to evolutionary, with changes occurring quickly versus changes occurring over a longer time frame.

Types of Change

Lipham, Rankin, and Hoeh (1985) conceptualized change as enforced, expedient, or essential. *Enforced change* is the result of needs identified from external forces. It would not have taken place if it were not for the external influence(s) involved. The task of leadership or management is to devise methods to cope with change, to act as a changemaster. But in this sense, the organization functions at the whims of those with more authority, influence, or political clout. Examples in the school environment could include state or federal mandates or the impact of community pressure groups.

Expedient change generally involves meeting immediate concerns of external sources and is generally short-term or reactionary. Although it can also be internally driven, it is more likely that expedient change in the organization will result from meeting external demands. In each case the school system adjusts to the disequilibrium present and seeks to reestablish a status quo. Examples in the school environment could include last-minute changes in the school budget, or storm damage to a school building.

Essential change is derived from internal rather than external sources. It is driven by the ability of the system to monitor itself and work toward improved performance. It requires that persons within the system work cooperatively to transform behavior or system components. In any system the ability to change is vital to the survival of the organism. Change may also be seen as planned or unplanned. *Planned change,* as defined by Owens (1987), is a deliberate attempt to direct change within a set of predetermined goals and values. *Unplanned change* is often enforced change, unanticipated, and often forced on a school system or an organization. It generally meets the needs of an external agent rather than the needs of the organization being changed. An example would be a merger of two small but functional school districts that resulted from the budgetary needs of the state rather than any dysfunction in the local districts. Expedient change is generally also unplanned, meeting operational needs as they arise but not causing deep adjustments in the nature or overall activities of the organization. Planned change, on the other hand, is foreseen and managed. It is brought about by persons directly connected within the system that is changing. Strategic planning in the school district is an example of planned change.

Resistance to Change

Change efforts may be long awaited by some and strike fear in others. Change should be viewed as not only an intellectual process but as a psychological process as well. Psychologically, change may be resisted because of interference with self-esteem needs, social status, and relationship fulfillment. The most obvious sources of personal resistance to change originate in the person's fear of the unknown. Organizational and individual routines have a high degree of certainty and are not easily altered without some opposition from an individual's or a group's concerns about the innovation's applicability, perceptions of their own abilities, concerns about other changes taking place at the same time, and the support that they are provided. People will resist change if they fear it will reduce their power and influence or make their knowledge and skills obsolete. Resistance arises in change situations.

Much of the interest in the stages of the change process is related to the issue of resistance to change, according to Simek (1997). She identifies a number of forces that produce resistance to change, including sunk costs (time, energy, and money), vested interests, misunderstandings, the existence of group norms and established procedures, and existing balances of power that may be threatened.

Resistance to change is an emotional–behavioral response to real or imagined threats to one's equilibrium or routine (Kreitner & Kinicki, 1989; Stanislao & Stanislao, 1983). Resistance can be manifest in overt or covert behaviors. Stanislao and Stanislao (1983) outlined eight reasons for employee resistance:

1. *Surprise and fear of the unknown.* This emerges when radically innovative changes are introduced without warning or official announcement. The rumor mill creates its own informal sources of information.

2. *Climate of mistrust.* Mistrust can come from prechange organizational climates as well as from climates arising from the change process. The best conceived changes can be doomed by mutual mistrust—mistrust perpetuates mistrust. Leaders and followers both suffer as the motivation necessary to change is absent.

3. *Fear of failure.* Self-doubt and lack of confidence drain growth and development when change participants are not allowed to prepare for change by participating in decision making or retraining.

4. *Loss of status and/or job security.* Resistance can quickly be triggered by real or perceived changes in power bases, loss of jobs, and loss of status due to administrative and technological changes.

5. *Peer pressure.* Resistance can arise not only in those directly affected by the proposed change but also in those who anticipate negative effects on peers, colleagues, or friends.

6. *Disruption of cultural traditions and/or group relationships.* If it is believed that the human element is the backbone of the organization, any modifications in work or personal relationships caused by transfers, promotions, or reassignments alter group dynamics and create disequilibrium.

7. *Personality conflicts.* The personality of the change agent can breed resistance if adversarial relationships develop between the change agent, the change-inducing system, and the target system.

8. *Lack of tact or poor planning.* The system's readiness is a key ingredient in successful change. A good idea may fall flat, not on its own merits, but due to poor timing or a poor manner of introduction.

Williams (1972) stated that resistance to change tends to focus on human relationships, in the sense that people resist change because it upsets their established routines or threatens their security. Harvey (1990) identified a number of sources of resistance: lack of ownership of the change, lack of benefits from the change, feelings of loneliness in dealing with the change, conflict with existing norms, and recognition gained by resisting the change.

The overall climate of the educational system will also have a major impact on the ability to create lasting change. Miskel and Ogawa (1988) defined climate as perceptions of expected work behavior. These perceptions are based on existing patterns of behavior and existing organizational characteristics, such as schedules and curricula. Organizational culture, according to Rossman, Corbett, and Firestone (1988), is knowledge of how things are and how things ought to be. This knowledge includes basic assumptions and beliefs shared by members of the organization. The shared assumptions and beliefs have often been developed over time as the organization produces resolutions to the problems of response to external demands and to the need for internal integration.

Climate and culture combine to provide a powerful matrix in which people function within the educational system. Because climate and culture are in one sense the organizational memory and an action context, they are also a powerfully conservative force within the organization. Therefore, during organizational change, attempts that do not address culture and climate are at great risk of failure.

Change is resisted if it does not adhere to preestablished norms and values. Norms are products of culture in organizations and, according to Watson (1969), correspond to people's habits, making it possible for members of an organization to work together. Norms, as representations of an invisible framework of standard beliefs and values, are valuable to an organization if they have worked well in the past, helped participants interpret daily occurrences, and minimized confusion. Strong norms that project integrity and sensibility in an organization and are shared by the participants across organizational roles are especially difficult to change.

Additional obstacles that may impede change include resource limitations, or the inability to increase production, augment services, purchase new equipment, or hire staff. In contemporary school districts, an additional barrier to change may be collective bargaining agreements, which commonly stipulate that specific changes in job descriptions may be subject to negotiation, thus placing added constraints on an administrator's ability to implement a desired change. Additionally, it is often the case that management and administrative responsibilities carry more importance than do leadership or change-agent roles. This barrier denigrates leadership and the ability of real change agents to act outside the normative–administrative functions of budgeting, scheduling, or even disciplining. Kowalski and Reitzug (1993) concurred and identified the structure of public schools as a quasimonopoly, where bureaucratic structures with their division of responsibility and concentration of power create a sense of disenchantment and alienation on the part of many staff members.

Sarason (1971) observed that cohesiveness (or lack of it) is an issue in effecting change in schools. Teachers are relatively autonomous, with little to do with one another during the normal school day. "They may identify with each other in terms of role or place of work, and they may have a feeling of loyalty to each other and the school, but it is rare that they feel part of a working group that discusses, plans, and helps make educational decisions" (p. 113).

Connor and Lake (1988) grouped barriers to change into three general categories: (1) barriers to understanding: not fully understanding what is proposed; (2) barriers to acceptance: those affected will not accept the change; and (3) barriers to acting: factors inhibiting implementation. Basom and Crandall (1991) identified seven common barriers that were specific to change in schools: (1) discontinuity of leadership, (2) managers' fears that change was unmanageable, (3) lack of training in management regarding change, (4) following a top-down model of decision making, (5) socialization and conditioning of school staff, which leads to the belief that the system is not the problem, (6) unresolved competing visions of what schools should be, and (7) inadequate time and resources.

Research on barriers to change indicates that resistance can be reduced significantly when planning is cognizant of the barriers as described above. Broad support from the change agent is also valuable. Additionally, Fullan (1982) found that four other characteristics enhance the potential for success with regard to change: (1) necessity, the need for change; (2) clarity of purpose, clear and consistent procedures and objectives; (3) complexity, whether change is worth the expanded effort; and (4) practicality, the capability of putting the change into practice. In each of the preceding lists about how to accomplish change, the primacy of integrative elements is critical as the change agents seek to define the complexity of change while demonstrating common action strategies.

Theoretical Implications of Change

Social thinking about change takes two different approaches. The first emphasizes a historical–deterministic thread that often reduces change to inexorable laws. In a second venue the human component is given center stage. Recognizing that greater knowledge and greater self-awareness leads to progressive improvement, the latter approach appears to have spearheaded the "widespread acceptance of change as a natural process and the equally widespread desire to mold that change in one direction or another—to imbue social change with human purpose" (Warren, 1977, p. 3).

Three major theoretical themes related to social change have emerged. In one view, change is seen on a grand scale, as a grand change theory. In this context, change explores a macroenvironment—total societies or total civilizations.

The second theme looks for the general laws that account for these changes—laws that have energized change in the past and would operate to shape the future as well. The third theme raises the question of whether deliberate intervention into social change processes is feasible or desirable. William Graham Sumner, an American sociologist and adherent of Herbert Spenser, saw direct intervention as undesirable and not feasible. Sumner wrote that change will occur as "the great stream of time and earthly things will sweep on just the same in spite of us" (Sumner, 1914, p. 209). Although human beings could attempt to modify and control, our efforts to create change would take a long time. The impact would at most be slight. Another American sociologist, Lester F. Ward, took the active approach to social change and saw as its end the entire development of knowledge and science serving to improve the human condition, the development of a better human society (Warren, 1977).

A sociologist more often cited by those interested in broad social planning and social intervention is Mannheim (1940). He cited three stages in the development of human society. The first is change by chance, discovery, trial, and error. The second is that of intervention, where intermediate processes and tools devised by human beings enable them to pursue systematic social adjustment rather than merely accept society as it is. The third stage encompasses democratic planning. In this stage, most often observed in Western society, various individual efforts are coordinated toward democratically agreed-upon ends. Both Mannheim and Ward, according to Warren (1977), were more interested in knowledge creation than in action or intervention strategies surrounding change.

Much of the action, intervention, and strategizing in social change literature focuses on three levels of social structure: across organizations, communities, and society. Organizational change literature falls into two camps. One focuses on the gradual change that formal organizations make over time and studies the complex processes that occur. The second focuses on planned or deliberate change and its outcomes. The intent is to learn how best to implement change objectives in organizations. Study of the formal organization, according to Warren, then forms the basis for understanding change at other levels of social structure, in communities and society. The second level of change literature is community development. Much of this literature evolves from the social action climate of the 1960s. Community organization and development projects emerged from attempts to bring about greater coordination among social service agencies. But this social action climate later broadened to include change in other parts of the community. Community change drives organizational change. The social macrocosm, national society, was the third level for planned social change. Societal change has a long history and is more closely related to the *grand theory* of social change (Warren, 1977). According to Warren, "most major social change goals, whether or not this is recognized by their proponents, include or presuppose major changes in organizations, often in large numbers and types of them" (p. 6).

The contexts of change in organizations are viewed through several frameworks. The first and most prominent practice is through management. Change is seen through the eyes of the change agent since it is the change agents, most often leaders and managers, who dominate decision making in most organizations. In another view, organizational change is assumed to occur from impetuses within an organization. Forces within the organization, scanning and responding to the environment, set the change process into motion. In this examination, change may be merely an adaptation to environmental changes, or it may be a comprehensive and more innovative approach intended to capitalize on opportunities presented from the environment.

Literature related to informal organizational structures centers about two schools of thought. Summarizing that literature, Warren (1977) noted that the work of such people as Bernard, Simon, Cyert, and March challenge the

bureaucratic–rational model first proposed by Weber. He stated that Bernard saw organizations as not always functioning as rational decision-making units, but as organizational subsystems vying for different outcomes and making highly political decisions. More recently, he said, Argyris and Bennis emphasized the human relations aspects of change among people at and between all levels of the organization.

Investigations of organizational change over the years reveal that change does not necessarily occur solely as a result of management manipulation of the formal structure. Organizational change can also be supported or resisted by the informal structure created by networks of people who may seek quite diverse ends. The study of organizational change should consider both formal and informal structures.

To minimize the importance of informal structures on change efforts would create an inaccurate model for change. The significance of informal organizational structures was brought to light by the Hawthorne experiments of the 1930s. Informal structures came to be seen as fulfilling the function of making life more bearable while meeting the demands of the formal organization. The importance of informal structure in organizational change is now widely recognized in the abstract, if not always in actual practice (Warren, 1977).

Strategies for Change

Change strategies developed by various authors emphasize a variety of aspects of the process. Some attempt to encompass the entire process, while others are restricted to a particular focus. Most tend to be very general or descriptive rather than prescriptive (Warren, 1977, p. 33).

Simek (1997) recommended a frame of reference which included knowledge of the stages that a change process may follow and awareness of potential resistance to change as helpful when deciding which change strategy to apply under given circumstances.

Chin and Benne (1969, 1976) trace change strategies to three basic roots: (1) rational–empirical, (2) normative–reeducative, and (3) power–coercive. The *rational–empirical model* that underlies liberal education, scientific approaches to management, and expert or authoritarian views of what is right is clearly deterministic in nature. *Normative–reeducative strategies* are patterned after Kurt Lewin's (1951) work and emphasize intervention in a client system. Intervention strategies are devised based on the system's perception of its own problems and need for change. These strategies involve a change agent in collaboration with a client system working together to discover elements that may impede change. In essence, the change agent and the client search for a pathology and its remedy. The *power–coercive strategy* applies political, economic, and moral power in order to manipulate or reconstitute power elites. This model underlies many of community development and sociopolitical change strategies. Many consider them overly disruptive. Several strategies and models are outlined for comparison.

Change strategy can be seen as normative–reeducative. These models have been explored across a wide range of client systems: individual, small group, organizations, and large communities. In these models, a client voluntarily engages a consultant as a change agent. In partnership, the client and consultant use a five-stage change model to invoke change. The steps of the model include definition of the need for change, establishment of the change–client relationship, implementation of change strategies, generalization and stabilization of change, and achievement of a terminal relationship. The model is premised, however, on the importance of information flow. Information must be shared freely and openly between the target system and the change agent. This information is useful only if it can be translated into action.

Others have developed models that closely parallel the above. Ross (1967) demonstrated a four-stage model very similar to most problem-solving models. Bennis (1966) also devised a parallel model that demonstrated added consideration to a broader set of variables and results in a more lengthy topology. He outlined, as a result, eight different types of change: (1) planned change, (2) indoctrinary change, (3) coercive change, (4) technocratic change, (5) interactional change, (6) socialization change, (7) emulative change, and (8) natural change.

Kreitner and Kinicki (1989) profiled a three-way topology of change. They believed their strategy applies to all types of change scenarios, including administrative and technical. Furthermore, radically innovative change involving high degrees of complexity, cost, and uncertainty also breed great difficulty in implementation and, additionally, pose the greatest threat to participants.

Nutt (1986) contributed a five-stage model of change he called the *transactional model*. In this strategy, management and a development team occupy a central role. The manager represents formal authority and maintains ultimate responsibility for the proposed change. Change development and implementation occur through the combined efforts of management and development committees or project teams. The manager and teams interact in each stage of the process: defining needs, clarifying premises and assumptions, weighing alternatives, and installing the change. Management ensures that needed structures and mechanisms are in place for the teams. The constituents of the developmental teams assist in problem identification, suggest objectives, recommend options and tentative plans, consider costs and benefits, and gather feedback information once the change has been installed (Kreitner & Kinicki, 1989).

Walton (1965) proposed two strategies related to social change: (1) a power strategy and (2) an attitude-change strategy. The underlying assumption of the *power strategy* is that attainment of change is built on a power base involving strategic manipulation of this power. *Attitude change* can best be achieved by developing mechanisms that promote trust and goodwill.

The change objective involves both a desired concession and a reduction of intergroup hostility. Although both strategies are useful, they may also demonstrate incompatibility. For example, hostile participants must learn to deal with power and trust, ambiguity and evasiveness, and bargaining through threat, and conversely, deal with openness and frankness and conciliatory gestures at the same time (Walton, 1965; cited in Warren, 1977, p. 29).

Meyerson and Banfield's (1964) experience with the Chicago Housing Authority demonstrated a deterministic model. Their model involved analysis of the situation, end reduction and elaboration, designing courses of action, and comparative evaluation of consequences. During analysis, attention is devoted to identifying opportunities and limiting conditions such that differentiation is possible between incidental ends and principal ends. As elaboration of principal ends occurs, developmental action can ensue to more specific levels. Consequences are then evaluated for effectiveness across cost–benefit criteria.

Lauer's process (1973) incorporated targets of change, agents of change, and methods of change. Targets of change may be individuals, groups, or societies, or a combination. Differing strategies are undertaken depending on the chosen target of change. For example, if the change target is a group, change may be sought through recomposition of the group itself. Two forms of change agents may emerge: authoritative or participative. Lauer, like Walton, also found a distinction between power and attitude strategies. Lauer asserted that attitude strategies are best directed at changing individuals and gaining mass support for developmental programs, whereas power strategies are applied more within social movements and organizational and interorganizational change.

Kostler's process (1973; cited in Lauer, 1973) is one of social action rather than social change. This strategy addresses three causes of social change: helping, protest, and revolution. These self-explanatory causes are the objectives or goals that those undertaking the change believe will remedy an identified problem. This discussion also addressed the concept of change agency, identifying two types: leaders and supporters. Kostler's strategies for change include power, persuasion, and reeducative strategies. Targets of change can be classified as ultimate targets and intermediate targets. These targets are acted upon through response or influence channels.

Lewin (1951) provided one of the earliest models of planned change. His model focuses on identifying and using sets of forces to bring about change. According to Lewin, states of equilibrium are maintained by two sets of forces, those maintaining the status quo and those that push for change. Both sets of forces must be present at relatively equal levels of tension for equilibrium to exist. To bring about change it is necessary to shift tension toward change forces and away from state-maintaining forces. Various combinations can be seen; for example, by pushing for change and decreasing maintenance forces, change should occur more rapidly. Lewin felt that tension and resistance related to change could be minimized if the chosen approach involved modifying state-maintaining forces. This modification of state-maintaining forces can be encouraged by instituting three steps: unfreezing, changing, and refreezing. Lewin's model provides a general framework for understanding organizational change.

Finally, the *action research model* of Huse and Cummings (1985) holds broad applicability and is adaptable to fit many different situations. This model focuses on planned change as a cyclic process involving collaboration between organization members and organizational development practitioners. It places strong emphasis on data collection and diagnosis as well as on careful evaluation of action results. The model involves seven steps:

1. *Problem identification.* Key organizational members who influence and hold power identify problems that might need attention.
2. *Consultation.* The change agent and the client begin developing a relationship

wherein the change agent, mindful of the assumptions and values of both systems, shares his or her frame of reference with the client. This sharing establishes a beginning, essential atmosphere of openness and collaboration.

3. *Data gathering and preliminary diagnosis.* This stage takes place in collaboration with the change agent and members of the organization. Four basic data collection tools may be used: interviews, questionnaires, process observations, and organizational performance. Using different data collection tools assures a more holistic set of data.

4. *Feedback.* Data gathered must be fed back to the client, usually in a group or work team meeting. The change agent provides the client with all relevant and useful data, which in turn help these groups to determine the strengths and weaknesses of the system or subsystem under study.

5. *Joint diagnosis of the problem.* To be useful, a diagnosis and recommendation must be understood and accepted. This occurs through an ongoing collaborative process by which data and diagnosis are shared with the group for validation and further diagnosis. Schein (1969) noted that the failure to establish a common frame of reference in the client–consultant relationship may lead to faulty diagnosis or a communication gap, whereby the client is sometimes unwilling to accept the diagnosis and recommendations (p. 98).

6. *Action.* A joint agreement is reached with regard to the action chosen. This is the beginning of the unfreezing process, as the organization moves toward a different state-maintaining equilibrium.

7. *Data gathering after action.* The cyclic process begins with the recollection of data as they relate to the actions taken. The action is monitored and measured to determine the effects of the action taken. Feedback of the results is communicated to the organization. This, in turn, leads to redefinition of the diagnosis and new action.

Models for Planned Change and Their Use

Beckhard and Harris (1977) presented a general model of change that encompasses a number of aspects of the planned change process. The general model had six facets: (1) diagnosing the present condition, including the need for change; (2) setting goals and defining the new state or condition after the change; (3) defining the transition state between the present and the future; (4) developing strategies and action plans for managing the transition; (5) evaluating the change effort; and (6) stabilizing the new conditions and establishing a balance between stability and flexibility.

Most models of change have steps similar to the Beckhard and Harris general model above. There are a variety of other strategies for initiating and managing models of planned change. Lipham et al. (1985) identified four models: problem solving, research–development–diffusion–utilization, social interaction, and linkage.

Problem-Solving Models

According to Lippett, Langseth, and Mossop (1985), all organizational change is directed toward a specific end. "They are all initiated in order to achieve some organizational objective and to solve problems" (p. 27). Hersey and Blanchard (1988) noted that a problem exists " . . . when there is a discrepancy between what is actually happening (the real) and what you or someone who hired you . . . would like to be happening (the ideal)" (p. 334). A problem situation in a school setting might involve a high level of absenteeism by students, a significant dropout rate, or poor achievement test scores.

Most problem-solving models involve the following elements: (1) diagnosis: the problem is noticed, identified, and defined; (2) alternative solutions: a variety of possible solutions are developed and the actions necessary to accomplish them are outlined; (3) selection and implementation: one possible solution is selected, based on its appropriateness and feasibility, and the solution is applied; and (4) evaluation: the results of the actions taken are monitored. If the problem has been resolved, action ceases except to consider how to avoid the problem in the future. If the problem is not resolved, further alternative solutions are considered and the model is recycled as appropriate.

According to Lipham et al. (1985), the most appropriate applications of the problem-solving model occur when problem solving is a norm within the system, when there is effective leadership to sustain the model, when problem solving is an agreed-upon vehicle for accomplishing change, and when time, space, and finances allow solution of the problem.

Research–Development–Diffusion–Utilization Models

Like the problem-solving models, research–development–diffusion–utilization (RDDU) is a rational–empirical approach to managing planned change. It provides a systematic framework for change. The RDDU model involves the following elements: (1) research: research leads to the discovery or invention of new knowledge, products, or techniques; (2) development: the new knowledge, product, or technique is validated through pilot testing and experimentation and then modified as appropriate for practical use; (3) diffusion: the new knowledge, product, or technique is packaged appropriately and marketed; and (4) utilization: if it is supported, encouraged, and accepted, the new knowledge, product, or technique becomes a new element in the overall system. This model is most applicable when there are cooperative arrangements among developers, users, and distributors, when research products are perceived as legitimate solutions to real-world problems, and when there is political support and leadership that encourages the use of research.

According to Havelock (1973), RDDU models are based on a series of assumptions. First, there should be a rational sequence in the evolution and application of the change. Second, because the innovations under consideration

are usually major, planning may take a long period of time. Third, the recipients of the changes are assumed to be passive but willing beneficiaries of the change.

Social Interaction Models

Social interaction models are also a rational approach to change. These models assess the need for change based on communication and information from outside the system and involve members of the change system in planning and implementation. Active participation in the process by the members of the system is the norm, unlike the passive role that members played in the RDDU models.

There are typically four stages in social interaction models: (1) knowledge: leaders and/or members of the system have information about a proposed innovation; (2) persuasion: members of the system are provided with information leading to positive (or negative) attitudes about the innovation proposed; (3) decision: members of the system can accept or reject the proposed innovation; and (4) confirmation: there is confirmation from peers that the decision to adopt or reject was appropriate.

The most effective use of social interaction models occurs when there is support to establish external contacts, when opportunities to gather external information, such as journals and conferences, are available, when there are funds to purchase products, and when there is a desire to gain status or recognition. The social interaction model is widely used in educational systems.

Linkage Models

Linkage models encompass elements of the problem solving, RDDU, and social interaction models. An agent within the system has an interest both within and outside the system, thereby serving as a link.

Stages involved in linkage models include the following: (1) identification: a problem is identified and defined; (2) communication: communication channels linking the system to outside resources are established; (3) research: external information and/or skills bearing on the problem defined are sought out and acquired; (4) solution: with the assistance of the external resource, a solution to the problem is identified or designed; (5) implementation: the solution is applied; and (6) evaluation: the applied solution is monitored, often in collaboration with the external resource, and appropriate action follows if necessary. Linkage models offer the best of all worlds in that they encompass many of the parameters of other models.

Organizational Variables within Models

A variety of organizational variables that have an impact on change were identified by Simek (1997). Major variables that were identified included goal setting, communication processes, decision making (which includes problem solving and action planning), leadership, utilization of human resources (which includes morale, cohesiveness, motivation, and attitudes), innovativeness, and adaptation. Effective use of human resources is a variable emphasized by Miles (1964), who stated that members of the organization must feel that they are growing and learning in order for them to be functional participants in the change process.

Leadership and Change

Throughout this book *leadership* and management have been defined and contrasted to management. *Leadership* is a process whereby leaders and followers intend mutually agreed upon changes, whereas *management* involves an authority relationship between a manager and at least one subordinate that is intended to meet a specific goal. Leadership may be a requisite factor to create and spearhead change, whereas management is necessary to maintain the stability of the educational system.

London (1988) suggested that change agents are leaders and managers who see a need for change, visualize what can be, and seek those strategies that will produce the required effect. The classical rational vista of leadership focuses on two groups: those who are in charge and those who are not. The classical theorists define roles and delineate hierarchical structures and patterns of interaction. The classical rational view is impersonal, formal, and task-centered. It focuses on optimizing organizational performance by optimizing organizational structure. It suggests a structural approach to change, with an emphasis on unilateral decision making, where people are assumed to be highly rational, and where authoritative directions are considered the best motivator of results (Grenier, 1989). It is assumed that compliance will lead to more effective results. The classical approach often uses leadership and management interchangeably. Similarly, change strategies in this arena are rational.

Participative leadership models, in contrast, view the organization as a democratic network having as its goal establishment of an environment that addresses the needs of its members and those functionally related to it (Lorsch & Trooboff, 1989). Supportive leadership, group decision making, and open channels of communication and information flow contribute to the maintenance of a healthy organization. This model suggests that key people be made a part of the change process. "According to participative designers, change should start by altering the most influential causal variables affecting what needs to be changed. Then there should be systematic plans prepared to modify all other affected parts of the organization in carefully coordinated steps" (Lorsch & Trooboff, 1989, p. 74). Authority may be present, but there is a sharing of power. Group decision making and group problem solving both reflect the participative approach to change.

Closely allied to the participative leadership models are human resources leadership models. Vroom and Yetton (1973) provide an example. They advocate being open, a sharer, a listener, a coach, and a participant in working with others. Empowerment of others is a major goal for such a leader.

Organizations, particularly educational organizations, are essentially bureaucratic in design and highly rational. However, leadership within the bureaucratic structure is a decidedly social concept "for it automatically presumes an interactive condition between leaders and followers" (Monahan & Hengst, 1982, p. 220). Leaders do not exist in a vacuum; leadership is a group phenomenon. Much of the literature on leadership focuses on how the leader views himself or herself in relation to followers or subordinates. The leader may assume an autocratic or democratic stance, or employ an interactional or situational approach to leadership and change.

Contingency and situational approaches recognize that position is not enough to ensure commitment or compliance. However, compliance may be enhanced through interpersonal interactions. The situational approach suggests that leadership in organizations is more dependent on its members and the nature of the circumstances that confront the organization. "The leadership task within this context is to relate specific behaviors to effective group performance and satisfaction" (Monahan & Hengst, 1982, p. 248). Change in this environment tends toward a rational and reeducative stance.

Senge (1990) proposed that leadership in a learning organization involves three roles: designer, teacher, and steward. As designer, the leader creates a vision and establishes the core values and principles of the organization. As teacher, the leader helps others to examine and restructure their views of organizational reality. As steward, the leader demonstrates commitment to the people being led and to the larger purposes of the organization. Through these roles, the leader functions as a change agent.

What Is a Change Agent or Change System?

A change agent is a person, group, or organization seeking to produce change in a system. The change agent may be external to the target system or may be an element in the target system. The change agent may initiate the change in question or may join a change process already under way and facilitate the activity. The change agent may be a chief executive officer, foreman, school superintendent, or principal.

Change agents, initiators of change, also may or may not hold formal leadership roles within the target system. In these instances it is vital to the success of the effort that significant elements of the formal leadership be incorporated into the change system. When that is not possible or when the leadership is in active opposition to the change effort, it may be necessary to supplement the existing leadership, change it, or force it into compliance with the effort.

A change system, according to Warren (1977), is the set of connections established between the change agent and the target system in which change is desired. This may be a system separate from the target system, or, in the case of self-change, the change system may be a subset of the target system.

Characteristics of Effective Change Agents

Effective change agents know about the task at hand, understand the cultural context in which the task must be performed, know their followers, and know themselves, according to Hodgkinson (1991). They are generally leaders who see a need for change, visualize what can be done, and move toward the strategies necessary to accomplish their ends. Effective leaders (change agents) possess high intellect, high initiative, strong orientation to both people and goal accomplishment, and a clear vision of what the organization can be (Mazarella & Grundy, 1988; Stogdill, 1974; Yukl, 1981).

Functions of Effective Change Agents

Change agents perform three functions in establishing an effective change-inducing system. These are recruitment, development, and control. Since the change agent working alone is unlikely to be successful in seeking change, one necessary function is recruitment of like-minded persons or subsystems. Warren (1977) pointed out that the larger and more complex the system, the more likely it is that there will be others either actively seeking change or predisposed toward it.

Development of a change-inducing system may involve creating a coalition or mobilizing already existing change-minded individuals or groups to take control of assets they did not control previously. In either case, as the process develops, three issues arise. One is to balance inclusion with coherence. That is, the more individuals or subgroups who are involved in the change effort the better, as long as the original purposes remain clear and coherent. The second is to balance the original goals with the interests and positions of new members of the change group and not to be diverted toward other and sometimes private ends. Third, the change-inducing system should not exist for its own sake but in order to accomplish a clearly defined end. If resources are diverted to maintain the change-inducing system for its own sake rather than meeting the original goals, that perverts the process.

The change agent's ability to balance control of the change process and share control when appropriate is the third function to consider. Once the change system is established, the change agent will begin to lose sole control of the process. Sharing of control is necessary to broaden the base of the effort. Ideally, shared values among the members of the change system will lead to shared understandings and effective decisions made by consensus. Fombrun (1992) considered the ability of the leader to recognize the need for change and the ability to gain consensus in that vision to be fundamental to success.

Another concern for the change agent is the appropriate degree of change to be undertaken. This issue leads to incremental change, planning for change in stages with careful checks at intermediate points. This may lead to reducing

the difficulty of the change objective while increasing the likelihood of success. Given these concerns, the change agent needs to be sensitive to what is possible as well as to what is desirable. Viewing the task in this way will lead the successful change agent to the development of allies, access to additional resources and sources of power when appropriate, and development of long-range multilevel plans that have an improved chance of success. Even in the best of situations, the change agent may well run into either passive or active resistance. There are a variety of tactics that the change agent may use to reduce that resistance.

Lunenberg and Ornstein (1991) stated that change agents use six methods to reduce resistance to change: (1) participation: involvement of those who will be affected by the change to participate in the planning, design, and implementation (participation establishes ownership, builds commitment, and reduces anxiety); (2) communication: employees need to know the purpose of the change and how it will affect them; (3) support: high-level support generates commitment; (4) rewards: resistance will be less if some benefit, tangible or intangible, is seen; (5) planning: well-thought-out infusion processes should be designed; and (6) coercion: though coercion may ensure that change occurs, it may also produce anger and resentment.

Kanter (1983) contended that "change brings pain when it comes as a jolt, when it is seemingly abrupt and shocking. The threat of change arouses anxiety when it is still just a threat and not an actuality, while too many possibilities are still open and before people can experience themselves in a new state" (p. 63). Feelings, thoughts, and actions that affect the lives of those who populate the system will influence how they react to change.

Huse (1975) cited several factors that aid in reducing resistance to change.

1. Any change process needs to take into account the needs, attitudes, and beliefs of the people involved, as well as the forces of organization.

The individual must perceive some personal benefit to be gained from the change before willingness to participate in the change process will be forthcoming.

2. The greater the prestige of the supervisor, the greater the influence that he or she can exert for change.

3. Strong pressure for changes in behavior can be established by providing specific information desired by the group about itself and its behavior. The more central, relevant, and meaningful the information, the greater the possibility for change.

4. Facts developed by the individual or the group, or the involvement and participation by the individual or the group in the planning, gathering, analysis, and interpretation of data, highly influence the change process.

5. Change that originates from within is much less threatening and creates less opposition than change that is proposed from the outside.

6. Information relating to the need for change, plans for change, and consequences of change must be shared by all relevant people in the group.

London (1988) also identified several factors that can aid in minimizing resistance to change.

1. Evaluate the characteristics of the change. Consider complexity, psychological and financial cost, the extent to which the purpose and intended outcome are clear, and the amount of mutual agreement.

2. Consider who and what is affected by the change. Try to determine how the change affects the work that is done and the working and personal relationships of those affected.

3. Envision how the change will be implemented. Reduce uncertainty to a minimum.

4. Be prepared for multiple interventions. As an example, training staff for new tasks will not necessarily be effective unless the social system and the reward structure reinforce the desirability of implementing the new behavior.

The key point is that planned change is most effective when human systems are an integral part of the change process. Whether it focuses on the introduction of new personnel or new technologies, planned change must be based on knowledge and must incorporate strategies derived from such knowledge (Chin & Benne, 1969).

Effective change agents are systems thinkers prepared for and planning for the complexities of multisystem interactions and long-term ripple effects once a change is implemented. Indeed, they should be prepared for such complexities once a change is suggested, since the anticipation of change will often produce an impact of its own.

Implementing this multisystem interactions perspective by the change agent involves development of clear answers to questions related to the situation, not only for the change agent but for all involved in the process. Essential questions for condition are: (1) What is to be changed? (2) Why is it to be changed? (3) How is it to be changed? (4) When is it to be changed? (5) Who will be involved in the change? (6) What barriers to the change will need to be overcome? (7) What impact can reasonably be expected on individuals, on subsystems, on the overall system, on the external environment? (8) What support for the change can be expected? (9) What will be the costs of the change? (10) What will be the benefits of the change?

Managing Planned Change

Beckhard and Harris (1977) presented a general model that outlines six aspects of management of the change process: (1) diagnose the present condition, including the need for change; (2) set goals and define the new state or condition after the change; (3) define the transition state between the present and the future; (4) develop strategies and action plans for managing this transition; (5) evaluate the change effort; and

(6) stabilize the new conditions and establish a balance between stability and flexibility.

Beckhard and Harris emphasized that there are two essential conditions for any change effort to be effectively managed. First, the organization leadership must be aware of the need for change and the consequences of their actions. Second, the desired end state must be relatively explicit. A clear differentiation between causes and symptoms is an essential component of the first aspect of the change process. What often occurs is poor system diagnosis that provides an inaccurate statement of the change problem. Change strategies can be effective if the symptom statement describes the fundamental condition needing change. Diagnosis must include probable causes of the problems as well as a goal statement. Such questions as "What would be different or better?" and "How much does it matter?" would provide clarity for the problem and goal statement. Problem definition and goal setting are interlinked and both must be explicit. It is important to recognize that although the concern for change is often triggered by the existence of some need or set of problem symptoms, it is the goal set by the leadership that should be the determining factor in defining both the strategy and direction for change (Beckhard & Harris, 1977, p. 20).

Detailed attention is required to define the present system and develop a description of what the system will appear to be when the desired change is achieved. In defining the present system, many organizations embark on a change process with erroneous assumptions about the current state of the organization. If action plans are developed on an inaccurate set of assumptions and then implemented, resistance, confusion, frustration, and general failure to achieve desired goals will result. Analyzing the present scenario involves analyzing what subsystems of the system are most significantly involved in the change process and what changes in their present attitudes or behavior or ways of work would have to occur if the desired goal is to be reached.

This requires a total organization perspective, since change in one part of the system will affect the total system. It is best to anticipate the degree and direction of anticipated change within the total system. This allows a proactive stance rather than a reactive stance to changes in subsystems that were not direct targets of the change process.

An additional focus is on the processes that would need to be changed for the overall innovation to be effective. These could include required changes in attitude, practices, policy, and structure, including rewards. Once a diagnosis is complete, priorities need to be set, keeping in mind the potential domino effect inherent in the change process.

Continuing the assessment process, there must be a clear understanding of each subsystem's readiness and capacity for change. Motivation to change is directly related to readiness and capability. The state of readiness to change is closely connected to attitudes of the system. Attitudes of the subsystem toward anticipated change will be influenced by assumptions, reality based or perceived, about the effect of the change as it relates directly to this subsystem. The success of change efforts is influenced as much by the processes of change as it is by the actual tasks involved. Capacity for change is related to readiness and encompasses analysis of available resources to support the change and offset negative consequences. Resources include not only personnel and equipment, but also technology, time, and funds.

Will the expected ends derived from the change offset the costs involved? This question can be answered accurately only if a whole system analysis is done. What may appear to have positive benefits for one part of the system may have immediate or long-term negative effects on other crucial elements.

The quality of input information in any decision-making process will directly affect the appropriateness of the decision. According to Beckhard and Harris (1977, p. 28), the input information includes determining (1) the degree of choice whether to change, (2) what needs changing, (3) where to intervene, and (4) intervention technologies.

Forces for change may be internal or external. Often, forces outside the system call for change. Under these circumstances the leadership may have limited control over events. This control may only extend to the means of making the change or coping with the results.

Decision Making

Change in any part of a system will create change requirements in other parts of the system. Given that, the question becomes: Which change is the best approach for solving a particular problem? This is a particularly important concept in considering change in an educational system that operates with multiple layers of subsystems, each with its own goals and objectives that must be taken into consideration if the effort to change is not to be self-defeating.

Decision making has been described elsewhere in this book as a matter of choosing among alternatives. These choices involve assessment of the level of risk involved, the amount of information available, some level of rationality (although most recent students of decision making note that rationality is not the only base for making individual choices), evaluation of preferences, identification of probable consequences, and communication of the decision.

According to French and Bell (1973), decision making includes the processes of problem solving and action planning. Conducting these processes successfully involves getting necessary information, establishing priorities, evaluating alternatives, and choosing one alternative over others.

Training educational leaders and managers has traditionally included efforts to improve decision-making skills. This is seen as particularly important since the educational decision maker functioning in a public arena makes decisions and communicates them in a highly politicized environment. Decision making in this situation often calls for the ability to bargain and negotiate in the manner described by Lindbloom (1965), as well as for significant communications skills.

Decision making in education has a heightened level of risk because full information is rarely available. Therefore, the educational decision maker generally operates on the basis of Simon's bounded rationality: considering the real-world situation as he or she sees it, reviewing the choices, and then constructing a simplified model through which a decision can be made. While the behavior is rational within the frame of reference of the model, the rationality is bounded in the sense that the effective decision maker understands the model to be limited by such factors as time and available information, and therefore is incomplete.

Once a choice has been made to initiate change, it remains to determine what needs changing and to increase the system's readiness and capacity for the change. Here the need for unfreezing and freezing techniques may be considered as a means of increasing readiness and capability. This is particularly true if a system's norms, attitudes, and ways of work are entrenched. Goal-setting exercises may be helpful if the system's goals are not shared. Structural change would be called for if the organizational chart does not reflect the new tasks to be done. New information or technical knowledge or skills may be required to achieve the change conditions.

Following the decision to initiate change and identification of change targets, there must be a determination of where to begin. Potential targets could include the top of the system, subsystems known to be ready for and capable of change, the "hurting system," or new teams or systems that may be more open to change because of a lack of history and experience in the old ways.

Change needs to be initiated and moved forward. This is accomplished by selecting the appropriate intervention techniques and technologies. Beckhard and Harris (1977) made several points about these choices. One is to identify and think through the most likely possible early activities and their consequences. They also warned against falling into the "quick fix" trap or the assumption that "we only need . . . [a management by objectives system, a planning exercise, new training programs]. . . . " What may be needed to initiate and move the change process forward is creation of a temporary system that can raise the possibility of novel solutions involving new approaches. It can be very difficult for a stable system to change itself.

Much can be accomplished through the use of planned change models, but there is no guarantee that these models will be appropriate. Problems may arise with the process: consultants can become wedded to one technique to the exclusion of others, organizations may not be willing to do what is necessary for success, or management may only want to buy into certain steps or may focus on validating their own or earlier positions. These and other problems may arise not from the change model but from its implementation.

Johansen (1967) investigated 59 school systems in Illinois to determine the relationship between teachers' perspective on the source of authoritative influence in local curriculum decision making and implementation of the resulting decisions. He noted that teacher participation in curriculum activities increased the chances of curriculum implementation. Perception on the part of teachers that they had been influential in decision making enhanced the chances of implementation, while perception that hierarchical authority was central to decisions decreased the chances of implementation.

Effecting Educational Change

Change is ever present in schools, as it is in any organization. Given the variety of challenges that educational systems face today, the ability to cope with change becomes even more of a necessity (Cetron & Gayle, 1991; Mauriel, 1989;

Millard, 1991). The shift of school ownership, advent of the information age, demographic shifts in funding, growing poverty among underclass children, demands of new market segments, and the quality of output of schools all have focused attention on reexamination of the efficiency and effectiveness of school systems.

Planned change in schools, however, is affected by the particular nature of educational systems. Schools tend to be loosely coupled with vague system boundaries, diffuse goals, relatively low technical capacity, a constrained decentralized structure, and a noncompetitive environment. These characteristics make effecting change in schools somewhat different from effecting change in other social organizations.

In the past, change in American education was viewed as an evolutionary process, a process of natural diffusion. As a result, the systems changed quite slowly. Mort and Ross (1957) reported that the average school in the United States lagged a quarter-century behind the best practice of the time. However, as the pace of change has increased in society, natural diffusion of educational change has given way to planned, managed diffusion (Owens, 1987). This shift has led to identification of a number of models for change that fit educational systems.

Models for Educational Change

"Educational change depends on what teachers do and think—it's as simple and as complex as that," said Fullan (1982, p. 107). He then went on to identify four categories of factors that affect implementation of educational change: (1) the characteristics of the change, (2) characteristics at the school district level, (3) characteristics at the school level, and (4) characteristics external to the local system. The greater the number of factors in those four sets that supported the innovation, the greater the chances were that the change would be implemented.

Fullan's view was supported by Waugh and Punch (1987), who concluded that variables to be considered before implementing educational change involving teachers included the practicality of the new system in the classroom, alleviation of fears and uncertainties concerning the change, articulation of perceived expectations associated with the change, and support of the teachers' role changes in reference to the change.

Educational change can be considered in terms of the problem-solving, social interaction, research–development–diffusion–utilization, and linkage models discussed in this chapter. In recent years, these models have been refined to fit the specific nature of educational systems.

The problem-solving model is based on a rational approach to change. It is user-centered, featuring user diagnosis of problems with emphasis on building the problem-solving capacity of users. There are four basic stages: (1) diagnosis of the problem, (2) development of a number of alternatives, (3) implementation of selected alternative(s), and (4) evaluation of the outcomes. This model is useful when there is sufficient time and funding, there is little controversy, and the staff has an open mind. School systems have used this approach to change frequently in the past. But as complexity has grown, so has the ineffectiveness of these simplistic models.

The social interaction model emphasizes communication channels and messages for diffusing innovations, interpersonal influence, and the impact of external stimuli for adoption of changes. Four stages are involved: (1) knowledge of the innovation, (2) persuasion leading to the formation of attitudes about the innovation, (3) a decision to adopt or reject the innovation, and (4) confirmation by peers of the decision. This model can be effective when the organization provides sufficient information, when the information is accessible, and when sound organizational communication networks exist. As society continues to change rapidly, schools will need to use these models more frequently, as constituents will demand greater and greater say.

The research–development–diffusion–utilization model identifies four stages in the change process: (1) research on a given topic; (2) frameworks formed from the research find-ings; (3) diffusion of the new knowledge, product, or techniques; and (4) implementation of the change. This model can be effective when planning on a massive scale is desirable, when rational division of labor and coordination of tasks is essential, when a cooperative arrangement exists among developers, distributors, and users, and when there is sufficient time to discover and implement new products or processes. The model can be particularly useful considering the overwhelming magnitude of change needed in education today.

The linkage model involves reciprocal change. This model emphasizes establishing communications networks among the sources and users of an innovation. The user establishes a reciprocal relationship with outside sources who are experiencing events that correspond with the events experienced by the user. There are three basic elements to this model: (1) identifying potential need for change, (2) establishing effective communication channels, and (3) transmitting new knowledge from researchers to potential users. This model is useful when the school administrator who must effect the change is able to connect with the larger educational community and serve as a change agent through all stages of the change process.

Phases of Educational Change

Effective educational change may come in a variety of sizes and shapes, depending on the system involved and the circumstances. However, the four models discussed above suggest a general model comprised of a combination of several stages: awareness, initiation, implementation, routinization, renewal, and evaluation (Lipham et al., 1985).

The awareness stage of this general model involves the discovery of problems that indicate anomalies in the present goals or programs. Participation of staff is helpful in clarifying goals, identifying discrepancies, defining problems, and identifying tentative alternatives for improving existing conditions. The initiation stage involves evaluation of current conditions and practices in terms of existing goals and exploring both expanded and ultimate goals, along with various means for achieving them. At this point, decisions are made for further action. Implementation is the next stage of this general model. Activities to assist the full staff in understanding and initiating change are begun. Approval, commitment, and cooperation of others are important. The basic problems, goals, and roles of change are identified at this stage. Once the change is implemented, routinization is the next stage. Change agents assist implementers in their efforts. A facilitative, supportive environment must be established. Decision making moves from the group to the individual level. In the renewal stage, implementers develop their ability to maintain the change and continue appropriate use without external help. A supportive climate will encourage high morale. Continuous feedback on the ongoing change continues the change moving toward the desired goal. Evaluation is the feedback loop that reveals ways to improve the change. With utilization of this model, the change process and outcomes are continually monitored and evaluated. Both formative and summative approaches to evaluation are employed. Criteria for evaluation are developed very early in the change process and are used to guide the evaluation efforts. Positive results open the way to routinization and renewal. Negative results point in the direction of other alternatives for change.

Effective Change Agents in Schools

Moving an educational system through a desired change requires the efforts of a leader who functions as a change agent. In most cases the person will either be a formal organizational leader or will be brought in from the external environment. External consultants have proven useful in developing and guiding educational change, particularly when the educational administrators involved have limited experience in implementing change.

A change agent must be able to identify and analyze complex organizational problems, must have insight into the effects of culture and climate on employees, must be able to conceptualize and implement broad plans for change, must be able to share power and develop consensus for collaborative decisions, must be able to maintain the openness of the educational system while monitoring the quality of input, output, and change, and must be able to maintain the positive aspects of the system while working toward improvement through change. Ultimately, since a leader (either system administrator or consultant) by definition does not work in isolation, the change agent must be able to assist others to develop appropriate goals, motivations, and behaviors that will lead to the desired ends. Effective change agents recognize that implementing major change takes time. Enough time must be allowed for modifying existing roles or creating new roles and then internalizing the changes.

As change agent, an educational administrator serves as catalyst, resources linker, solution giver, and process helper (Havelock, 1973; Lippett & Lippett, 1985). A change agent serves as a catalyst because of the built-in inertia of systems, leading to reluctance to change. The change agent can become a source of pressure, helping staff to see the need for change. As a resource linker, the change agent can bring human and nonhuman resources together, either external or internal to the system, and help to make the most effective use of those resources. During the process of change, the change agent can help set objectives, acquire resources, select solutions, adapt solutions, and evaluate the process and results.

Steeples (1990) elaborated on these tasks of the change agent in discussing management of change in higher education. He noted that the issue for leaders in higher education (and, by extension, in educational systems generally) is not whether or not to change, but which changes will be required. A first consideration is to understand the necessity of identifying goals and means to accomplish change. Even when it is clear that external or internal developments dictate a change, it is not always obvious what changes are appropriate. Therefore, decisions about change must be based on a strategic concept. The educational leader must create a strategic vision that must precede and help structure plans for innovation, so that the change meets more than short-term needs. "Properly undertaken, strategic planning can provide the vision which will show the way for meaningful, purposeful institutional change" (Steeples, 1990, p. 103).

Fullan (1991) held that change is a very personal experience, and the teachers who will be affected by change should be actively involved in the change experiences. They should be able to feel that the advantages of the change will exceed the disadvantages. Support for early efforts, which are often awkward, is vital.

Heisey (1997) focused on the building principal as a key change agent in education. According to Goldring and Rallis (1993), such a person should be able to articulate a vision, provide direction, facilitate those working for change, coordinate the effort, and balance forces affecting the effort.

Effective principals initiate change by using teacher leadership, Golding and Rallis said (1993). They do this through motivating teachers by creating a problem-solving climate, using participatory decision making, establishing collegial communication, providing for recognition and rewards, and obtaining the resources necessary to make and maintain the change.

In functioning as an effective change agent, the principal might well consider six questions posited by Fullan (1991): (1) Is the change appropriate to this specific situation? (2) Is the change understood, or do people just think that they understand? (3) Are both the goals and the implementation clear? (4) Will the status quo allow for change? (5) Does the change challenge a person's self-concept? (6) How do we know if the change is valuable?

Planning for a Changing Future in Education

Cunningham (1982) proposed that school administrators or managers of educational systems must work to anticipate the future. As decision makers today, their roles as change agents are critical. "Those who cannot project themselves into the future can only respond to the immediacy of the present, unable to envision and assess possible futures," he warned (p. 246). "The administrator cannot just decide whether or not to make decisions with futurity in mind; he or she must make them by the definition of the role" (p. 247). He argued for the skill of anticipation as a key element in the success of any administrator or manager. Anticipation is the ability to foresee and evaluate the medium- and long-range consequences of current decisions. It is a key to effective planning, and so to effective management of long-range change.

The Fate of Educational Changes

Even with the best intent in the world, no change can be considered permanent. Some take hold, flourish, meet long-term needs, and become an integral part of the original system. Some meet relatively short-term needs and disappear when the need is gone. Some flash brightly, but briefly, and are gone just as quickly.

Hogen (1994) noted that although teachers attend many workshops and training programs, little or no change is evident in the classrooms. Lack of effective instruction in how to use the innovation, and questions about the practicality of a new idea are among the factors that inhibit implementation that she identified.

Goodlad, reviewing the school reforms of the 1960s, commented that although much good could be found in many new practices, many suffered from unrealistic expectations on the part of practitioners, members of the school systems, and members of the general community. He called the period " . . . an extraordinarily innovative period in American education . . . [that]

ended in considerable disillusionment regarding the potency of schools, in large part [because] of unreasonable expectations" (Goodlad; cited in Knezevich, 1984, p. 112).

Problematic Features of Change

As may be assimilated from the brief comment by Goodlad, change may be problematic. As with all theorizing and praxis, models of change may be too rational, too constrained, and too systematic. Some have concluded that our understanding of change may be ill founded (Alderfer, 1977; Pettigrew, 1985).

Major organizational change generates four types of issues, according to Bolman and Deal (1997): (1) it affects a person's ability to feel effective, valued, and in control; (2) it produces uncertainty by disrupting existing roles and working relationships; (3) it creates winners and losers, which has the potential for conflict; and (4) it causes a loss of meaning for people on the receiving end of the change.

A brief review of problematic features follows (Srivastva et al., 1992).

1. Models of change frequently require practitioners to use a process that provides only brief glimpses of reality. Models are often too linear and forgo the dynamics of organizational life. Change may not be the phenomenon that begins, happens, and ends. It may be drastically more disorderly than theorized. Change agents need to be more cognizant of the daily complexity found in organizational life and adapt action methodologies that observe what choices are framed with why choices are made.

2. Equally critical are change scenarios that lack sufficient time horizons. Seldom are change intervention strategies concerned with lengths of time sufficient to display an alternative rationale for the events observed. In most studies of organizational culture, the broad history of basic assumptions is equally important to the constrained views that most models presume. Change must

be immersed in the totality of organizational life: its old practices and its new ones. Both are necessary if cohesion is to be satisfied.

3. Srivastva et al. (1992) also concluded that the study of change in organizations may lack true systemic understanding. More often than not, the study of change excludes interrelationships, interdependencies, environmental contingencies, and relationship factors. The context of change may be as important as identifying common characteristics or factors. As is often the case, the best change programs may be employed without understanding their context and, more inappropriately, with purposeful disregard for important contextual parameters. Organizational change must be linked to its total environment, along with assurance of continuity with social, technical, and ecological consequences of organizational action. Understanding the systemic context of change is paramount to thorough change modeling.

4. Concomitantly, change often is paralyzed in the existing, often limited paradigms. As is often the case in organizational change study, frames are bipolar. There is Theory X or Theory Y. There are democratic or authoritarian styles. In reality, multiplicity is evident, as change strategies often encompass situational or contingency approaches. Even multiplicity can be a trap. It is possible to comprehend what applications are available, but not why. A thorough understanding of change can seemingly be formative only if it is interpretive and interactive in its utilization of knowledge and conversion to praxis.

5. Finally, Srivastva et al. (1992) challenged the deterministic–outcome orientations of change strategies. This may also result from a highly systematic approach to change. Although we view organizations as open systems, we also tend to worry more about the effects of remaining a closed system. In this regard, we rarely mobilize energy to change, but more often draw attention to resistance factors. As a result, our models may be focused on reduction of barriers at the expense of equifinal methodologies.

In the forgoing display of problematic features, a distinctive summons can be noted for a more systemic understanding of change. The organizational world is full of examples that demonstrate the systemic nature of organizational functioning. Schools often exhibit their systemic proclivities despite their traditional bureaucratic form. For example, teachers ignore the mandates of curriculum, with results equal to or better than prescribed by mandates, alternative organizational structures increase teacher and administrator latitudes and work equally well, and new basics (critical thinking and creativity development) create better-rounded graduates. Our attention needs to focus on why these work and where they work as much as on what they are and the processes involved. Just as important, our search for whys must include thinking about new methodologies. As Srivastva et al. (1992) believe: "Our cup is partly full (with useful models, guidelines, and experiences); it is also partly empty" (p. 9).

CASE STUDIES

The Total Quality School

Many change programs have been started in the schools in response to seemingly unlimited claims of poor quality in education today. Total quality management (TQM) is an alternative technique that has come from the business/industrial community, adapted to the educational environment, and adopted in educational institutions. Some see these schools as "the ticket" for the future. However, as education has experimented with TQM, some in the business community have begun to sound alarms. They are labeling TQM efforts in industry as dead, another quick fix that has all but failed.

The following vignette relates the story of a fictitious school system that adopted TQM and sensed some problems. Read the case that follows. When you have finished reading, continue the discussion of the group. What options do you see for them?

TQM at the Falling Rock School District

Bill Shaller and Susan Asad, both principals in the Falling Rock School District, were carpooling together to a special meeting called by Superintendent Jean Kessler. Rumor had it that the superintendent was about to shut down the total quality management program in the district.

"I sure hope we don't go the way quality circles has gone in industry," said Susan. "I hear even industry is beginning to believe that TQM isn't all that it's touted to be. My neighbor was just caught in a restructuring at Xerox. Things were going great for them, but as the bottom fell out of the copier market, corporate management returned to their old habits and cut costs drastically. Their TQM effort wasn't the first to go, but the restructuring wasn't effectively planned and many well-functioning teams were broken up. Management couldn't resolve how to mend the team structures, so they put TQM on hold."

"I heard the same thing," said Bill. "They waited too long and TQM may never be reinstituted there."

At the district administration building they met Mike Rafferty, another principal, who was the designer of the TQM effort that the district had launched just over three years ago. "Good afternoon, you two," greeted Mike. "Wonder what Jean has up her sleeve today?"

"We heard the complete gamut" Susan replied. "Funding is down again, poorer than expected results came in from the spring testing, and the union is raising its hackles again. We even heard she may be considering shutting down TQM and entering another series of downsizing discussions with the school board, unions, and the parents. I sure don't envy what she has to do."

"I hope we can convince her to deal with this differently than she did last time," Mike said, as he opened the door to the superintendent's conference room. Seated in the room were the other eight principals from the district. Superintendent Jean Kessler entered the room.

"Good morning," said Jean as she sat down. "I'm glad you could make it on such short notice. I didn't expect to call this meeting so suddenly, but the school board wanted me to discuss all this with you before any final considerations were proposed. Funding is down drastically from the state this year, and we are not going to be able to continue operations without some pretty heavy downsizing. The form that this will take hasn't been decided yet, but I think you all should assume you'll each feel the effects."

"I've asked some of our educational administrators from the university to stop by this morning, so we could hear from them," continued Jean. "Ah, here they are now." Greetings were again exchanged and the discussion renewed.

"We are really at a loss," said Jean, "as to how to handle these continued problems that surface. Our TQM efforts have had profound effects at nearly all the schools. I think we'd all agree that the program was making good progress. But with an impending downsizing, I can't see how we're going to be able to justify the additional time we spend on extras like our TQM program."

Miles Bromberg, a professor in educational administration, was the first to speak. "I can really relate to what you're saying, Jean. We went through a similar exercise just last year when our enrollment figures declined. Administration and faculty alike voted with their pocketbooks. They couldn't justify the additional workloads they'd agreed to while our administration was having real problems. Rumors were rampant there, too. No pay raises, combining departments, even dropping some programs were considered."

Professor Nell Spires chimed in: "We didn't have anywhere near the investment you've had with TQM in our quality program, so most weren't overly concerned about the program dying. Your investment is much greater. I don't see how you can downsize to meet state goals and at the same time maintain the TQM program."

Mike Rafferty interrupted, as he couldn't listen to much more. "Nell, you and Miles were the real influences behind our adopting the quality focus here in our school district. Your guidance and counsel has been significant, and I, for one, am not ready to abandon those strengths we've achieved simply because there are problems. I think I can speak for most of us when I say that TQM is well liked across the board and most important, has really served to breathe new spirit into many of our teachers and students. They like their new latitudes. Although some of the cost of quality figures haven't been achieved and testing hasn't fully reversed itself, the trends are very positive. I, for one, wouldn't be in favor of dropping TQM. Let's find some other methods of cutting costs!"

Bill Shaller broke in. "I don't know where you're getting your figures from, Mike, but TQM hasn't been a bed of roses. In my school we're still having some significant problems. Having to measure all those new factors is time consuming. Some of the teachers are pretty upset, too. They've been saying for some time that TQM is just another way to get more from them for less."

Susan Asad chided Bill, "We all know that's because of that military command style you haven't been able to shed, Bill. You ought to lighten up some on those poor folks."

Bill, usually able to roll with jabs like this, wasn't as agreeable today. "You all may still be reading my style poorly, but I'm really concerned here. We cannot continue to ask more and more from our people and then turn around and yank the carrot away again."

"Nell and Miles, do either of you have any suggestions about how we can view this differently?" asked Jean Kessler as she regained control of the group.

"There are so many variables here," said Nell. "I think you may just need to take it on the chin with this one. We can't see many options. Even industry is smarting with the recent recession and all. Many have scrapped their TQM programs, returned to more centralization, taken away much of the latitudes they'd passed out, and worse, some are into their second and third downsizing attempts. Times are just tough!"

Jean had hoped for encouragement from the university staff, but didn't get it. "I'd like to see some discussion about this," she said. "I've got to meet with a couple of the school board members in a few minutes on another matter. Could you all begin some deliberation? I'll join in when I return. We've got to find some answers soon!"

Directions

Assume that you are the principal participants at this meeting and, as the superintendent has asked, discuss the situation further. What are the issues before the group? What alternatives are there for dealing with these issues? Is the TQM program at risk? It has only recently been instituted. Why are we so willing to do away with recent change? How does change affect us? How do we better cope with change from an administrative point of view? Can you articulate any change prescriptions that could benefit this group? What effects will be felt throughout the district by teachers? Students? Parents? The community?

The New Dean

When Dr. Jack Prince accepted the new post as Dean of the Business School at State College he knew the tasks ahead of him were formidable. Although he had had experience as a dean, all his experience had been at community colleges. State colleges were different institutions. Jack knew he would be replacing a dean who had stepped down after a vote of no confidence. She would be staying on for the time being, since she was tenured. It was also well known that some of the faculty of the Business School would pose problems that Jack would have to face.

Jack's new management staff included an associate dean and three department chairpersons. Two of the three department chairs had risen recently from within the faculty ranks, and the third chair, Dr. Bob Neuman, had held his position for over 10 years. The school had 45 faculty members, with the largest percentage in Bob Neuman's department.

After the announcement had been made concerning Jack's acceptance as dean, he had met with State College's provost and his long-time mentor, Dr. Amy Kim. Dr. Kim was an old friend and colleague and had herself moved to the state colleges from the community college environment. She knew that environment well. At their first meeting, Dr. Kim warned about some issues Jack would have to work through during the term. She said that the faculty in the Business School were, for the most part, very aggressive educators, liked by the student body, and considered highly competent, as indicated by evaluations of consulting industry. These faculty would be a pleasure to work with. But Bob Neuman led a small group of faculty who had become complacent. Their material was outdated, their participation as consultants was minimal, their classes were avoided by students except when required, and their instruction was less than inspiring. Bob Neuman himself was probably the worst of them all. However, Neuman was influential with his own faculty and exerted methods to control much of the younger faculty. For the past several years, he was also the faculty governance chairman.

Several days into the new fall semester, Jack contemplated how he would cope with his new challenge. It was too early to make any final judgments, but he was beginning to observe indications of exactly what Amy Kim had spoken about. After much thinking, Jack decided he would, in his words, "stir up the pot." During the first faculty meeting of the semester he would announce his intention to create quality teams. His intention was to give more power to all faculty and, at the same time, the student body. He had been a strong advocate of the quality movement in the community college environment, and he would begin developing exactly that in the state college.

Directions

This case poses some typical problems faced by a new administrator. Use the following questions to begin your discussion.

1. What do you think about the "pot stirring" the new dean decided upon?

2. How would you proceed in this situation? What would you have done?

3. Identify the following in the case: the change agent, potential supporters, and potential dissenters.

4. Identify a task that you as new dean might want to accomplish with your faculty. How would you go about this? What part might quality management play? How would you deal with potential supporters? Potential dissenters?

Discussion Case

A study in 1979 by the education section of the World Future Society and Old Dominion University developed a taxonomy of issues that were believed central to the future of education (Allen & Dede, 1979). These issues were grouped under six headings: responsibilities of different agents, content, process, improvement of the profession, interaction with the individual, and interface with society. Within these six headings there were 23 issues that can be examined when considering potential future educational changes.

Questions

1. Responsibilities of different agents

   a. *Schooling:* Rapid technological innovations and unstable financial and social conditions will require great sophistication and flexibility in education. Do schools, as now defined and operated, provide the best delivery system for educating children and adults?

   b. *Families:* In recent history, both the extended and the nuclear family structure have come under considerable strain because of changes in social values, and many educational tasks once the responsibility of the family are now seen as the function of the school system. Regardless of the allocation of responsibility, how can the school system work toward a position of educational partnership with the family?

   c. *Communities:* Should communities assume major educational responsibilities? If so, which ones?

   d. *Media:* Drastic changes in existing media delivery seem probable. To what extent will schools increase reliance on media to shape their concepts, programming, and delivery?

   e. *Industries/professions:* How can training best be structured to foresee and address short- and long-term variations in career goals? How should counseling best be done to maximize fit between individual abilities and interests and the types of work society needs? How should society coordinate training agents so as to minimize total cost?

2. Content

   a. *Social responsibility:* What values and attitudes are vital to successful cultural evolution into the twenty-first century, and by which educational agent is each best conveyed? How can and should instruction be individualized to respond to the diverse array of attitudes and values held by learners?

   b. *Basic cognitive skills:* What cognitive skills are needed by all citizens, and by which educational agent is each best conveyed? How can the expression of creativity be encouraged?

   c. *Basic affective skills:* Recent rapid and unexpected changes have caused many people to feel stressed, overwhelmed, and unable to control their futures. How can affective skills build self-awareness, personal esteem, and ability to resist diversity? How should the affective domain be interfaced with social responsibility?

d. *Values:* Should the educational system deliberately communicate values and attitudes beyond those needed for socialization? By what means? Is this desirable if at all possible? How should values education be integrated with instruction for social responsibility?

e. *Future thinking:* World support systems have become interdependent before world cultural systems have recognized this shift. How can education best convey an understanding of ecological, cultural, and social interdependence? In what ways should education build toward a "global consciousness"? To what extent can education prepare citizens for issues that may first become important in five years? A decade? A generation?

3. Process

a. *Diversity of learning:* Each learner has different needs, expectations, capacities, life experiences, and readiness—and all these attributes vary with time. To what extent and in which areas of instruction should individualized learning packages be developed? What needs to be done toward furthering understanding of the development and cultural basis of learning styles?

b. *Educational technology:* What major role can technology legitimately play in the educative process? What effect will large-scale uniform instructional programming have, and to what extent is specialization and individualization of technological instruction possible given high software production costs? What new types of training for educators will be required?

c. *Evaluation:* Evaluation in education is concerned with providing feedback on performance. For each type of educational agent, which evaluation techniques are most accurate, and in which manner should these be incorporated? How can evaluation validity be maximized? What are the best strategies for communicating results? By what methods can evaluation results of "work in progress" be incorporated into decision structures?

4. Improvement of the profession

a. *Professionalism:* How can the scope of education be more clearly delineated so that a more detailed analysis of the nature of the profession can be made? By what means can the most effective practitioner techniques be identified? What role differentiations are appropriate within the field, and what standards of technical and ethical training should each role meet? How can recognition of the importance and difficulty of education be increased?

b. *Staff development:* How can the image of the profession be improved? Given unionization, how can procedures be developed for removal of practitioners who have ceased to be effective? How can burnout be prevented? For each educational agent, how might professional development take place?

c. *Professional governance:* Leadership and cooperation are needed to meet the tremendous responsibilities and financial challenges society will place on education (in the foreseeable future). How can different educational agents (schooling system, family, community, media, industry) develop a framework for collaboration on common issues? What types of authority and power distribution systems will function most effectively?

5. Interaction with the individual

a. *Lifelong learning:* What types of educational experiences are important during infancy and early childhood, and by which educational agents would these best be delivered? What instructional systems can most effectively serve the needs of people and society for retraining, more sophisticated citizenship, and social interaction? How can instruction facilitate the fusion of work and leisure styles? By what means can this expansion in traditional instructional services best be staffed and financed?

b. *Credentialing:* Credentialing is a means of certifying future performance. How can educational credentialing systems be made a more effective means of determining quality without eliminating the diversity and individual uniqueness valued in a free society?

c. *Special needs:* Education is provided primarily for the middle-range-of-talent, physically and emotionally healthy individual in the majority culture. In as diverse a society as ours, this assumption means that many people are ill served by educational institutions. How can instructional settings be structured to incorporate the maximum range of learner needs, so that through direct experience our culture will lose its fear of physical, sexual, intellectual, behavioral, emotional, linguistic, racial, cultural, and chronological differences? How can learners with special needs best be given a sense of personal worth? At what point does the responsibility of educational systems cease for learners for whom no instructional strategy seems to function?

d. *Equity:* What biases in each type of educational agent need to be removed, and how can these agents act to promote equity of access, outcome, and staffing? What are the limits (if any) to the pluralism for which education is responsible? How can equality of outcome best be interpreted so as to allow for maximization of individual potential?

6. Interface with society

a. *Relation to other human services:* The field of human services is split into numerous specialties that encourage viewing a person only from certain perspectives rather than as a total human being. How can educational and other social services best be coordinated, and under what overall authority? How can administrative governance systems be evolved that will transcend the problems of hierarchical authority and allow human services to view the individual holistically?

b. *Funding:* What is the best mixture of educational funding sources: individual, local, state, national, international? Can new sources of funding be generated? How should resources be allocated among the educational agents? What should be the relationship between funding and policy control? How can the costs and benefits of education be delineated to society so that informed expenditure decisions can be made? What economies of scale in education are significant? What is the most likely means for improving educational productivity?

c. *External controls:* How can a coherent picture of the accomplishments and limits of the educational system, and the trade-offs between its duties and costs, be communicated to the public? What mix of governmental, community, family, and individual input should shape educational policy? Can these various groups be organized to coordinate demands and evaluation procedures, and what types of assessment can best be made from outside the profession? [The above excerpted from Allen and Dede (1979).]

Directions

This case provides an opportunity to develop a team approach to change. Utilize the case to formulate and create a plan for change for a specified school in a specified community, or for a school district.

References

Alderfer, C. (1977). Organizational development. *Annual Review of Psychology, 28,* 197–223.

Allen, D., & Dede, C. (1979). *An invitation to participate in creating better futures for education.* Norfolk, VA: Old Dominion University Press.

Basom, R. E., & Crandall, D. P. (1991). Implementing a redesign strategy: Lessons from educational change. *Educational Horizons, 69*(2), 73–77.

Beckhard, R., & Harris, R. T. (1977). *Organizational transitions: Managing complex change.* Reading, MA: Addison-Wesley.

Beer, M., Eisenstat, R., & Spector, B. (1990, November–December). Why change programs don't produce change. *Harvard Business Review, 90*(6), 158–166.

Bell, D. (1976). *The coming of the post-industrial society.* New York: Basic Books.

Bennis, W. (1966). *Changing organizations: Essays on the development and evolution of human organization.* New York: McGraw-Hill.

Bolman, L. G., & Deal, T. E. (1997). *Reframing organizations: Artistry, choice, and leadership* (2nd ed.). San Francisco: Jossey-Bass.

Bushnell, D. S. (1971). A systematic strategy for school renewal. In D. Bushnell & D. Rappaport, (Eds.), *Planned change in education: A systems approach.* New York: Harcourt Brace Jovanovich.

Caldwell, M. S. (1968, October). An approach to the assessment of educational planning. *Educational Technology, 8*(19), 5–12.

Cetron, M., & Gayle, M. (1991). *Educational resistance: Our schools at the turn of the century.* New York: St. Martin's Press.

Chin, R. (1976). The utility of systems models and developmental models for practitioners. In W. Bennis, K. D. Benne, R. Chin, & K. E. Corey (Eds.), *The planning of change* (2nd ed.). New York: Holt, Rinehart & Winston.

Chin, R., & Benne, K. S. (1969). General strategies for effecting change in human systems. In W. G. Bennis, K. D. Benne, & R. Chin (Eds.), *The planning of change* pp. 297–312. New York: Holt, Rinehart & Winston.

Chin, R., & Benne, K. S. (1976). General strategies for effecting changes in human systems. In W.

Bennis, K. Benne, R. Chin, and K. E. Corey (Eds.), *The planning of change* (2nd ed.). New York: Holt, Rinehart & Winston.

Connor, P. E., & Lake, K. L. (1988). *Managing organizational change.* New York: Praeger.

Cunningham, W. G. (1982). *Systematic planning for educational change.* Mountain View, CA: Mayfield.

Fombrun, C. J. (1992). *Turning points creating strategic change in corporations.* New York: McGraw-Hill.

French, W. L., & Bell, C. H. Jr. (1973). *Organization development.* Upper Saddle River, NJ: Prentice Hall.

Fullan, M. (1982). *The meaning of educational change.* New York: Teachers College Press, Columbia University.

Fullan, M. (1991). *The new meaning of educational change.* New York: Teachers College Press, Columbia University.

Goldring, E. B., & Rallis, S. F. (1993). Principals of dynamic schools: Taking charge of change. Newbury Park, CA: Corwin Press.

Goodlad, J. I. (1984). The dynamics of educational change: Toward responsive schools. In S. J. Knezevich (Ed.), *Administration of public education* (4th ed.). New York: Harper & Row.

Grenier, L. E. (1989). Common approaches to change. In R. McLennan (Ed.), *Managing organizational change* (pp. 138–140). Upper Saddle River, NJ: Prentice Hall.

Hahn, D. (1991). Strategic management: Tasks and challenges of the 1990's. *Long Range Planning, 24*(1), 26–39.

Hanson, E. M. (1985). *Educational administration and organizational behavior* (2nd ed.). Boston: Allyn & Bacon.

Harvey, T. R. (1990). *Checklist for change.* Boston: Allyn & Bacon.

Havelock, R. G. (1973). *The change agent's guide to innovation in education.* Upper Saddle River, NJ: Educational Technology.

Heisey, D. L. (1997). *Factors affecting the change process in three high schools that implemented intensive scheduling.* Unpublished dissertation, Widener University, Chester, PA.

Hersey, P., & Blanchard, K. H. (1988). *Management of organizational behavior utilizing human resources* (5th ed.). Upper Saddle River, NJ: Prentice Hall.

Hodgkinson, C. (1991). *Educational leadership: The moral art.* New York: State University of New York Press.

Hogen, E. A. O. (1994). *Exploring teacher change: A study of five first grade teachers immersed in three major areas of change.* Unpublished dissertation, University of South Dakota, Vermillion.

Huse, E. F. (1975). *Organizational development and change.* St. Paul, MN: West.

Huse, E. F., & Cummings, T. G. (1985). *Organizational development and change* (3rd ed.). St. Paul, MN: West.

Johansen, J. H. (1967). The relationship between teachers' perceptions of influence in local curriculum decision-making and curriculum implementation. *Journal of Educational Research, 61*(2), 81–88.

Kanter, R. M. (1983). *The change masters: Innovation and entrepreneurship in the American corporation.* New York: Simon and Schuster.

Kanter, R. M., Stein, B. A., & Jick, T. D. (1992). *The challenge of organizational change.* New York: Free Press.

Kohl, J. W. (1968, November). A conceptual tool for implementing change. *Journal of Secondary Education, 43*(7), 324–325.

Kostler, P. (1973). The elements of social action. In R. H. Lauer (Ed.), *Perspective on social change.* Boston: Allyn & Bacon.

Kowalski, T. J., & Reitzug, U. C. (1993). *Contemporary school administration: An introduction.* New York: Longman.

Kreitner, R., & Kinicki, A. (1989). *Organizational behavior.* Boston: BPI/Irwin.

Lauer, R. H. (1973). *Perspective on social change.* Boston: Allyn & Bacon.

Lewin, K. (1951). *Field theory in social sciences.* New York: Harper & Row.

Lindbloom, C. E. (1965). *The intelligence of democracy decision making through mutual adjustments.* New York: Free Press.

Lipham, J. M., Rankin, R., & Hoeh, J. (1985). *The principalship: Concepts, competencies, and cases.* New York: Longman.

Lippett, G. L., Langseth, P., & Mossop, J. (1985). *Implementing organizational change: A practical guide to managing change efforts.* San Francisco: Jossey-Bass.

Lippett, G. L., & Lippett, R. (1985). The consulting function of the human resource development professional. In L. Nadler (Ed.), *The handbook of human resource development* (pp. 5.1–5.27). New York: Wiley.

London, M. (1988). *New roles and innovation strategies for human resource professionals.* San Francisco: Jossey-Bass.

Lorsch, J. W., & Trooboff, S. (1989). Two universal models. In R. McLennan (Ed.), *Managing organizational change* (pp. 68–75). Upper Saddle River, NJ: Prentice Hall.

Lunenberg, F. C., & Ornstein, A. C. (1991). *Educational administration: Concepts and practices.* Belmont, CA: Wadsworth.

Mannheim, K. (1940). *Man and society in an age of reconstruction: Studies in modern social structure.* New York: Harcourt & Brace.

Mauriel, J. J. (1989). *Strategic leadership for schools: Creating and sustaining productive change.* San Francisco: Jossey-Bass.

Mazarella, J., & Grundy, T. (1988). Portrait of a leader. In S. C. Smith & P. K. Piele (Eds.), *School leaders' handbook for excellence* (2nd ed.). Eugene, OR: ERIC Clearinghouse on Educational Management, College of Education, University of Oregon.

Meyerson, M., & Banfield, E. C. (1964). *Politics, planning, and the public interest: The case of public housing in Chicago.* New York: Free Press of Glencoe.

Miles, M. B. (1964). Educational innovation: The nature of the problem. In M. B. Miles (Ed.), *Innovation in education.* New York: Teachers College Press, Columbia University.

Millard, R. M. (1991). *Today's myths and tomorrow's realities: Overcoming obstacles to academic leadership in the 21st century.* San Francisco: Jossey-Bass.

Miskel, C., & Ogawa, R. (1988). Work motivation, job satisfaction, and climate. In N. J. Boyan (Ed.), *Handbook of research on educational administration.* New York: Longman.

Monahan, W. G., & Hengst, H. R. (1982). *Contemporary educational administration.* New York: Macmillan.

Mort, P. R. (1962, October). Studies in educational administration from the Institute of Administrative Research. *IRA Research Bulletin, 3*(1), 1–8.

Mort, P. R., & Ross, D. H. (1957). *Principles of school administration*. New York: McGraw-Hill.

Nutt, P. (1986, June). Tactics of implementation. *Academy of Management Journal.*

Owens, R. G. (1987). *Organizational behavior in education* (3rd ed.). Upper Saddle River, NJ: Prentice Hall.

Perrow, C. (1961). An analysis of goals in complex organizations. *American Sociological Review, 26,* 854–866.

Pettigrew, A. (1985). *The awakening giant: Continuity and change in imperial chemical industries.* Oxford: Blackwell.

Pfeffer, J. & Salancik, G. R. (1978). *The external control of organizations.* New York: Harper & Row.

Ross, M. G. (1967). *Community organization: Theory and principles.* New York: Harper & Row.

Rossman, G. B., Corbett, H. D., & Firestone, W. A. (1988). *Change and effectiveness in schools: A cultural perspective.* New York: State University of New York Press.

Sarason, S. B. (1971). *The culture of the school and the problem of change.* Boston: Allyn & Bacon.

Schein, E. (1969). *Process consultations: Its role in organization development.* Reading, MA: Addison-Wesley.

Senge, P. (1990). The leader's new work: Building learning organizations. *Sloan Management Review, 32,*(1), 17–23.

Sheive, L. T. (1981). *A test and reformulation of three developmental models of organizational change in an organization of relative zero growth.* Unpublished dissertation, State University of New York at Buffalo.

Simek, R. (1997). *An investigation of the relationship between specific organizational variables and integration of emotionally disturbed and neurologically impaired students.* Unpublished dissertation, State University of New York at Buffalo.

Simsek, H., & Louis, K. S. (1994, November–December) Organizational change as paradigm shift: Analysis of the change process in a large public university. *Journal of Higher Education, 65*(6), 670.

Srivastva, S., Fry, R. E., & Associates. (1992). *Executive and organizational continuity: Managing the paradoxes of stability and change.* San Francisco: Jossey-Bass.

Stanislao, J., & Stanislao, B. C. (1983, July–August). Dealing with resistance to change. *Business Horizons,* 74–78.

Steeples, D. W. (Ed.). (1990). *Managing change in higher education.* San Francisco: Jossey-Bass.

Stogdill, R. (1974). *Handbook of leadership.* New York: Free Press.

Sumner, W. G. (1914). *War and other essays.* New Haven, CT: Yale University Press.

Thompson, V. A. (1965). Bureaucracy and innovation. *Administrative Science Quarterly, 10*(1), 1–20.

Vroom, V. H. & Yetton, P. W. (1973). *Leadership and decision making.* Pittsburgh, PA: University of Pittsburgh Press.

Walton, R. E. (Ed.). (1965). *A behavioral theory of labor negotiations: An analysis of a social interaction system.* New York: McGraw-Hill.

Warren, R. L. (1977). *Social change and human purpose: Toward understanding and action.* Chicago: Rand McNally College.

Watson, G. (1969). Resistance to change. In W. G. Bennis, K. D. Benne, & R. Chin (Eds.), *The planning of change* (2nd ed. pp. 488–498). New York: Holt, Rinehart & Winston.

Waugh, R. F., & Punch, K. F. (1987). Teacher receptivity to system-wide change in the implementation stage. *Review of Educational Research, 57*(3), 237–254.

Williams, E. (1972). Changing systems and behavior. In *Contemporary readings in organizational behavior.* New York: McGraw-Hill.

Yukl, G. A. (1981). *Leadership in organizations.* Upper Saddle River, NJ: Prentice Hall.

PART V

Strategy Formulation and Implementation

It is essential that members of an organization share a common understanding of the organization's purpose, values, and beliefs. Similarly, an essential function of leadership is to articulate and personify those values and beliefs. In Part V we emphasize traditional strategic and tactical planning arenas. We also speak to the effects of the information age, technological progression, and new approaches to preparing the educational practitioner for the future.

Chapter 12: The Impact of Universal Principles, Social Expectations, and Personal Values on Leadership. In this chapter we survey various philosophical points of view and then turn to social science perspectives on values. A person's philosophy determines how he or she interprets what is experienced. To be an effective tool of administrative behavior, however, it is preferable for this philosophy to be understood and intellectualized and for the values and beliefs that it implies to be made explicit. In this chapter we examine the importance of a person's values and beliefs and how these are integrated into the visions, missions, and goals of an organization. The role of megavalues held by society as a whole in shaping the policy-making process is explored.

Chapter 13: Strategy Formation and Planning at the District and School Levels. In Chapter 13 we seek to produce an understanding of how educational institutions develop a sense of direction and purpose, make decisions about organizing themselves in order to realize their purposes, and allocate resources available to them to further their purposes. Although the process is usually referred to as strategic planning, we distinguish between strategy formation and planning as two separate but equally important procedures. Planning is a convergent, logical process that attempts to formalize decision making, strategy making, and management through decomposition, articulation, and rationalization. Strategy formulation is a spontaneous, creative, and divergent process that cannot happen in isolation or on schedule and cannot be programmed. Because planning is an analytical process and strategy formulation is a synthesizing process, they must happen separately. We take the position that strategy is not the consequence of planning; rather, planning takes place within the framework formed by strategy. Planning helps to translate intended strategies into realized ones by taking the steps necessary for effective implementation.

Chapter 14: The Allocation of Resources for Education: Adequacy, Equity, and Efficiency.

An essential part of planning and implementation is allocation of resources. Demands for resources always exceed their availability. Therefore, it is incumbent upon society to use available resources to maximize productivity within the context of organizational priorities. In this chapter we address issues concerning the allocation of resources to the educational sector and within educational enterprises. Studies relating to the efficiency of public schools indicate with great consistency that schools are not using to full advantage resources entrusted to them. Other studies show that there are great inequities in the distribution of resources among schools and school districts.

We conclude that the greatest allocation problems facing educational leadership today and for years to come is designing instructional systems that are educationally effective and economically efficient. The second most urgent problem is improving equity in the distribution of resources to schools so that all children may have access to good facilities, competent instruction, and state-of-the-art materials and equipment. Equity issues are placed second only because of the overwhelming evidence that more resources are unlikely to improve achievement of at-risk children as schools are currently organized.

Chapter 15: The Role of Information and Technology.

The availability of appropriate information is critical to the development of wise strategies, effective plans, and efficient allocation of resources. The nature and importance of information systems to these processes is the subject considered in this chapter. Note is also taken of the astounding advances in information and communication technologies. The relevance of these changes to the organization of schools, a major segment of the information industry, is explored. Particular attention is paid to the changing nature of leadership as information technology has an impact across educational systems.

The Impact of Universal Principles, Social Expectations, and Personal Values on Leadership

Philosophy, in its broadest meaning, is a systematic attempt to make sense out of our individual and collective human experience (De George, 1990). The philosopher's primary intellectual tool is reason. Ethics is that part of philosophy concerned with morality, a complex of ideals showing how people should relate to one another in particular situations, to principles of conduct guiding those relationships, and to the kind of reasoning that one engages in when thinking about such ideals and principles (L. M. Smith, 1990).

Practically all of our activities occur within the context of decisions made about good and bad, right and wrong, or better and worse. Behavior is therefore a constant reflection of beliefs about how the world is structured and decisions are made, and how actions taken are based, implicitly or explicitly, on those philosophical considerations (Foster, 1986). Everyone has a philosophical view of life even though it may not have been thoroughly thought through and articulated (Nyberg, 1974). To be an effective guide to administrative behavior, however, it is best if this philosophy is understood and intellectualized. Such an understanding permits a leader to act consistently on pertinent issues and to reflect critically upon those actions. For this reason, it is important that persons in leadership roles learn "to do" philosophy for themselves rather than leave it by default to be done by others.

According to Hodgkinson (1983), the essence of the art of administration is the manipulation of people by people about goals.

He sees the most persuasive reason for doing philosophy in the field of executive action as being derived from the fact that administrators possess power; they make decisions that affect other people. "If morality is interpreted as a concern for others, then it follows that administration is a peculiarly moral activity" (p. 29).

> The field of executive action and the administrative endeavor which embraces it make philosophical demands. It is the highest function of the executive to develop a deep understanding of himself and his fellows, a knowledge of human nature which includes motivation but reaches beyond into the domain of value possibilities. . . . At its lowest level, organizational life is sort of a daily combat. Even here, however, the deadliest weapons in the administrative armory are philosophical: the skills of logical and critical analysis, conceptual synthesis, value analysis and commitment, rhetoric and most fundamentally, the depth understanding of human nature. So in the end philosophy becomes intrinsically practical. (Hodgkinson, 1983, p. 53)

Preparation programs for school administrators have been roundly criticized for emphasizing organizational, behavioral, and managerial theories while neglecting contextual considerations of culture, politics, morals, and ethics (Bolman & Deal, 1995; Foster, 1986; Osterman & Kottkamp, 1993). Cambron-McCabe (1993) saw in the current school debate a challenge to the technocratic perspective that has traditionally characterized administrative preparation programs. She pointed out that traditional programs taught administrators that organizations are rational, mechanistic structures that operate in a bureaucratic fashion. The programs focused on operational tasks, training administrators as management functionaries; consideration of moral, ethical, and values dimensions of leadership were largely absent. She observed that "[o]ne of the stances of the current reform effort is to make visible that leadership involves moral choices, not simply an adherence to technicism" (p. 157).

Sergiovanni (1992) holds a similar position. He charged that the dominating emphasis in contemporary programs on rationality, logic, objectivity, the importance of self-interest, explicitness, individuality, and detachment causes us to neglect the importance of group membership, sense and meaning, morality, self-sacrifice, duty, and obligation as additional values. "[W]e have come to view leadership as behavior rather than action, as something psychological rather than spiritual, as having to do with persons rather than ideas" (p. 3). To overcome this bias, he believes that it is necessary to give more attention in the preparatory curriculum to concepts of professional and moral authority.

The National Policy Board for Educational Administration (1989) recommended that the curriculum preparing school administrators be designed to provide frameworks and tools to assist students in assessing the moral and ethical implications of the decisions they make. According to the board, students of school administration must come to understand the concept of public trust and to realize how values affect behaviors and outcomes.

The board also recommended that students need to be encouraged to examine their own belief systems, their reasons for wanting to be administrators, and their images of the mission of schooling as a social process. Daresh (1988) referred to such understandings as *professional formation,* defined as an effort to enable a person to become aware of his or her own personal values and assumptions regarding the formal role of a school administrator (Daresh & Playko, 1992, p. 54). Professional formation addresses personal growth and development in the training of school administrators. It includes mentoring or coaching by experienced administrators and university faculty, the identification of one's personal administrative style, development of an ability to reflect in action, and commitment to constant self-preparation and taking moral and ethical stances.

In a similar vein, Sergiovanni (1984b) used the term *platform* as the articulation of one's principles into an operational framework. The platform governs a person's outlook and behavior in that it represents a set of criteria and an implicit standard from which decisions are made.

In studying trends in the reform of school administrator preparation programs, Murphy (1993) concluded that there is a new and general concern for including ethics in the curriculum. He hypothesizes that underlying this concern is a shared understanding among program staff that sound professional judgment and conduct are contingent on sound ethical judgment and conduct and that, in on-the-job contexts, routine practical decisions and ethical decisions are often indistinguishable. More specifically, these reformed programs acknowledge the fact that administrators are representatives of values and that the responsibility of principals to their students, teachers, and communities is to provide leadership based on an informed ethical reflection about education and public life. Murphy believes that unless leaders develop a moral and ethical conscience, they will find it difficult to make decisions and will lose a sense of purpose.

In this chapter we look at the importance of ethical considerations in the practice of educational leadership. We begin by describing selected philosophical views of the world and how they might influence executive behavior. Then, drawing also from social science perspectives, we focus on values and value hierarchies as they are found in individuals and organizations. How leaders analyze the world in the context of value systems is described. In the final section, we show how values in the form of metavalues shape the perception of reality in organizations and challenge administrative leaders to accept those value parameters or transform them to direct change.

Philosophical Guides to Leadership

To be effective, administrative behavior must rest on certain philosophical assumptions about such fundamental considerations as human nature, the nature of reality, conditions of knowledge, and the nature of value. Further, such behavior must be in harmony with great cultural movements and the ideas that impel them— ideas that are inevitably philosophical in character (Graff, Street, Kinbrough, & Dykes, 1966). Today's leaders must develop a holistic perspective that enables them to comprehend the myriad forces and conditions affecting important social, economic, scientific, and governmental institutions.

School administrators today are faced with pressures from all sides. Bewildering expectations are placed on the schools and the people who staff them. There is bitter conflict over what the purposes of education should be and how educational services should be delivered. The function of administration in relation to educational leadership is not clearly understood. School administrators desiring to provide effective leadership need a philosophical reference point from which to evaluate and base their actions. Without such a reference point, the administrator drifts like a rudderless ship on a stormy sea. In this section we provide a brief overview of some of the major philosophical systems that have been, or are, particularly influential in shaping our culture and the lives of individuals: idealism, liberalism, positivism and postpositivism, pragmatism, existentialism, critical theory, and constructivism. One system is not necessarily better than another, but the orientation to life and the behavior of a person subscribing to one system will be different from that of a person subscribing to another. Personal philosophies tend to be eclectic, having elements of several of the basic systems.

The roots of idealism can be traced back to ancient Greek scholars, who conceptualized the idea that there exists a system of perfect ideas that should serve to guide human decisions and behavior. Being highly compatible with the Judeo-Christian tradition enhanced idealism's influence on Western culture. Liberalism, which emphasizes individual freedom, began to emerge along with rationalism, scientific inquiry, free-market capitalism, and a growing middle class in the seventeenth and eighteenth centuries. It subscribes to universal natural laws and provided the intellectual basis for several political revolutions during the eighteenth and nineteenth centuries, including the American Revolution. It is largely the philosophy of liberalism that is expressed in the Declaration of Independence and the U.S. Constitution.

Positivism and postpositivism have dominated intellectual thought from the late nineteenth century until today. Both stem from the philosophy of science and subscribe to a reality that is independent of the human observer, but discoverable through science. The hegemony of postpositivism seems to be waning at the beginning of the twenty-first century, as we discuss at the end of this section. The claim to objectivity by the postpositivists (i.e., the separation of fact and value) is currently being challenged by critical theorists and constructivists. Critical theorists continue to hold along with postpositivists a belief in a reality independent of human experience; however, critical theorists reject the idea of the objectivity of science and claim that all inquiry is mediated by value considerations. Constructivists also reject the objectivity of science, and further, they reject the concept of any reality beyond that of individual human experience.

Pragmatism and existentialism are included as examples of two highly influential philosophies of the twentieth century. Pragmatism has much in common with postpositivism, but emphasizes the importance of utility or consequences in determining what is truth—or reality. John Dewey was a prominent pragmatist and, through him, pragmatism has had a strong influence on thinking about education—the progressive education movement in particular. Existentialism reached its zenith of influence beginning with World War I and continuing for several years following World War II. It has much in common with constructivism, accepting no reality other than individual human experience. It urges people to assume full responsibility for their own actions.

Table 12.1 has been developed as a summary and guide for the reader through the discussion on philosophies that follows. The table presents abbreviated statements for each philosophy considered as to how it tends to view the nature of reality (ontology), the relationship between the knower and the known (epistemology), conceptions of the desirable (values), and the nature of the schooling experience likely to be preferred.

Idealism

Idealism dominated learned thought until late in the nineteenth century, and it is still deeply ingrained in the thinking and institutions of Western civilization. There are many variations of idealistic thought, often identified with their originators, philosophers such as Plato, Kant, and Hegel.

The philosophy of idealism conceives the universe as being dualistic in nature. It assumes that the ultimate reality consists of a system of great ideas that transcend everyday experiences and are universal, enduring, and absolute. The world of everyday experience that is open to empirical or sensory exploration is not believed to be the real world, but a reflection of it. The ultimate reality is a system of perfect ideas. The world of everyday experiences is considered to be a world of illusions; the *real* world can only be reached through pure reason, intuition, or through revelation in the case of religion. Similarly, idealists assume a dualistic nature of humankind, the body and the mind (or soul), the latter being more important.

The elevation of universal truths over experience differentiates idealism from all other schools of philosophy. The idealist believes that absolute knowledge is obtained through the exercise of pure reason uncontaminated by empirical data. Thus, deductive logic becomes the primary intellectual tool in the search for truth. Since truth is not seen to exist in the world of experience, studying phenomena of this world is not a necessary source of knowledge. The idealist holds that the validity of truth is tested through one or more rigorous systems of logic (Graff et al., 1966); that is, does it stand the test of logic by the great minds of the ages? The application of idealism to education is best illustrated by the classical tradition, which gives priority to the "training of the mind."

The idealist assumes that there are ultimate and absolute values. The values of greatest worth are those that are identical to "truth." These true values are not to be questioned but to be accepted as guides for living. Idealism seeks the maintenance of the status quo; in the face of great social, economic, political, and technological changes, it looks to the past for solutions. Idealism resists change.

Liberalism

The central idea of liberalism is liberty; but the liberal's view of liberty is not absolute. Liberalism strives for a society that acts together freely to ensure the welfare of the many using methods that fortify the freedoms of individuals, enabling them to fulfill their potentials as each sees fit. Freedom is sought as a method and a policy of government, as an organizing principle in society, and as a way of life for the individual.

The golden age of liberalism dates roughly between the era of the French philosophers (ca. 1750) and the start of World War I. Many of the founders of the United States (e.g., Thomas Jefferson and Benjamin Franklin) were committed to liberalism, and the Declaration of Independence and U.S. Constitution are political expressions of liberalism. The emphasis of liberalism on liberty and freedom aligns naturally with economic concepts of free-market capitalism;

Table 12.1
Summary of the Beliefs of Selected Philosophies on Fundamental Philosophical Questions and the Type of Schooling Most Compatible with Those Beliefs

	Questions			
Philosophy	*Ontology:* What is the nature of the knowable "reality"?	*Epistemology:* What is the nature of the relationship between the knower and the known?	*Values: Conceptions of the desirable*	*Schooling preference*
Idealism	Universal, enduring, and absolute ideas that transcend everyday experience	Experienced world is a reflection of reality; humankind is dualistic in nature (i.e., the spiritual and the physical); understanding is gained from deductive logic removed from everyday experience	That which is identical with universal truths; coherence; stability; great minds	Training of the mind (i.e, the classical tradition), emphasizing Socratic Method; imitation; dialectics Liberal education to sharpen the tools of reason and to further the development of individuals; objective, experimental, and observational techniques
Liberalism	Universal laws rooted in nature; natural rights discoverable through science	Human and physical actions operate according to natural law; understanding is gained through rational inquiry	Liberty; freedom; reason/rationality/ scholarship; goodness; tolerance; human perfectibility	
Realism, postpositivism and logical positivism	Reality is in and of this world—governed by universal law which can be discovered through empirical research	*Objectivist:* value is separate from fact; human and physical interactions operate according to universal law; understanding is gained through empirical verification/scientific method	That which is in harmony with discoverable universal law/theory; objectivity; empiricism; reason/rationality/ scholarship	Clinical/laboratory/ experiential learning; basic skills

353

Table 12.1 (cont.)
Summary of the Beliefs of Selected Philosophies on Fundamental Philosophical Questions and the Type of Schooling Most Compatible with Those Beliefs

	Questions			
Philosophy	*Ontology:* What is the nature of the knowable "reality"?	*Epistemology:* What is the nature of the relationship between the knower and the known?	*Values:* Conceptions of the desirable	*Schooling preference*
Pragmatism	Truth is known though its practical consequences; it is a product of social practices	Knowledge is constructed in the minds of humankind through their collective experience; understanding is gained through rational inquiry/scientific method	Utility; experience; new ideas and newly discovered facts; reason/rationality/scholarship	Clinical/laboratory; problem-solving experiential learning; progressive education
Existentialism	The world is as it is experienced and interpreted by each person; there are no universal laws or principles of importance to humankind	Meaning and purpose are defined by each person through free choice; understanding is gained through introspection to find guidance and direction	Autonomy; authenticity; personal freedom and responsibility; human will; introspection	Arts and humanities; concern with emotions and feeling; personal relationship between teacher and student; enhance individuality
Critical theory	There is a reality independent of human existence, but it may never be fully understood	*Subjectivist:* values mediate inquiry; paradigms are human construction; understanding is gained through dialogic and transformative processes	Autonomy; responsibility, emancipation; commitment; reason/rationality/scholarship	The elimination of false consciousness and facilitating transformation
Constructivism	Socially and experientially based mental constructions by the person who holds them	*Subjectivist:* values mediate inquiry; understanding is gained through dialogical process between the self-understanding person and that which is encountered	Relativism; social consensus; personal experience; solidarity	Experiential, multicultural, self-reflection, relativistic, continuing

thus, it has had a particularly strong appeal to the middle class and to business interests. Liberalism experienced a relative decline in popularity and influence after World War I. With the recent failure of monolithic totalitarian and communist states, liberalism has gained new credibility and vitality. Among the European scholars contributing to liberal thought have been Voltaire, Locke, Rousseau, Hume, Kant, Adam Smith, and J. S. Mill.

In addition to holding liberty as a central value, liberalism perceives human beings as equipped with reason and goodness and endowed with certain natural rights, presented in the Declaration of Independence as "life, liberty and the pursuit of happiness." It is humankind's meddling with the natural order which, according to liberals, accounts for social disorder; it is the social structures of customs, traditions, and institutions that corrupt people. Therefore, for the most part, the best course of action is to leave things alone.

Other central concepts of liberalism include the creation of social conditions that allow people to maximize their freedom to think, to believe, to discuss, to act, to organize, to work, to carry on commerce, and to choose their rulers and their form of government—changing both rulers and government by revolution, if necessary. Liberalism stresses the importance of self-interest as a motivational force, reason as the instrument of science, and individual effort leading to self-realization (Lerner, 1972).

Liberalism does recognize, however, that while humankind is basically good, attributes such as ambition, desire for power, and political passions in excess can cause difficulty for others, and a majority gone awry can be as tyrannical as any other despot. Thus, the liberal view supports building safeguards into governmental structures to protect minority interests such as the Bill of Rights and the doctrine of separation of powers as found in the U.S. Constitution.

Liberalism dilutes the certitude of revealed religious dogma and emphasizes tolerance toward all religious and other philosophical ex-pression. It encourages free thought and scholarship and endorses rationalism and science. The focus is on human perfectibility—what humankind can achieve for itself to enhance the happiness of all. Removal of governmental, religious, and other traditional structural restrictions provides humankind with the freedom to function; but an educated populace is necessary to provide the tools by which reason can function and through which human perfectibility may be furthered. Thus, universal education is fundamental to the realization of liberal ideals.

Realism, Logical Positivism, and Postpositivism

Unlike idealism, the central tenet of the philosophy of logical positivism, or just positivism, is that reality is in and of this world. Realist truths are not figments of the mind; they are discovered in everyday experiences. There is confidence that answers to our problems can be discovered through studying experience. This philosophy gained influence with the rise of science, and some positivist philosophers view science as a substitute for philosophy. It has been the dominant philosophy during the mid- to late-twentieth century, although it is now being seriously challenged—at least in the social sciences—by critical theory and other interpretivistic paradigms. Positivism requires an empirical verification for all knowledge through use of the scientific method (i.e., hypotheses are stated in advance and subjected to empirical tests under carefully controlled conditions).

Positivists do not believe in a mind separate from the body as idealists do. The great truths of the universe are believed to be bound up in matter and can be discovered by using the methods of science whether studying natural, social, or human phenomena. The positivist assumes that human interactions operate according to universal law, as does the physical world, and can be discovered through research. The happiness and well-being of humankind depend on how well members of society keep in tune with those laws governing conduct, social relationships, and economic endeavors.

The positivist practices an objectivist epistemology (i.e., value is separated from fact). This is done using a manipulative methodology that controls for the inquirer's bias on the one hand and nature's propensity to confound on the other, and empirical methods that place the point of decision with nature rather than with the inquirer (Guba, 1990).

The positivist and the idealist assume the same rigidity regarding truth. Their difference is the process by which truth is discovered. In both philosophies it is assumed that truth has a universal quality (Graff et al., 1966).

Postpositivism is a modified version of positivism that moves away from what is now seen as a "naive" realist posture and toward a posture called *critical realism* (Guba, 1990). The essence of this position is that given their imperfect sensory and intellectual mechanisms, it is impossible for humans to perceive perfectly the real world, driven by real natural causes. Nevertheless, postpositivists maintain that there are universal truths, although no one can be sure that those ultimate truths have been discovered. Reality is driven by natural laws that can be only partially understood.

For postpositivists, objectivity remains a governing ideal, but with a recognition that it can only be approximated. They seek a modified objectivity that comes reasonably close to the ideal by striving to make their research designs as value-neutral as possible. This is accomplished by revealing one's own predispositions (biases), by requiring reports of any inquiry to be consistent with the existing scholarly tradition of the field, and by subjecting the results of every inquiry to the judgment of peers in the critical community (i.e., editors and referees of journals as well as their readers) (Guba, 1990).

Positivism and postpositivism deal only with what is, not what ought to be. Aims and value judgments cannot be made through analysis of purely empirical propositions. "Ought" issues remain within the realm of philosophy.

Pragmatism

Pragmatism developed out of traditional positivism. It holds that the real essence of ideas is to be found in their utilization as guides to action and behavior (i.e., truth can be known only through its practical consequences). Pragmatists have a basic distrust of the reliability of human ideas until they are tested by experience. Graff et al. (1966) refer to pragmatism as the American philosophy.

According to Graff et al. (1966), pragmatism makes the following assumptions: (1) it is impossible for human beings to gain knowledge of ultimate reality; (2) the universe is in a constant state of change and motion; (3) the world of ideas as we know it is incorporated in systems of symbols, letters, words, and mathematical formulas which have no reality in themselves but refer to items of practice and ways of doing things; (4) the scientific method is the most valid way of testing ideas; and (5) the social aspects of living are extremely important to the individual.

Pragmatism accepts the world of sense impressions and scientific study and rejects idealism's supernatural notions of an outside world of true and perfect ideas as the ultimate reality. In an evolving universe, the pragmatist finds it meaningless to speculate about the nature of reality. Instead, the pragmatist believes that to know reality, one must immerse oneself into all aspects of the world, experiencing it to the fullest. Thus, the pragmatist is always open to new ideas and newly discovered facts.

Pragmatists hold that all social institutions are servants and not masters of humankind and that educational institutions are among the most important. People are viewed as products of both heredity and environment (social and natural); they are neither "good" nor "bad" at birth, but may develop in either direction depending on their experiences with other people and social institutions. This concept of human beings as pliable entities places a heavy responsibility on schools and demands of them the best possible service (Graff et al., 1966).

Existentialism

Existentialism is a philosophical tendency or attitude rather than a philosophical school; thus there are few doctrines common to all its exponents. It grew out of the aftermath of World War I, the Great Depression, and World War II and concerns itself with the darker and more foreboding aspects of human life. It is a protest against views of the world and policies of action in which individual human beings are regarded as helpless creatures whose destinies are shaped wholly by historical forces or natural processes. Existentialism urges humankind to rid itself of the palliatives that have been devised to cushion the despair of human existence and to face up to the realities of a meaningless world full of anguish, loneliness, and death. Its fundamental tenets are autonomy, authenticity, and the complete freedom of the individual to choose a way to live. Reality is considered to be the world of the existing as it is experienced and interpreted by each person (Graff et al., 1966).

Existentialist writers seek to justify the freedom and importance of human personality. They emphasize the place of human will in contrast with reason. Each person is considered unique and inexplicable in terms of any metaphysical or scientific system. Because the person is totally free in making choices, his or her future is not wholly predictable and the burden of free choice generates personal suffering.

Existentialists believe that people must look within themselves to find guidance and direction through today's crises. It is believed that such direction cannot be derived from universal laws and principles, the lessons of history, government, other human beings, God, or modern science. They consider it a grievous error to view the world as possessing order and purpose that can or should determine the course of life. Such a course is the creation of the person living it.

Existentialists place the final responsibility on the individual for deciding who and what he or she is and, thereby, defining his or her own reality. They implore people to reject the escapism of social conformity and orthodox values and to face the stark reality of what it means to exist as a free person and the pain and suffering that such freedom entails.

Existentialists see education as a process of unfolding from within and are concerned with emotions, feelings, and matters that deal with the real existence of humankind. They tend to place greater emphasis on liberal education than on vocational and professional preparation. They emphasize a personal relationship between the teacher and student whereby the teacher reaches to the heart and mind of students, creating inner conflict and challenging and stimulating students' thinking (Graff et al., 1966). Existentialists warn against overemphasis on socialization and group togetherness in education. Believing in the preeminence of individuality, they look with disfavor on any educational arrangement that might impinge on the completely free development of the individual.

Critical Theory

Like the postpositivist, the critical theorist believes that there is a reality that exists independent of human experience, but that this reality may never be fully understood. Both share the assumption that theory possesses the power to affect progress positively and to transform human life. Here the similarities between the two philosophies end, however. The critical theorist is subjectivistic in epistemology, rejecting objectivity and claiming that values mediate inquiry. Because paradigms are human creations, critical theorists assert that paradigms inevitably reflect the values of those who created them. Nature cannot be seen as it "really is" except through a values window that distorts that reality.

The task of critical theory is to raise the consciousness of people (the oppressed) to the true nature of their condition and to the forces causing it. Appreciating how oppressed they are and why, people can then act to transform their world (Guba, 1990). Knowledge enlightens people by revealing the structural conditions of their existence, how these conditions came about, and the distortions and injustices they create. Such knowledge brings with it the power to stimulate action seeking greater autonomy, responsibility, and emancipation (Greene, 1990). Thus, the governing ideal for critical theory is the uniting of reason and commitment (i.e., the integration of knowledge and purposeful action). It seeks to make transparent the causes of distorted communication and understanding (House, 1990).

Critical theory focuses on the conceptualization of education as part of the social, political, cultural, and economic patterns by which schooling is formed. It gives reference to schooling as a socially constructed enterprise that contains continuing contradictions (Popkewitz, 1990).

Constructivism

The constructivist does not believe in a universal reality, but rather, in multiple social- and experience-based mental constructions that depend on the person holding them for form and content. These constructions are local and specific. As with critical theory, the epistemology of constructivism is subjectivist. The observer and the observed are fused into a single entity; observations are literally the creation of the process of interaction between the two. Constructivism does not pretend to predict and control the "real" world nor to transform it but rather, to reconstruct the world at the only point at which it is believed to exist: in the minds of the constructors. It is the mind that is to be transformed, not the "real" world (Guba, 1990). "Reality," as a social construction, can only be seen through windows of theory and values derived from human interactions. Theories and values are aimed at constructing meaning through social consensus among participants in a given context (Greene, 1990).

No unequivocal explanation is ever possible, according to constructivists. There can be many constructions but, for constructivists, there is no foundational way to choose among them. Unlike critical theory, constructivistic inquiry is not concerned directly with judging, evaluating, or condemning existing forms of social and political reality, or with changing the world; rather, it is concerned with describing and understanding their essence. Common goals of constructivistic inquiry are to enlarge and enrich human discourse by bringing experiences of strangers together with our own understandings and our own experiences (Greene, 1990). Since the constructivist rejects the concept of universal laws and principles, each person must determine for himself or herself the relevance of others' experiences to one's own experience.

Knowledge, as a human construction, is never certifiable as ultimately true, according to constructivists; knowledge is problematic and ever changing. Knowledge is the result of a dialogical process between the self-understanding person and that which is encountered—whether a text, a work of art, or the meaningful expressions of another person (J. K. Smith, 1990). Constructivist knowledge is grounded in experience and resembles context-specific working hypotheses more than generalizable propositions that warrant certainty or even probability (Greene, 1990). It constitutes holistic pattern theories or webs that reflect an intertwinement of part and whole and a view of knowledge that is more "circular" than hierarchical (Lincoln, 1990).

At the core of constructivism is the governing ideal of solidarity rather than objectivity. Thus, the constructivist position takes on many aspects of relativism. Relativism is seen as a key to openness and the search for more informed and sophisticated constructions (Guba, 1990).

The relativistic characteristics of constructivism has led to charges from idealists, postpositivists, and progressives that in rejecting foundational standards, constructivism takes on a form of irrationalism. Constructivists respond that if there is no foundation, there is no structure against which other positions can be judged "objectively" (Lather, 1990). According to Lather, relativism appears as a problem only for dominating groups at the point where the hegemony of their views is being challenged. "In sum, fears of relativism and its seeming attendant nihilism or Nietzschean anger seem to me an implosion of Western, White male, class-privileged arrogance—if we cannot know everything, then we can know nothing" (p. 321).

Nyberg (1993) also tends to discount the danger of runaway relativism because he saw that "even as values clash, there is a great deal of agreement within the moral universe about right and wrong, good and bad, which the majority of humankind assumes" (p. 208). There is much more that unites us than divides us.

Two Views of the World

The hegemony of postpositivist thinking directly affected the study of educational administration in the mid-1950s with the application of social science constructs and methodologies (in turn derived from the natural sciences). In embracing a postpositivist perspective, attention to the qualitative dimensions of educational administration was sorely neglected according to many critics of its "science" and practice (Foster, 1984; Greenfield, 1984; Hodgkinson, 1983; Lather, 1990; Sergiovanni, 1984a, 1992). The emphasis placed by the scientific method on quantitative measurement and value objectivity focused research and discussion on "what is" and the search for relationships among observable phenomena rather than on "what should be." Interest in the roles that values, emotions, meaning, and morality play in the practice of school administration had largely been absent until the relatively recent challenge to postpositivist thinking made by critical theorists and constructivists.

Greenfield (1978) was among the first educational administration theorists of the critical theory persuasion to attack the postpositivist hegemony, although others (e.g., Graff et al., 1966) had earlier pointed to the postpositivist insistence on the empirical verification of knowledge as a most serious error. Greenfield

challenged the perceptions of organizations as manifestations of natural order that are subject to universal and impersonal scientific laws (Greenfield, 1984). Rather, he argued, organizations are humanmade, arbitrary, ephemeral, and not universal; in other words, they are "nonnatural." Greenfield saw organizations as cultural artifacts and what goes on within them as products of individual action, intention, and will rather than of universal natural laws of social action. This view characterizes organizations as human creations that provide contexts for the negotiation and construction of meaning, moral order, and power (Bates, 1984).

Bates (1984, p. 260) is highly critical of mainstream theorists of educational administration for continuing to declare the incommensurability of fact and value and their pursuit of positivistic attempts to develop generalizable laws and principles to explain the structure and dynamics of organizations. He bases his criticisms on the contemporary positions of philosophers and social scientists. Philosophers, he points out, acknowledge the impossibility of eliminating evaluative judgments from the interpretive frameworks within which facts are both sought and understood and social theorists have largely abandoned the value-free science of society.

Foster (1984) pointed out that the "objectivity" of postpositivism is not objective at all; by removing reflective and dialectical thought from the province of meaningful expression, postpositivism is biased in perpetuating the existent social order unchallenged. In focusing on reflective and dialectical thought, however, Foster does not demean the relevance of an administrative science by saying, "it does a disservice to critical theory to suggest that such reflection must remain limited to subjectivistic impressions: empirical verification is required; data are necessary" (p. 249). Elsewhere, Foster (1986) proposed a three-tier model for the study of administration. The first tier involves the empirical study of organization and administration through descriptions of perceived reality and economic and political structures. The second tier consists of the development of individual constructions and interpretations of reality. The third tier is critical inquiry, a reflective process that includes dialogue intended to achieve true democratic participation by all members of the community.

Sergiovanni (1984a) joined Foster in calling for a multiple-perspective approach to the analysis of administration and organizations:

> Theories of administration, therefore, should not be viewed as competing, with the thought that one best view might emerge. Instead, the alternative and overlapping metaphor is offered. When viewed this way, each theory of administration is better able to illuminate and explain certain aspects of the problems administrators face but not others. Increased understanding depends upon the use of several theories, preferably in an integrated fashion. (p. 1)

Nyberg (1993) divided philosophers (and other people) into two broad orientations toward formulating moral judgments. The *moral-principle orientation* favors "ideas that are extensive, inclusive, universal and elegant in their simplicity" (p. 206). These would tend to include idealists and positivists. The *personal-value orientation* prefers to see "individuals with perfect clarity, in all their literal, particular, factual fullness . . . no matter how fragmented the world may then seem" (p. 206). These would include existentialists and constructivists.

The moral-principal orientation tends to view rationality as the striving for economy of means of thought by holding allegiance to a single conception or idea that can be applied broadly. The personal-value orientation's view of rationality is that "people can think and act in ways they themselves can understand and alter, that individuals are not merely victims of structural causes, and that justifications and explanations of human conduct must be in terms of personal, subjective motives and reasons, however idiosyncratic they may seem" (p. 198).

To close this section, we refer to an article by Gage (1989) entitled "The Paradigm Wars and Their Aftermath." In it, he addresses the continuing conflict among educational researchers who adhere to one of the competing philosophies of postpositivism, constructivism, critical theory, and antinaturalism. He issues an appeal to our educational intellectual leaders—philosophers, scientists, scholars, research workers—not to become bogged down in an intellectual no man's land and reminds us that "even as we debate whether any objectivity at all is possible, whether 'technical' research is merely trivial, whether your paradigm or mine should get more money, I feel that I should remember that the payoff inheres in what happens to the children, the students. This is our end concern" (p. 10). Our tasks carry with them moral obligations.

Thus, there seems to be a great divide between those who view the world in terms of a single paradigm and those who accept none as absolute, but are willing to be guided by insights provided by many. The authors of this book fall into the latter category. We recognize that educational administration is a moral pursuit and that the effective administrator must act with an understanding of the relevance of value structures to his or her executive actions. In this chapter we focus on such aspects of administration. We also appreciate, however, the contributions of the social sciences to the enlightenment of the practice of educational leadership, and these "scientific" aspects are highlighted in the next section of this chapter and elsewhere in the book.

Values and Value Systems

In this section our discussion is expanded to include insights gained from social scientists as well as philosophers.

Values Defined

Values are conceptions of the desirable (Hodgkinson, 1983; Hoy & Miskel, 1991; Parsons, 1951; Willower & Licata, 1997). A value is an enduring belief that a specific mode of conduct or state of existence is personally or socially preferable to an opposite or converse mode of conduct or state of existence. Values are synonymous with personal beliefs about the "good," the "just," and the "beautiful"; they propel us to a particular kind of behavior and lifestyle (Lewis, 1990). Values reflect the world view (philosophy) of an individual or organization (Hall, Kalven, Rosen, & Taylor, 1990). They are consciously or unconsciously held priorities that are expressed in all human activity. A value system is an enduring organization of values along a continuum of relative importance (Rokeach, 1973).

Values are subjective because they are concepts and they deal with the phenomenology of desire. We value things or states because we choose to attribute worth to them, not because of any innate worth. In so doing, we superimpose onto a thing a subjective element to indicate its level of importance for us (Beare, Caldwell, & Millikan, 1989). To be functional collectively, others must assign similar degrees of value to the same thing or state. "The essential point to grasp in thinking about value is that values do not exist in the real world. They are utterly phenomenological, subjective facts of the inner and personal experience . . ." (Hodgkinson, 1983, p. 31).

Rokeach made five assumptions about the nature of human values: (1) the total number of values that a person possesses is relatively small; (2) all people possess the same values to different degrees; (3) values are organized into value systems; (4) the antecedents of human values can be traced to culture, society and its institutions, and personality; and (5) the consequences of values will be manifested in virtually all phenomena that social scientists might consider worth investigating and understanding. A person holds countless beliefs that are organized into thousands of attitudes, several dozens of hierarchically arranged instrumental values, and several hierarchically arranged terminal val-

ues. Taken together, they form a belief system in which terminal values are more central than instrumental values and instrumental values are more central than attitudes. *Terminal values* refer to desired end states of existence; they can be either self-centered or society-centered. *Instrumental values* refer to morality (having an interpersonal focus) and competence (having a personal focus without interpersonal implications) aspects of modes of conduct. Terminal values are motivational in that they represent supergoals beyond immediate, biologically urgent goals. Since the total belief system is functionally interconnected, a change in any part of it should affect other parts and should ultimately affect behavior. To make a lasting change on human perception and behavior, the most central part of the system—terminal values—must be changed, according to Rokeach (1973).

Hodgkinson (1983) takes a different approach to differentiating among values by placing them into a hierarchy according to the approach implied in determining what is good or right. His four grounds or justifications for valuing are principles (type I), consequences (type IIA), consensus (type IIB), and preference (type III). The hierarchy is illustrated in Table 12.2.

Type I values are transrational; they go beyond reason, implying an act of faith or will as it is manifested in the acceptance of a principle. "Though such principles may often be defended by rational discourse they are essentially metaphysical in origin or location" (Hodgkinson, 1983, p. 39). Their philosophical orientations are found in religion and intuition. They are the universal ideas of the idealists and the natural law of liberalism.

Type III, preference, justifies a value on the grounds that the object or action is liked or preferred by the subject; these values may be innate or learned. All animals possess such values and such values are self-justifying. Type III values originate from affect, emotion, and feeling. Their philosophical orientations are found in behaviorism, positivism, and hedonism.

Table 12.2
Value Paradigm

Value Type	Grounds Value	Psychological Faculty	Philiosophical Orientations	Value Level	
I	Principles	Conation Willing	Religion Existentialism Intuition	I	Right
IIA	Consequence (A)	Cognition Reason	Utilitarianism Pragmatism Humanism Democratic	II	
IIB	Consensus (B)	Thinking	Liberalism		
III	Preference	Affect Emotion Feeling	Behaviorism Positivism Hedonism	III	Good

Source: C. Hodgkinson, *The philosophy of leadership,* (p. 38). Oxford: Basil Blackwell, 1983.

Type II values of both subsets A and B are justified on the ground of rationality. This can appear first as consensus (IIB). At the next-higher level of rational process, the value is established upon an analysis of the consequences (IIB) of holding it. The philosophical orientations of type II values lie in utilitarianism, pragmatism, humanism, democracy, and liberalism.

Type II values represent a middle ground between the commitments of ideology (type I) and the turbulence of affectivity (type III). At one extreme is immediate experience (type III) and at the other, ideology (type I); in between is the realm of pragmatics and common sense.

> This is fortunate for human nerve and tissue. Even at best the demands of ideology are rooted in abstraction and men do not live in intellectual abstractions, however much they may subscribe to them or be governed by them. As for affect, men cannot constantly be engaged in the internecine warfare of the ego. Between Type III realities and the Type I blueprints there lies the vast region of normality—the everyday, workaday world of organizational life. A banal world perhaps, but one in which man is at relative ease: habituated, conditioned, programmed, modest and content. (Hodgkinson, 1983, p. 121)

If values were completely stable, individual and social change would be impossible. If values were completely unstable, continuity of human personality and society would be impossible. The hierarchical conception of values enables us to define change as a reordering of priorities and, simultaneously, to see the total value system as relatively stable over time. Consensus is easier where type III values are involved and most difficult where type I values are present; indeed, in the latter case, conflicting type I commitments may be irreconcilable. Because of this, the practical person seeks to avoid engagement on matters of principles and searches instead for the politically possible (Hodgkinson, 1983; Lindblom, 1959). "Pragmatics will take us through the day but will not take us where we want to go" (Hodgkinson, 1983, p. 135).

Hall et al. (1990) take a different approach in developing a hierarchy of values. They hold that value development is a growth process that goes through eight stages to reach full maturity, a point that few reach. In the first four stages, authority is perceived by the person as originating outside the self, whereas in the last four stages, authority is perceived as originating within the person. The values associated with each stage from lowest to highest are self-preservation, security, self-worth, self-competence, independence, new order, interdependence, and rights and world order. At the lower stages, the individual is self-centered, seeking security in a world over which the person perceives no control. The ego stages grow into a recognition of a social world that must be accommodated; an external "they" is perceived as being in control and the person seeks acceptance, affirmation, approval, and achievement within the parameters set by "they." In the next stages, the person begins to assume control over his or her life and seeks to create his or her own identity. At the highest levels, the person assumes responsibility for others as well as himself or herself. In these upper stages, the person joins ranks with others seeking global harmony.

Value analysis neither implies nor entails any demands for logical closure where values are in contention. According to Hodgkinson (1983), true value conflict is always intrapersonal; the essential subjectivity of values dictates that any conflicts between values must occur within the individual consciousness. Hodgkinson views what is usually thought of as intervalue conflict as really a conflict of interests; ultimately, it is, in fact, a power struggle between value actors. Overt value actions of value actors tell us nothing of the value conflict within the individual actors. For example, does the loser of a war or a civil suit thereby change his or her conception of the desirable?

Nyberg (1993) holds a somewhat different position from Hodgkinson on the clash of values. Both agree on the intrapersonal conflict of values, but Nyberg also sees interpersonal and

intergroup value conflicts that are not merely conflicts of interests. Nyberg contends that the pluralism of competing values is as much a part of society as it is of each individual consciousness because it is human nature to see things differently. "This collision of values is the moral core of what it is to be human" (Nyberg, 1993, p. 198).

Archetypes of Leadership

Hodgkinson (1983) used several archetypes to describe leaders as they act within his value hierarchy (Table 12.2). The lowest archetype from the standpoint of moral or ethical regard is that of "careerist," which is characterized by the values of the ego, self-interest, primary affect, and motivation. Self-preservation and enhancement, self-centeredness, and self-concern are the dominant value traits. The careerist functions at the type I level in the values hierarchy. The basal form of the careerist archetype is predator, and the higher form is opportunist. Such persons may subscribe to the philosophical orientations of behaviorism or hedonism.

The second level of the value paradigm is the modal level for administration. Most administrators tend either to the politician (type IIB) or technician (type IIA) archetype. Hodgkinson (1983, p. 141) refers to politics as "administration by another name." The *politician archetype* is associated with the administrator whose interests have extended beyond those of self to the point where they embrace a collectivity or group. This group, typically the organization for which he or she is responsible, is then allowed to have some degree of influence over the establishment of organizational values, to the point of affecting the leader's own value structure and behavior. It thus refers to a value complex that takes into account the values of others, individually and corporately.

The politician is both moral and rational. The archetype is moral because his or her concern goes beyond that of self. The basic claim to rationality is that group preferences, if actualized, will advance the potential for individual realization of preference more than if laissez-faire pursuit of private desires are permitted. In all this, the politician has a relatively short-term orientation; it is the immediate problem that is pressing. "True politicians practicing the true art of the possible make the organizational world work. . . . But one can go beyond it" (Hodgkinson, 1983, p. 167). The politician, at worst, is a demagogue and, at best, a democrat. The politician's philosophical orientation tends toward that of liberalism, humanism, or pragmatism.

The *technician archetype* is primarily rational–cognitive and rational–legal. The values of Weberian bureaucracy, including dispassion, impartiality, logical analysis and problem solving, efficiency, effectiveness, goal accomplishment, planning, and maximization of the good, fit with this archetype. In contrast to the politician, the technician stresses institutional concerns over individual concerns. Utilitarian doctrines best reflect the philosophical orientation of the technician.

The technician "represents the highest of the archetypes that it is ordinarily possible for the administrator to aspire to and attain. This sets the safe limit to the moral ambitions and aspirations of administration" (Hodgkinson, 1983, p. 177). The technician can degenerate to the disengaged bureaucrat but also can aspire to the guardian–technocrat, as described below.

Hodgkinson (1983) called the archetype carrying type I values the *poet*. "The poet 'carries the fire,' makes things and men grow warm, extends the reach of language (and hence thought, concept, and rationality), steals fire from the gods, even—in the limit— reconciles the instant God and Man" (p. 178). Hodgkinson likens the poet to Plato's guardian or philosopher–king, whose moral base extended into the transrational domain of faith-activated will. The poet's *will* is the justification of right and the determinant of good. As a result, leadership of a poet may result in nirvana or in total destruction. At best, the poet is guardian, but at worst, megalomaniac. Or, in the words of Nyberg (1993): "Always to choose principles, or worse, The One Right Principle, over individual values and needs in resolving specific moral situations may sometimes be the road to martyrdom and sainthood, but it is also the road to inhumanity, which ironically is paved with illusions of perfection" (p. 205).

Hall et al. (1990) have also developed a leadership hierarchy that bears some resemblance to Hodgkinson's (1983), especially at the lower level. In their hierarchy, Hall et al. recognize the reciprocal relationship between leadership and followership. Their seven leadership cycles are reported in column II of Table 12.3. Each cycle is placed between two operative values for the cycle, which are reported in column I. Since value development is seen as a growth process, the leader experiences a tension between the two values as he or she shifts priority from the lower to the higher. The leadership mode is reported in column III. Leadership and followership characteristics are summarized in columns IV and V, respectively.

The lowest level of leadership in Hall et al.'s (1990) hierarchy, *primal,* operates from values of self-preservation and security. Such a leader functions in an autocratic mode, controlling the organization closely and making all major decisions. The primal leader maintains a discrete distance from subordinates and demands loyalty to himself or herself and to the organization. Followers respond with passivity and docility, exhibiting immature behavior. They view the leader as being unapproachable and as having an aura of infallibility. This type of leadership is preferred only at times of imminent danger.

In the *familial* cycle, the leader is a benevolent despot, assuming a parent–child relationship with subordinates. Such a leader operates from values of security and self-worth. While listening to subordinates, the familial leader still reserves all decisions to himself or herself. A personal loyalty to superiors and compliance with the rules of the organization are demanded. Followers develop a feeling of dependency. They

Table 12.3
Summary of Hall, Kalven, Rosen, and Taylor's Cycles and Educational Leadership

I Value Stage	II Leadership Cycle	III Leadership Mode	IV Leadership Characteristics	V Follower Characteristics
Self-preservation, security	Primal	Autocratic	Makes all major decisions; seeks absolute control; demands loyalty; maintains distance from followers	Docility, blind obedience, passivity; infantile; views leaders as distant and infallible
Self-worth	Familial	Benevolent authority	Listens, but makes all major decisions; demands loyalty; seeks adherence to rules	Feels cared for; dependency, views leaders as approachable, but in control
Self-competence	Institutional	Bureaucratic	Management by objectives; stresses order, clear policies, goals, and rules; demands loyalty to institution; delegates only to highly skilled and loyal employees	Exercises delegated authority; views leader as approachable and good listener
Independence	Intrapersonal	Enabling	Attempts to reconcile institutional demands and personal values; acts as listener/clarifier uncertain in making decisions	Confusion; willingness to express feelings; needs good interpersonal skills
New order	Collaborative	Charismatic	Democratic; clear vision about how to make institutions humane; modifies rules to personal conscience	Small group interactions; participation as peers in some decision making; group dynamic skills; conflict resolution skills
Interdependence	Mystical or integrative	Servant	Concern over impact on society and productivity; maximizes individual development; seeks agreement of values	Willing to assume responsibility; works at high levels of trust and intimacy; well-developed imaginal skills
Rights/world order	Prophetic	Interdependent	Leadership and followership are merged; collaborative efforts to improve balance between material and personal needs; seeks reconciliation among conflicting groups and the creative and humane use of technology	

Source: Adapted from B. P. Hall, J. Kalven, L. S. Rosen, and B. Taylor. *Developing human values*. Fond du Lac, WI: International Values Institute of Marian College, 1990.

view the leader as approachable, but recognize that he or she is clearly in charge. Leadership of this type is most appropriate when the leader is highly skilled and the followers are not. Relationships are based on fairness and mutual respect.

Managerial efficiency becomes a primary concern in the *institutional* cycle of leadership. This type of leader works from values of self-worth and self-competence. The institutional leader functions in a bureaucratic mode, managing by objectives and stressing the need for order and clear policies. Loyalty to the institution is demanded. There is some delegation of authority, but only to the skilled and to the loyal. Interpersonal, social, and technical skills are required at this level. This type of leader is likely to be rigid and resistant to change. Followers adhere to the clearly stated policies. They accept the delegation of authority and view the leader as being approachable and a good listener.

The *intrapersonal* cycle of leadership represents a transition from a self-oriented to a socially oriented philosophy. As a result, it is characterized by confusion and inconsistency in decision making and by conflict between values of organizational efficiency and human needs. The leader acts as a listener and clarifier and operates from the values of self-competence and independence. Followers exhibit confusion derived from the mixed signals given by the leadership. There is a general willingness to express feelings and there is a need among followers to display good interpersonal skills.

The *communal* or *collaborative* cycle works from the values of independence and new order. Its mode is charismatic. Hall et al. (1990) view this as being the ideal level of leadership for educational institutions, especially for secondary and postsecondary schools. "Individuals have passed successfully through the often paralyzing laissez-faire period and now have a new sense of personal creative energy and renewed vision of an institution that can be efficient, as well as dignifying, for its members" (p. 61). Leaders operating at this level are democratic in their style and

able to modify rules according to their personal conscience. Followers are characterized by small group interactions; they need well-developed skills in group dynamics and conflict resolution. Followers regularly participate as peers in some decision making. This level bears some resemblance to Hodgkinson's (1983) technician.

At the *mystical* or *integrative* cycle, values of new order and interdependence predominate. Leadership is interactive and collaborative, with the leader functioning as servant. In addition to organizational productivity, there is concern for the quality of organizational interactions and the organization's impact on society. Group decision making is the norm, with mutual responsibility and collegiality assumed by all members of the organization. Followers are willing to assume responsibility and they have well-developed inventive skills. All members work at high levels of trust and intimacy. The values of new order and interdependence are dominant.

Although both are rarely found, Hall et al.'s (1990) highest level of leadership, *prophetic,* is not nearly as doctrinaire as Hodgkinson's (1983) poet. At this level in Hall et al.'s hierarchy, the concepts of leadership and followership are merged. The mode of operation is interdependent or transformational. All persons are engaged in the task of improving the balance between material goods and human needs and dedicated to reconciling conflicts among groups and using technology in creative and humane ways. The values of interdependence and rights/world order dominate at this level (Bolman & Deal, 1995).

Values as Part of Organizational Cultures

Values are motivating determinants of behaviors (Spindler, 1955). Persons joined together by a similar set of values, beliefs, priorities, experiences, and traditions are said to form a common culture, whether it be in a small organization such as a school, a large nation such as the United States, or a group of nations such as the West or the Western world.

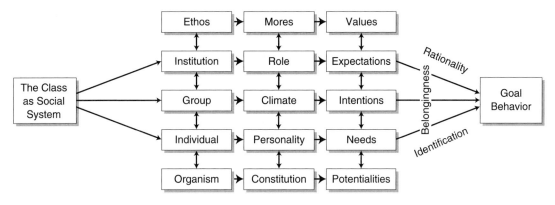

Figure 12.1
Getzels–Thelen model of the classroom as a social system

Source: "The classroom group as a social system." (p. 80) by J. W. Getzels and H. A. Thelen, in N. B. Henry (Ed.), *The dynamics of institutional groups,* 1960, 59th Yearbook of the National Society for the Study of Education. Used with the permission of the National Society for the Study of Education.

Shared values define the basic character of an organization and give it meaning (Hoy & Miskel, 1991; Wheatley, 1994; Wheatley & Kellner-Rogers, 1996). Ouchi (1981) argued that successful corporations in both Japan and the United States are energized by distinctive corporate cultures that are internally consistent and characterized by shared values of intimacy, trust, cooperation, teamwork, and equalitarianism. Similar observations have been made by Deal and Kennedy (1982), Peters and Waterman (1982), and Peters (1988).

Bates (1984) saw cultures also as providing the framework within which individuals establish meaning for themselves. He noted that part of culture is factual, but most is mythical. The latter part is concerned with meaning (i.e., the interpretive and prescriptive rules that provide the basis for understanding and action).

Getzels and Thelen (1960) portrayed the classroom as a social system and clearly demonstrated the function of values within the system. Their model is reproduced in Figure 12.1. The model represents the interplay among individuals, groups (e.g., classrooms), and institutions (e.g., schools). Schools as institutions are embedded within a culture holding certain mores

and values that influence institutional, group, and individual goals, roles, and social behavior. These are a function of continuing negotiations between individuals and their group, groups and their institution, and so on. Thus, value conflicts may develop within groups and institutions and between groups and institutions and institutions and the larger social culture. A primary function of leadership is to monitor these conflicts and to guide them in organizationally and socially positive directions.

Of primary concern to the administrator is the institutional or nomothetic dimension of the model, which seeks to link the organization with its goals by way of formally creating roles and role expectations (or jobs and job expectations). On the other hand, nonadministrative organization members are concerned primarily with the individual or ideographic dimension. The institutional dimension, for nonadministrative members, is viewed as constraints that limit their satisfactions while providing the rational–legal foundation for their contracts with the organization. The task of the executive is one of reconciliation: reconciliation of the organization to society and of organization members toward organizational goals.

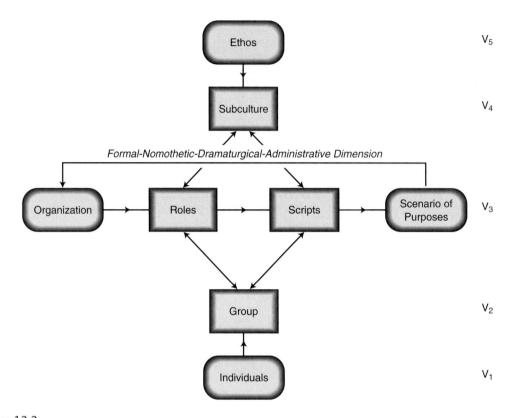

Figure 12.2
Total field of action
Source: C. Hodgkinson, *The philosophy of leadership* (p. 24). Oxford: Blackwell, 1983.

Sergiovanni and Carver (1973) observed that school executives too often avoid value confrontation by attempting to deal with conflict at the lowest level of abstraction possible—at the interpersonal level on a one-to-one basis. He believes, however, that the major problems concerning value differences that face most school executives are at the organizational level and are expressed in the form of competing organizational cultures. Such competition needs to be dealt with at the organizational level. According to Sergiovanni, administrative effectiveness requires continuous examination of internalized value assumptions, including comparing and testing value structures for goodness of fit and for overlap with those held by other educational

workers, students, and society at large. In the words of Hodgkinson (1991, p. 90), "An organization is, strictly speaking, an arrangement for conflict management through the device of superordinant or overriding goals."

Hodgkinson (1983) developed a model (Figure 12.2) that reconciles personal values with institutional elements such as those included in the Getzels and Thelen model (Figure 12.1). Level V_1 in the Hodgkinson model represents the value structure of the individual within the organization or the ideographic dimension; level V_2 represents the shared value structures of groups within the organization that modulate individual belief structures; level V_3 is the organizational or nomothetic dimension; V_4 represents the value structure of the subculture(s) that influence the organization's operations; and V_5 represents the overarching societal ethos.

The individual organization member (V_1) meets with the nomothetic dimension of the organization (V_3), not directly, but through workday encounters with formal and informal groups (V_2). These groups intervene between the member and the executive suite (V_3) and modulate the consciousness and experience of the member. In other words, the member's organizational perspective (V_1) is quite different from that of the administrator (V_3).

In a similar way, the prevailing ethos (V_5) does not impinge directly on the organization (V_3) but is modulated through intervening subcultures (V_4), such as professional organizations and local political groups. These levels overlap, intertwine, and interact in dynamic and contingent relationships (Hodgkinson, 1983).

Getzels (1957) differentiated values into only two levels: sacred and secular. National core or *sacred values* are relatively stable. These would correspond to Hodgkinson's ethos (V_5). *Secular values* are transient, subject to change and wide interpretation at the operational level. Examples of secular values are the work–success ethic, future orientation, independence, and Puritan morality. Such values govern one's everyday behavior with regard to work, time, relation to others, and personal morality. "[T]he fact that values do shift at least in emphasis and that individuals and groups do differ in the expression of the values may make for strains between generations and between school and community, with consequent problems and implications for the educational administrator" (Lipham, 1988, p. 177).

Organizational Leadership: Values and Vision

Greenfield (1984) postulated that "[o]rganizations are built on the unification of people around values. The business of being a leader is therefore the business of being an entrepreneur for values" (p. 166). Greenfield referred to or-

ganizations as cultural artifacts that are founded in meanings, in human intentions, actions, and experience. They are systems of meaning that can only be understood through the interpretation of meaning. The task of leaders is to act as interpreters, creating a moral order that binds them and the people around them.

Of the five leadership forces identified by Sergiovanni (1984c)—technical (management), human, educational, symbolic, and cultural—the last two are the most relevant in studying values. "The object of symbolic leadership is the setting of human consciousness, the articulation of key cultural strands that identify the substance of a school, and the linking of persons involved in the school's activities to them" (pp. 7–8). The symbolic leader signals to others what is of importance in the organization. In so doing, the leader gives to the organization purpose and direction. Vision becomes the substance of what is communicated through symbolic aspects of leadership. It provides a source of clarity, consensus, and commitment for students and teachers alike (Vaill, 1984).

The cultural leader seeks to define, strengthen, and articulate those enduring values, beliefs, and cultural strands that give a school its unique identity.

> The net effect of the cultural force of leadership is to bond together students, teachers, and others as believers in the work of the school. Indeed, the school and its purposes are somewhat revered as if they resembled an ideological system dedicated to a sacred mission. As persons become members of this strong and binding culture, they are provided with opportunities for enjoying a special sense of personal importance. (Sergiovanni, 1984a, p. 9)

Sergiovanni (1992, p. 102) noted that two important things happen when purpose, social contract, and school autonomy provide the foundation upon which to build the structure of schooling. The school is transformed from a mere organization to a covenantal community, and the basis of authority changes from an emphasis on bureaucratic and psychological authority to moral authority. In other words, the school changes from a secular to a sacred organization—changing from an instrument designed to achieve specific ends to a virtuous enterprise.

The mission of the cultural leader is to focus sharply the minds of the membership of a school organization on collectively held values, symbols, and beliefs. The more that these are understood and accepted, the better able the school is to move in concert toward the ideals it holds and the goals it wishes to pursue. A strong culture is characteristic of excellent schools. A tight value structure permits an otherwise loosely structured organization to allow wide discretion among the professionals working within the organization. Shared values and beliefs become the glue holding the organization together, not close managerial supervision (Wheatley, 1994; Wheatley & Kellner-Rogers, 1996).

Organizations need leaders who can provide a persuasive and durable sense of purpose and direction, rooted deeply in human values and spirit. Leaders need to be deeply reflective, actively thoughtful, and dramatically explicit about their core values and beliefs. The best managers and leaders create and sustain a tension-filled balance between core values and elastic strategies. They know what they stand for and what they want, and they communicate that vision clearly and forcefully. They also know that they must understand and respond to the complex array of forces that push and pull organizations in many different directions (Bolman and Deal, 1997).

Bennis (1984) aptly summarized the function of leadership within the context of organizational culture.

> In sum, the transformative power of leadership stems less from ingeniously crafted organizational structures, carefully constructed management designs and controls, elegantly rationalized planning formats, or skillfully articulated leadership tactics. Rather, it is the ability of the leader to reach the souls of others in a fashion which raises human consciousness, builds meanings, and inspires human intent that is the source of power. Within transformative leadership, therefore, it is vision, purposes, beliefs, and other aspects of organizational culture that are of prime importance. (p. 70)

Values, Democracy, and Followership

Maxcy (1991) proposed a pragmatic theory of value that stresses the importance of democratic cultural consensus in arriving at plans and policies that affect the school community. She argued that the quality of life is enhanced and pedagogical responsibility is fulfilled when the deliberative process is enlarged to include all those involved in or affected by schooling. She observed that leadership is always truncated and narrow when power is invested in the few.

With democratic cultural consensus, leadership needs the capacity to interact with self or others in terms of moving a discourse/practice toward an end based upon criteria that are at once rational and moral. "Leading is not so much telling others what is true or false, but rather helping them to come to know for themselves the merits and demerits of a case" (Maxcy, 1991, p. 195). Maxcy called for a reconstruction and reconceptualization of leadership as enlightened, critical, and pragmatic action—a notion of leadership that looks to everyone who participates in the teaching–learning process for the kinds of thought and effort that will result in a reformed education.

In a similar vein, Cambron-McCabe (1993) argued that moral principles guiding groups or organizations are not a matter of personal preference or intuition but must be subjected to a democratic deliberative process. She asserted that values must be determined in a democratic context for democratic ends.

Sergiovanni (1992) pointed out that leadership and followership are reciprocal in an empowered organization. He believes that in many ways, professionalism and leadership are antithetical insofar as, beyond a certain point, the more professionalism is emphasized, the less leadership is needed. Professionalism has a way of encouraging principals to be self-managers. Conversely, providing too much leadership, at least of the traditional type, discourages professionalism. Self-management and professionalism are complementary concepts. "If self-management is our goal, then leadership will have to be reinvented in a fashion that places 'followership' first" (p. 68).

Subordinates need external motivation. They do what they are supposed to do, but little else; they want to know exactly what is expected of them—they work to the rule. Followers, on the other hand, are self-motivated and work well without close supervision, assessing what needs to be done, when and how, and taking effective action on their own.

> Followers are people committed to purposes, a cause, a vision of what the school is and can become, beliefs about teaching and learning, values and standards to which they adhere, and convictions. . . . When followership and leadership are joined, the traditional hierarchy of the school is upset. It changes from a fixed form, with superintendents and principals at the top and teachers and students at the bottom, to one that is in flux. The only constant is that neither superintendents and principals nor teachers and students are at the apex; that position is reserved for ideas, values, and commitments at the heart of followership. Further, a transformation takes place, and emphasis shifts from bureaucratic, psychological, and technical rational authority to professional and moral authority. As a result, hierarchial position and personality are not enough to earn one the mantle of leader. Instead, it comes through one's demonstrated devotion and success as a follower. The true leader is the one who follows first. (Sergiovanni, 1992, pp. 71–72)

The interaction between leadership and followership was noted earlier in the presentation of the work of Hall et al. (1990) on developing human values (see Table 12.3). In their leadership hierarchy, the highest level was placed at the point where the concept of leadership and followership merge and the distinctions between them become meaningless.

Greenleaf (1977) wrote of the servant-leader. He referred to two polar types of leadership: that provided by persons naturally inclined to lead first, and that provided by persons naturally inclined to serve first but through service are endowed with leadership authority. Between the poles are many shadings. Leadership

is bestowed upon the servant-leader; it is sought by the leader-leader. Greenleaf noted a reassessment of the issues of power and authority whereby people are learning to relate to one another in less coercive and more creatively supporting ways. "A new moral principle is emerging which holds that the only authority deserving one's allegiance is that which is freely and knowingly granted by the led to the leader in response to, and in proportion to, the clearly evident servant stature of the leader" (p. 10). Servant leaders differ from other persons of goodwill because they act on what they believe. Greenleaf stressed the importance to the functioning leader of listening carefully and understanding. He expressed a strong bias that only a true natural servant responds automatically to any problem by listening first. Greenleaf saw the only viable institutions of the future as being predominantly servant-led.

These concepts of leadership, democracy, and followership were first developed by Burns (1978) and were summarized in the discussion of transformational leadership in Chapter 3. His foundational thoughts on leadership, particularly the moral implications of transforming leadership, are fundamental to this discussion. They place the reciprocal nature of transforming leadership in perspective as regards followers transforming leaders.

Values Analysis

Values analysis is complicated by the fact that values are very difficult to measure. Determining the espoused values [or theories (Argyris & Schön, 1974)] is relatively simple; you just ask. *Espoused theories* exist at the conscious level and they can be changed relatively easily with new information. They describe what we believe we believe; but they do not necessarily guide our actions. *Theories-in-use* (Argyris & Schön, 1974), however, are much more formidable to identify. These theories reside deeply within our subconscious and they are difficult for us to articulate; they are tacit. As such, they are hard to change, yet they are the values and beliefs that truly guide our actions. "Theories-in-use build up and solidify over a long period of time through acculturation and are reinforced by ongoing experience in the culture. They become such an integrated part of our beings that they are difficult to isolate. They disappear from our conscious foreground and become background (Osterman & Kottkamp, 1993, p. 10).

To change a theory-in-use, it is necessary to bring it into consciousness. We are usually unaware of differences between our espoused beliefs and our actions; and we are usually also unaware of discrepancies between our intended outcomes and the actual outcomes, especially when the outcomes deal with unmeasurable attributes such as attitudes. "Without this awareness, the individual may not personalize the new information or ideas to make the connection between the criticism and his or her own behavior" (Osterman & Kottkamp, 1993, p. 12).

Despite these difficulties, methods for analyzing and addressing the practical impact of values have been developed (with severe limitations) for application at three levels: the problem, the organization, and the individual. In this section we describe approaches that have been used at each level.

Reflection in Practice.   At the personal level, Sergiovanni (1984b) identifies several dimensions of leadership. One of these is *platform*, an articulation of one's principles into an operational framework. "Platforms are governing in the sense that they represent a set of criteria and an implicit standard from which decisions are made" (p. 109). The platform enables the determining of worth and separation of the trivial from the important. "More colloquially, it is one's philosophy of education or administration, a concise statement of what one intends to do, to accomplish, and how" (Osterman & Kottkamp, 1993, p. 67).

Osterman and Kottkamp (1993) have advocated a form of professional development that attempts to align implicit values and beliefs of individual professional educators with desired outcomes of school reform initiatives. Their process focuses on bringing beliefs and values into the conscious mind and comparing them with the beliefs and values implicit in a person's behavior. They begin the process by having people develop a written professional platform as defined earlier. The platform describes a person's beliefs about teaching, learning, and its context, and views about the orientations and means that are required to facilitate and support the learning process. More specifically, the platform may address aims of education, image of the learner, value of the curriculum, image of the teacher, preferred student–teacher relationship, purpose of supervision, and the preferred process of supervision as suggested by Sergiovanni and Starratt (1983).

The written platform is espoused theory, but writing it sets into motion a powerful reflective process. The writing process can be extremely difficult and emotionally intense. The platform could be developed in isolation, but Osterman and Kottkamp recommend that it be done with the assistance of at least one other person in whom the writer has complete trust. The colleague can react to the writings in a nonjudgmental way and analyze it for implicit beliefs and values.

Once the espoused theory has been documented, the next step is to gather information about theories-in-use by the individual. This can best be done through observing behavior and reflecting upon it to detect the assumptions that might have prompted it. The observations may be made by another, or they may be done by the individual through such means as keeping a journal or developing case records. Having carefully established the espoused theories and the theories-in-action, the stage is set for reflection and perhaps realignment of theories-in-use and behavior/actions.

Identifying Theories-in-Practice of Organizations.   Hall et al. (1990) saw the collection of reliable data about the values expressed implicitly or explicitly by an institution as critical to the process of organizational development. Comparisons and discrepancies can then be analyzed and compared using a consistent methodology. In their analytical scheme, organizational diagnosis consists of three parts: document analysis, personal values inventories, and group values analysis.

Documents examined include mission statements and statements of philosophy that express the intent and purpose of the organization, and policies and procedures focusing on stated behavioral expectations and sanctions. Using content analysis and looking for value clusters, a value profile of the organization can be developed. Values being reinforced, intentionally or unintentionally, can be identified through this process, enabling a school to develop strategies to help it become more consistent and more focused in what it does and says.

A number of instruments are available for assessing personal values such as the Hall–Tonna inventory (Hall et al., 1990). Such instruments generate personal values profiles that are useful for self-analysis and therapy or for aggregation by unit or organization permitting group analysis. Aggregated profiles can be compared with the intended values of the organization as revealed by the document analysis. Inconsistencies may reveal a need to restate the organizational values, to bring personal values in line with intended organizational values through staff development programs, or a combination of the two.

> Taken altogether, document analysis, individual and group analyses can provide insight into a number of critical aspects of the school's organizational culture. The information collected will reveal the possible stress areas between teachers and administrators as well as between administrators and board members. It will identify and measure current priority issues and values which can then be examined in an objective manner. The process will reveal operative leadership styles among teachers, administrators and school board members. It will identify, describe and analyze underlying value patterns in mission, philosophy and procedures, and will suggest ways in which these value patterns impact on a school's day-to-day culture. Finally, the data generated will indicate needed skills training for individuals and groups of teachers, administrators, or board members. (Hall et al., 1990, pp. 64–65)

Value Analysis of Problems. Hodgkinson (1983) focuses on applying value analysis to discrete problems. He asserted that a leader has a philosophical obligation to conduct a value analysis of significant problems being faced. In making such an analysis, the leader must separate personal interests and values from those of the organization, and the interest of others must be placed above his or her own. To exercise such control requires the leader to know the task, the situation, the group, and oneself. According to Hodgkinson (1983, p. 207), the following are among the questions to be answered in a value analysis: (1) What are the values in conflict, and can they be named? (2) What fields of values are most affected? (3) Who are the value actors? (4) How is the conflict distributed, interpersonally or intrapersonally? (5) Is the conflict interhierarchial or intrahierarchial? (6) What strategies for conflict resolution are most fitted to the case? (7) What are the metavalues involved in the case? (8) Is there a principle (type I value) raised or avoided? (9) Can the tension of nonresolution be accommodated? (10) What rational and pragmatic consequences attach to the possible and probable scenarios? (11) What bodies of value consensus and political interest, if relevant, are affected within and without the organization? (12) To what extent does the leader have control over the informative and affective media in the case (press, radio, television, lines of communication, informal organization, etc.)? (13) What is the extent of affect control among the parties in the case? (14) What is the extent of commitment among the parties in the case to their respective positions?

Willower and Licata (1997) have developed a similar approach called *moral valuation.* They justify the need for values and valuation in educational administration decision making by pointing out that the work of administrators is political and frequently rife with conflict. Administrators are generally engaged in a variety of brief, fragmented, and often interrupted activities, and they face an array of individuals and groups with special interests. The intense pressure for actions, often to conflicting ends, represents a continuing threat to distract the administrator from the guiding principles of the school.

They define *valuation* as "the process of choosing from and implementing conceptions of the desirable with an awareness of and sensitivity to their potential consequences for a variety of individuals and groups, as well as the multiplicity of values typically affected by implementation" (p. 26). The steps that they employ in valuation are those of ordinary scientific method applied to decision situations: a problem is formulated; alternative solutions are identified; the probable consequences of each alternative are elaborated conceptually; and a course of action is selected that seems most likely to attain the outcomes sought. In the analysis, they attempt to make the ethical considerations concrete and particular. They emphasize mitigating negative consequences as part of larger ethical decisions. Finally, they emphasize the utility of social science concepts and explanations in assisting administrators and others in their search for probable consequences and likely desirable outcomes.

Metavalues

Hodgkinson (1983) defined the term *metavalue* as "a concept of the desirable so vested and entrenched that it seems to be beyond dispute or contention—one that usually enters the ordinary value calculus of individual and collective life in the form of an unexpressed or unexamined assumption" (p. 43). In administration and organizational life, he identified the dominant metavalues as efficiency and effectiveness.

Nyberg (1993, p. 196) contended that "[t]he moral universe is the same for everyone in that it is based on concern for human dignity, decency, voluntary relations that are not oppressive, and some kind of spiritual fulfillment." The specifics differ from person to person, group to group, place to place, and time to time; but the basis of concern remains consistent. We are all similar, but each is unique.

Rokeach (1973) sought to identify ideals or values that are singled out for special consideration by all political ideologies. He hypothesized that the major variations in political ideology are fundamentally reducible to opposing value orientations concerning the political desirability or undesirability of freedom and equality in all their ramifications.

Getzels (1957, 1978) referred to national core values as "sacred." He identified four sacred values as being at the core of the American ethos: democracy, individualism, equality, and human perfectibility.

The literature on educational policy makes frequent explicit or implicit reference to these and similar values. Guthrie, Garms, and Pierce (1988) referred to equality, efficiency, and liberty as values of particular societal concern. Wirt (1987) referred to general agreement among nations that the major values in education are quality (excellence or human perfectibility), equity, efficiency, and choice (liberty or freedom). Boyd (1984) focused on liberty, equality, and efficiency as "three competing values" in educational policy and school governance in Western democracies (p. 4). Swanson (1989) identified five values that have been historically prominent in shaping Western societies and that are also particularly relevant to provision and consumption of educational services: liberty, equality, fraternity, efficiency, and economic growth. There is a good deal of overlap among the various lists with freedom and equality appearing on most.

The name of a metavalue may continue to be the same, but definitions may vary from place to place and over time. Nyberg (1981, Part II), for example, cautioned that *freedom* (or liberty) derives its meaning at least in part from the times in which it is used. He pointed out that the United States saw a transformation between 1787 and 1947, as "freedom as natural rights (rights *against* the government, rights of independence)" became "civil rights (rights to *participate* in civil government)" and later became "human freedoms (rights to the *help* of government in achieving protection from fear and want)" (pp. 97–98).

Parallel transformations took place in the meaning of equality (or equity). Initially, equality consisted only of rights and not conditions; that is, people were to be treated the same by law, custom, and tradition, with equality the instrument for guaranteeing liberty as originally defined. In recent times, the operational definition of equality has expanded to include factors of condition. For example, some persons are handicapped in enjoying liberty because of circumstances beyond their control, such as minority status, gender, poverty, and physical and psychological impediments. Although liberty and equality complemented one another as defined in 1787, the broader contemporary definition of equality brings it into direct conflict with the value of liberty (as originally defined) because the policies of remediation involve not only the disadvantaged person, but all others. Liberty requires an opportunity for expression through individual freedom, whereas equality of condition requires some curbing of individual freedom.

Because of the conceptual inconsistencies among values, it is not possible to emphasize all of them at the same time in public policy—or in individual lives—desirable though each may be. Individuals and societies must establish priorities. This is a dynamic process. Priorities of individuals change with circumstances, and where there has been a sufficient change among individuals, shifts in public priorities follow (Ravitch, 1985, p. 5). Agreement upon priorities is not necessary for private- or market-sector decisions beyond the family level. In the public sector, however, a singular decision is required involving

negotiations and compromises among interested partisans (subcultures and groups), generating significant social stress in the process. The higher the level of aggregation, the more difficult agreement becomes because of the greater amount of heterogeneity introduced.

Spindler (1955) explained the attacks on public education in the 1950s by citing major societal value shifts following World War II. (Reference to Spindler's analysis reminds us that this is not the first generation of educators to be the recipients of hostile public criticism.) Spindler saw the criticism of that day as products of an American culture that was experiencing a real shift in values. Populations going through cultural transition are characterized by conflict, and in its most severe form, demoralization and disorganization. The conflict goes beyond groups and institutions because individuals in a transformational society are likely to hold elements of both the dominant and the emerging value systems concomitantly. Such situations are not only confused by groups battling each other, but also by individuals fighting themselves.

Spindler (1955) described traditional values as Puritan morality, work-success ethic, individualism, achievement orientation, and future orientation. These values were being threatened by emergent values: sociability, relativistic moral attitudes, consideration for others, hedonistic present-time orientation, and conformity to the group. He concluded that there is a staunchness and a virility in the traditional value set that many viewed with nostalgia. But in his view, rugged individualism (in its expedient, ego-centered form) and rigid moralism (with its capacity for displaced hate) had become nonfunctional in a society where people are rubbing shoulders in polyglot masses and playing with technology that may destroy, or save, with the push of buttons.

More recently, Nyberg (1993) similarly concluded that a moral-principle or positivist orientation (described earlier) thrives in a supportive environment, but finds it difficult to adapt to new conditions when the environment changes. On the other hand, the personal-value or constructivist orientation (also described earlier) has a better chance of long-term survival in this moral world of constant changes because of its flexible adaptiveness and its willingness to live with uncertainty.

The shifting of values identified by Spindler and referred to by Nyberg is likely to continue into the foreseeable future. In addition, the geopolitical situation in the world has become fluid during the past decade. These, coupled with unparalleled technological advancements, actually seem to have accelerated the rate of major shifts in value priorities and in expressed dissatisfaction with the status quo. As a ripple effect, demands for educational reform have materialized. The old paradigms don't seem to fit anymore.

Major contemporary issues revolve around the competing social objectives of equality, personal liberty, and productive efficiency among others. The question of whether or not each can be furthered jointly through public policy is being hotly debated. The most likely scenario is that one or two values will be given priority, as in the past, to the jeopardy of the others. The ferment that we are experiencing today is a function of the dynamic political struggle to achieve the best balance among legitimate interests. The best balance has varied, and will continue to vary, from society to society and over time within a society as contexts and value definitions and priorities change (Wirt, 1986).

CASE STUDY[1]

Standardized Test Scores: A Potential Scandal

Analyze this case from the perspective of the director of pupil personnel services.

Part 1: Artificial Success

For the past several years, the results of the standardized tests for St. Stephen Elementary School have been considerably higher than the test results for the other elementary schools in the district. You are the district's test coordinator and have always found that fact curious. The students from St. Stephen's do not seem to do any better than the students from the other schools in the district when they get to high school. This year you decide to investigate the matter more closely.

You begin by speaking to St. Stephen's principal, Dana Winters. You are told that the scores went up after the school started taking a week to prepare the students for the exam. The teachers know that the tests cover specific areas, and they simply review the areas included on the tests. They also review the testing format and have the students take sample tests similar to the ones they will be given. The principal says that tests should measure students' academic achievement, not their level of test anxiety or test-taking ability.

Dana proudly shows you the test preparation materials the teachers use. For each grade there are thick compilations of questions in the same categories as those on the exam: math computation, vocabulary, spelling, math concepts, and so on. There are also answer sheets that correspond to the ones used on the actual exam. You ask if you can borrow the materials to look them over more closely in your office. Dana hesitates, but she agrees.

When you get back to your office, you read through the questions in the test preparation materials. They seem very reasonable. Then you get out a copy of the actual test corresponding to the preparation materials you are reviewing. About every third question in the preparation materials corresponds exactly to a question on the test. Your district owns the testing materials, and you have two sets of question booklets, Form A and Form B. You used Form B this year, but you find a copy of the Form A test. About a third of the questions on the test preparation materials come directly from the alternative form.

[1]Source: R. E. Kirschmann, *Educational administration: A collection of case studies* (pp. 127–129). Upper Saddle River, NJ: Merrill/Prentice Hall, 1996.

Questions

1. What will you do?

2. What will you say to the superintendent?

3. What additional information, if any, do you need?

4. What are the legal, moral, and ethical issues here?

5. Do you believe that the teachers at St. Stephen are involved in a conspiracy to cheat on the tests?

6. For years the local press and the community have commended St. Stephen for its test results. What will happen if this matter is discovered?

7. The test results are used to place students in the proper tracks when they get to seventh grade. A disproportionate number of students from St. Stephen are in the higher tracks. What, if anything, will you do about that matter?

Part 2: The Story Is Leaked

It has taken hours, but you have gone through all levels of the test preparation materials Dana gave you and all levels of both forms of the actual tests, highlighting all the questions on the preparation materials that duplicate actual test questions. The ratio has remained the same: one-third of the questions come from each form of the test, and the remaining one-third come from neither.

You take the fifth-grade materials in to show the superintendent, leaving the remainder on your desk. The superintendent knew about the week of test preparation and had even commended Dana for it. The superintendent did not know about the duplication of the actual test questions. The disclosure obviously would have many ramifications, and the two of you discuss how to handle the situation for some time. Before you come to any conclusions, the superintendent realizes that it is time to eat a quick supper and go to a school board meeting at Eastwick. You agree to consider the matter and decide on an approach the next day.

When you get home, you discuss the matter with your spouse, giving all details of the discussion between the superintendent and you. The next day is Friday, and the superintendent is out with a stomach virus. The question of the test preparation must wait. There does not seem to be any pressing need for immediate action. The tests for this year have already been completed and the results distributed. Your discussion will have to wait until Monday.

On Monday morning you are greeted by headlines in the local newspaper that read, "Standardized Tests Rigged at St. Stephen Elementary School." You have not even finished reading the article when the superintendent calls to ask who you told about the test situation. During the course of the conversation, it becomes apparent that neither of you said anything about this situation to anyone except your spouses. The highlighted test preparation materials and the tests themselves are still on top of the worktable in your office, except for the fifth-grade materials, which are on the superintendent's desk.

You search your memory to make sure that you did not mention the matter to anyone except your spouse. The superintendent does the same. Both of you also question your spouses. All four of you conclude that you have told no one or even made hints about the matter. The other people who might have known about the tests were the business manager, the assistant superintendent, the secretaries, and the custodian. The custodian comes in at night for a few hours and is an unlikely suspect.

The information in the newspaper is accurate and fairly detailed. It strongly suggests the possibility of a leak in the central office.

Questions

1. What moral and ethical questions do you now face?

2. What criteria are you going to use to place St. Stephen's sixth-graders in the junior–senior high school next year?

3. What measures will you take to deal with the faculty and principal of St. Stephen?

4. How will you protect your own reputation?

5. What will you say to the press?

6. How will you investigate the question of who leaked the information to the newspaper?

7. Who had anything to gain by disclosing the information at this time?

8. If you find out who told the press, what will you do?

9. What do you imagine is likely to happen now?

10. Now that the news is public, how will you handle the question of St. Stephen's test preparation? How can you carry on your internal investigation?

Activities

1. Everyone has a philosophical view of life even though it may not have been thoroughly articulated.

   a. Reflect on your philosophical view of life and summarize it in a few paragraphs.

   b. Is your philosophical view similar to any of those described in this chapter? Which one?

   c. How does your philosophy of life affect your professional behavior?

2. Develop for yourself a "professional platform" that can serve as an operational framework for decision making. Include:

   a. A description of your own system of beliefs

   b. A statement of your opinion as to the mission of schooling as a social process

   c. A statement as to the reasons you want to be a school administrator

   d. A statement of your views on the role of administrators in schools, their ideal relationships with other members of the school and system, and how they should implement their role

3. Numerous proposals have been presented for reforming education. Identify the macrovalues associated with each of the proposed reforms listed below and show how each marks a departure from macrovalues inherent in the status quo.

   a. Family choice of public schools

   b. Unconstrained educational vouchers

   c. Tax credits for private school tuition

   d. School-based decision making

   e. Full state funding of schooling

   f. Mandated state curriculum

References

Bates, R. J. (1984). Toward a critical practice of educational administration. In T. J. Sergiovanni & J. E. Corbally (Eds.), *Leadership and organizational culture* (pp. 64–71). Urbana, IL: University of Illinois Press.

Beare, H., Caldwell, B. J., & Millikan, R. H. (1989). *Creating an excellent school: Some new management techniques.* London: Routledge.

Bennis, W. (1984). Transformative power and leadership. In T. J. Sergiovanni & J. E. Corbally (Eds.), *Leadership and organizational culture* (pp. 64–71). Urbana, IL: University of Illinois Press.

Bolman, L. G., & Deal, T. E. (1995). *Leading with soul.* San Francisco: Jossey-Bass.

Bolman, L. G., & Deal, T. E. (1997). *Reframing organizations: Artistry, choice, and leadership.* San Francisco: Jossey-Bass.

Boyd, W. L. (1984). Competing values in educational policy and governance: Australian and American developments. *Educational Administration Review, 2* (2), 4–24.

Burns, J. M. (1978). *Leadership.* New York: Harper & Row.

Cambron-McCabe, N. H. (1993). Leadership for democratic authority. In J. Murphy (Ed.), *Preparing tomorrow's school leaders: Alternative designs.* University Park, PA: University Council for Educational Administration.

Daresh, J. C. (1988). *The preservice preparation of American educational administrators: Retrospect and prospect* (ERIC Document No. ED 294308, pp. 1–47). Cardiff, Wales: British Educational Management and Administration Society.

Daresh, J. C., & Playko, M. A. (1992). *The professional development of school administrators: Preservice, induction, and inservice applications.* Boston: Allyn & Bacon.

Deal, T. E., & Kennedy, A. A. (1982). *Corporate cultures: The rites and rituals of corporate life.* Reading, MA: Addison-Wesley.

De George, R. T. (1990). *Business ethics* (3rd ed.). New York: Macmillan.

Foster, W. P. (1984). Toward a critical theory of educational administration. In T. J. Sergiovanni & J. E. Corbally (Eds.), *Leadership and organizational culture* (pp. 240–259). Urbana, IL: University of Illinois Press.

Foster, W. P. (1986). *Paradigms and promises: New approaches to educational administration.* Buffalo, NY: Prometheus.

Gage, N. L. (1989). The paradigm wars and their aftermath: A "historical" sketch of research on teaching since 1989. *Educational Researcher, 18* (7), 4–10.

Getzels, J. W. (1957). Changing values challenge the schools. *School Review, 65,* 91–102.

Getzels, J. W. (1978). The school and the acquisition of values. In R. W. Tyler (Ed.), *From youth to constructive adult life: The role of the school* (pp. 43–66). Berkeley, CA: McCutchan.

Getzels, J. W., & Thelen, H. A. (1960). The classroom group as a unique social system. In N. B. Henry (Ed.), *The dynamics of instructional groups: The 59th yearbook of the National Society for the Study of Education* (pp. 53–82). Chicago: University of Chicago Press.

Graff, O. B., Street, C. M., Kimbrough, R. B., & Dykes, A. R. (1966). *Philosophic theory and practice in educational administration.* Belmont, CA: Wadsworth.

Greene, J. C. (1990). Three views on the nature and roles of knowledge in social science. In E. G. Guba (Ed.), *The paradigm dialog* (pp. 227–245). Newbury Park, CA: Sage.

Greenfield, T. B. (1978). Reflection on organization theory and the truth of irreconcilable realities. *Educational Administration Quarterly, 14* (2), 1–23.

Greenfield, T. B. (1984). Leaders and schools: Willfulness and nonnatural order in organizations. In T. J. Sergiovanni & J. E. Corbally (Eds.), *Leadership and organizational culture* (pp. 142–169). Urbana, IL: University of Illinois Press.

Greenleaf, R. K. (1977). *Servant leadership: A journey into the nature of legitimate power and greatness.* New York: Paulist Press.

Guba, E. G. (1990). The alternative paradigm dialog. In E. G. Guba (Ed.), *The paradigm dialog* (pp. 17–27). Newbury Park, CA: Sage.

Guthrie, J. W., Garms, W. I., & Pierce, L. C. (1988). *School finance and education policy: Enhancing educational efficiency, equality and choice.* Upper Saddle River, NJ: Prentice Hall.

Hall, B. P., Kalven, J., Rosen, L. S., & Taylor, B. (1990). *Developing human values.* Fond du Lac, WI: International Values Institute of Marian College.

Hodgkinson, C. (1983). *The philosophy of leadership.* Oxford: Blackwell.

Hodgkinson, C. (1991). *Educational leadership: The moral art.* Albany, NY: State University of New York Press.

House, E. R. (1990). An ethics of qualitative field studies. In E. G. Guba (Ed.), *The paradigm dialog* (pp. 17–27). Newbury Park, CA: Sage.

Hoy, W. K., & Miskel, C. G. (1991). *Educational administration: Theory, research and practice* (4th ed.). New York: McGraw-Hill.

Lather, P. A. (1990). Reinscribing otherwise: The play of values in the practices of the human sciences. In E. G. Guba (Ed.), *The paradigm dialog* (pp. 315–332). Newbury Park, CA: Sage.

Lerner, M. (1972). Liberalism. In *Encyclopaedia Britannica* (Vol. 13, pp. 1017–1020). Chicago: Benton.

Lewis, H. (1990). *A question of values: Six ways we make the personal choices that shape our lives.* New York: Harper & Row.

Lincoln, Y. S. (1990). The making of a constructivist: A remembrance of transformations past. In E. G. Guba (Ed.), *The paradigm dialog* (pp. 67–87). Newbury Park, CA: Sage.

Lindblom, C. E. (1959). The science of muddling through. *Public Administration Review, 19,* 79–88.

Lipham, J. M. (1988). Getzels' models in educational administration. In N. J. Boyan (Ed.), *Handbook on research on educational administration.* New York: Longman.

Maxcy, S. J. (1991). *Educational leadership: A critical pragmatic perspective.* New York: Bergin & Garvey.

Murphy, J. (Ed.). (1993). *Preparing tomorrow's school leaders: Alternative designs.* University Park, PA: University Council for Educational Administration.

National Policy Board for Educational Administration. (1989). *Improving the preparation of school administrators: The reform agenda.* Charlottesville, VA: NPBEA.

Nyberg, D. (1974). The inevitability of holding philosophical beliefs. *Metaphilosophy, 5* (1), 59–68.

Nyberg, D. (1981). *Power over power: What power means in ordinary life, how it is related to acting freely, and what it can contribute to a renovated ethics of education.* Ithaca, NY: Cornell University Press.

Nyberg, D. (1993). *The varnished truth: Truth telling and deceiving in ordinary life.* Chicago: University of Chicago Press.

Osterman, K. F., and Kottkamp, R. B. (1993). *Reflective practice for educators: Improving schooling through professional development.* Newbury Park, CA: Corwin Press.

Ouchi, W. G. (1981). *Theory Z: How American business can meet the Japanese challenge.* Reading, MA: Addison-Wesley.

Parsons, T. (1951). *The social system.* New York: Free Press.

Peters, T. J. (1988). *Thriving on chaos: Handbook for a management revolution.* New York: Knopf.

Peters, T. J., & Waterman, R. H., Jr. (1982). *In search of excellence: Lessons from America's best-run companies.* New York: Warner Books.

Popkewitz, T. S. (1990). Whose future? Whose past? Notes on critical theory and methodology. In E. G. Guba (Ed.), *The paradigm dialog* (pp. 46–66). Newbury Park, CA: Sage.

Ravitch, D. (1985). *The schools we deserve: Reflections on the educational crises of our times.* New York: Basic Books.

Rokeach, M. (1973). *The nature of human values.* New York: Free Press.

Sergiovanni, T. J. (1984a). Cultural and competing perspectives in administrative theory and practice. In T. J. Sergiovanni & J. E. Corbally (Eds.), *Leadership and organizational culture* (pp. 1–17). Urbana, IL: University of Illinois Press.

Sergiovanni, T. J. (1984b). Leadership as cultural expression. In T. J. Sergiovanni & J. E. Corbally (Eds.), *Leadership and organizational culture* (pp. 105–114). Urbana, IL: University of Illinois Press.

Sergiovanni, T. J. (1984c). Leadership and ex cellence in schooling. *Educational Leadership, 41*(5), 4–13.

Sergiovanni, T. J. (1992). *Moral leadership: Getting to the heart of school improvement.* San Francisco: Jossey-Bass.

Sergiovanni, T. J., & Carver, F. D. (1973). Applied science and the role of value judgement. In T. J. Sergiovanni & F. D. Carver, *The new school executive: A theory of administration.* New York: Dodd Mead.

Sergiovanni, T. J., & Starratt, R. J. (1983). *Supervision: Human perspectives* (3rd ed.). New York: McGraw-Hill.

Smith, J. K. (1990). Alternative research paradigms and the problem of criteria. In E. G. Guba (Ed.), *The paradigm dialog* (pp. 167–187). Newbury Park, CA: Sage.

Smith, L. M. (1990). Ethics, field studies, and the paradigm crisis. In E. G. Guba (Ed.), *The paradigm dialog* (pp. 139–157). Newbury Park, CA: Sage.

Spindler, G. D. (1955). Education in a transforming American culture. *Harvard Education Review, 25* (3), 145–156.

Swanson, A. (1989). Restructuring educational governance: A challenge of the 1990s. *Educational Administration Quarterly, 25* (3), 268–293.

Vaill, P. B. (1984). The purposing of high-performance systems. In T. J. Sergiovanni & J. E. Corbally (Eds.), *Leadership and organizational culture* (pp. 85–104). Urbana, IL: University of Illinois Press.

Wheatley, M. J. (1994). *Leadership and the new science: Learning about organizations from an orderly universe.* San Francisco: Berrett-Koehler.

Wheatley, M. J., & Kellner-Rogers, M. (1996). *A simpler way.* San Francisco: Berrett-Koehler.

Willower, D. J., & Licata, J. W. (1997) *Values and valuation in the practice of educational administration.* Thousand Oaks, CA: Corwin Press.

Wirt, F. M. (1986). *Multiple paths for understanding the role of values in state policy.* Paper presented at the Annual Meeting of the American Educational Research Association, San Francisco, CA (ERIC Document Reproduction Service No. ED278086).

Wirt, F. M. (1987). National Australia–United States education: A commentary. In W. L. Boyd & D. Smart (Eds.), *Educational policy in Australia and America: Comparative perspectives* (pp. 129–137). New York: Falmer Press.

Strategy Formation and Planning at the District and School Levels

This chapter seeks to produce an understanding of how educational institutions develop a sense of direction and purpose, make decisions about organizing themselves to realize their purpose(s), and allocate resources available to them to further their purpose(s). The process involves continuous monitoring of progress made toward organizational goals and objectives, adjusting implementation strategies to correct for unsatisfactory organizational performance, and adjusting direction and purpose(s) to accommodate changes in the sociopolitical environment.

Although the process is usually referred to as *strategic planning,* we accept Mintzberg's (1994) distinction between strategy formation and planning as two separate, but important procedures. He describes *planning* as a convergent, logical process that attempts to formalize decision making, strategy making, and management through decomposition, articulation, and rationalization. *Strategy formation* is described as a spontaneous, creative, and divergent process that cannot happen in isolation or on schedule and cannot be programmed. Because planning is an analytical process and strategy formulation is a synthesizing process, Mintzberg argues that they must happen separately. Strategy is thus not the consequence of planning; rather, planning takes place within the framework formed by strategy. Planning helps to translate intended strategies into realized ones by taking the first step that can lead to effective implementation.

We begin our discussion by first addressing issues of strategy formation, followed by issues of planning within the context of an existing strategy at the district level. Attention is then directed to these issues within the context of site-based management, including site-based budgeting. We close the chapter by describing an application of planning concepts as required of school districts by the New York State Education Department.

Strategy Formation

Strategy is a guide or course of action into the future that provides an organization with direction. It can be explicit, but it is more likely to be observed in consistency of behavior over time. It is the organization's perspective on how things should be done, its concept of the business. Strategy formation involves visioning, mission setting, and goal development. It is concerned with change and development.

There is a difference in opinion as to who should develop strategy and how it is shaped. The traditional view is that strategy formation is a function of leadership and must emanate from the top. Frazier (1997) identifies several reasons why this must be: (1) leaders are the only ones who have the best perspective on the big picture, (2) leaders have overall responsibility for management of the organization, (3) leaders have the authority to mold and arrange its various functions for strategic purposes, and (4) leaders have the power to make course corrections when needed (p. 105).

Wheatley and Kellner-Rogers (1996), on the other hand, stress the importance of interdependencies and interrelationships among members of an organization in establishing its identity and direction. They lament the impact of traditional institutional leadership on members of the organization and on the organization itself.

> It is strange to realize that most people have a desire to love their organization. . . . But then we take this vital passion and institutionalize it. We create an organization. The people who loved the purpose grow to disdain the institution that was created to fulfill it. Passion mutates into procedures, into rules and roles. Instead of purpose, we focus on policies. Instead of being free to create, we impose constraints that squeeze the life out of us. The organization no longer lives. We see its bloated form and resent it for what it stops us from doing. (p. 57)

Instead of a formal process, Wheatley and Kellner-Rogers advance the idea of an emergent process, one where a self gets organized, a world of shared meaning develops, networks of relationships take form, and information is noticed, interpreted, and transformed. "From these simple conditions emerge bodily different expressions of organizational forms" (p. 81).

Senge (1990) promotes the concept of the *learning organization,* "organizations where people continually expand their capacity to create the results they truly desire, where new and expansive patterns of thinking are nurtured, and where people are continually learning how to learn together" (p. 3). He characterizes a learning organization as a place where people are persistently discovering how they create their reality and how they can change it.

Mintzberg (1994) also notes that strategies need not originate from central management. He observes that big strategies can grow spontaneously from little ideas or initiatives. Anyone in the organization can prove to be a good strategist given a good idea and the freedom and resources to pursue it. This view is especially appropriate in professional organizations, such as schools, composed of well-educated members who are regularly required to apply discretionary judgment to solve problems within their areas of expertise. His grassroots model of strategy formation (Mintzberg, 1989, pp. 214–216) calls for letting patterns emerge rather than force an artificial consistency upon an organization prematurely. Such strategies become organizational when the patterns proliferate and pervade the behavior of the organization at large. Proliferation may be promoted consciously, but need not be, and they may or may not be managed. The management of such strategies is not to preconceive them but to recognize their emergence and to intervene as appropriate. Emergent strategies are more likely to happen during periods of change than during periods of stability.

In addition to emergent strategies, Mintzberg (1994) identifies four other types of strategies, as illustrated in Figure 13.1: intended, unrealized, deliberate, and realized. As the figure indicates, realized strategy takes on a different characteristic from that intended. This does not mean that the intended strategy is a failure. Quite the contrary, it served to launch the organization in what at the time was considered a desirable direction; but the organization was flexible in its implementation and took advantage of unforeseen opportunities (emergent strategy) and sloughed off unfruitful endeavors (unrealized strategy). In the end, a portion of the intended strategy was actually realized (deliberate strategy), enhanced by the emergent strategy. Mintzberg points out that few, if any, strategies are purely deliberate and few are purely emergent. "One suggests no learning, the other, no control. All real-world strategies need to mix these in some way—to attempt to control without stopping the learning process" (p. 25).

In this section we present strategy as an encompassing set of ideas and attitudes that permeate an organization's behavior and guides the decision-making process. In Figure 13.2 we have illustrated it as an umbrella under which all organizational activities take place. Strategy formation is discussed in four parts, although each is intermeshed with the others: visioning, mission statement, belief statements, and strategic policies.

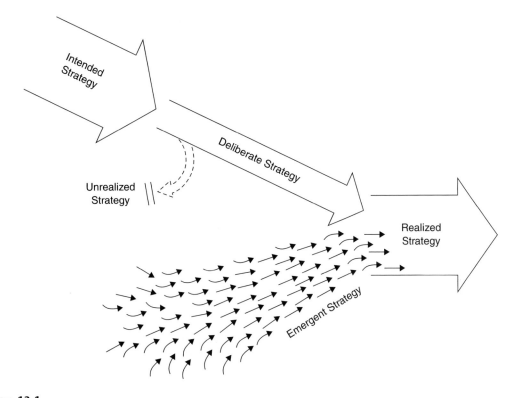

Figure 13.1
Mintzberg's forms of strategy
Source: H. Mintzberg, *The rise and fall of strategic planning* (p. 24). New York: Free Press, 1994.

Visioning

A *vision* is a mental image of a possible and desirable future state for an organization (Bennis & Nanus, 1985). It can be as vague as a dream or as precise as a goal or mission statement. The vision, however developed, must permeate the organization, being embedded in its structures, processes, and behaviors so that it shapes its operation and every decision made (Caldwell & Spinks, 1988). It creates a "consistency of purpose" throughout the organization (Deming, 1986). A vision sets the broad outlines of a strategy that leaves the specific details to be worked out later. Mintzberg (1994) argues that a visionary approach is a flexible way of dealing with an uncertain world so that when the unexpected happens, the organization can learn and adapt.

Wheatley (1994) metaphorically links vision in organizations to field theory in scientific thought. She sees the need for organizational clarity about purpose and direction as being more than creating a future destination for the organization. In addition, a vision of purpose needs to permeate the organization to take advantage of its formative properties serving to connect discrete and distant actions. Instead of controlling the organization through a myriad of policies and procedures, order is established through a shared vision embraced by all of its members; it is control by concept. According to Wheatley, when vision is seen as a field force, vision statements come off the walls and into the decisions and actions of the members of the organization.

Senge (1990) also portrays vision as a force of impressive power, a force in people's hearts.

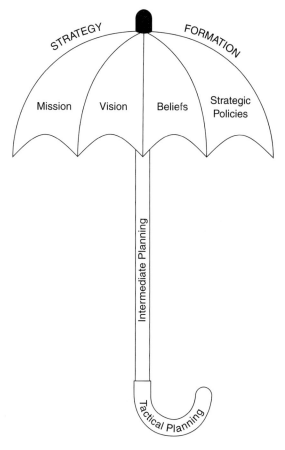

Figure 13.2
Relationship between strategy formation and intermediate and tactical planning

At its simplest level, a vision identifies what the members of the organization want to create. He points out that intrinsic visions can uplift people's aspiration; they can create a spark of excitement that elevates an organization above the mundane. A shared vision provides members with a feeling of ownership and encourages risk taking and experimentation in doing whatever is needed in pursuit of the vision. Without a shared vision pulling people toward a goal that they truly want to achieve, the forces in support of the status quo can become overwhelming.

Senge (1990) reminds us that shared visions must emerge from personal visions. "This is how

they derive their energy and how they foster commitment" (p. 211). According to Senge, the first step in building shared visions is to give up the traditional notion that visions must originate from the top of the organizational hierarchy or from its institutionalized planning process. Visions that are truly shared take time to emerge.

> They grow as a by-product of interactions of individual visions. Experience suggests that visions that are genuinely shared require ongoing conversation where individuals not only feel free to express their dreams, but learn to listen to each others' dreams. Out of this listening, new insights into what is possible gradually emerge. (Senge, 1990, pp. 217–218)

To facilitate the process, organizational leaders must be fully involved in the conversations and be willing to share their personal visions as well. They must also solicit the membership's endorsement rather than assume it.

Fullan (1993) warns that visions can blind as well as enlighten. "Having a sense of moral purpose and vision can be a decided advantage, but clarity of purpose can also be a liability if the vision is rigid and/or wrong, and if the process of vision building does not result in a *shared* sense of purpose" (p. 67). Fullan cautions that vision formation not be rushed for two reasons. First, vision emerges from action more than precedes it; reflective practice is needed before a plausible vision can be formed. Second, the sharing of a vision must evolve through the dynamic interaction of organizational members and leaders and this takes time. Vision seeking is an ongoing process. In avoiding premature formalization, visions may be pursued more authentically.

Mission Statements

A vision by its very nature is vague. In mobilizing the organization in pursuit of its vision, however, a time does come when it is useful to articulate the vision in more specific terms. This is commonly done through mission and belief statements.

The mission statement is a clear and concise expression of the district's purpose and func-

Figure 13.3
Mission statement of the West
Seneca, New York, Central
School District

> **MISSION**
>
> The mission of the West Seneca Central School District is to provide, under the guidance of a competent and committed staff and a supportive community, a diversified educational program which will produce literate, caring, responsible, and productive citizens who demonstrate positive ethical beliefs, possess self-discipline, exhibit dignity of character, and are capable of adapting to change.

Figure 13.4
Mission statement of the Maple
West Elementary School

> **MISSION STATEMENT**
> **MAPLE WEST ELEMENTARY**
>
> Our mission at Maple West Elementary is to be responsible for the preparation of children for the future by providing an educational setting that has a nurturing environment where learning is valued, individual differences accepted, and potential maximized.

tion. It should be a bold declaration of what the organization aspires to be. The mission statement should address the specific, local situation and represent the uniqueness of the district (school). Mission statements don't have to be feasible, only desirable. Missions exist at the boundary between the organization and its environment; they represent expectations that constituents have for the organization (O'Brien, 1991). The mission is the focus toward which the planning process is directed. Every person in the organization should know and understand it; it frequently is the only formal statement of the organization's vision. Figure 13.3 presents the mission statement for the West Seneca, New York, Central School District. Figure 13.4 presents the mission statement for the Maple West Elementary School.

Defining a district's mission is closely akin to what Drucker (1974) referred to as "knowing your business." According to Drucker, management must decide what its business is and what it should be. He argued that it is only upon the foundation of the basic purposes and missions

of the company that more detailed objectives, strategies, and tactical plans can be worked out. Schools and school districts often labor under the mistaken assumptions that their missions are rigidly set by law. In actuality, they have considerable flexibility, and defining their missions enables them to become emancipated from common preconceptions and to focus on a common purpose.

Belief Statements

Common beliefs held by members of the organization represent one of its primary bonding forces. The statement of beliefs is a formal expression of those fundamental principles that guide all district (or other unit, such as a school) decisions and activities. It describes the organization's moral character—its ethical code. The statement provides the value basis upon which subsequent portions of the planning process will develop and implementation will be evaluated; it is a public declaration of the moral essence of the district (Cook, 1990).

Figure 13.5
Belief statements of the West
Seneca, New York, Central
School District

BELIEFS

We believe that . . .

Excellence in education cannot be compromised.

Each student can learn and is entitled to an equal opportunity to reach his/her potential.

All members of the community have life-long educational needs.

Education is student centered.

A safe environment is essential.

A fundamental responsibility of the school community is to create and maintain an environment to foster the dignity and self-esteem of students, parents, and staff.

Discipline is essential.

Education is broad-based, encompassing intellectual, emotional, physical, and social growth.

Education promotes behaviors, attitudes and values inherent in a democratic society.

Learning is challenging, exciting, and rewarding.

Our educational system is vital to the community.

Education requires the responsible commitment of students, staff, parents, and the community at large.

All members of the community serve as role models.

Open communication with the community is essential.

Open communication within the educational system is essential.

Developing a statement of beliefs begins with what Goodstein, Nolan, and Pfeiffer (1992) call a *value scan*. It examines the personal values of those assigned to do the scan, the current values of the organization, the organization's philosophy of operations, the assumptions that usually guide the organization's operations, the organization's preferred culture, and the values of the stakeholders in the organization's future. (See the related discussion of values analysis in Chapter 12.) In conducting the values scan, the scanners move from an individual focus to a broader examination of the organization and how it works as a social system. It focuses attention on the frequently unacknowledged underpinnings that guide the behaviors and deci-

sions of organization members and, thereby, the organizational culture. Figure 13.5 illustrates a set of belief statements as developed by the West Seneca, New York, Central School District.

Strategic Policies

Strategic policies establish the parameters within which the district will operate. They specify the postures that the district will either always take, or never take. Policies act to channel thinking and to serve as guides to action. They set constraints within which discretion can be exercised. By adding the modifier *strategic,* the bulk of district policy that deals with the routine of daily operations is eliminated from

Figure 13.6
Strategic policies of the West
Seneca, New York, Central
School District

STRATEGIC POLICIES

No student will be automatically promoted.

No curriculum will be implemented or modified without the input of the staff who will be required to teach it.

We will never add or eliminate programs without careful analysis.

We will always provide programs which will assist all employees to perform more effectively.

Each employee will be evaluated and no employee will be granted permanent status unless he/she achieves an above-average rating.

No student will participate in any extracurricular activity who does not satisfy the eligibility requirements for that activity.

We will not compromise health and safety laws.

---

consideration. Cook (1990, p. 96) asserted that strategic policies "establish 'ground rules'; set in place protective mechanisms, ratios, formulas, and the like; dictate codes of behavior; define expectations; assert priorities; and define various boundaries." Policies focus the mission statement and prevent overzealous pursuit of them. Figure 13.6 illustrates strategic policies as developed by the West Seneca, New York, Central School District.

Planning

Strategy formation provides an organization with direction (vision and mission) and a set of governing principles (beliefs and strategic policies) that will guide the organization over the long term. Planning addresses the issues of mobilizing the resources of the organization to enable its mission.

Planning brings order to strategy by putting it into a form suitable for articulation to others. It makes specific the assumptions of strategy. It identifies the major hurdles that are likely to be realized in pursuing the strategy. It makes sure (or at least attempts) to take everything into account. Planning is alignment. Whereas strategy formation was characterized as a creative, spontaneous, intuitive, divergent process, planning is highly rational, logical, formal, and convergent. Strategy synthesizes; planning analyzes. Strategy integrates; planning decomposes. Planning designs the logistics necessary to implement strategy.

A well-organized planning system can provide an extremely useful communications network that links together all members of the organization. As plans approach completion, common understandings are generated about opportunities and problems that are important to individuals and to the organization. The choices made in the planning process are discussed in a common language and the issues are understood (or should be) by all those participating in decision making. According to Mintzberg (1994): ". . . planning sits toward the formal end of the continuum of organizational behavior. . . . It must be seen, not as decision making, not as strategy making, and certainly not as management, or as the preferred way of doing any of these things, but simply as the effort to formalize parts of them—through decomposition, articulation, and rationalization" (p. 15).

Planning must be recognized as a social–political process for coordinating and integrating the goals of the organization with those of the individual. (See discussion of values as part of organizational cultures in Chapter 12.) As a political process, planning may become a dynamic interaction and exchange involving bargaining, negotiations, and the exercise of power. Alternatively, as a social-consensual process, planning may be seen as developing uncoerced understanding and agreement among those involved through the free exchange of ideas. The latter is preferred to the exercise of power and adversarial bargaining assumed by the political model.

Throughout the planning process, individuals within the organization are constantly balancing their interests with those of the group (Lotto & Clark, 1986). Through negotiations, the preferences and activities of the organizational stakeholders are ordered and reordered, singularly and in groups. Underlying the process is a basic assumption that people who will be affected by a proposed plan will be extensively involved in its development because all members of the organization have relevant expertise, which will be translated into a better plan; also, the plan is more likely to be implemented successfully due to its enhanced pertinency and the sense of ownership on the part of stakeholders generated by involvement. The process strengthens the communal vision and understanding of the organization by its members.

Improved employee motivation and morale and community support are potential by-products of the planning process. Being involved in formulating organizational plans promotes a sense of satisfaction among participants gained from helping to shape—at least in part—their own destiny within the organization. Knowing what is expected of organizational members builds a sense of personal security and confidence. Taken together, these improved attitudes enable people to accept change more readily, a valuable attribute in any organization.

We divide the discussion of planning into two segments: (1) intermediate and (2) tactical. *Intermediate planning* has a time frame of three to five years, whereas *tactical planning* deals with the short term, usually one year. The process of intermediate planning asks and answers some key

questions in a way that might otherwise be easily overlooked and establishes a scale of priority and urgency for dealing with the answers. Questions addressed include: What opportunities or threats exist in the years ahead that we should exploit or avoid? What are our strategic objectives? What major changes are taking place in the environment that will affect us? What resources will be available to us over the next several years?

Intermediate planning identifies and addresses only those areas where change is critical to the welfare of the organization. Tactical planning addresses all activities of the organization in the short term.

Intermediate Planning

We divide the discussion of intermediate planning into four segments: internal and external analyses, gap analysis and the identification of critical issues, the development of strategic objectives, and the formation of action plans to address the critical issues. The relation of the segments is illustrated in Figure 13.7.

Internal and External Analyses. The internal analysis consists of a thorough and unbiased examination of the current and projected strengths and weaknesses of the district or school. Strengths are internal qualities, circumstances, or conditions that contribute to the district's/school's ability to achieve its mission with respect to such attributes as financial, personnel, organizational, physical, and social characteristics. Strengths relative to similar organizations are not of particular interest here, but rather, strengths relative to the potential for accomplishing the district's or school's mission. Strengths signal areas in which success may be most easily realized. Weaknesses, conversely, are internal qualities, circumstances, or conditions that impede the realization of the district's or school's mission. Data for the internal analysis are drawn from the organization's information system discussed in Chapter 15.

The external analysis looks beyond the district or school into its environment and into its

Figure 13.7
Components of intermediate
planning

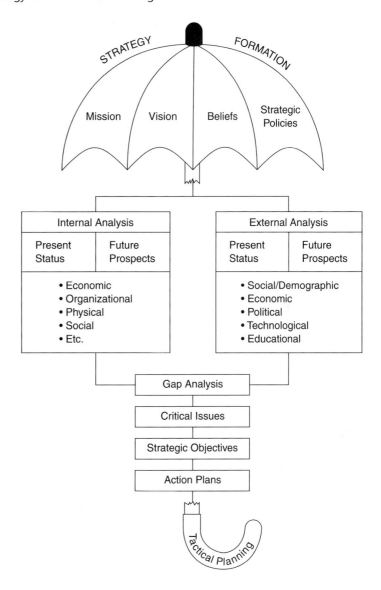

possible futures, anticipating events and conditions likely to occur that will have a significant impact on the organization. The purpose of the external analysis is to reduce the likelihood of surprises that may negatively affect the organization's ability to accomplish its mission and to identify opportunities the district or school may wish to exploit. The analysis needs to deal with five categories of influence: (1) social and demographic (e.g., family stability or instability, family structure, social structure, unemployment, general level of education, crime rate, size and composition of the population); (2) economic (e.g., economic trends, size of tax base, employment rate, salary levels); (3) political (e.g., agendas of special interest groups); (4) technological, scientific, and environmental (e.g., new inventions that may affect instruction or the life and employment of students, knowledge about human development and how people learn); and (5) educational trends and influences (Cook, 1990, p. 105).

The external analysis emphasizes the importance of systemic assessment of environmental impacts. Its major objective is to identify and analyze the key trends, forces, and phenomena having a potential impact on implementing strategies. It provides a forum for sharing and discussing divergent views about relevant environmental changes enabling vague opinions about different parts of the analysis to be made more explicit (Steiner, 1979). According to Steiner, such an analysis is not something that can or should be completed in the planning process solely on a formal basis. It should be done continuously in the personal surveillance of environments by the professional personnel. This type of environmental scanning is performed in a variety of ways from reading journals systematically to attending professional meetings, to conversing casually with fellow professionals. The results from environmental scanning may be useful in evaluating strategy as well as planning its implementation.

Gap Analysis.   The gap analysis determines "where we are" versus "where we want to be." It is an assessment by the school or district of its programs and services; the strengths, weaknesses, and adequacies of its staff and facilities; resources available in the community; and challenges being made to the status quo by internal weaknesses and trends, external community conditions, pressures exerted by external community interest groups, and forces at the state and national levels. It is an analysis within the documented social, political, and economic environments of the district's or school's capabilities to meet the challenges before they are realistically appraised given the resources available and the expectations of citizens and staff. Professional staff need to be proactive in looking for opportunities to serve its clients according to highest professional standards even when those standards are beyond the expectation or comprehension of its clients.

The gap analysis juxtaposes the internal and external analyses against the district's/school's mission. Data—past, present, and future—are analyzed in a fashion that provides a rationale for the formulation of strategic operating objectives and strategic commitment of resources. Organizations always represent states of inadequacy, the gap between the way things are and the way we want things to be (Hodgkinson, 1991).

Coming out of the gap analysis is an identification of critical issues that must be dealt with if the organization is to survive or re-create itself within the context of its stated mission. Identifying critical issues focuses attention on paramount threats and opportunities, thereby providing a compelling rationale for the deployment of resources (Cook, 1990).

Strategic Objectives.   Strategic objectives are statements that commit the organization to achieve specific measurable end results intended to address the critical issues identified in the gap analysis. The strategic objectives are what the district school must achieve in the next three to five years if it is to accomplish its mission and be true to its beliefs. Cook (1990) observes that most school districts experience difficulty in writing suitable objectives because most educators seem to be more process-oriented than results-oriented. True objectives create risks and impose accountability.

As much as possible, decisions should be made on facts rather than opinion. Numerical indicators help us to check our progress. Deming et al. (1992) identified two classifications for causes of variation in numerical indicators: (1) common and (2) special. *Common cause variations* are random fluctuations that are within normal control of management, for example, teacher absences. Common cause variations are usually within tolerable limits. *Special cause variations* are unpredictable and reflect more profound differences. Normally, we should respond to special cause variations before we attend to common cause variations.

Awkerman (1991) warned that in planning, we must clearly differentiate between means

Figure 13.8
Strategic objectives of the West
Seneca, New York, School
District

STRATEGIC OBJECTIVES

By June . . . , increase by 50% the number of people who have a
positive perception of the West Seneca Central School District.

By the year . . . , 90% of our students will participate in at least
one human service project annually.

By June . . . , 100% of our students will perform at their expected
achievement level.

By the year . . . , to have 100% of our students, within six months
after graduation, either gainfully employed or enrolled in an
institution of higher learning.

---

and ends. Too frequently we confuse the objectives of schools and school districts by expressing them in terms of means rather than ends. For example, we set goals for raising teachers' salaries or lowering class size when our true interest is in improving achievement or reducing dropout rates. Our assumption is that raising teachers' salaries will improve the caliber of teacher the district can hire, which, in turn, will have a positive effect on student achievement and retention. The truth is that the linkage among teachers' salaries, class size, and other input resources is, at best, tenuous and there are other means that should be considered for reaching the desired ends that may be just as effective and less costly. "The greater the clarity of a desired end, the greater the probability that any selected means will accomplish the same desired ends" (Awkerman, 1991, p. 206).

The strategic objectives list does not address all the outcomes for which a district or school is responsible. It only includes those that are to receive highest priority in the next three to five years. The list will change over time as strategic objectives are realized or as they are replaced by more urgent concerns. Strategic objectives for the West Seneca, New York, Central School district are illustrated in Figure 13.8.

Integrated Action Plans. Integrated action plans are the means by which a district or school will accomplish its strategic objectives in the process of implementing its mission. They specify the deployment of the district's resources in the quest of the organization's mission. They indicate its basic operational emphasis, its priorities, and the standards by which it will measure its own performance. They need to be stated conceptually and allow for practical flexibility as they are translated into action.

Action plans provide detailed descriptions of specific actions required in the short term to achieve specific results necessary for implementation of the strategic plan. They also address the ongoing business of the district or school in keeping with the statements of beliefs, mission, and strategic policies and giving special attention to strategic objectives. An effective action plan is conceived and written from an operations point of view. The content is predicated on progressive, direct cause-and-effect relationships and is immediately workable.

Tactical Planning Including Budgeting

Tactical Planning. Entering into tactical (or operational) planning, the time frame shifts from several years to one year or less. Strategy formulation has provided the school or district with its long-term direction and guiding principles. Intermediate planning has ascertained where the organization is in relation to where it wants to be and has determined some key tactics intended to put the school or district on

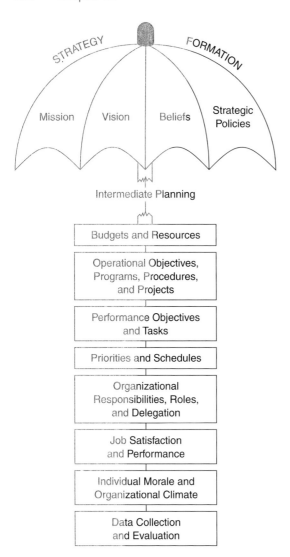

Figure 13.9
Components of tactical (or operational) planning

course to accomplish its mission. Tactical planning integrates these strategic initiatives into ongoing activities in the form of operational plans and budgets. Tactical planning addresses such issues as: (1) What programs, procedures, and projects are required? (2) What resources need to be committed? (3) What is the schedule of events? (4) Who will be responsible for implementing programs, procedures, and projects?

(5) What will be the impact on human resources? (6) What progress has been made toward realizing strategic objectives and mission?

The logistics of addressing these tasks is illustrated in Figure 13.9. It is important to keep in mind that any general planning model—of which there are many—must be adapted to the specific circumstances under which it will be applied. A planning process for a school district must be different from that for a school. The process and format for a high school must be different from that for an elementary school; and the processes and formats will vary among elementary schools and high schools.

In response to questions 1 and 2, strategic policies and objectives are translated into operational objectives, programs, procedures, projects, and budgets for immediate implementation and added to or integrated with the continuing operations of the school or district. Performance objectives are set and tasks are assigned. Deadlines are established (question 3, "What is the schedule of events?") and responsibilities for meeting those deadlines in the manner specified are placed with specific individuals (question 4, "Who will be responsible for implementing programs, procedures, and projects?").

New programs, projects, and directions frequently require new skills and new organizational configurations. The members of the district must be well prepared to deal with such changes or serious morale problems may develop, damaging the ability of the district or school to reach its goals. Providing those implementing the plan with the necessary knowledge and skills may require an extensive staff development program (responding to question 5, "What will be the impact on human resources?").

Evaluation of the success of implementation comes at the end of a tactical cycle (question 6, "What progress has been made toward realizing strategic objectives and mission?"), but deciding what data need to be collected to monitor success and the establishment of benchmarks need to be done before implementation begins. Measuring progress requires knowing the state of affairs before the plan was put into place; such information should have been part of the self assessment made during the intermediate planning process. By comparing the state of affairs periodically after implementation with the state of affairs prior to implementation, progress made toward goals can be monitored. If progress is unsatisfactory, corrective measures need to be taken in future operational plans. The information collected can also contribute to evaluation of the overarching strategy that needs to be reviewed every few years to make sure that changing conditions have not rendered it obsolete.

Tactical, or operational, planning is a process by which managers ensure that resources are obtained and used effectively and efficiently in the accomplishment of the organization's missions and strategic objectives (Cunningham, 1982, p. 12). Because of their focus on operations, the instructional and service units initiate tactical planning. These include not only the expected instructional programs, but also support services such as administration, maintenance of building and grounds, food service, transportation, and new initiatives established in the intermediate plan.

Perhaps the best way to describe tactical planning is to contrast it with strategy formulation. Although principals, teachers, students, and members of the community may be involved in strategy formulation, the process is usually initiated and monitored by the policy makers of the district, the board of education, and the superintendent. It is usually a top-down process. Tactical planning, on the other hand, is a decentralized process that takes place under the umbrella of the governing strategy where principals, supervisors, department heads, and teachers are the primary participants; it is a bottom-up process.

Tactical planning is bureaucratic in spirit; strategy formulation is entrepreneurial with intermediate planning serving as a transition between the two. Tactical planning focuses on current operating problems and realities in order to improve present performance, whereas strategy is directed toward long-term survival and devel-

opment to ensure future school system success. Unlike strategy formulation and intermediate planning, tactical planning is constrained by present conditions and resources. Tactical planning seeks to maintain efficiency and stability in the organization while strategy seeks to change it in order to develop future potential and flexibility. Tactical planning is based on information concerning teacher, parent, and student conditions. Strategy formulation uses such information as a baseline for making projections of future conditions, desires and values.

The responsibility for tactical planning is placed with line administrators, who have intimate understandings of the intricacies of day-to-day operations. In splitting the planning function, the basis for a two-way discourse is established. The discussion is initiated at the center that establishes the framework and sets the parameters in which tactical planning takes place. The detailed plans are developed by line administrators within the context provided by the center, which are, in turn, reviewed by the center to make sure that they are truly consistent with the established guidelines (Frazier, 1997).

The top-down, bottom-up approach requires much less need to modify and change plans and budgets developed at the operational level. When operational plans and budgets are initiated at the bottom in the absence of a strategic plan, major modifications are usually required through review by top administrators, due to incongruous goals and lack of organizational perspective. Frequent and major modifications place in question the efficacy of the entire planning process and encourage an attitude of cynicism throughout the organization.

The leadership style that is most compatible with tactical planning is conservative, placing high priority on that which has succeeded in the past. The leadership style most compatible with strategy formation is visionary, inspiring change to meet future needs. Tactical planning is oriented to solving problems through standard operating procedures that have been successful in the past. Strategy formation is more prone to approach problem solving with new techniques and ideas. Tactical planning is designed to minimize risk. Because of the great uncertainty associated with possible future events, strategy formation involves high risks; but the risks can be managed through continual monitoring and adjustments, a process toward which tactical planning contributes.

Budgeting. Budgeting is an integral part of tactical planning; but unfortunately, it is usually the only formal planning activity undertaken by many educational organizations. Typically, financial constraints are emphasized to the exclusion of educational plans and mission. Budgeting in the absence of a guiding strategy is directionless.

The primary purpose of a budget is to translate a district's or school's educational priorities and programs into financial terms within the context of available resources and legal constraints (answering question 2 above, "What resources need to be committed?"). The important decisions as to who gets what, when, and how are made through this process. Within the public sector, the budget is a legally adopted document that presents planned expenditures and anticipated revenues for a given fiscal year. It is this legal emphasis on financial aspects of the budget that largely explains the neglect of its programmatic aspects (Hartman, 1988).

The budget is one of the primary management tools of educational administrators and the major one in the fiscal area. In addition to its importance to the planning process, for public schools, the budget serves as a vehicle for public review and approval. Once approved, the budget becomes the legal basis for spending funds. During the course of the year, the budget serves as a management control document, providing specific spending limits that are not to be exceeded without prior authorization. Through careful monitoring, over-expenditures can be avoided and compensation for possible revenue shortfall can be made at the earliest possible point, allowing maximum flexibility for dealing with it (Hartman, 1988).

School-Based Management: Planning and Budgeting

Providing schools with greater authority to make critical decisions about their operations is a primary strategy of the school reform movement. It is presented here as a special case of strategy formation and planning.

School-based decision making (SBM) as a strategy of reform is founded on the premise that the school is the fundamental decision-making unit within the education system and that its administrators, teachers, and other professional and support staff constitute a natural decision-making and management team. Each school is considered a relatively autonomous unit with the principal in the role of chief executive officer. Shifting decision-making responsibilities from central administrative offices to schools means a redistribution of power among principals, teachers, parents, and community members under the assumption that involving key stakeholders in the decision-making process will make schools more responsive to the unique needs of local conditions and will more effectively harness their knowledge, creativity, and energy. The purpose of this strategy is to improve the instructional process and, implicitly, student outcomes (Summers & Johnson, 1996).

SBM is the product of decentralizing strategies that have been evolving over a quarter of a century beginning in the 1970s with the concept of school-based management and budgeting, and magnet schools. In the 1990s this trend led to self-governing charter schools. Organizational analysts have found that high-involvement decision-making structures are particularly appropriate in settings where the work is not routine and employees have to deal with great variation in inputs and where there is uncertainty about the relationships between means and outcomes (Lawler, 1986). It is also appropriate where the work and decisions of employees are interrelated in their impact and need to be coordinated in a manner that cannot be fully anticipated in advance. These conditions characterize education (Mohrman & Lawler, 1996).

Structures for making policy at the school level vary (Kirst, 1990). Authority may be placed with the principal alone (i.e., administrative decentralization), or the responsibility may be shared in some combination among administrators, teachers, parents, community representatives, and upper-grade students. Some manifestations of SBM place authority with a school-based governing board dominated by laypersons, for example, in Chicago; this is a form of political decentralization. When power is placed with lay boards, specific provision is usually made for formal professional involvement in the decision-making process. In administrative decentralization, authority is devolved from the district to members of the professional staffs in the schools. Political decentralization empowers those outside the traditional school structure such as parents and other community members (Ross, 1997).

Under SBM, school authorities may develop the budget, select staff, and refine the school's curriculum to meet specific needs of its pupils within legal constraints set by the school district or higher levels of government (Cawelti, 1989; U.S. General Accounting Office, 1994). The school district continues to set general priorities within which all schools must function, develop overarching educational objectives and the basic curriculum for meeting those objectives, allocate lump sums of money to schools based on student needs, negotiate labor contracts, and provide facilities and other support services, such as transportation, payroll, and accounting.

In actuality, there is little evidence that SBM leads directly to improved pupil achievement (Conway, 1984; Malen, Ogawa, & Kranz, 1990; Smylie, 1994; Summers & Johnson, 1996; Wohlstetter, Smyer, & Mohrman, 1994). Therefore, SBM must be viewed as an element of systemic reform if a connection with improved pupil achievement is to be made. Other elements need to involve higher performance expectations, more directed pedagogical demands, and clear accountability systems, and may include such reforms as national and state curricula, performance standards, and assessment; national teacher certification; and family choice of schools (Consortium on Renewing Education [CORE], 1998 Guthrie, 1998; Hannaway, 1996; Hannaway and Carnoy, 1993). Although not linked directly to improvement in student outcomes, SBM is credited with being an efficacious means of addressing conflicts over the distribution of scarce resources and enhancing the legitimacy of institutions authorized to make those decisions.

> The bottom line is that school based management is not an end in itself, although research indicates that it can help foster an improved school culture and higher quality decisions. School based management is, however, a potentially valuable tool for engaging the talents and enthusiasm of far more of a school's stake-holders than traditional, top-down governance systems. Moreover, once in place, school based management holds the promise of enabling schools to better address students' needs. (Wohlstetter & Mohrman, 1994, p. 1)

Arguments for Administrative Decentralization

Sizer (1985) claimed that hierarchical bureaucracy is paralyzing American education. "The structure is getting in the way of children's learning" (p. 206). Sizer's first imperative for better schools was to give room to teachers and students to work and learn in their own, appropriate ways. He saw decentralized authority as allowing teachers and principals to adapt their schools to the needs, learning styles, and learning rates of students individually. Although not denying the need to upgrade the overall quality of the educating profession, Sizer believed that, if empowered, there were enough fine teachers and administrators to lead a renaissance of American schools.

Goodlad (1984) identified the school as *the* unit for improvement. The approach to educational reform that Goodlad viewed to be most promising was the one "that will seek to cultivate the capacity of schools to deal with their own problems, to become largely self-renewing" (p. 31). He did not see the schools as being "cut loose," but rather, as being linked to the hub (district office) and to each other in a network. State officials should be responsible for developing "a common framework for schools within which there is room for some differences in interpretation at the district level and for some variations in schools resulting from differences in size, location, and perspective" (p. 275). According to Goodlad, the district should concern itself with the balance in curricula presented, the processes employed in planning, and the equitable distribution of funds. "What I am proposing is genuine decentralization of authority and responsibility to the local school within a framework designed to assure school-to-school equity and a measure of accountability" (Goodlad, 1984, p. 275).

Boyer (1983) also saw heavy doses of bureaucracy "stifling creativity in too many schools, and preventing principals and their staffs from exercising their best professional judgment on decisions that properly should be made at the local level" (p. 227). For Boyer, "rebuilding excellence in education meant reaffirming the importance of the local school and freeing leadership to lead" (p. 316).

Cuban (1988) argued that the bureaucratic organization of schooling is responsible for the lack of professional leadership. Autonomy is the necessary condition for leadership to arise.

> Without choice, there is no autonomy. Without autonomy, there is no leadership. . . . Schools as they are presently organized press teachers, principals, and superintendents toward managing rather than leading, toward maintaining what is rather than moving to what can be. The structures of schooling and the incentives buried within them produce a managerial imperative. (pp. xx–xxi)

Cuban also recognized the need for federal, state, and district regulations and their accompanying forms of accountability. He called for balanced procedures that permit sufficient discretion to those delivering a service while allowing prudent monitoring by higher levels of authority. Such procedures would focus "less on control through regulation and more on vesting individual schools and educators with the independence to alter basic organizational arrange-

ments (if necessary) to reach explicit goals and standards" (p. 248).

After an extensive review of the research on decentralization (SBM) and performance-based incentives such as holding schools accountable for meeting state standards, Hannaway (1996) concluded that incentives alone, such as decentralization alone, may do more harm than good; but in tandem, they hold great promise of raising achievement levels among elementary and secondary students. She points out that a major drawback of decentralization is that many schools, especially those serving disadvantaged students, may not have the capacity to guide school behavior effectively. Performance-based incentives can counter this weakness by directing a significant amount of school activity toward meeting societally defined academic achievement objectives even if those objectives are narrowly focused. Thus, schools with low capacity would not be left totally on their own to flounder aimlessly. On the other hand, the major drawback of performance-based incentives is curricular distortion, while an advantage of decentralization is that it provides a way to balance the system relatively easily when it becomes distorted because decentralization leaves the school largely unencumbered by bureaucratic red tape, procedures, and hierarchy.

Key elements in the strategy of the Consortium on Renewing Education (CORE) (1998) for doubling America's academic achievement scores by the year 2020 are focusing on student achievement and shifting the primary locus of control from districts to individual school sites. CORE argues that school control places decision-making authority for day-to-day instructional operations at the school site, empowering schools to make all legally permissible decisions that are professionally appropriate to meet specific state academic performance objectives. CORE proposes that the bulk of dollars spent on education be allocated directly to schools (about 75 percent of the total) and that schools be allowed to use these monies in ways they deem most productive in improving achievement. CORE does not rely solely on SBM, however, to meet its strategic objective; as recommended by Hannaway (1996), it couples SBM with an accountability scheme that involves high-stakes proficiency examinations for students graduating. Third graders would need to demonstrate their proficiency in reading before they can be promoted to fourth grade. Similarly, students would need to demonstrate proficiency in mathematics and algebra before they could enter high school.

Guthrie (1998) reminds us that the educational crisis lies primarily in the large urban school districts, where because of their size, governance reforms such as SBM are critical. He points out that 90 percent of school districts have fewer than 5000 pupils and 80 percent have fewer than 2500 pupils, making them small enough to avoid the most devastating effects of bureaucratic impairment. The problem lies with the 5 percent of the districts educating 50 percent of the nation's public school population. In these large, urban districts, decision making has become remote, diffuse, and divorced from the operating authority of the school. The enormous set of district, state, federal, and judicial rules by which those schools are expected to operate have made dysfunctional their operational integrity, increasing the difficulty for principals and staffs to forge a unified vision of the manner in which a school should operate or a strategy of implementation.

Guthrie sees site-based management as an idea that makes logical sense for overcoming these difficulties when coupled with other compatible reforms, such as a statewide or districtwide achievement accountability system. He fears, however, that genuine school-based management and related reforms are unlikely to happen because of the political controversy that they would probably promote. The ability of school boards to micromanage would be diminished. Many school principals fear the spotlight of accountability. Teacher union officials fear the erosion of their districtwide base of influence. Potential proponents of the reforms who would benefit most from them, students, parents and other citizens are ill informed regarding the idea and are unorganized for political action.

In summary, despite the political obstacles pointed out by Guthrie, analysts see SBM as an integral part of systemic school reform.

Strategy Formation and Planning at the School Level

Within a district planning scheme, the school is likely to be viewed as a program, one of the quasi-independent units within the system. With the growing practice of school-based management, schools themselves are becoming the primary planning unit. This practice is relatively new in the United States but is practiced extensively elsewhere, especially in England and Australia, where a valuable experience base has developed. One of the school-based management models that is built upon the collective experiences of schools in those countries is Caldwell and Spink's (1992, 1998) model for self-management (MSM). We feel that it offers an appropriate guide for U.S. schools and will describe it in some detail.

The MSM is illustrated in Figure 13.10. It integrates the annual management functions of design, budgeting, implementing, and evaluating with the strategic governance functions of direction and priority setting and policy making. MSM focuses on the central function of schools—learning and teaching—and is designed to involve administrators, teachers, and other staff; students; parents; and other members of the community. The management of the school is organized around programs that correspond to the preferred patterns of work in the school.

MSM attempts to dispel the confusion created by the simultaneous shifts in authority toward centralization of some decisions (e.g., state curricular mandates, standards, and assessment) and decentralization of others (e.g., school-based management and teacher and community empowerment). It acknowledges the influence of central authority, be it national or state government or local school district, through the "central framework" and the "charter." "Policies" and

Figure 13.10
Model for self-management
(MSM)

Source: B. J. Caldwell and J. M. Spinks,
Leading the self-managing school
(p. 33). London: Falmer Press, 1992.

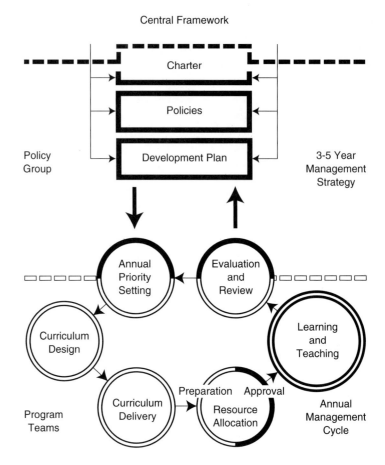

"development plan" are the points where the laws and regulations within which each school must operate are integrated with the school's unique characteristics, philosophy, and mission.

A school charter[1] is a document to which both government and school policy groups assent (Caldwell & Spinks, 1992, p. 40). It summarizes the centrally determined framework of priorities and standards and outlines the means by which the school will address this framework. It provides an account of the school's mission, vision, priorities, needs, and programs, and it specifies the process by which decisions will be made and approaches to evaluation.

The coordinating body for MSM is the policy group. The composition of the group varies according to the setting. In the Australian State of Victoria, it is the legally established School Council. In England, it is a school's Board of Governors. In the United States, where there is no universally established pattern of school governing boards, the nature of the policy group could be established by the state, as in the cases of Chicago and Kentucky; it could be established by the district, as in the case of Dade County; or it could be left to the discretion of the school. The policy group is solely responsible for goal setting, need identification, and policy making, although it is likely to seek advice broadly in carrying out these responsibilities. It must approve budgets prepared by program teams, assuring that the proposals reflect estab-

---

[1]Charters within the context of schools in England and in the state of Victoria in Australia are the rule rather than the exception as in the United States.

Figure 13.11
Sample program structures for elementary and secondary schools

---

AN ELEMENTARY SCHOOL

Kindergarten	Early Intervention
Primary Grades, 1–3	Special Education
Intermediate Grades, 4–6	Computer Studies
Art	Administration
Music	Food Service
Physical Education	Operations and Maintenance
Library and Media Center	Co-curricular Activities

A SECONDARY SCHOOL

English	Computer Studies
Mathematics	Special Education
Social Studies	Co-curricular Activities
Science	Administration
Business Studies	Food Service
Foreign Languages	Operations and Maintenance
History	Technology
Physical Education	Art
Music	Interscholastic Sports

---

lished policy and are supportable by the resources allocated to the school. The policy group is responsible for summative evaluation of programs, making judgments on the effectiveness of each program and on the effectiveness of policy supporting program efforts.

Caldwell and Spinks (1988) defined a policy as a statement of purpose accompanied by one or more guidelines as to how that purpose is to be achieved. A policy provides a framework for the operation of the school or a program, and it may allow discretion in its implementation. A policy's statement of purpose should be derived from the school's statement of philosophy as expressed in the school's charter or from a goal statement or statements. The guidelines should clearly state the intent of the policy and the desired pattern of action without becoming so specific as to prohibit professional judgment by those concerned with implementing the policy.

The development plan is adopted by the policy group as a strategic plan for improvement specifying in general terms priorities to be ad-

dressed in the next three to five years and the strategies to be employed. It includes a careful assessment of where the school is in relation to where it should be. A "need" exists when there is a significant gap between where the school is and where it desires to be. Schools typically have far more needs than their resources permit them to address, so priorities must be established as to which are the most pressing. Caldwell and Spinks (1988) suggest that one consideration in setting priorities is the extent of identifiable harm caused by each gap or need.

A program is defined as an area of learning and teaching, such as English, mathematics, art, and music, or a support service such as administration, audiovisual media, and maintenance of buildings and grounds (see Figure 13.11). A program team is usually composed of everyone involved in the delivery of the program service. Each team should have a designated leader, usually a person with formal authority related to the program, such as a subject coordinator or head of department. The teams prepare plans for their areas of responsibility within the parameters of the development plan and specify the resources needed to support those plans. The teams are responsible for the implementation of their plans as approved by the policy group. They are also responsible for formative evaluation of their respective programs and for submitting information to the policy group as required for their summative reviews. Although the division of responsibility is clear, some people are likely to serve on both the policy group and one or more program teams, thereby facilitating a high level of formal and informal communication.

On the surface, MSM resembles the largely discredited planning, programming, budgeting system (PPBS) model, which was popular in the United States during the 1960s and 1970s. Although they are similar in concept, they are very different in design. The creators of MSM learned much from the failures of PPBS and have largely succeeded in avoiding them. PPBS was very rigid, giving too much attention to the formal technology and minutia of planning and budgeting and requiring excessive paperwork.

> To these shortcomings may be added an inappropriate emphasis on the specification of performance requirements or criteria for evaluation. PPBS assumed a greater degree or capacity for rational or analytical planning than existed or was possible. In short, PPBS suffered from the 'paralysis through analysis' which is to be avoided if effectiveness along the lines studied by Peters and Waterman (1982) is to be attained. (Caldwell & Spinks, 1988, p. 68)

MSM keeps paperwork to a minimum. Each goal statement is limited to a single sentence; policies are limited to one page; program plans and budgets, to two pages; and evaluation reports, to one or two pages. Criteria for evaluation are kept simple and clearly related to learning and teaching. Priorities can be reordered quickly and simply as new needs emerge. All written material is to be free of technical jargon so that it can be easily read and understood by all members of the school community.

MSM recognizes three levels of planning: (1) program, (2) curricular, and (3) instructional.

> Program planning is determining in general terms how a program is to be implemented, specifying such things as the manner in which students will be grouped vertically (among grade or year levels) and horizontally (within a grade or year level); the number and nature of teachers and support staff associated with the program; the supplies, equipment and services required and initiatives (additions or deletions) which are noteworthy. Curriculum planning provides a relatively detailed specification of what will be taught, how it will be taught and when it will be taught. Instructional planning is considered here to be planning undertaken by individual teachers when implementing a curriculum plan in their own classrooms. (Caldwell & Spinks, 1988, pp. 43–44)

Cost of personnel allocated to specific tasks are made in program and school budgets, even though the actual salaries may be paid by the district. The salary rate used is the average salary for the district (plus cost of fringe benefits) rather than the actual salaries paid to personnel assigned to a program. Caldwell and Spinks (1988) noted that "the inclusion of such [salary] estimates is an acknowledgement that the major resource in a school is the staff" (pp. 46–48).

A program budget is a comprehensive plan for a program (Figure 13.12). It contains a statement of the program's purpose, a list of broad guidelines as to how the purpose is to be achieved, a plan for implementation with elements listed in order of priority, an estimate of resources required to support the plan, and a plan for evaluation. All must be reported in two pages or less.

The program budgets for all programs in the school are brought together in a single document for submission to the policy group for review, possible revision, and eventual approval (Figure 13.13). During the process of reconciliation, program expenditure requests are adjusted, if necessary, so that combined approved expenditures fall within the school's estimated income.

BUDGET FOR SPECIAL EDUCATION

ROSEBERY DISTRICT HIGH SCHOOL
PROGRAM: Special Education **RESPONSIBILITY: M.S.** **BUDGET CODE:173**

1. **Purpose:** We aim to have all children achieve their full potential in all areas of development during their school years. It is recognized, however, that some children fail to achieve their potential due to some specific disability which affects their capacity to learn. A purpose of the Special Education Program is to identify these children, determine the nature of their disability and to devise and implement plans to overcome the disability where possible.

    A further purpose of the program is to identify children who have overall a very low potential, and have great difficulty in learning, and to assist these children achieve their potential by designing individual programs for them and providing the necessary intensive help.

2. **Broad guidelines:** Children with specific disabilities or general low learning potential will be identified through consultation amongst the relevant people.

    Fundamental to the program is the philosophy that children should remain part of their peer group in as many respects as possible, and that by its very nature, special education requires a highly individualized approach to achieve maximum benefits. Those who design the teaching program must, therefore, ensure that the program is appropriate for each individual. A program could involve extraction as part of a group, or a totally individualized program to operate within the normal classroom.

    The main thrust of the program will be towards the younger children in need of special help so that problems can be overcome or reduced as early as possible. It is recognized, however, that older children can need special education, and that this need should be met if possible.

    It is vital that opportunities are provided for close liaison between the special education teachers and the classroom teacher of each child involved.

3. **Plan for implementation:**

    3.1 The equivalent of one full-time and one half-time special education teachers will be employed.
    Three rooms will be provided as teaching areas for extraction purposes, at least two of which will also be set up as resource centres for special education materials.

    3.2 Senior staff will supervise the program.

    3.3 A part-time aide will be provided for the program to assist in the preparation of learning materials.

    3.4 Sufficient materials and equipment will be provided for the effective operation of the program, including structured languages and maths, materials, manipulative equipment, art and craft supplies, and part-purchase of an additional large-print typewriter.

    3.5 Additional stocks of appropriate reading materials will be provided to enhance the effective operation of the program, particularly in the areas of high interest/low ability reading material of upper primary and lower secondary students, and teachers' resource material.

4. Resources required:

Planning elements	Teaching staff	Non-teaching staff	Materials & equipment	Books	Services
4.1 Teaching units provided by special education staff 37* units × $595/unit	22 015				
Related units of Planning, Marking and Organization (PMO) 9 units × $595/unit	5 355				
4.2 Senior supervision of the program by infant mistress 2 units × $738/unit		1 476			
4.3 Provision of teacher aide services to develop support materials 2 hrs × $7.22 × 40 weeks		577			
4.4 Support items for students' use			750		150
4.5 Books for students and staff to use, including a special focus for 1985				300	
	$28 846	577	750	300	150

Program total = $30 623

(*Units for 3–6 Regrouped Language Program included in Program 114)

5. **Evaluation (minor):** Keeping individual records for each child will provide the basis for evaluation reports. These reports will be given to teachers and parents although their form will vary according to the situation.
    The criteria used to determine children in need of the program may also be used to measure the progress of the total group and thus the effectiveness of the program.

Program team:
Liz Brient   Michele Davison   Trudy Drukin   Marilyn Spinks   Carol Titley

Figure 13.12
Example of a program budget as implemented by Rosebery District High School, Tasmania, Australia

Source: B. J. Caldwell and J. M Spinks, *The self-managing school* (pp. 254–255). London: Falmer Press, 1988.

ROSEBERY DISTRICT HIGH SCHOOL
PROGRAM BUDGET SUMMARY SHEET
RESOURCES REQUIRED

	Teaching staff	Non-teaching staff	Relief days	Materials & equipment	Book Services & hire	Minor materials	Travel	Services	Contingency reserve	Other	Program total
101 Extra-curricular activities							380		200		580
102 Art acquisition				410		60					470
103 Administration	109 791	36 456	760	7 000		250		5 400	523		160 180
104 Community bus											NRA*
105 Pastoral care	79 694			600			500				80 794
111 Curriculum resource	23 252	3 910		7 073					100		34 335
112 School council	1 618			10	100	100		200	100		2 128
113 K–10 Music	27 798		152	2 040	30	100		200		290	30 610
114 3–6 Regrouped language	41 102		228		500	50		250	100		42 230
121 Presentation Day				200		110		185	50		545
122 K–10 Physical education	44 077		152	2 530	300	100	600	300	200		48 259
122 K–10 Sport	2 427			900			2 260	600	100	480	6 767
124 Support Services	1 618	9 136						200			10 954
131 7–10 Social studies	56 193			1 350	1 800		500	30	168		60 041
132 9–10 History	6 688			500	150	260	50				7 648
133 7–10 Transition education	9 806					450	2 650	520			13 426
134 7–10 Teacher support service		7 859		600							8 459
141 7–10 English	61 405			600	2 200			425	200		64 830
142 3–10 Foreign languages	19 778			120	240						20 138
143 K–10 Speech & drama	26 466			596	200	180					27 442
144 Drama Festival	738										738
151 7–10 Mathematics	67 069			470	1 474	91		505	254		69 863
152 7–10 Science	55 764	1 444	152	3 300	1 775	405	400		300		63 540
153 K–10 Computer education	12 924		304	3 324	509			110	425		17 596

	Teaching staff	Non-teaching staff	Relief days	Materials & equipment	Book Services & hire	Minor materials	Travel	Services	Contingency reserve	Other	Program total
161 7–10 Technical subjects	79 707		152	7 200		500		1 300			88 859
162 7–10 Visual arts	19 326			860	100	270			200		20 756
163 7–10 Home economics	21 706			1 890	200	470			50		24 316
164 9–10 Commercial subjects	17 993		76	690	250	420			100		19 529
171 Early intervention	3 713			200							3 913
172 K–2 General studies	110 933	9 530	380	5 250		450		150	300		126 993
173 K–10 Special education	28 846	577		750	300			150			30 623
181 3–6 General studies	111 814	2 888		5 400		800			100	100	121 102
182 Public relations	738					40			10		788
191 Cleaning		65 651		4 467		223			50		70 391
192 Grounds		16 285		350		150			50		16 835
193 Canteen		591									591
194 Book sales		1 700									1 700
201 9–10 Journalism	11 900			830	200	150			100	300	13 480
202 School magazine				1 000							1 000
203 Student council	3 570		152	300				100			4 232
211 K–10 Talented students	+ 301 (R.F.)					110					310
TOTALS	1 058 764	156 027	2 508	60 810	10 328	5 739	7 340	10 625	3 680	1 170	1 316 991

*NRA (no resources allocated)

Figure 13.13
Example of a program budget summary sheet of resources required as implemented by
Rosebery District High School, Tasmania, Australia

Source: B. J. Caldwell and J. M. Spinks, *The self-managing school* (pp. 254–255). London: Falmer Press, 1988.

With the adoption of the program budget by the policy group, program teams are authorized to proceed with the implementation of their plans in the forthcoming year. There is no need for further reference to the policy group during the course of the year unless a program team desires to make a major change in its plan.

The final phase of the MSM cycle is evaluation and review, defined by Caldwell and Spinks (1988) as:

> . . . the gathering of information for the purpose of making a judgment and then making that judgment. Two kinds of evaluation should occur during or following the implementation of program plans. One is evaluation of learning, where information is gathered to form judgments about the progress or achievement of students. Another is evaluation of programs, when information is gathered to form judgments about the extent to which progress toward goals has been made, needs have been satisfied and policies have been implemented. (p. 49)

The policy group holds the major responsibility for program evaluation and may call in external authorities to assist it in the process. Planning teams have a similar, but more detailed interest and gather much of the information needed for program evaluation for their own purposes as formative evaluation. The school evaluation scheme may be coordinated with district and state evaluation schemes. Minor evaluations are carried out annually and their reports to the policy group are limited to one page (Figure 13.14). Major evaluations are scheduled for a three- to five-year frequency and their reports are limited to two pages (Figure 13.15). "The emphasis is on a manageable and usable approach to program evaluation, in contrast to the frequently exhausting approach to school review and evaluation which has been encountered in many schools in recent years" (Caldwell & Spinks, 1988, p. 50).

The MSM cycle is completed when judgments in program evaluation result in the setting of new goals, the identification of new needs, the formulation of new policies, or the introduction of new programs by the policy group. The model provides a comprehensive portrayal of all that eventually must be accomplished; but there seems to be no best point of entry to the model. A school may enter the cycle at any phase, completing the other phases in a manner appropriate for each setting. In a more recent volume, Caldwell and Spinks (1998) provide strategic guides for creating schools for the knowledge society, focusing on learning outcomes, and building systems of self-managing schools.

The mere existence of decentralization mechanisms will not guarantee positive results, however; the nature of the culture or attitudes/beliefs permeating the organization are also influential. Ross (1997) concluded that schemes resulting in effective participation by teachers "require new forms of collaborative and collegial involvement that shift the traditional isolated decision making environment to a team-based, power sharing one" (p. 317). A balanced centralization–decentralization approach supports a combined top-down, bottom-up planning process to meet the competing needs of the organization. "A co-existing loose–tight coupling between horizontal and vertical levels of the organization underlies a framework focused on systemic, rather than piecemeal, reform" (p. 319).

Ross (1997) found the greatest success in situations where teachers were offered a high-involvement form of participation, the power to influence decisions, and an enabling context for effective engagement of teachers. The pervading culture needs to be one of mutual respect and trust throughout all levels of the organization, nurtured by effective leadership and top-down commitment and support. It is critical that principal–teacher relationships be based on mutual influence in the decision-making process and that professional learning and staff development be focused on creating an ongoing capacity for school improvement responsive to student needs and meeting changes in the school community over time.

REPORT OF MINOR EVALUATION FOR SPECIAL EDUCATION

PROGRAM: Special Education   **RESPONSIBILITY: M.S.**   **CODE: 173**

EVALUATION REPORT FOR 19xx

This report should be read in conjunction with the policy and program plan for special education. Resources were allocated to implement fully the program plan.

SUCCESS INDICATORS

1. Many teachers have indicated that the Special Education Program is assisting them to deal more effectively with children who have special needs in the classroom. This has been particularly evident since the increase in provisions for special education at the beginning of this year.

2. Parent-teacher interviews conducted under the regular schedule have indicated strong support for the program.

3. A number of children on the program show evidence of increased self-esteem and ability to cope with learning tasks.

4. A small number of children in the early childhood area are likely to be coping well enough in the near future to come off the program.

AREAS OF CONCERN

1. There has been insufficient time for classroom teachers to consult with special education teachers on the progress of children.

2. Some classroom teachers are unaware of the need to consult, so that work can be followed up in the classroom.

3. Some children with problems 'slip through' and are put on the program too late, due to lack of continuity in monitoring their progress as they cross from one grade to another.

4. There are problems with the supply of books needed for teachers' resources due to:
   (a) lack of opportunity to select appropriate materials;
   (b) delays by suppliers in meeting orders.

COMMENTS AND RECOMMENDATIONS

- Senior staff need to create opportunities where possible for classroom teachers to consult with special education staff.

- Special education staff need to make themselves available at department meetings so that they can make teachers aware of the resources available. This includes resources in the form of support materials, and information about learning-teaching processes which take place through the individualized programs.

- Better liaison is needed between senior staff of the different grade areas to ensure that provisions for special education give continuity for particular children when they cross grade levels.

- The school should budget for professional development time so that special education staff can visit language and special education resource centres where they can select suitable materials and either purchase them or borrow them.

Prepared by members of the program team.

Figure 13.14

Example of a minor program evaluation as implemented by Rosebery District High School, Tasmania, Australia

Source: B. J. Caldwell and J. M. Spinks, *The self-managing school* (p. 256). London, England: Falmer Press, 1988.

REPORT OF MAJOR EVALUATION FOR SPECIAL EDUCATION

PROGRAM: Special Education   **RESPONSIBILITY: M.S.**   **CODE:173**

INTRODUCTION

For this year the Special Education Program was upgraded to provide an increased teacher component (1.5 teachers as compared to one teacher in the previous year). In evaluating the results of this program the evaluating group held a series of informal meetings with all teachers concerned, interviewed the guidance officer and speech pathologist connected with the school to ascertain objective indications of progress or otherwise of the children concerned, and interviewed a representative sample of parents who have children involved with the program. Child studies, with names removed to ensure anonymity, were also made available to the group. The findings of this evaluation are summarized below.

INADEQUACIES AND PROBLEM AREAS IDENTIFIED

1. The lack of ready access to some support staff (particularly guidance officer and speech pathologist) means that there are sometimes lengthy delays in obtaining information on which to base individual programs.
2. One parent interviewed was confused about the provision of 10 hours of teacher aide time (provided from an external source) to cater for mobility of the physically handicapped, and thought that this provision was teacher time to assist in overcoming intellectual handicap.
3. A very small minority of children show evidence of 'opting out' of the normal classroom, preferring the special education situation all the time, probably due to the greater feeling of security.
4. Children are sometimes not identified as being in need of special education until they are too old for their problems to be overcome.
5. There is insufficient time for classroom teachers to consult with special education teachers on the progress of children, and in some cases teachers are unaware of the special education resources available.

SUCCESSFUL OUTCOMES OF THE PROGRAM

1. Many teachers have indicated that the Special Education Program is assisting them to deal more effectively with children who have special needs in the classroom as they are given help with implementing individualized programs developed out of the work. The special education teachers do this with the children concerned. This feeling of receiving increased support is directly attributed to the increased provision.

2. A number of children on the program are showing evidence of increased self-esteem and ability to cope with learning tasks. Tests administered (refer guidance officer) give objective evidence of this.
3. A small number of children in the early childhood area are likely to be coping well enough in the near future to come off the program. This reinforces the benefits of early identification of children with problems and of early intensive help.

SUMMARY AND RECOMMENDATIONS

1. There is little if anything that can be done about the amount of the guidance officer's and speech pathologist's time provided to the school as this is an Education Department matter. The group feels that it is worth noting, however, that as yet the Special Education Program is in its infancy and that as the special education staff become more confident in their task of dealing with a wide range of disabilities and learning problems, the lack of ready access to support staff should be less of a problem.
2. The confusion that became evident about the nature of the provisions for special education for particular children points out the need for improved liaison between staff and parents. Consideration should be given to increasing the frequency of parent-teacher interviews with respect to children in the Special Education Program.
3. Particular staff members should be nominated to undertake special pastoral care of the small minority of children having unusual difficulty in coping with the normal classroom situation, particularly in the secondary years.
4. The need to identify children early and the benefits of early intensive help as previously outlined, underline the need to continue the main thrust of the program towards the early years. It is essential that continuity in monitoring children 'at risk' throughout the school is further developed and maintained.
5. Senior staff should create opportunities where possible for classroom teachers to consult with special education staff. The special education staff should make themselves available to department meetings so that they can make teachers aware of the resources available. This includes resources of the form of support materials, and information about learning-teaching processes which take place through individualized learning programs.

Prepared by the Evaluation Group including members of the Council and Program team.

Figure 13.15

Example of a major program evaluation as implemented by Rosebery District High School, Tasmania, Australia

Source: B. J. Caldwell and J. M. Spinks, *The self-managing school.*(pp. 257–258). London: Falmer Press, 1988.

School-Based Budgeting

School personnel cannot make meaningful curricular decisions without the authority also to make the necessary resource commitment decisions that enable the implementation of those curricular decisions (CORE, 1998; Guthrie, 1998; Odden & Busch, 1998). School-based decision making must include school-based budgeting as an integral component. The degree of empowerment of school staff is related directly to the proportion of the school budget under the control of school authorities. In this section we focus on issues related to school-based budgeting (SBB).

Wohlstetter and Buffett (1992) have described the differences between traditional centralized budgeting at the district level and school-based budgeting. Regardless of the level at which it takes place, the budgeting process involves formulation, adoption, and monitoring. Under the traditional mode, all three are accomplished at the district level with minimal involvement of school personnel. Human and physical resources are then assigned to schools for use in district-specified areas. Schools are usually given discretionary control over a small allocation, primarily for the purchase of instructional supplies and the provision of student enrichment experiences.

Where budgetary authority has been decentralized, the district still forecasts the resources that will be available at the district level. But from that point on, the procedures become quite different. Decentralized districts must first determine the extent of budgetary authority to be extended to schools. The primary issue is the degree of control to be granted to schools over personnel expenditures that account for between 60 and 80 percent of school and district budgets. Schools in Edmonton, Alberta, Canada, the state of Victoria in Australia, and in England are granted a lump-sum allocation covering virtually all costs encountered by schools with no specific amount designated for personnel—or any other expenditure category.

American school districts delegating to schools budgetary authority over half of the total cost per pupil include Broward County, Florida; Cincinnati; Pittsburgh; and Seattle (Odden, 1999). In Dade County, schools are allocated staff units, but these units may be exchanged for a monetary amount to be used for other purposes. Chicago schools do not have control over the resources assigned to the basic program, but they do have authority over funds provided by categorical aids in support of students; these funds may be used to purchase human and/or physical resources at the discretion of the school's council. In Kentucky, districts allocate monies to schools to hire certified and classified staff and to purchase instructional supplies and equipment (Dunn, James-Gross, & Trampe, 1998); but state and district constraints on how the monies can be spent severely limited school discretion (David, 1994). The limit of school discretion over school-based budgets was also noted by Goertz and Stiefel (1998) in a study of four large urban school districts (Chicago, Fort Worth, New York, and Rochester) that had implemented SBB to some degree; truly discretionary funds were found to be less than 20 percent of total school resources.

The second district-level decision is how much to allocate to schools and according to what unit. Some districts make their allocations by pupil units and others by staff units. In either case, the number of students in a school, their characteristics, previous performance, and the nature of the school (e.g., grade levels served and the presence of special programs) are primary determinants of the size of the school's allocation (Wohlstetter & Van Kirk, 1996).

Once an estimate of a school's allocation is determined by the district, action passes to school authorities to devise a detailed plan for using the funds in accordance with its curricular plan and within the constraints established by higher authority (Wohlstetter & Buffett, 1992). Whatever procedure is followed, budget building should be done within the context of a school's curricular plan.

With respect to budget adoption, the procedure between centralized and decentralized districts is similar. Final approval is by the board of education in either case. Wohlstetter and Buffett (1992) pointed out that the main difference is in the flow. While centralized districts may consult with school authorities, in the decentralized mode the school develops the budget and recommends its adoption to district officials. District review of school budgets is in terms of compliance with district and other strategic and legal constraints and not in terms of educational substance, philosophy, and so on.

Expenditures need to be monitored by both district and school personnel. The district role in the decentralized mode is primarily to provide information to the schools and to ensure that schools do not exceed their spending authorizations. In Chicago, Dade County, and, Edmonton, the district provides budgetary information to school personnel on a regular basis. Edmonton school officials have the option of being on-line to access financial information held in computer memory at any time and the flexibility of establishing their own accounting codes within the constraints of the district code structure.

In her study of the implementation of education reforms in Kentucky, David (1994) found that the biggest problem with the allocation process to schools was the lack of appropriate accounting systems and technological support by school districts. England and the State of Victoria in Australia faced a similar problem in moving to their systems of local management of schools, where schools now control directly 80 to 90 percent of a school's resources (Swanson & King, 1997; Gurr, 1999). Before financial allocations can be made to schools, it is necessary to know what the total resource requirement of schools is, and most current school accounting procedures are incapable of providing such information. Except for minor portions of the budget, such as instructional supplies, most ac-

counting systems do not link expenditures to buildings, programs, or classrooms. Computer and accounting technology permit such linkages, and our ability to trace all expenditures to the school level will improve as the practice of SBB spreads.

Although most accounting systems can be adapted to SBB, software is available that enable states and school districts to disaggregate their financial data to schools and programs with relative ease. One such software is In$ite,™ developed by the K–12 education team of Coopers and Lybrand LLP, based on developmental work done by Cooper and Sarrel (1993).

In$ite is a technology-based management information tool that can operate on a standard personal computer. The Finance Analysis Model for Education on which In$ite is based consists of a series of multidimensional spreadsheets that compile information on district and school expenditures. The three basic dimensions of the model are functional, program, and site-level (Speakman et al., 1996). The functional dimension is divided into five components: instruction, instructional support, operations, other commitments, and leadership. The program dimension is flexible and may include such programs as special education, bilingual education, gifted and talented, Title 1, summer school, and so on. The model requires that the time of persons working in more than one site be prorated according to the amount of time spent at each site. Salaries and fringe benefits are then prorated to the respective sites accordingly. Similarly, utility bills and other expenditures that are not normally distributed to cost centers are so prorated under this model. The components of the model are illustrated in Figure 13.16.

In$ite has been used by numerous school districts and the states of Hawaii and South Carolina to trace expenditures to the school, program, and grade levels. Other states with the ability to trace school expenditures to the school level are Florida, Ohio, and Texas (Busch & Odden, 1997).

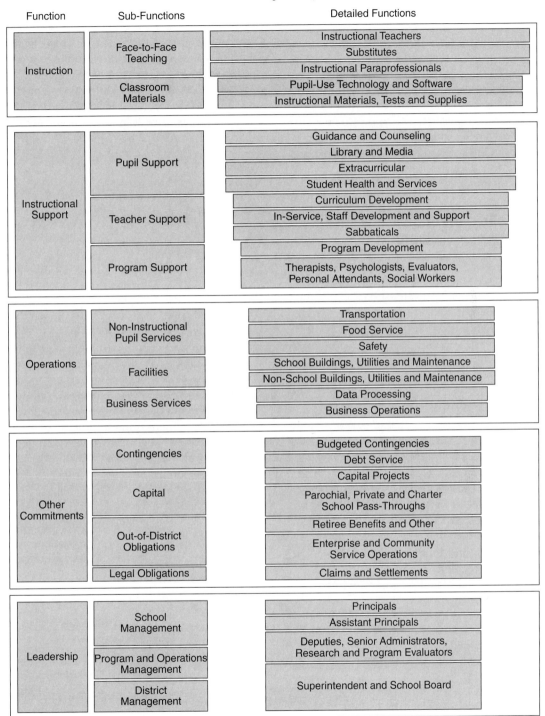

Figure 13.16 Finance analysis model for education

Source: In $ite™, a product of Fox River Learning Inc.

The type of resource allocation and expenditure distribution information provided by In$ite is critical to the successful functioning of SBM. Tracing resource demands to the school and classroom level is essential for informed decision making in SBM and SBB environments, and also holds the potential, with appropriate analysis, for advancing our understanding of the influences of inputs on educational outcomes and equity in the allocation of resources.

An Application of Strategy Formation and Planning at the District Level

A few schools and districts have well-established procedures for strategy formulation and planning of the nature outlined in the previous sections. Those school districts are the exceptions, however, not the rule. Some states are beginning to require all districts to follow similar procedures by mandating conformance to a prescribed format. Below we describe the format required by the State of New York.

It is open to question whether or not strategy formation and planning as we have presented it can be legislated. All districts will fill-in-the-blank spaces on the forms as required by the state. But the key to success is in its implementation, and this will vary markedly from district to district. What we have described is as much an attitude or a philosophy about how people should engage one another in common purpose as it is a formal process. Attitude and philosophy cannot be legislated, but must be freely embraced by the members of the organization themselves. While all districts will meet the letter of the law, few will meet its spirit, thereby failing to realize the full benefit of the process. Nevertheless, in promoting the process, the state endorses its legitimacy, thereby encouraging more districts to look into all of its aspects than would otherwise be done.

New York State was motivated into developing a standard strategic planning process because virtually all federal funds in support of education and much state support have been provided through categorical aids that require a separate proposal and budget for each program supported. This has meant a highly fragmented and poorly coordinated instructional program for many students, especially those in greatest educational need and whom the categorical aids were intended to help. As a result, it was not uncommon for categorical programs to work at cross purposes and not realize the achievement gains that were desired. Prior to implementation of the new procedures, New York State school districts had to submit separate plans under a dozen funding initiatives. Recognizing the inefficacy of this approach to school improvement, states and the federal government in recent years have broadened the definitions of categories (e.g., block grants) and have done much to enable schools and districts to combine funds from various sources to realize common objectives.

To permit school districts to focus all their available resources in an effective and efficient manner in helping all students reach new and high learning standards, the New York State Education Department is in the process of refining a unified procedure to satisfy the planning requirements of all programs. The procedure is called the Comprehensive District Education Plan (CDEP). Through CDEP, the State's goal is to focus school district energy and resources on improving student achievement through the use of data to:

- Facilitate a continuing discussion on improving student achievement
- Focus on results first, and then on means of realizing them
- Identify specific areas of need
- Prioritize those needs
- Identify root causes within district control
- Focus on improvement of systems rather than parts
- Measure, evaluate, and report results. (New York State Education Department, 1999, p. 1)

CDEP is a collaborative process that uses school improvement committees representative of the district's population to engage in discussions focused on improving achievement of all students from early childhood through adult. The plan is to be data driven using state and local data sources. All funding streams and other resources are aligned toward the resolution of specific needs as identified by the data. The plan is to indicate how student services and entitlements required by state and federal statutes are to be guaranteed and to make use of "best practices" and current research to determine strategies to resolve identified needs. The procedures used by the district are considered to be as important as the resulting document.

The plan submitted to the state must include: background/demographics; data analysis; identification of district strengths and successful interventions; district needs/areas for improvement; implementation plan; and assessing and reporting results. The state has developed a sophisticated software program enabling districts to quickly integrate existing databases and to conduct analyses in support of the planning process.

The background/demographics section includes vision, mission, and belief statements. A district statement is also required that sets forth any special or unique aspects of the school community that might clarify or influence the context of the plan.

In the data analysis section, the district documents its record over the past three years in meeting the state's benchmarks and state and local standards. The benchmarks, subject to modification, specify the minimum level of acceptable achievement and are listed in Figure 13.17. The state has developed generic standards for: Health, Physical Education, and Home Economics; Mathematics, Science, and Technology; English Language Arts; Languages Other Than English; The Arts; Career Development and Occupational Studies; and Social Studies. For illustrative purposes, the standards

for the English Language Arts are presented in Figure 13.18. These standards are subject to change as the process is refined.

In the next section of CDEP, the district identifies successful processes, programs, and interventions. This is followed by an identification of state and local standards and benchmarks where the district performance falls short of expectation and where improvement is needed. Analyses of the root causes of the discrepancies are presented (Bernhardt, 1998). The areas requiring improvement are prioritized and rationales for selecting the ones for immediate attention are given.

The implementation plan section includes an action plan for each need identified. An action plan describes the program of work to be undertaken on a particular need. The target population is identified, along with specific tasks and activities. A timeline is established and responsibilities are assigned for undertaking the activities and tasks. Funding sources available to accomplish the desired result are identified, as is the amount to be drawn from each source. Finally, the district assigns responsibility for undertaking the activities or tasks to complete the strategies by clearly specifying individuals by name and title.

In the section on assessing and reporting results, the district develops performance indicators for each action plan that measures its effectiveness in improving student achievement. The performance indicators are intended to enable the district to determine when it has remediated the identified need. This section also tells how the district will go about determining if strategies need to be revised and how it will periodically inform the public about how well its comprehensive plan is working.

The procedures specified in the Comprehensive District Education Plan follow fairly closely the steps described in the section of this chapter on intermediate planning. CDEP does not specify how strategy will be identified, but it does request that the district present the product of its strategy formulation process

✔ 90% of all students above SRP[1] in Grade 3 Reading

✔ 90% of all students above SRP in Grade 3 Mathematics

✔ District mean in Grade 4 Science/state mean: content

✔ District mean in Grade 4 Science/state mean: skills

✔ District mean in Grade 4 Science/state mean: manipulatives

✔ 90% of all students above SRP in Grade 5 Writing

✔ 90% of all students above SRP in Grade 6 Reading

✔ 90% of all students above SRP in Grade 6 Mathematics

✔ Percent of students above the mean: Grade 6 Social Studies

✔ Percent of students above the mean: Grade 8 Social Studies

✔ Percent of graduates obtaining a Regents diploma

✔ 90% of all students passing Comprehensive English Regents

✔ 90% of all students passing Math Course I Regents

✔ 90% of all students passing Biology Regents

✔ 90% of all students passing Social Studies II Regents

✔ 90% of all students passing Global Studies Regents

— An annual district-wide attendance rate in excess of 91%

— An annual district-wide suspension rate at 1% or less

— An annual drop-out rate of 3% or less

VESID GOALS

— 80% of SWDs[2] will exit with a local, Regents, or GED diploma

— Percentage of SWDs who drop out will decrease each year

— 95% of SWDs will participate in each PEP[3] administration

— 85% of SWDs will achieve the SRP on PEP tests

— SWDs will pass Occupational Education Proficiency Exams at the same rate as non-disabled peers (currently 81% of non-disabled students passed introductory exams)

— Percentage of SWDs receiving services in general education buildings will reach national average (95%)

— Percentage of SWDs receiving services in general education classrooms will exceed the national average (45%)

— Classification rate for SWDs will decrease (currently 11%)

[1]State reference point
[2]Students with disabilities
[3]State achievement tests
✔ Indicates a requirement of the New York State Education Department

Figure 13.17
New York State Assessment Standards: Benchmarks for Elementary, Middle, and Secondary Education

Standard 1   Language for Information and Understanding

Students will listen, speak, read, and write for information and understanding. As listeners and readers, students will collect data, facts, and ideas; discover relationships, concepts, and generalizations; and use knowledge generated from oral, written, and electronically produced texts. As speakers and writers, they will use oral and written language that follows the accepted conventions of the English language to acquire, interpret, apply, and transmit information.

Standard 2   Language for Literary Response and Expression

Students will read and listen to oral, written, and electronically produced texts and performances from American and world literature; relate texts and performances to their own lives; and develop an understanding of the diverse social, historical, and cultural dimensions the texts and performances represent. As speakers and writers, students will use oral and written language that follows the accepted conventions of the English language for self-expression and artistic creation.

Standard 3   Language for Critical Analysis and Evaluation

Students will listen, speak, read, and write for critical analysis and evaluation. As listeners and readers, students will analyze experiences, ideas, information, and issues presented by others using a variety of established criteria. As speakers and writers, they will use oral and written language that follows the accepted conventions of the English language to present, from a variety of perspectives, their opinions and judgments on experiences, ideas, information, and issues.

Standard 4   Language for Social Interaction

Students will listen, speak, read, and write for social interaction. Students will use oral and written language that follows the accepted conventions of the English language for effective social communication with a wide variety of people. As readers and listeners, they will use the social communications of others to enrich their understanding of people and their views.

Figure 13.18
New York State Learning Standards for English Language Arts

and vision/mission/belief statements. CDEP does not require the amount of detail that is required in a tactical plan.

Unfortunately, most schools and districts are adrift on the social and political seas of this world, helplessly battered by the winds and currents of special interest groups and circumstances. It is little wonder that their impact on the academic and behavioral development of our children falls short of national, state, and lo-

cal expectations. It is also not surprising that their operations are judged to be less than efficient. But this need not be the case. In this chapter, we have sought to provide an understanding of how educational institutions can develop a sense of direction and how they can mobilize the human resources at their disposal to move toward fulfillment of the vision of the organization. We have provided examples of operational systems of strategy formulation and planning at the school and state levels. Each school and district must work out the particulars for themselves, however. The way is not easy, but the rewards are substantial.

Activities

1. Select a school district (or a school if it has considerable autonomy over its budget) for the purpose of studying its planning, budgeting, and information systems.

   a. Is a formal set of policies and procedures followed in establishing a planning process for the district?

   (1) If such a policy exists, study it carefully and interview a number of key actors in the process to determine how closely the policy is adhered to; identify its perceived strengths and weaknesses.

   (2) If no such policy is in place, interview a number of persons whom you would expect to be involved in the planning process at all levels, including the board of education, the central office, principals, teachers, parents, and students. Describe the *de facto* process and its perceived strengths and weaknesses.

   b. Is a formal set of policies and procedures followed in establishing a budgeting process for the district?

   (1) If such a policy exists, study it carefully and interview a number of key actors in the process to determine how closely the policy is adhered to; identify its perceived strengths and weaknesses.

   (2) If no such policy is in place, interview a number of persons whom you would expect to be involved in the budgeting process at all levels, including the board of education, the central office, principals, and teachers. Describe the de facto process and its perceived strengths and weaknesses.

   (3) Examine the complete budget, popularized versions of it, the budget calendar, and related forms.

   c. Study the operating budget implementation process. How are purchases initiated, made, and paid for? How is payroll handled? How are expenditures monitored?

   d. What is the nature of the information system(s) that supports the planning and budgeting processes? Are all systems integrated?

2. Check your state education department's Web page. Look for performance indicators for schools and school districts. Has your state developed a set of educational standards and benchmarks for reaching them? What are they? How do these standards and benchmarks affect planning in your school and district?

3. Search the Web for home pages of other state education departments. Compare their treatment of educational standards and benchmarks with those of your state. What are the strengths and weaknesses of each?

References

Awkerman, G. (1991). Strategic ends planning: A commitment to focus. In R. V. Carlson & G. Awkerman (Eds.), *Educational planning: Concepts, strategies, and practices* (pp. 201–219). New York: Longman.

Bennis, W., & Nanus, B. (1985). *Leaders: The strategies for taking charge.* New York: Harper & Row.

Bernhardt, V. L. (1998). *Data analysis for comprehensive schoolwide improvement.* Larchmont, NY: Eye on Education.

Boyer, E. L. (1983). *High school: A report on secondary education in America.* New York: Harper & Row.

Busch, C., & Odden, A. (1997). Improving educational policy and results with school-level data: A synthesis of multiple perspectives. *Journal of Education Finance, 22* (3), pp. 225–245.

Caldwell, B. J., & Spinks, J. M. (1988). *The self-managing school.* London: Falmer Press.

Caldwell, B. J., & Spinks, J. M. (1992). *Leading the self-managing school.* London: Falmer Press.

Caldwell, B. J., & Spinks, J. M. (1998). *Beyond the self-managing school.* London: Falmer Press.

Cawelti, G. (1989). Key elements of site-based management. *Educational Leadership, 46,* 46.

Consortium on Renewing Education. (1998). *20/20 vision: A strategy for doubling America's academic achievement by the year 2020.* Nashville, TN: Peabody Center for Education Policy, Vanderbilt University.

Conway, J. A. (1984). The myth, mystery, and mastery of participative decision making in education. *Educational Administration Quarterly, 20*(3), 11–40.

Cook, W. J., Jr. (1990). *Bill Cook's strategic planning for America's schools* (rev. ed.). Arlington, VA: American Association of School Administrators.

Cooper, B. S., & Sarrel, R. (1993). Managing for school efficiency and effectiveness. *National Forum of Educational Administration and Supervision Journal, 8,* (3), 3–38.

Cuban, L. (1988). *The managerial imperative and the practice of leadership in schools.* Albany, NY: State University of New York Press.

Cunningham, W. G. (1982). *Systematic planning for educational change.* Palo Alto, CA: Mayfield.

David, J. L. (1994). School-based decision making: Kentucky's test of decentralization. *Phi Delta Kappan, 75,* 706–712.

Deming, E. W. (1986). *Out of the crisis.* Cambridge, MA: MIT Press.

Deming, W. E., et al. (1992). The new economics: For education, government, industry. In Quality Enhancement Seminars, *Instituting Dr. Deming's methods for management of productivity and quality* (notebook used in Deming seminars). Los Angeles: Author.

Drucker, P. (1974). *Management tasks, responsibilities, practices.* New York: Harper & Row.

Dunn, R. J., James-Gross, L., & Trampe, C. (1998). Decentralized budgeting: A study in implementation and implications. *Journal of School Business Management, 10* (1), 22–28.

Frazier, A. (1997). *A roadmap for quality transformation in education.* Boca Raton, FL: St. Lucie Press.

Fullan, M. (1993). *Change forces: Probing the depths of educational reform.* London: Falmer Press.

Goertz, M. E., & Stiefel, L. (1998). School-level resource allocation in urban schools. *Journal of Education Finance, 23*(4), 435–446.

Goodlad, J. I. (1984). *A place called school: Prospects for the future.* New York: McGraw-Hill.

Goodstein, L. D., Nolan, T. M., & Pfeiffer, J. (1992). *Applied strategic planning: A comprehensive guide.* San Diego, CA: Pfeiffer.

Gurr, D. (1999). *From supervision to quality assurance: The case of the State of Victoria (Australia).* Paris, France: International Institute for Educational Planning/UNESCO.

Guthrie, J. W. (1998). Reinventing education finance: Alternatives for allocating resources to individual schools. In W. J. Fowler, Jr. (Ed.), *Selected papers in school finance, 1996* (NCES98-217, pp. 85–107). Washington, DC: National Center for Education Statistics, U.S. Department of Education.

Hannaway, J. (1996). Management decentralization and performance-based incentives: Theoretical consideration for schools. In E. A. Hanushek & D. W. Jorgenson. *Improving America's schools: The role of incentives* (pp. 97–109). Washington, DC: National Academy Press.

Hannaway, J., & Carnoy, M. (1993). Preface. In J. Hannaway & M. Carnoy (Eds.). *Decentralization and school improvement: Can we fulfill the promise?* San Francisco, CA: Jossey-Bass.

Hartman, W. T. (1988). *School district budgeting.* Upper Saddle River, NJ: Prentice Hall.

Hodgkinson, C. (1991). *Educational leadership: The moral art.* Albany, NY: State University of New York Press.

Kirst, M. (1990). *Accountability: Implications for state and local policymakers* (Report 1590-982). Washington, DC: U.S. Department of Education.

Lawler, E. E., III. (1986). *High involvement management.* San Francisco: Jossey-Bass.

Lotto, L. S., & Clark, D. L. (1986). Understanding planning in educational organizations. *Planning and Changing, 17*(1), 9–18.

Malen, B., Ogawa, R., & Kranz, J. (1990). What do we know about school-based management? A case study of the literature—a call for research. In W. H. Clune & J. F. Witte (Eds.), *Choice and control in American education* (Vol. 2, pp. 289–342). Philadelphia: Falmer Press.

Mintzberg, H. (1989). *Mintzberg on management: Inside our strange world of organizations.* New York: Free Press.

Mintzberg, H. (1994). *The rise and fall of strategic planning*. New York: Free Press.

Mohrman, S. A., & Lawler, E. E., III. (1996). Motivation for school reform. In S. H. Fuhrman & J. A. O'Day, (Eds.). *Rewards and reform: Creating educational incentives that work* (pp. 115–143). San Francisco: Jossey-Bass.

New York State Education Department. (1999). *Comprehensive district education plan*. Unpublished monograph by the New York State Education Department, Albany, NY.

O'Brien, P. W. (1991). Strategic planning and management for organizations. In R. V. Carlson & G. Awkerman (Eds.), *Educational planning: Concepts, strategies, and practices* (pp. 163–176). New York: Longman.

Odden, A. (1999). Formula funding of schools in the United States of America and Canada. In K. N. Ross & R. L. Levačić, *Needs-based resource allocation in education via formula funding of schools*. Paris, France: UNESCO.

Odden, A., & Busch, C. (1998). *Financing schools for high performance: Strategies for improving the use of educational resources*. San Francisco: Jossey-Bass.

Peters, T. J., & Waterman, R. H., Jr. (1982). *In search of excellence: Lessons from America's best-run companies*. New York: Harper & Row.

Ross, M. L. (1997). *A comparative case study of teacher participation in planning in three types of decentralized schools*. Unpublished doctoral dissertation, State University of New York at Buffalo.

Senge, P. M. (1990). *The fifth discipline: The art and practice of the learning organization*. New York: Doubleday/Currency.

Sizer, T. R. (1985). *Horace's compromise: The dilemma of the American high school*. Boston: Houghton Mifflin.

Smylie, M. A. (1994). Redesigning teachers' work: Connections to the classroom. *Review of Research in Education, 20,* 129–177.

Speakman, S. T., Cooper, B. S., Sampieri, R., May, J., Holsomback, H., & Glass, B. (1996). Bringing money to the classroom: A systemic resource allocations model applied to the New York City public schools. In L. O. Picus & J. L. Wattenbarger (Eds.), *Where does the money go? Resource allocation in elementary and secondary schools (pp. 106–131).* Thousand Oaks, CA: Corwin Press.

Steiner, G. A. (1979). *Strategic planning: What every manager must know*. New York: Free Press.

Summers, A. A., & Johnson, A. W. (1996). The effects of school-based management plans. In E. A. Hanushek & D. W. Jorgenson (Eds.), *Improving America's schools: The role of incentives* (pp. 75–96). Washington, DC: National Academy Press.

Swanson, A. D., & King, R. A. (1997). *School finance: Its economics and politics*. New York: Longman.

U.S. General Accounting Office. (1994). *Education reform: School-based management results in changes in instruction and budgeting.* Washington, DC: GAO.

Wheatley, M. J. (1994). *Leadership and the new science: Learning about organizations from an orderly universe*. San Francisco: Berrett-Koehler.

Wheatley, M. J., & Kellner-Rogers, M. (1996). *A simpler way*. San Francisco: Berrett-Koehler.

Wohlstetter, P., & Buffett, T. M. (1992). Promoting school based management: Are dollars decentralized too? In A. R. Odden (Ed.), *Rethinking school finance: An agenda for the 1990s* (pp. 128–165). San Francisco: Jossey-Bass.

Wohlstetter, P., & Mohrman, S. A. (1994, December). School-based management: Promise and process. *CPRE Finance Briefs*.

Wohlstetter, P., Smyer, R., & Mohrman, S. A. (1994). New boundaries for school-based management: The high involvement model. *Educational Evaluation and Policy Analysis, 16,* 268–286.

Wohlstetter, P., & Van Kirk, A. (1996). Redefining school-based budgeting for high-involvement. In L. O. Picus & J. L. Wattenbarger (Eds.), *Where does the money go? Resource allocation in elementary and secondary schools* (pp. 212–235). Thousand Oaks, CA: Corwin Press.

CHAPTER 14

The Allocation of Resources for Education

Adequacy, Equity, and Efficiency

Education is big business. More than $350 billion is spent annually on public elementary and secondary schools, making expenditures for education the largest single budgetary component of state and local governments (National Center for Education Statistics [NCES], 1999). These expenditures represent nearly 4.3 percent of our nation's gross domestic product. More than 50 million children attend these schools, and they employ over 5 million professional educators and support personnel. No matter how one looks at it, schooling involves a highly significant portion of the nation's human and economic resources.

But education is much more than big business. Education deals with matters that relate to the hearts and souls of individual citizens and, at the same time, is critical to the political and economic welfare of the nation and its security. The quality of the decisions made about how much is spent on schooling (adequacy), how that spending is distributed among children (equity), and how the economic resources are transformed into educational delivery systems (efficiency) are the focus of this chapter.

We begin the chapter by looking at the equity of the distribution of financial resources among schools and school districts and the adequacy of the amounts provided. We then review the evidence of relationships between inputs to the schooling process and desired outcomes. We look at these relationships at two levels: societal, where we are interested in the impact of resources used for education on de-

sired social objectives such as economic growth; and the school or classroom, where we are interested in the impact of resources and their use on pupil behavior and pupil achievement. Such knowledge is necessary to improve the efficiency of educational institutions. The chapter concludes with a discussion of policy implications for improving the equity and efficiency of schooling.

Equity in the Allocation of Resources to Schooling

In a critical analysis of public education in the United States in 1943, Morrison (1943) referred to its structure disdainfully as "late New England colonial" (p. 258) and described the school district as "a little republic at every crossroads" (p. 75). Morrison was focusing on a characteristic of the system of U.S. public education that makes it unique among the school systems of the world—its extreme decentralization. Herein lay both its strengths and weaknesses.

Decentralized systems seem to be more adept than highly centralized and bureaucratic ones at mobilizing the energies of their constituents and adapting curricula and instructional systems to the diversity of their constituents. Yet decentralized systems have a tendency to become inequitable, providing an uneven quality of services. The good schools in a decentralized system tend to be very, very good; but such a system also generates—and tolerates—very poor schools. To bring about a greater degree of equity and set minimally acceptable social standards requires intervention of higher levels of government, (i.e., state and/or federal). This has been happening with increasing frequency over the 50 years since Morrison made his analysis.

Originally, "common" schools were financed primarily through locally levied property taxes, supplemented with voluntary contributions and some state subsidies. In 1920, 83 percent of elementary and secondary school expenditures were generated at the local level; less than 1 percent was provided by the federal government with the remaining 16.5 percent coming from state governments (NCES, 1999, p. 50). State-generated revenues now account for 47.5 percent of all school expenditures and the federal share is nearly 7 percent, leaving about 46 percent to be generated at the local level, still primarily through the property tax. Federal funds are provided primarily through categorical programs which direct monies and programs toward meeting the needs of children who are identified as being at risk, including those qualifying for compensatory reading and mathematics instruction as well as those with disabilities. The states make some use of categorical type aids, but most monies are channeled to local school districts as *equalized* general aid (i.e., distributed inversely to the taxing capacities of districts to compensate in part for the great differences in taxable wealth among districts).

Equality is defined as the state, ideal, or quality of being equal, as in enjoying equal social, political, and economic rights. The operational definition of equality within the sociopolitical context also includes factors of condition, placing emphasis on the *appropriateness* of treatment. As such, *equality* has taken on the broader connotations of *equity,* defined as "the state, ideal, or quality of being just, impartial and fair" (*American Heritage Dictionary of the English Language*). We use the term *equity* instead of *equality* as reflecting more accurately modern usage in reference to public policy.

In analyzing the impact of a policy on equity concerns, one must be fully aware of the level of equity the policy is intended to address and should consider the horizontal and vertical dimensions of equity. Horizontal equity refers to the equal treatment of equals—the traditional meaning of *equality.* Vertical equity recognizes that equal treatment is not always fair and just for persons (or school districts) experiencing abnormal conditions such as poverty and physical, psychological, and mental disabilities (or high costs of living, dispersed populations, and municipal overburden in the case of school districts). Thus, *vertical equity* refers to the appropriate unequal treatment of unequals. Some analysts add a third dimension, *equal opportunity,* defined in the negative as no differences in treatment according to characteristics (such as race or national origin) that are considered illegitimate (Berne & Stiefel, 1984, p. 17). Other analysts treat equal opportunity as a condition of horizontal equity, the position taken here.

Virtually all studies of resource allocation equity deal only with the horizontal dimension (including equal opportunity). The lack of agreement on what appropriate treatment is for exceptional populations makes analysis of vertical equity very difficult if not impossible; nevertheless, recognition of the concept is very important in designing school finance policy. Indeed, the concept is recognized in public policy through such programs as Head Start, special education, and compensatory education.

The Extent of Inequities in Resource Allocation

Despite the efforts to equalize resources available to school districts, great disparities remain. Table 14.1 shows the average per pupil current expenditures of school districts by quartile by state. The range in expenditures from high to low varies from $27,726 among New York State school districts to $1093 among Delaware districts. Hawaii is not included in the table because it operates as a state system and has no school districts. Except for Delaware and Indiana, the difference between the third-quartile expenditure and the highest expenditure is

Table 14.1
Average Current Cost per Pupil Expenditure by Quartile by State, 1995[a]

State	# of Districts	Low	First Quartile	Median	Third Quartile	High	Mean	Range
Alabama	127	2,680	3,031	3,262	3,557	5,618	3,347	3,138
Alaska	51	5,750	5,924	6,319	7,057	23,571	7,516	17,821
Arizona	207	2,861	3,579	3,700	4,061	10,826	3,933	7,965
Arkansas	310	2,727	3,142	3,372	3,632	7,253	3,471	4,526
California	976	2,808	4,062	4,403	4,845	17,933	4,488	15,125
Colorado	174	3,556	4,197	4,528	4,743	12,184	4,609	8,628
Connecticut	166	5,412	6,655	7,121	7,747	10,851	7,340	5,439
Delaware	16	4,909	5,285	5,543	5,786	6,002	5,556	1,093
Florida	67	3,868	4,359	4,584	5,035	5,943	4,688	2,075
Georgia	180	2,859	3,691	4,012	4,266	6,194	4,150	3,335
Idaho	109	2,652	2,984	3,236	3,686	10,250	3,349	7,598
Illinois	902	2,342	3,652	4,434	5,025	11,740	4,635	9,398
Indiana	28	3,430	4,553	4,773	5,104	5,785	4,836	2,355
Iowa	380	3,441	4,132	4,393	4,623	8,891	4,440	5,450
Kansas	304	2,901	4,080	4,573	4,823	11,054	4,544	8,153
Kentucky	NA	NA	NA	NA	NA	NA	NA	NA
Louisiana	66	2,976	3,738	4,112	4,379	6,332	4,107	3,356
Maine	223	2,524	4,439	4,779	5,154	9,968	4,880	7,444
Maryland	24	4,931	5,155	5,603	5,996	7,419	5,822	2,488
Massachusetts	295	3,078	4,537	5,063	5,938	12,669	5,362	9,591
Michigan	554	1,759	4,038	4,735	5,478	10,600	4,896	8,841
Minnesota	341	2,810	4,507	4,894	5,423	12,233	5,050	9,423
Mississippi	152	2,049	2,816	2,985	3,281	4,954	3,056	2,905
Missouri	527	2,331	3,271	3,769	4,329	10,300	4,152	7,969
Montana	455	2,286	3,500	3,926	4,784	21,774	4,473	19,488
Nebraska	641	1,909	4,129	4,761	5,208	15,844	4,762	13,935
Nevada	NA	NA	NA	NA	NA	NA	NA	NA
New Hampshire	160	3,398	4,482	5,052	5,870	10,711	5,228	7,313
New Jersey	551	3,976	6,431	7,059	8,001	14,691	7,254	10,715
New Mexico	89	3,007	3,378	3,803	3,842	9,984	3,788	6,977
New York	685	5,066	6,923	6,923	7,959	32,792	7,625	27,726
North Carolina	116	3,453	3,870	4,135	4,293	5,537	4,151	2,084
North Dakota	228	2,616	3,448	3,791	4,179	19,930	3,929	17,314
Ohio	610	2,543	3,702	4,330	5,266	15,000	4,576	12,457
Oklahoma	542	2,798	3,279	3,493	3,863	12,429	3,615	9,631
Oregon	240	3,296	4,596	4,966	5,547	18,750	5,155	15,454
Pennsylvania	NA	NA	NA	NA	NA	NA	NA	NA
Rhode Island	35	4,816	5,652	5,810	5,997	10,405	5,866	5,589
South Carolina	91	3,351	3,744	3,869	4,179	7,145	4,007	3,794
South Dakota	173	3,135	3,502	3,852	4,205	11,343	4,039	3,208
Tennessee	137	2,173	2,943	3,220	3,788	5,472	3,366	3,299
Texas	1,042	2,733	3,622	3,882	4,089	14,786	3,935	12,053
Utah	40	2,583	2,728	2,868	2,950	7,292	2,967	4,709
Vermont	238	2,991	4,987	5,612	6,439	14,667	5,793	11,676
Virginia	133	3,657	4,070	4,482	5,331	8,660	4,806	5,003
Washington	296	3,500	4,655	4,843	5,113	23,000	4,957	19,500
West Virginia	55	3,953	4,191	4,284	4,519	5,830	4,343	1,877
Wisconsin	425	3,693	5,136	5,540	6,207	10,214	5,667	6,521
Wyoming	49	4,687	4,858	5,043	5,297	19,475	5,395	14,788

Source: National Center for Education Statistics, State Equity Calculator, *http://216.181.15/ecalc/EcalaWeb.*
[a] NA, not available.

Table 14.2
Pupil and District Characteristics for Selected School Districts in the New York City Metropolitan Area

Districts

Item	New York City	Chappaqua	Cold Spring	Garden City	Great Neck
Enrollment[a]	992,992	3,022	1,480	3,044	5,462
Percentage White[a]	17.6	88.6	97.0	94.9	80.2
Percentage Black[a]	37.1	0.8	0.2	0.5	3.1
Percentage Hispanic[a]	36.1	1.6	0.7	1.1	6.7
Percentage Other[a]	9.2	9.1	2.1	3.5	10.0
Percentage Limited English[a]	15.8	1.9	0.8	0.9	2.5
1989 household income ($)[b]	29,823	107,319	111,515	74,506	66,385
1989 per capita income ($)[b]	20,186	47,197	52,447	33,224	39,316
Percentage households on public assistance[b]	13	1	1	2	2
Percentage age 16+ unemployed[b]	6	2	2	2	2
Percentage age 20+ high school dropouts[b]	31	4	4	5	9
Percentage age 20+ holding BA or above[b]	22	70	56	52	52
Percentage age 6–19 "at-risk"[b]	12	0	0	0	0
Annual attendance rate[a]	85.6	95.7	94.9	95.1	95.4
Pupils per teacher[a]	16	13	12	12	10
Median teacher salary ($)[a]	43,014	69,134	61,300	67,200	71,102
Expenditure per pupil ($)[a]	7,921	13,091	12,467	11,956	16,281
Combined wealth ratio[a]	1.0	2.5	3.1	3.0	3.9
Percentage enrolled in nonpublic schools[a]	23	20	24	23	16

[a]1993–94 school year.
[b]1989 (from U.S. Census).
[c]1992–1993 school year; no contract settlement for 1993–1994.
[d]1991–1992 school year; no contract settlement for 1993–1994 and 1992–1993.
Source: *School Finance: Its Economics and Politics,* 2nd ed., by Austin D. Swanson and Richard A. King. Copyright 1997, 1991 by Longman Publishers USA. Reprinted by permission of Addison-Wesley Educational Publishers, Inc.

larger than for any of the interquartile differences, suggesting that the greatest disparities are created by a relatively few very high spending districts with relatively large tax bases. State equalization policies are targeted primarily toward middle- and low-wealth districts.

Table 14.1 also illustrates that some states have done a better job of equalizing expenditures than others among middle- and low-spending districts. The differences in expenditures per pupil between the first- and third-quartile districts amount to less than $300

in Arkansas and Utah, but in New Jersey and Oklahoma, the differences are over $1500.

But equity is not the entire story; there is also the matter of adequacy. An analysis by the National Center for Education Statistics (1998, p. 101) pointed out that "although New York State is one of the lowest-ranking states in terms of intrastate equity, students at the lowest levels of revenue in that state (i.e., at the fifth percentile of district funding), received more than the median student (i.e., at the fiftieth percentile of district funding) in forty-five of the fifty

Hempstead	Malverne	Mt. Vernon	Roosevelt	Scarsdale	Sewanhaka	Yonkers
5,483	1,807	9,609	2,955	3,709	6,615	20,523
0.4	39.1	13.6	0.3	77.8	65.2	29.4
72.1	51.5	75.8	91.9	2.3	15.0	28.9
26.4	7.5	8.9	7.8	2.1	9.2	37.8
0.7	1.9	1.8	0.0	17.9	10.5	3.9
13.1	2.3	4.8	6.4	5.7	2.7	15.7
32,909	49,180	34,850	45,512	121,275	47,462	36,376
13,374	19,071	15,835	13,414	60,688	18,331	17,484
10	5	10	14	2	4	9
5	3	5	6	1	3	4
32	17	29	26	3	20	25
14	27	20	13	72	21	21
7	1	5	5	0	0	8
90.7	94.6	91.0	90.7	96.4	93.6	87.2
16	13	14	16	12	15	15
55,003	60,500[c]	60,909	39,004[d]	71,000	61,210	61,092
10,932	11,306	10,626	9,374	12,282	10,118	10,185
0.8	1.3	0.9	0.5	3.3	1.4	1.3
20	23	17	16	16	17	31

states." In an analysis of the school finance structures of four provinces of Atlantic Canada, Lake (1983) came up with a similar finding that in the quest for equity, adequacy of support may suffer. A more recent analysis by Paquette (1999) of Ontario's move to full provincial funding of elementary and secondary education found that the reforms "promise more equal but lower funding for Ontario boards" (p. 24).

To further illustrate the disparities among school districts, Table 14.2 provides information on the demographic and financial characteristics of selected school districts in the metropolitan New York City area. The data, derived from the 1989 federal census and 1993–1994 school district information, show the inequity created by the proliferation of small school districts in one of the most densely populated regions in the United States. Enrollment in these districts ranged from nearly 1 million pupils in New York City (NYC) to 1480 in Cold Spring. Median household income ranged from $29,823 in NYC to $121,275 in Scarsdale; median per capita income ranged from $13,414 in Roosevelt to $60,688 in Scarsdale.

Thirty-one percent of NYC's population over the age of 20 were high school dropouts, and only 22 percent held a bachelor's degree or higher. This compares with 3 percent and 72 percent, respectively, in Scarsdale.

Roosevelt, in Nassau County, Long Island, had an enrollment under 3000 pupils, of which 92 percent were African-American and 8 percent were of Hispanic origin. Nearby Garden City had 3000 pupils that were 95 percent white and less than 2 percent African-American or Hispanic. In the public schools of NYC, only 18 percent were classified as white, non-Hispanic; 37 percent were African-American, 36 percent were Hispanic, and 9 percent were classified as other. Only Sewanhaka had an enrollment distribution that reflected the distribution of the region as a whole. Under these circumstances, the ideal of the common school as a socially integrated institution is difficult to realize.

School district differences in demographic characteristics are reflected in their financial provision for instruction. NYC's per pupil expenditure, $7921, was among the lowest in the metropolitan area; Great Neck spent over twice as much per pupil, $16,281. Chappaqua, Cold Spring, Garden City, and Scarsdale spent at least 50 percent more per pupil than did New York City. The median teacher in Chappaqua, Garden City, Great Neck, and Scarsdale was paid at least $24,000 per year more than the median teacher in NYC. Of the districts listed in the table, only Roosevelt paid its teachers less than did NYC. NYC's pupil/teacher ratio was also among the highest in the region.

Intradistrict Equity Studies

During the 1990s, the policy emphasis in equity analyses shifted from inputs (e.g., spending levels) to outcomes (e.g., achievement), and from interdistrict equity to equity among schools, classrooms, and pupils. All equity analyses became more complicated as federal and state governments increased their use of categorical aids targeted to at-risk students as an instrument of public policy to promote vertical equity. Prior to the 1990s, categorical aids were small enough to be ignored or included with other revenue or expenditures in the evaluation of horizontal equity; such a procedure is no longer appropriate.

Berne and Stiefel (1994) set the pattern for the study of equity within districts in an analysis of the distribution of resources to New York City's more than 800 elementary and middle/junior high schools operated by the city's 32 community school districts. They found that the glaring inequities in vertical equity with respect to poverty that were commonplace at the state level did not exist within New York City. Even though elementary schools budgeted and spent more resources per pupil of general education funds in lower- than higher-poverty schools, categorical aids were sufficient to bring expenditures of high-poverty schools above those of low-poverty schools. Middle and junior high schools directed greater amounts of general education funds per pupil to higher-poverty schools. High-poverty schools, regardless of grade level, had greater access to most other resources (e.g., categorical aids) than did low-poverty schools.

They also found that average teacher salaries in high-poverty subdistricts of New York City were $4536 lower than in low-poverty subdistricts. This was because poorer students were taught by less experienced and less educated teachers and, as a result, the teachers were paid at a lower rate. Berne and Stiefel observed that "this raises the critical policy question of how to better allocate teacher resources within urban districts" (p. 419). These findings also suggested the methodological conclusion that "measures of dollars alone are not sufficient in an equity analysis and that to some degree the education process must be examined" (p. 419).

In 1246 New York State elementary schools in 300 school districts excluding New York City, Hyary (1994) found a different situation. She concluded that there was considerable variation across the districts in equity of intradistrict resource distribution. Districts with high levels of intradistrict inequality tended to have relatively large enrollments, numbers of schools, and percent of minority and/or poor children. There was no evidence that minority and/or poor children were being denied equal access to resources, however. The intradistrict inequities could be caused by deliberate district policy targeting compensatory resources to minority and/or poor children, but the study design did not permit the investigation of such possibility.

In California, Hertert (1994) analyzed the degree of disparity in per pupil expenditures at two levels, district and school. She concluded that judgments on the fairness of the distributions found is a matter of perspective. California has a fairly equitable system across districts; equalization across schools, however, is not so equitable. In a few of the districts studied, the variation among schools was substantial and could not be explained by school size or ethnicity. Noting that over the past several decades, a great deal of attention has been given to creating equity across districts, she concluded that these efforts might be more productive if attention were focused across schools rather than districts.

The equity of the distribution of resources among elementary schools within Dade County, Florida, the nation's third largest school district and containing the city of Miami, was studied by Owens (1994). He found that instructional expenditures in some elementary schools were much higher than in others. Unlike the New York City and California studies, however, he found that these differences were related to racial/ethnic and family income factors. High percentages of African-American and low-income students and large schools had lower instructional expenditures per pupil than schools without those characteristics. Owens attributed this inequity largely to the practice of permitting senior teachers to control where they will teach. As in the New York City study, less-experienced teachers and teachers with less education were more likely to be found in traditionally minority and low-SES schools.

There is a clear pattern of horizontal inequity among and within school districts in the United States. In at least some instances, however, the inequities within districts may be deliberate

policies to address issues of vertical equity by assigning more resources to pupils at risk of academic failure.

Conceptual Considerations

There was a marked shift in thinking about equity during the 1990s. It is no longer a matter of equity *or* high standards; it is a matter of equity *and* high standards. Although we continue to be interested in the equity of inputs into the educational process out of a sense of fairness, our ultimate concern is with student outputs and outcomes. Previously, there was an almost naive belief that if there was equity in terms of school district inputs, equity of student achievement would follow automatically. We now know better, as evidence presented in Chapter 1 has shown. We have come to know that the linkages between resources and outcomes are very tenuous (Monk, 1994). Merely adding resources to a failed system will not reform that system automatically; the resources have to be organized and used effectively for the singular purpose of improving student learning. Although we have scattered examples of this happening, they are few and far between.

Equity studies within districts centered on schools have shown us that there is inequitable distribution of resources within districts as well as among districts and states. The logical extension of the movement to school-centered studies is toward equity studies centering on programs, classrooms, and even individual children. We are moving from a concern over the equitable treatment of institutions to the equitable treatment of individuals.

Efficiency, Adequacy, and Economic Growth

Equity is only one (although a very important one) of many criteria used to evaluate resource allocation policies. In this section we turn our attention to other criteria: efficiency, adequacy, and economic growth.

A primary stimulus of the school reform movement launched in the 1980s was concern over the ability of the United States to compete in international markets. (Refer to the related discussion in Chapter 1.) Fears stemming from economic competition replaced the threat of military conflict as a fundamental stimulant of social action. The technological revolution that had been gaining momentum since World War II emerged into a new social and economic order that substantially upgraded educational requirements for those who were to participate in it fully. Coupled with the demographics of fewer entrants into the labor market and longer working careers, business and industrial leaders recognized how critical it is for workers to have the basic mathematical and language skills needed to provide a foundation for learning other skills (McDonnell & Fuhrman, 1986). As a result, improving the efficiency of the educational system was seen as critical to any strategy for strengthening the nation's economic condition.

Hanushek (1986, p. 1166) defined *economic efficiency* as "the correct share of input mix given the prices of inputs and the production function." *Production function* is the causal relationship between inputs and outcomes. He cautioned against confusing economic efficiency and technical efficiency. The latter considers only the *process* of combining inputs to produce outcomes and does not take into account the *prices* of inputs. Both concepts are important considerations in designing educational systems.

There are two aspects of economic efficiency, external and internal. *External efficiency* considers contributions to national economic growth made by the scarce resources allocated by society to various sectors of production, such as education. With respect to education, we are interested in the return on investments in education relative to return from other investment opportunities. *Internal efficiency* relates to the allocation of resources within educational enterprises in order to maximize output (e.g., achievement, skill develop-

ment, and behavioral and attitudinal changes among students) from the resources committed. Analyses of external efficiency assist in making decisions about the amount of resources to be committed to and among educational services and in determining the level of societal investment in population quality in order to promote economic growth.

In other words, studying external efficiencies addresses the issues of how much to spend for educational services and of which kinds of services to provide in order to create the greatest amount of economic benefit. Internal efficiency relates to the means by which educational services are provided. The study of internal efficiency is directed toward gaining the maximum benefit from the resources committed to an institution. Whereas internal efficiency is studied through educational production functions and cost-benefit and cost-effectiveness analysis, external efficiency is studied through rate of return analysis.

External Efficiency

Since approximately 90 percent of expenditures for elementary and secondary education are provided through the public sector in the United States, deciding how much to spend for educational services is largely a political process, and the decisions made may not be efficient from an economic or technical perspective. (See complementary discussion in Chapter 9.) Economic analysis can estimate the efficiency by which we are using scarce resources for educational services; but in the political process, economic efficiency is only one of many, often conflicting objectives of social policy. Concerns for improving economic efficiency must be balanced against other social concerns, and when other concerns take precedence, policies adopted may be inefficient for good reasons. Too often, however, public policy is adopted not fully knowing its economic ramifications.

The economic benefit of investments in education has been studied at two levels: the individual and society. The human capital approach assumes that schooling endows a person with knowledge and skills that enable him or her to be more productive and thereby receive higher earnings. This is, of course, beneficial to the person. The accumulation of benefits derived by all persons is beneficial to society as a whole through greater total production, higher tax yields, and possible spillover benefits which may contribute to a generally improved quality of life for all.

Causes of Economic Growth. In analyzing causes of economic growth, economists had traditionally considered only increases in the *quantity* of labor and physical capital and largely ignored improvements in their *quality*. Schultz (1981, p. 11) condemned this assumption that capital is qualitatively homogeneous. Claiming that each form of capital has specific properties, he introduced the concept of variation in quality of both physical and human capital. The seeds for the concept of human capital were planted in Adam Smith's defining work on economics, *The Wealth of Nations,* published in 1776, but the concept had been largely ignored by economists until Schultz.

Schultz, who received the Nobel Prize in Economics in 1979 for his work with developing countries, is generally credited with sparking a renewed interest in human capital theory. He turned attention to the economics of education, observing that the concepts commonly used to "measure capital and labor were close to being empty in explaining the increases in production that occur over time" (Schultz, 1963, p. viii). Schultz was referring to the fact that quantitative increases in labor and physical capital explained less than one-third of the rate of economic growth in the United States.

In attempting to explain the cause of the remaining two-thirds of growth, called the *residual,* Schultz drew an analogy between additions of stock to physical capital and increases in the amount of education available in the population at large. Schultz's (1963) thesis was that traditional measures of labor and capital understated the true investment. Schultz concluded that the unexplained economic growth "originates out of forms of capital that have not been measured and consists mainly of human capital. . . . [T]he economic capabilities of man are predominantly a produced means of production and . . . most of the differences in earnings are a consequence of differences in the amounts that have been invested in people" (pp. 64–65). Extending Schultz's analysis, Benson (1978, p. 72) estimated that the net "investment" through education accounted for approximately one-fifth of the growth in real national income of the United States.

Hanushek and Kim (1995) took Schultz's qualitative differentiation theory one step further. In addition to the quantity of education achieved by a country's population, they investigated the impact of differences in the quality of that education on national economic growth. They used as their quality measures comparative tests of mathematics and scientific skills of school children from 39 countries participating in various international testing programs over the past three decades. They concluded that quality of education has a "consistent, stable, and strong influence on economic growth. . . . [T]he impact of quality indicates that one standard deviation in mathematics and science skills translates into one percentage point in average annual real growth" (p. 34).

These studies show that education contributes significantly to national economic growth; but they did not address the *adequacy* of investment in education. To address the adequacy issue, another analytical procedure is used, *rate-of-return analysis.* With respect to education, rate-of-return analysis is intended to inform policy makers about whether to spend on different kinds of programs (Benson, 1978, p. 91). Rate-of-return analysis compares the profit (increased earnings) to the expense of acquiring knowledge and skills, including earnings forgone in the process.

In a free market, when supply and demand for persons possessing a particular set of knowledge and skills are in equilibrium, the rate of return approximates that which is generally expected from other types of investments. If the rate is much higher, there is an apparent shortage of persons with these skills, permitting them to command higher wages. This encourages more people to acquire similar training and enter the workforce until wages and the rate of return drop to the expected level. If, on the other hand, the rate of return is much lower than that which can be obtained from other investments, there is a surplus of persons with similar skills—more than the market can absorb. Competition for employment drives wages down, discouraging people from acquiring such skills until supply again equals demand and the rate of return from earnings over expenditures equals the expected. Market effects may be dampened by constraints placed on them through such vehicles as union contracts, which are quite common among public school districts. (See the complementary discussion in Chapter 9.)

Evaluating social policy by computing internal rates of return for investments in education was the focus of the pioneering work by Becker (1960, 1964). He estimated the social rate of return for white male college graduates to be between 10 and 13 percent. Assuming that rates for college dropouts and nonwhites would be lower, he estimated the rate for all college entrants to be between 8 and 11 percent. Becker (1964, p. 121) concluded that "the rates on business capital and college education seem, therefore, to fall within the same range." Rates of return for high school graduates were higher, and they were highest for elementary school graduates. Becker cautioned, however, that adjustments for differential ability would probably reduce or eliminate the differences in rates among levels of schooling.

Higher rates of return for lower levels of education may be changing, however. An analysis by Pierce and Welch (1996) has found that the returns to schooling and labor market experience for white males in the United States over the past 25 years have risen along with wage inequality. In 1992, men with a college degree earned about 50 percent per week more than high school graduates and they were more likely to be fully employed year round. "This period witnessed a pause in the convergence of wages between black and white men as well as the beginnings of rapid wage gains for white women relative to white men" (p. 54). They also found that, increasingly, secondary-level schooling results in higher earnings only as it prepares students for college. The increased importance of education as a determinant of labor market outcomes is at least partly due to economywide factors that have acted to increase the demand for relatively skilled workers. Paquette (1991) found similar results for Canada. He concluded that with regard to average employment income, the incremental earning advantage of lower levels of educational attainment was diminishing rapidly.

Spending Levels for Education.   When 14 economically advanced countries were compared in terms of elementary and secondary school expenditures from public sources as a percentage of gross domestic product (GDP) in 1994, the United States ranked about in the middle, consuming 3.6 percent. Educational spending consumed more of the GDP in Sweden (4.5 percent), Denmark (4.3 percent), Norway and Switzerland (4.1 percent), France (4.0 percent), New Zealand and Portugal (3.9 percent), and Belgium and the United Kingdom (3.8 percent). Countries that devoted proportionally less included Australia (3.2 percent), the Netherlands (3.0 percent), and Japan and Germany (2.9 percent) (NCES, 1999, p. 469).

Investment in education by level in the United States for the period 1959 through 1997 is reported in Table 14.3 along with the percentage of the total population enrolled in precollegiate and higher education. The percentage of

Table 14.3
Percentage of Gross Domestic Product (GDP) Spent on Education and Percentage of Total Population Enrolled in Educational Institutions by Level, 1959–1997

Year	Elementary and Secondary Schools		Higher Education		Total	
	Percentage of GDP	*Percentage Enrollment of Population*	*Percentage of GDP*	*Percentage Enrollment of Population*	*Percentage of GDP*	*Percentage Enrollment of Population*
1959	3.3	23.0	1.4	2.0	4.7	25.0
1965	3.9	24.9	2.2	3.0	6.1	28.0
1970	4.7	25.1	2.7	4.2	7.3	29.3
1975	4.6	23.1	2.7	5.2	7.3	28.3
1980	4.0	20.3	2.5	5.3	6.6	25.7
1985	3.9	18.9	2.6	5.1	6.4	24.1
1990	4.3	18.6	2.9	5.5	7.2	24.2
1995	4.4	19.2	2.9	5.4	7.3	24.7
1997	4.3	19.4	2.9	5.4	7.2	24.7

Source: National Center for Education Statistics, *Digest of Education Statistics*. Washington, DC: U.S. Department of Education, 1999.

GDP spent for all educational institutions rose steadily from 4.7 percent in 1959 to 7.3 percent in 1970 through 1975. It then declined to 6.4 percent in 1985, rising again to 7.3 percent in 1995. The earlier peak allocation of GDP to education (1970) corresponds to the peak in the percentage of the population enrolled in educational institutions (29.3 percent). The 1997 allocation of GDP to education (7.2 percent) is for a smaller cohort than was the case in 1970 (24.7 percent of the total population), meaning that per pupil expenditures have grown faster than the GDP (and inflation for that matter).

For elementary and secondary school expenditures, the percentage of GDP rose from 3.3 percent in 1959 to 4.7 percent in 1970. Although expenditure per pupil continued to increase in current and constant dollars, the percentage of GDP declined to 3.9 percent in 1985, but has since risen to 4.3 percent. The rise and fall in the percentage of GDP spent for precollegiate education parallels the fluctuation in the proportion

of the total population attending elementary and secondary schools. Enrollment peaked in 1970 at 25.1 percent of the total population, subsequently declining to 18.6 percent in 1990 and then increasing to 19.4 percent in 1997.

The percentage of GDP spent on colleges and universities rose steadily from 1.4 percent in 1959 to 2.9 percent from 1990 on. Actual enrollments in postsecondary education have steadily risen from 3,640,000 in 1959 to over 14,350,000 in 1997. The percentage of the population enrolled in higher education in 1959 was 2.0 percent. It rose to 5.5 percent in 1990, dropping back to 5.4 percent in 1995 and 1997.

Percent of gross domestic product spent on elementary and secondary education is only one aspect of our interest. Also of interest is the *amount* spent and the *adequacy* of that amount. Figure 14.1 shows the increase in current expenditures per pupil in average daily attendance between 1971 and 1998 in constant 1996–1997 dollars and in current dollars. The

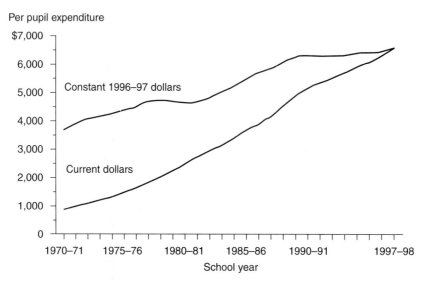

Figure 14.1
Current expenditure per pupil in average daily attendance in public elementary and secondary schools, 1970–1971 to 1997–1998

Source: National Center for Education Statistics, *Digest of Education Statistics* (NCES 1999-036, p. 49), Washington, DC: U.S. Department of Education, 1999.

amount spent in 1970–1971, in inflationary-adjusted dollars, was $3710, growing to $6624 in 1997–1998. Looking at the figure, one can detect an acceleration in the rate of growth in per pupil expenditures beginning about 1981–1982 and a leveling off beginning about 1989–1990. During the first eight-year period, which corresponds with the early stages of the current reform movement, growth averaged about 4 percent per year; for the subsequent eight-year period, it was approximately 0.5 percent.

The gradual increase in inflation-adjusted expenditures since mid-twentieth century has sparked much interest and a number of investigations into "Where has the money gone?" Rothstein and Miles's (1995) study found that the bulk of the increase went into special education programs. The share of special education spending of all spending increased from 4 percent in 1967 to 17 percent by 1991. The share of expenditures for regular education actually declined from 80 percent in 1967 to 59 percent in 1991.

Another study of the distribution of new resources allocated to public schools over a 5-year period ending in the early 1990s is reported by Odden, Monk, Nakib, and Picus (1995). Their conclusion is that the funds have been distributed unfairly and used ineffectively and that the public education system needs to be restructured so that new resources can be strategically linked to improved student achievement. They found that the largest portion of increased spending had been used to hire more teachers to reduce class size and to provide more out-of-classroom services, primarily "pull-out" instruction for disabled and low-achieving students. Funds were also used to increase teacher salaries, but not in a fashion that would enhance teacher expertise. Large portions of increased revenues were also used to expand special education services. The authors contend that the long-term task of reform is to get schools to act more like producers of high levels of student achievement than like consumers of educational resources.

Guthrie (1997) came to similar conclusions. Whether in special education, general education, or elsewhere in the schools, he identified the principal factor contributing to higher expenditures as more people working in the schools and being paid at higher levels. He notes that in 1950, there was one school employee for every 19.3 pupils; this ratio has now dropped to one employee for every 9.1 pupils. Some of these additional people are working in expanded special education programs, while others are required because of fewer dropouts at the secondary level, full-day kindergarten, preschool programs, and compensatory education. Also contributing to higher costs is an increase in the salaries of teachers because more hold advanced degrees and are generally more experienced than they were a few years back. The relative number of administrators has not grown over the years and may actually have shrunk slightly.

As expenditures per unit rise, so do questions about the effectiveness and efficiency of the programs in which those resources are expended. The rate-of-return studies reviewed earlier suggest that advanced countries, including the United States, are probably spending at or near the optimal rate for educational services *given the existing state of employed educational technology.* If this is the case, educational performance in the United States is more likely to be improved by improving the efficiency of the present system or deploying improved technology than by increasing expenditures (Burtless, 1996; Swanson & King, 1997).

Internal Efficiency

We now turn to consideration of the efficiency with which resources allocated to schools are used in the education of children. The ability of such resources to improve individual and societal welfare will be enhanced or diminished according to the efficiency with which they are used.

Fuller and Clarke (1994) divide educators and researchers into two camps when it comes to defining and studying school effectiveness and

efficiency: policy mechanics and classroom culturalists. *Policy mechanics,* working from a production function metaphor, attempt to identify instructional inputs and uniform teaching practices that yield higher achievement; that is, their focus is on economic efficiency. They search for universal determinants of effective schools that can be manipulated by central agencies (e.g., state education departments) and assume that the same instructional materials and practices will produce similar results across diverse settings.

Classroom culturalists reject this orientation and "focus on the normative socialization that occurs within classrooms: the value children come to place on individualistic versus cooperative work, legitimated forms of adult authority and power, and acquired attitudes toward achievement and modern forms of status" (p. 120). The classroom culturalists tend to ignore narrower forms of cognitive achievement and have not been particularly interested in antecedent inputs and classroom rules that are manipulable by central authority. Although they do not normally use the term, their focus is on what economists refer to as *technical efficiency.* Fuller and Clarke conclude:

> The classroom culturalists have advanced researchers' understanding of how motivated learning occurs within particular social contexts, like classrooms. The production function gurus continue to hold comparative advantage in empirically linking classroom tools to achievement. But this advantage will only be retained if these inputs and teaching practices are awarded real cultural meaning—within a particular context which is energized by variable forms of teacher authority, social participation, and classroom tasks. (p. 143)

In this section we review the findings of both camps. We begin by examining production function and scale studies of economic efficiency done by policy mechanics and then consider research and applications relating to technical efficiency as revealed by effective schools research, program evaluations, and evaluations of whole-school reform models. Finally, we consider policy implications for improving internal efficiency of schools among schools and students.

Economic Efficiency.   In looking for evidence concerning economic efficiency of schools and school districts, we turn to studies of educational production functions and economies of scale.

Production Function Studies.   Studies of the economic efficiency of schooling that relate outcomes to inputs have been classified by several terms, including *educational production functions, input–output analysis,* and *cost–quality studies.* Such research has been pursued by researchers from a variety of disciplines in an effort to improve educational productivity. In this section we refer to them by the economic classification *production function.*

A production function may be conceptualized as a set of relations among possible inputs and a corresponding set of outputs for a firm or industry—in this case, schools and education (Burkhead, 1967, p. 18). According to Hanushek (1987), "a firm's production possibilities are assumed to be governed by certain technical relationships, and the production function describes the maximum feasible output that can be obtained from a set of inputs" (p. 33). Monk (1989, p. 31) states that a production function tells what is currently possible: "It provides a standard against which practice can be evaluated on productivity grounds." Monk goes on to identify two traditions with respect to the study of the production of education services. The first attempts to estimate the parameters of the educational production function. The second uses the production function as a metaphor, allowing for application of broader economic theories and reasoning that can be used to guide inquiry. He argues that the latter is the more appropriate application in education.

An educational production function may be expressed simply as output (O) being a function of inputs consisting of student characteristics (S), schooling inputs (I), and instructional processes (P):

$$O = f(S, I, P)$$

Outputs (O) include behavioral and attitudinal changes in pupils induced through school activities. Outputs are usually measured by standardized test scores but occasionally include other measures, such as high school graduation rate, attendance rate, and rate of graduates continuing on to postsecondary education. Student characteristics (S) range from socioeconomic status of family and student IQ to previous achievement. Schooling inputs (I) include expenditures, teacher characteristics, class size, characteristics of buildings, and so on. Instructional processes (P) include student time on task, teaching methods, student–teacher interactions, and so on.

If, indeed, there is an educational production function, there must also be a common underlying technology of education, an assumption that may come as a surprise to many educators because production technologies in education are inexact. Nevertheless, the sameness of schools in the United States (and around the world, for that matter) lend credibility to an assumption of an implicit technology. School buildings are typically arranged with classrooms and certain ancillary spaces, such as libraries, auditoriums, and gymnasiums. Each classroom is usually presided over by one teacher only, and there is a large degree of similarity in the ways that teachers organize and manage classrooms.

A most significant finding of the production function studies, beginning with the *Equality of Educational Opportunity* (EEO) study (Coleman, 1966), is the very strong relationship between family background and pupil achievement. The relationship is so strong that findings of these studies have frequently been misinterpreted to mean that schools have relatively little impact on pupil achievement. It is well documented that schools have not been very effective in closing achievement gaps among racial and ethnic groups and among socioeconomic classes [although gains are being made (Grissmer, Flanagan, & Williamson, 1998)]; nevertheless, schools do have enormous impacts on the development of all children.

Even the most gifted of children learn—or at least develop—their basic academic skills in schools. Most children come into schools as non-readers and leave with varying levels of literacy skills. Similar statements could be made about mathematics, writing, and other academic skills, as well as about knowledge and attitudinal development. Mayeski et al. (1972) stated it very well in a reanalysis of the EEO data: "Schools are indeed important. It is equally clear, however, that their influence is bound up with that of the student's background" (p. ix). Very little influence of schools can be separated from the social backgrounds of their students, and very little of the influence of social background on learning can be separated from the influence of the schools. Dealing with the collinearity of variables is a major challenge to researchers making production function analyses in education.

Some of the most influential writings involving production function research have been done by Hanushek (1986, 1991, 1994, 1996). Based on a meta-analysis of 187 production function studies published in 38 articles or books, he concluded that "there is no systematic relationship between school expenditures and student performance" (1991, p. 425). More recently, Hanushek (1996) wrote:

> The central issue in all policy discussions is usually not whether to spend more or less on school resources but how to get the most out of marginal expenditures. Nobody would advocate zero expenditures on schooling, as nobody would argue for infinite spending on schooling. The issue is getting productive uses from current and added spending. The existing evidence simply indicates that the typical school system today does not use resources well (at least if promoting student achievement is their purpose). . . . In essence U.S. schools are unlikely to improve in terms of either student outcomes or costs unless much stronger incentives for improved student performance are instituted. (p. 69)

Hanushek's methodology and conclusion have been bitterly challenged by Hedges, Laine, and Greenwald (1994a, 1994b; also, Greenwald,

Hedges, & Laine, 1994; Hedges & Greenwald, 1996), who claim that although the methods that Hanushek used were accepted as adequate when he began his research more than 15 years ago, they "are now regarded as inadequate synthesis procedures. When examined using more adequate methods, the data upon which his finding is based support exactly the opposite inference: the amount of resources are positively related to the accomplishments of students" (Greenwald et al., 1994, p. 2). Because of more stringent standards for including studies in their reanalysis, it involved fewer cases than did Hanushek's original study. Also, Hanushek employed an analytic method known as vote counting, while Greenwald et al. used combined significance tests and combined estimation methods.

In a rebuttal to Greenwald et al.'s challenge, Hanushek (1994) retorted that the challengers had made the larger error in asking the wrong question. According to Hanushek, the challengers posed the fundamental issue as one of using the right statistical method, while he saw it as one of identifying correct policies: "It is important that the policy significance not be lost in the technical details. . . . Most importantly, the policy interpretations do not depend really on the statistical issues" (p. 5). Some credence is given to Hanushek's rebuttal in Greenwald et al.'s (1994) conclusion that: "Even if the conclusions drawn from the studies analyzed in this paper are correct, we would not argue that 'throwing money at schools' is the most efficient method of increasing educational achievement. It certainly is not. Greater emphasis must be placed on the manner in which resources are utilized, not simply the provision of those resources" (p. 20). Later, as the argument continued, Hedges and Greenwald (1996) wrote, "We hope that the emphasis will shift from the question of 'does money matter?' to the issue of how resources matter in specific circumstances."

Another review of the literature on educational production functions by King and MacPhail-Wilcox (1994, p. 47) summarized the

prevailing thinking about the relationships between school inputs and outputs: "A safe conclusion is that the way in which schools, teachers, and students take advantage of whatever
materials are available matters as much or more
than the actual human, physical and fiscal resources present in schools."

Ferguson (1991) completed a most promising
study of a large and particularly rich data source
that he assembled for the state of Texas. The
data included information on nearly 900 school
districts serving over 2.4 million students and
employing 150,000 teachers. Because of the
comprehensive database and the careful, systematic preparation of the data, Ferguson found
a much larger school effect than had been
found by similar studies in the past. Between
one-fourth and one-third of the variation among
Texas school districts in students' scores on the
reading examination were explained by school
effects, primarily teachers' knowledge scores. A
major weakness of the Ferguson study is that
data were aggregated at the district level.

The power of teachers' knowledge scores to
predict student achievement is of particular interest and is in keeping with the findings of
other studies, beginning with the EEO study,
which found that the strongest school effect on
pupil achievement was teachers' verbal ability.
Ferguson also found that class size matters as
well. His analysis showed that reducing the
number of students per teachers in districts to
18—which approximates an average class size
of 23—is very important for performance in the
primary grades. Dropping the ratio below the
threshold of 18 showed no relationship to test
scores. Similarly, there was a threshold effect for
teacher experience; up to five years of experience at the primary level and up to nine years
at the secondary level had a positive influence
on student performance. He found no upper
limit for the positive effect of teachers' knowledge scores, however. Ferguson concluded:

> The teacher supply results, when combined with
> the results for student test scores, demonstrate that
> hiring teachers with stronger literacy skills, hiring

more teachers (when students-per-teacher exceeds eighteen), retaining experienced teachers,
and attracting more teachers with advanced training are all measures that produce higher test
scores in exchange for more money. (Ferguson,
1991, p. 485)

Based on his findings, Ferguson makes the
policy recommendation that apart from the
common focus by states on equalizing spending
per pupil, a serious equalization policy should
equalize the most important of all schooling inputs, teacher quality. Similar recommendations
were made in the equity studies of New York
City (Berne & Stiefel, 1994) and Dade County,
Florida (Owens, 1994).

The Consortium on Renewing Education,
(CRE) (1998) identified Texas as the most persuasive example that reform can be productive.
In 1993, a high-stakes testing and accountability
system was introduced in Texas that includes a
comprehensive database facilitating analyses at
the building and grade levels, overcoming one
of the limitations of the Ferguson (1991) database. Among those taking advantage of this
new and rich data resource are Hanushek, Kain,
and Rivkin (1998). In their study they found
large differences in the quality of schooling in a
way that ruled out the possibility that the differences were driven by nonschool factors; but
the researchers concluded that "resource differences explain at most a small part of the difference in school quality, raising serious doubts
that additional expenditures would substantially
raise achievement under current institutional
structure" (p. 31). As did Ferguson (1991), the
most significant factor they found explaining
variation in student achievement was variation
in teacher characteristics. Although most of the
specific attributes relating to student achievement remained unidentified, they were able to
draw some conclusions with policy implications. For example, they found no evidence that
holding a master's degree was related to pupil
achievement. They did find a relationship between achievement and up to two years of
teaching experience, but not thereafter. They

noted that "the estimated relationship between achievement and graduate degrees and experience opens questions about the prevalence of teacher pay scales that reward these characteristics" (p. 34). They also found some advantage to small class size for children from low-income families in grades 4 and 5 but the effect declined with grade level.

Although we are growing in our understanding of the relationships between educational inputs and outputs, the causal relationships between school inputs and processes on pupil achievement are largely unknown. This high degree of ignorance has serious policy implications for deploying strategies to improve student equity, and it places in serious question the efficacy of the provision in the 1994 Educate America Act encouraging states to develop "opportunity-to-learn" standards. At this point, the posture of the classroom culturalists looks quite wise, focusing on the normative socialization that occurs within classrooms. There is not sufficient knowledge to specify a one best way for the organization, management, and operation of schools from the center, be it the state or the federal government.

Economies and Diseconomies of Scale.

Assuming a universal educational production function, economies of scale are realized when average production costs decline as more units (e.g., pupils) are produced or serviced. Conversely, there are diseconomies of scale when average production costs increase as more units are produced or serviced. These are important concepts in the efficient organization of educational enterprises.

Policies concerning school district consolidation are directed toward realizing economies of scale, whereas policies decentralizing large-city school districts are directed toward avoiding diseconomies of scale. Similarly, during periods of declining enrollments, closing underutilized buildings is a strategy for minimizing operating costs. Reorganizing very large schools into "houses" or "schools within schools" is a strategy

for realizing the benefits of both large and small units while minimizing their disadvantages. Interest in scale economies derive from concern over economic efficiency.

Policy implications drawn from studies on relationships between school and district size, pupil achievement, and cost have taken a dramatic turn in recent years. From the beginning of the twentieth century through the 1960s, the overwhelming evidence seemed to support large schools and school districts in terms of economies and the higher number, diversity, and caliber of professional and administrative personnel they could attract. These early studies were concerned primarily with inputs (costs) and gave little, if any, attention to outputs and ratios of outputs to inputs. As researchers began to take into account total cost and socioeconomic status of pupils, and to include measures of output such as achievement, pupil self-image, and success in college, economies of scale evaporated at relatively low numbers of pupils. The disadvantages of large size became readily apparent. It now appears that given present assumptions about how schools (and school districts) should organize, the relationships between size and quality of schooling are curvilinear. The benefits brought by larger enrollments increase to an optimal point and then decline following an inverted U-shaped curve (Engert, 1995; Fox, 1981; Riew, 1981, 1986). Ballou (1998) concluded that the evidence strongly suggests that urban districts exceed the size to realize scale economies. "It would appear that scale economies at the district level are exhausted somewhere between the typical suburban size (about 5000 students) and the average urban enrollment of 15,000" (pp. 69–70).

Scale research has two foci: the district and the school. For very small districts, these are the same thing. Large districts have choices, however, as they may operate schools over a wide range of sizes. Thus, a large district may operate small schools as a matter of district policy, although most do not. Large districts may also formulate most policy centrally, or they may empower schools to make policy within general parameters established at the center. Large schools can operate as a single unit, or organize "schools within schools" to secure the advantages inherent in both large and small schools.

Rogers (1992) provided an explanation for the advantage of small schools over large ones.

> When kids belong, they are engaged, they are "available" to learn and be taught. However, behind the pedagogical justification which argues for small schools where kids can be easily known, there is a psychological advantage as well. Adolescence is a time of craving acceptance, ways to fit in, a sense of *belonging*. In a large school where anonymity is the rule, kids go to what we might consider foolish lengths in order to gain attention and acceptance. . . . The lack of connection that leads some kids to join gangs is frighteningly pervasive, invading even those communities we think of as "safe." (pp. 103–105)

New York City found the value of small schools combined with parental choice and community involvement in its Central Park East Project in East Harlem, one of the poorest sections of the city. Over 30 small schools of choice were created. The concept is now being replicated throughout the city (Bradley, 1995). Rather than try to fit all students into a standard school, a variety of schools have been designed so that there is a school to fit every student (Fliegel & MacGuire, 1993; Meier, 1995a, 1995b, 1998).

Meier (1995b) stressed the importance of smallness for the success of the pedagogical innovations implemented in the schools she founded in Central Park East. She recommended a maximum size for elementary schools of 300 pupils, and for high schools of 400. She contended that small and focused educational communities enhance the climate of trust between families and schools and facilitate deep ongoing discussions in ways that produce change and involve the entire faculty. Small schools enable the faculty to know students and their work individually and they permit adults to play a significant role in the development of a positive school culture. They more easily provide for the physical

safety of all and are more readily made accountable to parents and to the public.

Through her work in Philadelphia, Fine (1993) saw large schools as promoting a general, rather than a particularistic perspective on students. "They encourage passivity rather than participation, and they stress, by definition, the need to control students rather than to engage them critically" (p. 273). To address the concerns of Philadelphia school officials over low student achievement and high dropout rates, the city is following a strategy similar to that being pursued in New York; big secondary schools are being broken up into "Charter Schools" of 200 to 400 students with 10 to 12 core faculty working with students from ninth grade through graduation. This restructuring aims to care for the emotional and social needs and wants of students and to engage the intellects and passions of educators and scholars. According to Fine, accomplishing these goals is much more difficult in large settings.

Citing supporting research, Darling-Hammond (1996) identified small size as one of the important characteristics of high-performing schools. All else being equal, small schools in the range of 300 to 500 students are associated with higher achievement, better attendance rates, fewer dropouts, and lower levels of misbehavior. Because they are less fragmented, more personalized, and facilitate frequent and purposeful interaction among and between students and staff, "they are more effective in allowing students to become bonded to important adults in a learning community that can play the roles that families and communities find harder and harder to play" (p. 148).

Economist Ronald Coase (1988), who received the Nobel Prize in Economics in 1991, developed a theory of transaction costs to explain the impact of large size on organizations in general. Transaction costs are costs of communication, coordination, and deciding. Eventually, expansion of an organization (e.g., school or district) can lead to diseconomies and higher unit costs because of managerial problems that are characteristic of large operations. The problems develop because as more people become involved, the complexity of communications increases exponentially. Building on Coase's earlier work, Williamson (1975) argued that conventional estimates of economies of scale have vastly underestimated *transactional costs*. Peters and Waterman (1982), in their study of "America's best-run companies," found that divisions, plants, and branches were smaller than any cost analysis would suggest they should be. Decentralization of function was practiced where classic economics would ordain otherwise. "The excellent companies understand that beyond a certain surprisingly small size, *diseconomies* of scale seem to set in with a vengeance" (p. 112).

Optimum school and district size is a function of desired standards, available technology, and governing structures. The criteria defining these characteristics change over time. In the past, providing diversity in curriculum and support services at an affordable cost were the primary justifications for large urban schools and suburban and rural school consolidation. Now, the disadvantages of bigness and the virtues of smallness have been well documented. Additionally, technological advances characteristic of the Information Age have made it possible for any person in almost any place to access curricular diversity easily. These developments combine to impel a reassessment of the large school policies of central cities and state school consolidation policies for rural areas. Fowler (1989) concluded:

> It is apparent that public school size and district size both influence schooling outcomes, and although other evidence of this relationship has accumulated, policy makers seem to ignore the finding and its significance. Much litigation has been undertaken to equalize expenditures per pupil, or to assure equivalent staff characteristics in an effort to increase learning; however, it appears that keeping schools relatively small might be more efficacious. (p. 21)

Although there are disadvantages in being very small, there are also disadvantages in being very large. There is little agreement on an optimal size, and optimal size appears to be a function of circumstances. The challenge before us is to provide stimulating learning environments with broad educational programs characteristic of large schools along with the supportive social structure characteristic of small schools.

Technical Efficiency. In addressing the issue of technical efficiency, we review two types of studies, effective schools research and program evaluations. The growing practice by school districts of using externally developed school organizational strategies is discussed as whole-school reform networks.

Effective Schools Research. Effective schools research constituted a reaction to the findings of the EEO and other production function studies that schools had little impact on closing the gap between minority- and majority-pupil achievement. Whereas education production function research takes a normative approach in studying school efficiency, effective schools research focuses on exceptions to the norm. It consists largely of case studies of schools and classrooms that have unusually positive effects on pupil achievement in order to identify practices which might cause or contribute to that effectiveness (Brookover & Lezotte, 1979; Edmonds, 1979; Jackson, Logsdon, & Taylor, 1983; Reed, 1985; Venezsky & Winfield, 1980; Weber, 1971). Effective schools research usually ignores cost considerations; thus, its findings relate more to technical efficiency than to economic efficiency and to the philosophy of the classroom culturalists.

Effective schools have been found to be characterized by effective classroom teaching practices that include high teacher expectations, good classroom management techniques, and greater time on task than one would find in most schools. These schools are also characterized by strong leadership, usually in the person of the principal, who provides for the coordination of the instructional program at the building level in a manner that is tightly coupled but not bureaucratic. The principal appears to be a key factor in establishing a common school culture and sense of community, consisting of "shared goals; high expectations for student performance; mechanisms to sustain motivation and commitment; collegiality among teachers, students, and the principal; and a school-wide focus on continuous improvement" (Odden & Webb, 1983, p. xiv). Given current assumptions about schooling, effective schools research identified some ways for schools to make more efficient use of the resources they already have.

Monk (1989) referred to effective schools research as "backwards-looking." He called effective schools "sites of excellence . . . making exemplary use of traditional, labor intensive instructional technologies" (p. 38). According to him, effective schools accept all the parameters of the present system and the methodology condemns them only to refine the current system's very labor-intensive and expensive organization and practice rather than to permit them to break through into the discovery and use of new technologies.

Evaluation Studies. Evaluation studies of schooling also have important implications for technical efficiency of schools. For the most part, like effective schools research, evaluation studies do not take into account the price of inputs. Evaluation studies have produced results that provide ground for greater optimism about the impact of schools on pupil achievement than those conducted by economists and sociologists.

Walberg (1984) analyzed nearly 3000 investigations of the productive factors in learning conducted during the 1970s. Table 14.4 summarizes his synthesis of effects of various approaches to improve teaching and learning. Relationships between achievement and socioeconomic status [0.25 standard deviation (s.d.)] and peer groups (0.24 s.d.) are relatively small compared with many of the instructional interventions reported in the table.

Reinforcement (1.17 s.d.) and instructional cues and feedback (0.97), both of which are psycho-logical components of mastery learning, ranked first and third in effect. Acceleration programs (1.00), which provide advanced activities to high-achieving students, ranked second. Also, ranking third was reading training (0.97), which involves skimming, comprehension, finding answers to questions, and adjusting reading speeds. Other highly effective techniques included cooperative learning (0.76), graded homework (0.79), and various approaches to individualized instruction. High teacher expectations (0.28) had a moderate impact, as did time on task, advanced organizing techniques, morale or climate of the classroom, and home interventions. Reduced class size had little impact. Walberg (1984) concluded:

> Synthesis of educational and psychological research in ordinary schools shows that improving the amount and quality of instruction can result in vastly more effective and efficient academic learning. Educators can do even more by also enlisting families as partners and engaging them directly and indirectly in their efforts (p. 26).

Most of the techniques identified by Walberg as effectively improving student achievement require few, if any, new economic resources, but rather, a redirection of already committed resources.

Walberg's conclusion about the relation between class size and achievement has been challenged and supported by other research. At best, the evidence is conflicting. Although Hanushek's (1986) meta-analysis of 112 studies investigating student/teacher ratios found only nine that discovered positive, statistically significant relationships with achievement, his own research (Hanushek et al., 1998) did find a weak link between small classes and improved achievement for children coming from poor families. On the other hand, a meta-analysis by Glass and Smith (1979) found little relationship between class size and achievement over the normal range of classes. Glass and Smith did find, however, that *where instruction was individualized* in small classes, better achievement resulted; otherwise, the potential of small classes was not realized. In a major study conducted in Tennessee schools, Finn and Achilles (1990) found that small classes (13 to 17

Table 14.4
Walberg's Syntheses of Effects on Learning

Method	Effect	Size[a]
Reinforcement	1.17	XXXXXXXXXXXX
Acceleration	1.00	XXXXXXXXXX
Reading training	.97	XXXXXXXXXX
Cues and feedback	.97	XXXXXXXXXX
Science mastery learning	.81	XXXXXXXX
Graded homework	.79	XXXXXXXX
Cooperative learning	.76	XXXXXXXX
Class morale	.60	XXXXXX
Reading experiments	.60	XXXXXX
Personalized instruction	.57	XXXXXX
Home interventions	.50	XXXXX
Adaptive instruction	.45	XXXXX
Tutoring	.40	XXXX
Instructional time	.38	XXXX
Individualized science	.35	XXXX
Higher-order questions	.34	XXX
Diagnostic prescriptive methods	.33	XXX
Individualized instruction	.32	XXX
Individualized mathematics	.32	XXX
New science curricula	.31	XXX
Teacher expectations	.28	XXX
Computer assisted instruction	.24	XX
Sequenced lessons	.24	XX
Advance organizers	.23	XX
New mathematics curricula	.18	XX
Inquiry biology	.16	XX
Homogeneous groups	.10	X
Class size	.09	X
Programmed instruction	−.03	−.
Mainstreaming	−.12	−X.

Source: H. J. Walberg, "Improving the productivity of America's schools," *Educational Leadership, 41*(8), 1984, Figures 3–4 p. 24. Reprinted with permission of the Association for Supervision and Curriculum Development.
[a]The x symbols represent the sizes of effects in tenths of standard deviations.

students per teacher) were definitely related with higher achievement in the primary grades in reading and mathematics (Finn & Achilles, 1999; Nye, Hedges, & Konstantopoulos, 1999). Follow-up studies indicated that these gains were sustained in higher grades and that students at risk were the greatest benefactors of small classes. As noted previously, Ferguson (1991) detected an improve-ment in achievement when average class size was reduced to 23 students, but further reduction did not appear to be fruitful.

The relationships between class size, pupil/teacher ratios, and pupil achievement have enormous implications for the allocation of resources; but existing evidence is not sufficient to make definitive policy judgments. It is important to note that none of the studies of class size cited take into account the *cost* of smaller classes. It is possible—and likely—that there are other means of producing academic gains that are as effective and less costly than reducing class size. Certainly, Walberg's (1984) research suggests this.

Whole-School Reform Networks.

A number of organizational strategies intended to make schools more effective have been developed over the past decade and a half. Fashola and Slavin (1998) pointed out that classroom-level change cannot be dictated from above; however, not every school must reinvent the wheel. School staffs and community representatives can select among a variety of existing, well-designed methods and materials that have been shown to be effective with children. Schools subscribing to a given set of organizing principles frequently form networks, usually under the direction of the model designer. These reform models took on new importance with the passage by Congress of the 1994 Title I [of the Elementary and Secondary Education Act (ESEA)] Reauthorization Act, which made it easier for high-poverty schools to be designated a schoolwide Title I Project. This designation, which can be obtained by any school with at least 50 percent of its students in poverty, allows a school to use Title I funds for schoolwide change, not just for changes that serve individual students having difficulties.

The release of a national evaluation of Chapter I of the Elementary and Secondary Education Act (subsequently changed to Title I) (Puma et al., 1997) called into question the effectiveness of the entire program and contributed to the documentation of the need for Congress to take further action, which it did with the passage of the Comprehensive School Reform Demonstration Program in 1997. This bill authorized $150 million in federal grants to schools to undertake whole-school reform; 17 models were listed in the bill as examples of the types of reforms that could be considered for funding.

Fashola and Slavin (1998) point out the advantages to schools and school districts in adopting these "off the shelf" instructional models.

> Organizations behind each of the school-wide models provide professional development, materials, and networks of fellow users. These reform organizations bring to a school broad experience working with high-poverty schools in many contexts. Unlike district or state staff development offices, external reform networks are invited in only if they are felt to meet a need, and they can be invited back out again if they fail to deliver. Their services can be expensive, but the costs are typically within the Title I resources available to high-poverty school-wide projects. (p. 371)

Fashola and Slavin (1997, 1998) evaluated thirteen school-wide models for elementary and middle schools which they considered to be "promising, ambitious, comprehensive, and widely available." Subsequently, the American Institutes for Research (AIR) (1999) released *An Educators' Guide to Schoolwide Reform* rating 24 designs of whole-school reform. The development of the guide was commissioned by the National Education Association, the American Association of School Administrators, the American Federation of Teachers, the American Association of Elementary School Principals, and the American Association of Secondary School Principals. The guide is intended to provide reliable information to school officials as they seek proven solutions to low-performing schools. The reform models are rated according to whether they improve achievement in such measurable ways as higher test scores and attendance rates. It also evaluates the level of assistance provided by model developers to schools that implement the models and compares first-year costs of the programs.

Aligning Economic and Technical Efficiency.

The analyses of economic and technical efficiency have presented us with conflicting results. Analyses of economic efficiency suggest that schools are using the resources allocated to them inefficiently and that there are, at best, tenuous links between financial inputs and student outcomes. Analyses into the technical efficiency of programs and even whole-school reform models, however, show that some approaches work much better than others and that students experience significant educational gains. The disparity of the results suggests at least two possible explanations. Schools, in general, are not using what has been shown to be best practice. Or, since evaluation studies of technical efficiency do not consider the *cost* of resources as do studies of economic efficiency, the problem may lie with the pricing and distribution of resources commonly used in the instructional process. Of particular interest is paying for and distributing professional staff since they represent over half of all school expenditures. In this section we focus on the latter explanation.

Current Practice. Teachers, with few exceptions, are paid according to a single salary schedule that has two dimensions: length of service and amount of formal education beyond the bachelor's degree. Thus, a teacher with 20 years of experience and 30 graduate credit hours beyond the master's degree is likely to earn about twice as much as a beginning teacher with a bachelor's degree. Yet research, some of which was cited earlier in the section on production functions, has shown that there is little evidence of any relationship between the number of graduate hours a teacher has accumulated and student achievement. Further, length of teaching service is unrelated to student performance after the first three or four years; yet commonly, school districts provide salary increments for length of service up to 15 years—and sometimes more.

In assigning teaching duties, school districts recognize the lack of relationships between education level and longevity in that beginning teachers with a bachelor's degree are given responsibilities identical to those given to teachers with long tenure and much graduate education. Thus, one first-grade teacher may be earning $30,000 per year, while the first-grade teacher in the adjoining classroom may be earning $60,000. To make matters even more bizarre, it is not unusual for teachers to have gained the right through collective bargaining to transfer to open teaching positions on the basis of their seniority in service. This frequently results in the schools with the best working conditions (i.e., schools enrolling high-achieving and well-disciplined children) having the most senior and expensive staffs while the schools with large portions of children at risk educationally have the least experienced and least expensive teachers. In effect, because of the higher salaries paid to teachers in the more attractive schools, proportionally more economic resources are placed in those schools than in schools with greater need, although physical resources (e.g., the numbers of teachers) in each school may be the same (Guthrie, 1997). Illustrations of this phenomenon were given earlier in this chapter for studies done in Texas, New York City, and Dade County, Florida.

Another practice that contributes to the disparity in results between analyses of economic and technical efficiency is the growing use of specialists and support staff. Although some research has indicated the importance of small class size and the continuity of relationship between teacher and student, school districts have added relatively fewer regular classroom teachers than they have professional specialists to supervise and consult with classroom teachers and to operate *pullout programs*. The latter practice has been shown to weaken the relationships and influence of classroom teachers on their students while adding greatly to the cost of public schooling.

From 1960 to 1998, the number of pupils per teacher (classroom and special teachers in grades K–12) dropped from 25.8 to 17.2 (down 33 percent) while average class size at the elementary level dropped from 29 to 24 (down 17 percent). At the secondary level, average class size actually increased from 28 to 31 (up 11 percent), although the mean number of students taught per day dropped from 138 to 97 (down 30 percent)

(NCES, 1999). From 1960 to 1996, the number of pupils per staff member (including classroom and special teachers, administrators, and support staff) declined from 16.8 to 8.9 (down 47 percent), indicating that support staff have been added at a faster rate than professional staff.

Looking at the trends from a different perspective, the National Commission on Teaching and America's Future (NCTAF) (1996) reported that the proportion of professional staff classified as teachers declined from more than 70 percent in 1950 to 52 percent in 1993. Of the 52 percent, more than 10 percent were specialists not engaged in classroom teaching. For every four classroom teachers, there are nearly six other school employees. By contrast, NCTAF reports that in other developed countries, teaching staffs represent from 60 to 80 percent of public education employees. In defense of school districts, in adding specialists and support staff to their rosters, they have been responding to state and federal categorical aid programs and mandates that are only now beginning to allow greater discretion at the local level.

Miles (1995) identified four managerial and educational practices behind these staffing trends: (1) large numbers of specialized teachers working outside regular classrooms with specifically defined classifications of students; (2) the practice of providing teachers with planning time in short, fragmented periods during the school day and using other classroom teachers to cover instruction at these times; (3) a formula-driven approach to grouping students for instruction that is guided by formal student classification and contract guidelines rather than school-level decisions; and, (4) the fragmented daily schedule at the secondary school level in which teachers instruct five completely different groups of students for less than an hour each day (pp. 477–478). NCTAF has soundly criticized the resulting bureaucracy:

> Far too many people sit in offices at the sidelines of the core work, managing routines rather than promoting innovation aimed at improving quality.

A bureaucratic school spends substantial resources on controlling its staff; a thoughtful school invests in knowledge and supports that liberate staff members to do their jobs well. A traditional school administers rules and procedures; a learning organization develops shared goals and talents. Our inherited school anticipates the worst from students and teachers; the school of the future expects and enables the best. (p. 101)

NCTAF has expressed well the case for whole-school and, indeed, systemic reform.

Rethinking the Allocation of Teacher Resources.

This situation has led a number of analysts to call for a reallocation of teaching resources. Miles and Darling-Hammond (1998) have observed six strategies of resource reallocation used by schools trying to improve achievement within general constraints of existing resources. These include reduction of specialized programs, more flexible student grouping by school-level professionals, structures that create more personalized environments, longer and varied blocks of instructional time, more common planning time for staff, and creative definition of staff roles and work schedules.

The NCTAF (1996) is more specific. It has developed a five-pronged strategy for ensuring that all communities have teachers with the knowledge and skills they need so that all children can learn and that all school systems are organized to support teachers in this work. Two are particularly relevant to the concerns of this section: encourage and reward teacher knowledge and skill, and create schools that are organized for student and teacher success.

Figure 14.2 illustrates how a typical elementary school of 600 pupils can be reorganized following NCTAF's guidelines. The plan reduces average class sizes from 25 students to 16 or 17 and increases teachers' planning time from less than four hours per week to at least 10 hours. *All of this is accomplished using only the personnel normally assigned to such a school.* They do this by creating teams of teachers who share students. Almost all adults in these teaching

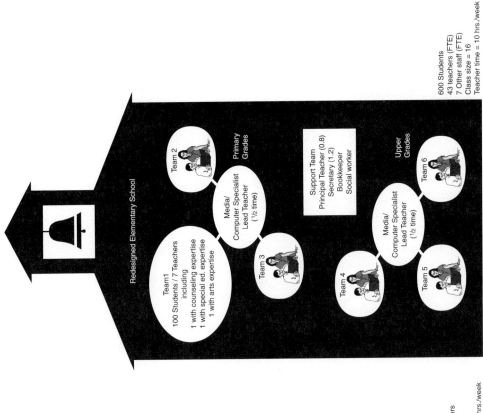

Traditional Elementary School

Principal	Assistant Principal	Dean of Discipline	Secretary	Book-keeper	Office Clerk
Special Program for Under-achievers					Counselor
Bilingual/ ESL Pullout					Counselor
Music Specialist					Counselor
Art Specialist					Social Worker
Media Clerk					Psychologist
Media Specialist		2 Title I Aides (1/2 time)	Title I Pullout	Title I Pullout	Special Education Pullout
Reading Specialist					Speech Pullout
Math Specialist	Science Specialist				Resource Room

600 Students
24 Classroom teachers
26 Other staff
Class size = 25
Teacher time = 3.75 hrs./week

Redesigned Elementary School

Team1
100 Students / 7 Teachers including
1 with counseling expertise
1 with special ed. expertise
1 with arts expertise

Media/ Computer Specialist
Lead Teacher (½ time)

Team 2

Team 3

Primary Grades

Support Team
Principal Teacher (0.8)
Secretary (1.2)
Bookkeeper
Social worker

Team 4

Media/ Computer Specialist
Lead Teacher (½ time)

Team 5

Team 6

Upper Grades

600 Students
43 teachers (FTE)
7 Other staff (FTE)
Class size = 16
Teacher time = 10 hrs./week

Figure 14.2
Traditional and redesigned elementary schools as developed by the National Commission on Teaching and America's Future

Source: National Commission on Teaching and America's Future, *What matters most: Teaching for America's future* (p. 106). New York: NCTAF, 1996.

441

teams are engaged in a way by which they can share expertise directly with one another, and can reduce pullouts and nonteaching jobs. "The school's resources are pushed into the core classroom structure where they can be used in the context of extended relationships with students rather than sitting around the periphery of the school to be applied in brief encounters with students or in coordinative rather than teaching roles" (p. 105).

The school is divided into two divisions, one for primary grades and one for intermediate grades. Each division has three instructional teams, consisting of seven teachers, including one with counseling expertise, one with special education expertise, and one with arts expertise. Each team serves 100 students representative of all ages within a given division, permitting the team and students to remain together for at least a three-year period (Osin & Lesgold, 1996; Veenman, 1995). The teams in each division share a media/computer specialist and a lead teacher who is released from teaching half-time to facilitate planning and to cover classes while other teachers visit and observe one another. Support staff for the school consists of a principal, secretary/bookkeeper, and a social worker. NCTAF also urges that the investment in teachers be accompanied by investments in technology that extend the capacity of every teacher and child to connect with an infinite variety of resources and tools for learning. NCTAF proposes that principals come from the ranks of highly skilled teachers and that they should continue to have some teaching responsibilities.

Odden (1996) notes that compensation theory counsels policy makers on the importance of matching pay practices to the strategic needs of organizations. NCTAF does this through linking teacher salaries to a progressive demonstration of growing knowledge and skills that mark a career continuum. They start with the presumption that teachers will be hired only after completing a high-quality NCATE (National Council for Accreditation of Teacher Education)-accredited preparation program and pass-

ing tests of subject matter knowledge and teaching knowledge to receive an initial license. NCATE established new standards in 1995 reflecting the evolution of a much stronger knowledge base for teaching and requiring schools of education to demonstrate how they are incorporating these higher expectations into their preparation programs. NCTAF recommends that licensing examinations be based on the standards set by the Interstate New Teacher Assessment and Support Consortium (INTASC), a consortium of more than 30 states that has tackled the question of what beginning teachers must know and be able to do to teach in the ways new student standards demand. INTASC standards are aligned with NCATE standards. Once hired, it is proposed that a new teacher go through a one- or two-year induction period during which the teacher receives mentoring and will be closely evaluated. After passing an assessment of teaching skills, recognition of *professional* teacher status is granted along with a substantial salary increment.

NCTAF recommends that teachers be encouraged through additional salary increments to become certified in more than one subject area. This would acknowledge the value to the school of being able to teach expertly in two or more subject areas or of bringing counseling or special education expertise to a teaching team. Having teachers certified in more than one area provides schools greater flexibility in organizing instructional teams.

For experienced teachers to gain the highest level of recognition, advanced certification from the National Board for Professional Teaching Standards would be recognized through additional salary increments. The National Board's standards are aligned with those of NCATE and INTASC. National Board certification would also be a prerequisite for qualification as lead teacher and principal.

There are numerous barriers to implementing reallocation of resources as proposed by NCTAF and others. Most teacher–district labor agreements would have to be changed with respect to definitions of teacher workday and seniority transfers. Some state and federal policies might need to be relaxed to enable breaking down barriers between programs, subjects, and age groupings. Teacher, parent, and student attitudes and expectations might also have to be changed (Miles, 1995; Miles & Darling-Hammond, 1998). Tradition dies hard and it has many allies.

Linking Equity, Efficiency, and Adequacy Considerations

There is some encouraging evidence that the higher academic standards set by states as part of the education reform movement, and their corresponding assessment strategies, are serving to reduce, if not eliminate, the inequities in outputs experienced by at-risk children. These initiatives have been relatively inexpensive to implement. Between 1973 and 1990, the percentage of academic course taking by all students jumped from 59 percent to over two-thirds (Mirel & Angus, 1994). In 1982, only 2 percent of all high school graduates met the standards recommended by the National Commission on Excellence in Education (four Carnegie units of English, three of social studies, three of mathematics, two of a foreign language, and one-half of computer science); by 1994, this percentage had increased to 25.3. The percentage of Hispanic and Asian students meeting this standard exceeded that of whites. Even though the percentage of African-American graduates meeting that standard increased dramatically (from 0.9 percent to 19.5 percent), it was still below the 26.5 percent for whites (NCES, 1999).

While high school students take more rigorous courses of study, the national percent of dropouts among persons 16 to 24 continues to drop, from 13.9 percent in 1981 to 11.0 percent in 1997. The absolute decrease was greater for minority groups than that for whites, but their rate remained much higher (7.6 percent for whites in 1997, 13.4 percent for African Americans, and 25.3 percent for Hispanics).

Growing numbers of minority students are taking advanced placement examinations. For African-American students, the number grew from 10,000 in 1988 to more than 15,000 in 1993; for Hispanic students, the number increased from 10,000 to nearly 30,000 (Mirel & Angus, 1994). Minority students are also performing better on national standardized examinations. Between 1976 and 1993, scores for African-American students rose 21 points for the verbal section of the SAT and 34 points for the math section; similar progress was shown by Hispanic students. And larger proportions are going to college. The percentage of African-Americans 18 to 24 years of age enrolled in postsecondary institutions increased from 19.9 percent in 1981 to 29.8 percent in 1997 (NCES, 1999). For Hispanics, the percentage grew from 16.6 to 22.4. Both groups still lagged far behind the college participation rate for whites, however, which grew from 27.7 percent to 40.6 percent.

Mirel and Angus (1994) commented on these overall gains:

> [F]or more than half a century, educational policy makers have made decisions based on the presumption that tougher course requirements automatically increase the dropout rate, especially among poor and minority students. Moreover, these policy makers assumed that the only way to keep the dropout rate from soaring was to make the high school curriculum less challenging and more entertaining. . . . [P]oor and minority students have been the most frequent casualties of such standard-lowering policies as allowing less rigorous courses to meet academic requirements for graduation or diluting course content in academic courses while keeping course titles the same. . . . Much of the failure of American K–12 education lies in our avoiding the formidable task of discovering how to teach difficult subjects in ways that are both accessible to young people and yet still true to the complexity and richness of the material. (pp. 40–42)

Levin (1994) listed what he considered to be the necessary and sufficient conditions for equity in education outcomes. The necessary conditions "are to provide access to all children of a full range of appropriate programs as well as to the funding and other resources that will enable them to benefit from those programs" (p. 172). Traditional equity studies have focused on one or more of these conditions, but this approach does not lead to equity if schools are differentially effective.

In discussing the sufficient conditions of equity, Levin (1994) cited several studies that have shown large variations in outcomes of schools with apparently similar resource and student characteristics and noted that the inefficiencies seem to be greatest among schools serving populations that are most at-risk educationally. To rectify this situation, Levin's sufficient condition for achieving education equity "is that schools are maximally effective with all children in that resources are used optimally to meet their educational needs" (p. 172). Effectiveness of educational programs have not been a focus of equity studies until recently, however; but one of the reasons for moving from input to output objectives of equity is the growing realization that when input equity has been achieved, it has not necessarily resulted in output equity.

Hanushek (1994) followed a line of argument similar to Levin's when he observed that "the flaw in the traditional school finance debate is that the entire discussion centers on funding and school spending. Spending is (often implicitly) equated to school quality or performance" (p. 464). He went on to note that inflation adjusted increases in expenditure per pupil between 1970 and 1990 were absorbed largely by the old, failing structure of schooling and were not allocated to programmatic innovations shown to improve student performance. He concluded that "the chances for improving the performance of the schools are closely linked to changes in the incentive structure, and these changes are at odds with much of the recent finance discussion" (p. 461).

Others also see the lack of productivity and incentives as being an impediment to the realization of equity (Fuhrman & O'Day, 1996;

Hanushek & Jorgenson, 1996). Behind the problem of productivity and incentives is a problem of knowledge and practice (Elmore, 1996). Porter (1994) proposed teacher, school, school district, and state accountability with serious consequences as incentives for improving productivity and reaching outcome equity. "For most . . . there are no consequences for excellence or for failure" (p. 493). Darling-Hammond (1994) observed, "To provide such incentives, schools' success must be gaged by the quality of teaching and learning experiences they provide to all students rather than by measures of aggregate outcomes that may be substantially manipulated by changes in the students admitted or retained" (p. 195).

Summary

Based on the evidence summarized in this chapter, we have concluded that the United States devotes about the optimal proportion of its resources (GDP) to education given the current state of educational technology. If there are to be improvements in educational outcomes, those improvements will be primarily as a result of improvements in internal efficiency—not through the application of additional resources (CRE, 1998).

Studies relating to the economic efficiency of public schools indicate with great consistency that schools are not using the resources entrusted to them to full advantage. Given current organization and practice, the problem is not so much the lack of resources but rather the nature of available resources and the ways in which they are being used. Although there is inequity in the distribution of resources among schools and school districts, improving the equity of the flow of funds to schools is not likely to improve the educational experiences of all children unless the application of those resources within schools is radically changed.

The greatest resource allocation problem facing policy makers during the twenty-first century is designing instructional systems that are educationally effective and economically efficient. The second most important problem is improving equity of distribution of resources to schools so that all children have access to good facilities, competent instruction, and state-of-the-art learning materials (Swanson & King, 1997). Equity issues are placed second only because of the extreme harm being done currently to educationally at-risk children as a result of the inefficiencies of existing schooling arrangements.

Activities

1. Interview your superintendent of schools and members of your board of education about how resource allocation decisions are made in your school district. Compare the expenditures in this district with those in comparable districts. (See Activity 6 for instructions as to how this may be done on a national scale.)

2. In this chapter the authors conclude that the United States is already devoting an adequate proportion of its resources to formal education and that any improvements in education will have to come from using those resources more wisely (more efficiently). Do you agree with this position? List and discuss arguments supporting it and those that do not.

3. Using the information provided in the section on internal efficiency, devise a configuration or configurations for using public school resources that are likely to be more efficient than configurations typically employed at the present time.

4. Visit a large school and a small school serving the same grade levels and seek answers to the questions that follow. Alternatively, form a study group made up of persons with experience in different-size schools and compare experiences as you discuss the questions below.

   a. Do you find any differences between schools that can be attributed to their variation in size?

   b. What are the advantages and disadvantages of large schools? Of small schools?

   c. What strategies might best neutralize the negative effects of school size?

5. Investigate several whole-school reform models and identify the strengths and weakness of each for a particular school with which you are familiar. In your investigation, search for information and evaluations on the Internet. For example, check *www.aasa.org, www.aft.org, www.nea.org,* and/or *www.ecs.org.*

6. Investigate the Web site of the Education Finance Statistics Center, National Center for Education Statistics, U.S. Department of Education (http://nces.ed.gov/edfin/). Do a "Peer Search," allowing you to compare the finances of a school district of your choice with districts which share similar characteristics.

7. This chapter challenges the efficacy of the Single Salary Schedule by which most teachers are paid (i.e., salary being determined by education level and years of teaching experience) and seniority provisions in many teacher union contracts. Devise another remuneration policy for teachers that would link salary to responsibility and that would ensure the best qualified teachers be available to the students in greatest academic need.

References

American Institutes for Research. (1999). *An educators' guide to schoolwide reform.* Arlington, VA: Educational Research Service.

Ballou, D. (1998). The condition of urban school finance: Efficient research allocation in urban schools. In W. J. Fowler, Jr. (Ed.), *Selected papers in school finance, 1996* (NCES 98–217, pp. 65–83). Washington, DC: National Center for Education Statistics, U.S. Department of Education.

Becker, G. S. (1960). Underinvestment in college education? *American Economic Review* (Papers and Proceedings), *50,* 345–354.

Becker, G. S. (1964). *Human capital: A theoretical and empirical analysis, with special reference to education*. New York: National Bureau of Economic Research.

Benson, C. S. (1978). *The economics of public education* (3rd ed.). Boston: Houghton Mifflin.

Berne, R., & Stiefel, L. (1984). *The measurement of equity in school finance: Conceptual, methodological, and empirical dimensions*. Baltimore: The Johns Hopkins University Press.

Berne, R., & Stiefel, L. (1994). Measuring equity at the school level: The finance perspective. *Educational Evaluation and Policy Analysis, 16,* 405–421.

Bradley, A. (1995). Thinking small. *Education Week, 14*(26), 37–41.

Brookover, W., & Lezotte, L. (1979). *Changes in school characteristics coincident with changes in student achievement*. East Lansing, MI: College of Urban Development, State University.

Burkhead, J. (1967). *Input and output in large-city high schools*. Syracuse, NY: Syracuse University Press.

Burtless, G. (1996). Introduction and summary. In G. Burtless (Ed.), *Does money matter? The effect of school resources on student achievement and adult success* (pp. 1–42). Washington, DC: Brookings Institution Press.

Coase, R. H. (1988). *The firm, the market, and the law*. Chicago: University of Chicago Press.

Coleman, J. S. (1966). *Equality of educational opportunity*. Washington, DC: U.S. Government Printing Office.

Consortium on Renewing Education. CRE (1998). *20/20 vision: A strategy for doubling America's academic achievement by the year 2020*. Nashville, TN: Peabody Center for Education Policy, Vanderbilt University.

Darling-Hammond, L. (1994). Standards of practice for learner-centered schools. In R. Berne & L. O. Picus (Eds.), *Outcome equity in education* (pp. 191–223). Thousand Oaks, CA: Corwin Press.

Darling-Hammond, L. (1996). Restructuring schools for high performance. In S. H. Fuhrman & J. A. O'Day (Eds.), *Rewards and reform: Creating educational incentives that work* (pp. 144–192). San Francisco: Jossey-Bass.

Edmonds, R. (1979). Effective schools for the urban poor. *Educational Leadership, 37,* 15–24.

Elmore, R. F. (1996). Getting to scale with successful educational practices. In S. H. Fuhrman & J. A. O'Day (Eds.), *Rewards and reform: Creating educational incentives that work* (pp. 294–329). San Francisco: Jossey-Bass.

Engert, F. (1995). *Efficiency analysis of school districts using multiple inputs and outputs: An application of data envelopment analysis*. Unpublished doctoral dissertation, State University of New York at Buffalo.

Fashola, O. S., & Slavin, R. E. (1997). Promising programs for elementary and middle schools: Evidence of effectiveness and replicability. *Journal of Education for Students Placed at Risk, 2,* 251–307.

Fashola, O. S., & Slavin, R. E. (1998). Schoolwide reform models: What works? *Phi Delta Kappan, 79*(5), 370–379.

Ferguson, R. F. (1991). Paying for public education: New evidence on how and why money matters. *Harvard Journal on Legislation, 28,* 465–498.

Fine, M. (1993). Democratizing choice: Reinventing, not retreating from, public education. In E. Rasell & R. Rothstein (Eds.), *School choice: Examining the evidence* (pp. 269–300). Washington, DC: Economic Policy Institute.

Finn, J. D., & Achilles, C. M. (1990). Answers and questions about class size: A statewide experiment. *American Educational Research Journal, 27,* 557–577.

Finn, J. D., & Achilles, C. M. (1999). Tennessee's class size study: Findings, implications, misconceptions. *Educational Evaluation and Policy Analysis, 21,* 93–109.

Fliegel, S., & MacGuire, J. (1993). *Miracle in East Harlem: The fight for choice in public education*. New York: Random House.

Fowler, W. J., Jr. (1989). *School size, school characteristics, and school outcomes*. Paper presented at the annual meeting of the American Educational Research Association, San Francisco.

Fox, W. F. (1981). Reviewing economies of size in education. *Journal of Education Finance, 6,* 273–296.

Fuhrman, S. H., & O'Day, J. A. (Eds.). *Rewards and reforms: Creating educational incentives that work*. San Francisco: Jossey-Bass.

Fuller, B., & Clarke, P. (1994). Raising school effects while ignoring culture? Local conditions and the influence of classroom tools, rules, and pedagogy. *Review of Educational Research, 64*(1), 119–157.

Glass, G. V., & Smith, M. L. (1979). Meta-analysis of research on the relationship of class-size and achievement. *Educational Evaluation and Policy Analysis, 1,* 2–16.

Greenwald, R., Hedges, L. V., & Laine, R. D. (1994). When reinventing the wheel is not necessary: A case study in the use of meta-analysis in education finance. *Journal of Education Finance, 20,* 1–20.

Grissmer, D., Flanagan, A., & Williamson, S. (1998). Does money matter for minority and disadvantaged students? Assessing new evidence. In W. J. Fowler, Jr. (Ed.), *Developments in school finance, 1997* (NCES 98-212, pp. 15–30). Washington, DC: National Center for Education Statistics, U.S. Department of Education.

Guthrie, J. W. (1997). School finance: Fifty years of expansion. *The Future of Children, 7*(3), 24–38.

Hanushek, E. A. (1986). The economics of schooling: Production and efficiency in public schools. *Journal of Economic Literature, 24,* 1141–1177.

Hanushek, E. A. (1987). Education production functions. In G. Psacharopoulos (Ed.), *Economics of education: Research and studies* (pp. 33–42). Oxford: Pergamon Press.

Hanushek, E. A. (1991). When school finance "reform" may not be good policy. *Harvard Journal on Education, 28,* 423–456.

Hanushek, E. A. (1994). Money might matter somewhere: A response to Hedges, Laine, and Greenwald. *Educational Researcher, 23*(4), 5–8.

Hanushek, E. A. (1996). School resources and student performance. In G. Burtless (Ed.), *Does money matter? The effect of school resources on student achievement and adult success* (pp. 43–73). Washington, DC: Brookings Institution Press.

Hanushek, E. A., & Jorgenson, D. W. (Eds.). (1996). *Improving America's schools: The role of incentives.* Washington, DC: National Academy Press.

Hanushek, E. A., Kain, J. F., & Rivkin, S. G. (1998). *Teachers, schools, and academic achievement* (Working Paper 6691). Cambridge, MA: National Bureau of Economic Research.

Hanushek, E. A., & Kim, D. (1995). *Schooling, labor force quality, and economic growth* (Working Paper 5399). Cambridge, MA: National Bureau of Economic Research.

Hedges, L. V., & Greenwald, R. (1996). Have times changed? The relation between school resources and student performance. In G. Burtless (Ed.), *Does money matter? The effect of school resources on student achievement and adult success* (pp. 74–92). Washington, DC: Brookings Institution Press.

Hedges, L. V., Laine, R. D., & Greenwald, R. (1994a). Does money matter? A meta-analysis of studies of the effects of differential school inputs on student outcomes. *Educational Researcher, 23*(3), 5–14.

Hedges, L. V., Laine, R. D., & Greenwald, R. (1994b). Money does matter somewhere: A reply to Hanushek. *Educational Researcher, 23*(4), 9–10.

Hertert, L. (1994). *Equalizing dollars across schools: A study of district and school-level fiscal equity in California.* Paper delivered at the American Education Finance Association Annual Meeting, Nashville, TN.

Hyary, A. (1994). *Intra-district distribution of educational resources in New York State elementary schools.* Paper delivered at the American Education Finance Association Annual Meeting, Nashville, TN.

Jackson, S., Logsdon, D., & Taylor, N. (1983). Instructional leadership behaviors: Differentiating effective from ineffective low-income urban schools. *Urban Education, 18,* 59–70.

King, R. A., & MacPhail-Wilcox, B. (1994). Unraveling the production equation: The continuing quest for resources that make a difference. *Journal of Education Finance, 20,* 47–65.

Lake, P. (1983). Expenditure equity in the public schools of Atlantic Canada. *Journal of Education Finance, 8,* 449–460.

Levin, H. M. (1994). The necessary and sufficient conditions for achieving educational equity. In R. Berne & L. O. Picus (Eds.), *Outcome equity in education.* Thousand Oaks, CA: Corwin Press.

Mayeski, G. W., Wisler, C. E., Beaton, A. E., Jr., Weinfeld, F. D., Cohen, W. M., Okada, T., Proshek, J. M., & Tabler, K. A. (1972). *A study of our nation's schools.* Washington, DC: U.S. Government Printing Office.

McDonnell, L. M., & Fuhrman, S. (1986). The political context of school reform. In V. D. Mueller & M. P. McKeown (Eds.), *The fiscal, legal, and political aspects of state reform of elementary and secondary education* (pp. 43–64). Cambridge, MA: Ballinger.

Meier, D. (1995a). How our schools could be. *Phi Delta Kappan, 76,* 369–373.

Meier, D. (1995b). *The power of their ideas: Lessons for America from a small school in Harlem.* Boston: Beacon.

Meier, D. (1998). Can the odds be changed? *Phi Delta Kappan, 79,* 358–362.

Miles, K. H. (1995). Freeing resources for improving schools: A case study of teacher allocation in Boston Public Schools. *Educational Evaluation and Policy Analysis, 17,* 476–493.

Miles, K. H, & Darling-Hammond, L. (1998). Rethinking the allocation of teaching resources: Some lessons from high performing schools. In W. J. Fowler, Jr. (Ed.), *Developments in school finance, 1997.* Washington, DC: National Center for Education Statistics, U.S. Department of Education.

Mirel, J., & Angus, D. (1994). High standards for all? The struggle for equality in the American high school curriculum, 1890–1990. *American Educator, 18 (2),* 4–9, 40–42.

Monk, D. H. (1989). The education production function: Its evolving role in policy analysis. *Educational Evaluation and Policy Analysis, 11,* 31–45.

Monk, D. H. (1994). Policy challenges surrounding the shift toward outcome-oriented school finance equity standards. *Educational Policy, 8,* 471–488.

Morrison, H. C. (1943). *American schools: A critical study of our school system.* Chicago: University of Chicago Press.

National Center for Education Statistics. (1998). *Inequalities in Public School District Revenues* (NCES 98-210). Washington, DC: U.S. Department of Education.

National Center for Education Statistics. (1999). *Digest of education statistics* (NCES 1999-036). Washington, DC: U.S. Department of Education.

National Commission on Teaching and America's Future. (1996). *What matters most: Teaching for America's future.* New York: NCTAF.

Nye, B., Hedges, L. V., & Konstantopoulos, S. (1999). The long-term effects of small classes: A five year follow-up of the Tennessee class size experiment. *Educational Evaluation and Policy Analysis, 21,* 127–142.

Odden, A. (1996). Incentives, school organization, and teacher compensation. In S. H. Fuhrman & J. A. O'Day (Eds.), *Rewards and reform: Creating educational incentives that work* (pp. 226–256). San Francisco: Jossey-Bass.

Odden, A., Monk, D., Nakib, Y., & Picus, L. (1995). The story of the education dollar: No academy awards and no fiscal smoking guns. *Phi Delta Kappan, 77,* 161–168.

Odden, A., & Webb, L. D. (1983). Introduction: The linkages between school finance and school improvement. In A. Odden & L. D. Webb (Eds.), *School finance and school improvement: Linkages for the 1980s* (pp. xiii–xxi). Cambridge, MA: Ballinger.

Osin, L., & Lesgold, A. (1996). A proposal for reengineering of the educational system. *Review of Educational Research, 66,* 621–656.

Owens, J. T., Jr. (1994). *Intradistrict resource allocation in Dade County, Florida: An analysis of equality of educational opportunity.* Paper delivered at the American Education Finance Association Annual Meeting, Nashville, TN.

Paquette, J. (1991). Why should I stay in school? Quantizing private educational returns. *Journal of Education Finance, 16,* 458–477.

Paquette, J. (1999, March). *The Ontario approach to restraint: From burgeoning local share to full funding and central control.* Paper presented at the Annual Conference of the American Education Finance Association, Seattle, WA.

Peters, T. J., & Waterman, R. H., Jr. (1982). *In search of excellence: Lessons from America's best-run companies.* New York: Warner Books.

Pierce, B., & Welch, F. (1996). Changes in structures of wages. In E. A. Hanushek & D. W. Jorgenson (Eds.), *Improving America's schools: The role of incentives* (pp. 53–73). Washington, DC: National Academy Press.

Porter, A. C. (1994). *National equity and school autonomy. Educational Policy, 8,* 489–500.

Puma, M. J., Karweit, N., Price, C., Ricciuti, A., Thompson, W., & Vaden-Kiernan, M. (1997). *Prospects: Final report on student outcomes.* Cambridge, MA: Abt Associates.

Reed, L. (1985). *An inquiry into the specific school-based practices involving principals that distinguish unusually effective elementary schools from effective elementary schools.* Unpublished doctoral dissertation, State University of New York at Buffalo.

Riew, J. (1981). Enrollment decline and school reorganization: A cost efficiency analysis. *Economics of Education Review, 1,* 53–73.

Riew, J. (1986). Scale economies, capacity utilization, and school costs: A comparative analysis of secondary and elementary schools. *Journal of Education Finance, 11,* 433–446.

Rogers, B. (1992). Small is beautiful. In D. Durrett & J. Nathan (Eds.), *Source book on school and district size, cost, and quality.* Minneapolis, MN: North Central Regional Educational Laboratory.

Rothstein, R., & Miles, K. H. (1995). *Where's the money gone? Changes in the level and composition of education spending, 1967–1991.* Washington, DC: Economic Policy Institute.

Schultz, T. W. (1963). *The economic value of education.* New York: Columbia University Press.

Schultz, T. W. (1981). *Investing in people: The economics of population quality.* Berkeley, CA: University of California Press.

Smith, A. (1776/1993). *An inquiry into the nature and causes of the wealth of nations.* Oxford: Oxford University Press.

Swanson, A. D., & King, R. A. (1997). *School finance: Its economics and policy.* New York: Longman.

Veenman, S. (1995). Cognitive and noncognitive effects of multigrade and multi-age classes: A best-evidence synthesis. *Review of Educational Research, 65,* 319–381.

Venezsky, R., & Winfield, L. (1980). *Schools that exceed beyond expectations in the teaching of reading* (Studies on Education, Tech. Rep. 1). Newark, DE: University of Delaware Press.

Walberg, H. J. (1984, May). Improving the productivity of America's schools. *Educational Leadership, 41,* 19–27.

Weber, G. (1971). *Inner-city children can be taught to read: Four successful schools.* Washington, DC: Council for Basic Education.

Williamson, O. E. (1975). *Markets and hierarchies: Analysis and antitrust implications.* New York: Free Press.

CHAPTER 15

The Role of
Information and Technology

Our age has been dubbed the *information society* and educational institutions at all levels and of all types represent a major segment of the *information industry*. A primary function of schooling is to pass the information of past generations to the youngest generation. But schools, colleges, and universities go beyond the mere transmission of information and provide students with constructs to organize data into useful knowledge and to enable them to make new discoveries. At the same time, schools depend on information and information processing to carry out their missions effectively.

The task of managing information has burgeoned in recent decades with the increasing amount of information available and with the growing sophistication of information technology. Supercomputers, fiber-optic cable, communication satellites, and related technology have fueled this information explosion, changing the way we live, work, and do business. The fabric and meaning of culture, time, distance, and space are being changed (Westbrook, 1998).

The greater availability of information can assist in making better plans and in monitoring implementation of those plans; alternatively, policy makers and administrators can be paralyzed into inaction with an overload of information or misled by faulty analyses of the data. Good plans need to be built on good information, and good information is required to monitor implementation. A district's information systems are critical elements in making decisions and in maintaining organizational memory.

The primary focus of this chapter is on formal and integrated information systems; but we begin with a discussion of the nature of infor-

mation and the importance of informal information systems. Following the discussion of the structure of formal information systems, we examine the issue of the interface between information technology, the instructional process, and the structure of schooling. We conclude with the presentation of an integrated information system that centers on the learning progress of individual students with links to the supporting instructional, business, personnel, and community resource systems.

Informal Information Systems

A learning or self-renewing organization can only maintain its fluidity (and stability) if it has continuing access to new information about external factors and internal resources. The information available to us affects the way we form our organizations—and reform them as necessary (Wheatley, 1994).

> A system needs to access itself. It needs to understand who it is, where it is, what it believes, what it knows. These needs are nourished by information. Information is one of the primary conditions that spawns the organization we see. If it moves through a system freely, individuals learn and change and their discoveries can be integrated by the system. The system becomes both resilient and flexible. But if information is restricted, held tightly in certain regions, the system can neither learn nor respond. (Wheatley & Kellner-Rogers, 1996, p. 82)

When we speak of information sources, we are usually thinking in terms of formal information systems. Although such systems are important and useful, they have, nevertheless, a bias of treating information as linear and inert, devoid of the vitality that Wheatley describes. In truth, much important information is tacit or gained from structured and casual exchanges among individuals and not recorded in any formal system. This type of information is usually referred to as *soft information,* while the quantified facts usually found in formal information systems are referred to as *hard information* or data. Unfortunately, there is a general tendency to discount the value of soft information.

Much of the information used in strategy formulation, discussed in Chapter 13, and by managers of day-to-day operations is of the soft type. Whereas hard information may be available to every trusted party, soft information cannot be captured by formal systems and is available only to those exposed to it directly. "[T]he decisions so quickly available from intuition must sometimes be checked for accuracy by formal analysis, while those produced by careful analysis must generally be confirmed intuitively for face validity" (Mintzberg, 1994, p. 328). Thus, while structuring formal information systems, it is also important to design organizations and nurture organizational cultures that allow for and encourage the informal sharing of information among members and provide them discretionary freedom to exercise their tacit understandings.

Formal Information Systems

With respect to formal information systems, school districts routinely collect all kinds of data—from birth dates and achievement test results to records of measles vaccinations. But data are not information. Data consist of raw facts such as an employee's name, social security number, address, salary, and number of dependents. Such data must be retained by the employer as a routine business procedure in order to make payrolls and to comply with governmental regulations concerning withholding income and payroll taxes. When facts or data are organized in a meaningful manner, they become information. *Information* is a collection

of facts organized in such a way that they have additional value beyond the value of the facts themselves (Stair, 1992).

For example, in collective negotiations, the superintendent and union negotiators need to know the total cost of salaries, their distribution, their average cost, and how all relate to salaries paid in similar districts. The raw data, except for the comparative information, are available in the payroll office, but organized for a different purpose. To serve the negotiators' purposes, it is not necessary to collect the data again, but only to organize the existing data differently.

Similarly, teachers need to know by name and date what students in their classes are absent so that the students can make up missed instructional opportunities. As the administrator of compulsory attendance laws, however, the superintendent needs to know who the individual truants are, but does not need to know about those who are legally absent. Thus, the same data can be organized in numerous ways to meet the information needs of a variety of decision makers.

Information management has been achieved successfully for thousands of years without the availability of computers, telecommunications, and networks. *Information systems,* however, as they are emerging today are a product of the last 30 years (Rowley, 1996). An information system is a set of interrelated elements or components that collect (input), manipulate and store (process), and disseminate to targeted persons data and information (output). An information system also typically has a feedback process whereby adjustments can be made to input and processing activities to enhance the efficiency of the system.

Types of Information Systems

Rowley (1996) identifies six types of information systems: (1) transaction processing systems, (2) management information systems, (3) decision support systems, (4) executive information systems, (5) expert systems, and (6) office information systems.

Transaction processing systems are dominated by accounting applications, recording data about events or transactions. Most district financial transactions, for example, would be of this nature, as are inventories, attendance, report cards, and library management (checking out and in of books) systems. Data are captured, usually through on-line computer terminals, as events occur. The data entered update master files and are validated and checked for errors through the master files. Input can take many forms, from employee time cards to teacher grade sheets to a message taken by a telephone receptionist. An efficient information system will collect each data element only once for the entire system and eliminate the redundancy of having each department and office collect similar data from the same people over and over again. Outputs are usually in the form of documents and reports but can take a variety of other forms, including that of paychecks, report cards, tuition billing, letters, or computer display screens.

Management information systems (MISs) provide information on computer screen or hard copy to managers in support of decisions they have to make. MISs are used when the information requirements can be determined in advance and where the need for information occurs on a regular basis. Data used in MISs may be drawn from many parts of the organization and are usually collected through the transaction processing system. School districts typically use MISs to manage their business functions. MISs could be equally effective for teachers in managing instructional functions, although currently, such use is not widespread.

Decision support systems (DSSs) are designed to address those special situations where an MIS does not provide the information required. Analyses are produced that assist managers with unique, nonrecurring, and relatively unstructured decisions. DSSs build mathematical, statistical, or financial models that permit what-if, sensitivity, optimization, and simulation analyses (Taylor, 1995; Wholeben, 1995). These models provide managers with great flexibility in evaluating alternative solutions to problems. DSSs are relied on in strategic and tactical situations where the risk associated with error is high and the consequences of a mistake are serious.

Executive information systems are similar to MISs but are tailored to provide top management (superintendent) and policy makers (board of education) with the broad picture of the district's operations without overloading them unnecessarily with detail. Executive systems provide access to all databases within an organization for those occasions when detail is needed and to external databases for comparison purposes. "Typically, EIS seek to combine the power and data storage capacity of an organizational information system, with ease of use and graphics capability" (Rowley, 1996, p. 14).

Expert Systems fall within the field of artificial intelligence and are likely to draw on computerized knowledge bases from outside the organization through networks. Expert systems do not make decisions, but offer decision support in situations where data are incomplete and where it is necessary to take into account the effects of uncertainty and judgment.

Rowley's (1996) last category is *office information systems*. These support the daily functioning of an office; some of the information captured may be entered into master files, but much is maintained only for the convenience of a specific person to assist him or her in carrying out job-related activities. Components include word processing, scanners, voice mail, facsimile transmission, e-mail, Internet access, electronic filing, and diaries.

Fulmer (1995) argues for an integrated information system in education. He notes that school districts, state education departments, and the federal education department tend to archive information to meet legal requirements rather than to place it in databases to facilitate analysis and support decision making. Data pertinent to employee salaries are collected and maintained by the payroll office. Other financial data are maintained in the business office. Teacher-assigned grades may be found only in a student's file while his or her scores on state required tests may be recorded in an electronic file and transmitted to the state education department. Records concerning student disabilities may be in a file held by the committee for special education, and attendance information may be maintained by the attendance officer independently of any other file. To understand a school or district thoroughly and to monitor its operations effectively, all information sources need to be linked so that information may flow freely from one to another and so that analysts may draw data from any combination of sources in undertaking new analyses. Although few districts are currently doing this, the number is growing slowly.

Fulmer (1995) envisions an integrated system that would facilitate analysis and support decision making by teachers and administrators. Such a system would have multiple input ports, allowing teachers, administrators, and clerks to record transactions (attendance, disciplinary actions, grades and other accomplishments, assignments, etc.) at the point where the action takes place. The system would need to be designed to accommodate multiple types and forms of data, including normative, ordinal, interval, ratio, qualitative, feedback, self-evaluation, samples of writing, student journals, parent feedback, and other forms of student attitude, performance, and behavior. Teachers and administrators should be able to access the total database when faced with a decision to be made about an individual student (Rowley's management information system) or collectively in the development of school policy. The system would need to be designed so that the data may be aggregated into alternative units of analysis (Rowley's decision support systems). A prototype of such an integrated system is presented in the last section of this chapter.

Using Information Systems

A district's information system comes into play throughout the processes of strategy formation and planning. It is particularly important in providing information for the internal analysis of assessing strengths and weaknesses of the organization. It comes into play again in designing action plans and in building and administering the budget. It can be useful in strategy formulation. The information system plays a critical role in contrasting actual accomplishments against expectations. Most important, a good information system enables all members of an organization to monitor the effect of their actions and decisions. Without good information, an organization is blind to its past achievements and failures and to its future potential.

That which cannot be measured cannot be controlled or understood. This understanding is driving the standards movement. In the past it has been common practice for educators to claim success on very little tangible evidence other than the intuitive feeling of those professionals involved in designing and implementing a program. Now higher levels of government, the state in particular and the public in general, are asking, "How do you know? What evidence do you have that supports your perceptions and opinions?"

One of the most articulate champions of management (and decision making) by fact was W. Edwards Deming (1986). The Deming principles were originally applied to the management of business organizations, first in Japan and subsequently in the United States. Now they are being applied to the organization and management of schools, school districts, and other educational organizations (Frazier, 1997; Schmoker & Wilson, 1993). Deming contended that collecting and analyzing data around an organization's priority objectives is essential for improvement, for validating efforts, and for refining strategies. What is more important to schools, to parents, and to the public in general than the quality of student outcomes? Equally important to the taxpayers who pay for the personnel, facilities, equipment, and supplies used in developing those outcomes is the assurance that those resources are being applied efficiently and are not being wasted in any way.

The information system is critically important in monitoring, evaluating, and adjusting the implementation and effectiveness of action plans and programs. The proper use of statistics, for example, is central to Deming's (1986) philosophy of *total quality management* (TQM). According to him, management in any form is prediction. Statistical data are essential to improvement; facts, reasoning, and evidence should drive operational decisions, not power or authority or personality.

We need to look to data continually in checking our progress. Research, experimentation, and data gathering are built into the daily routine of learning organizations. Such organizations are able to anticipate and to accept new knowledge and to modify old organizational premises in order to optimize processes and achieve excellence in schooling (Schmoker & Wilson, 1993).

Deming (1986) identified the individual worker as key to program quality. The only proper use of data, according to him, is to help employees to perform better and to provide them with a basis for taking pride in their workmanship. The workers (e.g., principals, teachers, secretaries, bus drivers, cleaners) are the experts in what they do and are fully capable of improving their own performance when given feedback that enables them to monitor their own work. Deming placed much importance on the gathering of numerical data, but he emphasized that it must never be used to place blame on any employee or group of employees. Data are to be used to isolate problem areas, to design corrective action, and to identify staff training needs. Data do not have to be of the standard statistical variety, however; the most useful kinds of data are frequently those generated by the employees themselves.

Data Included in an Educational Information System

Learning is a very complex function and the causes and effects are not clearly understood. Adding to the complexity is the fact that learning is an ubiquitous process; it takes place everywhere. Although schools only have substantial control over that which takes place within them, in order to design successful curricula and evaluate the effectiveness of programs, teachers need comprehensive information about the students themselves and the environments in which they live their out-of-school lives.

Bernhardt (1998) proposes four major classifications of data to be included in an information system designed to improve student achievement: (1) demographics, (2) perceptions, (3) student learning, and (4) school processes. These are illustrated as overlapping circles in Figure 15.1. The figure reports the type of information that can be gained from individual measures and the enhanced information that can be gained through analyses suggested by the intersection of measures.

Demographic data are about student characteristics. They help us to know our "clients" and the context of the school. Included would be the name and special needs of each student. Other information would include gender, ethnicity, age, grade in school, attendance record, and years in this school and in previous schools. Socioeconomic characteristics should also be kept, usually as characteristics of the parents' education levels, employment, and income. Information would also be maintained with respect to name, address, and telephone numbers of parents or guardians. Demographics are generally measured with hard data.

Learning is strongly influenced by the attitudes and the likes and dislikes of the learners. In designing and evaluating learning experiences, it is important to know what these perceptions are. Perceptions are much more difficult to measure than demographics because they are subjective, and clues to their existence can be obtained only indirectly through such devices as questionnaires, surveys, observations, interviews, and analysis of written or oral expressions.

To bring about student learning is the *raison d'etre* of the schools; it is the outcome, the end product. The type of information collected here

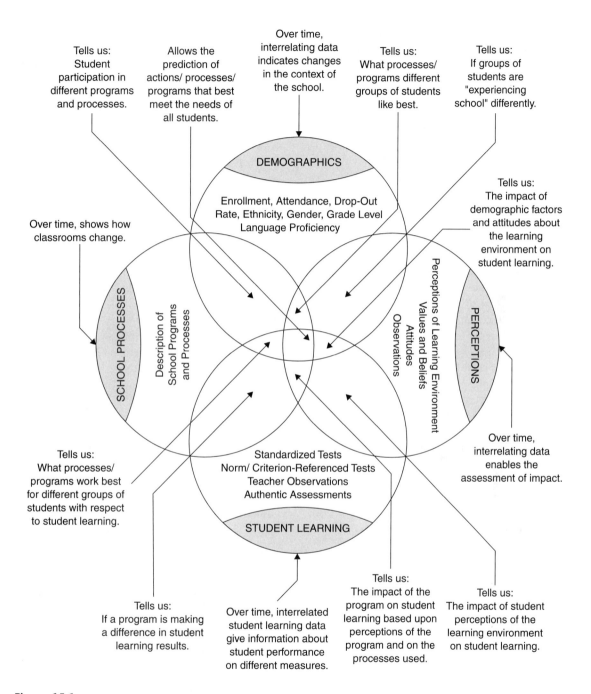

Tells us:
Student participation in different programs and processes.

Allows the prediction of actions/ processes/ programs that best meet the needs of all students.

Over time, interrelating data indicates changes in the context of the school.

Tells us:
What processes/ programs different groups of students like best.

Tells us:
If groups of students are "experiencing school" differently.

Tells us:
The impact of demographic factors and attitudes about the learning environment on student learning.

Over time, shows how classrooms change.

DEMOGRAPHICS

Enrollment, Attendance, Drop-Out Rate, Ethnicity, Gender, Grade Level Language Proficiency

SCHOOL PROCESSES

Description of School Programs and Processes

PERCEPTIONS

Perceptions of Learning Environment Values and Beliefs Attitudes Observations

Tells us:
What processes/ programs work best for different groups of students with respect to student learning.

Standardized Tests
Norm/ Criterion-Referenced Tests
Teacher Observations
Authentic Assessments

STUDENT LEARNING

Over time, interrelating data enables the assessment of impact.

Tells us:
If a program is making a difference in student learning results.

Over time, interrelated student learning data give information about student performance on different measures.

Tells us:
The impact of the program on student learning based upon perceptions of the program and on the processes used.

Tells us:
The impact of student perceptions of the learning environment on student learning.

Figure 15.1
Bernhardt's four major classifications of data to be included in an information system designed to improve student achievement

Source: V. L. Bernhardt. *Data analysis for comprehensive schoolwide improvement* (p. 15). Larchmont, NY: Eye on Education, 1998.

will be guided by school mission as well as performance standards set by the school, the district, and the state. Student learning measures usually recorded in a formal information system consist of teacher-assigned grades, standardized tests, norm-referenced tests, and criterion-referenced tests, including teacher-made tests. Authentic assessments may also be included in the form of samples of student work and video and audio recordings of student performance (Fulmer, 1995).

The nature of school processes and programs provided are the only learning experiences directly under the control of school officials. Presumably they have been designed and implemented to influence student behavior as envisioned in the school or district mission statement and in derived goals and objectives. Appropriate measures from Bernhardt's other three categories need to be drawn upon to evaluate the effectiveness of each process and program for students having various characteristics and attitudes (proclivities) of interest. In describing the processes, it is important that the nature and amount of resources used be recorded to permit cost analyses. Resources applied would include teacher and student time, equipment (textbooks, computers, etc.), supplies, and space. Educators are inclined to overlook cost factors, but if two procedures are equally effective, the less expensive one is preferred from a policy standpoint.

The Role of Information Technology in Instruction and Learning

Because educational institutions are an integral part of the information industry, the remarkable advances in information and communication technologies hold enormous potential for revolutionizing schooling. To date, however, that potential is largely unrealized (Dede, 1998; Fullerton, 1998; Trotter, 1997); but building external pressures for change cannot be delayed much longer by a largely reluctant profession.

Technological Change and Education

Educational technology is the application of scientific knowledge, including learning theory, to the solution of problems in education. Education and technology are concurrently cause and effect vis-à-vis the other. Technological developments place continuing pressure on educators to keep curriculum and instructional methods up to date. At the same time, educational institutions are essential to the generation and assimilation of new technology.

Although society in general has tended toward enhanced technological sophistication and increased capital intensity, the education sector has retained a traditional, labor-intensive, craft-oriented technology (Bolton, 1994; Butzin, 1992; Cuban, 1988; Goodlad, 1984; Murphy, 1993). This "standing still" creates both sociological and economic problems. From an economic standpoint, labor-intensive education is unnecessarily expensive and it, in general, does not produce a workforce with prerequisite attitudes and skills needed for a rapidly changing workplace. From a sociological standpoint, technologically unsophisticated schools are losing their credibility and thereby their effectiveness with pupils because they are no longer congruent with the larger societal context.

Nonservice industries (e.g., manufacturing) generally understand that technological structure is not inalterably fixed, especially under competitive market conditions. Instead, there is an ongoing search for alternative, more efficient production methods that require different mixes of human and nonhuman resources. These alternatives are judged by their potential costs and effectiveness. Education, however, which is largely a state monopoly with weak market incentives for efficiency, appears to be locked into one labor-intensive mode of production. (Consult related discussions in Chapters 9 and 14.) Even when parents enter the educational marketplace, they exercise choice among public and private schools that differ in size and philosophies but are remarkably similar in the teaching technologies employed. Glennan and Melmed (1996) note that:

> Compared with the private sector, [social service providers in general and educational agencies in particular] lack an investment mentality. School districts do not regularly set aside a specified portion of their revenues for investing in activities to improve school performance. The reasons for this are found in the *political* nature of resource allocation in public education. (p. 2, emphasis added)

Baumol (1967, p. 415) argued that "inherent in the technological structure" of such service industries as education "are forces working almost unavoidably for progressive and cumulative increases in the real costs incurred in supplying them." If productivity is to be enhanced in education (and other service industries), there must be a willingness to develop alternative means of providing services, including modifications in their technological structures. The purpose of technology is to make labor go further by replacing it, to the extent possible, with mechanical devices and more efficient organization in order to produce a better product or service and/or to reduce the costs of production (Benson, 1961).

It isn't that schools have totally neglected new technologies; the concern expressed is over the way in which schools have chosen to accommodate them. Technological devices have been used as add-ons to assist or supplement teacher efforts rather than as integral parts of new learning systems that combine the capabilities and energy of students and teachers with those devices to achieve results superior to that which could be achieved without them or to achieve equal results at a lower cost (Dede, 1998; Willett, Swanson, & Nelson, 1979). When technology is used as an add-on or as enrichment, costs are increased and efficiency is decreased unless there is evidence of greatly improved outcomes (Butzin, 1992).

Using technology in school as an add-on is not a recent phenomenon. In a 1972 study, Vaizey, Norris, and Sheehan noted that teacher costs accounted for at least half of all school costs and that unless increases in pupil/teacher ratios took place as a result of the use of new technologies, new technologies would necessarily add to total costs. The authors accurately predicted that increases in pupil/teacher ratios would not happen: "[I]t seems unlikely that any teacher substitution will occur—certainly none has yet taken place. Thus for new methods to be used on a wider scale, the decision will have to be taken that the educational benefits are worth the resulting increases in costs" (p. 234).

Because educators have used technology almost exclusively as an add-on to traditional instructional procedures, there is a tendency for them to think of instructional technology as being very expensive, but this is the case only when technology is not used for labor substitution. One of the most telling shortcomings of current leadership in the public schools is its failure to understand the role of technology. Employing new technologies has only one purpose: to increase productivity. This is the reason that most of the rest of the economy spends billions of dollars annually on new technological devices in order to remain competitive by keeping unit production costs low. Public schools need to learn from the practice of other organizations and squarely address the issue of productivity (Doyle, 1994). (Consult the discussion of the concepts of efficiency and educational production functions in Chapter 14.)

Another explanation for the generic failure of educational technologies in the past is being due largely "to a misplaced obsession with hardware and neglect of software, other resources, and instructional setting [including teacher readiness] that are necessary to successful implementation" (H. Levin & Meister, 1985, p. 9). Levin and Meister (1985) provide a rule of thumb that the purchase of equipment should represent only about 10 percent of the total cost of an innovation if that innovation is to be effective. A substantial proportion of the remaining 90 percent needs to be invested in the involvement of the persons who must operate the systems in designing those systems and in staff development (Zehr, 1997).

Bromley (1998) points out that one of the most significant mistakes made by designers and implementers of new instructional technologies is the assumption that the issues are only technical and can be solved by technicians. Rather than being technological, he argues that the dominating issues are social and cultural.

Emerging Information Age Schools

In an increasingly literate and sophisticated society, ways are being found to meet the unique needs of individual students at current or reduced costs. No longer need these two goals be mutually exclusive. They are being obtained concurrently in a few new schools designed specifically for the information age. These schools (1) place the learner in a role of active participant, (2) restructure the ratio of human and capital inputs in the schooling process, and (3) take advantage of existing information and communication technologies. To make them cost effective, these schools are designed systemically (Dede, 1998), making the use of instructional technology an integral part of the teaching–learning process. Innovations in pedagogy, curriculum, assessment, and school organization are developed simultaneously with innovations in instructional technology.

Individualization of Instruction.
Our system of schooling began to develop 150 years ago to make "book learning" available to every person. Most of the schools we have today are remnants of the Industrial Age, when we lived in communities that were nearly self-contained, served by local newspapers, local merchants, and locally owned factories (Mecklenburger, 1994). Ideas of that period about how the industrial world worked were adapted to schooling, and those industrial concepts of standardization and economies of scale continue to dominate thinking about the organization and administration of schools even though modern technology has rendered them virtually irrelevant. Large schools are still believed necessary for enabling variety in course offerings and specialization. This Industrial Age thinking has made today's schools so rigid that they cannot adequately respond to individual differences of students or changing conditions in the environment.

In our current school organization, too little recognition is given to the fact that learning is primarily a function of the interest, motivation, and hard work of the student (B. Levin, 1994). We frequently assume that learning takes place best in the physical presence of a teacher to guide and supervise learning activities from moment to moment. The practical effect of this assumption has been to claim that for a child to learn, a course has to be established. More critically, the course requires a certified teacher, and cost considerations require approximately 20 or more pupils per class. Under these assumptions, individualization requires many courses, many teachers, and many students.

Contemporary schooling is too often rigidified and standardized in ways that actually thwart learning and fail to educate young people for productive lives in a society now facing accelerating change and diversity. Rather than create self-directed learners who can function independently and interpret change, the school has continued to create teacher-dependent role players. The Industrial Age school assumes that students are raw materials to be "processed" by schools according to specifications dictated by schedules, programs, courses, and exit tests (Darling-Hammond, 1993). It further assumes that children are passive instead of active, incapable instead of capable, directed instead of self-directed, acquiescent instead of assertive, dependent rather than independent (Des Dixon, 1994).

Only a handful of entirely new schooling efforts are actually in operation. Darling-Hammond (1993) described emerging Information Age schools as assuming that students are not standardized and that teaching is not routine:

[T]his view acknowledges that effective teaching techniques will vary for students with different learning styles, with differently developed intelligences, or at different stages of cognitive and psychological development; for different subject areas; and for different instructional goals. Far from following standardized instructional packages, teachers must base their judgments on knowledge of learning theory and pedagogy, of child development and cognition, and of curriculum and assessment. They must then connect this knowledge to the understandings, dispositions, and conceptions that individual students bring with them to the classroom. (p. 758)

The emerging schools provide regimens and instructional methods that are flexible enough to provide students with programs and content that are individualized according to their learning abilities and personal interests. A constructivist view of learning has replaced a positivist view. Learning is no longer considered a linear process; rather, it is recognized that stimuli are received largely at random and that the role of the teacher is to help the learner develop procedures for processing the stimuli and for constructing meaning (Butzin, 1992; Mecklenburger, 1994). School curricula are becoming interrelated across subject boundaries in order to permit the integration of ideas and to emphasize the interrelatedness of problems.

New Roles for Teachers.   In an information-rich society, the teacher's role as purveyor of information is rapidly becoming obsolete. Communication and computer technologies provide the means whereby any student knowing how to read and to use these resources can obtain most information needed in a manner of presentation that is at least as effective as today's typical teaching (Butzin, 1992). This portends new roles for educational professionals. In the Information Age schools, teachers—if we continue to call them that—become experts in managing information resources and in designing learning experiences for individual students relevant to their needs, growth, and development. They are involved primarily in diagnosing individual learning needs, prescripting individualized learning experiences (i.e., curriculum design), motivating each student and evaluating the results (B. Levin, 1994). In carrying out these functions, the primary interaction with students is, of necessity, on a one-to-one basis, in essence eliminating the classroom as we have known it.

The emerging schools focus on learning rather than teaching. With the nearly unlimited accounting capabilities of computer networks, emphasis is placed on *continuous* rather than discontinuous learning that is *individualized* to capitalize on student strengths and to remedy student weaknesses as these are diagnosed. For over three decades, it has been the law of the land that children with learning disabilities and other disabling conditions receive individual diagnoses and education prescriptions; all children are so treated in Information Age schools.

A multimedia approach to learning does not eliminate traditional teaching, but traditional teaching becomes only *one* of many methods. Other media include books, drill, computer-assisted instruction (CAI), Internet access, videodisk enhanced by computer, audiodisk, lecture (large group), discussion (small group), drama, chorus, band, athletic teams, tutors (teacher, aide, volunteer, or other student), collaborative learning, laboratory, and field experiences (Halal & Liebowitz, 1994). In these schools, student/teacher ratios are relevant only where particular group sizes can be shown to contribute to greater efficiency in the *learning* process.

The learning experience is viewed as a function of all life experiences, not just those in school. A school building is viewed as a *place* of learning but not the *center* of learning, which is the student. Kozma and Schank (1998) argue that technology can be the instrument for breaking the relative isolation of schools and firmly linking them with the outside world.

Schools, homes, and workplaces today function separately—connected always by geography and circumstance, but only infrequently by common purpose and collaborative action. In our vision of communities of understanding, digital technologies are used to interweave schools, home, workplaces, libraries, museums, and social services to integrate education into the fabric of the community. Learning is no longer encapsulated by time, place, and age, but has become a pervasive activity and attitude that continues throughout life and is supported by all segments of society. Teaching is no longer defined as the transfer of information; learning is no longer defined as the retention of facts. Rather, teachers challenge students to achieve deeper levels of understanding and guide students in collaborative construction and application of knowledge in the context of real-world problems, situations, and tasks. Education is no longer the exclusive responsibility of teachers; it benefits from the participation and collaboration of parents, business people, scientists, seniors, and students across age groups.

How can technology support this transformation? First, the Internet is connecting schools with one another and with homes, businesses, libraries, museums, and community resources. This connection between school and home will help students extend their academic day, allow teachers to draw on significant experiences from students' everyday lives, and enable parents to become more involved with the education of their children and find extended educational opportunities for themselves. Connections between school and work will allow students to learn in the context of real-life problems and will allow teachers to draw on the resources of other teachers, a range of professional development providers, and technical and business experts. Connections among schools, homes, and the rest of the community will enable students to relate what is happening in the world outside to what is happening in school, will allow teachers to coordinate formal education with informal learning, and will allow the community to reintegrate education into daily life. (p. 5)

In a similar vein, Dede (1998) proposes that schools deliberately take advantage of the non-formal instructional experiences that already exist in the home, workplaces, and community and tie them in with the formal curriculum of the school. He notes that people spend lots of money on astonishingly powerful and inexpensive devices purchased for entertainment and information services such as televisions, video

recorders, computers, and video games—"many ubiquitous in rich and poor homes, urban and rural areas" (p. 203). He notes that by removing from classroom settings some of the burden of presenting material and inducing motivation, learning activities that use the technology infrastructure outside schools would reduce the amount of money needed for adequate levels of classroom-based technology.

To take full advantage of available technology, Information Age schools rely on computers for their complete range of capabilities, but these machines are subject to human direction, planning, and control. Teachers are still absolutely essential, but their role is changed from one of director, leader, and final authority to one of diagnostician, prescriber, motivator, facilitator, and evaluator. Teachers, students, and aides are seen as multidimensional human resources leading to specialization and division of labor, breaking the self-contained classroom mold of today's schools. Tasks requiring professional judgment are separated from those that are routine. High-cost, professionally trained persons are assigned to the former, and lower-cost paraprofessionals are assigned to the latter. The pupil/teacher ratio is likely to increase over time, but the pupil/adult ratio is likely to remain the same or even decline from current levels as more paraprofessionals assume routine tasks.

Staffing.   Intelligent direction for these emerging schools depends on the professional educators associated with them, and school-based decision making is the norm for them. Their teachers have become experts in learning theory, curriculum design, motivational techniques, and developmental procedures. They have highly specialized skills in diagnosing the strengths and weaknesses of individual students with various intellectual skills and backgrounds and in prescribing best combinations of available learning experiences and resources (Darling-Hammond, 1993; Des Dixon, 1994).

The use of teaching teams results in distinct advantages to the professional personnel. Each professional can specialize in the areas of expertise to which that person is best suited by personality and training. The required "omniscience in the classroom," assumed under the present system as necessary for the professional, is relaxed.

Student assistants (Johnson & Johnson, 1987; Lippitt, 1975) and paraprofessional adults have become valuable staff members in these schools. The roles of both are arranged to complement, and supplement, that of the highly trained professionals who have the prime responsibility for guiding student instruction. For a long time, teacher supply was so abundant and teacher salaries were so low that little attention was given to maximizing teacher time available for making decisions that required professional discretion. As a result, teachers have been expected to assume assignments such as collecting lunch money, typing worksheets, and monitoring cafeterias, lavatories, and hallways, which could be accomplished as well or better by persons without professional teacher training. With a growing shortage of well-qualified teachers and salaries that are reaching professional levels in some districts, it becomes imperative that teachers' time be concentrated on tasks requiring professional discretion. Less expensive persons can be employed to carry out clerical and routine tasks.

A Prototype Integrated Information System to Manage Individualized Instruction

Figure 15.2 illustrates an information system designed to be used within the context of a learning environment committed to individualized instruction in support of the Information Age schools described in the preceding section. At the center of this model is depicted a teacher and a student meeting together on a regular basis to develop, monitor, and update an instructional plan for the student. During this meeting, the teacher evaluates the student's progress, drawing on the teacher's professional knowledge and tacit understandings, supported by information drawn from the *student information system,* containing

descriptive information about the student and his or her background and the student's achievement to date compared to expected standards and objectives as determined by the school, district, and state and augmented by the student, teacher, and family. Descriptive information about the student includes the student's needs, capabilities, attitudes, perceptions, inclinations, likes, and dislikes.

Based on the available information and the teacher's professional judgment, a diagnosis of the student's current situation is made by the teacher, possibly in consultation with an expert system in particularly troublesome situations. Referring to the available instructional tools and strategies as recorded in the *instructional resource management system* (IRMS), the teacher prescribes an appropriate individualized experience to take the student on the next leg of the journey toward the eventual mastery of the educational standards set for him or her. Each item in the instructional resource inventory is classified according to content, pedagogical approach, and instructional objectives (Osin, 1995).

Each of the subcomponents of the system parallels the essential functions which the teacher must perform as an instructional manager. The first tasks are needs assessment and accounting for the progress of the student. Both are combined in one system, the *student information system,* for they deal with portrayal of student growth before and after specific instructional activities. Whether one emphasizes this portrayal as a process of needs assessment or evaluation is relatively unimportant. The important concept is that educational planning requires a comprehensive picture of the student's "growth status," with sufficient information regarding his or her strengths and weaknesses.

Given this information, the second function of instructional management is to identify the types of instructional resources and/or learning experiences available for accomplishing the developmental tasks using the IRMs, the related computer support system. Again, this concept is a simple one, although laborious to

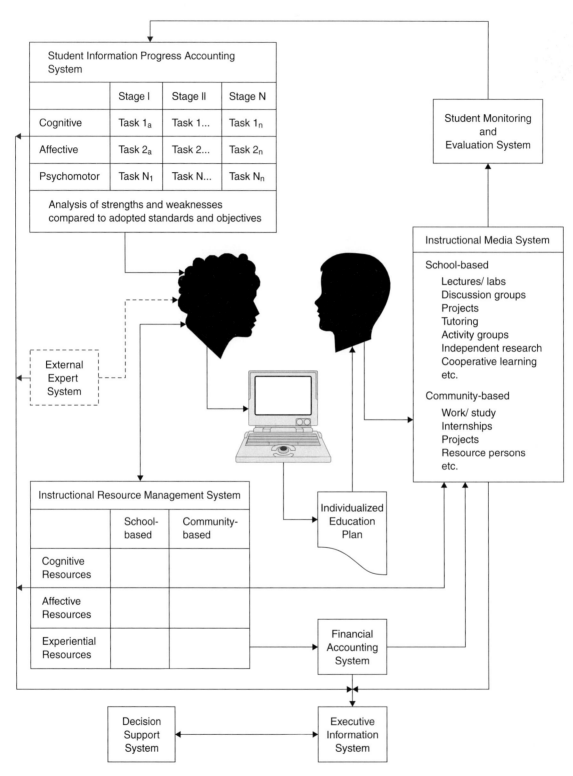

Figure 15.2
Prototype integrated information system for individualized instruction

implement. For each task or objective, the resource management system would list the "lessons," instructional packages, or structured learning experiences that the school has at its disposal for providing instruction through the *instructional media system* (IMS). The IMS could include projects, lectures, discussion groups, books, independent research, cooperative learning, tutoring, activity groups (e.g., athletic, music, drama, debate), and so on. The important trend toward using community resources outside the school could be accommodated. Employers willing to participate in cooperative work experience could be listed, as could available internships or opportunities for youth participation in community projects. Instructional programs offered by museums, art galleries, and other cultural institutions would be included.

Once an event (or events) is authorized through the IMS, assuring that needed personnel, space, supplies and equipment, software, and so on, are available at the appropriate time and place, the student is scheduled for the experience in the IMS; the financial accounting system is notified simultaneously of resources committed. Finally, the student is provided with his or her individualized education plan reporting the learning goals and objectives, time and place of activities, and the nature of the assessment.

The result of combining input from the needs assessment and resource management system is to make possible the development of an individualized education plan for each student. But simultaneously, the individualization of instruction increases the problems of scheduling and control. In existing high school systems, it is typically the task of the guidance counselor to assist the student in the selection and scheduling of courses to be taken over the course of a semester. When the teacher assumes the role of instructional manager, as has been more typical of primary and intermediate teachers, the function of counseling is assumed as well. Because scheduling will be on an individual and objective-by-objective basis, a capability must be built into the system for handling the far greater complexities of scheduling, but many prototypes are currently in operation, although not necessarily in education.

An important aspect of control is to know that activities are being pursued according to plan. In this sense, the planning capability provided by the needs assessment and resource management systems contribute to the school's control capability. Nevertheless, even greater control is necessary; a means must be provided to ensure that students actually engage in the learning activities prescribed. Whether the unit of study is an individualized learning packet that can be completed in one hour, or a full-semester internship, controls can be built into the student information system via the student monitoring and evaluation system. End-of-unit test results or other performance measures are implicit in every unit of instruction and can be entered as evidence that the activity was completed satisfactorily. A computerized system for comparing projected completion dates with end-of-unit notifications can easily alert teachers to difficulties and the need for modifications in the individualized educational plan. Linking this system with systems containing information on district finances and school and community demographic information opens the possibility to types of analyses to inform policy formulation impossible for virtually all schools and districts to do with the information systems available today.

The Department of Education in the State of Victoria, Australia (of which Melbourne is the capital city), has developed an integration of several specialized information systems similar to that conceived in the prototype presented above to support its program of school-based decision making within the context of state standards and assessment instruments (Gurr, 1999). The system is illustrated in Figure 15.3. KIDMAP is designed primarily for teacher use and is similar to the student information system and the IRMS in the prototype model. It is a commercially developed product adapted to Victorian requirements. KIDMAP provides for student assessment and recording, analysis and profiling

Figure 15.3
Integrated information systems
of the Department of Education,
State of Victoria, Australia

Source: Adapted from Gurr, 1999, Fig.
10, p. 66.

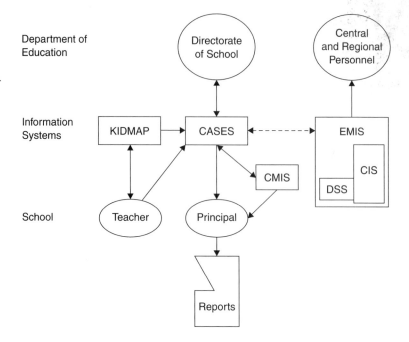

of student progress or needs, access to teaching resources, and preparation of reports for parents. It interfaces with information systems designed to serve the management and policy-making needs of the school and the state system.

CASES (Computerized Administrative Systems Environment for Schools), developed by the Victoria Department of Education, is the platform that provides a standard administrative system for the state's reform initiative, known as *Schools for the Future.* CASES stores and processes a range of school-generated data, including student records and financial, physical, and human resource data. Some data are drawn directly from the KIDMAP system. CASES is designed for principal use and provides a direct link to the Department of Education in support of policy analyses at the state level and an indirect link through the department's primary information system. CMIS is an add-on software to CASES designed to produce a range of summary reports, including graphics of school performance measures, primarily for use by school principals.

EMIS (Education Management Information System) is the system used by the Department of Education and its regional offices. It is linked to the CASES system, but most data are entered by the department. EMIS consists of two subsystems: the corporate information system (CIS) and the decision support system (DSS). CIS contains the database and DSS facilitates analysis. The EMIS is what Rowley (1996) referred to as an *executive information system,* containing aggregate information on schools.

Although operational, the interfaced system is subject to continual refinement and upgrade. In particular, efforts are under way to enhance the ability of the system to share information among components.

Summary

According to Wheatley (1994), information forms us as individuals and our organizations. For an organization to be true to its mission, information must flow freely within that organization and between it and its environment. For most of recorded history, information developed slowly and linearly, making the task of assimilation relatively simple. Today, information is expanding at exponential rates, and individuals and organizations are bombarded with overwhelming amounts of data at random. Separating the relevant from the nonrelevant and making sense of it all has become an essential task of individuals and of organizations. Information systems have been developed to assist the process, supported by a burgeoning information and communications technology.

Educational institutions were precursors of the Information Age. Ironically, however, schools have not kept pace with the rest of society in adapting to that age. This is the source of much of the current public dissatisfaction with schools. Most of today's schools were designed for another era, a simpler era. To accommodate the educational needs of an Information Age, schools themselves must be reinvented.

In this chapter we have discussed the role of information in organizations and how data are processed into policy and amalgamated into performance through information systems. We have presented a description of new schools that are emerging to meet the challenges of the Information Age. Finally, we presented a prototype of an information system to serve Information Age schools.

Activities

1. Study the information systems in your school and district. How many of the types identified by Rowley are used? Are they integrated? Develop a set of recommendations with rationale for the school board for improving their effectiveness.

2. What kinds of instructional technology are used in your school? Is the technology an integral part of the instructional system or does it stand apart? Develop a set of recommendations with rationale for the school principal for improving the use of instructional technology.

References

Baumol, W. J. (1967). Macroeconomics of unbalanced growth: The anatomy of urban crisis. *American Economic Review, 57*(3), 415–426.

Benson, C. (1961). *The economics of public education.* Boston: Houghton Mifflin.

Bernhardt, V. L. (1998). *Data analysis for comprehensive schoolwide improvement.* Larchmont, NY: Eye on Education.

Bolton, W. R. (1994). *Factors that may influence the use of computer technology in the teaching and learning process.* Unpublished doctoral dissertation, State University of New York at Buffalo.

Bromley, H. (1998). Introduction: Data-driven democracy? Social assessment of educational computing. In H. Bromley & M. W. Apple, *Education/technology/power: Educational computing as a social practice* (pp. 1–25). Albany, NY: State University of New York Press.

Butzin, S. M. (1992). Integrating technology into the classroom: Lessons from the Project CHILD experience. *Phi Delta Kappan, 74,* 330–333.

Cuban, L. (1988). *The managerial imperative and the practice of leadership in schools.* Albany, NY: State University of New York Press.

Darling-Hammond, L. (1993). Reframing the school reform agenda: Developing capacity for school transformation. *Phi Delta Kappan, 74,* 752–761.

Dede, C. (1998). The scaling-up process for technology-based educational innovations. In C. Dede (Ed.), *Learning with technology: Association for Supervision and Curriculum Development Yearbook* (pp. 199–215). Alexandria, VA: ASCD.

Deming, W. E. (1986). *Out of the crisis.* Cambridge, MA: MIT Press.

Des Dixon, R. G. (1994). Future schools: How to get there from here. *Phi Delta Kappan, 75,* 360–365.

Doyle, D. P. (1994). The role of private sector management in public education. *Phi Delta Kappan, 76,* 128–132.

Frazier, A. (1997). *A roadmap for quality transformation in education.* Boca Raton, FL: St. Lucie Press.

Fullerton, K. (1998). Common "mythstakes" in technology planning. In K. C. Westbrook (Ed.), *Technology and the educational workplace: Understanding fiscal impacts* (pp. 63–76). Thousand Oaks, CA: Corwin Press.

Fulmer, C. L. (1995). Maximizing the potential of information technology for management. In B.-Z. Barta, M. Telem, & Y Gev (Eds.), *Information technology in educational management* (pp. 3–8). Padstow, Cornwall, England: TJ Press.

Glennan, T. K., & Melmed, A. (1996). *Fostering the use of educational technology: Elements of a national strategy*. Santa Monica, CA: RAND Corporation. *http://www.rand.org/publications/MR/MR682/contents.html*

Goodlad, J. I. (1984). *A place called school: Prospects for the future*. New York: McGraw-Hill.

Gurr, D. (1999). *From supervision to quality assurance: The case of the State of Victoria (Australia)*. Paris: International Institute for Educational Planning/UNESCO.

Halal, W. E., & Liebowitz, J. (1994). Telelearning: The multimedia revolution in education. *Futurist, 28*(6), 21–26.

Johnson, D. W., & Johnson, R. (1987). *Learning together and alone: Cooperative, competitive, and individualistic learning* (2nd ed.). Upper Saddle River, NJ: Prentice Hall.

Kozma, R., & Schank, P. (1998). Connecting with the 21st century: Technology in support of educational reform. In C. Dede (Ed.), *Learning with technology: Association for Supervision and Curriculum Development Yearbook* (pp. 3–21). Alexandria, VA: ASCD.

Levin, B. (1994). Improving educational productivity: Putting students at the center. *Phi Delta Kappan, 75,* 758–760.

Levin, H., & Meister, G. (1985). *Educational technology and computers: Promises, promises, always promises* (Project Report 85-A13). Stanford, CA: Stanford Education Policy Institute, Stanford University.

Lippitt, P. (1975). *Students teach students*. Bloomington IN: Phi Delta Kappa Educational Foundation.

Mecklenburger, J. A. (1994). Thinking about schooling in The Global Village: We can see into the future of schooling, now. And its name is not just "reform." *Inventing Tomorrow's Schools, 4*(2), 2–9.

Mintzberg, H. (1994). *The rise and fall of strategic planning*. New York: Free Press.

Murphy, J. (1993). What's in? What's out? American education in the nineties. *Phi Delta Kappan, 74,* 641–646.

Osin, L. (1995). Educational management in Israeli elementary schools. In B.-Z. Barta, M. Telem, & Y Gev (Eds.), *Information technology in educational management* (pp. 209–214). Padstow, Cornwall, England: TJ Press.

Rowley, J. (1996). *The basics of information systems* (2nd ed.). London: Library Association Publishing.

Schmoker, M. J., & Wilson, R. B. (1993). *Total quality education: Profiles of schools that demonstrate the power of Deming's management principles*. Bloomington, IN: Phi Delta Kappa Educational Foundation.

Stair, R. M. (1992). *Principles of information systems: A managerial approach*. Boston: Boyd & Frazier.

Taylor, R. G. (1995). Graphic information and school facility planning. In B.-Z. Barta, M. Telem, & Y Gev (Eds.), *Information technology in educational management* (pp. 153–161). Padstow, Cornwall, England: TJ Press.

Trotter, A. (1997). Taking technology's measure. *Education Week, XVII*(11), 12–18.

Vaizey, J., Norris, K., & Sheehan, J. (1972). *The political economy of education*. New York: Wiley.

Westbrook, K. C. (1998). *Technology and the educational workplace: Understanding fiscal impacts*. Thousand Oaks, CA: Corwin Press.

Wheatley, M. J. (1994). *Leadership and the new science: Learning about organizations from an orderly universe*. San Francisco: Berrett-Koehler.

Wheatley, M. J., & Kellner-Rogers, M. (1996). *A simpler way*. San Francisco: Berrett-Koehler.

Wholeben, B. E. (1995). Interactive simulation for planning, coordination, and control: Mathematical decision support systems in education. In B.-Z. Barta, M. Telem, & Y Gev (Eds.), *Information technology in educational management* (pp. 162–169). Padstow, Cornwall, England: TJ Press.

Willett, E., Swanson, A., & Nelson, E. (1979). *Modernizing the little red schoolhouse: The economics of improved schooling*. Englewood Cliffs, NJ: Educational Technology.

Zehr, M. A. (1997). Teaching the teachers. *Education Week, XVII*(11), 24–29.

PART VI

Leadership for a New Millennium

Leaders of the future will be people who possess the broad variety of skills that enable them to function comfortably in changing environments. In these new environments change becomes the constant. Understanding this reality of educational systems and the means of working within it is the focus of this last part and chapter.

Chapter 16: Educational Leadership for a Systemic Change. In this chapter we build a composite view of the complete work by synthesizing all discussions of previous chapters. In this final discussion we provide further illustrations of how education must contend with emerging issues and conditions and discuss possible scenarios that portray possible futures of education.

Educational Leadership for Systemic Change

We are nearing the end of our treatise on the fundamental concepts of educational leadership and administration. We have addressed the general principles underlying the knowledge base of leadership and management as specifically applied to educational institutions. The review of current scholarship in a wide range of areas was intended to compel the reader to consider critically the theoretical underpinnings of the subject within the context of current issues, problems, and proposed solutions.

Our approach has been an analytical one—thinking between paradigms—and mapping the theoretical and practical worlds of leadership and management. Four dimensions of leadership were examined (inquiry, communication and human interaction, analysis and planning, and decision making and change) from several perspectives (human inquiry, observation, philosophy, human relations, communication, organization, environmental interaction, planning, allocation of resources, evaluation, decision making, policy formulation, and change). In this concluding chapter, we look back on that which has preceded and reflect on its significance for leadership in contemporary educational institutions.

Interlinking Concepts

We have turned to an expanded version of systems theory to serve as a vehicle for integrating the many faces of leadership. It was observed that the levels of traditional systems discourse had hit a glass ceiling imposed between biological-based systems and human social systems. As things stood, nothing learned or seen above that ceiling could be valued by systems scientists unless it yielded both positivistic and predictive systems knowledge. Flood's (1990) argument for a complementarist theoretical position that is open and conciliatory overcomes the theoretical fortress mentality of traditional systems thinking and encompasses the emancipatory forces of critical self-reflection. Critical reflection views all theories and methodologies as complementary. Intellectual tension among competing theories and methodologies can lead to new understandings, whereas universality and convergence lead to complacency with what is known.

This pioneering approach allows researchers and practitioners to deal with such issues as employee empowerment, workplace diversity, cultural abnormalities, coercion, ideologies, and ownership of values in a deliberative normative way. Subjectivity is openly acknowledged, not as antithetical to system science but as part of its legitimate discourse. Postulating a role for critical systems theory immediately removes most of the two-value (either–or) constraints that have plagued systems literature on educational administration. Machine images as metaphors for social systems can be complemented by contextual analysis. In this spirit, the aspects of leadership discussed previously can be viewed as subsystems, with the concept of leadership serving as the system.

Each aspect of organizational leadership is related to every other aspect to some degree.

The philosophy, values, and ethics of the leader guide what is observed, his or her approach to inquiry, and the way the leader deals with other people (human relations). Leadership philosophy also has a strong influence on what decisions and policies are made and how resources are allocated.

Inquiry, the process of finding and knowing, was discussed as a key component of leadership. It was viewed as a philosophical issue, beginning with a discussion of the various philosophical points of view that shape a person's interpretation of experience. The process of inquiry was considered directly, and the impact of the traditional scientific paradigm was balanced against the possibility of new ways of gathering and interpreting data. There was discussion of the possibility of taking an eclectic approach and drawing on several paradigms when working in the fields of education. This was considered further in the discussion of observation, which is a fundamental element in the ability of the school leader to detect and recognize relevant events and information.

Communication was referred to as the breath of the organization. The means and networks of communication reflecting the value placed on human interactions and the extent to which leadership is open or closed to inputs from members of the organization and the community (environmental interactions) was considered. The function of communication as a significant element of school systems was explored, and communication was considered as the binding agent in human interaction on the personal and group levels.

Analysis and planning as the prerequisites for rational decision making and management of change were considered. Strategic planning, a process that moves from development of a vision to sharing the vision to implementation of the vision, was considered from the perspective of the educational leader who will have to implement that process. The relation of a variety of paradigms held by the leader and/or by the members of the organization was explored, and

the effects of these paradigms and the related planning models on the allocation of resources were discussed. Planning grows out of the values held collectively by members of the organization and from the evaluation of the successes and failures of current efforts. Allocation of resources is a product of rational planning and political policy formulation. The problem of effective resource allocation and the concomitant need to monitor results was identified as a major concern for leaders at all levels of the educational enterprise.

Educational decision making—the *raison d'etre* for all that has gone before—was considered with respect to collective policy formulation and with respect to individuals and groups. A variety of approaches to decision making that are applicable in a public setting were considered and evaluated. Decision making as the process of choosing among alternatives was identified as one of the most crucial skills needed by an effective educational leader. A circular model appropriate to the view of education as an open general system was proposed. Each activity of the organization requires innumerable decisions made informally by individuals with varying degrees of discretion and formally by the bureaucratic hierarchy. The impact of constant change within and outside educational systems on decision making and on the systems themselves was discussed. For the organization to adapt to ever-shifting environments (internally and externally), organizational change must take place. The success or failure of the change process depends to a large extent on the collective philosophy of the organization and the nature of its human relations and communication networks.

We have reviewed the scholarship on leadership in general terms. In this chapter we are focusing more specifically on leadership in educational institutions. In earlier discussion we found that there was little agreement on how leadership should be defined or how it works. For our purposes we have defined leadership quite broadly as influencing others' actions in achieving mutually desired ends. Leadership provides direction to an organization, concentrating on doing the right things. Leadership involves philosophy, values, and ethics. Leaders are people who shape the goals, motivations, and actions of others. Frequently, they initiate change to reach existing and new goals. Occasionally, they lead in order to preserve what is valuable, such as to protect core organizational functions. We have not viewed leadership as being role specific since the roles of leader and follower are interchangeable. Both roles are critical to an organization's success. Some roles, however, offer greater opportunities for exercising leadership, such as the role of principal or superintendent.

We do differentiate between leadership and management. Management is concerned with doing things right; it focuses on the technology of administration. Leadership provides purpose and direction (i.e., doing the right things). Although leadership and management/administration are different, both are important. The success of modern organizations requires the objective perspective of the manager *and* the vision and commitment that wise leadership provides (Bolman & Deal, 1997). It may be possible to be an effective manager without strong leadership skills, but it is not possible to be an effective leader without good management skills. Superficial managerial tasks can be transformed by skilled leaders into opportunities for communicating organizational meaning and purpose in the context of the routine and the mundane (Sergiovanni, 1992).

The Traditional Role of Principal

Foster (1989) identified two foci for leadership research: (1) the bureaucratic–managerial and (2) the political–historical models. The *bureaucratic–managerial model* is based on business practices and assumes that (1) leadership is a function of position; (2) leadership is goal centered with goals driven by organizational, not social or follower needs; and (3) the leader's role is to motivate workers to perform and thus achieve organizational goals. The leader's focus in this model becomes one of assuring employee conformance to managerial desires. Leadership resides not in an individual but in a hierarchical power position where manipulation is used to control tasks, people, and structures. It was once believed that tasks, people, and structures could be strictly controlled to safeguard goal achievement. Leadership, however, can no longer be equated with organizational management.

Today, according to Foster (1989), the concept of leadership seems to focus narrowly on such a bureaucratic definition. Vision and follower empowerment is translated into profit, growth, and illusory power for followers through extrinsic rewards. In today's society, teachers act as therapists adjusting students to social conditions *and* as managers controlling situations for personal and organizational gain. Loose coupling of educational organizations makes rational and goal-oriented control of schools illusory. Leadership in schools cannot be achieved neatly through managerial techniques that are unable to control and predict human action. Instead, Foster argued that leadership should be critical, focused on social vision and change, not organizational goals.

The *political–historical model* is a study of power, politics, and historical facts. People possessing qualities, values, and vision are capable of achieving new and different social orders through transactional or transformative leadership. Transactional leadership, employing exchange relationships between followers and leaders, uses concessions, negotiations, and accommodations to manipulate and integrate social variables. Transformational leadership deals with the leader's ability to create a new social situation, communicate that vision to followers, and engage followers in the pursuit and accomplishment of that vision. Infusing leader and follower with goals and aspirations leads to a higher level of social reality, a new social morality. Leadership becomes a moral and value-driven elevation of the social group with transformational leadership rather than a technocratic, managerial tool for goal achievement.

Foster (1989) criticized today's emphasis on instrumentality that portrays people as "instruments for the achievement of organizational goals" (p. 59). Instrumentality is evidenced in education by practices that judge students by SAT scores, basic skills scores, and employability measures and judge schools by comprehensive assessment reports. Instead, school districts should identify what they want students to achieve at the end of their schooling experience as whole people and members of a community.

Over three decades ago, Parsons (1959) contended that a functionalist perspective has dominated thinking about public education that views the primary role of schools as socializing students to adapt to and share basic norms and values, thus assuring the continuance and survival of society and maintenance of the social power and economic status quo. More recently, Smyth (1989) and Angus (1989) have taken positions similar to that of Parsons.

A functionalist perspective that maintains the status quo assures that power remains in the hands of those who already possess it. Compulsory education is valued by functionalists, for it provides a system that ensures that youth will be educated to assume the existing and emerging adult work roles of a technological society and develop values to assure societal solidarity. This sociological perspective is reflected in educational leaders who practice a top-down, hierarchical, authoritarian, Weberian leadership style. These educational leaders may rely on incremental changes, certification through testing, and increased requirements to foster educational improvement by fixing the participants (teachers and students) while maintaining the management system's structure and status quo.

Similarly, Codd (1989) asserted that a socialization process dominates elementary and secondary education. Students are led to conform to accepted, preset standards; traditional common beliefs and values are imparted in both the for-mal and informal curriculum; and willing acceptance of their role in school and society is ingrained in students. At the tertiary level, students are called upon to examine critically, reflect upon, and challenge accepted values, theories, and practices in society. Codd warned that this dichotomy of socialization and education must not be allowed to persist.

The socialization function of schools is reflected in the typical roles performed by the titular school leader, the principal. For the past 30 years the principal's central role has been interpreted as "building manager, administrator, politician, change agent, boundary spanner, and instructional leader" (W. F. Smith & Andrew, 1989, p. 1). Depending on school district policy, building principals' authority can range from empowered site management and leadership to rote implementation and maintenance of district policies and programs (Guthrie & Reed, 1991, p. 87). Building administrators spend most of their time on noninstructional activities: supervising students between classes in the hallways, at lunch, at various extracurricular events, before and after school, during bus loading and unloading; responding to parental and community concerns; preparing reports and responding to central office requests; resolving conflicts between students and between students and teachers; handling student discipline; requiring and distributing teacher resources; scheduling classes and other school activities; supervising staff; meeting with individual and small groups of students, teachers, and parents; and responding to any number of unexpected school emergencies that may arise during the day (Guthrie & Reed, 1991, p. 230). Instructional leadership activities (teacher supervision, classroom observation, curriculum development, staff development, and technical support) are not the predominant focus of the building principal's routine, for principals are faced with unpredictable, varied situations each day. Although principals regret their inability to spend more time on instructional matters, research has shown that teachers prefer the absence of principals from the teachers' private, quasiautonomous classrooms (W. F. Smith & Andrew, 1989).

These tasks cast the principal as an administrator–manager rather than as an instructional leader (Cuban, 1988). Subordinates value administrative behavior that conducts these tasks efficiently while giving attention to human relations and school politics (Bredeserl, 1989). Firestone and Wilson (1989), however, among many others, have criticized principals for leaving instruction wholly to teachers and not trying to shape thinking about what should be taught and how.

Effective Schools and Reform Literature

The publication in 1966 of the Coleman Report, *Equality of Educational Opportunity,* dominated thinking about elementary and secondary education for over a decade. In many respects it was a very pessimistic report. It documented the gap in academic achievement between minorities and the majority population and concluded that the primary means of social intervention, the schools, was ineffective in closing the gap. Low achievement was attributed chiefly to family background and peer-group associations. Many interpreted the findings as saying that "schools don't make a difference." In 1979, Brookover and Lezotte published the results of a study they had made of inner-city schools with relatively high-achieving pupils. Although acknowledging that achievement levels of such schools were, in general, unacceptably low, they identified several intervention strategies that appeared to narrow the achievement gap. This approach of studying urban schools that differed positively from the norm was developed into the "effective schools movement" by other researchers, such as Edmonds (1979).

Cunningham (1990) observed that since the educational reform era began in the 1980s, "principals and superintendents have been cited in the spate of national reports over and over again as both [the] Achilles heel of American ed-

ucation and the Adonis for improved performance of the nation's schools" (p. 2). The literature clearly identifies the principal as essential to school improvement and reform. In effective school programs, as discovered by Edmonds (1979) and Brookover and Lezotte (1979), staff and students formulate mission and vision statements that develop consensus about and ownership of the school's goals and purposes. As the key educational actor, the effective school principal is seen as the one who is primarily responsible for school improvement and who ensures an atmosphere of order, discipline, and purpose; a climate of high expectations for staff and students; collegial and collaborative staff relationships; commitment among staff and students to school goals; adequate time for instruction; and adequate staff development.

After examination of varied definitions of instructional leadership, Weber (1989) stated that they were rooted in the general goal to improve or maintain conditions that encourage student learning. Achievement of this goal, according to Weber, requires instructional leadership that involves "long-term dedication to instructional excellence, not a one-time resolution to 'get more involved instruction' " (p. 192). He further concluded that leading the instructional program requires both an understanding of educational techniques and a personal vision of academic excellence that can be translated into effective classroom strategies.

Principals perform numerous activities that have varied impact on the instructional program, but Weber (1989) identified several that seem to be particularly critical for directly influencing the instructional program. According to Weber, principals must define the school's mission and develop common goals and a vision to establish a shared sense of direction for employees. Visions and missions are made a reality by articulating and demonstrating a commitment to these ideals. In managing curriculum and instruction, the principal must have knowledge of trends in content areas, media, instructional processes/programs, and instructional strategies/approaches. A positive learning climate is promoted by raising teacher expectations of students' achievement abilities, establishing a link between daily activities and student achievement, and rewarding and recognizing academic achievement. Time devoted to instruction must be protected while ensuring that the quality of this time is maintained or improved. Principals need to manage instruction through observation and evaluation of teachers' instructional strategies. The instructional program needs to be assessed regularly through formative and summative evaluation, matching the intended curricula to the actual curricula and classroom practices; teachers' perceptions of the program's effectiveness should be solicited and program revisions should be made as needed.

Also, Weber (1989) found three leadership traits common to principals carrying out the foregoing tasks successfully: (1) they exercised style flexibility in varied situations involving student needs; (2) they displayed a willingness to attempt various innovative strategies while consistently trying to achieve the goal of improved student achievement; and (3) they imbued their vision, mission, and goals for their schools in the performance of daily school activities, thus connecting and reinforcing their instructional program with the entire school program.

Similar findings have resulted from other research, including Peterson (1987), E. C. Smith and Piele (1989), and W. F. Smith and Andrew (1989). In addition, Smith and Piele asserted that teachers are not influenced by a principal's status or position or ability to reward and punish, but by the teachers' perception that the principal is expert, competent, and able to empower and inspire others. An examination of principals' daily activities by Smith and Andrew found that in most cases, effective principals are strong instructional leaders as well as strong building managers. Principals who are effective instructional leaders are capable of managing their time so that instructional matters are the focus of their discretionary time.

Criticism of Effective Schools Research

Criticism of the effective schools research and literature takes two forms: (1) criticism of its conceptualization, and (2) criticisms of its research designs. Beginning with the research design issues, Deal (1987) contended that the effective schools literature's emphasis on the principal as the key and crucial ingredient for school and curriculum improvement has created a mythological representation of the principal as the instructional leader. Although education reformists identify building-level leadership focused on instruction as a key indicator of school effectiveness, research has been unable to establish a clear relationship between leadership and school effectiveness (Anderson, 1989; Angus, 1989; Burlingame, 1987; Codd, 1989; Deal, 1987; Hallinger & Murphy, 1987). Burlingame further charged that the research has been hasty to make generalizations and has tended to ignore contextual issues. By ignoring context, researchers disregard the influence of the community on school goals, leadership, and teaching. In a similar vein, Hallinger and Murphy (1987) stressed that leadership is situational and that selecting the appropriate style of instructional leadership will be influenced by organizational and environmental factors. Most effective schools research focuses on poor, urban elementary schools and advocates strong instructional leadership as necessary for school improvement.

Hallinger and Murphy (1987) identified other limitations in the effective schools research. Most studies have been conducted at a single point in time; case studies are usually limited to one year. Researchers focus on identifiable characteristics of effective schools and neglect investigation of the processes used by principals to effect these improvements. Most studies focus on poor, urban elementary schools and use student achievement as the sole criterion for assessing effectiveness. There is no clear evidence that this research can be generalized to high schools, to schools of differing socioeconomic conditions, or to educational goals other than student achievement. Finally, lack of a uniform operational definition of instructional leadership restricts researchers' abilities to make comparisons among various research studies.

Moving into conceptual considerations, many researchers contend that educational leadership must be defined more broadly than effective schools researchers have tended to do. Definitions of leadership should include rational, reflective, and deliberate action and should not be confined narrowly to management strategies.

Burlingame (1987) saw three incompatible images of leadership projected by effective schools research. In the first image, the principal is the key figure, possessing traits of supreme rationality (intellectually able to develop appropriate goals, review alternatives, weigh consequences, choose appropriate solutions) and supreme pragmatism (when solutions are ineffective, evaluates the situation and develops an alternative plan). Leadership is top-down. Goals are aimed at raising basic skills test results, and scores are improved by providing a stable, orderly environment and raising teachers' expectations of student academic achievement. This image portrays the leader as dominant and the follower as passive.

In the second image, cultural context is emphasized as leaders model and set goals that align with the community's goals, mores, and norms. Leaders act rationally and pragmatically to be certain that their leadership behavior and goals conform to community expectations. Thus, leadership is constrained by cultural context. Reproduction of the status quo prohibits any predictions of the school's leadership and schooling practices to education in general. Both leaders and followers are portrayed as conformists in this image.

In the third image, the leadership style focuses on faculty consensus in decision making and planning and uses a bottom-up leadership approach. This image portrays leaders as followers and followers as leaders.

These incompatible images of leadership produce several problems for the effective schools literature. One set of problems is that influence flows from the principal to teachers, and a benign relationship exists between school and classrooms. The principal is not influenced by the environment, and he or she isolates the school from negative community influences just as teachers control external influences within the classroom (Angus, 1989; Burlingame, 1987). Another set of problems involves search for the one best system of schooling; educators have overestimated the power of prescribed strategies (Madeline Hunter, Lezotte) and ignored the abilities of external groups to define education and schooling (parents, business). These strategies are used by some to control teaching and make it "foolproof" by insisting on one best and accepted way. Such strategies limit and constrict teacher autonomy in the classroom.

Blind acceptance of the first leadership image may have two problematic consequences. Principals are encouraged to believe that they must define school goals, create a stable environment, raise teacher expectations, and maintain a dominant leadership role. However, teachers view these strategies as an encroachment upon their professional roles. Parents and students protest these changes in routine community actions and activities and cultural constraints of the school act to limit principal-initiated change strategies.

With any of the images, there is a real danger of blind acceptance of coined slogans that are meant to represent the philosophy of education within a school. These slogans are likely to be ambiguous and vague. The word *effective*, for example, can imply a description of a condition or a prescription for a condition. Slogans reduce complex educational concerns to simplistic terms that gloss over ambiguities, turn complex situations into simple, misleading models, highlight commonalities, and deemphasize differences (Burlingame, 1987). Slogans restrict the uses of power and authority to promote uniform, universal educational practices.

Angus (1989) charged that the effective schools research has shifted the focus of education from providing educational equality for all students to achieving excellence in education. Attention is focused on analysis of educational factors and variables while ignoring the political and social context of education—the people. He criticized the common view of leadership that ignores the complexity of administrator and teacher roles and the social, cultural, and political contexts within which they operate. It assumes a functionalist approach to education, described earlier, in which the society's power structures and social systems are maintained and perpetuated through the prescribed socialization of students in the schooling process. Angus argued that the leadership of the principal is not unilaterally controlled and determined by the principal but that it is influenced by teachers, the reputation and history of the school, and institutionalized expectations of the school and community. Leadership is influenced by interactions of organizational subsystems, situational factors, and intervening variables.

Monk (1989) made a similar criticism of the effective schools research. He charged that the research has focused our attention on institutions using an outdated technology directed toward outmoded goals in a highly efficient manner. Instead, he believed we should be designing radically new schools directed toward meeting contemporary conditions and needs that make full use of our new communications technology.

The simplistic interpretation of the school as a stable, consensually shared goal-oriented organization holds teachers and administrators responsible for school outcomes while ignoring the influence of other subsystems in the internal and external environment. This is evidenced by the shift in educational focus from curriculum improvement to the matching of students' skills, attitudes, and beliefs to the work ethic required by business's agenda to achieve economic superiority.

A limited, traditional view of school effectiveness, corroborated by statistical data—basic skills tests results—ignores the skills, habits, and attitudes that are a part of education but cannot be captured and measured by traditional, quantitative testing methods. Thus, instructional leadership, as defined by the effective schools movement, addresses the lower levels of Bloom's taxonomy. This numerical representation of education, basic skills test results, focuses on maintenance of the status quo, where minimum competency is interpreted as excellence in educational endeavors. This type of leadership values control, predictability, and efficiency in the educational process (Angus, 1989).

According to Angus, the effective schools literature conceptualizes schools as an educational contest wherein the principal is encouraged to manipulate teachers and situations to ensure that they share the same visions. Leadership creates and reinforces beliefs, values, and norms within the organization as a subtle form of control in a loosely coupled organization in which direct, authoritarian control is ineffective. Control is achieved through perception modifications, monitoring and reinforcing actions and statements, and appropriate behavior modeling. The literature assumes the passive, docile acceptance of this form of control by the members of the educational organization. It also assumes that the person whose authority is legitimated by position is the only leader in the school organization.

In summary, effective schools research has focused on instructional leadership as a technical, rational function related to supervising, evaluating, and improving the instructional delivery within the school building. This results in a perspective of leadership that engages the instructional leader in roles that emphasize a human resource view (focused on people, organizational effectiveness, and morale) or structural view (focused on productivity, role specialization, goals, and instructional technology) of the school organization (Deal, 1987, p. 235). However, if instructional leadership is defined to include the culture, politics, and power relationships within schools perceived as social organizations, the instructional leader, through negotiation, conflict resolution, and culture building (values, symbols, ceremonies, rituals), performs a role that is complex, directly and indirectly influencing school performance. We broaden the views of educational leadership considered in the next section to include these aspects. Much has been learned from the effective schools research, and it helped to remove the blinders of pessimism that dominated the thinking of policy makers during the 1970s about the potential positive influence of schools, but it is not sufficient to inform the type of leadership required to meet the challenges facing schools today.

Emerging Views of Leadership for Schools

Educational Leadership as Transformative Leadership

Sergiovanni (1989) defined *leadership* as "the process of persuasion by which a leader or leadership group . . . induces followers to act in a manner that enhances the leader's purposes or shared purposes" (p. 213). For some policy makers and administrators, leadership is expressed in ideas and symbols that inspire and create meaning in followers. Leadership also is conveyed in the leader's ability to analyze situations and people, psychologically affect followers, and control the environment.

Sergiovanni (1989) viewed effective schools as organizations that are culturally tight (controlled by norms, group mores, patterns of beliefs, values, socialization, and socially constructed reality) and structurally loose (less emphasis on bureaucratic rules, management rules, contingency trade-offs, and rational reality). Teachers respond better to informal traditions and norms than to management systems. Schools that are loosely structured and culturally tight respond better to transformative leadership for school improvement where order and direction help coordinate efforts and develop shared

values. On the other hand, school improvement programs that attempt to prescribe teacher actions and behaviors are based on transactional leadership premises that respond well to tightly structured, culturally loose environments. Transactional leaders attempt to affect improvement by tightly managing and controlling objectives, curriculum, teaching strategies, and evaluation. By contrast, transformational leaders realize that autonomy in classrooms and schools is a prerequisite to fundamental change. In schools, transformative leadership is able to coordinate and order followers through shared beliefs, culture, and imitation—not management—to achieve shared goals.

Sergiovanni stated that "authentic accountability can be achieved only when teachers and principals are provided with authority to match their responsibility" (1989, p. 223). The overmanagement and under-leading of schools impede the goal of quality schooling. Emphasis on leadership is evidenced in long-range planning, attention to and manipulation of the external environment to achieve goals, attention to vision and values, ability to cope with conflict and complexity, and desire to initiate change. Transformative leadership produces a broad value perspective that includes "justice, community, excellence, democracy, and equality" (Sergiovanni, 1989, p. 224) and enables schools to achieve excellence.

Transformative leadership develops shared meanings and significance that leads to increased motivation and commitment. Bennis (cited in Sergiovanni and Corbally, 1989) identified vision, which is creation and communication of a desired state of affairs that explains the present and assures future commitment as a requirement of purposive leadership because it reflects the needs, desires, values, and beliefs of the group.

Attaining the empowerment of transformative leadership requires the leader to delegate and surrender power over people and events in order to achieve power over accomplishments and goal achievement. Empowerment coupled with purposing leads to increased motivation and commitment in teachers and administrators.

Leadership density, the extent of leadership role sharing and leadership exercise, relates to the school principal as the leader of a collegial team of administrators and teachers. Principals maintain their hierarchical position of accountability. Because of the loosely coupled nature of subsystems in schools, dispersed individuals within schools may perform leadership functions. Understanding the gap between those who have the ability and those who have the authority to make decisions that is present in schools, if it is acknowledged by school leaders, will help to develop situations where leaders lend their authority to teachers in order to borrow teachers' ability.

Transformative leadership views as mandatory a commitment to a shared core of beliefs about the school by administrators, teachers, and students but allows discretion in implementing these values in teaching, supervision, and administration. Transformative leaders shape school culture and protect school values, thus validating the importance and meaning of these cultural imperatives.

Developing attributes such as community, established patterns of living based on mutual need, affection, development, and protection requires transformational leaders capable of changing community structures, forms, and order (Foster, 1989). To succeed, leaders must be able to evaluate critically present social conditions and envision and forge an emancipatory community free of social, economic, and discriminatory constraints. Because leadership occurs within the community (such as a school), it resides in the community and is developed through communal relationships. Leadership is shared and exchanged among leaders and followers and does not reside permanently in a power position.

Moral Leadership

Sergiovanni (1992) proposed that the present "effective schools" emphasis on instructional leadership in education, which requires strong, forceful, direct leadership from principals, may not be the type of leadership that can effectively improve schools. Although instructional leadership is capable of initiating large-scale, school-wide instructional programs that involve teachers in curriculum redesign, instructional leadership alone is not capable of sustaining these initiatives over an extended period of time. Sergiovanni, instead, espoused moral leadership that relies on the development of substitutes for leadership that are capable of initiating and sustaining changes in the school through the actions of and values held by the workers (i.e., the teachers).

Sergiovanni (1992) argued that in addition to the traditional bases of authority that rely on bureaucracy, psychological knowledge, and technical rationality that emerges from theory and research, professional and moral authority need to be added. Acting as a school community, the members of the school need to form a covenant based on their shared values that unite the members to act in a morally responsive way to satisfy the needs of the school. He maintains that there remains a place for command leadership, instructional leadership, and interpersonal leadership, but the heart of one's leadership practice is to become the embodiment of one's ministerial role.

Sergiovanni asserted that authority based on bureaucratic, psychological, or technical—rational authority requires an external force to induce people to comply. However, professional authority (craft knowledge and personal expertise) and moral authority (obligations and duties resulting from shared values and ideas) derive from an inner responsibility, shared commitment, and communal interdependence. Thus, emphasis is placed on the teacher as being superordinate to the knowledge base. Teachers who are skilled and able to reflect and understand knowledge and experiences exercise professional authority by integrating these diverse inputs and applying this newly derived knowledge to practice.

Sergiovanni (1992) identified four substitutes for leadership that can provide those who work in the school community with an inner motivation or meaning to respond to and achieve the shared goals of the school. These include (1) school norms, a connectedness that binds school members around a shared set of values and beliefs; (2) the professional ideal, responsibility for one's professional development and serving one's students; (3) rewarding work, teachers' perception that their work is meaningful, that they are accountable for results, and that they are able to evaluate the results of their efforts; and (4) collegiality, connects teachers together with shared support and aid while developing self-management and self-leadership skills. The substitutes make principal leadership less necessary. By implementing these substitutes for leadership, teachers are empowered and administrators become facilitators as schools develop the capacity to improve from within. However, when schools rely predominantly on command and instructional leadership, teachers become dependent subordinates who do what is required of them and little more.

Servant leadership is evidenced when professional competence and community values are the basis for defining the leader's actions rather than personal interests and commitments (Greenleaf, 1977). Moral leadership, Sergiovanni (1992) asserted, necessitates the replacement of the traditional hierarchical structure of schools where those in positions of authority reside at the apex with a structure in which leaders and followers have equal status and the apex is reserved for the values, commitments, vision, and covenants that guide community actions.

Moral Imagination or Visioning

According to Greenfield (1987), most researchers agree that successful principals have a vision of what they want to accomplish and that the vision guides them in managing and leading activities. Situations and dilemmas addressed by principals require them to assign values to facts, evaluate alternative actions, and reach decisions. "The ability to see the discrepancy between how things are and how they might be—not in terms of the ideal, but in terms of what is possible" (p. 16)—is called *moral imagination*

by Greenfield. The term *moral* refers to the application of an accepted standard of goodness.

Once the principal has been able to analyze the school situation and formulate a moral vision, the principal must be able to convey this vision and enlist the supportive actions of the school community members. Through situational identity, the principal is able to influence others to a desired response. To achieve this, the principal must help develop a consensus among teachers in defining the situation and prescribing actions. To be successful in this endeavor, it is critical that principals be able to view and understand situations from other participants' perspectives. Interpersonal competency thus requires sensitivity to others' views and work situations to elicit desired actions.

Qualities of interpersonal competence and moral imagination are developed through formal socialization processes (administrative preparation programs, staff development programs, and in-service education) and informal socialization processes (norms, values, and orientations of groups). Moral outcomes of socialization are the sentiments, beliefs, standards, and values of the reference group to which one belongs or aspires (Greenfield, 1987). Technical outcomes of socialization are knowledge and skills necessary for satisfactory role performance. Moral and technical outcomes are influenced by both formal and informal socialization processes. "Moral imagination requires technical skills in observation and analysis as well as formal knowledge about standards of good practice" (p. 68). Greenfield believed that interpersonal competence requires interpersonal communication skills and knowledge about teachers, tasks, and teacher perspectives.

School Culture and Participatory Democracy

Participatory democracy in education requires (1) an administration that deals with self-criticism, ethics, transformation, and education; (2) appropriate use of participative and leader decision-making strategies where participants are educated to their democratic responsibilities; and (3) an attitude of respecting the past while challenging the future. In their research, W. F. Smith and Andrew (1989) found that many principals perceive an imbalance of authority and responsibility between district-level and building-level administrators that prohibits the implementation of broad participatory practices. Building principals claim that their authority is inadequate to operate their buildings as effective instructional organizations in the sense being discussed, while being held accountable for operating efficient, well-managed schools at the district level.

School-based management is one technique that may facilitate a participatory, or transformative, style of leadership. School-based management is a strategy of school governance that allows each school to act as a relatively autonomous unit, being responsible for budget, curricula, and personnel decisions. These decisions are made at the building level by building personnel and may include participation by parents, students, and community representatives. When school-based management is employed, the school board's role remains that of providing general goals and policies to guide decisions made throughout the district. "By establishing the principal as the 'total educational leader,' one person becomes truly accountable for what takes place in each building" (Lindelow & Heynderick, 1989, p. 127). Through school-based management, principals gain the authority and control necessary to lead and manage their buildings, and the opportunities for involving others in the decision-making process are greatly enhanced.

Rallis (1990) contended that the dichotomy that exists between principals and teachers will erode as administrators and teachers collaboratively identify and meet the needs of diverse ethnic groups and student populations. Eliminating the isolation and hierarchical structuring of schools will require administrators who can deftly build an organizational culture that connects the varied members into a cohesive, collaborative network where expertise and leadership are shared willingly. The principal is often the only person who has access to all the varied systems operating more or less independently in the loosely coupled school.

In Foster's (1989) interpretation of leadership as a consensual task (i.e., a sharing of ideas and a sharing of responsibilities), a "leader" is a leader for the moment only. Leadership lies in the struggles of a school community to find meaning for itself; it must be validated by the consent of followers. Rallis (1990) described the reconceptualized view of leadership as being more context-oriented than person- or role-specific. Leadership is a process of bringing people together, helping them to belong, so that they may do the work of the organization. They belong by accepting and sharing the norms, values, and beliefs of the organizational culture, however large or small the organization may be.

Emphasizing that schools are simultaneously tightly and loosely coupled organizations, Sergiovanni (1984) contended that excellent schools need to have a clear sense of purpose while providing staff members with the freedom to determine how they will achieve that purpose. Firestone and Wilson (1989) acknowledged the loose coupling of schools but argued that principals can provide a tighter structure by using cultural linkages to influence the delivery of the instructional program in their schools. Cultural linkages can be used to influence task definition and task commitment through principals' manipulation of symbols, icons, and rituals. Icons and rituals provide opportunities for principals to demonstrate and communicate school culture. Through stories, events, and symbols, principals can emphasize values, portray school members as heroes, and monitor the information that flows through the school.

In most cases, instructional leaders start with a preexisting program. They must be able to recognize the existing norms, culture, and resources of a school and apply strategies of persuasion and change to maintain and/or enhance the school culture and norms, thus having a positive impact on the instructional program. Principals can become a cultural expression of their schools through demonstrated modeling, daily routines, and commitment. For culture manipulation to be effective, principals must be able to weave both bureaucratic and cultural linkages to create an impact on curriculum and its delivery. Limits may be placed on the principal's authority, however, by external policies (district policies, judicial decisions, legislated mandates) and superordinate and subordinate members' inclusion in the decision-making process. To ameliorate these influences, principals can capitalize on the ambiguity that exists in school organizations. Principals may interpret policies to influence favorably their instructional program and intercede on behalf of teachers to improve and/or protect the instructional climate (Firestone & Wilson, 1989).

Situational Variations

The technology of schools, the curricula and instructional strategies employed, vary in clarity and complexity and thus influence the amount of coordination and control over teacher tasks exerted by principals (Hallinger & Murphy, 1987). Clarity is the extent to which the instructional process is understood and can be specified. Traditionally, it has been difficult for teachers to determine the best instructional strategies and curricular content for each situation. Complexity, the degree to which the instructional processes of the school require interdependence and coordination among the teaching staff, is exhibited in the way that schools organize, such as departmentalized curricula, funded programs, and team teaching.

Three staff characteristics that influence the way principals exercise and adapt leadership have been identified by Hallinger and Murphy (1987). Structural factors, such as age of staff, educational level, experience, and staff stability, affect principals' ability to coordinate the work of teachers. Leadership styles change from formal, directive styles to informal, indirective styles as faculties mature and stabilize. When considering faculty intellectual ability, teachers with greater abstract thinking skills require a less directive leadership style than those with lower abstract thinking skills. Directive leadership styles are appropriate when staff commitment to organizational goals is low, and more directive styles are appropriate when staff commitment is low. Weak commitment requires more control; high commitment requires more collaborative behavior.

Differences between elementary and secondary school organization also influence the way that instructional leadership is practiced. Research has not addressed this concern sufficiently. Because of the complexity of structure and operation at the secondary level, secondary principals cannot exercise the same leadership style used by elementary principals. This complexity and the size of the school limit principals' ability to be involved directly in all instructional management activities. This necessitates delegation of some of these responsibilities.

In schools serving communities of low socioeconomic status (SES), principals tend to assume a directive role closely supervising classroom instruction and establishing expectations and standards (Hallinger & Murphy, 1987). In high-SES schools, principals tend to exercise less control, providing teachers with more autonomy over instructional decision making and monitoring student outcomes. In low-SES schools, time is allocated to basic skills instruction. The staffs in both high- and low-SES effective schools need to hold high academic expectations for their students. However, in low-SES schools, the principal may be the key figure in setting, developing, and accepting responsibility for these expectations.

Critical Theory

Angus (1989) proposed an alternative concept of leadership that addresses education's complexity, critically scrutinizes school issues, and relates school to society. The "new" leadership rhetoric that is based on business administration theory and research emphasizes organizational change to overcome mediocre levels of performance. Business asserts that improved productivity can be achieved by organizational members if they work within the boundaries of the leader's vision. Educational leadership thus becomes the ability to transform an educational organization into a successful, excellent "enterprise." Principals become the main actors in developing effective schools, affirming a productive organizational culture, and assuring teacher and student performance. Angus believes that an interventionist leadership is needed in today's schools rather than the autocratic, hierarchical, formal position power that the effective schools literature assumes.

Like Angus (1989) and Sergiovanni (1992), Codd (1989) asserted that educational leadership is a form of moral action. An educational leader's philosophical perspective, influenced by a sociological premise, will determine how the person defines the purpose and goals of education. This may lead to a functionalist's orientation in which socialization and competency in basic skills becomes the major thrust in education, and thus society is preserved and reproduced. Or it may lead to a critical theorist's orientation in which education in critical skills, problem solving, and open inquiry becomes the major thrust. Society may thereby be challenged, improved, and redefined through rational, reflective thought and action.

Codd (1989) predicted that as educational leaders relinquish reliance on the managerial orientation to leadership and develop a critical, philosophical approach, they will be capable of reforming both the structure and functions of schools. Managerial approaches to educational leadership, which place little importance on the values inherent in education, result in teacher compliance in achieving minimal performance levels that demonstrate efficiency without necessarily achieving excellence. Codd urges that educational leaders not only facilitate learning and socialization, but that they also embody

and impart educational values. In Codd's view, educational leaders need to develop a commitment to a defined set of values, not merely to a specific organization.

Codd (1989) identified three ways by which administrators evolve theories that influence and determine their practices: (1) developing a body of theories formulated through the scientific study of educational administration; (2) acting on personal experience and common sense through habit, convention, and intuition; and (3) critiquing practices philosophically through empirical and interpretive modes of inquiry. The third alternative—and Codd's preference—calls for the integration of theory and practice.

Analytical philosophy attempts to clarify the way that people think about human activity by identifying concepts, influences, and choices that are made and by questioning premises, consequences, and alternatives (Codd, 1989). *Common sense* is defined as those beliefs that people share unquestionably and that shape the way they view reality, relations, and ideals. Common sense is formed to a large extent through social institutions such as schools, mass media, religion, and culture, yielding enormous influence to those who control them. Philosophy challenges common sense's complacency and tradition through the exercise of skepticism and reason. Ultimately, philosophy and common sense are two different ways of thinking. Actions can be derived from philosophical thought, commonsense thought, or a combination.

The critical theorist uses philosophy to criticize and reformulate common sense. Thus, philosophy becomes a method of reflecting on societal conditions and practices and rationally addressing issues through creative and critical inquiry and theoretical perspective. Codd (1989) argued that educational leadership is distinguished from management because of its commitment to educational values and principles for practice rather than skill competency. He also contended that educational leadership must serve to preserve democratic administrative values by practicing within schools moral principles of justice, freedom, and respect. According to Codd and other critical theorists, education should not support social conformity but rather, be an active informed social critic.

Administrators following the model of philosophical conjecture are able to reflect on the organizational actions and structures of schools to initiate reforms that change both the structure and functions of school. Managerial perspectives that focus on preserving present social structures will be replaced by reflection in action that challenges the status quo and leads to excellence in education and society. Critical theorists strive for an educational system that will influence society rather than permit society to dominate and control educational and other social institutions.

Leadership at the District Level

Current population increases, continued school district consolidation, intensified public expectations for schools, growth of suburban school districts, and a general trend toward societal bureaucratization have contributed to the contemporary widespread use of school administrators at many organizational levels: superintendent, central office, school site, county, state, and federal agencies. For educational leaders to be successful today and in the future, these leaders must be able to blend their visions, actions, and analyses in order to evaluate their organizations' missions and effectiveness and to determine whether instituting change or maintaining the status quo is appropriate and effective for their organizations (Guthrie & Reed, 1991). Because schools are affected continually by changes and pressures from their internal and external environments, educational leaders must be able to anticipate change, develop a broad knowledge base, and be cognizant of external and internal dynamics throughout the world, not just those of their local communities. Although state and federal government agencies have assumed a more active role in the regulation and policy

formulation of schools since 1950, the local school board is still considered the major and predominant unit for forming policy and making decisions.

The superintendent of schools, the school board's chief operating officer, possesses a position of high visibility within the community which is both practical and symbolic. However, only 20 to 25 percent of the superintendent's time actually is devoted to instructional or student matters; budgetary, financial, personnel, facilities, and public relations activities consume most of the superintendent's time (Guthrie & Reed, 1991).

DeYoung (1989) argued that school superintendents play a critical role in formulating district policy and programs to achieve educational excellence. Superintendents must be able to balance external political forces that call for change with the needs of pupils in district schools and with organizational needs. Although the superintendent maintains the role of chief administrator and is still responsible to the board for all administrative decisions, other central administrators assume roles of developing standards concerning student and staff performance, providing technical assistance to building personnel, and monitoring and evaluating instructional effectiveness through standardized testing.

History has demonstrated the ineffectiveness of top-down, mandated reform efforts imposed on local educational agencies by state and federal edict that threaten local control. Yet local control provides a dilemma. On the one hand, it provides a vitality and a sense of school district ownership that is lost in a monolithic organization; on the other hand, great inequalities are created. Because of the Balkanization of our school governance, some districts, the ready and the able, are well in advance of state and federal leadership; other districts are neither ready nor able, however, and fall far behind state and national aspirations. If governance is decentralized further, the possibility of even greater inequalities and disparities looms large.

Issues of equality and coordination can still best be handled at the district, state, and federal levels under a system of school-based management. However, the last 30 years have witnessed the erosion of superintendents' ability to influence public school policy by public-interest groups, state and federal mandates, teacher unions, and mass-media criticism of the U.S. educational system.

Peterson (1987) addressed the issue of administrative control exercised by district-level leaders. He noted that it can shape, constrain, or support the activities, goals, and beliefs of building-level principals. Recent research indicates that control is zoned and can be loosely or tightly linked to constrain and shape principal behavior. These controls are designed to ensure principals' coordination, cooperation, goal achievement, and motivation. Six mechanisms of control are commonly used to influence decisions, behaviors, and norms of principals (Peterson, 1987): (1) supervision, the direct observation of subordinates' work, is followed by positive or corrective feedback; (2) input control, control over the amount, use, and flow of money and human resources, influences managerial autonomy at the building level; (3) behavior (bureaucratic) control, standardization of work through rules, directives, and task specifications, has limited use as a control; (4) output control, monitoring and evaluating outputs or outcomes and providing feedback, are more difficult to apply because of ambiguous, difficult-to-measure outcomes of the work of principals and schools; (5) selection-socialization control, nonhierarchical and derived from internal norms and values, ensures that the subordinates are socialized to the norms and values held by district-level leaders; and (6) environmental control, nonhierarchical and originating from agents outside the school, is exercised when superiors allow outside agents to bring school-related information to the district administration.

Application of these six controls comprise the districts' control system over principals. Administrative tasks are more tightly controlled than instructional leadership tasks. A balance of control and autonomy is achieved when principals' administrative tasks or outcomes are strictly controlled while allowing autonomy in selecting methods to achieve ends. For example, research supports the prevalent use of input control over teacher transfers but not over teacher hiring. Behavior controls are used predominantly over reports, meetings, evaluations, and curriculum objectives; normally, these controls are employed on tasks that are specific and standard (Peterson, 1987).

Although the six mechanisms of control can individually apply to directive, restrictive, or formative control, these mechanisms can be modified to address more than one form of control; for example, supervisory mechanisms that are directive can also be used in a formative control context to shape values and goals. In effective districts, these controls are used to provide a coordinated, directive style for setting goals; develop specific models of instruction and curricular objectives on which to base training, supervision, and evaluation of subordinates; and model proactive leadership and address district-level mission statements. In effective districts, emphasis is placed on supervisory, behavioral, and output controls (Peterson, 1987). District superiors need to increase formative control in order to enhance instructional leadership in principals. Socialization to district expectations and norms and provision of technical expertise will result in attention to instructional leadership behaviors.

Wimpelberg (1987) contended that for significant instructional leadership and school improvement, there must be a collaboration between intermediate central office administrators and the individual school units. He felt that there is a paucity of successful schools in the nation and that number will not increase significantly if school-by-school reform continues.

The typical principal, lacking adequate training to assume instructional leadership roles, spends little time on curricular or instructional matters, concentrating, rather, on managerial functions (Cuban, 1988). There is scant research about the influence exerted by central office administrators on successful schools (Hallinger & Murphy, 1987; Wimpelberg, 1987). Nevertheless, as the principal has become the key agent for change according to effective schools research and teachers have increased their pedagogical knowledge and skills, central office administrators have to assume an integrator role. As the superintendency has shifted to a more political, statesmanship role, little direct attention is focused on instruction by that office.

Because of the loose coupling in school organizations, coordination of activities can be lost without district-level intervention. This can best be accomplished by midlevel central office administrators. They can provide linkages that facilitate change and promote improvement strategies among all schools. Hierarchical, top-down decision making can be replaced by an interactive top-down and bottom-up process.

Wimpelberg (1987) outlined five roles that the central office can assume in support of school improvement through school-based management and shared decision making.

1. District-level leadership develops linkages between central office, schools, among schools, and among building teachers; cooperative learning among the different units is cultivated, coordinated, and networked by district administrators.

2. To effect positive linkages, central office administrators and principals collaboratively determine how improvement will be defined and achieved.

3. Intermediary central office administrators supervise and evaluate principals and supplement the expert knowledge and expertise (referent authority) available to principals in support of their actions.

4. Intermediary district administrators assist principals in developing technical management expertise required by school-based management and shared decision making.

5. District instructional leadership encourages a shared relationship between district and school personnel; the central administrator must be knowledgeable about positive and negative school conditions, provide communication networks among schools for professional information exchanges, and devote time of sufficient frequency and duration for consultations with the schools.

The development of a mission and goals statement for a school can help to achieve a school culture conducive to academic achievement; development of a districtwide mission and goals statement is equally important. Such statements can be used to select administrators, to define administrative team composition, and to socialize administrators to share district goals. In addition, supervision, output, and environment control mechanisms are used to disseminate district goals among subordinates. Some of these control mechanisms, such as output control, foster rapid goal orientation, whereas others, such as selection-socialization control, may require more time to achieve results.

Without strong, internal motivation, principals will not become effective instructional leaders. Motivation increases commitment and persistence to achieve instructional goals and improve instructional programs. Limited motivation results in leaders who focus primarily on maintenance and stability behaviors. Directive controls used with management by objectives can lower principals' expectations of their effectiveness and lower their motivation. To ensure effective instructional leadership, superiors should initially exercise supervisory control to help shape values, provide feedback, and communicate high expectations. With increased subordinate experience, superiors should adopt less directive, more formative controls to reinforce values and provide supportive feedback. As district administrators develop an optional mix of controls for their districts, a balance between control and autonomy will result that enables principals to be effective instructional leaders working toward a shared vision and goals and focused on instructional program and improvement of student performance.

Reforming Leadership Preparation Programs

Recognizing the principal as the key player in achieving excellence in schools, Anderson (1989) critically examined present training and selecting practices. He found that university programs do not address adequately the complexity of this position, nor do school districts invest sufficient resources to identify, select, orient, and train principals.

Research, through behavioral and situational approaches, affirms that leadership can be learned. However, practicing administrators are critical of the adequacy of their preparation. Many find that university programs place emphasis on theory and knowledge but do not bridge effectively the transition from theoretical perspectives to practical applications. Anderson (1989) contended that although present research emphasis on the principal as a critical ingredient for school improvement cannot be proven empirically, it has led to demands for universities, school districts, and training institutes to collaboratively address and bridge the gap between theoretical and technical education and the practical requirements of the job. He advocated activities that will emphasize improvement of the ability of administrators to develop critical analytical skills for application in reflective activities. He called for a partnership between universities, school districts, and training institutes to ensure that principals have adequate technical and theoretical bases, meaningful and relevant training experiences, and smooth transition and continued assistance in developing skills while performing their jobs.

Greenfield (1987) discussed the role that professional development programs and school districts play in training and preparing potential educational leaders. Identification of the personal qualities and technical skills needed for

successful leadership can influence what and how skills and knowledge are transmitted and developed in administrative students. It also guides in selecting, orienting, and promoting growth of leadership capabilities in school administrators.

Murphy (1993) made an extensive survey for the University Council Educational Administration (UCEA) of the restructuring taking place in university programs providing preservice preparation for school administrators. Programs undergoing restructuring were redefining curricular content to include recommendations by the National Policy Board for Educational Administration (NPBEA) (1989): societal and cultural influences on schooling, teaching and learning processes and school improvement, organizational theory, methodologies of organizational studies and policy analysis, leadership and managerial processes and functions; policy studies and politics of education, and the moral and ethical dimensions of schooling.

Reforming programs based their changes on a set of normative assumptions that constituted a programmatic ideology. A new concern for ethics is prevalent, acknowledging the fact that administrators are representatives of values and that the responsibility for the education of children and adolescents is a moral one. There is a greater emphasis than in the past on social and cultural trends that affect various understandings and expectations about schooling. In many of the reformed programs, there is a commitment to critical inquiry and evaluation of educational practice. There is greater correspondence between the work of students and administrators and there is a reconnection between the practice and academic arms of the profession; these endeavors are of two types: stronger field-based components and stronger connections with district- and school-based educators.

Murphy (1993) concluded: "The preparation programs that we currently have simply are not good enough. They need to be made better. The task ahead of us is an important one, both at the individual department level and across the profession as a whole" (p. 252).

Persons preparing for roles of educational leadership are faced with the reality of pervasive social change. Although these changes affect persons in all walks of life, there is bound to be greater impact on those in positions of greater social visibility and concern. Thus, the spotlight of social responsibility rests on those persons holding responsibility for educational systems. Society has the right to expect competent performance in those positions; preparatory programs and the state have an obligation to assure it as far as humanly possible. Under these circumstances, competent leadership behavior cannot be a matter of copying conventional behavior. To advance education, there is a clear need for its leadership to have the ability to comprehend the dynamics of human affairs as a basis for relevant action under novel conditions, the need for better understanding of issues and processes in educational institutions, and the need for greater originality in designing instructional and administrative strategies.

It is no longer enough to be aware of educational issues and problems and their theoretical remedies. In these times of sophisticated technological development and change there is increased need for systematic understanding in all content areas with particular emphasis on methods of analysis and synthesis, and flexibility in adapting to the variety of individual interests and social needs. Educational leaders also need to have an understanding of shifting social issues and developments that form the context in which educational institutions function. Finally, educational leaders need on-the-job skills to act effectively.

In sum, educational leadership includes the ability (1) to have a vision of the future, (2) to see into the intentions of others, and (3) to take effective action. Clearly, there is much to discover about the dynamics of human leadership; the approach needs to remain hypothetical and open-ended so that more may be learned by what is done.

Looking Ahead: The Educational Leader and the New Millennium

Challenges for the educational leader at the dawn of the new millennium are driven by changes at all levels of the educational system. Some indicators of the broad nature of those changes include the following.

A significant number of schools are implementing team approaches to teaching, to learning, and to governance. The variety of approaches in this regard is as wide as the number of schools and groups attempting it. Examples include students teaching students, teachers collaborating in a variety of ways, team-taught classes, and bodies of teachers performing significant governance roles. Traditional models of schooling are being broken down and replaced by highly effective technological and human technology systems. The relevance of learning in these new environments has taken on new meaning.

Schools are becoming highly connected. They are using this connectivity to enhance classroom instruction, bringing greater global variety to experiential activities in the classroom and connecting diverse learners from across the globe. Davis and Botkin (1994) and Davis and Meyer (1998) are among those who have identified this trend. This connectivity has enabled other dramatic shifts. No longer is the electronic classroom merely an arena where more knowledge is available. Now it is an arena where knowledge is used in broad situational activities. Problem-based learning is the result of greater connectivity. Learners are exposed to real-life scenarios. They must seek to understand the purpose of the problem, target various approaches and outcomes, and achieve closure by implementing specifically designed action steps. These learners are being exposed to a lesson in diversity as they work collectively with a wide variety of learners across the globe. Boundaries fade as learners observe and participate in highly constructive settings that achieve unique and powerful cultural, political, and economic awareness. No longer must the learner wait to experience new thinking and practice—an opportunity that our parents may never have had or thought about.

Knoke, Knoke, and Turner (1996) are among those who have attested to the necessity of changing how education is delivered and practiced. As the learner-centered environment takes shape, teachers will learn to be less structured and provide services as mentor, coach, or steward. No longer will the teacher be the center of the learning environment. New roles are being created as teachers take steps to eliminate impractical methods that they have learned and practiced. In their place new methods and role models seek to establish responsibility and accountability. These changes will result in producing the highly productive learners and thinkers who will be needed in the new millennium.

Access to information is enhancing the role of the teacher in new ways while making the teacher of old antiquated. The teaching profession will need to adapt to a continuous learning environment. If we ask what the teaching profession will look like in 30 years, the answer is that it will be changed in some ways that we can foresee and some that we cannot. We can predict, however, that the teaching profession must not rest on past laurels but constantly change and perfect its own practices.

Broad changes in competency are occurring as the national population realizes the inadequacy of its approaches to teaching and learning. There are some powerful examples of countries and school systems that "have a better mousetrap": England is well into the process of connecting its complete school system, and Singapore and Korea provide examples of new beliefs about educating their constituencies. At the same time, there are many examples of outmoded school systems and educational practices across the globe. As broad changes take place in these nations, the needs of future learners and educators will come to the fore.

Without viable educational leadership across the globe, educational practice will ill serve its audiences.

Certification and accreditation bodies are being pressed to change bureaucratic practices as educational organizations are remaking the face of how we educate. Traditional-thinking bodies face a dim future. Changes occurring globally in K–12 education will necessitate changes in the realms of educational practice, governance, certification, and accreditation. Certifying and accrediting bodies will need to make themselves more fluid, more connected, more responsive to the needs of the future learner, teacher, and school system.

So will the teaching profession go the way of the hotel dishwasher? Future thinkers such as McRae (1994) and Knoke et al. (1997) argue that the current state of educational systems is part of a cycle of decline going on in many parts of the globe. It was apparent during the latter portions of the industrial age that populations were being created who would not be able to compete as the knowledge revolution and global markets continued to expand. Modernization of industrial and service organizations has been displacing human capital as broader educational needs have surfaced. A growing population of workers needs new or changed skills and abilities. The age of the knowledge worker has arrived and traditional school systems are not positioned to respond to these new needs. Similarly, traditionally minded teaching and learning professionals may not be ready to meet the requirements of these new learners.

The challenge of the new millennium, then, is whether we will simply replace aging professionals with mechanistic systems, with more integrated learning systems, or with automated, highly responsive and flexible learning and teaching processes and programs? Will our body of professionals be capable of responding to the new demands? The evolving system will place great demands upon the educational leaders of the next generation. Will they be ready?

References

Anderson, M. E. (1989). Training and selecting school leaders. In S. C. Smith & P. K. Piele (Eds.), *Leadership: Handbook for excellence* (2nd ed., pp. 53–86). Eugene, OR: ERIC Clearinghouse on Educational Management, University of Oregon.

Angus, L. (1989). "New" leadership and the possibility of educational reform. In J. Smyth (Ed.), *Critical perspectives on educational leadership* (pp. 63–92). Philadelphia: Falmer Press.

Bennis, W. (1989). Transformative power and leadership. In T. J. Sergiovanni & J. E Corbally (Eds.), *Leadership and Organizational Culture.* Urbana, IL: University of Illinois Press, pp. 67–71.

Bolman, L. G., & Deal, T. E. (1997). *Reframing organizations: Artistry, choice, and leadership* (2nd ed.). San Francisco: Jossey-Bass.

Bredeserl, P. V. (1989). An analysis of the metaphorical perspectives of school principals. In J. L. Burdin (Ed.), *Leadership: A contemporary reader* (pp. 297–317). Newbury Park, CA: Sage.

Brookover, W., & Lezotte, L. (1979). *Changes in school characteristics coincident with changes in student achievement.* East Lansing MI: College of Urban Development, Michigan State University.

Burlingame, M. (1987). Images of leadership in effective schools literature. In H. Greenfield (Ed.), *Instructional leadership: concepts, issues, and controversies* (pp. 3–16). Boston: Allyn & Bacon.

Codd, J. (1989). Educational leadership as reflective action. In J. Smyth (Ed.), *Critical perspectives on educational leadership* (pp. 157–178). Philadelphia: Falmer Press.

Coleman, J. S., Campbell, E. Q., Hohson, C. J., McPartland, J., Mood, A. M., Weinfeld, F. D., & York, R. L. (1966). *Equality of educational opportunity.* Washington, DC: Office of Education, U.S. Department of Health, Education, and Welfare.

Cuban, L. (1988). *The managerial imperative and the practice of leadership in schools.* Albany, NY: State University of New York Press.

Cunningham, L. L. (1990). Education leadership and administration: Retrospective and prospective views. In B. Mitchell & L. L. Cunningham (Eds.), *Educational leadership and changing of families, communities and schools* (pp. 1–17). Chicago: National Society for the Study of Education.

Davis, S., & Botkin, J. (1994). *The monster under the bed.* New York: Touchstone.

Davis, S., & Meyer, C. (1998*). Blur: The speed of change in the connected economy.* Reading, MA: Addison-Wesley.

Deal, T. (1987). Effective school principals: Counselors, engineers, pawnbrokers, poets . . . or instructional leaders. In W. Greenfield (Ed.), *Instructional leadership: Concepts, issues, and controversies* (pp. 230–246). Boston: Allyn & Bacon.

DeYoung, A. J. (1989). Excellence in education: The opportunity for school superintendents to become ambitious. In J. L. Burdin (Ed.), *School leadership: A contemporary reader* (pp. 34–55). Newbury Park, CA: Sage.

Edmonds, R. (1979). Effective schools for the urban poor. *Educational Leadership, 37,* 15–24.

Firestone, I. J., & Wilson, B. L. (1989). Using bureaucratic and cultural linkages to improve instruction: The principal's contribution. In J. L. Burdin (Ed.), *School leadership: A contemporary reader* (pp. 275–296). Newbury Park, CA: Sage.

Flood, R. L. (1990). *Liberating systems theory.* New York: Plenum Press.

Foster, W. (1989). Toward a critical practice of leadership. In J. Smyth (Ed.), *Critical perspectives on educational leadership* (pp. 39–62). Philadelphia: Falmer Press.

Greenfield, W. (1987). Moral imagination and interpersonal competence: Antecedents to instructional leadership. In W. Greenfield (Ed.), *Instructional leadership: Concepts, issues, and controversies* (pp. 56–73). Boston: Allyn & Bacon.

Greenleaf, R. K. (1977). *Servant leadership: A journey into the nature of legitimate power and greatness.* New York: Paulist Press.

Guthrie, J. W., & Reed, R. J. (1991). *Educational administration and policy: Effective for American education* (2nd ed.). Boston: Allyn & Bacon.

Hallinger, P., & Murphy, J. (1987). Instructional leadership in the school context. In W. Greenfield (Ed.), *Instructional leadership: Concepts, issues and controversies* (pp. 179–207). Boston: Allyn & Bacon.

Knoke, W., Knoke, B., & Turner, P. (1996). *Bold new world: The essential road map for the twenty-first century*. New York: Kodansha International.

Lindelow, J., & Heynderick, J. (1989). School-based management. In E. C. Smith & P. K. Piele (Eds.), *School leadership for excellence* (2nd ed., pp. 109–134). Eugene OR: ERIC Clearing House on Educational Management, University of Oregon.

McRae, H. (1994). *The world in 2020*. Boston: Harvard Business School Press.

Monk, D. (1989). The education production function: Its evolving role in policy analysis. *Educational Evaluation and Policy Analysis, 11*, 31–45.

Murphy, J. (Ed.). (1993). *Preparing tomorrow's school leaders: alternative designs*. University Park, PA: University Council for Educational Administration.

National Policy Board for Educational Administration. (1989). *Improving the preparation of school administrators: The reform agenda*. Charlottesville, VA: NPBEA.

Parsons, T. (1959). The school class as a social system: Some of its functions in American society. *Harvard Educational Review, 2*, 297–318.

Peterson, K. D. (1987). Administrative control and instructional leadership. In W. Greenfield (Ed.), *Instructional leadership: Concepts, issues, and controversies* (pp. 139–152). Boston: Allyn & Bacon.

Rallis, S. (1990). Professional teachers and restructured schools: Leadership challenges. In B. Mitchell & L. L. Cunningham (Eds.), *Educational leadership and changing contexts of families, communities and schools* (pp. 184–209). Chicago: National Society for the Study of Education.

Sergiovanni, T. J. (1984). Leadership and excellence in schooling. *Phi Delta Kappan, 41*, 4–13.

Sergiovanni, T. J. (1989). The leadership needed for quality schooling. In T. J. Sergiovanni & J. H. Moore (Eds.), *Schooling for tomorrow: Directing reforms to issues that count* (pp. 213–226). Boston: Allyn & Bacon.

Sergiovanni, T. J. (1992). *Moral leadership: Getting to the heart of school improvement*. San Francisco: Jossey-Bass.

Sergiovanni, T. J., and Moore, J. H. (Eds.). (1989). *Schooling for tomorrow: Directing reforms to issues that count*. Boston: Allyn & Bacon.

Smith, E. C., & Piele, P. K. (Eds.). (1989). *School leadership: handbook for excellence* (2nd ed.). Eugene, OR: ERIC Clearing House on Educational Management, University of Oregon.

Smith, W. F., & Andrew, R. L. (1989). *Instructional leadership: How principals make a difference*. Alexandria, VA: Association for Supervision and Curriculum Development.

Smyth, J. (Ed.). (1989). *Critical perspectives on educational leadership*. Philadelphia: Falmer Press.

Weber, J. R. (1989). Leading the instructional program. In E. C. Smith & P. K. Piele (Eds.), *School leadership: Handbook for excellence* (2nd ed., pp. 191–224). Eugene, OR: ERIC Clearinghouse on Educational Management, University of Oregon.

Wimpelberg, R. K. (1987). The dilemma of instructional leadership and a central role for central office. In W. Greenfield (Ed.), *Instructional leadership: concepts, issues, and controversies* (pp. 100–117). Boston: Allyn & Bacon.

Name Index

Abbott, M., 64, 65
Aburdene, P., 5
Achilles, C. M., 437
Ackoff, R. L., 33, 46, 52
Adelman, L., 293
Adorno, T. W., 203
Agarawala, R., 272
Agger, B., 202, 203, 204, 205, 210
Albrecht, T. L., 123
Albrow, M., 101
Aldag, R. J., 172, 176
Alderfer, C., 170, 336
Alexander, W. M., 238
Allen, D., 87, 88, 121, 340, 342
Allport, G., 12
Alter, S. L., 293
Anderson, C. A., 305, 309
Anderson, D. R., 292
Anderson, M. E., 474, 486
Andrew, R. L., 472, 473, 474, 480
Angus, D., 443
Angus, L., 472, 474, 475, 476, 481, 482
Anthony, W. P., 33, 34, 37, 41
Ardrey, R., 171
Argyris, C., 51, 90, 99, 103, 127, 157, 158, 162, 210, 306, 371
Aron, R., 200
Ashmos, D. P., 29
Astuto, T. A., 106
Atkinson, J. W., 170
Atkinson, R. C., 283, 296
Awad, R. M., 294
Awkerman, G., 390, 391
Ayers, J. B., 156
Ayers, W., 109

Babbie, E., 206
Bacharach, S. B., 268
Baeshen, N., 142
Baird, B. F., 281, 282, 284, 285, 289, 295
Bales, R. F., 176, 177
Ballou, D., 433
Banathy, B. H., 34
Bandura, A., 167, 168
Banner, T. K., 89
Banta, R. W., 250
Banta, T. W., 229
Barker, J., 105
Barnard, C., 40, 89, 137, 142, 158, 295
Baron, J., 281, 282, 283, 296
Barr, S. H., 172
Barrett, R., 294

Barrow, R., 197
Bartlett, F. C., 217
Basom, R. E., 319
Bass, B. M., 62, 77, 95, 184
Bates, R. J., 359
Bateson, G., 51
Baumol, W. J., 457
Bazerman, M. H., 281, 284, 302, 303, 304, 305, 309
Beare, H., 276, 361
Beaton, A. E., 8, 15
Beaton, A. E., Jr., 431
Beatty, W. H., 239, 240
Bebe, E., 198
Becker, G. S., 426
Beckett, J., 95
Beckhard, R., 98, 324, 329, 330, 331
Beeby, 225
Beer, M., 315
Beer, S., 46, 53
Bell, A., 129, 130, 131, 133, 134
Bell, C. H., Jr., 331
Bell, D., 282, 283, 284, 285, 295, 296, 297, 300, 315
Benge, E., 174, 175
Benjamin, 292
Benne, K. D., 39, 48
Benne, K. S., 322, 329
Bennett, W. J., 88
Bennion, J. W., 178, 181
Bennis, W., 39, 60, 68, 77, 186, 322, 370, 383, 477
Benson, C., 268, 425, 457
Benton, T., 200
Berelson, B., 128
Bergquist, W., 100, 104, 106
Berk, R. A., 224, 226, 235
Berlew, D. E., 163
Berliner, D., 6, 9, 217
Berliner, R. F., 6, 9
Berlo, D. K., 125
Berne, R., 418, 422, 432
Berney, M. F., 156
Bernhardt, V. L., 411, 454, 455
Bernstein, B., 13
Bertalanffy, L. von, 30, 31, 33, 38, 39, 44, 101, 216, 217
Best, J. H., 233, 235, 241, 242, 244
Biddle, B. J., 6, 9
Bierlein, L., 17
Bion, W. R., 105
Bittel, L. R., 283

Bittel, M. A., 283
Blake, R. R., 64, 66, 72, 73, 74, 90, 158
Blanchard, K. H., 71, 72, 324
Blase, J., 212, 214, 217
Blau, P. M., 98
Bloom, F. E., 300
Blumberg, A., 50
Bodily, S. E., 289, 290
Boje, D. M., 50
Bolman, L. G., 53, 90, 95, 181, 182, 336, 349, 366, 370, 471
Bolton, W. R., 456
Bordage, G., 283, 305
Borg, W. R., 206
Borich, G. D., 227, 243
Botkin, J., 49, 487
Bougon, M. G., 125
Boulding, K. E., 34, 35, 47
Bowditch, J., 40
Bowers, 63
Boyd, W. L., 374
Boyer, E. L., 396
Bradley, A., 434
Bradley, R., 15
Brandt, R. S., 230
Bredeserl, P. V., 473
Bredeson, P. V., 49, 50, 51
Bridge, R. G., 268
Brief, A. P., 172
Brief, E. P., 176
Bromley, H., 458
Brookover, W., 435, 473
Brophy, J. E., 163
Brown, A. F., 43
Brown, F., 12
Brown, J., 110
Brown, M., 92
Brown, P. R., 277
Brown, S. L., 45
Bryant, H. D., 282, 284, 287, 300, 301, 306
Buede, D. M., 295, 296, 297
Buffett, P. M., 407, 408
Burkhead, J., 430
Burless, G., 429
Burlingame, M., 50–51, 53, 474, 475
Burns, J. M., 60, 75, 76, 77, 78, 184, 371
Burns, T., 91, 94
Burtless, G., 429
Busch, C., 407, 408
Bushnell, D. S., 316
Butzin, S. M., 456, 457, 459

Caldwell, B. J., 15, 276, 361, 383, 397, 398, 399, 400, 401, 402, 403, 404, 405, 406
Caldwell, M. S., 316
Cambron-McCabe, N. H., 349, 370
Cameron, K., 89, 98
Campbell, D. E., 135
Campbell, E. Q., 473
Campbell, J. D., 165
Campbell, R. F., 178, 181
Campbell, T. A., 135
Caracheo, F., 64, 65
Carlson, B. W., 304
Carlson, C., 292
Carnevale, A. P., 142
Carnoy, M., 395
Carraway, R. L., 289, 290
Carroll, G. R., 39, 45
Carroll, J. S., 283, 287
Carroll, S., 80
Carson, R., 288
Carter, M. W., 294
Carver, F. D., 183, 368
Catton, W. B., 179
Cawalti, G., 395
Centra, J. A., 242
Cetron, M., 110, 315, 332
Champagne, P. J., 176
Chapman, J. P., 283, 302
Chapman, L. J., 283, 302
Charnes, A., 292
Chatov, R., 105
Checkland, P. B., 52
Cheney, P. K., 96
Childress, J. R., 60, 80
Chin, R., 39, 245, 322, 329
Chinneck, J. W., 294
Chubb, J. E., 108
Churchman, C. W., 37, 52
Cibulka, J. G., 272
Clancy, J. J., 47
Clark, D. L., 106, 388
Clark, R., 12, 170
Clarke, P., 429
Clayton, E. R., 292
Clegg, S. R., 88, 95, 100, 101, 106, 109
Clift, P., 230
Clinton, D., 20
Coase, R. H., 434
Codd, J., 472, 474, 482
Cohen, M., 106
Cohen, W. M., 431
Coker, H., 239
Colapinto, S. J., 89
Coleman, D., 294
Coleman, J. S., 15, 16, 276, 430, 473
Coleman, P., 243
Comer, J., 15
Conner, D. R., 100
Connor, P. E., 319
Conway, J. A., 51, 281, 287, 288, 395

Cook, T. D., 225, 227
Cook, W. J., Jr., 385, 387, 390
Coombs, A. W., 87
Coombs, F. D., 50–51, 53
Coons, A., 63
Coons, J. E., 268, 276
Cooper, B. S., 408
Cooper, W. W., 292
Corbally, J. E., 78, 477
Corbett, H. D., 319
Corcoran, T. B., 16
Cornell, A. H., 281, 283, 284
Cornell, F. G., 91
Coulmad, F., 188
Cox, K., 227
Cragan, J. F., 124
Crandall, D. P., 319
Cremin, L. A., 276
Cronbach, L. J., 224, 225, 230, 232
Cuban, L., 18, 19, 396, 456, 473, 485
Cubberley, E. P., 20
Culler, J., 203
Cummings, T. G., 323
Cunningham, L. L., 473
Cunningham, W. G., 335, 393
Cyert, R., 281
Cziko, G., 209, 216

Dachler, H. P., 165
Daft, R. L., 141
Damme, S. R., 95, 96
Dance, F. E. X., 124
Daresh, J. C., 350
Darling-Hammond, L., 238, 239, 241, 242, 243, 244, 434, 440, 443, 444, 458, 460
Datcher-Loury, L., 12
David, J. L., 407, 408
Davidson, D. H., 95
Davies, P. C., 110
Davis, B. G., 230
Davis, K., 157, 159, 160, 161, 162, 176, 177, 178
Davis, S., 45, 47, 49, 487
Davis, S. M., 95
Deal, T. E., 53, 90, 95, 99, 181, 182, 336, 349, 366, 367, 370, 471, 474, 476
Dede, C., 340, 342, 456, 457, 458, 460
DeGeorge, R. T., 349
DeGreene, K. B., 53
Deming, E. W., 383
Deming, W. E., 106, 390, 453, 454
Dennison, H., 157
DePree, M., 45, 112
Derrida, J., 203
Des Dixon, R. G., 458, 460
Dessler, 70
Deutsch, M., 13
Dewey, J., 178, 198, 199, 200, 202
DeYoung, A. J., 21, 483

Dickson, W. J., 157, 176
Dijnozka, E. L., 283
Diminnie, 292
Donnelon, A. G., 125
Dorsey-Gaines, C., 12
Downs, A., 262
Doyle, D. P., 457
Dressel, P. L., 244
Dror, Y., 269, 271
Drucker, P., 251, 385
Drucker, P. F., 5, 89
Dryfoos, J. G., 16
Duchon, D., 163
Duignan, D. A., 156
Dunn, R. J., 17, 407
Durkin, D., 15
Dye, T. R., 257, 270
Dykes, A. R., 351, 352, 356, 357, 359

Easton, D., 259, 266, 267
Eckstein, O., 273
Eddy, D. M., 283
Eden, D., 163
Edmonds, R., 182, 435, 473
Edwards, P. A., 12
Edwards, W., 227, 229
Ehie, 292
Einhorn, H. J., 283, 295, 304, 305, 309
Eisenhardt, K. M., 45
Eisenhart, E. M., 96
Eisenhart, M., 209
Eisenstat, R., 315
Eisner, E., 110, 198, 199, 210, 218
Eitzen, D. S., 12
Elam, S. M., 109, 238
Elazar, D. J., 264
Eleey, M. F., 150
Elmore, R. F., 16, 277, 444
Elstein, A. S., 283, 305
Emery, F. E., 31
Emery, F. F., 91, 101, 107
Emihovich, C., 14
Engdahl, R. A., 44
Engert, F., 433
Engleberg, J., 49
Eom, H. B., 293
Eppen, G. D., 289, 290
Eraker, S. A., 299
Erickson, F., 197
Etzioni, A., 88, 96, 126, 172, 174
Evers, C. W., 209
Ewell, P. T., 300

Fagen, R. E., 33, 37
Farace, R. V., 137
Farmer, C. H., 245, 246, 247
Fashola, O. S., 438
Fayol, H., 88, 89, 100
Fedor, D. B., 50
Feinstein, C. D., 290
Feldman, J. M., 165–166

Ferguson, J., 51
Ferguson, R. F., 432, 437
Ferland, J., 294
Fiedler, F. E., 70, 158
Fiegenbaum, 298
Fine, M., 434
Fink, A., 229, 232
Finn, C. E., Jr., 17
Finn, J. D., 437
Firestone, I. J., 473, 480, 481
Firestone, W. A., 202, 216, 319
Fischhoff, B., 282, 283, 284, 297, 298, 299, 300, 303, 305
Fishburn, P. C., 297
Fisher, A., 135
Fitzpatrick, J. L., 227, 251
Fitzpatrick, M. A., 80
Flanagan, A., 430
Flanders, J. P., 168
Fleisher, A., 157
Fleming, T., 178, 181
Fleurent, C., 294
Fliegel, S., 434
Flood, R. L., 52, 469
Follett, M. P., 157
Fombrun, C. J., 328
Fong, G. T., 283
Forsyth, P. B., 156
Foster, H. L., 13
Foster, W., 349, 359, 471, 472, 478, 480
Foucault, M., 204
Fowler, W. J., Jr., 435
Fox, W. F., 433
Frame, J. D., 48
Francke, D. C., 141
Frankel, L. K., 157
Frazier, A., 381, 393, 453
Fredrickson, M. P., 132
Freeman, J., 91, 99
French, J., 65, 68
French, W. L., 331
Frey, S. C., 289, 290
Friedlander, F., 51
Friedman, M., 276
Fry, R. E., 315, 336, 337
Fuhrman, S., 16, 277, 424, 444
Fullan, M., 320, 332, 335, 384
Fuller, B., 429
Fullerton, K., 456
Fulmer, C. L., 452, 453, 456

Gabler, J. E., 80
Gage, N. L., 198, 214, 360
Gagne, T. E., 89
Gainer, L. J., 142
Galbraith, J. K., 5
Gall, M. D., 206
Gallup, A. M., 109, 238
Gallup, G. H., 238
Gantt, H. L., 157
Gardner, J. W., 62, 68

Garfenckel, H., 105
Garms, W. I., 374
Gatto, J., 110
Gayle, M., 110, 315, 332
Genova, W. H., 245
George, J. F., 293
George, P. S., 16
Getzels, J. W., 35, 50, 107, 180, 367, 369, 374
Giorgi, A., 207
Glaser, E. M., 175
Glasman, N. S., 225, 227, 229, 230, 231, 249, 250
Glass, B., 408
Glass, G. V., 436
Glasser, W., 110
Gleick, J., 46
Glennan, T. K., 457
Goertz, M. E., 407
Gold, S. D., 23
Golden, B. L., 293
Goldring, E. B., 335
Goodlad, J. I., 335, 336, 395, 396, 456
Goodman, N., 216
Goodstein, L. D., 386
Goodwin, 246
Gorry, G. A., 293
Gould, F. J., 289, 290
Graen, G. B., 163
Graff, O. B., 351, 352, 356, 357, 359
Graham, P. A., 4
Grandori, A., 295
Graves, 294
Gray, B., 125
Gray, L. N., 283, 284
Gray, P., 250
Green, S. G., 163
Greenberg, P. D., 175
Greene, J. C., 358
Greenfield, T. B., 359, 369
Greenfield, W., 50, 148, 184, 479, 486
Greenleaf, R. K., 371, 479
Greenwald, R., 431
Grenier, L. E., 41, 326
Griffin, R. W., 172
Griffith, H., 156
Griffiths, D. E., 156, 180
Grissmer, D., 430
Grodzins, M., 264
Grundy, T., 64, 327
Guba, E. G., 107, 198, 201, 202, 203, 205, 206, 207, 208, 209, 210, 211, 212, 214, 216, 225, 356, 357, 358
Guimaraes, 293
Gumpert, 72
Gurr, D., 408, 463, 464
Guskey, T. R., 17, 266
Guthrie, J. W., 156, 374, 397, 407, 428, 439, 472, 483
Guttentag, M., 227

Habermas, J., 202
Hackman, J. R., 172, 176
Haefele, D. L., 241, 242
Haertel, G. D., 227, 231, 251
Hahn, D., 315
Haig, R. M., 22
Halal, W. E., 459
Hall, 68
Hall, A. D., 33, 37
Hall, B. P., 361, 364, 365, 366, 371, 372, 373
Hall, D. T., 163
Hall, J., 163
Hall, R. H., 128, 135
Hallinger, P., 474, 481, 485
Halloran, K., 159, 161
Hambleton, 72
Hamel, G., 113
Hammond, K. R., 163
Hamner, E. P., 167
Hamner, W. C., 158, 167
Hamreck, H., 15
Hannan, M. T., 91, 99
Hannaway, J., 395, 396, 397
Hanson, E. M., 276, 315
Hansot, E., 22
Hanushek, E. A., 424, 425, 430, 431, 432, 436, 444
Harker, P. T., 293
Harmon, F. G., 44
Harris, P., 15
Harris, R. T., 324, 329, 330, 331
Hartman, W. T., 394
Harvey, T. R., 318
Haugland, M., 144
Havelock, R. G., 324, 334
Hawes, L. C., 53
Hearn, G., 43
Heath, S. B., 13, 15
Hedges, L. V., 431, 437
Heisey, D. L., 335
Helgeson, S., 80, 128, 135
Hellriegel, D., 133, 176
Hempel, C., 202
Hengst, H. R., 327
Hentges, K., 132
Hentschke, G. C., 87, 88
Herman, J., 257
Hernstein, R. J., 283, 296
Hersey, P., 71, 72, 324
Hertert, L., 423
Herzberg, F., 88, 90, 158, 172
Hess, G. A., Jr., 17, 266
Hess, J. K., Jr., 17
Hesusius, L., 200, 206
Heynderick, J., 480
Hickley, J., 174, 175
Hickman, E. P., 292
Hicks, J. R., 285
Hickson, D., 67, 88, 90, 101
Hill, G. W., 287

Hill, H., 179
Hillier, F. S., 289, 290, 291
Hinings, C., 67
Hiterman, R. J., 165–166
Hodge, B. J., 33, 34, 37, 41
Hodgkinson, C., 88, 103, 107, 257, 327,
  349, 359, 360, 361, 362, 363, 364,
  366, 368, 369, 373, 374, 390
Hodgkinson, H., 8, 9, 10, 11, 16
Hoeh, J., 317, 325, 333
Hoeh, J. A., Jr., 50
Hoff, D. J., 3
Hoffer, T., 15, 16, 276
Hogarth, R., 283, 284, 295, 300, 304,
  305, 309
Hogen, E. A. O., 335
Hohson, C. J., 473
Holloway, C. A., 284
Holloway, M. L., 230
Holsapple, C. W., 293
Holsomback, H., 408
Holt, M., 230
Holtzman, S., 299
Homans, G. C., 40
Hooker, C. A., 281, 284
Hopkins, D., 228
Horkheimer, M., 203
Houdeshel, G., 293
House, E. R., 230, 233, 235, 236, 243,
  244, 358
House, R. J., 68, 70, 166
Howe, K., 209
Hoy, W. K., 51, 108, 129, 212, 281, 307,
  360, 367
Hoyt, D. P., 244, 245
Huber, G. P., 29, 283
Huberman, A. M., 206
Huelskamp, R. M., 6, 11
Huff, A. S., 211
Hughes, K. N., 87, 88
Hunt, J., 75, 217
Huse, E. F., 40, 323, 328
Husen, T., 14
Hwang, 293
Hyary, A., 422

Iannaccone, L., 276
Igbaria, 293
Ignizio, J. P., 292
Ijiri, Y., 292
Immegart, G. L., 35, 41
Imrie, B. W., 227
Iran-Nejad, A., 217

Jackson, D., 228
Jackson, M. C., 52
Jackson, S., 435
Jacobson, L., 163
Jacques, E., 105
Jago, A., 74, 75, 287
James-Gross, L., 17, 407

Janis, I. L., 287, 297, 298
Jaques, E., 30
Jay, M., 203
Jefferson, T., 20
Jepson, C., 302
Jermier, 91, 105
Jessup, L. M., 294
Jick, T. D., 316
Johansen, J. H., 332
Johnson, A. W., 394, 395
Johnson, C., 19
Johnson, D. W., 461
Johnson, E. J., 283, 287
Johnson, H. J., 41
Johnson, M. S., 300
Johnson, R., 461
Johnson, S., 12
Johnston, R. C., 4
Jorgenson, D. W., 444

Kahn, R. L., 39
Kahneman, D., 281, 283, 284, 297, 298,
  299, 300, 301, 302, 303, 304, 305
Kain, J. F., 432, 436
Kalven, J., 361, 364, 365, 366, 371, 372,
  373
Kanfer, F. H., 168
Kanter, R., 106, 124, 316, 328
Kapel, D. E., 283
Karoly, P., 168
Karweit, N., 438
Kast, F. E., 33
Katz, D., 39
Katz, R., 171
Kauchak, D., 242, 243
Kaufman, R., 257
Kearns, D. T., 18
Keen, P. G. W., 293
Keeney, R. L., 282, 291
Kefalas, A., 134, 136
Kefalas, A. G., 38, 42
Kellner-Rogers, M., 367, 370, 382, 450
Kennedy, A. A., 99, 367
Kets de Vries, M. F. R., 37
Keys, P., 52
Khairullah, Z. Y., 292, 293
Khandwalla, P., 130, 131, 132, 133, 135,
  144
Kiechel, W., 47
Kim, D., 425
Kimbrough, R. B., 35, 40, 42, 351, 352,
  356, 357, 359
King, J. A., 241
King, R. A., 267, 268, 277, 408, 420,
  429, 431, 445
Kinicki, A., 318, 322
Kirst, M., 9, 264, 265, 275, 395
Kleiner, A., 217
Kmetz, J. T., 50
Knapp, M. S., 244
Knezevich, S., 50, 95, 160, 336

Knoke, B., 488
Knoke, W., 488
Koestenbaum, 75
Kohl, J. W., 316
Komaki, J. I., 164
Konstantopoulos, S., 437
Kossen, S., 159, 174, 175, 176, 177, 188
Kostler, P., 323
Kottkamp, R. B., 349, 372
Kouzes, J. M., 156
Kovacic, B., 123, 124
Kowalski, T. J., 107, 317, 319
Kowalski, T. T., 226
Kozma, R., 459
Kozol, J., 21, 22
Krantz, D. H., 283, 302
Kranz, J., 395
Kreitner, R., 318, 322
Krepel, T. L., 281, 289
Krippendorff, K., 150
Krivonos, P., 134
Kuhn, T. S., 5, 50, 105, 197, 198, 201
Kunda, Z., 302
Kwak, 292
Kwong, S. S., 288

Labaree, D. F., 258
Laine, R. D., 431
Lakatos, I., 217
Lake, K. L., 319
Lakomski, G., 209
Lamm, H., 287, 301
Lancione, F., 294
Langemann, E. C., 8
Langseth, P., 324
Laporte, G., 294
Lather, P. A., 358, 359
Lauer, R. H., 323
Lavoie, D., 272
Lawler, E. E., 158, 166
Lawler, E. E., III, 176, 394
Lawrence, P. R., 91, 102
Lawton, D., 276
Lawton, S. B., 23
Lazerson, A., 300
Leach, J. J., 281, 284
Lee, C., 12, 67
Lee, S. M., 292, 293
Lengel, R. H., 141
Lepper, M. R., 305, 309
Lerner, M., 355
Lesgold, A., 442
Levin, B., 458, 459
Levin, H., 259, 443, 444, 457
Levine, A., 87, 88
Levine, H. G., 206
Leviton, L. C., 225
Lewin, K., 40, 99, 127, 165, 322, 323
Lewis, H., 361
Lewy, A., 227
Lezotte, L., 435, 473

Liberatore, M. J., 292
Licata, J. W., 361, 373
Lichtenstein, S., 282, 283, 284, 297, 299, 300, 303, 304, 305
Lieberman, G. J., 289, 290, 291
Liebowitz, J., 459
Likert, R., 63, 64, 70, 90, 96, 138, 158, 164
Lincoln, Y. S., 198, 207, 208, 209, 210, 211, 212, 214, 216, 225, 358
Lindblom, C. E., 269, 272, 362
Lindbloom, C. E., 93, 307, 331
Lindelow, J., 480
Lindzey, G., 283, 296
Link, A. S., 179
Lipham, J. M., 50, 141, 317, 325, 333, 369
Lippett, G. L., 324, 334
Lippett, R., 334
Lippitt, P., 461
Lippitt, R., 40, 62
Little, J. W., 182
Littlejohn, S. W., 96, 125, 136, 137, 138, 198
Litwin, G. H., 91
Logsdon, D., 435
London, M., 326, 329
London, N. A., 288
Loomes, G., 298
Lorsch, J. W., 91, 102, 326
Lotto, L. S., 388
Louis, K. S., 315
Lowe, R., 22
Lowell, E. L., 170
Lu, 293
Lunenburg, F. C., 62, 63, 64, 70, 328
Luthans, F., 167

MacGuire, J., 434
MacPhail-Wilcox, B., 282, 284, 287, 300, 301, 306, 431
Macpherson, R. J. S., 156
Madaus, G. F., 223
Madoff, M. K., 245
Mahoney, M. J., 167
Malen, B., 395
Mangieri, J. N., 156
Mann, 298
Mannheim, K., 320
Manno, B. V., 17
March, F., 281
March, J. G., 93, 106, 281
Mark, D. L. H., 12
Mark, M. M., 227
Marney, M. C., 43
Marsh, D., 266
Marsick, V. J., 127
Martin, W. J., 50
Maruyama, M., 112
Maslow, A. H., 158, 169
Massell, D., 16

Maturana, H., 111
Mauriel, J., 332
Mausner, B., 158, 172
Maxcy, S. J., 156, 370
May, J., 408
Mayeski, G. W., 15, 431
Mayo, E., 88, 90, 157
Mazarella, J., 64, 327
McAfee, R. B., 176
McClelland, D. C., 170, 171
McClennen, E. F., 281, 284
McCormick, R., 230
McDonnell, L. M., 424
McFarland, L. J., 60, 80
McGee, V. H., 229
McGinn, N., 276
McGregor, D., 68, 69, 70, 88, 90, 158, 163
McGuire, C. H., 283, 300
Mckeachie, W., 217
McKean, K., 303, 304
McKinsey, J. C., 285
McLaughlin, M. W., 13, 15
McNeil, B., 281, 283, 284, 297, 299, 300
McNeil, L. M., 276
McPartland, J., 473
McPhee, R. D., 96, 139
McRae, H., 488
Mecklenburger, J. A., 18, 458, 459
Medley, D., 239
Mehrens, W. A., 226
Meier, D., 434
Meisel, A., 299
Meister, G., 457
Melmed, A., 457
Merton, R. K., 163
Meyer, C., 45, 47, 487
Meyer, J. W., 109
Meyerson, D. E., 95
Miklos, E., 50
Miles, J. K., 206
Miles, K. H., 428, 440, 443
Miles, M., 108, 326
Miles, R. E., 158
Millard, R. M., 332
Miller, A. H., 227
Miller, D., 37
Miller, J. G., 135, 145
Miller, R. I., 231, 244
Millikan, R. H., 276, 361
Millman, J., 239, 241, 243
Mintzberg, H., 89, 93, 97, 100, 106, 109, 284, 381, 382, 383, 387, 451
Mintzberg, J., 80
Mirel, J., 443
Mischell, W., 167
Miskel, C., 108, 129, 212, 281, 307, 319, 360, 367
Mitchell, 75
Mitchell, D. E., 268
Mitchell, T. R., 166

Mitchell, V. F., 171
Mitzel, H. E., 232, 233, 234, 235, 241, 242, 244
Mobley, W., 165
Moe, T. E., 108
Moehlman, A. B., 179
Mohr, B. J., 45
Mohrman, S. A., 394, 395
Mollaghesemi, M., 293
Monahan, W. G., 327
Monge, P. R., 96, 137
Monk, D., 423, 428, 430, 436, 476
Montgomery, H., 296
Mood, A. M., 473
Moore, J. H., 107, 156, 289, 290
Moreno, 177
Morgan, G., 89, 94, 100, 101, 102, 103, 105, 109, 111, 127, 128
Morgenstern, O., 285
Morrison, H. C., 417
Mort, P. R., 315, 332
Mossop, J., 324
Moudgill, P., 171
Mouton, J. S., 64, 66, 72, 73, 74, 90, 158
Murphy, H., 129
Murphy, J., 350, 456, 474, 481, 485, 486
Murray, H. A., 170
Myers, D. G., 287, 301
Myrdal, G., 12

Naisbitt, J., 5
Nakib, Y., 428
Nanus, B., 60, 62, 77, 186, 383
Nebecker, 75
Neel, A., 295, 296, 297
Nelson, E., 457
Nevo, D., 225, 227, 229, 230, 231, 243, 249, 250
Newell, L. J., 178, 181
Nickols, F. W., 46
Nisbett, R., 283, 302, 305
Nolan, T. M., 386
Norris, K., 457
Norris, N., 226
Nosek, J., 294
Novak, M. A., 163
Nunnery, M. Y., 35, 40, 42
Nutall, D., 230
Nutt, P., 322
Nyberg, D., 349, 359, 360, 363, 364, 374, 375
Nydick, R. L., 292
Nye, B., 437

O'Brien, P. W., 385
O'Day, J. A., 444
Odden, A., 266, 407, 408, 428, 436
O'Donnell-Trujillo, 140
Ogawa, R., 319, 395
Ogbu, J., 12
Ohmae, K., 45

Okada, T., 431
Oldaker, L. L., 16
Oldham, G. R., 172
Olfman, L., 294
Olgivy, J., 214
Olsen, J., 106
Olsen, L., 108
Olson, L., 18
Omurtag, 292
O'Reilly, C. A., 140
Ornstein, A. C., 62, 63, 64, 70, 328
Orton, J. D., 53
Osborn, R., 75
Osin, L., 442, 461
Oskamp, 305
Osterman, K. F., 349, 372
O'Toole, J., 106, 175
Ott, S., 88
Otteman, R., 167
Ouchi, W., 69, 70
Ouchi, W. A., 89
Ouchi, W. G., 159
Ouchi, W. J., 367
Outhwaite, W., 200
Owen, R., 106
Owens, J. T., Jr., 423
Owens, R. G., 166, 181, 317, 332

Pacanowsky, 140
Packham, R., 92
Palomba, C. A., 229
Paquette, J., 421, 426
Parsons, T., 37, 40, 51, 212, 360–361, 472
Patton, M. Q., 225
Pauker, S., 281, 283, 284, 297, 299, 300
Pease, S. R., 238, 239, 241, 242, 243, 244
Peck, C., 129
Pegels, C. C., 128
Pennings, J., 67
Perrow, C., 316
Pet-Edwards, J., 293
Peters, T., 89, 106, 127, 276, 367, 400, 435
Peterson, K., 242, 243, 474, 484
Peterson, M. F., 62, 64, 68, 70, 71, 74, 78, 79
Petrie, H. G., 18
Pettigrew, A., 336
Pfeffer, J., 67, 316
Pfeifer, P. E., 289, 290
Pfeiffer, J., 386
Philipsen, G., 123
Phillips, D. C., 202
Phillips, M. E., 95
Picus, L., 428
Piele, P. K., 133, 474
Pierce, B., 426
Pierce, L. C., 374
Pilecki, F. J., 35, 41

Pinder, C. C., 171, 172, 176
Playko, M. A., 350
Plous, F. K., 176
Polkinghorne, D., 199, 200
Pondy, L. R., 140
Poole, M. S., 96, 139
Popham, J. W., 223, 229, 230
Popkewitz, T. S., 204, 358
Porter, A. C., 444
Porter, L. W., 158, 166, 169
Posner, B. Z., 156
Potter, D. A., 242
Prahalad, C. K., 113
Price, C., 438
Prigogine, I., 111
Pritchard, R. D., 165
Prom-Jackson, S., 12
Proshek, J. M., 431
Pugh, D. S., 88, 90, 101
Puma, M. J., 438
Punch, K. F., 332
Putnam, R., 81, 90, 99, 103

Quinn, J. B., 100
Quinn, R. E., 89, 98

Rabinowitz, W., 232, 233, 235, 241, 242, 244
Ragan, L., 144
Raiffa, H., 282, 283, 284, 285, 286, 295, 296, 297, 300
Rainer, R. K., Jr., 293
Rallis, S., 335, 480
Rankin, R., 317, 325, 333
Raven, B., 65, 68
Ravitch, D., 17, 375
Raywid, M. A., 275
Reavis, C. A., 156
Reed, L., 435
Reed, R. J., 156, 472, 483
Reeves, G. R., 292
Reigeluth, C., 54, 113
Reitz, H. J., 130, 133, 134, 135, 136, 161, 162, 165–166, 167, 175, 176, 282, 287, 289, 291, 295, 296, 300
Reitzug, U. C., 107, 317, 319
Render, B., 289, 290, 292
Reynolds, A., 15
Ricciuti, A., 438
Rice, 287
Ricotta, M. C., 98
Riew, J., 433
Rivkin, S. G., 432, 436
Robb, F. F., 53
Roberts, C., 217, 289
Robertson, P. J., 288
Rock, S., 15
Roethlisberger, F. J., 157, 176
Rogers, B., 434
Rokeach, M., 361, 374
Rose, L. C., 109, 238

Rosen, L. S., 361, 364, 365, 366, 371, 372, 373
Rosenthal, R., 163, 164
Rosenzweig, J. E., 33
Rosner, M., 186
Ross, D. H., 332
Ross, J., 298, 305
Ross, L., 305, 309
Ross, M. G., 322
Ross, M. L., 395, 404
Ross, R., 217
Rossi, P. H., 207
Rossman, G. B., 319
Rost, J., 60, 70, 71, 81, 91, 95, 217
Roth, L. H., 299
Rothstein, R., 428
Roufa, S. A., 98
Rowland, K. M., 50
Rowley, J., 451, 452, 464
Ruben, B. D., 177
Runkel, P. J., 108
Rusche, P. J., 43
Russell, H., 137

Saaty, T., 292
Sackmann, S. A., 94
Salancik, G., 67, 316
Salisbury, D. F., 29
Salomon, G., 214, 215, 216, 217
Saltonstall, R., 159
Sampieri, R., 408
Samuelson, P. A., 260
Sanchez, P. M., 292
Sanders, J. R., 227, 248, 251
Sandham, J. L., 4
Sanford, A. C., 157, 161, 162, 177
Sankaran, 294
Sarason, S. B., 319
Sarrel, R., 408
Satzinger, J. W., 294
Sauter, V., 293
Savage. P. M., 183
Saylor, J. G., 238
Scandura, T. A., 163
Schank, P., 459
Schein, E., 44, 79, 90, 94, 99, 124, 127, 138, 146, 324
Schlechty, P. C., 156
Schmidt, C. P., 289, 290
Schmidt, G. L., 183
Schmidt, W. H., 158
Schmoker, M. J., 453, 454
Schmuck, R. A., 108
Schneck, R., 67
Schneider, 287
Schoderbek, C. G., 38, 42
Schoderbek, P. P., 38, 42
Schön, D., 51, 99, 127, 371
Schrage, 294
Schuck, G,, 121, 150
Schultz, C. L., 272

Schultz, T. W., 261, 425
Schurr, P. H., 298
Schwartz, P., 214
Scott, J. T., 281, 288, 292
Scott-Jones, D., 12
Scott Morton, M. S., 293
Scott, W. G., 159, 160
Scott, W. R., 177, 178
Scriven, M. S., 223, 225, 226, 227, 231
Seashore, 63
Selye, H., 43
Senge, P., 47, 103, 108, 111, 112, 186,
    217, 306, 308, 327, 382, 383, 384
Senn, L. E., 60, 80
Sergiovanni, J. J., 50–51, 53
Sergiovanni, T. J., 78, 87, 89, 107, 110,
    156, 183, 184, 350, 359, 360, 368,
    369, 370, 371, 372, 471, 477, 478,
    479, 480, 482
Sexton, 294
Shade, B. J., 12
Shadish, W. R., 225
Shafritz, J., 88
Shakeshaft, C., 81
Shamir, B., 172, 174
Shavelson, R., 239
Shedd, J. B., 268
Sheehan, J., 457
Sheive, L. T., 316
Shelling, T. C., 286
Shephard, G., 294
Shetty, Y., 67
Shields, C., 132
Shields, D. C., 124
Shockley-Zalabak, P., 126, 133, 136, 137
Shubick, M., 286
Sigband, N., 129, 130, 131, 133, 134
Silverman, D., 92, 157
Simek, R., 318, 321, 326
Simey, T., 200
Simon, H. A., 35, 40, 93, 129, 281, 282,
    284, 295, 297, 298, 307
Simsek, H., 315
Sizer, T. R., 395
Skinner, B. F., 167
Skrtic, T. M., 205
Slavin, R. E., 438
Sleeper, 294
Slocum, J., 133
Slocum, J. W., Jr., 176
Slovic, P., 282, 283, 284, 297, 299, 300,
    303, 304, 305
Small, J. F., 51
Smer, R., 395
Smith, 246
Smith, A., 20
Smith, B., 217
Smith, D. M., 23, 90, 99, 103
Smith, E. C., 474
Smith, J., 200, 206
Smith, J. K., 212, 214, 217, 358

Smith, L. M., 349
Smith, M. L., 436
Smith, N. M., 43
Smith, P. B., 62, 64, 68, 70, 71, 74, 78,
    79
Smith, S. C., 133
Smith, W. F., 472, 473, 474, 480
Smylie, M. A., 395
Smyth, J., 472
Snapper, K., 227
Snyderman, B. B., 158, 172
Soar, R., 239
Solomon, L. C., 87, 88
Soltis, J., 202
Sox, H. C., 299
Speakman, S. T., 408
Spector, B., 315
Spencer, D. G., 170
Spindler, G. D., 366, 375
Spinks, J. M., 383, 397, 398, 399, 400,
    401, 402, 403, 404, 405, 406
Sprague, R. H., Jr., 293
Spreigel, W. R., 89
Srivastva, S., 315, 336, 337
Staats, A. W., 167
Stair, R. M., 451
Stair, R. M., Jr., 289, 290, 292
Stake, R. E., 239, 240
Stanislao, B. C., 318
Stanislao, J., 318
Starbach, W. H., 99
Starratt, R. J., 372
Staw, B. M., 298, 305
Steeples, D. W., 334, 335
Steers, R. M., 51, 170
Stein, B. A., 316
Steiner, G., 128, 390
Steinmetz, J. L., 305, 309
Stengers, I., 111
Stephens, M., 124
Stern, P., 239
Stevens, T., 20
Stevenson, H. W., 182
Stevenson, R. B., 215
Stiefel, L., 407, 418, 422, 432
Stigler, J. W., 182
Stogdill, R., 62, 63, 327
Stout, R. T., 156
Strack, F., 305, 309
Strayer, G. D., 22
Street, C. M., 351, 352, 356, 357, 359
Street, S., 276
Striplin, P., 129
Stufflebeam, D. L., 223, 225, 235, 248,
    249
Sugarman, S. D., 268, 276
Sugden, R., 298
Summers, A. A., 394, 395
Sumner, W. G., 320
Swanson, A., 14, 267, 268, 277, 374,
    408, 420, 429, 445, 457

Sweeney, D. J., 292

Taber, T. D., 163
Tabler, K. A., 431
Taggart, 294
Tagiuri, R., 91
Tallman, I., 283, 284
Tanenbaum, R., 158
Tannebaum, A. S., 93
Taylor, B., 361, 364, 365, 366, 371, 372,
    373
Taylor, B. W., III, 289, 290, 292
Taylor, D., 12, 285, 287, 295
Taylor, F. W., 88, 89, 101, 157, 224
Taylor, N., 435
Taylor, R. G., 452
Terrell, I., 228
Tetlock, 298
Thelen, H. A., 367
Therborn, G., 101
Thomas, 298
Thomas, G. B., 245
Thomas, K. W., 94
Thompkins, P. K., 96
Thompson, J. D., 91
Thompson, V. A., 315
Thompson, W., 438
Thurston, P. W., 50–51, 53
Toffler, A., 5, 44
Tolman, E. C., 165
Tom, A., 197
Tosi, H. L., 158
Trampe, C., 17, 407
Trist, E. L., 91, 101, 107
Trooboff, S., 326
Trotter, A., 456
Truman, D. B., 269
Tuckman, B., 227
Turner, P., 488
Tversky, A., 281, 282, 283, 284, 285,
    295, 296, 297, 298, 299, 300, 301,
    302, 303, 304, 305
Tyack, D., 22, 108, 109
Tyler, R. T., 180
Tyler, R. W., 223, 225

Ulrich, W., 52
Ure, A., 157

Vaden-Kiernan, M., 438
Vaill, P. B., 369
Vaizey, J., 457
Valacich, J. S., 294
Van Kirk, A., 407
Varela, F., 111
Veenman, S., 442
Venezsky, R., 435
Von Neumann, J., 285
Vroom, V., 74, 75, 158, 165, 287, 326

Wagner, H. M., 289, 290

Wainer, H., 7
Walberg, H. J., 11, 12, 15, 436, 437
Walberg, J. J., 227, 231, 251
Walden, P., 292
Walker, D. B., 264
Walker, L. J., 16
Wallace, M., 12
Wallace, R. C., Jr., 182
Wallenius, J., 293
Walters, R. H., 168
Walton, R. E., 175, 322, 323
Warren, R. L., 320, 321, 323, 327, 328
Wartenberg, M., 144
Wasil, E. A., 293
Waterman, R. H., 276
Waterman, R. H., Jr., 367, 400, 435
Watkins, K., 127
Watson, G., 319
Watson, H. G., 293
Watson, H. J., 293
Watson, J., 40, 167
Watson, S. R., 295, 296, 297
Waugh, R. F., 332
Wayson, W. W., 51
Weatherford, L. R., 289, 290
Webb, L. D., 436
Weber, G., 435
Weber, J. R., 473, 474
Weber, M., 87, 89, 100, 101
Weick, C., 281
Weick, K. E., 45, 53, 96, 103, 111, 113, 139
Weiler, H. N., 272

Weiner, N., 39
Weinfield, F. D., 431, 473
Weisbord, M. R., 45
Welch, F., 426
West, W., 228
Westbrook, K. C., 450
Westley, B., 40
Wheatley, M. J., 367, 370, 382, 383, 450, 464
Whinston, A. B., 293
White, D. J., 281
White, J. L., 16
White, R., 62
Whitty, G., 276
Wholeben, B. E., 452
Wickstrom, R. A., 183
Wiener, N., 132
Wilbur, K., 212
Wildavsky, A., 272
Wildstrom, S. H., 188
Willett, E., 457
Williams, E., 318
Williams, R. L., 13
Williams, T. A., 292
Williamson, O. E., 435
Williamson, S., 430
Willis, V. J., 38
Willower, D. J., 50, 361, 373
Wilson, B. L., 473, 480, 481
Wilson, J. D., 230
Wilson, R. B., 453, 454
Wimpelberg, R. K., 484, 485
Winfield, L., 435

Wirt, F. M., 264, 265, 275, 276, 374, 375
Wise, A. E., 238, 239, 241, 242, 243, 244, 272, 276
Wisler, C. E., 431
Wohlstetter, P., 395, 407
Wolf, R. M., 225, 229, 232, 251
Wolman, B., 177
Woodman, R., 133
Woodward, J., 89
Worthen, B., 223, 227, 235, 237, 248, 251

Yaney, J., 132
Yauch, W., 180
Yetton, P., 74, 287, 326
Yoon, 293
York, R. L., 473
Young, O. R., 42
Yu, 293
Yukl, G. A., 61, 62, 63, 65, 66, 67, 70, 71, 95, 130, 138, 327

Zalesznik, A., 105
Zehr, M. A., 458
Zeigler, H., 270
Zeleny, M., 291, 292, 293
Zigarmi, D., 71
Zigarmi, P., 71
Zionts, S., 292, 293
Zohar, D., 110
Zuboff, S., 150

Subject Index

Absolute information, 137
Accuracy standards for evaluation, 248
Achievement
 classroom size and, 436–438
 declining, 6–9
 effective schools research findings, 435–436
 evaluation studies findings, 436–438
 internal economic efficiency and, 432–435
 measurement of, 227–228
 motives for, 170
 teacher evaluations and, 242
Achievement-oriented leadership, 71
Action component of education, 111
Action planning and decisionmaking, 331
Action research model of change, 323
Action-rich environment in classrooms, 14–15
Ad hoc committees for evaluations, 247
Adaptation aspects of systems, 39, 42, 102
Adequacy of investment in education, 425–428
Adhocracy, 97
Administration/administrators, 242–244.
 See also Management/managers;
 Principals
 communication and, 122–124, 129–133, 136, 140–144, 149
 evaluation of, 231–232, 244–247
 evaluations by, 249–250
 human relations theory, 178–189
 inquiry process and, 209–210
 interaction with teachers, 18–19, 179, 474
 metaphor and system modeling, 47–50
 systems theory and, 29–30
Administrator model of decisionmaking, 297–298
Administrative Behavior, 295
Affiliation needs, 170–171
Affiliate decision rules, 297–298
African-Americans, 12, 13, 188,
Aggregate nonsystems, 32
Aggregate thinking, 31–33
Alderfer's need categories, 170
Allocation of resources, 417. *See also*
 Budgeting process
 efficiency, adequacy, and economic growth criteria, 423–444

equity in education, 417–423, 443–445
 expenditures per pupil, 418–422, 428
 private/public funding of schools, 17–18, 21–22, 259–260, 395, 407–408
 reallocating teacher resources, 440–442
Alternative-focused thinking, 291
America 2000, 17
American College Testing (ACT) scores, 6
American Federation of Teachers (AFT), 268
Analytic hierarchy process (AHP), 292–293
Anchoring and adjustment heuristic in decisionmaking, 304–305
Androgynous communication, 80
Antipositivist movement, 200
Ardrey's territorial theory, 171
Assembly to morphogenesis inquiry paradigm, 213–214
Assessment. *See* Evaluation, educational
At-risk children, 11–15, 422
Attitude change strategy, 322–323
Authenticity criteria in research, 208–209
Authoritarian leadership, 62, 64–65, 478
Authority allocation in policy formulation, 395
Authority-compliance management, 73
Autonomy
 of individuals, 169
 of schools, 19, 23–24, 396
Availability heuristic in decisionmaking, 302
Awareness phase of change, 333

Back-to-basics school movements, 109
Base rate heuristic in decisionmaking, 303
Behavior
 communication and, 138–139
 motivation and, 160–161
 rational choice and, 282–283
 theory of, 62–64
Behaviorist models of motivation, 167, 186
Benevolent-authoritative leadership, 63–64, 138
Biologically based systems, 111
Black English, 13

Blake and Mouton's managerial grid, 72–74
Boundaries of systems, 36, 41
Bounded rationality, 282–283, 297
Brain metaphor for organizations, 102–103, 147
Brown v. Board of Education, 179, 276–278
Budgeting process. *See also* Allocation of resources
 model for self-management and, 400–404
 school-based management and, 394–395, 407–410
Bureaucratic-managerial model for leadership, 471
Bureaucratic models of organizations, 89, 97, 109
Bush, George, 17
Business sector funding of public schools, 18

Calculative dimensions of worker motivation, 172–173
Cancellation in decisionmaking, 296–297
Capitalism, social legislation and, 5
Careerist archetype of leadership, 363
Cartesian philosophy of certainty, 199, 200
Centralized administrative control, 108–109, 484–485
Centralized communication networks, 135
Certainty and decisionmaking, 289–290
Certification/accreditation, 4, 442, 488
Change, 315
 barriers to, 319–320
 case studies, 337–342
 decisionmaking and, 331–332
 defined, 315–317
 effecting educational, 332–337
 fate of, 335–336
 leadership and, 326–329, 469–471
 managing planned, 329–331
 models for, 316, 322–326, 332–333
 organizing process and, 99–100
 phases of, 333–334
 problematic features of, 336–337
 resistance to, 177, 186, 211, 317–320, 328–329
 strategies for, 321–324
 theoretical implications of, 320–321
 types of, 317–318

Change agents, 334–335
Change systems, 327
Charismatic power, 65
Charter schools, 17
Charters, for schools, 398
Chief state school officer (CSSO), 23
CIPP model for program evaluation,
    235–237
Circle-pattern communication
    networks, 135
Circles of causality in organizational
    study, 111–112
Clarity of communication, 130–133
Class stratification, 14–15
Classroom culturalist research on
    efficiency, 428
Classroom observation of teachers,
    241–242
Classroom size, 439–441
Climate, organizational, 140, 319
Clinical dimension of human relations
    theory, 160
Clinton, William, 3, 17
Closed system in systems theory, 32,
    102, 111, 136–137
Coercive power, 65
Cognitive-behavioral communication
    theories, 125–126
Cohesiveness and communication, 135
Collaborative power relationships, 66
Collective efficacy, 173
Collectivistic motivation theory,
    172–174
Common cause variations, 390
Common sense, 482
Communal/collaborative cycle of
    leadership, 365–366
Communication codes, 13–15
Communication, organizational, 96–97,
    121–123, 135–136, 470
    barriers to, 131–133
    behavioral approaches to, 138–139
    case study, 151–153
    clarity, credibility, and directionality
        in, 130–133
    distinguishing features, 127–130
    external, 134–135
    formal channels, 131, 133, 136, 142,
        144
    future for, 142–144, 148–151
    gender differences, 80
    human relations aspects, 182
    informal (grapevine) channels, 131,
        141–142, 144, 162, 177, 186
    message directionality and, 133–135
    metaphors for, 122–123, 126–128,
        146–148
    sociopsychological perspective on,
        140–142
    structural/functional approaches to,
        136–138

synthesizing principles of, 144–146
theories on, 123–126, 139–140
Communication skills, 129–130,
    142–143
Community
    communicating with, 134–135
    control of public schools, 19–20
    involvement in educational affairs,
        179
Community development, literature on,
    321
Comparability in decisionmaking,
    295–296
Competitive power relationships, 66
Comprehensive District Education Plan
    (CDEP), 410–414
Comprehensive School Reform
    Demonstration Program, 18
Computerized Administrative Systems
    Environment for Schools
    (CASES), 464
Computers, 460
    for budget monitoring, 408
    for decisionmaking, 294
    for individualized instruction, 460
Confirmation bias in decisionmaking,
    305
Conflict resolution, 81, 182
Conflict theory in decisionmaking, 298
Conjunctive/disjunctive events bias in
    decisionmaking, 305
Consensual decisionmaking/planning,
    69–70
Consortium on Renewing Education
    (CORE), 396–397, 432
Constructionalist model for change, 99
Constructivism, 354, 358
Consultative leadership, 138
Contingency theory/models of
    leadership, 42, 70–75, 327
Continuous feedback, 43
Continuous learning, 459, 488
Control function of change agents,
    327–328
Cost-benefit perspective on educational
    evaluation, 233, 234–235
Council for Basic Education (CBE), 268
Country club management, 73
Covenantal relationships, 45
Craftsman metaphor for administrators,
    215
Credibility of communication, 130–133,
    140
Credibility of evaluations, 245
Creeping determinism, 305
Crisis management, 108
Critical awareness, 92
Critical-reflective system theory, 52
Critical systems thinking, 92
Critical theory, 202–205, 354, 357–358,
    481–483

critical science and, 204
interpretivistic criticism of, 205–206
relationships investigated in, 197
Culture
    as barrier to communication,
        132–133
    leadership and, 77–80, 369–370
    organizational, 94–95, 99–100,
        104–105, 146–147, 319
    of schools, 479–481
Cybernetic aspects of systems, 37, 39

Data. See also Information (knowledge)
    classifications of, 454–455
    collecting and analyzing, 451–456,
        453–454
Data envelopment analysis (DEA), 294
Decentralization/centralization of
    school governance, 108–109,
        264, 275–276, 395–397
    Chicago school system, 17, 24
    equity concerns, 417–418
Decentralized communication
    networks, 135
Decision-facilitation evaluation models,
    230–231
Decision theory, 284–287
Decisionmaking, 281–282, 470
    approaches to, 282–283
    case studies, 308–309
    change and, 331–332
    classifying decision types, 289–290
    consensual, 69–70
    four-quadrant research, 42
    gender differences, 81
    by groups, 287–289
    heuristics and bias in, 283–284,
        301–305
    human relations aspects, 182
    idiographic factors in, 300–301
    implications in educational practice,
        307–308, 331
    information support systems,
        451–452
    models of, 74–75, 264–273, 295–300
    multicriteria, 291–293
    organizing process and, 92–93
    patterns of, 93
    political systems and, 264–273
    problem solving and, 283–284
    school-based, 394–395, 460
    support systems (DSS), 293–294
    systems theory and, 306–308
    tools and techniques, 290–291
    training in, 283
    Vroom and Jago's model, 74–75
    Vroom and Yetton's model, 74
Deconstruction, 203–204
Deference in critical theory, 204
Deliberate strategies, 382–383
Democratic cultural consensus, 370–371

Democratic educational administration, 178–179, 479–481
Demographic data on students, 419–422, 454–455
Describers approach to program evaluation, 233–234
Descriptive approach to decisionmaking, 282, 295, 297
Determinacy to indeterminacy inquiry paradigm, 212–213
Deterministic models of decisionmaking, 289
Deutero-learning, 51
Development function of change agents, 327–328
Dialectical analysis of organizations, 112
Differentiation/specialization in systems, 38
Directionality of communication, 130–133
Directive leadership, 71
Disabled persons, 273–274
Diseconomies and government intervention, 273–274
Diseconomies of scale, 433–435
Disjointed incrementalism, 93
Disorder, managing, 112–113
Dissipative structures, 111–112
Distributed information, 137
Divorce, 12
Dominance. See also Power
  decisionmaking and, 296, 297
  principle of critical theory, 203
  program evaluation and, 233
Double-loop learning, 51
Downward communication, 133–134
Dropouts, school, 8, 273, 443
Dyad level of organizational communication, 137
Dynamic homeostasis/equilibrium, 38, 40, 99

Ebonics, 13
Eclectic approach to program evaluation, 233–234
Economic efficiency, 424
  alignment with technical efficiency, 438–443
  external, 424–429
  internal, 424, 429–443
Economic model of decisionmaking, 296
Economic model of management, 41
Economics. See also Allocation of resources
  census, 1990, 9–11
  circular flow of resources, 260, 263
  cost-benefit perspective on educational evaluation, 233–235
  disparity between rich and poor, 5, 9–11

family influences vs. socioeconomic status, 12–15
free market, 260–262, 426
policy formulation and, 259–260
systems thinking and, 45
Economies of scale, 433–435
Edison Project, 18
Educate America Act (1994), 17
Education Management Information System (EMIS), 464
Educators' Guide to Schoolwide Reform, 438
Effective schools research, 435–436, 474–477
Effectiveness models for schools, 51–52
Efficiency and testing age of educational evaluation, 224
Elementary and Secondary Education Act (ESEA), 22, 438
Elite theory of policymaking, 270–271
Emergent strategies, 382–383
Emotive rules in decisionmaking, 298
Empirically based organizational change, 99
Employment, education and, 8–9, 16, 258–259, 261, 426
Enforced change, 317
Entrepreneurial organization structure, 97
Entry-level skills, 1, 4, 11–13
Environment of systems, 36–37
Environmental factors, student success and, 12–15
Equality of Educational Opportunity (EEO) study, 430, 473
Equifinality in systems, 42, 92
Equilibrium of organizations, 99
Equity
  in educational policy, 22, 273–277, 417–423, 443–445
  and program evaluation, 233
Espoused values/theories, 371–372
Essential change, 317
Esteem needs, 169
Ethical dimensions of human relations theory, 160
Ethics. See Values
Ethnic groups. See also Minority groups
  changes in school enrollment, 11
  conflict among, 5
  discrimination and, 188
  disparity in performance among, 7–8
  equity in education, 4
  NAEP scores of, 6–7
  risk factors and, 11
  SAT scores of, 6
Ethos of organizations, 104
Evaluation, educational, 222–223, 225–228. See also Testing
  of administrators, 231–232, 244–247

case study, 252
core processes, 229
correctional, 228
fairness of, 245–246
future of, 250–251
history of, 223–225
motivational, 228
perspectives and models, 230–231
of programs, 232–238
requirements for conducting, 249–250
standards for, 247–249
targets of, 228–229
of teachers, 238–244
Evaluation phase of change, 333–334
Ex post facto evaluation, 227
Executive information systems, 451–452, 464
Existence needs, 170
Existentialism, 351–352, 354, 357
Expansion age of educational evaluation, 224
Expectancy models of motivation, 165–167, 186
Expected utility model in decisionmaking, 296–297
Expedient change, 317
Expenditures for education. See Allocation of resources
Experimentalist approach to program evaluation, 233–234
Expert information systems, 452
Expert power, 65
Exploitative-authoritative leadership, 63–64, 96, 138
External analyses for strategic planning, 388–390
External communication, 134–135
External economies and government intervention, 273–274
Extraordinary risks and government intervention, 274

Face-to-face communication, 136, 141, 144
Factors of production, 260–261
Fairness in interpretivistic paradigm, 209
Familial cycle of leadership, 364–366
Family
  household characteristics of, 10–11
  school success and, 11–15
  socioeconomic status and, 12–15
Feasibility standards for evaluation, 248
Federal role in education, 19–20, 24
Feedback, 132–133, 144–145
  circles of causality and, 112
  decisionmaking and, 306
  decline of systems and, 43
  input-throughput-output model, 35–37

negative, 48, 167
negentropy of systems, 39
in political systems, 267
positive, 167
Pygmalion leadership and, 164
situational noise and, 141
types of, 43–44
variety and, 46–47
Feminine communication, 80
Financial analysis model for education, 408–409
Followership, 370–371
Force-field analysis, 40
Forgotten Half, 12
Formal communication, 131, 133, 136, 141–144
Formal organizational structures, 89, 162, 168
Formative evaluation, 226–228, 245
Four-quadrant research into decisionmaking, 42
Frameworks level in systems, 33–35
Framing in decisionmaking, 299–300
Frankfurt School, 202–203
Free market
    influence on public policy, 260–262
    training of labor force in, 426
Freezing/unfreezing organizations, 99
Functionalism in systems, 34–35, 37, 472
Funding of schools. *See* Allocation of resources
Futuring, 45

Gallup Poll/Phi Delta Kappan Poll, 109
Game metaphor for organizations, 47–48
Game theory, 285–287
Gap analyses for strategic planning, 390–391
Gender
    communication and, 80
    decisionmaking/power and, 80–81, 168, 186
    discrimination based on, 188
    equity in education, 4
General Systems Theory (GST), 29–30, 91
    case study, 54–56
    communication and, 123
    critical inquiry framework, 52–54
    decisionmaking and, 306–308
    definitions, 31–33
    feedback requirements, 35–37, 39, 43–44
    frameworks for, 33–35
    future of, 49–52
    history of, 30–31
    interventions in, 42–43, 45
    management roles and contexts, 40–41

metaphor and system modeling in educational administration, 47–50
organizational implications, 39–41
organizational stages, 42
political systems and, 266–269
properties of systems, 35–39
unrest in organizations, 44–46
variety in organizations, 46–47, 49
Goal-attainment evaluation models, 230–231
Goal programming, 292
Goal-seeking systems, 34
Goals, 39, 129, 177–178, 186, 331
Goals 2000: Educate America Act, 3–4
Government
    allocation of resources, 262–263
    federal role in education, 19–20, 24
    intervention by, 257–259, 262–264, 273–276
    state role in education, 20–23
    structure of educational governance, 19–24
Graduate Record Examination (GRE) scores, 9
Great man theory of leadership, 62
Greek inquiry processes, 199
Gross domestic product (GDP) and educational spending, 426–429
Group communication, 126, 135, 137
Group decisionmaking, 287–289, 294
Group dynamics and resistance to change, 177, 186, 211, 317–320, 328–329
Group maturity, 72
Group theory of policymaking, 269–270
Groupware, 294
Growth contracting and evaluations, 247
Growth needs, 170

Hard information, 451
Hawthorne studies, 138, 157–158, 162, 321
Hermeneutic/dialectic process in research, 208
Herzberg's motivator-hygiene theory, 171–172
Heuristic theory, 264
Heuristics and bias in decisionmaking, 283–284, 301–305
Hierarchical to heterarchical inquiry paradigm, 212
Hierarchy of systems, 34–35
Hindsight bias in decisionmaking, 305
Holism, 33, 35
Hologram metaphor for schools, 212
Horizontal equity, 418, 423
Households in a mixed economy, 260–262
House's path-goal theory of leadership, 71–72, 166–167

Human capital theory, 425
Human nature, 160, 163
Human relations theory, 138–139, 156–157, 168
    case studies, 189–190
    classical thinking stage, 157
    conceptualizing theories on, 159–162
    contemporary issues, 188–189
    decline stage, 158–159
    definitions, 159–160
    in educational administration, 178–182
    historical development of, 157–159, 179–181
    of management, 41
    productivity and, 138
    refinement stage, 158
    revolving stage, 159
    systematic development stage, 157–158
    teaching and practice stage, 158
    theoretical perspectives of, 162–165, 187
Human resources development (HRD) theories, 127
Human resources leadership models, 326–327
Hygiene factors of worker motivation, 172

Idealism, 351, 352, 353
Identity needs, 171, 173, 174
Idiographic factors in decisionmaking, 300–301
Illusion of validity bias in decisionmaking, 303, 304
Imaginability bias in decisionmaking, 302
Immigrants, 4, 11, 13, 14
Immunizations, 12
Implementation phase of change, 333–334
Impoverished management, 73–74
Incrementalism model for policymaking, 269
Independence in decisionmaking, 296
Individual behavior model of management, 41
Individual communication level, 135, 137, 140–142
Individualized instruction, 458–459, 461–464
Informal communication, 131, 142–144, 162, 177, 186
Informal information systems, 450–451
Informal organizations, 89, 162, 168
    advantages of, 177–178, 186
    disadvantages of, 177, 186
    inevitability of, 178, 186
    leaders of, 177
    literature on, 321

Informated organizations, 43–44, 121–122, 148, 150
Information age schools, 458–461
Information (knowledge), 450. *See also* Data
    access to, 121–122
    control and power, 94, 122–123, 145
    credibility of, 132–133
    transmitting false, 177, 186
    types of, 137
Information systems
    formal systems, 451
    informal systems, 450–451
    managing, 450, 451
    technology and, 456–458
    types of, 451–453
    use of, 453–454
Initiation phase of change, 333–334
Innocence age of educational evaluation, 224
Innovation management model for change, 99
Input-throughput-output feedback model, 35–37, 102, 137
Inquiry process, 197–198, 200–201
    case study, 217–218
    critical theory, 202–205
    educational administration and, 209–210, 470
    historical development of, 198–200, 209–210
    interpretivistic theory, 205–209
    paradigm debates, 214–217
    positivism/postpositivism and, 200, 201–202
    research limitations, 210–214
Insensitivity to predictability bias in decisionmaking, 303, 304
Insensitivity to sample size bias in decisionmaking, 303
In$ite software, 408
Institutional/community systems, 40
Institutional evaluation functions, 245
Institutional power, 64–65, 67
Institutionalism, 264–266
Instruction and technology, 456–458
Instructional media system (IMS), 463
Instructional resource management system (IRMS), 461, 463
Instrumental values, 361
Integrated action plans, 391
Integrated information systems, 452–453
    model for individualized instruction, 461–464
Integration principle, 69
Integrative study, 49, 49–50
Intended strategies, 382–383
Interactional-conventional communication theories, 125–126

Intermediate planning/leadership, 388–391
Intermediate school districts, 24
Intermittent feedback, 43
Internal analyses for strategic planning, 388–390
International comparisons, of education, 8
Interpersonal communication, 126
Interpretive-critical communication theories, 125–126
Interpretivistic approach to knowledge, 52, 197, 205–209
Interschool competitions, 16
Interstate New Teacher Assessment and Support Consortium (INTASC), 442
Intervention, systemic, 42–43, 45
Intrapersonal cycle of leadership, 365–366
IQ scores, 9
Iron cage metaphor for schools, 212
Irrelevance in decisionmaking, 296
Isomorphic structures in systems, 38
Isomorphic team, 48

Japanese human relations concepts, 159
Job rotation/enlargement/enrichment, 176
Job satisfaction, 66–67, 175. *See also* Morale
Joint Committee on Standards for Educational Evaluation, 248, 249
Journey metaphor for organizations, 47–48
Judgmental evaluation models, 230–231
Judicial influence on educational policy, 276–278

KIDMAP, 463–464
Knowledge. *See* Information (knowledge); Inquiry process
Koestenbaum's leadership model, 75

Laissez-faire leadership, 62
Language
    integrative study and, 50
    poststructuralist perspective, 203–204, 205
Latchkey children, 13
Lateral (horizontal) communication, 134
Law of requisite variety, Ashby, 46
Leaders for America's Schools, 156
Leadership, 60–61, 129, 142–144
    archetypes of, 363–366
    behavioral theory and, 62–64
    case study, 82–83
    change and, 60, 326–329, 469–471
    communication by, 122–124, 129–130, 148–151

congruence of, 168
consideration of worker needs, 171
contingency/situational theories on, 42, 70–75
    within a cultural context, 77–80
    cycles of, 364–366, 365–366
    density of, 478
    at district level, 483–486
    effective schools research and, 156–157
    empirical vs. hermeneutic studies of, 214–215
    future of, 143–144, 148–151, 181–183, 487–488
    grid of Blake and Mouton, 72–74
    of informal organizations, 177
    vs. management, 19, 61–62, 130, 326, 471
    managing internal/external relationships, 68, 70
    by members of minority groups, 168
    models, 63, 75, 78
    motivation and, 183–188
    new paradigms for, 5–6, 48, 81–82
    path-goal theory of, 71–72, 166–167
    power-influence perspective on, 64–68
    preparation programs for, 486–487
    Pygmalion, 163–165
    situational determinants theories on, 75
    styles of, 62–64, 68–74, 80–81, 163, 287
    trait theories on, 62, 64
    transactional, 75–78, 184, 471
    transformational, 75–77, 184–185, 471, 477–478
    values of, 349–352, 369–370, 478–479
    women in authority, 80–81, 168, 186
Leading parts in systems, 37–38
Learning
    organizational models for, 51
    social, 167–168
    student perceptions and, 454–455
    technology and, 456–458
Learning organizations, 47, 92, 127–128, 147–148, 382
    information technology and, 450–451
    leadership role in, 327
    model for change, 99
Legislative influence on educational policy, 276–278
Legitimate power, 64–65, 94
Levels of discourse in systems thinking, 34
Liberalism, 351, 352–353, 355
Likert's four-systems organizational concept, 69–70, 96, 138

Linchpin/liaison structures for communicating, 145
Linear causality to mutual causality inquiry paradigm, 213
Linear communication model, 130
Linkage models of change, 325–326, 333
Load concept in communication processes, 137
Local school districts, 20–21, 23, 109
  budgeting process and, 407–408
  control by, 17, 18, 22, 265
  decisionmaking by, 288
  demographic and financial characteristics, 419–422
  and educational spending, 264–265, 421–423
  intradistrict equity studies, 422–423
  leadership of, 483–486
  vs. national curriculum, 17
  policy formulation by, 397–398
  size of, 433–435
Logical positivism. See Positivism/postpositivism

Machine bureaucracy, 41, 97
Machine metaphor for organizations, 53, 97, 100–101, 109, 212
Magnet schools, 109, 275
Majority distribution and program evaluation, 233
Management by objectives (MBO), 244, 247
Management information systems, 451–452
Management/managers. See also Administration/administrators; Leadership
  applying human relations concepts, 162, 180–181
  approaches to power, 67–68
  as decisionmakers, 287
  grid of Blake and Mouton, 72–74
  internal/external relationships and, 68, 70
  vs. leaders, 19, 61–62, 130, 326, 471
  Likert's four-systems organizational concept, 69–70, 96
  models, 41
  roles/contexts in systems thinking, 40–41, 50–51, 136
Managerialism, 210–211
Manatt's mutual benefit evaluation model, 242–244
Map of systems education, 34
Marketplace influence on public policy, 260–264
Masculine communication, 80
Maslow's need hierarchy, 169
Mass communication, 126
Mathematics, national standards for, 17

Maturity of subordinates/groups, 71–72
McClelland's social motives, 170–171
McGregor's theory on assumptions about workers, 68–69
Means vs. ends argument, 201
Measurement vs. evaluative research practices, 207, 209–210, 225–226
Mechanical to holographic inquiry paradigm, 212
Mechanized continuous feedback, 43
Messages
  directionality of, 133–135
  erosion/filtering of, 133–134, 136, 140, 145, 148–149
  meaning of, 140
  medium for sending, 141
Metaphor and system modeling, 47–50
Metaphors for communication, 122–123
Metaphors for organizations, 96, 100–106, 126–128
Metavalues, 374–376
Methodological pluralism, 92
Micronetwork of group interactions, 137
Middle ages, inquiry processes in, 199
Minimax and program evaluation, 233
Minimum competency testing programs, 4
Minority groups. See also Ethnic groups
  advanced placement examinations and, 443
  leadership and, 168
Misconceptions of chance bias in decisionmaking, 303–304
Mission statements, 384–386, 485
Missionary organization, 97–98
Model for self-management (MSM), 397–398
  budgeting process, 400–404
  development plans, 399
  policy formulation and, 398–400
  program development/evaluation, 399–400, 404–406
Modeling and social learning, 167–168
Models
  of administrative evaluation, 246–247
  of change, 99, 316, 322–326, 332–333
  of classroom as social system, 367
  of decisionmaking, 74–75, 264–273, 295–300
  of educational evaluation, 230–231
  of effective schools, 51–52
  of human relations, 165–169
  of leadership, 183–188, 471
  of management, 41
  of organizational communication, 80, 124–126, 130, 142, 144
  organizational variables within, 326
  of organizations, 87–88, 89

of planning, 394–406
of problem solving, 325–326
for program evaluation, 233–238
for teacher evaluation, 242–244
of work design, 89–90
Moral leadership, 349–352, 478–479
Moral principle orientation, 360
Moral valuation, 373–374
Morale, 138–139, 174–175
  approaches to studying, 175
  productivity and, 158, 162
  quality of work life, 175–176, 186
Morality, 349–351, 479. See also Values
Morphogenesis, 212
Morrill Act (1862), 22
Mothers, working, 13
Motivation
  behavior and, 160–161
  behaviorist models, 167, 186
  content models, 168–174, 186
  expectancy models, 165–167, 186
  model for educational leadership, 183–188
  performance and, 46, 161
  process models, 165–168
  social learning models, 167–168, 186
  sociotechnical systems for, 176
  of workers, 157–158, 168, 171–174, 176–178
Motivator-hygiene theory, 171–172
Multiattribute decisionmaking (MADM), 291–293
Multicriteria decisionmaking (MCDM), 291–293
Multiple literacy concept, 14
Myers-Briggs type indicators, 301
Mystical/integrative cycle of leadership, 365–366
Mythmaking in organizational development, 50

National Academy of Sciences, 17
National Assessment of Educational Progress (NAEP), 6–7
National Assessment Governing Board, 17
National Board for Professional Teaching Standards, 442
National Center for Education Statistics (NCES), 4, 6–10, 21, 417, 419–420
National Commission on Excellence in Education, 4
National Commission on Teaching and America's Future (NCTAF), 440–442
National Congress of Parents and Teachers (PTA), 268
National Council for Accreditation of Teacher Education (NCATE), 442

National Council of Teachers of Mathematics (NCTM), 17
National Council on Educational Standards and Testing (NCEST), 17
National Education Association (NEA), 268
National Education Goals Panel (NEGP), 4, 12, 17
National Governors' Association, 17, 18
National Policy Board for Educational Administration (NPBEA), 350, 486
National standards
    vs. local control, 17, 18, 22
    in mathematics, 17
    in science, 17
    for teachers, 442–443
National Teacher Examination (NTE) competency tests, 241
Natural monopolies and government intervention, 274
Naturalistic evaluation models, 230–231
Naturalistic research, 206–207
Needs, human, 158, 160–161, 169–171
Negentropy of systems, 39
Negotiation/bargaining, in game theory, 286
Networks communication metaphor, 96
Networks of communication, 135, 145, 149
New American Schools Development Corporation, 17–18
New Compact for Learning, 184
New scientist, 199
New York State's strategic planning process, 410–414
Nonformal instruction, 460
Nonverbal communication, 125, 131–132, 136, 141
Normative approach to decisionmaking, 282, 295–296
Normative-reeducative change strategies, 322
Norms, 319
Notes on the State of Virginia, 20

Objective to perspectival inquiry paradigm, 214
Objectivity, 199, 208
Office of Educational Research and Improvement, 17
Office information systems, 452
Ohio State University leadership studies, 63
Open enrollment, 275
Open system in system theory, 32–33, 136–137
Operational planning. See Tactical leadership/planning
Operations research/management science (OR/MS), 290–292

Organism metaphor for organizations, 101–102, 110, 126, 146
Organization-as-art metaphor, 127, 147
Organization-as-psychoentity metaphor, 127, 147, 148
Organizational change literature, 106–107, 473–474
Organizational climate, 91, 97
Organizational identification theory, 96
Organizational life cycles, 89, 98–99
Organizational/managerial systems, 40
Organizational systems, schools as, 87–88, 141–142
    case study, 114–116
    change and, 41–42, 99–100, 316–317, 332–337
    culture and, 94–95, 104–105, 127, 140, 184
    decisionmaking and, 92–93, 307–308
    future of, 44–54, 110–114, 124–125, 335–337
    health and effectiveness of, 98–99
    leadership and, 48, 78
    metaphor and system modeling, 47–50, 100–103, 126–128
    political systems and power, 93–94, 103–104
    as psychic prisons, 105–106
    restructuring education and, 108, 150
    size, structure, and complexity, 97–98, 128–129, 139, 481
    traditional ways of viewing, 88–92, 106–108, 212
    values of, 366–369
Organizational theory, 39–41, 44–45
Outcomes assessment movement, 250–251

Paraprofessionals, 461
Parent-teacher cooperation, 15
Parents
    impact on public policy, 268
    involvement of, 49
    responsibility of, 18
    school choice by, 264, 266
Pareto optimality and program evaluation, 233
Participative
    leadership/decisionmaking, 62–64, 71, 79, 138, 326, 479–481
Partisan analysis, 269
Path-goal theory of leadership, 71–72, 166–167
Peer groups, 14–16
Peer review of teachers, 242
Performance. See Achievement; Motivation: performance and
Person-environment fit, 98
Personal power, 65–66

Personal value orientation, 360
Personnel Evaluation Standards, 248
Philosophy, 349–352
    conflicting world views, 359–360
    constructivism, 354, 358
    critical theory, 197, 202–206, 354, 357–358
    existentialism, 351–352, 354, 357
    idealism, 351, 352, 353
    leadership and, 482–483
    liberalism, 351, 352–353, 355
    positivism/postpositivism, 351, 353, 355–356
    pragmatism, 351–352, 354, 356
    realism, 353, 355–356
Physical capital, 260–261
Physical/psychological distance and communication, 135
Physiological needs/perspective, 169, 174
Planned change, 317–318
Planning, programming, budgeting system (PPBS) model, 400
Platforms of principles, 350, 372
Poet archetype of leadership, 364
Policy formulation
    equity in education, 417–423
    judicial/legislative influence on, 276–278
    models, 264–273, 398–399
    political interactions in, 257, 266–269
    public/private sector differences, 259–260, 262–264
    school-based management and, 395
Policy mechanics research on efficiency, 428
Political-economic perspective on educational evaluation, 233
Political-historical model for leadership, 471
Political metaphor for organizations, 104
Political power/leadership, 65–66, 77, 103–104
    policy formulation, 257, 264–273
    strategic planning and, 387–388
Politician archetype of leadership, 363–364
Polyhedron organizational model, 53
Population ecology, 91, 102
Porter-Lawler model of motivation, 166
Porter's need hierarchy, 169–170
Position power, 65–66, 68
Positivism/postpositivism, 52–53, 200–202, 351, 353–356
    critical theory's criticism of, 203
    interpretivistic criticism of, 205–206
Postmodernism, 204, 205
Poststructuralism, 203–204, 205
Poverty, 9–11

Power. *See also* Political
  power/leadership
  change and, 99
  information control and, 94,
    122–123, 145
  management and, 41
  as motive, 170–171
  organizing process and, 93–94
  student perception of, 48
  work satisfaction and, 66–67
Power-coercive change strategies, 322
Power-influence perspective on
  leadership, 64–68
Power strategy for change, 322–323
Powerlessness, 66
Pragmatism, 351–352, 354, 356
Pregnancy, smoking and drinking
  during, 12
Prescriptive approach to
  decisionmaking, 282
Prestige power, 64–65
Presumed associations bias in
  decisionmaking, 302
Primal archetype of leadership, 364,
  365
Principals
  case study, 82–83
  as change agents, 335
  communication by, 129
  effective schools research and,
    474–475
  leadership traits of, 474
  pupil achievement and, 435–436
  traditional role of, 50–51, 471–474,
    484–485
Private schools, 24
Private sector funding of public
  schools, 17–18
Probability theory, 284
Problem solving, 373–374
  decisionmaking and, 283–284, 331
  models, 324–325, 333
Process models of motivation, 165
Producers in a mixed economy,
  260–262
Production function studies of
  economic efficiency, 424,
  430–433
Productivity, 138
  human relations aspects, 157–158
  leadership and, 78
  in machine organizations, 100–101
  morale and, 162, 175
  motivation and, 172
  vs. relationship-building, 74
Professional bureaucracy, 97
Professionalism age of educational
  evaluation, 224–225
Program evaluation, 232–238
Progressive mechanization/segregation
  of systems, 38

Prophetic cycle of leadership, 365–366
Proportional feedback, 43
Propriety standards for evaluation, 248
Prospect theory in decisionmaking,
  298–300
Provus model for program evaluation,
  235, 238
Psychic prisons, 105–106
Psychological perspectives of morale,
  174
Public/private sector differences
  allocation of resources, 259–260
  policy formulation, 262–264
Public schools
  accomplishments in twentieth
    century, 4
  causes for concern, 6–16
  diversity of, 11, 179
  governance of, 23–24
  government intervention, 257–259
  historical development, 19–22
  private-sector funding, 17–18
  public and private benefits of,
    258–260
  revenue sources for, 265
  taxation and, 10, 21, 418
Punctuated equilibrium, 99
Pupil-teacher ratios/relationships, 16,
  113–114, 437–443
Purposeful systems, 34–35
Pygmalion leadership, 163–165

Quality circles, 159
Quality of work life, 175–176
Quantum science and understanding of
  organizations, 110–111
Quasimechanical communication
  model, 130, 140

Racial discrimination, 188
Rate of return on investment in
  education, 425–426
Rating scales and evaluations, 246–247
Rational choice, behavioral model of,
  282–283
Rational-empirical change strategies,
  322
Rationalism theory of policymaking,
  271–273
Realism, 353, 355–356
Reality
  interpretivistic perspective, 205–206
  positivist/postpositivist perspective,
    201–202
  poststructuralist perspective, 205
Realized strategies, 382–383
Reconstructive learning, 51
Recruitment function of change agents,
  327–328
Redfern's management by objectives
  evaluation model, 242–244

Referent power, 65
Reflective approach in decisionmaking,
  298
Reform age of educational evaluation,
  224
Reform movement in education, 16–19,
  224–225, 335–336, 424, 438
Regret payoff, 285
Reinforcement, 167–168. *See also*
  Feedback
Relatedness needs, 170
Relationship-building vs. production
  concerns, 74
Relationship-oriented leadership, 63, 78
Relay feedback, 43
Reliability in interpretivistic paradigm,
  208
Religious schools, 24
Renewal phase of change, 333–334
Representations of knowledge, 199
Representativeness heuristic in
  decisionmaking, 302–304
Research. *See also* Inquiry process
  authenticity criteria, 208–209
  educational, 197
  hermeneutic/dialectic process, 208
  limitations of, 210–214
  naturalistic inquiry approach,
    206–207
  positivist principles of, 202
  trustworthiness criteria, 208
Research-development-diffusion-
  utilization (RDDU) models, 325,
  333
Restructuring education, 108, 150
Reward power, 65
Risk and decisionmaking, 289–290
Routinization phase of change, 333–334
Rules concept of communication
  processes, 137
Rural schools, 21

Safety needs, 169
Sandia study, 6
SAPHIR decisionmaking software, 294
Satisficing, 93
Scalar principle, 69
Scholastic aptitude test (SAT) scores, 6,
  9, 15
School-based budgeting, 407–410
School-based management (SBM),
  394–395, 460, 480
School-business partnerships, 18
School environment, culture of,
  479–481
School governance, scope and
  structure, 19, 265–266
School size and achievement, 433–435
Schools for the Future, 464
"Schools That Work," 109–110
Schrödinger boxes, 110